Simply Heavenly!

Simply Heavenly!

THE MONASTERY VEGETARIAN COOKBOOK

Abbot George Burke

Macmillan • USA

MACMILLAN
A Simon & Schuster Macmillan Company
1633 Broadway
New York, NY 10019-6785

Library of Congress Cataloging-in-Publication Data

Burke, George, 1940–
Simply heavenly!: the monastery vegetarian cookbook / George Burke.
p. cm.
Includes index.
ISBN 0-02-861267-1 (alk. paper)
1. Vegetarian cookery. I. Title.
TX837.B922 1997
641.5'636—DC20 96-23979
CIP

Manufactured in the United States of America

10 9 8 7 6 5 4 3 2 1

Design by Amy Peppler Adams—designLab, Seattle

Contents

Introduction 1

Salad Dressings 10

Salads 25

Potato Salads 42

Bread and Such 49

Crackers 59

Soups 61

Chili 90

Dairy Substitutes 93

Gluten: For Goodness' Sake! 98

UnBeef Substitutes and Dishes 109

Burgers 118

UnPork Substitutes and Dishes 122

UnHam Substitutes and Dishes 130

UnSausage Substitutes and Dishes 132

UnBacon Substitutes and Dishes 136

UnChicken Substitutes and Dishes 137

UnTurkey Substitutes and Dishes 147

UnSeafood Substitutes and Dishes 149

Flavoring Broths 155

Heavenly Broth 157

Vegetables 159

Casseroles 192

Dried Beans 228

Grains 242

Tofu Dishes 249

Gravies 253

Sauces 256

Pasta Sauces 263

Pasta 266

Pizza 278

Focaccia 282

Square Meals 284

Pickles, Relish, Salsa, Etc. 290

Sandwiches and Spreads 298

N'eggs 302

Seasonings 303

Desserts 305

N'Ice Kreem 314

Cake 316

Cookies 322

Pies 328

Sweet Pastry 334

Etc. 337

Index 343

Introduction

Originally Christians, like their Jewish spiritual antecedents, the Essenes, were vegetarians, but in time the insistence on a vegetarian diet became confined to the monasteries. One of the most interesting monastic "relics" of the early Christian era is a letter written by a monk of Egypt to one of his disciples who had gone to Alexandria on some project and there had begun to eat meat.

Learning of this, the monk immediately wrote to him, exhorting him to return to his vegetarian ways, reminding him that in Paradise Adam and Eve had been told: "Behold, I have given you every herb bearing seed, which is upon the face of all the earth, and every tree, in the which is the fruit of a tree yielding seed; to you it shall be for meat" (Gen. 1:29). This being so, the monk wrote that those who aspire to return to that pristine state of purity and communion with God must eat the diet of Paradise while on the earth in order to prepare themselves to regain that lost blessedness.

At times, especially in the West, this ideal has been forgotten. Whenever there was a resurgence of spiritual consciousness and reform among the monastics, the absolute first principle would be that of total abstinence from animal flesh (including eggs) in all forms. Usually this abstinence would be extended to dairy products as well.

In the Eastern and Oriental Orthodox Churches this principle is still evident in the requirement for all Orthodox Christians, lay as well as monastic, to totally abstain from meat, fish, eggs, and dairy products on nearly all Wednesdays and Fridays, as well as all days in the seasons of abstinence such as the forty days of Lent and Advent. In the Oriental Orthodox Churches these days of abstinence comprise more than half of the calendar year.

But many of the Eastern Christian monastics, and some nonmonastics as well, prefer to observe this abstinence all the time. This is because in the Eastern Church such abstinence is not regarded as penitential self-denial or "mortification of the flesh," but rather as an aid to interior prayer (Hesychia, *The Silence*).

The Fathers of the East taught that diet had a formative influence on the mind, which they saw as a field of energy, not merely the physical brain, which they considered to be only the organ of the mind. They observed that some foods made the mental processes (movements of noetic energies) heavy, whereas other foods made the mind light and quick in movement. Topping the list of "heavy" foods were all animal proteins, including dairy. In contrast, vegetables, grains, and fruits, the food of Paradise, were seen to make the mind fluid and able to grasp the subtleties of spiritual thought and experience (theoria).

In this approach to vegetarianism they were maintaining the principle to be found in the Aramaic text of the Evangelion Da-Mepharreshe, the oldest text of the Gospels known to exist. There, in the Gospel of Luke (21:34), Jesus says most forthrightly: "See that you do not make your minds heavy, by never eating meat or drinking wine." In our own century, Saint John of Kronstadt (+1908) wrote that the more we live in the spirit the less will we live on animal flesh, the implication being that those who live fully in the spirit abstain completely from animal food. Saint John, a nonmonastic parish priest, insisted that his spiritual children abstain at all times from animal foods, thus keeping a perpetual Lent. Those priests who were under his spiritual aegis did the same in relation to those under their spiritual care.

Now that more detailed, and honest, research and information regarding diet and health are becoming widely spread, many clergy and laity of the Orthodox Church who had previously held an indifferent attitude toward observance of the traditional rules of abstinence are realizing the wisdom of the ancient ways.

So much excellent material has been written on the material and spiritual "why" of vegetarianism that I will not add any more here. (I would, though, like to recommend two books: *What's Wrong with Eating Meat*, by Vistara Parham, and *Diet for a New America*, by John Robbins.)

But I do want to say a word about the quality of vegetarian food—at least what I think it should be. From the first day I became a vegetarian I have been convinced that vegetarian food should not just be healthful in a theoretical sense and eaten like medicine, but that it should be really good food—in taste and appearance. In fact, since it is better for us than nonvegetarian food, it should taste even better than nonvegetarian food. Accomplishing that is not so simple. This cookbook is a result of more than twenty years' endeavor to do so.

One of the best ways to motivate others to consider becoming vegetarian is to feed them good vegetarian food. I am glad to say that by means of the recipes in this book our monastery has done so for many years. And so can you. Every recipe in this book has been put to the ultimate test: eating!

We always eat together with those who attend our Sunday church service, so we cook several experimental dishes for the Sunday lunch. Then we vote on whether or not to pass them on to you. This way I can make sure that each recipe that goes into this book is one that produces really good food, and not just some mediocre mess that can get by merely because it does not nauseate the eaters. That may seem strong language, but I am increasingly unhappy with the low quality of the recipes that usually appear in vegan publications. Why a vegan should be subsisting on fare that would have been dished up in the Cro-Magnon era when Dad's spear missed the bison is beyond me.

When I quit eating meat the quality of my food got better—not just from the health aspect, but from the flavor aspect as well. No longer relying on a main dish of death to distract the attention of the diners from the insipidity of the vegetables, I had to get competitive with the carnivore cooks, of which I had been one. And I easily surpassed them, much to their and my surprise. Things went along quite well for years until it became evident that a vegetarian had to be just that, and dairy needed to be eliminated. The result was that we "ate better" than ever before.

So much has been written on the subject of vegetarian and vegan diet (no dairy or egg products) that there is no need to repeat it here. The proof is in the eating and in the resulting health benefits.

One last word: God did not write this cookbook. Nor can I claim to be His instrument in the writing lest that prove me to be slightly bent, if not broken. So don't think these recipes are infallible or inflexible. Feel free to use them as a basis for your own creativity. As Justin Wilson says, good cooking is a combination of imagination and common sense.

And speaking of eating: the kind and quality of the ingredients used in the recipes will have a determining effect on the flavor of a dish. So I am going to share my ideas and experience with you by commenting on some of the ingredients called for in the recipes.

Apples

We prefer to use Granny Smith apples in the recipes that call for apples. They are a bit tart, and the recipes reflect this in the amount of Sucanat (a trade name for a sweetener made by dehydrating sugar cane juice; see below) used, so you might want to experiment with cutting it down when you use other kinds of apples.

Cheese Substitutes

This book has three wonderful cheese alternatives: Yeast Cheez, Pimiento Cheez, and Notzarella Cheez. We use them frequently and find them more than satisfactory. However, some may not care to bother with making them or may want a more "melty" or "cheesy" type of ingredient. Most soy-based cheese substitutes are awful, but I can wholeheartedly recommend Soy Kass, made by Soy Kass, Inc., Atlanta, Georgia, and distributed by American Natural Snacks, St. Augustine, FL 32085. Soy Kass comes in several types: Mozzarella, Cheddar, Smoked Cheddar, Jalapeño, Garlic and Herb, and Monterey Jack. All, but the Monterey Jack, which is also fat-free, contain sodium caseinate (a derivative of milk which many vegans may not wish to use, and which those with an allergy to milk may find irritating).

There are some recipes in which the Parmesan Cheez given in this book just does not work, giving too lemony a taste to the dish. But I have just discovered a perfect Parmesan made from tofu that tastes exactly like the real thing, but has nowhere the amount of sodium. So it is a double-plus. The brand is Lite and Less made by Soyco. For information write to: Soyco Foods, 2441 Viscount Row, Orlando, FL 32809.

Flour

Most recipes in this book call for unbleached white flour. This may be surprising to some, but whole wheat flour is often simply too strong in its taste and interferes with the desired flavor. Although unbleached white flour does not contain all the nutrients of whole wheat flour, it is not devoid of food value. Bleached flour, however, is both worthless and poisonous.

Gluten Substitute

Those who have trouble with gluten can make just about all of the meat substitutes given in this book by using an equal amount of tofu that has been frozen, thawed, pressed, and cut into slices or pieces and then cooked in the flavoring broth.

Jalapeño Peppers

You will often find jalapeño peppers listed as an ingredient. If you don't like them, just leave them out. Also, keep in mind that throughout the growing season jalapeños vary in their degree of hotness, so the amount may have to be adjusted some. You may find it simpler to use cayenne pepper instead since it is consistent. But the distinctive taste of jalapeños is worth the trouble.

Kitchen Bouquet

Kitchen Bouquet has been around for many decades. I know, because as a child attracted by the name and the smell I took a gigantic swig from my "aunt" Suzy Snow's bottle! Brown lightning! It was my first introduction to flavorings that, no kidding, are supposed to be used sparingly! Only when I was a seasoned vegetarian did I overcome my trauma and agree to try it in cooking.

Kitchen Bouquet imparts a richer flavor (and color) to dishes that accommodate a beeflike flavor. While it is no substitute for UnBeef Broth (page 155) or other "beef" flavorings, it does sometimes give that added touch and body that makes a recipe just right. You can buy Kitchen Bouquet at just about any grocery store.

Lea and Perrins Steak Sauce

Many recipes need the boost that Worcestershire sauce can give, but when this cookbook was first printed the only two vegetarian versions I knew of (unnamed out of Christian charity) tasted terrible. Now I am glad to tell you that there is one source of a really good sauce: Harvest Direct, P.O. Box 4514, Decatur, IL 62525 (800/835-2867). When using Harvest Direct instead of Lea and Perrins Steak Sauce in a recipe from this book, cut the amount in half.

But I still somewhat prefer Lea and Perrins Steak Sauce (their Worcestershire sauce contains anchovies) as an excellent substitute. When you are cooking from another book and a recipe calls for Worcestershire sauce, use twice the amount of Lea and Perrins Steak Sauce, as it is not as pungent as Worcestershire.

Liquid Smoke

I recommend only Wright's Liquid Smoke, as it alone is made from all natural ingredients.

Louisiana Hot Sauce and Tabasco Sauce

When the recipe calls for Louisiana Hot Sauce, I mean the real Louisiana Hot Sauce made by Bruce Foods Corporation in New Iberia, Louisiana, not any of the imitations, all of which are poor. The purpose of this sauce is to impart both a red pepper "heat" and a good vinegary tang that brings out the other flavors in the dish. (If you are watching your salt intake, be aware that all hot pepper sauces of this type contain large amounts of salt.) Also, Louisiana Hot Sauce (the real thing, remember) does not mask any flavors, but only adds a dimension of its own.

Tabasco is of course known throughout the world, and rightly so. Tabasco, however, is much hotter than Louisiana Hot Sauce and tends to impart the heat of red pepper more than any tangy flavor. Yet there are times when that is needed in preference to the effect of Louisiana Hot Sauce. Therefore in these recipes the two are not interchangeable, but each is called for according to its characteristic effect on the dish. If you are in a pinch, however, use what you have, but remember: if the recipe calls for Louisiana Hot Sauce, use only half the amount of Tabasco; if the recipe calls for Tabasco, use twice the amount of Louisiana Hot Sauce.

Measurements

One of my pet peeves is the encountering of a recipe in which I find terms like "a large bell pepper," "a medium potato," and "a small onion," not to mention "a scant cup" or a "heaping spoon." Grrrrrrr! So I have not done this to you—unless it has slipped by me or refers to packages of frozen vegetables, raw grains, or pasta. However, this may mean that you will have a little of some ingredient left over in the measuring. Put it in. Live!

Milk Substitutes

In this book I give recipes for Soy Milk (page 96), Cashew Milk (page 93), and Almond Milk (page 93). But in the recipes you will see that I always recommend Cashew Milk. This is because I feel that soy and almond milks do not have the body or flavor I prefer in cooking. But go ahead and try the other two if Cashew Milk does not appeal to you. Try Soy Milk if you have an allergy to nuts.

For those who want an easy way, I suggest two excellent products: Vitamite and Solait. In some places Vitamite is available in the dairy sections of stores, packaged just like milk. It is the nearest thing to milk we have found and when cold, is a delicious drink. However it does contain sodium caseinate. It is made by Diehl Specialties International, 24 N. Clinton St., Defiance, OH 43512 (419/782-8219).

Solait is a soy milk powder that is beyond excellent and is also wonderful by itself when cold. It also works perfectly (as does Vitamite) in recipes that call for Cashew Milk. Solait makes by far the best soy milk we have ever tasted. It is available from Devansoy Farms, Inc., P.O. Box 885, Carroll, IA 51401 (800/747-8605).

Molasses

Barbados molasses is recommended in these recipes, unless you like the heavier taste of Blackstrap molasses. This really must be obtained from health food stores or suppliers. (Be warned: A very famous "natural" brand of "unsulphured molasses" found in regular supermarkets contains a high percentage of white sugar, but is not required to be labeled so since white sugar is considered "natural.")

Monosodium Glutamate (MSG)

Now here is something really important. A vegan friend of ours with a doctorate in chemistry provided the following information: "MSG is a flavor-enhancing food product made from gluten, usually wheat gluten. The gluten is simply hydrolized with hot, dilute hydrochloric acid, about in the same concentration as stomach acid. After digestion is complete, the gluten has been broken down into its main amino acid component, glutamic acid, whereupon the glutamic acid is simply neutralized with baking soda, filtered, and crystallized from the solution by slow evaporation.

"Monosodium glutamate is a natural food product, but a number of people react badly to it mainly because they are sensitive to wheat gluten, and while they may not react to wheat all the time, the highly soluble MSG gets into the bloodstream very rapidly and causes them problems.

"To most adults, MSG acts as a brain nutrient and actually improves brain function such as concentration and memory. However, babies are not adults and their systems usually cannot handle glutamates, and soluble glutamates may cause brain lesions in severe cases. Of course all mothers know babies should not be fed wheat products until after the first year, so they should be doubly careful of soluble wheat derivatives such as MSG.

"And all this goes without saying that for some people the sodium part must cause this food to be used somewhat sparingly." So people with MSG problems should find out if they might actually have a problem with wheat gluten itself.

Our friend who wrote us the above was intrigued as to how Asians can eat so much MSG and have no problems at all—actually be in better health than most of us in the West. His investigations revealed that even infants are not harmed by it unless they are also being fed adulterated foods. The combination with the adulterants produces an allergy that persists into adulthood and causes them to experience "Chinese restaurant syndrome." So the culprit is not MSG, but the adulteration of our food!

Our experience has carried this research one step further. When we used dairy products we, too, would sometimes get "MSG hangovers" after eating in an Asian restaurant. But after becoming vegans we never had any such reactions. In fact, we eat more Asian food than before, since we are safe. Apparently animal protein of any kind, including that from eggs and milk, is considered an adulterant by the body and causes an allergic reaction when MSG meets any residue of it in the body of the eater.

Realizing how tricky this whole matter of MSG can be, it is only listed in a recipe when the flavor desired cannot be obtained any other way. If you wish, you can substitute salt in the soups, but in a couple of the flavoring broths it is just not possible to get a satisfactory flavor without it. Even in the recipes that contain MSG, not much really goes into a serving since it is diluted in the broth that flavors the dish. And also it will usually only be in one dish at a meal.

Mushrooms: A Substitute

Those who do not care for mushrooms will find that in most recipes sliced or chopped black olives will substitute quite well.

Nondairy Margarine

Read the labels of supposedly "nondairy margarine" carefully, keeping in mind that ingredients such as sodium caseinate are really elements taken from milk.

Oil can be used if you do not have nondairy margarine or prefer not to use it.

Nonoil Cooking

Some of these recipes just will not work without some oil, but most of them will do just fine. Simply leave the oil out! But in cases where sautéeing can really enhance the flavor, use Heavenly Broth (page 158) instead of oil. Here is a table for substitutions.

1 tablespoon oil = 1/4 cup Heavenly Broth

2 tablespoons oil = 1/3 cup Heavenly Broth

3 tablespoons oil = 1/2 cup Heavenly Broth

1/4 cup oil = 2/3 cup Heavenly Broth

5 tablespoons oil = 3/4 cup Heavenly Broth

6 tablespoons oil = 1 cup Heavenly Broth

When a recipe says to fry something, broil or grill it instead.

Nutritional Yeast

First of all, nutritional yeast is not brewer's yeast. I mention this because friends of ours have wanted to try the recipes in this book and have been told at health food stores that the two yeasts are one and the same, and their culinary attempts were disasters! (Recently "Betty Crocker" assured readers in "her" column that the two were the same.) Nutritional yeast (saccharomyces cerevisiae) is a food yeast grown in a molasses solution. It gives a "cheesy" taste to food, and is the basis for the Yeast Cheez (page 97). It can be stirred into or sprinkled on many things, and is especially good in adding flavor to soups. It contains several B vitamins, including the elusive B_{12} that is so important for those who eat no dairy products.

Nutritional yeast can be obtained from a health food store or by mail from: The Farm, Summertown, TN 38483, or from the Red Star Yeast Company. There may be other sources, as well.

Oil

Once a Theravadin Buddhist monk, commenting on a rival school of Buddhism, said to me: "It is a jungle!" So is the world of "healthful eating"! More so, I expect. The question of oil—how much, if any, and what kind—is a truly vexing question. Especially since I have had the vexation of going through every recipe in this book and looking carefully at the quantities of oil prescribed!

As an Orthodox monk I have had much experience of totally oilless cooking, and am not interested. For I can say with Huck Finn: "I've done been there." However, I have tried to reduce the oil to the minimum that will still (to my palate) produce something that tastes good, yet is not (to my mind) unhealthful. Some "ethnic" dishes, such as Indian, demand oiliness—otherwise they are just not the dish. But I have done what I could without violating their basic nature.

There is also quite a good chance that I have managed to skip or overlook a recipe. If so, cut down the oil and forgive me (and if you would let me know about it I would be most appreciative.) But believe me, I have gone through the jungle of this book with an oil-hacking machete and done my best.

Olive oil is an excellent food. It is the only monosaturate among oils, and has been found to actively remove cholesterol deposits from arteries. It is best used raw as in salad dressings, and in cooked dishes where its distinctive flavor is desired.

Corn oil is excellent in cooking, since it loses very little of its nutritional value from the heat. Mazola is the best brand beyond a doubt.

Onions

Onions, despite some medicinal elements, do contain some toxins that can affect the heart action. This is why the yogis of India avoid them. Red onions, however, contain the least of these elements and are also easier to digest, so I recommend that you try them. However, you can use any type of onion you prefer in the recipes. Chives, leeks, scallions, or shallots are good substitutes for onions.

Recipe Comments

Under the headings of many recipes I have made comments about the dish. This is because I am aware how easy it is to pass up a really good dish simply because it does not sound interesting. But please do not think that those without comments are not as good as those with them—they are! Sometimes I just could not think of anything clever to say about them. Often I have been tempted to put, "Please try this! Please!" under many headings, because I know how much you will like it if you do.

Red Pepper Flakes

When the ingredients list says "red pepper flakes" I mean crushed hot red pepper flakes, not red bell pepper flakes.

Rice

Whenever a recipe in this book calls for rice, natural white rice is intended, not the white rice usually found in grocery stores, which has neither fragrance nor taste. True natural rice has a definite fragrance and a distinct, though delicate, taste. The best sources for rice are Indian or Asian grocery stores. The best rice from India is basmati rice, but my favorite is jasmine rice from Thailand. "Jasmine" is a type of rice, not a brand name, and don't be disturbed if the bag says the rice is "scented." The producers (whose English is not the best) only mean that it smells good when cooked. Also be assured that the rice does not smell or taste like jasmine—a pretty awful idea.

If you have no Indian or Asian stores in your town from which to obtain good quality rice, there are quite a few Asian food companies that will sell to you through the mail. Asain cookbooks often list such companies, or your local library should be able to help you locate them.

Those who prefer brown rice can substitute it, but they should keep in mind that cooking time will need to be adjusted since brown rice takes about four times longer to cook. This is because brown rice is really white rice that has been steamed in the husk before its removal. This causes some of the nutrients and color from the husk to enter the grain. But when the partially cooked grain dries out it becomes very hard, much like what occurs when beans are dried, so longer cooking time is needed.

Salt

Sea salt is always recommended in these recipes because it is more easily assimilated by the body.

Sovex and Vegex

Sovex and Vegex are the brand names for a dark, saltish paste that is a yeast extract used for flavoring. Some large grocery stores carry it in the section where they have bouillon cubes, but usually it must be bought from health food stores.

Soy Sauce

In the recipes calling for soy sauce I prefer to use low-sodium soy sauce, for not only is it better for us (it has been estimated that in the "normal" American diet we eat twenty to thirty times more salt than we need), but also I find that the low-sodium soy sauce has a stronger-bodied and better flavor. If possible, a naturally brewed sauce should be used rather than the "common garden variety" brands we grew up with.

Angostura Low Sodium Soy Sauce is lower in sodium than any others I know of, and the flavor is incomparably better. Also, some other brands are much less flavorful, so the amount will have to be increased in the recipe to get the desired taste. However, this will increase the overall amount of sodium. So get Angostura if you can.

Not all soy sauces, low-sodium or regular, are equal in strength, so you may need to adjust the amounts used according to the brand, which can vary from batch to batch.

Spices

Spices and herbs are important ingredients in cooking, both for flavor and for health. But not all brands are the same in quality. I recommend that you use the excellent products produced by the Watkins company. They have been around for generations and deserve their fine reputation. We have found no other poultry seasoning that "delivers" like theirs—especially in making UnChicken (page 137) and UnChicken Broth (page 155). So many of their products are good that I can't list them all. (Be aware, though, that not everything made by Watkins is animal-free.)

Sweeteners (Sucanat)

The latest, and best, word on sweeteners is a product called "granulated sugar cane juice," which, despite the odd name, is actually a sweetener made by dehydrating sugar cane juice. Completely unrefined, the resulting powder contains all the nutrients of the sugar cane juice with none of the negative qualities of refined sugar. The brand I am familiar with and use is Sucanat, which is produced by Nutra-Cane, 58 Meadowbrook Pkwy., Milford, NH 03055 (603/672-2801). In the Etc. chapter I give the formula for making Powdered Sucanat (page 340) when powdered sugar is needed in a recipe.

Since Sucanat can give a "brown sugar" taste to recipes, you might want to try a couple of alternatives that are, however, not as healthful. One is turbinado sugar that is not as refined as white sugar, and is filtered through wood charcoal, not bone char. The other is palm sugar, which, as its name indicates, comes from the sap of the palm tree. It usually comes in a soft but solid form (sometimes not so soft!) that looks like crystallized honey. Turbinado can be found at health food stores, and palm sugar from either health food or Asian stores.

Tahini

Tahini is a paste made from sesame seeds. It has a "smoky" or "bacon" taste that adds much to recipes. You can buy it in health food and import grocery stores.

Tomatoes

Our ancestors thought tomatoes were deadly poison. They were mistaken, but tomatoes do contain some elements that are toxic to a degree. It has been my experience that these elements are not in Italian (sometimes called roma or plum) tomatoes, and that Italian tomatoes are better in flavor when cooked. Nor are they as acidic as other tomatoes. As with the onions, if you prefer or do not have Italian tomatoes, simply use whatever is available.

Vitamin B_{12}

There is far more misinformation than fact being given out regarding Vitamin B_{12}, and as vegans it is important that we get the facts straight.

Vitamin B_{12} is not available from vegetable sources, but is made only by bacteria. Those who ingest animal proteins get the vitamin that way. Do not be misled by the fear propaganda from the carnivores. The truth is, most cases of severe vitamin B_{12} deficiency develop in nonvegetarians. But we vegans are the ones who get pointed at.

How to get Vitamin B_{12}? Well, have you heard the old adage "eat dirt"? That's pretty good advice in this case. People with their own gardens used to get plenty of ? from the dirt that was on the vegetables they ate. Go out, pull up a radish or carrot (from an organic garden, please), knock off the more obvious dirt, and eat it. You will get plenty of B_{12}, or would have, in a normal ecology. Fermented soy foods at one time supplied plenty of B_{12}, but there, too, it was the dirt involved. Now that governments have imposed stringent sanitation measures in their manufacture they no longer contain the vitamin to any significant degree. Cleanliness is obviously not always next to healthiness.

What to do, then? We do two things. First, nutritional yeast is always on the table, and we sprinkle it generously on our food (if it is not already in the dish). Here, too, because of sanitation, the yeast can vary from batch to batch in its B_{12} content. But if you eat a lot you will surely manage. The second thing we do is take a vitamin supplement three times a week. We prefer MEGA B-150 made by Nature's Plus. We suspect that the nutritional yeast alone would do, but prefer to be sure.

If you want more information on vitamin B_{12}, Dr. Michael Klaper's books *Vegan Nutrition: Pure and Simple* and *Pregnancy, Children, and the Vegan Diet* give the whole and true picture.

Zatarain's Crab Boil

"Crab Boil" is a mixture of spices put in the water used to boil crab or shrimp in Louisiana creole and Cajun cooking. While it is not absolutely necessary to have it in making UnShrimp (page 150) according to the recipe given in the UnSeafood chapter, I greatly recommend it.

There are several brands of Crab Boil available in supermarkets, but I have found that Zatarain's is by far the best, and more than a century of satisfied users agree with me. If you cannot find it in a local store, call Zatarain's at 504/367-2950 and ask where it might be sold near you. If there is no store nearby that stocks it, don't worry—Zatarain's will sell it to you directly through the mail (UPS, actually) by the case. That may seem like a lot to buy, but when you taste "shrimp" made with it, it won't take long to use it up. Or you can split a case with friends.

Zatarain's sells three forms of Crab Boil: dry (whole spices in a bag), liquid, and preseasoned (powdered in a box). I recommend the dry whole spices in the bag.

Salad Dressings

Alfalfa Sprout Dressing

½ cup alfalfa sprouts
2 teaspoons celery seed
2 tablespoons olive oil
2 tablespoons water
⅓ cup lemon juice or white vinegar
½ teaspoon soy sauce
1 teaspoon onion powder, or 1 tablespoon scallion, shallot, or leek
1 tablespoon sesame seeds

Mix well by hand, or blend in a blender, according to your taste.

Almond Dressing

¼ cup almonds
¼ teaspoon garlic powder
½ teaspoon sea salt
½ cup chopped tomato
2 tablespoons lemon juice or white vinegar
3 tablespoons olive oil

Mix well by hand, or blend in a blender, according to your taste.

Avocado-Cashew Dressing

½ cup raw cashews
1½ cups hot water
2 ripe avocados, peeled and pitted
2 teaspoons lemon juice or white vinegar
¼ cup chopped onion
½ teaspoon sea salt

Blend cashews and hot water until smooth. Add remaining ingredients and continue to blend. Cool before using.

Avocado Dressing 1

1 ripe avocado, peeled, pitted, and cut into chunks
1 tomato, chopped
¼ teaspoon sea salt
2 tablespoons lemon juice
¼ cup chopped onion
1 tablespoon nutritional yeast
1 tablespoon olive oil

Mix well by hand, or blend in a blender, according to your taste.

VARIATION: *Add ⅔ cup Tofu Mayonnaise (page 22), Cashew Mayonnaise (page 12), or Miraculous Whip (page 17).*

Avocado Dressing 2

1/2 teaspoon garlic powder
1/2 ripe avocado, peeled and pitted
2 tablespoons lemon juice
1/4 cup Tofu Mayonnaise (page 22), Cashew Mayonnaise (page 12), or Miraculous Whip (page 17)

Mix well by hand, or blend in a blender, according to your taste.

VARIATION: *Add 1/4 teaspoon dill.*

Avocado Dressing 3

This does not keep well. Use up at one meal, if possible.

4 ripe avocados, peeled, pitted, and mashed
1 tablespoon olive oil
1 1/2 tablespoons soy sauce
1/4 teaspoon onion powder
1/4 teaspoon oregano
1/4 teaspoon basil
1/4 teaspoon garlic powder
1/4 teaspoon sea salt

Mix well by hand, or blend in a blender, according to your taste.

Avocado Dressing 4

3 ripe avocados, peeled, pitted, and mashed
1 cup Cashew Sour Kreem (page 94) or Tofu Sour Kreem (page 97)
1 teaspoon sea salt
2 tablespoons lemon or lime juice

Mix well by hand, or blend in a blender, according to your taste.

Avocado Dressing 5

2 ripe avocados, peeled, pitted, and mashed
1 1/3 cup Cashew Sour Kreem (page 94) or Tofu Sour Kreem (page 97)
1 teaspoon sea salt
1/2 teaspoon chives
1/8 teaspoon onion powder
4 teaspoons lemon juice or white vinegar

Mix well by hand, or blend in a blender, according to your taste.

Avocado Dressing 6

1 ripe avocado, peeled, pitted, and mashed
1 tablespoon lemon juice or white vinegar
2 tablespoons minced onion
2 tablespoons chopped bell pepper or pimiento
1/2 teaspoon sea salt
2 tablespoons Cashew Sour Kreem (page 94) or Tofu Sour Kreem (page 97)
1/4 teaspoon dill

Mix well by hand, or blend in a blender, according to your taste.

Avocado-Olive Dressing

1 ripe avocado, peeled, pitted, and mashed
1/4 cup ripe olives, sliced or chopped
1 cup Cashew Mayonnaise (page 12) or Tofu Mayonnaise (page 22), Miraculous Whip (page 17), or Cashew Sour Kreem (page 94) or Tofu Sour Kreem (page 97)

Mix well by hand, or blend in a blender, according to your taste.

Avocado Mayonnaise

1/4 cup peeled, pitted, and mashed ripe avocado
1 1/2 teaspoons lemon juice or white vinegar
1 tablespoon corn oil

Mix well by hand, or blend in a blender, according to your taste.

Simple Avocado Dressing

Mash avocado(s) and gradually add lemon juice (or white vinegar, or tomato juice), beating until it is creamy. Mix well by hand, or blend in a blender, according to your taste.

Bitters Dressing

3/4 cup lime juice
3 tablespoons olive oil
1/4 teaspoon garlic powder
1 1/2 teaspoons sea salt
1 teaspoon aromatic bitters

Mix well by hand, or blend in a blender, according to your taste.

Caper French Dressing

1 cup French Dressing (page 14)
1/3 cup capers, minced

Mix well by hand, or blend in a blender, according to your taste.

Caraway Dressing

1/3 cup Cashew Mayonnaise (see below) or Tofu Mayonnaise (page 22), Miraculous Whip (page 17), or Cashew Sour Kreem (page 94) or Tofu Sour Kreem (page 97)
3/4 teaspoon caraway seeds
1 tablespoon sesame seeds
1 1/2 teaspoons lemon juice or white vinegar
1/4 teaspoon sea salt
1/4 teaspoon paprika

Mix well by hand, or blend in a blender, according to your taste.

Carrot Dressing

4 medium carrots, grated
2 tablespoons olive oil
1/2 teaspoon garlic powder
1/2 teaspoon onion powder
1 cup water
1 tablespoon soy sauce
2 tablespoons tahini or nut butter

Mix well by hand or blend in a blender, according to your taste.

Cashew Cheez Dressing

Superb!

3/4 cup cashews
1/2 cup water
3/4 teaspoon sea salt
3/4 teaspoon onion powder
2 tablespoons lemon juice or white vinegar
1/4 cup canned pimientos
4 1/2 teaspoons olive oil

Put the nuts in a blender (Vita-Mix is best) and grind them as fine as possible. Add the rest of the ingredients and continue blending until everything is smooth, about 1 minute.

VARIATION: *Add 3 tablespoons of nutritional yeast.*

Cashew Mayonnaise

2 cups water
6 tablespoons cornstarch or arrowroot powder
2 cups hot water
2 cups cashews
1/3 cup lemon juice or white vinegar
1 teaspoon garlic powder
2 teaspoons onion powder
1 tablespoon sea salt
1 tablespoon Sucanat
1/8 teaspoon paprika

Mix the 2 cups of water with the cornstarch or arrowroot and boil until it thickens. Set aside to cool slightly. Blend the 2 cups hot water and cashews well. Add the rest of the ingredients to the cashew liquid. Add this to the cornstarch mixture and combine thoroughly. Cool before using.

Chive Dressing

2/3 cup French Dressing (page 14)
1/4 cup chopped fresh chives

Mix well by hand, or blend in a blender, according to your taste.

VARIATION: *Add 1/4 cup Cashew Mayonnaise (see above) or Tofu Mayonnaise (page 22), Miraculous Whip (page 17), or Cashew Sour Kreem (page 94) or Tofu Sour Kreem (page 97).*

Kreem French Dressing

When French Dressing 1 is used, this is marvelous—good enough to eat by the spoonful.

½ cup French Dressing 1 (page 14)
¼ cup Cashew Mayonnaise (page 12) or Tofu Mayonnaise (page 22), Miraculous Whip (page 17), or Cashew Sour Kreem (page 94) or Tofu Sour Kreem (page 97)

Mix well by hand, or blend in a blender, according to your taste.

Crunchy Kreem Dressing

½ cup finely chopped cucumber
2 tablespoons finely chopped bell pepper
2 tablespoons finely chopped fresh chives
2 tablespoons thinly sliced radishes
1 cup Cashew Sour Kreem (page 94) or Tofu Sour Kreem (page 97)
½ teaspoon sea salt
¼ teaspoon paprika

Mix well by hand, or blend in a blender, according to your taste.

VARIATION: *Add 1 or 2 teaspoons of soy sauce.*

Cucumber Dressing

1 cup chopped cucumber
½ teaspoon sea salt
1 tablespoon lemon juice
1 tablespoon fresh dill, minced, or 1 teaspoon dried
1 cup Cashew Mayonnaise (page 12) or Tofu Mayonnaise (page 22), Miraculous Whip (page 17), or Cashew Sour Kreem (page 94) or Tofu Sour Kreem (page 97)

Mix well by hand, or blend in a blender, according to your taste.

VARIATION: *Add 2 or 3 tablespoons of finely chopped onion.*

Curry Mayonnaise

1½ cups Cashew Mayonnaise (page 12) or Tofu Mayonnaise (page 22), or Miraculous Whip (page 17)
1½ teaspoons curry powder

Mix well by hand, or blend in a blender, according to your taste.

Dill Dressing

Outstanding!

¾ cup tofu, mashed
2 tablespoons corn oil
2 tablespoons wine vinegar
½ teaspoon sea salt
1 teaspoon Sucanat
1 teaspoon dill
⅛ teaspoon freshly ground black pepper
1 tablespoon minced onion

Blend in a blender until smooth and creamy.

Dried Bean Dressing

Unusual, but equally tasty.

1 cup dried beans, cooked
2 tablespoons minced onion
1 cup UnBeef Broth (page 155)
1 teaspoon garlic powder
½ teaspoon oregano
½ teaspoon basil
½ teaspoon paprika

Mix well by hand, or blend in a blender, according to your taste.

French Dressing 1

3 tablespoons olive oil
3 tablespoons corn oil
2 tablespoons water
3 tablespoons lemon juice
1/2 teaspoon sea salt
1/4 cup cashews
1/2 teaspoon paprika
1/4 teaspoon garlic powder
1/2 teaspoon onion powder
1/4 teaspoon dill
1/4 teaspoon basil

Mix well by hand, or blend in a blender, according to your taste.

French Dressing 2

1/3 cup corn oil
2 tablespoons vinegar
2 tablespoons lemon juice
2 teaspoons Sucanat
1/2 teaspoon sea salt
1/2 teaspoon dried mustard
1/2 teaspoon paprika

Mix well by hand, or blend in a blender, according to your taste.

French Dressing 3

1 1/2 cups chopped tomato
1/2 cup tahini
1/8 cup soy sauce
1/4 teaspoon oregano
1/4 teaspoon garlic powder
1/4 teaspoon parsley
1/4 teaspoon sea salt
1/4 teaspoon basil

Mix well by hand, or blend in a blender, according to your taste.

Fresh Herb Dressing

1 tablespoon minced garlic
1/2 cup chopped fresh herbs, such as chives or green onions, basil or oregano, spearmint or peppermint
2/3 cup corn oil
1/3 cup lemon juice
2 tablespoons soy sauce
1/4 teaspoon sea salt

Put everything in a blender and blend for 10 to 15 seconds.

Fresh Tomato Dressing

1 1/2 cups Tahini/Oil Dressing (page 21)
3/4 cup chopped tomato
2 tablespoons chopped bell pepper
3 tablespoons chopped black olives
2 tablespoons minced onion

Mix well by hand, or blend in a blender, according to your taste.

Fresh Vegetable Dressing

1 cup pureed fresh tomatoes
1/4 cup chopped spinach or other greens
2 tablespoons chopped squash
2 tablespoons minced bean sprouts

Mix well by hand, or blend in a blender, according to your taste.

Garlic Dressing

1 cup tofu, mashed
2 tablespoons corn oil
2 tablespoons lemon juice
1/2 teaspoon Sucanat
3/4 teaspoon sea salt
2 teaspoons minced garlic

Blend in a blender until smooth and creamy.

Garlic and Dill Dressing

1/4 cup red wine vinegar
3 tablespoons water
1 teaspoon Sucanat
3 tablespoons olive oil
1/8 teaspoon garlic powder
2 tablespoons chopped fresh parsley
2 tablespoons chopped chives
2 tablespoons Parmesan Cheez (page 94)

½ teaspoon dill
½ teaspoon sea salt
⅛ teaspoon freshly ground black pepper

Put all ingredients in a glass jar with a tight-fitting lid and shake until blended. Refrigerate.

Green Dressing 1

1½ cups Tahini/Oil Dressing (page 21)
2 tablespoons chopped bell pepper
¼ cup chopped spinach or bok choy
1 tablespoon parsley

Mix well by hand, or blend in a blender, according to your taste.

Green Dressing 2

¼ cup finely chopped bell pepper
¼ cup finely chopped fresh parsley
2 tablespoons finely chopped celery
1 tablespoon finely chopped onion
1 tablespoon finely chopped pimiento
1 tablespoon capers, finely chopped
½ teaspoon sea salt
⅛ teaspoon basil
2 tablespoons olive oil

Mix well by hand, or blend in a blender, according to your taste.

Green Gazpacho Dressing

2 tablespoons chopped onion
1 teaspoon garlic powder
¼ cup chopped bell pepper
1 tablespoon chopped fresh basil, or ¾ teaspoon dried
2 teaspoons chopped fresh parsley
1 cup quartered tomato
3 tablespoons lemon juice or white vinegar
2 tablespoons olive oil
½ teaspoon sea salt

Mix well by hand, or blend in a blender, according to your taste.

Green Goddess Dressing

For those who love both flavor and tang!

1 cup Cashew Mayonnaise (page 12) or Tofu Mayonnaise (page 22), Miraculous Whip (page 17), or Cashew Sour Kreem (page 94) or Tofu Sour Kreem (page 97)
2 tablespoons corn oil
½ tablespoon chives
½ cup chopped fresh parsley
2 tablespoons tarragon vinegar
1 teaspoon onion powder
⅛ teaspoon freshly ground black pepper
⅛ teaspoon garlic powder
½ teaspoon sea salt

Put all in a blender and blend until smooth and creamy.

Green Onion Salad Dressing

1 bunch green onions, ends and dark tops removed, sliced as thin as possible
2¼ teaspoons chopped garlic
3 tablespoons lemon juice
1 teaspoon sea salt
½ teaspoon freshly ground black pepper
¾ cup Tofu Yogurt (page 97)

Put everything in a blender and puree until very smooth. Chill thoroughly.

Herb Dressing 1

3 tablespoons olive oil
2 tablespoons lemon or lime juice
½ teaspoon chervil
½ teaspoon thyme
½ teaspoon oregano
½ teaspoon savory
¼ teaspoon coriander
⅛ teaspoon sage
½ teaspoon sea salt
1 tablespoon Cashew Sour Kreem (page 94) or Tofu Sour Kreem (page 97)

Mix well by hand, or blend in a blender, according to your taste.

Herb Dressing 2

¼ cup finely chopped celery
3 tablespoons finely chopped onion
2 tablespoons chopped fresh parsley
½ teaspoon sea salt
1 teaspoon paprika
¼ teaspoon basil
⅛ teaspoon marjoram or rosemary
⅔ cup olive oil
⅔ cup lemon juice or white vinegar

Mix well by hand, or blend in a blender, according to your taste.

Herb Mayonnaise Dressing

1½ cups Cashew Mayonnaise (page 12) or Tofu Mayonnaise (page 22), or Miraculous Whip (page 17)
¼ teaspoon paprika
1 teaspoon herbs
¼ teaspoon onion powder
⅛ teaspoon curry powder

Mix well by hand, or blend in a blender, according to your taste.

Hot Cheez and Cider Dressing

Something special!

½ cup apple cider
1 cup Yeast Cheez (page 97) or Pimiento Cheez (page 94)
½ teaspoon sea salt
⅛ teaspoon cayenne pepper
¼ teaspoon finely chopped fresh parsley or chives
Pinch garlic salt

Heat the cider to the boiling point, then reduce to a simmer. Stir the Cheez gradually into the cider until well blended. Add the seasonings.

Hummus Dressing

An excellent way to boost protein when eating salad. Tastes good, too!

1⅓ cups dried garbanzo beans
2 tablespoons olive oil
1 tablespoon sea salt
1 tablespoon minced garlic
¼ cup lemon juice or white vinegar
1 cup tahini

Pressure-cook the garbanzos, drain and mash them, reserving garbanzo water. Add the remaining ingredients except the garbanzo water to the mashed garbanzos. Using the garbanzo water, blend everything in a blender until smooth and of the consistency of a medium-thick sauce.

Italian Dressing 1

½ cup olive oil
½ cup white vinegar or lemon juice
½ teaspoon sea salt
¼ teaspoon celery seed
¼ teaspoon basil
¼ teaspoon oregano
¼ teaspoon onion powder
⅛ teaspoon garlic powder

Mix well by hand, or blend in a blender, according to your taste.

Italian Dressing 2

½ cup olive oil
½ cup white vinegar or lemon juice
½ teaspoon sea salt
¼ teaspoon basil
¼ teaspoon oregano
2 tablespoons minced onion

Mix well by hand, or blend in a blender, according to your taste.

Lemon Dressing

1 teaspoon sea salt
⅛ teaspoon freshly ground black pepper
Pinch cayenne pepper
¼ teaspoon paprika
1½ tablespoons lemon juice
3 tablespoons olive oil
1 tablespoon finely chopped pimiento
1 tablespoon finely chopped cucumber
¾ tablespoons finely chopped bell pepper
½ tablespoon finely chopped fresh parsley
¼ cup finely chopped onion

Combine first four ingredients. Slowly add the lemon juice and olive oil and beat thoroughly. Add remaining ingredients and mix well by hand, or blend in a blender, according to your taste.

Lemon Garlic Dressing

1/3 cup olive oil
6 tablespoons lemon juice
2 tablespoons red wine vinegar
1/3 cup finely chopped green onions
2 tablespoons chopped fresh parsley
1 tablespoon minced garlic
1 teaspoon Dijon-style mustard
1/4 teaspoon sea salt
1/8 teaspoon freshly ground black pepper

Combine all ingredients in a jar with a tight lid. Shake vigorously until the mixture is blended. Store in the refrigerator.

Lorenzo Dressing

1 cup French Dressing (page 14)
1/4 cup Tomato Relish (page 295), semiliquefied
1/4 cup chopped fresh parsley

Mix well by hand, or blend in a blender, according to your taste.

Marinade Dressing

2 tablespoons olive oil
1/4 cup lemon juice or white vinegar
1/2 cup water
2 teaspoons soy sauce
3 tablespoons nutritional yeast
2 tablespoons tahini
1/4 teaspoon onion powder
1/4 teaspoon garlic powder
1/2 teaspoon sea salt

Mix well by hand, or blend in a blender, according to your taste.

Mayonnaise Dressing

1 cup Cashew Mayonnaise (page 12) or Tofu Mayonnaise (page 22), or Miraculous Whip (see below)
1 tablespoon chopped cucumber
1 tablespoon chopped pimiento
1 tablespoon chopped bell pepper
1 tablespoon chopped fresh parsley
2 tablespoons chopped black olives
2 tablespoons chopped onion
Sea salt to taste

Mix well by hand, or blend in a blender, according to your taste.

Mexican Tomato Dressing

1 cup chopped tomato
2 tablespoons minced onion
2 tablespoons lemon juice or white vinegar
2 tablespoons olive oil
1 teaspoon cayenne pepper
1 teaspoon nutritional yeast

Mix well by hand, or blend in a blender, according to your taste.

Mexican Tomato Vinaigrette

1/2 tablespoon tomato paste
2 tablespoons minced onion
1 tablespoon lemon juice or white vinegar
2 tablespoons olive oil
1/2 teaspoon chili powder

Mix well by hand, or blend in a blender, according to your taste.

Miraculous Whip

Tastes as much like the real thing as the real thing itself!

1 1/2 cups firm tofu
3 tablespoons corn oil
1 tablespoon apple cider vinegar
1/2 cup water
1 1/2 teaspoons prepared yellow mustard
1 teaspoon minced garlic
1/4 cup minced onion
1/4 teaspoon white pepper
1 1/4 teaspoons sea salt
1 tablespoon lemon juice or white vinegar
1 tablespoon cashew nuts, ground fine

Put everything in a blender and blend until completely smooth. Refrigerate.

VARIATION: *For dishes such as fruit salads in which you do not want the flavors of onion, garlic, and mustard, leave them out.*

Nut Butter Dressing 1

½ cup nut butter
1 cup water
1 tablespoon lemon juice or white vinegar
¼ teaspoon sea salt

Mix well by hand, or blend in a blender, according to your taste.

VARIATION: *Add ¼ cup of Tofu Mayonnaise (page 22), Cashew Mayonnaise (page 12), Miraculous Whip (page 17), or Cashew Sour Kreem (page 94).*

Nut Butter Dressing 2

¼ cup nut butter
¼ cup Cashew Sour Kreem (page 94) or Tofu Sour Kreem (page 97)
1 teaspoon lemon juice or white vinegar
¼ teaspoon basil or parsley

Mix well by hand, or blend in a blender, according to your taste.

Nut Butter Dressing 3

¼ cup nut butter
2 tablespoons corn oil
2 tablespoons lemon juice or white vinegar
2 tablespoons water
½ teaspoon sea salt
⅛ teaspoon paprika

Mix well by hand, or blend in a blender, according to your taste.

Nut Butter Dressing 4

¼ cup nut butter
⅓ cup tomato juice
2 tablespoons corn oil
¼ teaspoon sea salt

Mix well by hand, or blend in a blender, according to your taste.

Nutritional Yeast Dressing

½ cup nutritional yeast
2 tablespoons corn oil
½ cup UnBeef Broth (page 155)
½ teaspoon onion powder
½ teaspoon garlic powder
¼ teaspoon basil
¼ teaspoon oregano
¼ teaspoon paprika

Mix well by hand, or blend in a blender, according to your taste.

Oil and Lemon Juice Dressing

½ cup lemon juice
½ cup olive oil
¼ teaspoon sea salt

Mix well by hand, or blend in a blender, according to your taste.

Oil and Vinegar Dressing

½ cup olive oil
¼ cup red wine vinegar
1 clove garlic, peeled and minced
¼ teaspoon basil
1 teaspoon Sucanat
1 teaspoon Dijon-style mustard
½ teaspoon sea salt
¼ teaspoon freshly ground black pepper

Combine all ingredients in a jar with a tight lid. Shake vigorously until the mixture is blended. Store in the refrigerator.

Old-Fashioned Boiled Dressing

1 tablespoon nondairy margarine
2 tablespoons unbleached white flour
1 cup Cashew Milk (page 93)
1 teaspoon dried mustard
⅛ teaspoon cayenne pepper
¼ cup cider vinegar

Heat the margarine in a saucepan until it melts. Sprinkle in the flour, stirring carefully until it is smoothly blended with the margarine. Add the Cashew Milk, 1/4 cup at a time, stirring briskly to avoid lumping. Stir in the mustard and cayenne pepper. Let the sauce bubble gently until it is thick, 8 to 10 minutes. Slowly stir in the vinegar and bring the mixture to a gentle boil. Let the dressing cool before using.

Olive Dressing

3/4 cup French Dressing (page 14)
1/4 cup chopped ripe olives

Mix well by hand, or blend in a blender, according to your taste.

Oregano-Mint Dressing

3 tablespoons olive oil
1/4 cup lemon juice or white vinegar
1/4 teaspoon chopped fresh mint
1/4 teaspoon oregano
1/3 cup Cashew Mayonnaise (page 12) or Tofu Mayonnaise (page 22), Miraculous Whip (page 17), or Cashew Sour Kreem (page 94) or Tofu Sour Kreem (page 97)

Mix well by hand, or blend in a blender, according to your taste.

Parsley Dressing

2 tablespoons olive oil
2 tablespoons lemon juice or white vinegar
1/4 teaspoon sea salt
1/4 teaspoon onion powder
2 tablespoons chopped fresh parsley

Mix well by hand, or blend in a blender, according to your taste.

Potato Dressing 1

1/2 cup French Dressing (page 14)
1/3 cup baked and mashed potato

Mix well by hand, or blend in a blender, according to your taste.

Potato Dressing 2

1 cup Cashew Sour Kreem (page 94) or Tofu Sour Kreem (page 97)
1 cup baked and mashed potato
2 tablespoons minced onion

Mix well by hand, or blend in a blender, according to your taste.

Potato Dressing 3

1/2 cup chopped onion
5 cups mashed potato
1 1/2 cups flavoring broth of choice (see Flavoring Broths chapter), or water from cooking the potatoes
3 tablespoons olive oil
2 tablespoons lemon juice or white vinegar

Mix well by hand, or blend in a blender, according to your taste.

VARIATION: *Use 4 teaspoons of garlic powder instead of onion. Add 1/2 to 1 cup of chopped ripe olives.*

Potato Mayonnaise

1 cup Cashew Mayonnaise (page 12) or Tofu Mayonnaise (page 22), or Miraculous Whip (page 17)
1 cup baked and mashed potato

Mix well by hand, or blend in a blender, according to your taste.

Russian Dressing 1

1 cup Cashew Mayonnaise (page 12) or Tofu Mayonnaise (page 22), Miraculous Whip (page 17), or Cashew Sour Kreem (page 94) or Tofu Sour Kreem (page 97)
2 tablespoons finely chopped bell pepper
2 tablespoons finely chopped celery
2 tablespoons finely chopped black olives
1 tablespoon finely chopped pimiento
1/4 cup Tomato Relish (page 295)

Mix well by hand, or blend in a blender, according to your taste.

Russian Dressing 2

1 cup chopped tomato
2 tablespoons olive oil
1 tablespoon lemon juice or white vinegar
2 tablespoons finely minced onion
½ teaspoon sea salt
1 teaspoon paprika
1 teaspoon garlic powder

Mix well by hand, or blend in a blender, according to your taste.

Sour Kreem Dressing 1

½ cup Cashew Sour Kreem (page 94) or Tofu Sour Kreem (page 97)
3 tablespoons corn oil
½ cup wine vinegar
2 tablespoons Sucanat
½ teaspoon sea salt
2 tablespoons minced onion

Mix well by hand, or blend in a blender, according to your taste.

Sour Kreem Dressing 2

1 cup Cashew Sour Kreem (page 94) or Tofu Sour Kreem (page 97)
1 tablespoon chopped pimiento
1 tablespoon chopped bell pepper
1 tablespoon chopped fresh parsley
2 tablespoons lemon juice or white vinegar
2 tablespoons chopped black olives
2 tablespoons minced onion
Sea salt to taste

Mix well by hand, or blend in a blender, according to your taste.

Sweet Basil Dressing

1 cup hot water
½ cup cashews
¼ cup chopped onion
½ teaspoon sea salt
1 teaspoon basil
2 tablespoons lemon juice or white vinegar
¼ cup minced black olives

Blend well in a blender.

Tahini Dressing 1

3 tablespoons tahini
3 tablespoons UnChicken Broth (page 155) or UnBeef Broth (page 155), or soy sauce

Mix well by hand, or blend in a blender, according to your taste.

Tahini Dressing 2

¼ cup tahini
2 tablespoons lemon juice or white vinegar
2 tablespoons olive oil
¼ cup UnBeef Broth (page 155)
⅛ teaspoon sea salt
1 tablespoon chopped fresh parsley

Mix well by hand, or blend in a blender, according to your taste.

Tahini Dressing 3

¼ cup finely chopped celery
½ cup tahini
1 tablespoon lemon juice or white vinegar
Water, if needed, to thin the dressing

Mix well by hand, or blend in a blender, according to your taste.

Tahini Dressing 4

1 teaspoon garlic powder
1 cup tahini
¾ cup water
¼ cup lemon juice or white vinegar
1 teaspoon sea salt

Mix well by hand, or blend in a blender, according to your taste.

Tahini Dressing 5

½ cup tahini
⅔ cup water
1 tablespoon soy sauce
¼ teaspoon garlic powder
⅓ teaspoon paprika
⅛ teaspoon basil
⅛ teaspoon oregano
1 teaspoon onion powder

Mix well by hand, or blend in a blender, according to your taste.

Tahini Dressing 6

1 cup tahini
1 cup water
1 teaspoon sea salt
2 tablespoons finely chopped onion
1/4 cup lemon juice or white vinegar
1/4 teaspoon basil
1/4 teaspoon oregano

Mix well by hand, or blend in a blender, according to your taste.

Tahini/Oil Dressing

2 cups tahini or olive oil
1 teaspoon sea salt
3 tablespoons chopped onion
1/4 cup chopped black olives
1/8 teaspoon cayenne pepper
2 tablespoons finely chopped bell pepper
1 tablespoon lemon juice or white vinegar
1/2 teaspoon basil
1/2 teaspoon oregano
1 1/2 cups water

Mix well by hand, or blend in a blender, according to your taste.

Tartar Dressing

1 cup Cashew Mayonnaise (page 12) or Tofu Mayonnaise (page 22), Miraculous Whip (page 17), or Cashew Sour Kreem (page 94) or Tofu Sour Kreem (page 97)
2 tablespoons finely chopped ripe olives
1 tablespoon finely chopped cucumber
1 tablespoon finely chopped pimiento
1 tablespoon finely chopped bell pepper
2 tablespoons finely chopped onion
1 tablespoon finely chopped fresh parsley
1/4 teaspoon sea salt

Mix well by hand, or blend in a blender, according to your taste.

VARIATIONS: *Add 1 tablespoon of capers, chopped very fine. Add 2 tablespoons of lemon juice or white vinegar.*

Thousand Island Dressing 1

3 cups Cashew Mayonnaise (page 12) or Tofu Mayonnaise (page 22), Miraculous Whip (page 17), or Cashew Sour Kreem (page 94) or Tofu Sour Kreem (page 97)
1/2 cup catsup or Tomato Relish (page 295), liquefied
1/4 cup finely chopped bell pepper
4 teaspoons chopped pimiento
2 tablespoons minced onion
2 tablespoons minced black olives

Mix well by hand, or blend in a blender, according to your taste.

Thousand Island Dressing 2

1 cup French Dressing (page 14)
2 tablespoons chopped bell pepper
3 tablespoons chopped pimiento
2 tablespoons chopped black olives
1/2 teaspoon soy sauce

Mix well by hand, or blend in a blender, according to your taste.

Thousand Island Dressing 3

1 cup Cashew Mayonnaise (page 12) or Tofu Mayonnaise (page 22), or Miraculous Whip (page 17)
3 tablespoons catsup
1 tablespoon chopped bell pepper
1 teaspoon chopped pimiento
1 teaspoon chopped fresh chives

Mix well by hand, or blend in a blender, according to your taste.

Tofu Mayonnaise 1

Adding the lemon in stages and the oil as slowly as possible is the secret of making good thick mayonnaise with this recipe.

1 cup firm tofu
1 teaspoon Dijon-style mustard
1/2 teaspoon sea salt
Pinch paprika
1 tablespoon plus 1 1/2 teaspoons lemon juice or white vinegar
2 tablespoons corn oil

Put the tofu, mustard, salt, and paprika in a blender with 1 tablespoon of the lemon juice (or vinegar). Blend at high speed, stopping frequently to scrape down the sides of the blender, until well combined. Still blending, add the oil a few drops at a time, increasing to a steady stream, until about 1/3 of the oil is used. Slowly add another teaspoon of lemon juice while blending. Dribble in another 1/3 of the oil. Add the rest of the lemon juice the same way as before. Continue adding the oil until it is gone.

Tofu Mayonnaise 2

1 1/2 cups firm tofu
2 tablespoons corn oil
1 tablespoon cider vinegar
2 tablespoons water
1 1/2 teaspoons prepared mustard
1/2 teaspoon minced garlic
1/4 cup minced onion
1/4 teaspoon white pepper
1 1/4 teaspoons sea salt
1 tablespoon lemon juice or white vinegar
1 tablespoon cashew nuts, ground fine

Put everything in a blender and blend until smooth. Refrigerate.

Tofu Mayonnaise 3

1 1/2 cups firm tofu
1/2 teaspoon garlic powder
1 teaspoon prepared mustard
1 1/2 tablespoons lemon juice or white vinegar
2 tablespoons corn oil
1 teaspoon sea salt
1/8 teaspoon white pepper

Put everything in a blender and blend until smooth. Refrigerate.

Tofu Mayonnaise Dressing 1

3 tablespoons Tofu Mayonnaise (see above)
3 tablespoons UnChicken Broth (page 155) or UnBeef Broth (page 155), or soy sauce

Mix well by hand, or blend in a blender, according to your taste.

Tofu Mayonnaise Dressing 2

1/4 cup Tofu Mayonnaise (see above)
2 tablespoons white vinegar
3 tablespoons water
1/4 cup UnBeef Broth (page 155)
1/8 teaspoon sea salt
1 tablespoon chopped fresh parsley

Mix well by hand, or blend in a blender, according to your taste.

Tofu Mayonnaise Dressing 3

1/4 cup finely chopped celery
1/2 cup Tofu Mayonnaise (see above)
1 tablespoon white vinegar
Water, if needed, to thin the dressing

Mix well by hand, or blend in a blender, according to your taste.

Tofu Mayonnaise Dressing 4

1 teaspoon garlic powder
1 cup Tofu Mayonnaise (see above)
3/4 cup water
1/4 cup white vinegar
1 teaspoon sea salt

Mix well by hand, or blend in a blender, according to your taste.

Tofu Mayonnaise Dressing 5

1/2 cup Tofu Mayonnaise (see above)
2/3 cup water

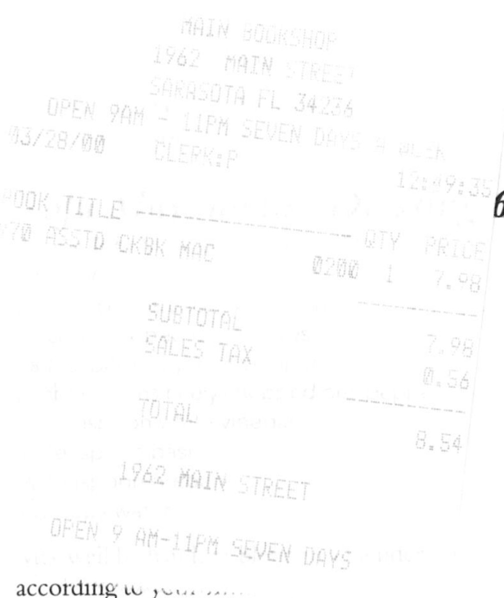
MAIN BOOKSHOP
1962 MAIN STREET
SARASOTA FL 34236
OPEN 9AM - 11PM SEVEN DAYS A WEEK
03/28/00 CLERK:P
12:49:35

BOOK TITLE		QTY	PRICE
ASSTD CKBK MAC	0200	1	7.98
SUBTOTAL			7.98
SALES TAX			0.56
TOTAL			8.54

1962 MAIN STREET
OPEN 9 AM-11PM SEVEN DAYS

6

according

Tofu Mayonnaise Dressing 7

1 cup Tofu Mayonnaise (page 22)
1 cup water
1 teaspoon sea salt
2 tablespoons finely chopped onion
¼ cup white vinegar
¼ teaspoon basil
¼ teaspoon oregano

Mix well by hand, or blend in a blender, according to your taste.

Tomato Dressing 1

½ cup canned tomato puree (or blend raw tomatoes well)
1 tablespoon dill
2 tablespoons minced onion
2 teaspoons minced bell pepper
2 tablespoons lemon juice or white vinegar
¼ teaspoon tarragon
1 tablespoon soy sauce
½ teaspoon basil
½ teaspoon garlic powder

Mix well by hand, or blend in a blender, according to your taste.

Tomato Dressing 2

2 quarts tomatoes, chopped
1 cup chopped celery
½ cup chopped bell pepper
1 cup chopped onion
¼ teaspoon garlic powder
2 teaspoons sea salt
1 cup lemon juice or white vinegar

Blend all ingredients. Use up in a few days.

Tomato-Cashew Dressing

½ cup raw cashews
½ cup chopped onion
1 teaspoon garlic powder
1 teaspoon celery salt
1 teaspoon paprika
1 teaspoon marjoram
2 cups tomato juice
2 tablespoons olive oil
Sea salt, if needed

Blend well in a blender.

Tomato Mayonnaise

1 cup Cashew Mayonnaise (page 12) or Tofu Mayonnaise (page 22), Miraculous Whip (page 17), or Cashew Sour Kreem (page 94) or Tofu Sour Kreem (page 97)
⅓ cup tomato juice or puree
1 teaspoon minced onion
⅛ teaspoon garlic powder
½ teaspoon sea salt

Mix well by hand, or blend in a blender, according to your taste.

Tomato French Dressing

1 cup French Dressing (page 14)
½ cup tomato juice, or 2 or 3 tomatoes, chopped

Mix well by hand, or blend in a blender, according to your taste.

Vinaigrette Dressing 1

2½ tablespoons white vinegar or lemon juice
2½ tablespoons olive oil
1 tablespoon chopped fresh parsley
½ teaspoon sea salt

Mix well by hand, or blend in a blender, according to your taste.

Vinaigrette Dressing 2

2 tablespoons olive oil
2 tablespoons white vinegar or lemon juice
¼ cup UnBeef Broth (page 155)
1 teaspoon basil
1 teaspoon oregano
½ teaspoon garlic powder

Mix well by hand, or blend in a blender, according to your taste.

Zesty French Dressing

1 garlic clove, crushed
¼ teaspoon sea salt
2 tablespoons olive oil
1 tablespoon lemon juice
¼ cup wine vinegar
4 teaspoons Lea and Perrins Steak Sauce
½ teaspoon Louisiana Hot Sauce

Blend together in a blender.

Salads

I have not given any recipes for fruit salad, simply because fruit looks, smells, and tastes wonderful just as it is. To my way of thinking, the trouble of cutting it up and mixing it seems pointless. Also, since the fruits have such natural good taste and juiciness, it seems a shame to mask them with some kind of dressing, whereas vegetables need a dressing since they are so dry.

Another big "absent" in most of these recipes is lettuce. We should indeed eat lettuce, but a lot of people (including me) consider a salad that is mostly lettuce just plain uninteresting. Therefore I have listed the nonlettuce ingredients only, and you can put in the amount of lettuce you like, or leave it out altogether. But when you do use lettuce, be sure it is not iceberg or "head" lettuce. That stuff is wet cellulose, not worth the trouble—a waste of time for your stomach, which deserves something real. Romaine lettuce is the staple, but other types are good, too. I always prefer spinach to lettuce in salad, and I recommend it.

Consider sometimes using cabbage instead of lettuce. Bok choy, "Chinese cabbage," is excellent, too.

I also have not listed lettuce so you can use the recipes to make salads with grains—an option well worth trying. Instead of lettuce, mix the salad ingredients with rice, tabouli wheat, cracked wheat, barley, or millet. Tabouli wheat need not be cooked, just soaked adequately, but cracked, or bulghur, wheat must be cooked (see Grains chapter).

In case you prefer your grain in another form, any salad goes well stuffed in fresh pocket bread. People who dislike lettuce salad often find they like it very much when eaten this way as a sandwich.

You can use these recipes four ways: (1) just as given, (2) with lettuce, (3) with grains, and (4) in pocket bread.

Except for potatoes, grains, and beans, all the vegetables listed in these recipes should be raw.

Peas should be frozen first, as this makes them soft and easy to eat, as well as especially delicious. But be sure to drain them or put them on paper towels so they won't be wet and clammy. To bring them to room temperature in a hurry, run tap water over them, then drain and dry.

Corn, if not frozen, may need to be lightly steamed before using.

If you are not familiar with the different types of bean sprouts, start out using alfalfa sprouts.

When good avocados are not available, substitute mashed green peas.

Most of these salads should be served with a dressing from the Salad Dressings chapter. Those salads that have their own dressing or one recommended can be varied by substituting another dressing.

Anne Goldstein's Tabouli

Gourmet simplicity!

1 cup bulgur wheat, uncooked
1 1/4 cup chopped fresh parsley
1 cup chopped mint
1 cup chopped onion
2 bunches of finely chopped green onions
2 cups chopped canned tomatoes
1/2 cup lemon juice
1/3 cup olive oil
1 teaspoon sea salt
1 teaspoon freshly ground black pepper

Wash the wheat, then soak it in enough water so there are 2 inches of water above the wheat. Soak until the wheat is soft. Drain and squeeze dry. Combine with the rest of the ingredients. Refrigerate 2 to 8 hours.

Avocado Salad 1

2 large ripe avocados, peeled, pitted, and diced
2 large tomatoes, diced
1/4 cup finely chopped bell pepper
1/4 cup finely chopped onion
2 tablespoons lemon juice
1 teaspoon olive oil
1/2 teaspoon sea salt

Combine all the ingredients in a bowl.

Avocado Salad 2

2 ripe avocados, peeled, pitted, and mashed
1/4 cup chopped onion
1/4 cup chopped fresh parsley
1/2 teaspoon sea salt
2 tablespoons lemon juice
1 1/4 cups Cashew Sour Kreem (page 94) or Tofu Sour Kreem (page 97)
1 teaspoon soy sauce

Combine all the ingredients in a bowl.

Barbecue Bean Salad

Mix together 1 part of Barbecue Beans (page 230) and 2 parts of Cottage Cheez Salad 1 (page 29).

Bean Salad

6 cups water
1 cup corn
1 cup finely diced carrots
1 cup finely diced celery
2 1/2 cups cooked beans or black-eyed peas
1 cup finely diced bell pepper
1 1/2 teaspoons minced red onion
1/3 cup balsamic vinegar
2 teaspoons corn oil
1/2 cup chopped fresh parsley
1 teaspoon sea salt
1/2 teaspoon freshly ground black pepper

Bring the water to a boil. Add the corn, carrots, and celery. Blanch for 1 minute or until just tender. Drain, rinse under cold water, and drain well again. Combine the beans, blanched vegetables, bell pepper, and onion. Pour the vinegar and oil over and toss well. Let stand at least 30 minutes at room temperature. Half an hour before serving, add the parsley, salt, and pepper and toss well.

Bean Sprout Salad 1

1/2 cup finely chopped celery
1/2 cup chopped bell pepper
2 1/2 cups bean sprouts
1/4 cup chopped onion
1/2 cup chopped cucumber
2 cups chopped tomato
2 cups garbanzo beans, cooked
1 cup French Dressing (page 14)

Combine all the ingredients in a bowl.

Bean Sprout Salad 2

2 cups bean sprouts
1 cup shredded carrots
1 cup diced ripe avocado

Combine all the ingredients in a bowl.

Broccoli, Potato, and Garbanzo Salad

3 medium potatoes, cut into 1-inch cubes, steamed, and drained
2 tablespoons tarragon vinegar
2½ teaspoons corn oil
½ teaspoon freshly ground black pepper
1 teaspoon sea salt
6 cups broccoli florets, steamed, drained, and rinsed under cold running water and drained
1 cup garbanzo beans, cooked
½ cup tofu yogurt
3 tablespoons lemon juice
1 tablespoon balsamic vinegar
1 teaspoon Dijon-style mustard
¾ teaspoon minced garlic

Toss the potatoes with the vinegar, oil, pepper, and salt. Toss the broccoli with the rest of the ingredients (not the potatoes). Combine the potatoes and broccoli mixture and toss gently to mix completely. Serve warm or at room temperature.

Cabbage-Pineapple Salad

3 cups shredded cabbage
1 cup pineapple chunks
1 cup shredded carrots
¼ cup raisins
¼ cup sunflower seeds (unsalted)
¾ cup Miraculous Whip made according to the variation for fruit salad (page 17)

Combine everything well.

Cabbage and Pepper Salad

1 red bell pepper, seeded and thinly sliced
1 green bell pepper, seeded and thinly sliced
1 onion, thinly sliced and pushed out into rings
1 cucumber, cut into ½-inch cubes
2 tomatoes, thinly sliced
½ white cabbage, thinly sliced
2 tablespoons Sucanat
3 tablespoons lemon juice
½ cup olive oil
¼ cup red wine vinegar
2 teaspoons sea salt
1 teaspoon freshly ground black pepper

Combine the vegetables in a large bowl. Put the other ingredients in a blender or jar and blend or shake until well mixed. Pour over the vegetables and toss well.

Cabbage and Lima Bean Salad

1 small head of cabbage, shredded
½ cup sliced radishes
½ cup finely chopped fresh parsley
One 10-ounce package frozen green lima beans, thawed
½ cup chopped scallions, shallots or leeks
½ teaspoon sea salt

Combine all ingredients in a bowl.

Cabbage Slaw 1

4 cups shredded cabbage
1½ cups shredded carrots
1 cup chopped bell pepper
1 cup chopped celery
½ cup chopped onion
1½ cups Cashew Sour Kreem (page 94) or Tofu Sour Kreem (page 97)
1¼ tablespoons lemon juice
½ teaspoon dill
½ teaspoon sea salt

Combine all the ingredients in a bowl.

VARIATIONS: *Slice tomatoes and put the slaw on top of the slices. Sprinkle with chopped ripe olives. Add 3 cups of cooked beans to the slaw. Add ½ teaspoon caraway seed.*

Cabbage Slaw 2

5 cups shredded cabbage
1 cup shredded carrots
1 cup Cashew Mayonnaise (page 12) or Tofu Mayonnaise (page 22), or Miraculous Whip (page 17)
2½ tablespoons white vinegar
1 tablespoon prepared mustard
1 tablespoon celery seed
1 teaspoon sea salt

Combine cabbage and carrots and set aside. Blend the mayonnaise, vinegar, mustard, celery seed, and salt, and mix with the cabbage and carrots. Let sit for an hour or so for flavors to blend.

VARIATION: *For extra zest, add ½ to 1 teaspoon of Louisiana Hot Sauce.*

Cajun Cole Slaw

Fun on the bayou, I tell you!

½ cup Cashew Mayonnaise (page 12) or Tofu Mayonnaise (page 22), or Miraculous Whip (page 17)
3 tablespoons prepared mustard
1 tablespoon olive oil
2 tablespoons Lea and Perrins Steak Sauce
1 teaspoon Louisiana Hot Sauce
2 tablespoons catsup
2 teaspoons sea salt
1 teaspoon garlic salt
1 tablespoon red or white wine vinegar
2 tablespoons lemon juice
1 large head of cabbage, very finely shredded
4 bell peppers, shredded fine
2 medium onions, shredded very thin

Put the mayonnaise and mustard in a bowl. Beat together with a fork until combined. Slowly add the olive oil, beating all the time, until the mixture has returned to the thickness of the original mayonnaise. Still beating, add steak sauce, hot sauce, then the catsup, the salt and garlic salt, vinegar, and then the lemon juice. Place the cabbage, peppers, and onion in a large bowl, pour the sauce over, and toss well. This should sit at least an hour before serving, and tastes even better the next day.

Chef's Bean Salad

5 cups white beans
½ teaspoon minced garlic
½ cup Italian Dressing (page 16)
¼ cup minced onion
½ cup diced celery
½ cup diced dill pickle
¼ cup Cashew Mayonnaise (page 12) or Tofu Mayonnaise (page 22), or Miraculous Whip (page 17)
½ cup Pimiento Cheez (page 94)
1 teaspoon minced jalapeños
4 teaspoons white vinegar.

Combine all and chill for several hours or overnight.

Corn Salad 1

2 cups corn
½ cups finely chopped bell pepper
⅓ cup chopped onion
1 cup finely chopped tomato

Combine all the ingredients in a bowl.

VARIATIONS: *Add 1 to 2 cups of shredded cabbage. Omit the tomatoes and put the Mexican Tomato Dressing (page 17) over it.*

Corn Salad 2

3 cups corn
1½ cups chopped tomato
¼ cup chopped onion
⅓ cup Cashew Sour Kreem (page 94) or Tofu Sour Kreem (page 97)
1 tablespoon lemon juice
½ teaspoon sea salt
¼ teaspoon mustard seed
¼ teaspoon celery seed

Combine all the ingredients in a bowl.

Corn, Rice, and Bean Salad

1 1/2 cups corn
1/2 cup dried beans, pressure-cooked and drained
2 cups chopped tomato
2 tablespoons chopped fresh parsley
1/4 cup chopped bell pepper
1 teaspoon sea salt
1/2 cup Cashew Mayonnaise (page 12) or Tofu Mayonnaise (page 22), or Miraculous Whip (page 17)
1 1/2 teaspoons lemon juice
1 1/2 teaspoons olive oil
1/4 teaspoon cayenne pepper
2 cups rice, cooked

Mix the corn, beans, tomato, parsley, bell pepper, and salt. Let this sit for 30 minutes at room temperature. Combine the mayonnaise, lemon juice, olive oil, and pepper. On a serving plate, place the rice, then the corn-bean mixture, and spoon the dressing over.

Cottage Cheez Salad 1

4 1/2 cups Tofu Cottage Cheez (page 96)
3 cups finely chopped tomato
1/4 cup chopped onion
1/2 cup chopped black olives
1/2 cup finely chopped bell pepper
1 1/2 teaspoon minced jalapeños
1/4 teaspoon dried basil
1/8 teaspoon dill
1 1/2 teaspoons sea salt

Combine all the ingredients in a bowl.

Cottage Cheez Salad 2

2 cups Tofu Cottage Cheez (page 96)
1 cup Cashew Sour Kreem (page 94) or Tofu Sour Kreem (page 97)
1 cup frozen mixed vegetables, steamed and cooled
1/3 cup finely minced onion
1/2 teaspoon finely minced jalapeños
1/2 teaspoon sea salt
1/4 teaspoon dill or dried basil

Combine all the ingredients in a bowl.

Country Rice Salad

Dressing

1/2 cup Miraculous Whip (page 17)
1/4 cup prepared mustard
2 tablespoons Sucanat
1 teaspoon balsamic vinegar
1/4 teaspoon sea salt
1/8 teaspoon freshly ground black pepper
1 to 2 tablespoons Cashew Milk (page 93) (if needed)

Salad

3 cups cooked rice, chilled
1/4 cup sweet pickle relish
One 2-ounce jar of pimientos, drained and chopped
1/3 cup finely chopped green onions (tops, too)
1/4 cup finely chopped bell pepper
1/4 cup finely chopped celery
Parsley
Cherry tomatoes

Mix well the dressing ingredients, except for the "milk," and set aside. Combine the salad ingredients. Pour the dressing over them and toss gently, adding the "milk" if it is too dry. Chill several hours before serving. Top with parsley and cherry tomatoes.

Cucumber Salad 1

3 cups sliced cucumbers, about 1/8 inch thick
1 teaspoon sea salt
2 teaspoons lemon juice
1 cup Cashew Sour Kreem (page 94) or Tofu Sour Kreem (page 97)
1/4 teaspoon dill

Combine all the ingredients in a bowl.

Cucumber Salad 2

4 cups thinly sliced cucumbers
2 cups chopped tomato
1/3 cup chopped onion
1/4 cup fresh basil, or 1 teaspoon dried
1 1/2 teaspoons olive oil
1 tablespoon lemon juice
1/4 teaspoon sea salt

Combine all the ingredients in a bowl.

VARIATIONS: *Substitute dill or parsley for the basil. Add 1/4 or 1/2 cup of chopped ripe olives.*

Couscous Salad

2 1/2 cups couscous, cooked
2 cups diced tomato
1/2 cup minced onion
1/2 cup diced cucumber
3/4 cup chopped fresh parsley
1/4 cup lemon juice
2 teaspoons corn oil
3/4 teaspoon minced garlic
1/2 teaspoon ground cumin
1/2 teaspoon ground coriander seed
3/4 teaspoon sea salt
1/2 teaspoon freshly ground black pepper

Combine everything. Let sit for a while for flavors to meld.

Dilled Cucumbers

2 cups peeled and thinly sliced cucumbers
1/2 teaspoon sea salt
1/2 cup Cashew Sour Kreem (page 94) or Tofu Sour Kreem (page 97)
1 tablespoon lemon juice
2 tablespoons finely chopped green onions
1/8 teaspoon freshly ground black pepper
1/4 teaspoon Sucanat
1/2 teaspoon dried dill

Toss the cucumbers with the salt. Let stand for 10 minutes. Meanwhile, combine all the other ingredients. Drain the cucumbers and combine with the other ingredients. Chill until ready to serve.

Dried Bean Salad

4 cups cooked dried beans (one type or more), drained
1/4 cup chopped onion
2 tablespoons lemon juice
2 teaspoons olive oil
1/2 teaspoon dried oregano
1/4 teaspoon cumin
1/2 teaspoon sea salt
2 tablespoons minced fresh parsley
1/4 cup chopped bell pepper
2 cups diced tomato
1/2 cup peeled and diced cucumbers

Combine and let sit for a few hours.

Garbanzo Bean Salad 1

1/2 teaspoon olive oil
1/4 cup lemon juice
1/2 teaspoon sea salt
1 cup garbanzo beans, cooked
2 tablespoons chopped fresh parsley
1 cup chopped celery
1/4 cup chopped onion

Combine all the ingredients in a bowl.

Garbanzo Bean Salad 2

2 1/2 cups garbanzo beans, cooked and drained
2 tablespoons finely chopped fresh parsley
2 tablespoons chopped onion
1/8 teaspoon garlic powder
1 tablespoon lemon juice
1/2 teaspoon olive oil
1/2 teaspoon sea salt

Combine all the ingredients in a bowl.

Garbanzo and Cabbage Salad

2 cups shredded cabbage
1 cup garbanzo beans, cooked
3 tablespoons chopped onion
1/4 cup chopped pimiento
2 teaspoons fresh basil, or 1/2 teaspoon dried
1/2 teaspoon sea salt
3 tablespoons lemon juice
1 teaspoon olive oil
1/4 cup Cashew Sour Kreem (page 94) or Tofu Sour Kreem (page 97)

Combine all the ingredients in a bowl.

Garbanzo Salad 1

1 cup garbanzo beans, pressure-cooked and drained
2 tablespoons chopped onion

1 tablespoon minced fresh parsley
2 teaspoons lemon juice
1/4 teaspoon olive oil
1/4 teaspoon ground cumin
1/2 teaspoon sea salt

In a glass or enamel bowl combine the beans, onion, and parsley. In a separate bowl, whisk the lemon juice with the oil, cumin, and salt. Pour over the bean mixture.

Garbanzo Salad 2

1 cup garbanzo beans, cooked and drained
1 tablespoon chopped green onions (not the tops)
1/4 teaspoon ground cumin
1 tablespoon minced fresh parsley
2 teaspoons lemon juice
1/4 teaspoon olive oil
1/2 teaspoon sea salt

In a glass or enamel bowl combine the beans, onions, cumin, and parsley. In a separate bowl, whisk the lemon juice with the oil and salt. Pour over the bean mixture.

Garbanzo-Tomato Salad

1 teaspoon olive oil
2 tablespoons lemon juice
1 teaspoon sea salt
1/2 teaspoon dried oregano
1 cup garbanzo beans, cooked
2 cups chopped tomato
3/4 cup chopped bell pepper
12 ripe olives, sliced
3/4 cup chopped onion
1/4 cup chopped fresh parsley

Combine all the ingredients in a bowl.

Gazpacho Salad

Dressing

3 tablespoons olive oil
2 tablespoons lemon juice
2 tablespoons chopped fresh parsley
1/4 teaspoon garlic powder

1 cup chopped bell peppers
4 cups chopped tomato
2 cups chopped cucumbers
1/3 cup chopped onion
1/2 teaspoon sea salt

Combine the dressing ingredients in a bowl. In a separate bowl, combine the remaining ingredients. Add the dressing, and mix well to combine.

VARIATION: *Add 3 cups of mashed ripe avocado to the dressing and mix thoroughly.*

Gluten Salad

You can trust this to please every time!

2 1/2 cups flavored gluten, ground or chopped
1/4 cup finely chopped celery
1/4 cup finely chopped bell pepper
1/3 cup finely chopped onion
3/4 cup fresh dill or sweet pickle, chopped fine
1 tablespoon finely chopped fresh parsley
2 cups Miraculous Whip (page 17), Cashew Sour Kreem (page 94) or Tofu Sour Kreem (page 97)
1/4 teaspoon Louisiana Hot Sauce
1/8 teaspoon garlic powder
1/8 teaspoon freshly ground black pepper
1 tablespoon white vinegar

Combine and chill for a few hours to let flavors mix.

VARIATION: *Use frozen tofu, either flavored beef, chicken, ham, sausage, or fish.*

Green Pea Salad 1

Two 10-ounce packages of frozen peas, thawed
1 1/2 cups coarsely chopped medium tomato
1 cup Cashew Mayonnaise (page 12) or Tofu Mayonnaise (page 22), Miraculous Whip (page 17), or Cashew Sour Kreem (page 94) or Tofu Sour Kreem (page 97)
1/3 cup chopped onion
1 1/2 tablespoons lemon juice
1 teaspoon sea salt

Combine all the ingredients in a bowl.

Green Pea Salad 2

Two 10-ounce packages frozen green peas, thawed
1 cup thinly sliced celery
1/2 teaspoon dried dill
1/3 cup French Dressing (page 14) or Italian Dressing (page 16)

Combine all the ingredients in a bowl.

Green Vegetable Salad

1 cup peas
1 cup lima beans, cooked
1 cup chopped celery
1/2 cups chopped bell pepper
1/2 cups finely chopped onion

Combine all the ingredients in a bowl.

Guacamole 1

I doubt that guacamole is really holy, but every one of these certainly is heavenly!

2 large, ripe avocados, peeled, pitted, and mashed
1/4 cup chopped onion
1/2 cup chopped tomato
1/2 teaspoon sea salt
1/8 teaspoon pepper
2 1/2 teaspoons lemon juice

Combine all the ingredients in a bowl.

Guacamole 2

3 ripe avocados, peeled, pitted, and mashed
1/3 cup Cashew Mayonnaise (page 12) or Tofu Mayonnaise (page 22), Miraculous Whip (page 17), or Cashew Sour Kreem (page 94) or Tofu Sour Kreem (page 97)
1 teaspoon sea salt
1/4 teaspoon garlic powder
2 tablespoons lemon juice
1 tomato, chopped
1/4 cup chopped onion
1/3 cup sliced celery
1/2 cups chopped bell pepper

Combine all the ingredients in a bowl.

Guacamole 3

2 ripe avocados, peeled, pitted, and mashed
1/4 cup Cashew Mayonnaise (page 12) or Tofu Mayonnaise (page 22), Miraculous Whip (page 17), or Cashew Sour Kreem (page 94) or Tofu Sour Kreem (page 97)
2 tablespoons chopped onion
1/2 teaspoon sea salt
1/2 teaspoon garlic powder
4 teaspoons lemon juice
2 tomatoes, chopped

Combine all the ingredients in a bowl.

Guacamole 4

4 ripe avocados, peeled, pitted, and mashed
1/2 teaspoon sea salt
2 tablespoons lemon or lime juice
1/2 teaspoon soy sauce
1 teaspoon garlic powder

Combine all the ingredients in a bowl.

Guacamole 5

2 large ripe avocados, peeled, pitted, and mashed to a puree
1 tablespoon finely chopped onion
1/2 cup chopped tomato
1/2 teaspoon sea salt
1/8 teaspoon freshly ground black pepper
2 teaspoons lemon juice
3 tablespoons Tomato Salsa (page 296) or Taco Sauce (page 260)

Combine all the ingredients in a bowl.

Kidney Bean Salad 1

This is almost a meal in itself, and is excellent in pocket bread.

1/4 cup apple cider vinegar or lemon juice
2 1/2 teaspoons olive oil
1 tablespoon sea salt
1/2 teaspoon dried mustard
1/4 teaspoon freshly ground black pepper
1/8 teaspoon cayenne pepper
1/4 teaspoon dill

5 cups kidney beans, cooked and drained
3/4 cup chopped onion
2 cups chopped cucumber
2 cups chopped tomato
1/2 cup chopped celery
1/2 cup chopped bell pepper

Blend the vinegar (or lemon juice), oil and spices. Mix with all other ingredients. Serve cold.

VARIATIONS: *Use some type of beans other than kidney. Use mayonnaise instead of vinegar (or lemon juice) and olive oil. Add 1 cup of cooked lentils.*

Kidney Bean Salad 2

2 cups kidney beans, cooked and drained
1 lemon, juiced and peel grated
1/2 teaspoon corn or olive oil
1/4 teaspoon sage
3 tablespoons chopped fresh parsley
1/2 teaspoon sea salt
1/4 teaspoon cayenne pepper

Combine everything, cover, and marinate for several hours.

Lentil Salad 1

3 cups lentils, cooked and chilled
3 tablespoons chopped onion
1 cup chopped tomato
1/4 cup chopped bell pepper
1/2 cup peas
2 tablespoons lemon juice
1/2 cup Cashew Mayonnaise (page 12) or Tofu Mayonnaise (page 22), Miraculous Whip (page 17), or Cashew Sour Kreem (page 94) or Tofu Sour Kreem (page 97)
1/4 teaspoon celery seed
1/4 teaspoon sesame seed
1/4 teaspoon sea salt
1/4 teaspoon garlic powder
1/4 teaspoon marjoram
1/4 teaspoon dried basil

Combine all the ingredients in a bowl.

Lentil Salad 2

2 cups lentils, cooked and chilled
1/2 cup French Dressing (page 14)
1/4 cup chopped bell pepper
3/4 cup chopped onion
1/2 cup chopped celery
2 tablespoons chopped fresh parsley

Lentil Salad 3

Dressing
1 tablespoon lemon juice
2 tablespoons olive oil
1 teaspoon sea salt
1/8 teaspoon garlic powder

2 cups lentils, cooked and chilled
1/4 cup chopped onion
1 cup grated carrots
1/2 cup chopped radishes

Combine the dressing ingredients in a bowl. In a separate bowl, combine the remaining ingredients, add the dressing, and mix well to combine.

Lentil Salad 4

1 cup lentils
1 small yellow onion
3 3/4 cups finely chopped tomato, drained in a fine sieve over a bowl
1/2 cup finely chopped celery
1/2 cup finely chopped carrot
1/4 cup finely chopped red onion
1/4 teaspoon ground ginger
1 1/2 tablespoons lemon juice
1 1/2 tablespoons soy sauce
1/4 teaspoon freshly ground black pepper
1/4 teaspoon cayenne pepper
3/4 teaspoon sea salt
1 1/2 cups peeled, seeded, and diced cucumber
1 1/2 teaspoons balsamic vinegar
1 tablespoon corn oil
3/4 teaspoon dried dill
1/2 teaspoon Dijon-style mustard

Wash and gently cook the lentils with the whole yellow onion for 45 minutes or until done. Drain, discard the onion, and cool. Combine the lentils with the tomato, celery, carrots, red onion, ginger, lemon juice, soy sauce, pepper, cayenne, and salt. Mix well and set aside. Put the cucumber in a blender with the vinegar, oil, dill, and mustard. Process until very smooth. Season to taste with black pepper and salt. Combine everything and serve.

Lima Bean Salad 1

This is good with Potato Dressing 1.

2 cups green lima beans, cooked, drained, and cooled
1 cup chopped celery
2 cups frozen green peas, thawed
¼ cup chopped onion

Combine all the ingredients in a bowl.

VARIATIONS: *Add 1 cup of chopped tomato and ½ cup of chopped bell pepper. Add 2 cups of corn.*

Lima Bean Salad 2

2 packages frozen lima beans, cooked, drained, and cooled
1 tablespoon lemon juice
¼ teaspoon garlic powder
1½ teaspoons olive oil
2 tablespoons chopped fresh parsley
½ teaspoon sea salt
1 cup Cashew Sour Kreem (page 94) or Tofu Sour Kreem (page 97)

Combine all the ingredients in a bowl.

VARIATIONS: *Add ½ cup of chopped celery. Add ½ cup of chopped bell pepper.*

Lima Bean and Garbanzo Salad

1½ cups garbanzo beans, cooked
1½ cups cooked lima beans
¼ cup chopped onion
¼ cup chopped pimiento

Combine all the ingredients in a bowl.

Lima Bean Gazpacho Salad

2 cups cooked lima beans, fresh, frozen, or dried
2 cups chopped tomato
½ cup chopped cucumber
½ cup chopped bell pepper
½ cup chopped celery
½ cup chopped onion
½ teaspoon garlic powder
½ teaspoon dried oregano
½ teaspoon dried basil
⅛ teaspoon cumin
2 cups French Dressing (page 14) or Italian Dressing (page 16)

Combine all the ingredients in a bowl.

Macaroni and Cheez Salad

2 cups macaroni, cooked and drained
1½ cups peas, cooked and drained
2 cups yeast or Pimiento Cheez (page 94)
½ cup chopped black olives
½ cup Cashew Mayonnaise (page 12) or Tofu Mayonnaise (page 22), Miraculous Whip (page 17), or Cashew Sour Kreem (page 94) or Tofu Sour Kreem (page 97)
2 tablespoons chopped onion
½ teaspoon sea salt

Combine all the ingredients in a bowl.

Marinated Zucchini Salad

3 cups thinly sliced zucchini
½ cup chopped bell pepper
½ cup diced celery
½ cup diced onion
¼ cup diced pimiento
¾ cup balsamic vinegar
⅓ cup olive or corn oil
½ cup Sucanat
½ teaspoon sea salt
½ teaspoon freshly ground black pepper

Combine the zucchini, bell pepper, celery, onion, and pimiento and set aside. Combine the rest of the ingredients in a jar, cover, and shake well. Pour over the vegetables and toss gently. Cover and chill 8 hours or overnight.

Mexican Corn Salad

2½ cups corn
½ cup chopped pimiento
1 cup chopped onion
½ cup chopped bell pepper
1 cup chopped cucumber

Combine all the ingredients in a bowl.

Mexican Bean and Corn Salad

1 cup corn
1½ cups kidney or pinto beans, cooked and drained
2 cups shredded lettuce
¼ cup black olives, sliced or chopped
2 tablespoons finely chopped bell pepper
3 tablespoons minced onion
½ cup Mexican Tomato Vinaigrette (page 17)

Combine all the ingredients in a bowl.

Mixed Vegetable Salad 1

¾ cup grated carrots
¾ cup chopped cauliflower
1 cup peas
¼ cup sliced ripe olives

Combine all the ingredients in a bowl.

Mixed Vegetable Salad 2

2 cups cooked and cubed potatoes
2 cups peas
2 cups corn
2 cups lima beans
2 cups cubed carrots
½ cup sunflower seeds

Combine all the ingredients in a bowl.

VARIATION: *Add 2 or 3 cups of chopped tomato.*

Monastery Tomato Salad

4 cups diced tomato
1 cup nondairy soy cheese (Soy Kaas), cubed
1½ cups chopped bell pepper
¾ cup chopped onion
2 tablespoons lemon juice
2 tablespoons balsamic vinegar
4 teaspoons chopped fresh basil, or 1 teaspoon dried
1 cup sliced olives
1½ teaspoons sea salt
¼ teaspoon pepper
1 teaspoon paprika
½ teaspoon celery seed
2 teaspoons olive oil

Put tomato, cheese, bell pepper, and onion into a bowl and set aside. Combine the remaining ingredients, pour into the vegetable mixture, and toss well.

VARIATION: *Use flavored gluten instead of cheese.*

Mushroom Salad

Fantabulous!

4⅔ cups sliced mushrooms
½ cup thinly sliced bell pepper (red preferred)
¼ cup chopped green onions
3 tablespoons chopped fresh parsley
½ cup olive oil
¼ cup raspberry vinegar
1 teaspoon sea salt
½ teaspoon freshly ground black pepper

Combine the mushrooms, bell pepper, onions, and parsley. In a separate bowl, whisk together the oil, vinegar, salt, and pepper until well blended. Add to the mushroom mixture and toss thoroughly to coat.

Pasta Salad Vinaigrette

2 cups vermicelli, cooked and chilled
2 cups sliced black olives
1¼ teaspoons olive oil
4 teaspoons wine vinegar
1 tablespoon lemon juice
1 teaspoon sea salt
2 teaspoons Sucanat
1 teaspoon dried dill
½ cup peas
½ cup bell pepper, cut in strips
Lettuce or spinach

Toss together all the ingredients except the peas, bell pepper, and greens. Let it marinate for 20 minutes in the refrigerator. Mix in the peas and bell pepper. Serve on the lettuce or spinach.

Peanut Pasta Salad

2 cups dry pasta (bow-tie, macaroni, etc.)
4 cups coarsely chopped Chinese cabbage (bok choy)
¼ cup diced bell pepper (red preferred), cut into ¼-inch dice
¼ cup thinly sliced green onions
½ cup peanut butter
¼ cup vinegar
3 tablespoons low-sodium soy sauce
2 tablespoons genuine maple syrup
1 tablespoon oriental sesame oil
¼ cup water
¾ teaspoon cayenne pepper
¾ cup roasted peanuts

Cook the pasta, drain, rinse with cold water, and drain again. Put into a large bowl and add the bok choy, bell pepper, and onions and toss well. In a separate bowl, whisk together the peanut butter, vinegar, soy sauce, maple syrup, and sesame oil until smooth. Whisk in the water and cayenne. Pour this dressing over the salad, add the peanuts, and toss well.

Pecos Bean Salad

4 cups cooked dried beans, drained
⅓ cup chopped onion
¼ teaspoon garlic powder
½ cup chopped bell pepper
1½ teaspoons olive oil
1 tablespoon lemon juice
½ teaspoon dried oregano
½ teaspoon dried basil
1 teaspoon sea salt

Combine all the ingredients in a bowl.

Piquant Cauliflower

2 cups cauliflower flowerets
½ teaspoon corn oil
3 tablespoons white vinegar
⅓ cup chopped tomato
4 teaspoons chopped pimiento
2 teaspoons chopped green olives
1 tablespoon chopped dill pickle
1 teaspoon Sucanat
1 teaspoon sea salt
1 teaspoon paprika
⅛ teaspoon cayenne pepper

Separate the cauliflower into flowerets and cook in boiling water until tender, about 10 minutes. Combine the rest of the ingredients and pour over the cauliflower. Chill 2 to 3 hours, stirring occasionally. At serving time drain off the excess liquid.

Pink Beans and Red Cabbage Salad

3 cups pink or pinto beans, cooked
1 cup grated celery
1 cup grated radishes
1 cup grated cucumber
2 cups shredded red cabbage
¼ cup finely chopped onion

Combine all the ingredients in a bowl.

Rice Salad 1

Basic, but never dull!

2 cups rice, cooked
1 teaspoon sea salt

1¼ teaspoons olive oil
1½ tablespoons lemon juice
¼ cup chopped fresh parsley
⅓ cup chopped onion
1 cup chopped tomato
1 cup total of one or more of the following (singly or in combination):
- Bean sprouts
- Bell pepper, chopped
- Cabbage, shredded
- Celery, diced
- Corn
- Cucumber, diced
- Dried beans, cooked
- Green beans, cooked
- Lima beans, cooked
- Peas
- Radishes, sliced or chopped
- Thin carrot slices

"Greens" of any type, chopped

Combine everything. If it seems too dry, add more oil and lemon. Let stand for flavors to meld.

VARIATION: *Cook the rice in a Flavoring Broth (page 155).*

Rice Salad 2

2 cups cooked rice
½ cup corn
½ cup diced bell pepper (red preferred)
½ cup chopped tomato
¼ cup cooked peas
¼ cup diced red onion
¼ cup green beans, cut into pieces and cooked
2 tablespoons balsamic vinegar
2 teaspoons corn oil
2 tablespoons chopped fresh basil, or ¼ teaspoon dried
2 tablespoons chopped fresh parsley
1 tablespoon lime juice
⅛ teaspoon freshly ground black pepper
4 teaspoons sea salt

Combine everything and toss well.

Rice and Avocado Salad

1 cup ripe avocado, mashed
½ teaspoon crushed garlic
1 teaspoon sea salt
1½ teaspoons olive oil
2 teaspoons lemon juice
2 teaspoons wine vinegar
2 teaspoons Louisiana Hot Sauce
4 teaspoons Lea and Perrins Steak Sauce
1 tablespoon Dijon-style mustard
½ cup chopped fresh parsley
1 cup chopped tomato
3 cups rice, cooked and chilled

Combine all the ingredients in a bowl.

Rice and Bean Salad

½ cup chopped onion
½ cup chopped cucumber
½ cup chopped bell pepper
½ cup black olives, halved
1½ cups beans, cooked
2½ cups rice, cooked
½ teaspoon sea salt
2 tablespoons lemon juice
1½ teaspoons olive oil

Combine all the ingredients in a bowl.

Rice Salad Especial

1½ cups rice, uncooked
1 cup chopped black olives
1 teaspoon olive oil
¼ cup chopped pimientos
1 cup chopped tomato
2 tablespoons wine vinegar
½ teaspoon dried oregano
½ teaspoon marjoram

Cook the rice. Add the remaining ingredients, mixing well. Chill at least 2 hours.

Rice Salad Southern Style

Even Yankees will like this!

2 cups rice, uncooked
1 cup chopped green onions
1 cup chopped dill pickles
1 cup chopped sweet pickles
1 cup chopped celery
1 cup chopped bell pepper
1 cup chopped green olives, stuffed with pimientos
1 1/4 cups Cashew Mayonnaise (page 12) or Tofu Mayonnaise (page 22), or Miraculous Whip (page 17)
3 tablespoons prepared mustard
1/4 teaspoon cayenne pepper
2 teaspoons olive oil
2 teaspoons wine vinegar

Cook the rice, cool, and then combine with the vegetables. In a separate bowl, combine the mayonnaise, mustard, pepper, oil, and vinegar. Mix well with the rice mixture. Refrigerate.

Rice Salad with Black-Eyed Peas

5 cups black-eyed peas, cooked
1 tablespoon olive oil
1/8 cup lemon juice
1 teaspoon sea salt
3 cups rice, cooked
1/2 cup finely chopped onion
3/4 cup chopped celery
3/4 cup grated carrot
1/2 cup chopped bell pepper
1/3 cup chopped pimiento

Combine all the ingredients in a bowl.

Rice Salad with Olives and Capers

4 1/2 teaspoons Dijon-style mustard
1/4 cup and 1 1/2 teaspoons balsamic vinegar
1/2 teaspoon Sucanat
1/2 teaspoon sea salt
1/2 teaspoon freshly ground black pepper
1/4 cup and 1 1/2 teaspoons olive oil
3 cups cooked rice, warm
1 cup bell pepper (different colors, if possible), cut into strips
1/2 cup diced onion (red preferred)
1/2 cup capers, rinsed and drained
1/4 cup thinly sliced green onions
1/2 cup chopped black olives
1/4 cup chopped fresh parsley
1/4 cup chopped fresh dill, or 1 tablespoon dried

Combine the mustard, vinegar, and Sucanat. Whisk in the salt and pepper, then the oil. Pour this over the rice and toss well. Add the rest of the ingredients and toss again. Serve warm or cold.

Russian Potato and Beet Salad

2 1/2 cups beets, peeled, cooked, and diced
2 1/2 cups potatoes, peeled, cooked, and diced
1 cup peeled, seeded, and chopped cucumber
6 tablespoons finely chopped green onions
1/2 teaspoon dried mustard
1 teaspoon Sucanat
1 teaspoon sea salt
1/2 teaspoon freshly ground black pepper
2 tablespoons balsamic vinegar
1 cup Tofu Yogurt (page 97)
1/3 cup Cashew Sour Kreem (page 94) or Tofu Sour Kreem (page 97)
2 tablespoons chopped fresh dill

Mix everything thoroughly and refrigerate for a few hours before serving.

Salad Nicoise 1

Outstanding!

2 tablespoons lemon juice
1 teaspoon crushed garlic
1 tablespoon olive oil
1/2 teaspoon sea salt
1 teaspoon minced fresh chives
2 cups potatoes, cooked and sliced
1 cup chopped tomato
3/4 cup chopped onion

¾ cup chopped celery
½ cup chopped bell pepper
¼ cup chopped black olives or sliced
4 cups chopped romaine lettuce

Blend the lemon juice, garlic, oil, and salt. Toss with all the ingredients except the lettuce. Just before serving, mix in the lettuce.

VARIATION: *Add 1 cup of cooked white or northern beans.*

Salad Nicoise 2

You must try this!

¼ cup lemon juice or balsamic vinegar
¼ cup olive oil
½ teaspoon sea salt
½ teaspoon chervil
1 teaspoon crushed garlic
2 cups potatoes, peeled, cooked and sliced
2 cups green beans, cooked and cut into l-inch pieces
1 cup chopped tomato
1 cup sliced onion
¼ cup black olives
4 cups chopped romaine lettuce

Blend the lemon juice or vinegar, oil, salt, chervil, and garlic. While the potatoes and beans are still warm, combine them and mix in the dressing. Let sit for a few hours or refrigerate overnight. When ready to serve add the rest of the ingredients and mix well.

Summer Crock Salad

Ideal!

8 bell peppers, sliced
6 cups thinly sliced tomato
8 cups sliced onion, separated into rings
3 cups apple cider vinegar
1 cup Sucanat
2 tablespoons sea salt
2 teaspoons celery seed
3 cups corn oil

Put the vegetables in layers in a deep glass bowl, jar, crock, or enamelware pan. In another bowl combine the vinegar, Sucanat, salt, and celery seed until the Sucanat is dissolved. Then stir in the oil. Pour this over the vegetables, cover, and marinate overnight in the refrigerator.

VARIATION: *Use fresh dill or basil instead of celery seeds.*

Summer Tomato Salad

2 cups tomato wedges
¼ cup sliced onion
2 tablespoons olive or corn oil
2 tablespoons balsamic vinegar
½ teaspoon garlic salt
¼ teaspoon coarse ground black pepper
1 tablespoon chopped fresh basil, or ½ teaspoon dried

Combine everything.

Sunshine Salad

2 cups garbanzo beans, cooked
2 cups corn
1 cup diced celery
¼ cup chopped onion
¼ cup chopped bell pepper
3 tablespoons diced pimiento

Combine all the ingredients in a bowl.

Tabouli Salad

Put this in pocket bread and you have magic!

3 cups tabouli wheat (this is not cracked wheat—see Grains section)
½ cup lemon juice
1 tablespoon olive oil
2 cups finely diced cucumbers
½ cups minced bell pepper
¼ cup finely chopped fresh parsley
4 cups diced tomato
1 cup finely chopped onion
½ teaspoon cayenne pepper
2 teaspoons sea salt

Place the cracked wheat in a bowl and cover with water. Let it soak for 15 minutes, then drain. Add the lemon juice to the wheat and combine all the ingredients and mix well.

Three-Bean Salad 1

1 cup lima beans or green beans, cooked
1 cup kidney or pinto beans, pressure-cooked, drained, and cooled
1 cup garbanzo beans or white beans, pressure-cooked, drained, and cooled
1/3 cup chopped onion
1/2 teaspoon minced jalapeños
2 tablespoons lemon juice
1 teaspoon olive oil
1/4 teaspoon sea salt

Combine the beans, onions, and jalapeños. In a separate bowl, blend the lemon juice, oil, and salt. Pour over the beans and let them marinate at room temperature for 30 minutes.

Three-Bean Salad 2

2 cups garbanzo beans, cooked
1 cup kidney beans, cooked
1 cup lima beans or green beans, cooked
1/4 cup chopped bell pepper
1/2 cup chopped celery
1/2 cup chopped black olives
3/4 cup chopped onion
1 1/2 teaspoons olive oil
3 tablespoons lemon juice
1 teaspoon sea salt
1 teaspoon celery seed
1 teaspoon grated lemon peel
1 teaspoon mustard seed
1 teaspoon garlic powder
1 teaspoon dill seeds

Combine all the ingredients in a bowl.

Three-Bean Salad 3

2 cups kidney beans, cooked and drained
2 cups garbanzo beans, cooked and drained
2 cups green beans, cooked and drained
1/2 small chopped red onion
2 to 4 tablespoons finely chopped fresh parsley
1/2 cup balsamic vinegar
1/3 cup olive oil
3 garlic cloves
1/2 teaspoon dried basil
1/2 teaspoon dried oregano
1/2 teaspoon marjoram
1/2 teaspoon freshly ground black pepper
1 teaspoon sea salt

Combine beans, onion, and parsley. Combine the dressing ingredients, add to beans and mix. Refrigerate for 2 to 3 hours.

Tomato Salad

I love tomatoes, and this is my favorite!

4 cups diced tomato
1 1/2 cups chopped bell pepper
3/4 cup chopped onion
2 teaspoons olive oil
2 tablespoons lemon juice
2 tablespoons red wine vinegar
4 teaspoons chopped fresh basil, or 1 teaspoon dried
1 cup thinly sliced cucumber
1 1/2 teaspoons sea salt
1/4 teaspoon pepper
1 teaspoon paprika
1/2 teaspoon celery seed

Put tomato, bell pepper, and onion into a bowl. Add the olive oil and toss to coat evenly. Add the remaining ingredients and toss well. Refrigerate 30 minutes before serving.

Tomato and Bean Salad

1 1/2 teaspoons olive oil
4 1/4 cups plus 1/2 teaspoon lemon juice
1 teaspoon sea salt
1/2 teaspoon dried oregano
2 cups cooked dried beans
1 1/2 cups chopped tomato
3/4 cup chopped bell pepper
12 black olives, sliced
3 tablespoons chopped onion
2 tablespoons chopped fresh parsley

Combine all the ingredients in a bowl.

Tomato Slaw

2 cups shredded cabbage
1 cup diced tomato
1/4 cup chopped bell pepper

¼ cup chopped cucumber
1 teaspoon sea salt

Combine all the ingredients in a bowl.

Tossed Salad

2 tomatoes, chopped
1 bell pepper, chopped
1 carrot, chopped
1 celery stalk, chopped
1 cucumber, chopped
1 head of romaine lettuce

Combine all the ingredients in a bowl.

VARIATION: *Put in whatever you please. Experiment!*

UnShrimp Salad

3 cups macaroni
5 cups UnShrimp (page 150)
2 cups finely chopped onion
1 cup finely chopped celery
2 cups chopped black olives fine
2 cups chopped dill pickles
1 quart Miraculous Whip (page 17)
4 teaspoons olive oil
2 teaspoons Louisiana Hot Sauce or ½ teaspoon cayenne pepper
2 tablespoons lemon juice
2 tablespoons Lea and Perrins Steak Sauce
1 tablespoon mustard
2 tablespoons seafood cocktail sauce

Cook the macaroni, drain it, and let it cool. In a large bowl combine the macaroni, UnShrimp, onion, celery, olives, and pickles, and toss well. In a separate bowl, combine the mayonnaise, oil, hot sauce, lemon juice, steak sauce, mustard, and cocktail sauce. Pour this over the macaroni mixture and mix well. If the salad seems too dry, make some more sauce and mix it in. Refrigerate for 1 hour before serving.

White Bean Salad 1

1 cup dried white beans, soaked overnight in cold water
¼ onion (yellow preferred), peeled
½ cup carrot, peeled and cut into large chunks
½ teaspoon dried basil
Pinch oregano
¼ bay leaf
Enough UnChicken Broth (page 155) to cover the beans
8 garlic cloves
1 teaspoon sea salt
¾ teaspoon freshly ground black pepper
1 cup chopped celery
1¼ cup diced tomato
2 tablespoons chopped fresh basil or 1 teaspoon dried
2 tablespoons balsamic vinegar
2 teaspoons corn oil
¼ cup sliced green onions
2 tablespoons coarsely chopped fresh parsley
1 tablespoon lemon juice
1 tablespoon capers, rinsed and chopped

Drain the beans and cover them with cold water in a saucepan. Bring to a boil, drain, return to the pan, and add the onions, carrot, basil, oregano, bay leaf, broth, garlic, a pinch of the salt and ½ teaspoon of the black pepper. Bring to a boil, reduce heat, cover, and simmer gently until the beans are tender, about 2 hours, adding more broth if needed. Drain and cool. Combine the rest of the ingredients in a bowl and then mix with the beans.

White Bean Salad 2

5 cups white beans, pressure-cooked and cooled
¾ cup Italian Dressing (page 16)
½ cup chopped onion
½ cup chopped bell pepper
¼ cup chopped fresh parsley
¼ cup Cashew Mayonnaise (page 12) or Tofu Mayonnaise (page 22), Cashew Sour Kreem (page 94) or Tofu Sour Kreem (page 97), or Miraculous Whip (page 17)
1 teaspoon sea salt
½ teaspoon Louisiana Hot Sauce

Combine all the ingredients in a bowl.

VARIATION: *Add 3 cups of Pimiento Cheez (page 94).*

Potato Salads

Austrian Potato Salad

2 cups sliced potatoes, cooked and chilled
1/3 cup minced onion
1/2 teaspoon minced garlic
1/2 teaspoon sea salt
1/4 teaspoon cayenne or freshly ground black pepper
1 tablespoon minced fresh parsley
1/2 teaspoon olive oil
4 teaspoons tarragon vinegar
1/2 teaspoon prepared mustard

Combine the potatoes in a bowl with the onion, garlic, salt, pepper, and parsley. In a saucepan, bring the oil, vinegar, and mustard to a boil and pour over the salad. Mix and serve cold.

Cajun Potato Salad

A real zinger! It is best to make this a day ahead of time so the flavors will meld.

10 cups potatoes
1 1/2 cups Cashew Mayonnaise (page 12) or Tofu Mayonnaise (page 22), or Miraculous Whip (page 17)
1/4 cup prepared yellow mustard (the "American" type)
2 teaspoons sea salt
1/4 cup Louisiana Hot Sauce
1 cup dill relish
1/2 cup sweet relish
1 cup chopped green olives
1 cup finely chopped onion
1/2 cup finely chopped celery
1/2 cup finely chopped fresh parsley

Boil the potatoes in their skins, cool them, peel them, and chop in large chunks. Mix the mayonnaise, mustard, salt, and hot sauce. Combine with the potatoes and the rest of the ingredients and mix well.

Dilled Potato Salad

1 pound potatoes, cut into chunks and cooked
2 cups brussels sprouts (or a 10-ounce package frozen, thawed), halved and cooked
1 cup cherry tomatoes, halved, or chopped regular tomatoes
2 tablespoons sliced green onions
1/2 cup balsamic vinegar
2 tablespoons olive or corn oil
2 teaspoons fresh dill, snipped, or 1/4 teaspoon dried
1 teaspoon Sucanat
1/4 teaspoon sea salt

Cook the potatoes and brussels sprouts together, covered, in a small amount of boiling water for about 12 minutes, or until the potatoes are tender. (If you are using frozen sprouts, then add them after 7 minutes of cooking the potatoes.)

Drain and transfer to a bowl. Add the tomatoes and onions. Put the vinegar, oil, dill, Sucanat, and salt together in a jar and shake well to combine. Pour over the potatoes and toss everything to mix and coat well. Serve warm or cold.

French-Style Potato Salad 1

4 cups diced potatoes, cooked
½ cup chopped onion
1 cup French Dressing (page 14)
½ teaspoon sea salt
½ teaspoon paprika
¼ cup fresh parsley

Combine all of the ingredients except parsley, cover, and chill. Just before serving, stir in the parsley.

French-Style Potato Salad 2

2 pounds potatoes, peeled
¼ cup tarragon vinegar
¾ teaspoon sea salt
½ teaspoon freshly ground black pepper
1 tablespoon Dijon-style mustard
¼ cup minced onion
6 tablespoons olive oil
3 tablespoons minced fresh parsley
1 tablespoon minced fresh tarragon

Put the potatoes in a pot and cover with water. Bring to a boil, cover, and simmer, stirring once or twice to ensure even cooking, until a thin-bladed paring knife or a metal cake tester inserted into a potato can be removed with no resistance. Drain, cool the potatoes slightly, and cut them into slices while still warm, rinsing the knife occasionally in warm water. Layer warm potato slices in medium bowl, sprinkling with 2 tablespoons of the vinegar and the salt and pepper as you go. Let stand at room temperature while preparing the dressing. Combine the rest of the vinegar, mustard, and onion. Gradually whisk in the oil. Pour over potatoes and toss lightly. Refrigerate until ready to serve. Bring to room temperature and toss with the parsley and tarragon and serve.

German Potato Salad 1

½ cup chopped onion
1¾ teaspoons corn oil
2 tablespoons unbleached white flour
1 teaspoon celery seed
2 tablespoons Sucanat
1½ teaspoons sea salt
½ cup wine vinegar
1 cup water
6 cups sliced potatoes, cooked
¼ cup UnBacon (page 136), chopped fine, or imitation bacon bits
½ teaspoon paprika
¼ cup diced canned pimiento
1 tablespoon chopped fresh parsley

Sauté the onion in the oil until tender. Blend in the flour, celery seed, Sucanat, and salt. Add the vinegar and water. Cook and stir until thickened and bubbly. Add the potatoes and UnBacon and heat thoroughly, tossing lightly. Garnish with paprika, pimiento, and parsley.

German Potato Salad 2

As good as it is simple!

¾ cup chopped onion
2 tablespoons corn oil
2 tablespoons unbleached white flour
⅔ cup cider vinegar
1⅓ cup water
¼ cup Sucanat
1 teaspoon sea salt
⅛ teaspoon freshly ground black pepper
10 tablespoons UnBacon (page 136), ground
6 cups potatoes, cooked, peeled, and sliced

Sauté the onion in the oil until soft. Stir in the flour and blend well. Add the vinegar and water. Cook and stir until bubbly and slightly thick. Add the Sucanat and stir until it dissolves. Add salt and pepper. Gently stir in the UnBacon and potatoes. Heat through, stirring carefully to coat the potato slices. Serve warm.

German Potato Salad 3

7 medium potatoes, peeled, cooked, drained, and sliced
1 cup UnBacon (page 136), chopped
2 tablespoons corn oil
1/2 cup chopped onion
1/2 cup diced celery
3 tablespoons unbleached white flour
3 tablespoons Sucanat
3/4 cup water
3/4 cup vinegar
1 teaspoon sea salt
1/2 teaspoon freshly ground black pepper

Put the potatoes in a large bowl. Brown the UnBacon in the oil and take out with a slotted spoon. In remaining oil sauté the onion and celery until tender. Add the flour, Sucanat, water, vinegar, salt, and pepper. Cook and stir until it bubbles and thickens. Add the UnBacon and sauce to the potatoes. Toss gently to coat. Serve warm or at room temperature.

Grandma's Potato Salad

When I was growing up in a small town in Illinois, this was potato salad!

3 cups Miraculous Whip (page 17)
2 1/2 tablespoons Sucanat
3/4 teaspoon vanilla
1/4 teaspoon prepared mustard
1/4 cup Cashew Milk (page 93)
5 pounds potatoes, cooked, peeled, and cubed
1 cup chopped celery
3 radishes, sliced
1/2 cup chopped onion
3 tablespoons chopped bell pepper
2 1/4 teaspoons sea salt
1/2 teaspoon freshly ground black pepper
1/2 teaspoon paprika
1 1/2 tablespoons chopped fresh parsley

Combine the Miraculous Whip, Sucanat, vanilla, and mustard. Stir in the "milk." Gently fold in the potatoes, celery, radishes, onion, bell pepper, salt, and pepper. Chill for several hours or overnight. Before serving sprinkle the paprika and parsley over the top.

Herbed Potato Salad

Salad

6 cups potatoes, cooked, peeled, and cubed
1/4 cup chopped fresh parsley
1/2 cup chopped celery
2 tablespoons chopped green onions
1/2 cup diced bell pepper

Dressing

3/4 cup Fresh Herb Dressing (page 14)
1/4 cup Miraculous Whip (page 17)
1/2 teaspoon prepared mustard
1/4 teaspoon sea salt
Dash black or white pepper

Combine salad ingredients. In a separate bowl, combine dressing ingredients thoroughly, pour over the salad ingredients, and toss.

Hot Potato Salad

4 cups potatoes, quartered lengthwise and cut crosswise into 3/4-inch pieces
1/2 cup finely chopped onion
2 teaspoons corn oil
1 cup sausage gluten of choice, cut in 1/4-inch cubes (page 132)
1/2 cup white vinegar
1/2 cup UnBeef Broth (page 155)
1/2 teaspoon sea salt
1/4 teaspoon freshly ground black pepper
1/3 cup minced fresh parsley

Steam the potatoes until they are just tender. Put in a bowl and let them cool to room temperature. While steaming the potatoes, in a skillet sauté the onion in the oil until soft. Remove the skillet from the heat and add the gluten, vinegar, broth, salt, and pepper. Bring this to a boil until the liquid is reduced to about 2/3 cup. Add this to the potatoes with the parsley and combine well. Let sit for a few hours. Reheat before serving.

Mexican Potato Salad

1/2 cup salsa
1/4 cup lime juice
2 tablespoons corn oil
1/2 teaspoon sea salt

1/4 teaspoon cayenne pepper
2 pounds potatoes, cut into chunks and cooked until tender
2 1/2 cups chopped tomato
1 cup sliced mushrooms
1/2 cup sliced green onions
2 tablespoons chopped fresh parsley (or cilantro)

Combine the salsa, lime juice, oil, salt, and cayenne. Cook, uncovered, until heated through. Add to the cooked potatoes along with the rest of the ingredients and toss together to coat well.

Parsleyed Potato Salad

4 cups potatoes, cooked and diced
1/4 cup chopped celery
1/4 cup chopped fresh parsley
1/4 cup chopped bell pepper
1/2 cup chopped onion
1/4 cup chopped dill pickle
1 3/4 cups Miraculous Whip (page 17) or other "mayonnaise"
3/4 cup French Dressing 1 (page 14)
2 teaspoons prepared mustard
1 1/2 teaspoons sea salt

Combine all the ingredients in a bowl.

Potato-Cucumber Salad

Dressing
1 cup Tofu Yogurt (page 97)
1 teaspoon minced garlic
1/4 teaspoon ground ginger
1/2 teaspoon ground cumin
1 1/2 cups cucumbers, peeled, quartered, and sliced 1/4 inch thick
1 cup diced tomato
1/4 cup chopped onion
1 tablespoon seeded and minced jalapeño
2 tablespoons chopped fresh parsley, or 1 tablespoon parsley and 1 tablespoon mint
3 tablespoons nutritional yeast
1/4 cup balsamic vinegar, lemon juice, or juice from some type of pickle
1 teaspoon Sucanat
1/4 teaspoon freshly ground black pepper
1/2 teaspoon sea salt

Vegetables
5 cups potatoes, peeled, cubed, and boiled in UnChicken Broth (page 155) until just cooked
1/4 cup finely chopped bell pepper

Put dressing ingredients in a blender or food processor and blend until smooth, but not liquefied. Toss with the vegetables.

Potato Salad 1

Good with Cashew Sour Kreem (page 94) or Tofu Sour Kreem (page 97) or French Dressing (page 14).

6 cups potatoes, cooked and cubed
1 cup chopped cucumber
1/2 cup finely diced celery
3/4 cup chopped onion
1/2 cup finely chopped bell pepper
1/4 cup chopped black olives
2 to 3 tablespoons chopped fresh parsley or dill, or some of both
1 teaspoon sea salt

Combine all the ingredients in a bowl.

VARIATION: *Add 1/2 head of cabbage.*

Potato Salad 2

4 cups potatoes, boiled and sliced
1 cup chopped celery
1/2 cup chopped onion
1 tablespoon chopped pimiento
2 tablespoons chopped fresh parsley
1 teaspoon sea salt
Caper French Dressing (page 12)

Combine all the ingredients in a bowl.

Potato Salad 3

8 cups cooked and cubed potatoes
6 tablespoons finely chopped fresh parsley
1/2 cup finely chopped bell pepper
1/3 cup finely chopped black olives
1/4 cup finely chopped pimientos
3 tablespoons finely chopped onion
1/4 teaspoon cayenne pepper
3 cups Cashew Sour Kreem (page 94) or Tofu Sour Kreem (page 97)
2 1/4 teaspoons corn oil
1 tablespoon wine vinegar
1 1/2 teaspoons sea salt

Combine all the ingredients in a bowl.

VARIATION: *Use French Dressing (page 14), Cashew Mayonnaise (page 12) or Tofu Mayonnaise (page 22), or Miraculous Whip (page 17) instead of Sour Kreem.*

Potato Salad 4

3 tablespoons plus 1 teaspoon balsamic vinegar
1/4 teaspoon sea salt
1 teaspoon chopped fresh thyme, or 1/2 teaspoon dried
2 teaspoons Dijon-style mustard
1 tablespoon corn oil
1/8 teaspoon freshly ground black pepper
1/4 cup water
1 tablespoon chopped green onions
4 1/2 cups potatoes, sliced and cooked in salted water

Whisk together everything but the potatoes, pour over the potatoes, and toss to coat well.

Potato Salad with Mustard Dressing

4 cups potatoes, quartered lengthwise and cut crosswise into 3/4-inch pieces
1 tablespoon balsamic vinegar
2 tablespoons Dijon-style mustard
1/2 teaspoon sea salt
1/4 teaspoon freshly ground black pepper
1/4 cup olive oil
1/4 cup finely chopped onion
1/4 cup finely chopped bell pepper
2 tablespoons finely chopped sweet gherkin

Steam the potatoes until they are just tender. Put in a bowl and let them cool to room temperature. Whisk together the vinegar, mustard, sea salt, and pepper. Add the oil in a stream, whisking until it is emulsified. Add the dressing to the potatoes along with the onion, bell pepper, and gherkin, and combine well.

Potato Salad with Peas

2 cups peas
3 cups cubed potatoes, cooked
1/4 cup chopped onion
3/4 teaspoon sea salt
1 tablespoon parsley
1/3 cup ripe olives, sliced or chopped
1 1/2 teaspoons olive oil
2 teaspoons lemon juice

Combine all the ingredients in a bowl.

Red Potato Salad

3/4 cup Cashew Sour Kreem (page 94) or Tofu Sour Kreem (page 97)
1/2 cup Miraculous Whip (page 17)
2 tablespoons herb or balsamic vinegar
1 1/2 teaspoons sea salt
1 teaspoon celery seed
4 cups red potatoes, peeled, cooked, and cubed
3/4 cup sliced green onions
1/3 cup sliced radishes
1/4 cup chopped celery

Combine the Sour Kreem, mayonnaise, vinegar, salt, and celery seed, and set aside. Combine the rest of the ingredients. Add the dressing and toss lightly. Cover and chill.

Roast Potato Salad with Green Beans and Onions

2/3 cup olive oil
6 cups potatoes, halved and cut into 1-inch wedges
3/4 teaspoon minced garlic
1/4 cup red wine vinegar
2 teaspoons rosemary
1 1/2 teaspoons sea salt
1 1/2 cups onion, halved lengthwise and sliced thin lengthwise
6 cups green beans, cut into 1-inch pieces
24 black olives, pitted and halved

Heat 1/3 cup of the oil in a large roasting pan in a 425° oven for 5 minutes. Add the potatoes, tossing them to coat. Roast them, stirring every 10 minutes, for 30 minutes, or until they are tender. Let the potatoes cool in the pan. In a blender purée the garlic, vinegar, rosemary, and salt. Add the other 1/3 cup of the oil in a stream and blend the dressing until it is emulsified. Soak the onion in a small bowl of ice and cold water for 5 minutes. Drain it well and pat dry. Bring some water to a boil and boil the beans for 5 minutes or until crisp-tender, and drain in a colander. Rinse the beans under cold water and pat dry. Combine everything and toss gently. Serve at room temperature.

Tangy Potato Salad

Genteel fare!

12 medium red potatoes
1 cup chopped onion
2 dill pickles, chopped fine
2 tablespoons minced fresh parsley
3/4 cup UnChicken Broth (page 155)
3/4 cup Miraculous Whip (page 17)
1 1/2 teaspoons sea salt
1/2 teaspoon freshly ground black pepper
1/4 teaspoon garlic powder
2 cups cubed tomatoes
3/4 cup bacon gluten, chopped fine

Cook the potatoes in boiling salted water until tender. Drain and let cool slightly. Peel and slice. Combine with the onion, pickles, and parsley. Set aside. Heat the broth to warm, not hot. Take from heat and add the Miraculous Whip, salt, pepper, and garlic powder. Mix until smooth. Pour over the potato mixture and mix lightly. Cover and chill. Just before serving, gently stir in the tomatoes and gluten.

Tunisian Potato Salad

Truly something completely different!

3 cups potatoes, peeled and cut into 1/4-inch cubes
3/4 teaspoon cayenne pepper
1/4 teaspoon ground cumin
4 1/2 teaspoons lemon juice, strained
1/4 cup olive or corn oil
1 teaspoon ground caraway
3/4 teaspoon sea salt

Put the diced potatoes in lightly salted boiling water (enough to cover the potatoes completely), and cook briskly, uncovered, until they are tender but still intact. Drain off the water and, sliding the pan back and forth constantly, cook over low heat for a minute or so until the potatoes are dry. In a separate bowl combine the cayenne, cumin, and lemon juice thoroughly. Heat the oil in a skillet, then add the lemon juice mixture, caraway, and salt. Stirring occasionally, cook until most of the liquid has evaporated. Remove from heat, add potatoes, and turn them about gently with a spoon until they are evenly coated. Transfer to a serving bowl and cool to room temperature before serving.

Warm Potato Salad with Garlic UnSausage

4½ cups potatoes, peeled
UnSausage Broth (page 156)—enough to cover the potatoes
2 cups Garlic UnSausage (page 133), cubed
4 teaspoons balsamic vinegar
2 teaspoons Dijon-style mustard
⅓ cup olive oil
¼ cup UnSausage Broth (use some of what the potatoes were cooked in)
¼ teaspoon sea salt
⅛ teaspoon freshly ground black pepper
4 teaspoons finely chopped fresh tarragon
2 teaspoons finely chopped fresh chives
2 teaspoons finely chopped fresh parsley
2 tablespoons Parmesan Cheez (page 94)

Put the potatoes into a saucepan of broth, bring to a boil, and simmer until the potatoes are tender, about 15 minutes. Remove the potatoes, reserving the broth, let them cool, and slice them thinly. Combine with the cubed gluten. Whisk all the rest of the ingredients together. Pour over the potatoes and mix thoroughly. Serve at room temperature, or warm in an oven before serving.

Bread and Such

Anadama Bread

You might as well know—I did not like bread. Then one day I tried this. Revelation! It was so good that we began baking and selling it in stores, and from that came a successful bakery that we operated for several years.

½ cup corn meal
3 tablespoons corn oil
¼ cup Barbados molasses
2 teaspoons sea salt
¾ cup boiling water
1 package yeast
¼ cup warm water
3 cups flour

Combine the corn meal, oil, molasses, salt, and boiling water. Let stand until lukewarm. Sprinkle yeast over the ¼ cup of warm water to dissolve. Stir yeast and half of the flour into the corn meal mix. Beat. Stir in remaining flour. Knead until smooth and elastic, about 10 minutes. Transfer to a greased loaf pan, cover with a cloth, and set in a warm place until dough is 1 inch above the top of the pan. Sprinkle with a little corn meal and salt, if desired. Bake at 350°F for 50 to 60 minutes.

Apple and Banana Bread

1 apple
4 cups unbleached white flour
2½ teaspoons dry yeast
½ cup warm water
1 cup Sucanat
1 teaspoon sea salt
1 teaspoon ground cinnamon
1 teaspoon ground nutmeg
⅓ cup golden seedless raisins, soaked in apple juice
2 bananas, mashed
⅛ teaspoon grated lemon peel

Chop and steam the apple until tender. Press through a sieve to make a puree and let cool. Mix together 1 cup of flour, yeast, and warm water until smooth. Leave in a warm place until frothy. Combine remaining flour, Sucanat, salt, spices, and raisins in a bowl. Stir in yeast mixture, apple puree, mashed bananas, and lemon peel, and beat well. Divide the mixture between 2 greased loaf pans. Let rise in a warm place until mixture reaches top of pans. Bake at 375°F for about 35 minutes.

Apple Icing Bread

¾ cup warm water
2½ teaspoons Sucanat
1 tablespoon yeast
1 teaspoon sea salt
1 tablespoon corn oil
2½ cups unbleached white flour
6 cups applesauce, slightly warm
¼ cup unsweetened coconut

Mix the water, Sucanat, and yeast together and let it sit for 10 to 15 minutes. Then add the salt, oil, and flour. Squeeze between your fingers until all is mixed and the dough begins to stop sticking to your fingers. (You may need to add more flour, but do not be too quick to do so.) Turn onto an oiled board and knead well. Roll the dough out ½ inch thick. Place in a large, flat baking pan, lining it with the dough, including the sides. Prick the dough with a fork. Pour on the warm applesauce. Sprinkle with the coconut. Cover with a flat pan or kneading board. Let rise until the dough is double in thickness. Bake 1¼ hours at 350°F. Leave in the pan for one or more days. Heat before serving. Slice as a pie.

Baking Powder Biscuits

4 cups unbleached white flour
2 tablespoons baking powder
1 teaspoon sea salt
1 cup corn oil
1½ cups water

Sift the dry ingredients into a bowl. Cut in the oil until the whole thing is like coarse crumbs. Make a depression in the mass and put in the water all at once. Stir quickly with a fork just until the dough follows the fork around the bowl. Do not overmix! The dough should be soft. Turn onto a lightly floured surface. Knead gently 10 to 12 strokes. Roll or pat the dough into ½-inch thickness. Dip a cutter in flour and cut the dough straight down—no twisting! Bake on an ungreased baking sheet at 450°F for 12 to 15 minutes.

Biscuit Dumplings

2¼ cups Biscuit Mix (see below)
⅔ cup Cashew Milk (page 93) or water

Biscuit Mix
6 cups unbleached white flour
3 tablespoons baking powder
3 tablespoons Sucanat
1 tablespoon sea salt
1 cup nondairy margarine

For Biscuit Mix: In a large mixing bowl combine thoroughly the dry ingredients. Sift it all together 6 to 8 times. Work in the margarine with your fingers until the mixture is the consistency of very fine gravel. (Store in a tightly covered container at room temperature for up to 4 months. Tape 2 or 3 whole bay leaves to the inside of the lid to keep away any bugs.) Mix with Cashew Milk into a soft dough. Drop by spoonfuls into boiling liquid. Cook uncovered over low heat for 10 minutes. Cover and cook 10 minutes more.

Biscuits

2 cups unbleached white flour
1 tablespoon baking powder
½ teaspoon sea salt
¼ cup corn oil
¾ cup Cashew Milk (page 93)

Sift the dry ingredients into a bowl. Cut in the oil until the mixture is like coarse crumbs. Make a well in the mixture and add the Cashew Milk all at once. Stir quickly with a fork just until dough follows the fork around the bowl. Turn onto a lightly floured surface. (The dough should be soft.) Knead gently 10 to 12 strokes. Roll or pat the dough ½ inch thick. Dip a cutter in flour and cut the dough straight down—no twisting. Bake on an ungreased baking sheet at 450°F for 12 to 15 minutes.

Breadsticks

A satisfying change from ordinary bread or crackers. Also a great crunchy snack when you want that little something that is also good for you!

2 tablespoons yeast
1 cup warm water
1 teaspoon Sucanat
¼ cup corn oil
3 cups unbleached white flour
½ teaspoon garlic powder
1½ teaspoons sea salt
¼ cup nutritional yeast
½ cup finely minced onion

Mix the yeast, water, and Sucanat. Let stand in a warm place for 10 to 15 minutes until risen and foamy. Whisk in the oil. In another bowl sift together the flour, garlic powder, salt, and nutritional yeast, and mix well. Add this, in small amounts at a time, with a whisk, to the yeast mixture, alternating with the onion. Continue to mix it with a spoon till it is smooth. Knead it for a while, just until it is a nice soft ball. Roll it out to about pencil thickness, and cut in strips with a pizza cutter. Put strips in lightly oiled baking pans with some space between. Let stand in a warm place until they rise. Bake in a 400°F oven for 10 to 15 minutes, or until golden brown on both sides, turning them over once.

For hard breadsticks: Put breadsticks in a warm oven overnight or in a 200°F oven for 2 to 3 hours, or until hard.

"Buttered" Bread Crumbs

Sauté 1 cup of bread crumbs in 1/3 cup of nondairy margarine. You may add minced onion, if you like.

Cheez Bread

Make the recipe for White Bread (page 57), except put in 1 cup of nutritional yeast.

Corn Bread 1

The same as White Bread (page 57), except add these ingredients:

4 cups white flour
1 3/4 cups corn flour
2 3/4 cups water

The kneading time must be 15 minutes.

Corn Bread 2

2 cups cornmeal
2 cups unbleached white flour
5 teaspoons baking powder
1 1/2 teaspoons sea salt
2 tablespoons Sucanat
2 3/4 cups water
1/3 cup corn oil

Mix all dry ingredients, then add all liquid ingredients and mix. Pour into greased and floured pan. Bake at 425°F for about 45 minutes or until top is browned.

VARIATION: *For crispy corn bread, add water until a thin batter is formed, pour out until batter covers the bottom of the pan or cookie sheet, and then bake.*

Corn Bread 3

1/2 cup finely chopped onion
Corn oil
1 1/4 cups unbleached white flour
3/4 cup cornmeal
2 tablespoons Sucanat
1 tablespoon baking powder
1 teaspoon sea salt
1 tablespoon nutritional yeast
3 tablespoons nondairy margarine
1 cup Cashew Milk (page 93)
1/2 cup bacon gluten, chopped fine

Sauté the onion in as little corn oil as possible. Mix the flour, cornmeal, Sucanat, baking powder, salt, and yeast together and set aside. Melt the margarine and add the Cashew Milk to it. Stir that into the dry ingredients. Stir in the onion and gluten. Pour into greased and floured pan. Bake at 425°F for about 45 minutes or until top is browned.

Corn Chips

The commercial cardboard-tasting chips just cannot equal these!

1/2 cup Cashew Milk (page 93) or water
3 tablespoons corn oil
1/2 cup yellow cornmeal
1/2 cup toasted cornmeal
1/2 cup unbleached white flour
3/4 teaspoon sea salt
1/4 teaspoon baking soda
1/8 teaspoon cayenne pepper
1/2 teaspoon chili powder
1/4 teaspoon onion powder
Salt or paprika

Combine the Cashew Milk and oil and set aside. Stir the dry ingredients together in a mixing bowl. Add the Cashew Milk mixture and stir until the dough forms a ball. Knead on a floured board (adding a little more flour if necessary) about 5 minutes. Divide the dough in half. Roll each half into a 12-inch square. Cut into 1-inch squares. Sprinkle with salt or paprika. Bake on a lightly oiled baking sheet for 15 minutes or until lightly brown around the edges. Cool slightly before removing from the baking sheet, and transfer to a wire rack.

Corn Tortillas

3 cups unbleached white flour
3 cups corn flour (not meal)
1 teaspoon sea salt
1 teaspoon baking powder
1/4 cup corn oil or nondairy margarine, melted
1 1/4 cups warm water

Mix the flours, salt, and baking powder. Make a depression and put in the oil (or margarine). Mix with a spoon. Add 1/2 cup of warm water and mix again. Add about 3/4 cup more warm water, or enough to knead it into bread dough consistency. Let it rest for about 5 minutes. Form into balls about 1 1/2 inches in diameter and dip each ball into flour before rolling it out on a lightly floured board. Cook on a hot, dry griddle until bubbly and brown-flecked on each side. (This will not take long—only a few seconds on a really hot griddle.)

VARIATION: *For deep-fried tortillas, omit the baking powder.*

Cranberry Bread

This makes a special gift, but bake some for yourself, too!

2 cups unbleached white flour, sifted
1 teaspoon sea salt
1/2 teaspoon baking soda
1 1/2 teaspoons baking powder
1 1/4 cups Sucanat, or genuine maple syrup
1/4 cup corn oil
1 N'egg (page 302)
3/4 cup orange juice
1 tablespoon grated orange rind (optional)
1/2 cup chopped nuts
1 cup chopped cranberries

Sift together the dry ingredients. Cut in the oil. Pour the N'egg, orange juice, and grated rind all at once into the dry ingredients, mixing just enough to dampen. Carefully fold in the nuts and cranberries. Spoon into a greased loaf pan. Spread the corners and sides slightly higher than the center. Bake at 350°F about 1 hour.

Drop Biscuits

2 1/4 cups Biscuit Mix (page 50)
2/3 cup Cashew Milk (page 93) or water

Mix into a dough and beat for 30 seconds. Drop by spoonfuls onto an ungreased baking sheet. Bake at 450°F 8 to 10 minutes until golden brown.

Flat Bread

This doesn't look like much on the page, but it is excellent! We much prefer this to chapatis or puris when eating Indian food.

1 cup rye flour
2 cups unbleached white flour
2/3 cup soy flour
1/3 cup wheat bran
1 teaspoon sea salt
1/4 cup corn oil
1 1/4 cups boiling water

Mix the flours, bran, and salt in a bowl. Add the oil. Stir in only enough of the boiling water to make a stiff dough. Knead to mix thoroughly. Roll out small pieces of dough paper-thin to about 8 inches in diameter. Bake directly on top of an ungreased griddle, or place on an ungreased cookie sheet in an oven set at 250°F until thoroughly dried and slightly browned.

Flour Tortillas

6 cups unbleached white flour
1 teaspoon sea salt

1 teaspoon baking powder
1/4 cup corn oil or nondairy margarine, melted
1/2 cup warm water
3/4 cup warm water

Mix together the flour, salt, and baking powder. Make a well and pour in the oil or margarine and mix again with a spoon. Add 1/2 cup of warm water and mix again. Add about 3/4 cup more warm water—enough to knead it into bread dough consistency. Let it rest for 5 minutes. Form into balls about 1 1/2 inches in diameter and dip each ball into flour before rolling it out very thin on an unfloured board. Cook on a hot, dry griddle until bubbly and brown-flecked on each side.

French Bread

1 package dry yeast
1 teaspoon Sucanat
2 cups warm water (100°F–103°F)
3 1/3 cups unbleached white flour
1 1/2 teaspoons sea salt
1 tablespoon corn oil

In a glass measuring cup, stir together the yeast, Sucanat, and 1/2 cup of warm water. Allow it to stand until foamy. In a large bowl of an electric mixer, place the yeast mixture, rest of water, flour, and salt, and beat for 5 to 7 minutes or until the dough is smooth and elastic. It should be very soft and sticky. Drizzle the oil evenly over the dough. Cover the bowl with plastic wrap and then a towel and set it in a warm place (75°F–80°F) until it is doubled in bulk. With a spatula, scrape the dough down into the bowl, cover it as before, and let it rise again until doubled. Grease a 3-loaf baguette pan, 8 1/2x17 inches. With a large kitchen spoon, scoop out 1/3 of the dough into each section and spread it out evenly. Brush the tops with a little oil. Cover the pan loosely with plastic wrap and allow the dough to rise again until almost doubled. Remove the plastic wrap and bake in a preheated 425°F oven about 25 minutes, until the tops are a beautiful golden brown and the bread sounds hollow when tapped. Remove the bread from the pan and cool on a rack.

Fried Cheez Balls

1 cup Biscuit Mix (page 50)
1 1/2 cups yeast or Notzarella Cheez (page 94)
1/2 cup chopped onion
Oil

Mix everything together, adding a little water if needed, and form into balls and fry them in oil.

Fried Cornmeal Cakes

Versatile. Can be a side dish or can take the place of corn bread, regular bread, biscuits, etc. Good with syrup, too!

2 tablespoons nondairy margarine, softened
2 cups Cashew Milk (page 93)
2 cups water
1 tablespoon corn oil
1 1/3 cups yellow cornmeal
1 teaspoon sea salt

Spread the margarine over the bottom and sides of a shallow baking dish with a pastry brush. Set aside. In a saucepan bring the "milk," water, and corn oil to a boil. Stirring constantly with a wooden spoon, pour in the cornmeal in a slow, thin stream so the water continues to boil as the cornmeal is absorbed. Stir in the salt, reduce heat to low, and, stirring frequently, simmer until the cornmeal is so thick that the spoon will stand unsupported in the middle of the pan, 15 to 20 minutes. While the cornmeal is still hot, spoon it into the baking dish, spreading it out to 1/2-inch thickness, smoothing the top with a spatula. Cover with wax paper and refrigerate overnight or for at least 6 hours. Or spread the cornmeal into a pan with sides and cool in a freezer for 15 or more minutes, until the cornmeal is firm to the touch. With a pastry wheel or sharp knife, divide the chilled cornmeal into 2-inch squares and carefully lift them out of the pan with a small metal spatula. In a skillet melt 2 tablespoons of nondairy margarine. Fry 4 or 5 of the cornmeal squares for 2 or 3 minutes on each side, turning them over gently with a spatula until brown. Fry the remaining squares, adding more margarine as needed.

Garlic Bread

Melt two cups of nondairy margarine with 1 tablespoon of garlic powder. Spread on bread slices. Toast the bread in the oven under the broiler.

Garlic Croutons

1 loaf of bread
2 cups nondairy margarine
1 tablespoon garlic powder

Cube the bread (about ½-inch cubes). Toast in the oven at 550°F, turning often until the edges brown, about 10 minutes. Melt the margarine with the garlic powder. Roll the toasted bread cubes in the margarine.

Hamburger Buns

Make Whole Wheat Bread (page 57) or White Bread (page 57) recipe. Roll out dough thickly on a lightly floured surface and cut into six 4-inch rounds. Place on a baking sheet, brush lightly with apple juice, and bake at 400°F for 20 to 25 minutes.

Herb Bread

Make the recipe for White Bread (page 57), except put in 1 teaspoon oregano, 1½ teaspoons rosemary, 1 teaspoon turmeric, and ½ teaspoon sage.

Herb and Onion Bread

Make the recipe for White Bread (page 57), except put in 1 cup of finely chopped onion and ½ teaspoon of dill weed.

Hush Puppies

Even Yankees like these! Try using different kinds of chopped vegetables.

2 cups cornmeal
1 cup unbleached white flour
1 teaspoon baking powder
1 teaspoon sea salt
½ teaspoon baking soda
½ teaspoon garlic powder
½ cup finely chopped fresh parsley
¼ teaspoon cayenne pepper
2 N'eggs (page 302)
1 cup Cashew Milk (page 93) or Tofu Buttermilk (page 96)
1 cup finely chopped green onions
2 tablespoons corn oil

Combine the cornmeal, flour, baking powder, salt, baking soda, and garlic powder. Add the rest of the ingredients and mix well. Drop by spoonfuls into hot oil and deep-fry until brown on all sides. Remove and drain on paper towels.

Mexican Bread

1 package yeast
1¼ cups warm water
3 cups unbleached white flour
¾ cup yellow cornmeal
½ cup corn
1 tablespoon chopped jalapeños
1 N'egg (page 302)
1 tablespoon nondairy margarine
½ teaspoon sea salt
4 teaspoons Sucanat

Dissolve yeast in ¼ cup warm water until it starts to foam. Combine the rest of the ingredients except for the remaining cup of water. Add the yeast mixture and water. Knead into a dough. Place in a nonstick loaf pan and allow to rise until doubled in size. Bake at 400°F until golden brown.

Mexican Corn Bread

1 cup unbleached white flour
1½ cups cornmeal
3 teaspoons baking powder
1 teaspoon sea salt
½ teaspoon baking soda
1 teaspoon Sucanat
1 cup corn
2 N'eggs (page 302)
2 jalapeño peppers, chopped
2 tablespoons finely chopped bell pepper
1 cup Cashew Sour Kreem (page 94) or Tofu Sour Kreem (page 97), or Cashew Buttermilk (page 93) or Tofu Buttermilk (page 96)

1 cup Yeast Cheez (page 97)
2 teaspoons corn oil

Mix everything together and pour into a hot skillet. Bake at 400°F for 1 hour or until brown.

Oatcakes

Something truly different. I like these just by themselves, but they can be used in place of crackers, biscuits, and regular bread. A backpacker's delight!

1¾ cups oatmeal
¼ teaspoon baking powder
¼ teaspoon sea salt
1 tablespoon nondairy margarine, melted
5 to 8 teaspoons hot water

Half a cup at a time, pulverize 1 cup of the oatmeal by blending at high speed in a blender until you have a gritty "flour." Combine the pulverized oatmeal, baking powder, and salt in a bowl. Stir in the melted margarine. When all the margarine has been absorbed, add the hot water, a teaspoon at a time, stirring constantly, to make a smooth but firm paste. Gather the mixture into a ball and place it on a board or table lightly sprinkled with ¼ cup of the remaining oatmeal. Roll the ball into the oatmeal until it is completely covered with the flakes. Spread another ¼ cup of oatmeal evenly over the board and, with a rolling pin, roll the ball out into an 8-inch circle about ⅛ inch thick. With a pastry wheel or sharp knife, cut the circle into 8 pie-shaped wedges. Scatter the remaining ¼ cup of oatmeal on a baking sheet and, with a large metal spatula, carefully transfer the wedges to the sheet. Bake the cakes in the middle of the oven for about 15 minutes at 350°F. When the wedges are light brown, turn off the heat and open the door of the oven. Leave the oatcakes in the oven until they become firm and crisp, 4 to 5 minutes. Serve at once.

One-Hour Whole Wheat Bread

Everything—including the flour—must be measured, warm, and ready to go. (Warm the flour by putting it in a 275°F oven for 3 to 5 minutes.)

1 cup warm water
3 packages yeast
1 tablespoon molasses (unsulphured)
3 cups hot water
⅓ cup Sucanat
1½ cups whole wheat flour
1½ tablespoons salt
¼ cup oil
Approximately 7½ cups whole wheat flour—just enough to make a soft dough consistency

Combine the 1 cup of warm water, yeast, and molasses, and let it stand for 10 minutes. While the yeast mixture is standing, combine the 3 cups of hot water, Sucanat, and 1½ cups of whole wheat flour. After the 10 minutes, or when this has cooled to lukewarm, add the yeast mixture and let it stand for 15 minutes. Add the salt, oil, and flour. Mix so it makes a soft dough—not too stiff. If you want, you can knead it for up to 10 minutes, but you may knead it just until it is smooth. Put directly into loaf pans (3 or 4, according to the size of loaf you want). Let sit in a warm place until doubled in bulk. Bake at 350°F until done.

Onion Bread

Make the recipe for White Bread (page 57), except put in 1½ cups of chopped onion.

Pocket Bread

We struggled for years to succeed in making pita (pocket) bread, and here is the success!

1½ teaspoons dry active yeast
1½ cups warm water
1 tablespoon Sucanat, genuine maple syrup, or Barbados molasses
¼ cup corn oil
4 cups unbleached white flour
½ teaspoon sea salt
Oil

Preheat your oven to 550°F. Dissolve the yeast in warm water, and add the sweetener and oil. Set aside for a few minutes. It should foam up. Sift together the flour and salt. Add the yeast mixture to the flour and salt and knead 5 minutes. Shape the dough into a ball and place it in an oiled bowl. Coat the dough ball lightly with oil. Cover the bowl with a dry towel and place it in a warm place until it is doubled in bulk, about one hour. Again knead for 5 minutes. Separate the dough into 4 parts. Divide each of those parts into 6 small balls, so you have 24 total. (If you desire a larger size pocket bread, divide the parts into larger balls.) Roll all of the balls out into round shapes about 1/8 to 1/4 inch thick. Then beginning again in the order you originally rolled them out, roll the rounds out slightly thinner (somewhere between 1/8 and 1/4 inch thick). This may seem unnecessary, but it is important. Cover them all with a dry cloth and then with a damp cloth over the dry. Let the rounds rise for 20 minutes. While the rounds are rising, put your ungreased baking pans (or cookie sheets) in the oven so they will get hot. After 20 minutes, take the pans out of the oven and quickly and gently transfer the rounds to the pans. Place the pans on the bottom rack of the oven for about 2 minutes. Then transfer the pans to the middle of the oven for 1 to 2 minutes more. Remove the pans, cool the rounds, and cut in half. If you are not going to serve the bread immediately, cover the rounds with a damp cloth so they will not dry out.

Tips

If you wish the tops of the bread to be more browned, transfer the pans to a rack in the middle of the oven and leave them there for two more minutes. If the bread is a day or more old, you can steam it to soften it before serving.

Pumpernickel Bread

1 quart water, warm enough to warm up the molasses
1 cup Barbados molasses
1 tablespoon oil
1 tablespoon salt
1 package of yeast
3 cups rye flour
6 cups whole wheat flour

Mix the water, molasses, oil, salt, and yeast, and let them stand for 10 minutes. Slightly warm the flour in the oven. Add the flour to the other ingredients. Mix. Let stand for 15 minutes. Knead until smooth and elastic. Cover and put in a warm place until it is doubled in bulk. Form into small loaves and place in pans. Let rise again until doubled in size. Bake for one hour at 350°F.

Puris

1/2 teaspoon sea salt
1 cup whole wheat flour
1 cup unbleached white flour
1 1/2 teaspoons nondairy margarine
1 1/2 teaspoons corn oil
1 cup warm water (all this may not be used)

Combine the salt, flour, margarine, and oil and mix until it looks like coarse meal. Add the minimum amount of water and knead well, adding water slowly. Use only enough water so as to form a firm compact ball. Knead about 7 minutes, or until the dough becomes smooth and elastic. Cover the dough with a damp towel and let it sit for at least 30 minutes. Break off pieces about 2 tablespoons in size. Roll out each piece on a lightly floured surface into a 5- or 6-inch circle. Deep fry until it starts to brown, turning occasionally. They will puff up some. Set to drain in a colander or on paper towels. Keep them covered if they are to sit for any length of time. Taste-test the first few. If they are raw, either the oil is too hot or the puri is rolled too thick. If it is too crisp, then it has been rolled too thin.

"Sourdough" Bread

Use one of the recipes for Whole Wheat Bread (see below) or White Bread (see below), but instead of water use Tofu Yogurt (page 97), in the same amount as the recipe calls for water.

Soy Bread

7 cups warm water
½ cup plus 2 tablespoons Barbados molasses
3 tablespoons yeast (dry; or 2 yeast cakes)
½ cup corn oil
2 tablespoons sea salt
14 cups unbleached white flour
4 cups soy flour

Combine the water, 2 tablespoons of molasses, and yeast. Let it stand until dissolved. Add the ½ cup of molasses, oil, and salt. Stirring, slowly add the flours. Mix with a spoon and then knead for 10 minutes. Let rise in warm place until doubled. Shape into loaves. Brush with oil and let rise till very light. Bake at 350°F until brown on top, about 1 hour.

Sweet Muffins

2 cups Biscuit Mix (page 50)
⅓ cup Sucanat
⅔ cup Cashew Milk (page 93)
2 tablespoons corn oil

Mix all ingredients together until just moistened. Spoon into greased muffin pans and bake at 400°F for about 15 minutes, until brown.

VARIATION: *After mixing muffin batter, fold in ¾ cup blueberries.*

Toast Points

Trim the crust from thin slices of bread. Cut the bread slices diagonally in half. Brush one side of each slice with melted margarine. Put the bread, margarine side up, on a baking sheet. Bake at 450°F for 3 minutes. Turn the bread over and bake until golden brown, 2 to 3 minutes.

White Bread

1 package dry yeast
2¼ cups warm water
2 teaspoons sea salt
2 tablespoons corn oil
1 tablespoon Sucanat, genuine maple syrup, or Barbados molasses
6¼ cups unbleached white flour (or a combination of white and whole wheat flours)

Soften the yeast in the ¼ cup of warm water. Combine all the rest of the ingredients with the yeast. Turn out on floured board and knead until smooth and satiny, about 10 minutes. Cover and let sit in a warm place for about 20 to 30 minutes. Punch down and separate into three equal parts. Put the dough into loaf pans and shape. Wipe their tops with more oil and let rise 30 to 45 minutes. Bake in 400°F oven until well brown so there will be a heavy crust.

Whole Wheat Bread

A lot of whole wheat bread ought to be sold to the roads department to fill holes in the pavement. But this is what it ought to be!

3 cups warm water (105°F–110°F)
3 tablespoons yeast
3 tablespoons Sucanat, genuine maple syrup, or Barbados molasses
3 teaspoons sea salt
3 tablespoons corn oil
8 cups whole wheat flour (warmed in a 275°F oven for 3 to 5 minutes)

Mix the water, yeast, and sweetener together. Add the salt, oil, and flour. Knead for 10 minutes. Let rise in the bowl in a warm place, covered, until doubled in bulk. Cut into 3 parts with a sharp knife, place in loaf pans, and shape. Allow to rise until doubled in bulk. Bake in a 425°F oven for 15 minutes. Reduce heat to 350°F and bake about 30 minutes more. Remove from pans and cool on a wire rack so the air can circulate around them.

VARIATIONS: *For Raisin Bread, add 1½ cups of raisins to the dough. For a single loaf, use only ⅓ of the ingredients, except use 2½ cups of flour.*

Whole Wheat Buns

Make the Whole Wheat Bread recipe (page 57). Roll out the dough thickly on a lightly floured surface and cut into six 4-inch rounds. Put on a baking sheet, brush lightly with apple juice, and bake at 400°F for 20 to 25 minutes.

Yeast Biscuits 1

A good idea!

1 1/3 cups warm water
1 tablespoon yeast
4 cups unbleached white flour
1 teaspoon sea salt
2 tablespoons Sucanat
1/4 cup corn oil

Mix all ingredients, but only barely enough to get them wet, as overhandling makes the biscuits more like rolls. Oil your hands and shape the biscuits. Place on an oiled pan 1/2 inch apart. Let them rise only about 1/4 inch or the texture will resemble that of buns instead of biscuits. Bake at 400°F for 20 to 30 minutes.

Yeast Biscuits 2

1 tablespoon dry yeast
1 cup warm water
1 tablespoon Sucanat or Barbados molasses
2 1/2 cups unbleached white flour
1 teaspoon sea salt
5 tablespoons nondairy margarine or corn oil

Dissolve the yeast in 1/2 cup of warm water with the sweetener. Sift together the flour and salt. Cut shortening and remaining warm water into the flour and salt. Add the yeast mixture and mix lightly. Roll out 1 inch thick. Cut with biscuit cutter. Place on an oiled pan 1/2 inch apart. Let rise 20 minutes. Bake at 400°F–425°F for 25 to 30 minutes.

Crackers

Crackers

This makes good pizza dough, too.

1½ tablespoons yeast
1 cup warm water
1 teaspoon Sucanat
⅓ cup corn oil
1 teaspoon sea salt
3½ cups unbleached white flour

Combine the yeast, water, and Sucanat in a medium-sized bowl. Let sit until foamy. Add the oil, salt, and flour to the yeast mixture and knead lightly together. Let rise at least 5 minutes. Roll out thin. Put in a baking pan that has not been oiled. Cut or score into squares or diamonds. Bake at 450°F–500°F until light brown.

Cheez Crackers

My favorite cracker to eat straight or in soup. Make these good and crispy.

2 cups unbleached white flour
2 teaspoons baking powder
½ teaspoon sea salt
2 tablespoons corn oil
¾ cup water
½ cup nutritional yeast
1 teaspoon garlic powder
1 teaspoon chili powder (optional)

Mix all ingredients into a stiff dough, adding more water as needed. Knead lightly. Roll dough as thin as possible. Oil the top of the dough and sprinkle with salt. Cut into squares. Bake 5 to 7 minutes at 375°F or until brown on both sides.

Coconut Crackers

As good as they are unusual.

⅓ cup coconut
¼ cup Barbados molasses
1 teaspoon sea salt
3 tablespoons corn oil
¾ cup water
3 cups unbleached white flour

Blend the coconut, molasses, salt, oil, and water in a blender until the coconut is chopped. Pour this into the flour and mix into a dough. Roll out very thin on cookie sheets. Score and prick with a fork. Bake at 275°F until well browned, about 45 minutes.

Graham Crackers

Better than the "real thing"!

2 cups whole wheat flour
1 1/2 cups unbleached white flour
2 tablespoons cornstarch or arrowroot
1/2 teaspoon sea salt
1/2 cup water
1/3 cup corn oil
1/2 cup Barbados molasses

Mix all the dry ingredients. In a blender, mix all the wet ingredients. Combine with dry ingredients. Knead a little. Roll out to 1/4 inch thick. Cut, and prick with a fork. Bake at 275°F for 35 minutes.

Rye Crisps

3 cups rolled oats
1 cup rye flour
1/2 teaspoon sea salt
1/4 cup corn oil
1 cup water

Grind the oats to a course flour in a blender. Combine with other dry ingredients. Add the oil to the water in a blender and whirl to emulsify. Pour it over the dry mixture while stirring to distribute the moisture evenly. Divide into three equal portions and place each on an ungreased cookie sheet. Press out flat with your fingers. Sprinkle lightly with flour to prevent sticking to the rolling pin, and then roll out until thin and even. Cut into squares or diamond shapes. Bake at 300°F for 50 minutes. Watch carefully when nearly done. Or bake at 250°F for 1 1/4 hours to be sure the crisps do not burn.

Soups

Abbot George's Low-Calorie Soup

9 cups tomato juice
3 cups cubed potatoes
1 cup chopped onion
½ cup chopped bell pepper
6 tablespoons finely chopped jalapeño
1 cup lima beans
1 tablespoon fresh parsley, minced
1¼ cups cubed gluten (plain or flavored)
⅓ cup chopped carrot
¾ teaspoon sea salt
¼ teaspoon basil
⅛ teaspoon garlic powder

Combine and cook until potatoes are good and soft, about 30 minutes or more.

VARIATION: *Substitute 2 cups of Snap-E-Tom for 2 cups of the tomato juice.*

Almost Instant Vegetable Soup 1

6 cups frozen vegetables of choice, thawed
⅛ teaspoon freshly ground black pepper
¼ teaspoon onion powder
⅛ teaspoon garlic powder
1½ teaspoons corn oil
½ teaspoon sea salt
1 teaspoon monosodium glutamate (MSG)
½ teaspoon poultry seasoning
3 tablespoons nutritional yeast
4 cups water

Combine all ingredients, heat, and serve.

VARIATIONS: *Include 3 cups of canned tomatoes, blended slightly to break them up (in which case use 2 teaspoons of oil). Omit the MSG and add 1 teaspoon of salt.*

Almost Instant Vegetable Soup 2

¾ cup chopped onion
2 teaspoons corn oil
4 cups frozen vegetables
3 cups chopped canned tomatoes (reserve liquid)
1 teaspoon basil
3 tablespoons soy sauce
½ teaspoon cayenne pepper
4 cups UnBeef Broth (page 155)

Sauté the onion in the oil. Combine all ingredients and cook together for 20 to 30 minutes. If more liquid is needed, use the tomato liquid or more broth.

Avocado and Tomato Soup

6 medium tomatoes, chopped and pureed
2/3 cup Cashew Sour Kreem (page 94) or Tofu Sour Kreem (page 97)
1/2 cup Cashew Milk (page 93)
3 tablespoons lemon juice
2 tablespoons Italian tomato paste
1 1/2 teaspoons olive oil
3 tablespoons chopped fresh parsley
1 1/2 teaspoons sea salt
1/4 teaspoon white pepper
1 small ripe avocado, peeled, pitted, and pureed or mashed

Combine everything, except the avocado, until well blended. Cover tightly and refrigerate for at least 2 hours, until thoroughly chilled. Just before serving, blend the avocado into it.

Baked Bean Soup

3 cups Barbecue Baked Beans (page 230)
1/2 cup canned tomatoes, blended
2 cups water
1 tablespoon soy sauce
1/4 teaspoon cayenne pepper

Combine everything and simmer for 30 minutes. Add more water or tomato juice if it gets too thick.

Basque Vegetable Soup

2 1/2 cups chopped onion
3/4 teaspoon minced garlic
1 tablespoon corn oil
1 1/2 cups sliced sausage gluten of choice (page 132)
2 cups cubed UnChicken (page 137)
1 cup sliced carrot
1 large turnip, peeled and cubed
1 1/4 cups peeled and cubed potatoes
1 1/2 teaspoons sea salt
1/2 teaspoon freshly ground black pepper
1 tablespoon chopped fresh parsley
1 teaspoon thyme
1 cup shredded cabbage
2 cups cooked navy or great northern beans
6 cups UnChicken Broth (page 155)

Sauté the onion and garlic in the oil until soft. Combine everything, bring to a boil, reduce heat, cover, and simmer for 30 minutes.

Black Bean and Spinach Soup

2/3 cup black beans
3 tablespoons chopped onion
2 tablespoons chopped celery
1 teaspoon finely chopped garlic
2 teaspoons corn oil
1/4 teaspoon ground ginger
1/2 teaspoon sea salt
1/4 teaspoon freshly ground black pepper
4 cups water
5 ounces spinach leaves, stemmed and rinsed
4 tablespoons Tofu Yogurt (page 97)

Sort, wash well, and drain the black beans. Sauté the onion, celery, and garlic in the oil until soft. Combine with the beans, ginger, salt, pepper, and water and bring to a boil, stirring occasionally. Reduce heat and simmer, covered, until the beans are fully cooked, about 1 hour. Meanwhile, wash the spinach leaves to remove all sand and grit. Put them in a skillet and sauté in a small amount of corn oil until they are wilted but still bright green, 2 to 3 minutes. Cool. Mince the spinach and set aside. Put 1/3 of the beans into a blender or food processor. Puree until completely smooth and transfer back to the soup. Stir the spinach into the soup, return to a simmer. Take from the heat and stir in the yogurt.

Black Bean Soup 1

2 1/2 cups dried black beans
1 cup chopped bell pepper
3 tablespoons chopped onion
2 teaspoons corn oil
6 cups UnBeef Broth (page 155) or UnChicken Broth (page 155)
3/4 teaspoon sea salt
1/8 teaspoon cayenne pepper
2 cups chopped tomato
1/4 teaspoon summer savory

Pressure-cook the beans. Sauté the bell pepper and onion in the oil. Combine with rest of ingredients and cook about 30 minutes more. If needed, add more broth or water to keep a soup consistency.

Black Bean Soup 2

2 cups dried black beans
1/3 cup chopped onion
1/2 cup chopped celery
1/2 teaspoon minced garlic
2 teaspoons corn oil
1/8 teaspoon Italian herb seasoning
1/4 teaspoon sage
1 bay leaf
1/4 teaspoon cayenne pepper
2 cups cooked and diced potatoes
1 cup carrots, cooked and sliced into rounds
1 cup finely chopped UnBacon (page 136)
4 cups UnChicken Broth (page 155)

Pressure-cook the beans. Sauté the onion, celery, and garlic in the corn oil. Combine all ingredients and cook for 30 minutes.

VARIATIONS: *Omit the gluten and use UnBeef Broth (page 155) instead.*

Black Bean Soup 3

1 cup dried black beans
3/4 cup chopped onion
1 teaspoon nondairy margarine
2 cups UnBeef Broth (page 155) or UnChicken Broth (page 155)
1/4 teaspoon cayenne pepper

Pressure-cook the beans. Sauté the onion in the margarine. Combine all ingredients and simmer for 1 hour.

Borscht 1

Peeling the beets ensures that they will not have their usual "earthy" taste that many people dislike.

2 cups peeled and diced beets
1 cup peeled and diced carrots
4 cups peeled and diced potatoes
1/2 cup diced celery
1/2 cup chopped onion
1/2 cup chopped tomato
1 bay leaf
1 teaspoon sea salt
1/4 teaspoon freshly ground black pepper
4 cups UnBeef Broth (page 155)
1 tablespoon corn oil

Combine everything, bring to a boil, reduce heat, and simmer until the potatoes start to fall apart. Serve with Cashew Sour Kreem (page 94) or Tofu Sour Kreem (page 97).

Borscht 2

1 cup chopped onion
1 tablespoon corn oil
1/2 cup chopped carrot
1/4 cup chopped celery
1/4 teaspoon freshly ground black pepper
1 cup tomato puree
1 teaspoon dill
2 cups peeled and grated beets
1 cup peeled and grated potato
2 1/2 cups shredded cabbage
8 cups UnBeef Broth (page 155)
2 tablespoons lemon juice

Sauté the onion in the oil until it is transparent. Add the carrot, celery, and pepper, and sauté until they are soft. Add the tomato puree and dill and simmer 10 minutes. Add the beets, potato, cabbage, and broth. Bring to a boil, reduce heat, and simmer until the vegetables are tender. Add the lemon juice.

Broccoli, Bean, and Spaghetti Soup

1/3 cup chopped onion
1/2 teaspoon minced garlic
3 1/2 teaspoons corn oil
2 cups cooked dried beans
4 cups chopped broccoli
6 cups chopped tomato
1/2 teaspoon basil
1/2 teaspoon oregano
1/8 teaspoon cayenne pepper
1/2 teaspoon sea salt
2 cups UnChicken Broth (page 155)
1 cup spaghetti, uncooked, broken in pieces

Sauté the onion and garlic in the oil. Combine all the ingredients, except the spaghetti, and cook for 30 minutes. While this is being done, cook and drain the spaghetti. When the soup has cooked for 30 minutes, add the spaghetti and cook for 5 minutes more.

Budapest Bean Soup

Every spoonful of this is a delight!

1 pound dried white beans
9 cups UnChicken Broth (page 155)
1 bay leaf
½ teaspoon oregano
1 cup chopped onion
½ cup chopped celery
1 tablespoon olive oil
2 tablespoons paprika (or ½ teaspoon hot paprika)
¼ teaspoon cayenne pepper
4 cups cubed zucchini
½ teaspoon freshly ground black pepper

Pressure-cook the beans in 6 cups of the UnChicken Broth with the bay leaf and oregano. Put half the beans through a food mill or puree them in a food processor and mix back in with the rest of the beans. Sauté the onion and celery in the oil until the onion is translucent. Stir in the paprika, cayenne, zucchini, and rest of broth. Cook for 5 minutes. Combine with the beans and add the black pepper. Cook 5 more minutes, adding more broth or water if it gets too thick.

Cabbage and Cheez Soup 1

1 cup shredded cabbage
1½ cups grated potatoes
2 cups Cashew Milk (page 93)
¾ teaspoon nondairy margarine
2 cups water
½ teaspoon sea salt
¼ teaspoon black or cayenne pepper
¼ cup Pimiento Cheez (page 94) , Yeast Cheez (page 97), or Notzarella Cheez (page 94)

Cook the cabbage and potato together until soft. Drain off the cooking liquid and reserve 2 cups of it. If it is not 2 cups, add enough water to complete that measure. Mash the cooked cabbage and potatoes with the "milk" and margarine. Gradually add the reserved liquid, salt, and pepper. Cook slowly for 15 minutes, stirring occasionally. Stir in the Cheez just before serving.

VARIATION: *Make the Cashew Milk with UnChicken Broth (page 155) or UnBeef Broth (page 155) and cut the salt in half.*

Cabbage and Cheez Soup 2

⅓ cup chopped onion
1 cup shredded cabbage
1½ cups grated potatoes
2 cups Cashew Milk (page 93)
¾ teaspoon nondairy margarine
2 cups UnChicken Broth (page 155)
¼ teaspoon sea salt
¼ teaspoon cayenne pepper
¼ cup Pimiento Cheez (page 94), Yeast Cheez (page 97), or Notzarella Cheez (page 94)

Cook the onion, cabbage, and potato together until soft. Drain. Mash them with the "milk" and margarine. Gradually add the broth, salt, and pepper. Cook slowly for 15 minutes, stirring occasionally. Add the Cheez and stir in well.

Cabbage and Potato Soup

1 cup chopped onion
1 tablespoon corn oil
4 cups coarsely shredded cabbage
2 cups potatoes, cut into ½-inch pieces
4 cups chopped canned tomatoes, with juice
3 tablespoons lemon juice
2 tablespoons Sucanat
¼ teaspoon thyme
1 teaspoon sea salt
½ teaspoon freshly ground black pepper

Sauté the onion in the oil until soft. Combine everything and simmer 1 hour or until the cabbage and potatoes are tender.

Cabbage and Tomato Soup

1 cup chopped or ground UnBeef (page 109)
2 cups grated or coarsely cut cabbage
½ cup sauerkraut, drained
1 cup chopped canned tomatoes, drained
2 cups UnChicken Broth (page 155)
½ cup UnBeef Broth (page 155)
1½ teaspoons soy sauce
1¼ cups chopped onion
¾ teaspoon minced garlic
⅓ cup finely grated carrot
⅛ teaspoon freshly ground black pepper
1½ teaspoons corn oil

Combine all the ingredients, bring to a boil, lower the heat, and simmer with the lid slightly off for about 1 hour.

Cabbage Borscht

Although a long-standing beet-hater, I love this, and I think you will, too!

¾ cup peeled and chopped beet
⅔ cup chopped red onion
¾ cup grated carrot
2½ cups thinly sliced cabbage
1 tablespoon nondairy margarine
8 cups UnBeef Broth (page 155)
1¼ cups chopped tomato
⅛ teaspoon sea salt
¼ teaspoon cayenne pepper
2 cups peeled and diced potatoes

Combine everything and simmer for 1½ hours. This is good served with Cashew Sour Kreem (page 94) or Tofu Sour Kreem (page 97).

Cabbage Soup 1

⅓ cup chopped onion
2 tablespoons nondairy margarine
2 tablespoons unbleached white flour
4 cups UnBeef Broth (page 155)
1 cup diced potatoes
8 cups shredded cabbage
1 cup Cashew Sour Kreem (page 94) or Tofu Sour Kreem (page 97)

Sauté the onion in the margarine until light yellow—not brown. Add the flour, mix well, and then add the broth, potatoes, and cabbage. Cook until the potatoes are soft. Add a bit of the hot soup liquid to the Sour Kreem and mix well. Add this to the soup (it should not curdle).

Cabbage Soup 2

Not what you might expect!

1 cup chopped onion
1½ teaspoons minced garlic
2 tablespoons corn oil
4 cups cubed UnBeef (page 109)
1 cup pared and coarsely chopped carrots
1 bay leaf
1 teaspoon thyme
½ teaspoon paprika
4 cups UnBeef Broth (page 155)
4 cups water
8 cups coarsely chopped cabbage
4 cups canned tomatoes
2 teaspoons sea salt
½ teaspoon Tabasco
¼ cup chopped fresh parsley
3 tablespoons lemon juice
3 tablespoons Sucanat
2 cups sauerkraut

Sauté the onion and garlic in the oil until soft. Combine everything and cook until the vegetables are tender.

Calsoup

½ cup chopped bell pepper
⅓ cup chopped onion
2 tablespoons corn oil
6 cups chopped tomato
4 tablespoons flour
1 to 2 tablespoons lemon juice
½ teaspoon sea salt

Sauté the bell pepper and onion in the oil. Combine with rest of ingredients and cook.

Carrot Soup

3/4 cup chopped onion
1 teaspoon minced garlic
1 3/4 teaspoons nondairy margarine
2 cups chopped carrot
2 cups chopped potatoes
1/4 teaspoon sage
1/4 teaspoon thyme
4 cups UnBeef Broth (page 155) or UnChicken Broth (page 155)
1/4 teaspoon sea salt
1/4 teaspoon cayenne pepper

Sauté the onion and garlic in the margarine until the onion is transparent. Add the rest of ingredients. Bring to a boil, reduce heat, and simmer, covered, 30 minutes. Cool a bit, then blend in a blender. Reheat if need be.

Cheez Soup 1

1/2 cup finely chopped bell pepper
1 cup sliced or chopped mushrooms
3 tablespoons chopped onion
1/8 teaspoon cayenne
1/2 teaspoon nondairy margarine
1 1/2 cups UnChicken Broth (page 155)
3 cups Cheez Sauce (page 257), warm

Combine everything but the Cheez Sauce and cook until the vegetables are done. Sir in the Cheez Sauce.

VARIATIONS: *Add 1 cup of chopped canned tomatoes. Add 1/3 cup of cooked Tomato Salsa (page 296). Add Cashew Sour Kreem (page 94) or Tofu Sour Kreem (page 97).*

Cheez Soup 2

3/4 cup chopped onion
1 cup chopped potatoes
1 cup chopped carrot
2 cups UnBeef Broth (page 155)
3/4 teaspoon nondairy margarine
1/4 teaspoon thyme
1 cup Cashew Milk (page 93)
1 1/2 cups Yeast Cheez (page 97) or Pimiento Cheez (page 94)
1/4 teaspoon sea salt
1/4 teaspoon cayenne pepper

Combine the vegetables, broth, margarine, and thyme. Bring to a boil, reduce heat, cover, and simmer for 25 minutes. Add the rest of the ingredients and allow to cool slightly. Blend until smooth. Reheat, if need be, but do not boil.

Cheez and Onion Soup

1 1/2 cups coarsely chopped onion
1/2 teaspoon minced garlic
1/2 teaspoon nondairy margarine
2 tablespoons unbleached white flour
2 cups Cashew Milk (page 93)
1 teaspoon sea salt
1/4 teaspoon freshly ground black pepper or cayenne pepper
1/2 cups Pimiento Cheez (page 94), Yeast Cheez (page 97), or Notzarella Cheez (page 94)

Combine everything but the Cheez and cook till the onion is soft. Stir in the Cheez.

Chili Potato Soup

6 cups peeled and diced potatoes
3 cups UnChicken Broth (page 155)
1 1/2 cups chopped onion
1/4 cup finely chopped green onions, including the tops
1/2 teaspoon sea salt
1/2 teaspoon ground cumin
1 teaspoon basil
1/2 teaspoon freshly ground black pepper
2 garlic cloves, minced
3/4 cup finely diced bell pepper
2 tablespoons chopped jalapeño, or 1 1/2 teaspoons hot pepper flakes
2 cups Cashew Milk (page 93) made with UnChicken Broth (page 155)

Combine everything but the "milk" and cook for 15 minutes or until the potatoes start to fall apart. Add the "milk" and cook 15 more minutes.

Chilled Tomato and Bell Pepper Soup

4 red bell peppers
2 teaspoons corn oil
1 cup chopped onion

2 teaspoons chopped garlic
5 cups chopped tomato
Pinch thyme
8 basil leaves
1 teaspoon genuine maple syrup
¼ teaspoon freshly ground black pepper
½ teaspoon sea salt
6 cups Vegetable Consommé (page 88)
1 tablespoon balsamic vinegar
¾ cup Tofu Yogurt (page 97)

Put the bell peppers on a baking sheet and roast them in the top third of the oven at 500°F, turning them frequently, until they blacken and blister. Immediately put them in a bowl and seal it, airtight, with plastic wrap. Let them steam for 30 minutes. Remove and discard the skin, stem, and seeds. (For difficult spots, use a paring knife.) As you do this, dip your fingers occasionally in water. Keep any juice that may be released from the peppers. Chop them and set aside in their juice (if any). Heat the oil in a pan and sauté the onion until translucent. Add the garlic, tomato, bell peppers, thyme, basil, syrup, pepper, and salt. Cook slowly for 5 minutes. Add the Vegetable Consommé and bring to a boil. Reduce the heat and simmer for 15 to 20 minutes. Put in a blender or food processor and puree until completely smooth, in batches if necessary. Cool to room temperature and refrigerate. Just before serving, stir in the vinegar and yogurt. Thin with more yogurt if needed.

Cold Kreem of Squash Soup

1½ teaspoons nondairy margarine
3 tablespoons finely chopped onion
¾ cup finely chopped carrot
1 tablespoon finely chopped bell pepper
3½ cups yellow crookneck squash, cut into ½-inch dice
1 cup potatoes, peeled and cut into ½-inch dice
4 cups UnChicken Broth (page 155) made with Cashew Milk (page 93)
½ teaspoon dill
¼ teaspoon cayenne pepper

Melt the margarine and sauté the onion, carrot, and bell pepper, and cook for 5 to 6 minutes until the vegetables are soft but not brown. Stir in the diced squash and potatoes, and pour in the broth. Bring to a boil, reduce heat and simmer, partially covered, for about 20 minutes, or until the squash is tender and offers no resistance when pierced with the tip of a sharp knife. Strain through a fine sieve set over a large mixing bowl, and puree the vegetables through a food mill or by pushing them through the sieve with the back of a large wooden spoon. Combine the puree and the soup liquid and, when the soup has cooled to room temperature, stir in the dill and cayenne. Cover tightly with plastic wrap and refrigerate for at least 2 hours, or until thoroughly chilled.

Cold Kreem of Tomato Soup

Unusual—and unusually good!

2 teaspoons olive oil (do not use "extra virgin" olive oil, as the taste will be too strong in this dish).
1½ cups chopped onion
1½ teaspoons minced garlic
¼ teaspoon ground mace
3 tablespoons unbleached white flour
3 cups UnChicken Broth (page 155)
4 cups coarsely chopped tomato
½ teaspoon Sucanat
½ cup Cashew Sour Kreem (page 94) or Tofu Sour Kreem (page 97)
½ teaspoon sea salt
⅛ teaspoon freshly ground black pepper
Chopped chives for garnish

Heat the oil in a heavy saucepan over low heat. Add the onion, garlic, and mace. Cook, covered, for 5 minutes. Do not let brown. Sprinkle the flour over the onion mixture, and cook while stirring for 2 minutes. Whisk in the broth. Add the tomato and Sucanat. Bring to a boil, reduce heat, and simmer, uncovered, for 20 minutes. Let cool to room temperature. Puree in batches in a blender or food processor. Combine and stir together until smooth, then pour through a sieve into a bowl. Whisk in the Sour Kreem, salt, and pepper. Chill thoroughly. Sprinkle with chopped chives before serving.

Cool-As-A-Cucumber Soup

1 tablespoon cornstarch
1 cup cold Cashew Milk (page 93)
3/4 teaspoon sea salt
1/8 teaspoon freshly ground black pepper
2 cups peeled and finely diced cucumbers
1/4 cup finely chopped onion
1 tablespoon corn oil
1 cup UnChicken Broth (page 155)
1 teaspoon dried mint
1 cup Cashew Sour Kreem (page 94) or Tofu Sour Kreem (page 97)

Combine the cornstarch, "milk," salt, and pepper. Bring to a boil, stirring constantly. Boil for 1 minute and set aside. Sauté the cucumbers and onion in the oil for 5 minutes. Combine with the "milk" sauce, broth, and mint. Cool. Blend 2 cups of this on high heat for 30 seconds until smooth. Mix with the rest. Stir in the Sour Kreem. Chill.

Corn and Potato Chowder 1

1/2 cup chopped onion
1 1/4 teaspoons corn oil
6 cups UnChicken Broth (page 155)
2 cups cooked and cubed potatoes
2 1/2 cups corn
1/8 teaspoon cayenne pepper
1/2 teaspoon savory

Sauté the onion in the oil. Combine with rest of ingredients and cook.

Corn and Potato Chowder 2

1/2 cup diced onion
1/2 cup diced celery
1/4 cup chopped bell pepper
1 teaspoon corn oil
1 cup raw and cubed potatoes
3/4 cup UnBeef Broth (page 155)
2 cups creamed style corn
1 1/2 cups UnBeef Broth (page 155) made with Cashew Milk (page 93)

Sauté the onion, celery, and bell pepper in the corn oil. Stir in the potatoes and plain broth. Heat to boiling. Reduce heat and simmer until tender, but do not overcook. Add the corn and milk-broth and heat to the boiling point.

Corn and Tomato Chowder

1/2 teaspoon nondairy margarine
2 tablespoons chopped onion
2 tablespoons unbleached white flour
1 cup tomato juice
2 cups canned tomatoes
1 1/2 cups corn
1/2 teaspoon sea salt
Pinch cayenne pepper
1/2 cup Yeast Cheez (page 97), Pimiento Cheez (page 94), or Notzarella Cheez (page 94)

Melt the margarine and sauté the onion. Blend in the flour. Gradually add the tomato juice. Stir in the rest of the ingredients except for the Cheez. Simmer for 10 minutes. Stir in the Cheez well.

Corn Chowder 1

1/4 cup chopped bell pepper
3 tablespoons chopped onion
1 teaspoon corn oil
1 cup cooked and cubed potato
Pinch cayenne pepper
1/2 cup UnChicken Broth (page 155)
2 cups creamed corn
1 1/2 cups corn milk (equal parts of corn and UnChicken Broth [page 155] well blended in a blender)
1/4 teaspoon sea salt

Sauté the bell pepper and onion in the oil. Combine with rest of ingredients and cook until it thickens.

Corn Chowder 2

1/2 cup chopped onion
2 teaspoons corn oil
6 cups UnChicken Broth (page 155)
2 cups cooked and cubed potatoes
5 cups corn
1/8 teaspoon cayenne pepper
1/2 teaspoon savory

Sauté the onion in the oil until soft. Combine all ingredients and cook until the potatoes start to fall apart, about 30 minutes.

Corn Chowder Deluxe

1 cup cubed Mexican Chorizo UnSausage (page 134)
2 tablespoons corn oil
1 cup chopped onion
½ cup chopped celery
1 cup chopped red bell pepper
½ cup chopped green bell pepper
3 cups corn
1 bay leaf
4 cups UnChicken Broth (page 155)
2½ cups potatoes, peeled and cut into ½-inch cubes
1 cup Cashew Kreem (page 93)
½ teaspoon sea salt
¼ teaspoon freshly ground black pepper

Brown the gluten in the oil. Add the onion, celery, and bell pepper and cook until the vegetables are softened. Add the corn and bay leaf, and cook, stirring, for 1 minute. Add the broth and simmer, stirring occasionally, for 30 minutes. Add the potatoes, Kreem, salt, and pepper and simmer, stirring occasionally, for 25 minutes, or until the potatoes are tender. Discard the bay leaf.

VARIATION: *Use Italian UnSausage (page 133).*

Corn Soup

1 cup chopped bell pepper
3 tablespoons minced onion
1 teaspoon nondairy margarine
4 cups corn
3 cups UnChicken Broth (page 155)
¼ teaspoon cayenne pepper
½ teaspoon sea salt

Sauté the bell pepper and onion in the margarine. Combine corn and broth in a blender, and blend slightly until "cream corn" consistency. Combine everything and cook for 20 minutes.

VARIATIONS: *When done, add 2 cups of Yeast Cheez (page 97) or Pimiento Cheez (page 94) and stir over low heat until the Cheez is mixed in. Add 3 cups of cubed potatoes and 2 more cups of UnChicken broth to ingredients. Add 2 cups of squash or pumpkin to ingredients.*

Creamed Lentil-Celery Soup

2 cups diced onion
1 cup chopped celery
2 garlic cloves, mashed
1 tablespoon corn oil
1½ cups lentils, sorted through and rinsed well
2 bay leaves
¼ cup chopped fresh parsley
1½ teaspoons sea salt
2 teaspoons Dijon-style mustard
1 tablespoon balsamic vinegar

Sauté the onion, celery, and garlic in the oil until soft. Combine everything but the mustard and vinegar. Bring to a boil, reduce heat, and simmer, partially covered, until the lentils are completely tender, about 45 minutes, stirring occasionally. Let cool a bit, puree in batches in a blender, then pass the puree through a food mill to remove the lentil skins. Put back in the pot, return to the heat, and stir in the mustard and vinegar. Thin with some water if necessary.

Creamy Onion Soup

2¾ cups chopped onion
1½ teaspoons minced garlic
1 teaspoon nondairy margarine
1 cup chopped potato
2 cups Cashew Milk (page 93)
1 cup UnBeef Broth (page 155), UnChicken Broth (page 155), UnHam Broth (page 156), or UnSausage Broth (page 156)
1 bay leaf
¼ teaspoon sea salt
¼ teaspoon cayenne pepper

Combine everything, bring to a boil, reduce heat, cover, and simmer for 20 minutes. Remove the bay leaf. Cool slightly, then run through a blender. Reheat if need be.

Creole Soup

This really is something different!

1 tablespoon chopped bell pepper
1 tablespoon chopped red onion
1 teaspoon nondairy margarine
2 tablespoons unbleached white flour
1 cup Italian tomato, cooked
3 cups UnBeef Broth (page 155)
1/8 teaspoon sea salt
1/8 teaspoon cayenne pepper
1/2 teaspoon balsamic vinegar

Sauté the bell pepper and onion in the margarine for 5 minutes. Stir in the flour and add the tomato and broth. Simmer for 15 minutes, then strain and add the salt, pepper, and vinegar.

Curried Mushroom Soup

This is best made one day before so the flavors will mingle!

1/4 cup unbleached white flour
2 cups chopped onion
2 teaspoons minced or crushed garlic
2 teaspoons corn oil
3 cups mushrooms, cleaned, stemmed, and sliced or chopped
41/2 teaspoons curry powder
1/4 teaspoon cayenne pepper
1/4 teaspoon sea salt
4 cups UnChicken Broth (page 155) or UnBeef Broth (page 155)

Put the flour in a heavy skillet, spreading it out. Put it on low heat. Stir with a wooden spoon occasionally. Within a few minutes the flour will turn a slightly darker shade and begin to smell "nutty." Then begin stirring continuously to prevent burning. When the flour has toasted and developed a rich aroma, remove it from the pan immediately and set aside. Sauté the onion and garlic in the oil over medium heat for 3 to 5 minutes. Add the mushrooms and sauté 2 to 3 minutes more. Sprinkle the curry powder, cayenne, and salt over the vegetables and stir gently. Add the toasted flour and stir to coat all the vegetables. Stir in the broth. Bring to a boil, lower the heat, and simmer for 15 to 20 minutes. When the vegetables are soft, transfer the soup, 2 cups at a time, to a blender and puree it.

VARIATIONS: *Instead of mushrooms, try cauliflower, broccoli, or zucchini. Stir in 1/3 cup of Cashew Milk (page 93) before serving.*

Curried Split Pea Soup

1 cup minced onion
2 teaspoons minced garlic
1 tablespoon curry powder
1/2 teaspoon turmeric
1 teaspoon mustard seeds (black preferred)
1 tablespoon corn oil
8 cups UnChicken Broth (page 155)
2 cups yellow split peas
1 bay leaf
2 teaspoons sea salt
1 teaspoon cayenne
1/2 cups Tofu Yogurt (page 97)
21/2 tablespoons lemon juice

Sauté the onion, garlic, curry powder, turmeric, and mustard seeds in the oil until the onion is soft. Combine everything but the yogurt and lemon juice. Bring to a boil, reduce heat and simmer, covered, until the peas are tender, 45 to 60 minutes. Cool a bit, take out bay leaf, then process in a blender or food processor to a coarse puree. Return to the saucepan. Just before serving, heat through and stir in the yogurt and lemon juice.

Curry Stew

Our version of a Vietnamese-Indian recipe.

11/2 cups onion, cut in large chunks
1 teaspoon crushed garlic
11/4 teaspoons corn oil
3 tablespoons curry powder
3 cups UnChicken Broth (page 155)
2 cups cubed potatoes
11/2 cups sliced carrot
11/2 cups coconut milk

Sauté the onion and garlic in the oil. When the onion is transparent, add the curry powder and sauté for 2 more minutes, stirring constantly. Add the rest of ingredients except the coconut milk and cook until the vegetables are done. Add the coconut milk and cook for 10 more minutes.

Dal Soup

1/4 cup finely chopped bell pepper
3 tablespoons chopped onion
1 1/2 teaspoons corn oil
2 cups dried dal
3/4 teaspoon sea salt
1/8 teaspoon crushed red pepper
1 cup chopped tomato
4 1/2 cups UnChicken Broth (page 155)

Sauté the bell pepper and onion in the oil. Combine with rest of ingredients and cook.

Dieter's Broth

This is a tremendous help for those wanting to cut down on calories. However, if water retention is also a problem, you might want to omit either the salt or the soy sauce.

1/4 cup soy sauce
1/2 cup tomato juice
1 1/2 teaspoons sea salt or salt substitute
1/2 teaspoon garlic powder
4 cups cabbage
1 1/2 cups celery
2 cups onion
3/4 cup chopped bell pepper
2 cups tomato
3 quarts water
1/4 teaspoon cayenne pepper
1 1/2 teaspoons nutritional yeast

Combine everything except the nutritional yeast in a pot. Cook for 40 minutes. Take from heat and stir in the yeast. Puree in a blender or food processor if you like.

Easy Days Vegetable Soup

One 10-ounce package frozen cut green beans
One 10-ounce package frozen peas and carrots
One 10-ounce package frozen lima beans
One 10-ounce package frozen corn
One 10-ounce package frozen chopped spinach
4 cups canned tomatoes
1 1/4 cup cooked kidney beans, drained and rinsed
1 cup tomato sauce
1 tablespoon minced onion flakes
1 bay leaf
1/2 teaspoon thyme
1 1/2 teaspoons basil
1/4 teaspoon garlic powder
1 1/2 teaspoons sea salt
1/2 teaspoon freshly ground black pepper
5 cups UnBeef Broth (page 155) or UnChicken Broth (page 155), or water
1 tablespoon corn oil
1 cup orzo, or other small pasta

Put everything but the pasta in a pot and bring to a boil, stirring occasionally, using a spoon to break up any clumps of frozen vegetables as well as the tomatoes. Cover, reduce heat, and simmer 45 minutes or until the vegetables are tender. Add the pasta, cover, and cook until the pasta is tender, 10 to 15 more minutes. Remove and discard the bay leaf before serving.

Fresh Tomato Soup

1 1/2 cups chopped onion
1 1/4 teaspoon nondairy margarine
1 cup chopped potatoes
2 cups chopped tomato
1/2 teaspoon basil
1 bay leaf
2 tablespoons tomato paste
2 cups UnBeef Broth (page 155)
1/2 teaspoon sea salt
1/4 teaspoon cayenne pepper
2 cups Cashew Milk (page 93), hot

Sauté the onion in the margarine until transparent. Add the rest of the ingredients except for the "milk." Cover and simmer for 20 minutes. Remove from the heat, take out the bay leaf, and stir in the "milk."

VARIATION: *Instead of Cashew Milk, use UnBeef Broth (page 155), UnChicken Broth (page 155), or UnSausage Broth (page 156), or plain water. If broth is used, cut the salt in half.*

Garbanzo and Cabbage Soup

3 tablespoons chopped onion
1 tablespoon corn oil
1½ cups diced tomato
2 cups finely shredded cabbage
1½ cups diced potatoes
4 cups water
5 cups garbanzos beans, cooked
Juice of half a lemon
1 teaspoon paprika
½ cup minced fresh parsley
1 teaspoon sea salt

Sauté the onion in the oil until soft. Add tomato and cabbage, stir well, then cover and simmer until the cabbage is cooked, about 10 minutes. Set aside. In a pot cook the potatoes in the water until tender, about 15 minutes. Strain off 2 cups of the liquid and puree the potatoes in a blender with 1 cup of the garbanzos until smooth. Add the blended beans and sautéed vegetables to the potatoes. Stir in the remaining beans. Add lemon juice, paprika, parsley, and salt. If needed, thin the soup with extra water to the desired consistency.

Garbanzo Soup

1 cup chopped onion
1 cup chopped celery
1 cup sliced carrot
2 tablespoons corn oil
2 teaspoons minced garlic
1 cup diced potatoes
5 cups UnChicken Broth (page 155)
½ teaspoon sea salt
¼ teaspoon cayenne
3¾ cups garbanzos beans, cooked and drained

Sauté the onion, celery, and carrot in the oil until soft. Add garlic and sauté 2 more minutes. Put everything together and simmer until everything is well cooked. Puree half of this in a blender or food processor before serving.

Gazpacho 1

3 tablespoons minced onion
2 teaspoons corn oil
3 tablespoons soy sauce
1 teaspoon Kitchen Bouquet
1 tablespoon nutritional yeast
⅛ teaspoon rubbed sage
2 cups tomato juice
2 cups finely chopped tomato
2 cups chopped tomato and then pureed
3 tablespoons finely chopped onion
¼ cup finely chopped bell pepper
½ cup finely chopped celery
¼ cup cooked Tomato Salsa (page 296)
¼ teaspoon sea salt

Sauté the onion in oil until transparent. Add soy sauce, Kitchen Bouquet, nutritional yeast, sage, and tomato juice. Simmer for 5 minutes. Cool to room temperature. Combine all ingredients and chill for a few hours. Serve with Cashew Sour Kreem (page 94) or Tofu Sour Kreem (page 97).

Gazpacho 2

1 cup crushed canned tomatoes, or chopped fresh tomatoes
4 cups tomato juice
½ cup finely chopped onion
½ cup finely chopped cucumbers
½ cup finely chopped bell pepper
½ cup salsa
4 teaspoons soy sauce
⅛ teaspoon garlic powder

Combine all (you may need to blend the garlic powder with some of the tomato juice in a blender to make sure it mixes) and chill for a few hours.

Gazpacho 3

2 cups canned tomatoes with juice
¾ cup tomato juice
¾ teaspoon minced garlic
½ cup chopped bell pepper
2 tablespoons minced green onion
3 tablespoons chopped fresh parsley
¼ cup chopped watercress
⅓ cup finely chopped celery
2 teaspoons olive oil
2 tablespoons low-sodium soy sauce
3 tablespoons lemon juice
⅓ cup sliced black olives

In a blender puree the tomatoes, juice, and garlic. Add the rest of the ingredients and blend thoroughly.

VARIATION: *Serve with nutritional yeast so each one can mix in to taste.*

Golden Corn Soup

3/4 cup chopped onion
1 teaspoon nondairy margarine
2 cups corn
3/4 cup UnChicken Broth (page 155) made with Cashew Milk (page 93)
1/2 teaspoon sea salt
Pinch cayenne pepper
1 cup chopped tomato
3/4 cup UnChicken Broth (page 155)
1/2 teaspoon oregano

Sauté the onion in the margarine, put all together, and cook.

Green Pea Soup

1/3 cup coarsely chopped onion
1/2 teaspoon minced garlic
3/4 teaspoon nondairy margarine
1 1/2 cups green peas (if frozen, thawed, if fresh, lightly steamed)
1 cup coarsely chopped potatoes
2 1/2 cups UnChicken Broth (page 155) or UnBeef Broth (page 155)
1/8 teaspoon sea salt
1/8 teaspoon cayenne pepper
1/2 cups Cashew Milk (page 93)

Sauté the onion and garlic in the margarine until the onion is transparent. Add the peas, potatoes, broth, salt, and pepper, and bring to a boil. Reduce heat, cover, and simmer for 20 minutes. Remove from heat and stir in the "milk." Cool a bit, then blend in a blender. Reheat if need be.

VARIATION: *May be served chilled. If so, chill before adding the "milk," which should also be cold.*

Hungarian UnChicken Stew

1/3 cup finely chopped UnBacon (page 136)
Oil
2 cups thinly sliced onion
4 cups cubed UnChicken (page 137)
2 tablespoons paprika
1/2 teaspoon sea salt
1/2 teaspoon caraway seeds
1 teaspoon crushed garlic
1/2 cup tomato slices
1 cup sliced bell pepper (half red and half green if possible)
4 cups potatoes, cut into small chunks
2 cups UnChicken Broth (page 155)

Brown the UnBacon in some oil and set aside. Sauté the onion until soft and set aside. Brown the UnChicken. Add the rest of the ingredients and simmer, covered, for 20 minutes or until the potatoes are done, adding extra broth if needed.

Kreem of Broccoli Soup

This tastes very much like oyster soup!

3/4 teaspoon nondairy margarine
4 cups Cashew Milk (page 93)
1/4 teaspoon garlic powder
1/4 teaspoon onion salt
Dash cayenne pepper
3 cups broccoli, cooked in UnChicken Broth (page 155) and drained

Puree all ingredients together in a blender. Simmer for 5 minutes.

VARIATION: *During the 5 minutes of simmering, stir in 1 cup of Yeast Cheez (page 97) or Pimiento Cheez (page 94).*

Kreem of Carrot Soup

1 1/2 cups chopped onion
1 teaspoon minced garlic
1 teaspoon corn oil
3 cups chopped carrot, cooked
4 cups UnChicken Broth (page 155) made with Cashew Milk (page 93)
1/2 teaspoon sea salt
1/4 teaspoon cayenne pepper

Combine all ingredients, cook, and run through a blender until smooth. Heat just to the boiling point.

Kreem of Cauliflower Soup

2 cups cauliflower, broken or cut into flowerets
2 tablespoons chopped onion
1/4 teaspoon minced garlic
1 cup chopped celery
3/4 teaspoon nondairy margarine
1/4 cup unbleached white flour
4 cups UnChicken Broth (page 155)
2 cups Cashew Milk (page 93)

Cook the cauliflower in boiling salted water until barely tender. Reserve 1/3 of the flowerets. Chop the rest of the cauliflower fine or run through a sieve or puree strainer. Sauté the onion, garlic, and celery in the margarine. Add the flour. Slowly add the broth. Add all the cauliflower and "milk" and heat through.

Kreem of Celery Soup

1 1/2 cups diced celery
1/3 cup chopped onion
1/4 teaspoon minced garlic
1 cup salted boiling water
3 1/2 cups Medium White Sauce (page 262), made with UnChicken Broth (page 155)

Cook the celery, onion, and garlic, covered, in the cup of boiling water until tender, about 13 minutes. Drain off the water, stir in the White Sauce, and heat through.

Kreem of Corn Soup

1 cup cooked corn
2 cups Thin White Sauce (page 262)
1 tablespoon chopped onion
2 teaspoons nondairy margarine
1/4 teaspoon sea salt
1/4 teaspoon paprika
1/8 teaspoon cayenne

Blend together in a blender, heat, and serve.

Kreem of Mushroom Soup

1/4 cup chopped onion
2 cups chopped mushrooms
1 teaspoon minced garlic
1 tablespoon nondairy margarine
1 tablespoon cornstarch
2 cups UnBeef Broth (page 155) made with Cashew Milk (page 93)

Sauté the onion, mushrooms, and garlic in the margarine until the onion is soft. Combine the cornstarch and broth. Add to the vegetables and cook until it thickens.

Kreem of Onion Soup

1 1/2 cups sliced onion
2 teaspoons nondairy margarine
5 cups Thin White Sauce (page 262) made with UnChicken Broth (page 155)

Sauté the onion in the margarine. Add the White Sauce and cook slowly for 30 minutes.

Kreem of Pea Soup 1

4 cups peas (if frozen, thawed; if fresh, lightly steamed)
2 cups UnChicken Broth (page 155) or UnBeef Broth (page 155) made with Cashew Milk (page 93)
4 1/2 teaspoons nondairy margarine

Blend the peas with the broth and margarine. Heat and serve.

VARIATION: *Use 2 cups of Thin White Sauce (page 262) made with UnChicken Broth (page 155) or UnBeef Broth (page 155).*

Kreem of Pea Soup 2

1 teaspoon nondairy margarine
1 tablespoon chopped onion
2 cups peas, fresh or frozen, cooked
1/2 teaspoon sea salt
1 teaspoon Sucanat
3 cups Thin White Sauce (page 262)
Paprika

Sauté the onion in the margarine. Combine all ingredients and process in a blender, then heat through.

Kreem of Pinto Bean and Tomato Soup

1/4 cup sliced onion
1 teaspoon corn oil
1 cup pinto beans, cooked
1 cup chopped canned tomatoes
3 cups Thin White Sauce (page 262)

Sauté the onion in the oil. Combine with beans and tomatoes and heat together. Put through a sieve or blender. Combine with the White Sauce just before serving.

Kreem of Potato Soup 1

1 cup finely chopped onion
1 teaspoon minced garlic
2 tablespoons finely chopped bell pepper
2 tablespoons finely chopped celery
2 teaspoons nondairy margarine
1 tablespoon unbleached white flour
4 cups UnChicken Broth (page 155) made with Cashew Milk (page 93)
3 cups peeled, cooked, and cubed potatoes
1/4 cup minced UnBacon (page 136), or imitation bacon bits
1 tablespoon minced fresh parsley
1/8 teaspoon black or cayenne pepper

Sauté the onion, garlic, bell pepper, and celery in the margarine until soft. Stir in the flour well. Combine everything and cook until the soup thickens, about 15 minutes.

Kreem of Potato Soup 2

1 cup mashed potatoes
2 cups Thin White Sauce (page 262) made with UnBeef Broth (page 155) or UnChicken Broth (page 155)
Paprika

Combine and heat through.

Kreem of UnChicken Soup

1 tablespoon nondairy margarine
1/3 cup chopped onion
1 teaspoon minced garlic
1 cup UnChicken Broth (page 155)
2 cups Medium White Sauce (page 262), omitting the salt, made with UnChicken Broth (page 155)
1/8 teaspoon freshly ground black or white pepper
1 1/2 cups UnChicken (page 137), chopped and browned in corn oil

Melt the margarine and sauté the onion until soft. Add the garlic and sauté 1 more minute. Add the rest of the ingredients and simmer until it begins to thicken, about 10 minutes.

VARIATION: *Sauté 2 tablespoons of curry powder with the onion.*

Lentil and Tomato Soup

1/2 cup dried lentils
3/4 cup chopped onion
1 teaspoon minced garlic
1 1/2 teaspoons corn oil
4 cups chopped tomato
1 cup tomato juice
3 3/4 cups UnBeef Broth (page 155)
1/4 teaspoon sea salt
1/4 teaspoon cayenne pepper

Pressure-cook the lentils. Sauté the onion and garlic in the oil until the onion is transparent. Add the rest of the ingredients, cover, and simmer for 30 minutes.

Lentil Soup 1

2 1/2 cups dried lentils
Enough UnBeef Broth (page 155) or UnChicken Broth (page 155) to cover the lentils with 2 inches of broth
1 cup chopped bell pepper
3 tablespoons chopped onion
2 teaspoons corn oil
3/4 teaspoon sea salt
1/8 teaspoon cayenne pepper
2 cups chopped tomato
1/4 teaspoon summer savory

Cook the lentils in the broth for about 30 minutes until they are soft. Sauté the bell pepper and onion in the oil. Combine with rest of ingredients and cook about 30 minutes more. If needed, add more broth or water to keep a soup consistency.

Lentil Soup 2

2 cups dried lentils
1/3 cup chopped onion
1/2 cup chopped celery
1/2 teaspoon minced garlic
2 teaspoons corn oil
1/8 teaspoon Italian herb seasoning
1/4 teaspoon sage
1 bay leaf
1/4 teaspoon cayenne pepper
2 cups cooked and diced potatoes
1 cup carrots, cooked and sliced into rounds
1 cup finely chopped UnBacon (page 136)
4 cups UnChicken Broth (page 155)

Pressure-cook the lentils. Sauté the onion, celery, and garlic in the corn oil. Combine all ingredients and cook for 30 minutes.

VARIATION: *Omit the gluten and use UnBeef Broth (page 155) instead.*

Lentil Soup 3

1 cup dried lentils
3/4 cup chopped onion
1 teaspoon nondairy margarine
2 cups UnBeef broth (page 155) or UnChicken Broth (page 155)
1/4 teaspoon cayenne pepper

Pressure-cook the lentils. Sauté the onion in the margarine. Combine all ingredients and simmer for 1 hour.

Lentil Soup 4

1 cup dried lentils
3/4 cup chopped onion
3/4 cup chopped celery
1/4 teaspoon minced garlic
1 1/2 teaspoons corn oil
3/4 cup chopped carrot
1 cup chopped tomato
1/8 teaspoon basil
1/8 teaspoon oregano
1 bay leaf
1 teaspoon sea salt
3/4 cup diced potato
3 cups UnBeef Broth (page 155) or UnChicken Broth (page 155)

Pressure-cook the lentils for 5 minutes. Sauté the onion, celery, and garlic in the oil. Put everything together and cook for 30 minutes.

Lima Bean Soup

2 tablespoons minced UnBacon (page 136)
1 tablespoon corn oil
1/2 cup finely chopped onion
2 cups UnChicken Broth (page 155)
1 3/4 cup lima beans, fresh or frozen (thawed)
Sea salt
Freshly ground black pepper
1/3 cup thinly sliced green onions

Brown the gluten in some oil until crisp, and drain on paper towels. In the 1 tablespoon of oil sauté the onion until soft. Add the broth and beans and simmer for 8 minutes or until the beans are tender. Add the salt and pepper. Puree the soup in a food processor or blender, return to the pan, and heat until hot. Serve with the gluten and green onions to be sprinkled on the soup as desired.

Mashed Potato and Cheez Soup

1 cup finely chopped bell pepper
1/4 cup chopped onion
1 teaspoon nondairy margarine
3 cups mashed potatoes
4 cups UnBeef Broth (page 155) or UnChicken Broth (page 155)
1/8 teaspoon cayenne pepper
1/4 teaspoon sea salt
1 cup Yeast Cheez (page 97), Pimiento Cheez (page 94), or Notzarella Cheez (page 94)

Sauté the bell pepper and onion in the margarine. Combine all ingredients except the Cheez, and simmer 30 minutes, adding more broth if needed. Add the Cheez and stir in well.

VARIATION: *Make the broth with Cashew Milk (page 93) instead of water.*

Mexican Summer Stew

2 cups sliced onion, 1/4 inch thick
2 teaspoons minced garlic
2 tablespoons corn oil
1 quart water, or UnChicken Broth (page 155) or UnBeef Broth (page 155)
4 cups sliced zucchini, 1/2 inch thick
2 2/3 cups sliced yellow squash
2/3 cup diced bell pepper, 1/2-inch dice
2 cups peas
3 cups chopped tomato
3 tablespoons soy sauce
3 tablespoons chili powder
1 tablespoon ground cumin
3 cups chopped UnBeef (page 109), UnChicken (page 137), or UnPork (page 122)
1 tablespoon catsup
2 cups corn
1 tablespoon cornstarch or arrowroot
1/4 cup cold water

Sauté the onion and garlic in the oil until soft. Combine everything but the cornstarch and water. Simmer 30 minutes. During the final minutes, dissolve the cornstarch in the water and add to the stew. Stir until thickened.

Minestrone 1

1 1/2 teaspoons nondairy margarine
1/4 cup chopped onion
1 1/2 teaspoons minced garlic
1/2 cup peas
1/2 cups zucchini or other squash, scrubbed and sliced (not peeled)
1/2 cup diced potatoes
1/2 cup diced carrot
3 tablespoons thinly sliced celery
1 1/2 cups coarsely chopped tomato
4 cups UnChicken Broth (page 155)
1/2 teaspoon basil
1 bay leaf
1 1/2 teaspoons parsley
1/8 teaspoon sea salt
Dash black or cayenne pepper
2 tablespoons uncooked spaghetti broken in 1-inch pieces
1/4 cup cooked dried beans of choice, drained
1/8 cup finely chopped UnBacon (page 136)
2 cups ground UnHam (page 130) or UnSausage (page 132), fried

Melt the margarine in a skillet and sauté the onion and garlic until the onion is soft and lightly browned. Stir in the peas, zucchini, potatoes, carrot, celery, tomato, broth, basil, bay leaf, parsley, salt, and pepper. Bring to a boil, reduce heat and simmer partially covered for 25 minutes. Add spaghetti, beans, and gluten and cook until the spaghetti is done, 15 to 20 minutes more.

Minestrone 2

1 cup cooked white beans
1/4 cup green split peas
1/4 cup yellow split peas
1/2 cup shredded cabbage
1 cup chopped onion
1 cup diced mushrooms
1 teaspoon minced garlic
1/3 cup tomato paste
4 1/2 cups UnChicken Broth (page 155) or UnBeef Broth (page 155)
2 tablespoons low-sodium soy sauce (omit if using UnBeef Broth)
2 teaspoons corn oil
1/4 cup macaroni, small

Combine everything but the macaroni and cook for 30 minutes. Add the macaroni and simmer until it is done.

"Mock" Cream of Mushroom Soup

1 cup minced celery
1/2 cups minced onion
2 teaspoons corn oil
2 tablespoons unbleached white flour
2 cups garbanzos beans, cooked
4 cups Thin White Sauce (page 262)
1/2 teaspoon sea salt
1/4 cup minced fresh parsley
1 tablespoon nutritional yeast

Sauté the celery and onion in the oil until tender. Stir in the flour well. Add the remaining ingredients and heat through.

Monastery Potato Soup

3/4 cup chopped onion
1 teaspoon minced garlic
1 1/4 teaspoons corn oil
1/4 cup finely chopped celery
1 cup chopped mushrooms
1 1/2 teaspoons minced jalapeños
2 cups cubed potatoes
1 cup finely chopped carrots
1/2 teaspoon sea salt
2 cups water
1/4 cup nutritional yeast

Sauté the onion and garlic in the oil until the onion is transparent. Combine with rest of ingredients, bring to a boil, reduce heat, and simmer for 30 minutes. Take off the heat and stir in the nutritional yeast.

VARIATION: *When sautéing the vegetables, add 2 tablespoons of curry powder, and do not add the nutritional yeast at the end.*

Monastery Vegetable Soup

1 cup chopped onion
1/4 cup finely chopped celery
1/2 cups chopped bell pepper
1 cup chopped mushrooms
3 cups cubed UnBeef (page 109) or UnChicken (page 137)
4 teaspoons corn oil
2 teaspoons minced garlic
3 cups cubed potatoes
1 1/2 cups cubed yellow squash
1 cup green beans
3/4 cup lima beans
3/4 cup finely chopped carrot
3/4 teaspoon crushed red pepper flakes
6 cups water
3 cups mashed canned tomatoes (use juice)
1/4 cup tomato paste
3 tablespoons chopped fresh parsley
1/4 teaspoon basil
1/4 teaspoon oregano
1 1/2 teaspoons sea salt

Sauté the onion, celery, bell pepper, mushrooms, and gluten in the oil until the onions are transparent. Add the garlic and sauté a little more. Combine with rest of ingredients, bring to a boil, reduce heat, and simmer until the potatoes begin to fall apart, about 45 minutes.

Mulligatawny Soup

1 1/2 cups chopped onion
1 teaspoon minced garlic
2 teaspoons curry powder (Madras style preferred)
2 teaspoons corn oil
1 cup chopped carrot
2 cups chopped potatoes
1 cup tomato juice
5 cups UnBeef Broth (page 155)
1/2 teaspoon sea salt
1/4 teaspoon cayenne pepper

Sauté the onion, garlic, and curry powder in the oil until the onions are transparent. Add the rest of the ingredients and bring to a boil. Reduce heat, cover, and simmer for 30 minutes. Cool a bit, then blend in a blender. Reheat if need be.

Onion Soup

1 teaspoon corn oil
4 cups thinly sliced onion
2 teaspoons minced garlic
1 quart UnBeef Broth (page 155), UnChicken Broth (page 155), UnHam Broth (page 156), or UnSausage Broth (page 156)

Combine everything and cook uncovered over low heat, stirring occasionally, for 20 to 30 minutes. Add the broth and cook for 20 minutes or more, until done.

Pease Porridge

Remember the nursery rhyme? Well, here it is!

2 cups dried green split peas
2 cups water
1 teaspoon sea salt
2 teaspoons nondairy margarine
1/4 teaspoon paprika

Pick over the split peas and discard any discolored ones. Wash them thoroughly under cold running water and continue to wash until the draining water runs clear. In a heavy 3- to 4-quart saucepan, bring the water to a boil. Drop in the peas slowly so the water continues to boil. Reduce the heat and simmer, partially covered, for 1 1/2 hours, or until the peas can be easily mashed against the side of the pan with a spoon. Drain the peas in a colander and puree them in a food mill or force them through a fine sieve set over a large bowl. Return the peas to the pan, stir in salt, margarine, and paprika, and cook over low heat, stirring constantly, until the puree is heated through. Serve at once from a heated dish.

Potato Soup

3/4 cup chopped onion
1 teaspoon minced garlic
3 tablespoons chopped bell pepper
1 teaspoon corn oil
3 cups cubed potatoes
Pinch cayenne pepper
1/4 teaspoon sea salt
3 cups UnBeef Broth (page 155)

Sauté the onion, garlic, and bell pepper in the oil. Combine ingredients and cook until the vegetables are done.

VARIATION: *Add 2 cups of corn and omit the garlic.*

Portuguese Bean Soup

Goodness with a difference.

4 cups cooked beans (preferably red beans)
1/4 cup sliced red onions
1 1/2 cups diced potatoes
1 1/2 teaspoons sea salt
1 teaspoon paprika
1/4 teaspoon cayenne pepper
1 tablespoon corn oil
1/2 cup uncooked macaroni
1 cup tomato sauce
5 cups water
2 cups chopped cabbage
2 tablespoons lemon juice

Combine and cook 25 to 30 minutes.

Potato and Mushroom Soup

6 cups diced potatoes
2 quarts water
2 teaspoons sea salt
1 cup well-chopped red onion
2 teaspoons minced garlic
2 cups sliced mushrooms
2 1/2 teaspoons nondairy margarine
2 tablespoons unbleached white flour
1/2 teaspoon freshly ground black pepper
2 teaspoons poultry seasoning
3 tablespoons monosodium glutamate
2/3 cup nutritional yeast flakes
1/2 teaspoon caraway seed

Begin to boil the potatoes in the water with the salt. Sauté the onion, garlic, and mushrooms in the margarine. Add the flour and stir it in well. Add this and all the rest of the ingredients to the boiling potatoes. Cook until the potatoes start to fall apart.

Potato Soup with Garlic and Greens

2 cups diced onion
4 garlic cloves, peeled
2 tablespoons seeded and minced jalapeños
4 teaspoons corn oil
5 cups cubed potatoes
3 cups coarsely chopped Swiss chard or spinach
3 cups coarsely chopped tomato
2 cups canned tomatoes
1 quart UnChicken Broth (page 155) or UnBeef Broth (page 155)
1 teaspoon sea salt
1/2 teaspoon freshly ground black pepper
3 tablespoons balsamic vinegar

Sauté the onion, garlic, and jalapeños in the oil until the onion is soft. Combine everything in a big pot and cover. Bring to a boil over high heat, reduce heat, and simmer, covered, for 35 minutes, or until the potatoes are soft. Cool slightly and puree in blender or food processor.

Potato-Cabbage Soup

1/2 cup chopped bell pepper
1/4 cup chopped onion
1 1/4 teaspoons corn oil
2 cups chopped cabbage
2 cups peeled and chopped potatoes, in pieces no bigger than 1 inch
1/4 teaspoon sea salt
1/8 teaspoon cayenne pepper
2 1/4 cups UnBeef broth (page 155) or UnChicken Broth (page 155)

Sauté the bell pepper and onion in the oil until the onion is soft. Combine with the rest of the ingredients and cook for about 30 minutes or until the potatoes are done.

VARIATION: *Use squash instead of cabbage.*

Potato-Onion Soup

3 cups cubed onion
1 tablespoon nondairy margarine
2 teaspoons minced garlic
4 cups cubed potatoes
7 cups UnChicken Broth (page 155) made with Cashew Milk (page 93)
1/4 teaspoon cayenne pepper

Sauté the onion in the margarine until soft. Add the garlic and sauté 1 more minute. Add everything else and cook until the potatoes start to fall apart.

Potato-Spinach Soup

1 1/2 teaspoons minced garlic
1 cup chopped onion
3 cups potatoes, peeled and cut into 2-inch pieces
2 tablespoons corn oil
2 1/2 cups cubed Mexican Chorizo UnSausage (page 134)
1 bay leaf
3/4 teaspoon sea salt
1/4 teaspoon cayenne pepper
4 cups UnSausage Broth (page 156)
2 cups water
2 cups spinach

Sauté the garlic, onion, and potatoes in the oil until the onion is soft. Add the UnSausage, bay leaf, salt, pepper, UnSausage Broth, and water, and bring to a boil. Simmer, uncovered, stirring occasionally, for 45 minutes. Stir in the spinach and simmer 10 more minutes.

Roasted Tomato Soup

Something different and worthwhile.

6 pounds tomatoes, cored
1/4 cup olive oil
2 1/4 teaspoons minced garlic cloves
1 teaspoon thyme
1 1/2 cups chopped onion
2 teaspoons olive oil
2 1/4 teaspoons basil
2 cups UnChicken Broth (page 155)
1/2 cup Cashew Kreem (page 93)
3 1/2 teaspoon sea salt
1/4 teaspoon freshly ground black pepper
1/4 cup fresh basil

Put the tomatoes in a baking pan large enough to place them in one layer. Drizzle them with 1/4 cup of the oil and sprinkle them with the garlic and thyme. Roast the tomatoes at 350°F, turning them occasionally, for 1 hour. Sauté the onion in the 2 teaspoons of oil until it is soft. Add the tomatoes and dried basil, and cook, stirring, for 5 minutes. Add the broth, bring to a boil, and simmer, stirring, for 5 minutes. Force the mixture through a food mill (medium disk) into a bowl, or process in a blender or food processor for 10 seconds (in batches) and return it to the cooking pot. Stir in the Cashew Kreem, salt, and pepper. Keep the soup warm. Put a little broth or water with the fresh basil in a blender and blend thoroughly. Stir into the soup.

Russian Vegetable Soup

1/3 cup chopped onion
1/2 cup shredded cabbage
1 1/4 teaspoon nondairy margarine
2 cups chopped potatoes
1 cup chopped parsnips or carrots, if none are available or if you don't like parsnips
1 cup chopped carrot
2 tablespoons chopped fresh parsley
1/4 teaspoon basil
1/4 teaspoon oregano
5 cups UnBeef Broth (page 155)
1/4 teaspoon sea salt
1/4 teaspoon cayenne pepper

Sauté the onion and cabbage in the margarine until they are transparent. Add the rest of the ingredients, bring to a boil, reduce heat, cover, and simmer for 30 minutes. Let cool a bit, then run through a blender until smooth.

Savannah UnBeef and Okra Stew

2 cups cubed UnBeef (page 109)
3 tablespoons olive oil
1 1/2 cups chopped onion
2 teaspoons minced garlic
2 cups chopped canned tomatoes, drained (reserving 1 cup of juice)
3 cups UnBeef Broth (page 155)
1/2 teaspoon sea salt
1 bay leaf
1/2 teaspoon oregano, crumbled
2 teaspoons Louisiana Hot Sauce
1 1/2 cups okra, cut into 3/4-inch pieces

Brown the UnBeef in the oil. Add the onions and sauté until soft. Add the garlic and sauté 1 more minute. Combine everything but the okra and simmer together, stirring occasionally, for 30 minutes. Add the okra and simmer 15 more minutes, stirring occasionally, until the okra is tender.

Shchi 1

1 can Loma Linda "Big Franks"
1 quart sauerkraut, drained
1 cup finely minced onion
4 cups UnBeef Broth (page 155)
2 1/2 teaspoons corn oil
1 bay leaf
1/4 teaspoon freshly ground black pepper
2 cups diced potatoes
1/2 teaspoon caraway seeds
Liquid from the "Big Franks"

Pour off the liquid from the Big Franks and reserve it. Grind the franks in a food processor or grinder. Add all the ingredients, including the Big Frank liquid, and cook for 45 minutes.

VARIATION: *Instead of Big Franks use 2 cups of UnSausage (page 132), but retain the UnBeef Broth.*

Shchi 2

2 cups coarsely shredded cabbage
1/3 cup wine vinegar
1 teaspoon sea salt
2 cups water
1/2 cup chopped onion
2 teaspoons corn oil
2 cups canned tomatoes
5 cups UnBeef Broth (page 155)
1 bay leaf
1/2 cup grated carrot
1 teaspoon caraway seeds
1/8 teaspoon white pepper
2 cups diced potatoes

Combine the cabbage, vinegar, salt, and water. Bring to a boil and cook, partially covered, for 20 minutes. While cabbage is cooking, sauté onion in the oil. Add tomatoes, broth, bay leaf, carrot, caraway, and pepper. Simmer. When cabbage is done, drain it, saving the liquid. Add cabbage to simmering soup along with the potatoes. Simmer at least 30 to 45 minutes. If soup is not tart enough, add some of the reserved cabbage juice. Serve with Cashew Sour Kreem (page 94) or Tofu Sour Kreem (page 97).

Smoky Black Bean and Vegetable Soup

This delivers!

1½ cups coarsely chopped onion
¾ cup thinly sliced celery
¾ cup chopped carrot
2 tablespoons olive oil
1 tablespoon minced garlic
1½ tablespoons canned or dried seeded and minced chipotle chile
2 bay leaves
2 teaspoons ground cumin
2 teaspoons basil
1 teaspoon chili powder
1 teaspoon oregano
4 cups cooked black beans
3½ cups canned chopped tomatoes, with liquid
4 cups UnChicken Broth (page 155)
4 cups water
1 teaspoon sea salt

In a large soup pot sauté the onion, celery, and carrot in the oil until the onion is soft. Add the garlic and sauté 1 more minute. Add the chile, bay leaves, cumin, basil, chili powder, and oregano and sauté 2 more minutes. Stir in the rest of the ingredients and bring to a boil. Lower heat and cook, partially covered, for 1 to 2 hours.

Soup Thickener

For each 2 cups of soup, melt 1 tablespoon of margarine and stir in 1 teaspoon of potato flour (this is best), or 1 tablespoon of unbleached white flour. Cook slowly until smooth, stirring constantly, about 5 minutes. Add a little of the hot soup, stir well, and pour into the rest of the soup. Reheat the soup, stirring constantly.

Sour Kreem Tomato Soup

2 tablespoons finely minced onion
1 teaspoon corn oil
2 cups tomato juice
¼ teaspoon sea salt
Pinch cayenne pepper
Pinch dill
1 cup Cashew Sour Kreem (page 94) or Tofu Sour Kreem (page 97)

Sauté the onion in the oil. Add rest of ingredients except the Sour Kreem and simmer for 30 minutes. Just before serving blend in the Sour Kreem.

Spicy Tomato Soup

¼ cup chopped onion
¼ teaspoon minced garlic
1 teaspoon minced jalapeños
2 tablespoons chopped bell pepper
1 teaspoon nondairy margarine
1 tablespoon unbleached white flour
2 cups hot water
1 cup chopped tomato
¼ teaspoon sea salt

Sauté the onion, garlic, jalapeños, and bell pepper in the margarine for 6 minutes. Add flour and blend, then add the hot water gradually while stirring. Add tomato and salt. Simmer for 15 minutes.

Spicy Vegetable Soup

2½ cups sliced onion
2 tablespoons corn oil
1 tablespoon minced garlic
3 cups cooked garbanzo or white beans, drained
1 bay leaf
6 cups UnChicken Broth (page 155)
3 cups coarsely chopped tomato, canned or fresh
1 tablespoon sliced jalapeño
2¼ cups coarsely chopped carrot
2¼ cups coarsely chopped potatoes

½ teaspoon sea salt
¼ teaspoon freshly ground black pepper
3 cups thickly sliced zucchini
¼ teaspoon cayenne
1 cup chopped fresh parsley

Sauté the onion in the oil until soft. Add the garlic and cook 1 more minute. Combine everything in a pot. Bring to a boil, reduce heat, and simmer, covered, for 30 minutes.

Spinach Soup

¾ cup chopped onion
1 teaspoon minced garlic
1½ teaspoons nondairy margarine
½ cup chopped potatoes
¼ cup chopped carrot
1 cup chopped tomato
2 tablespoons parsley
1 bay leaf
2½ cups UnBeef Broth (page 155) or UnChicken Broth (page 155)
⅛ teaspoon sea salt
¼ teaspoon cayenne pepper
2 cups spinach, finely shredded

Sauté the onion and garlic in the margarine until transparent. Add everything else except the spinach. Bring to a boil, reduce heat, cover, and simmer for 30 minutes. Let cool a bit, then run through a blender until smooth. Return to saucepan, add the spinach, and simmer for 10 minutes.

Split Pea Soup 1

2½ cups dried split peas
Enough UnBeef Broth (page 155) or UnChicken Broth (page 155) to cover the peas with 2 inches of broth
1 cup chopped bell pepper
3 tablespoons chopped onion
2 teaspoons corn oil
¾ teaspoon sea salt
⅛ teaspoon cayenne pepper
2 cups chopped tomato
¼ teaspoon summer savory

Cook the peas in the broth for about 30 minutes until they are soft. Sauté the bell pepper and onion in the oil. Combine with rest of ingredients and cook about 30 minutes more. When done the peas will be "dissolved." If needed, add more broth or water to keep a soup consistency.

Split Pea Soup 2

2 cups split peas
⅓ cup chopped onion
½ cup chopped celery
½ teaspoon minced garlic
2 teaspoons corn oil
⅛ teaspoon Italian herb seasoning
¼ teaspoon sage
1 bay leaf
¼ teaspoon cayenne pepper
2 cups diced potatoes, cooked in water
1 cup sliced carrots, in rounds and cooked in water
1 cup minced or finely chopped UnBacon (page 136)
4 cups UnChicken Broth (page 155)

Pressure-cook the split peas. Sauté the onion, celery, and garlic in the corn oil. Combine all ingredients and cook for 30 minutes.

VARIATIONS: *Omit the UnBacon and use UnBeef Broth (page 155) instead. Use lentils instead of split peas.*

Split Pea Soup 3

1 cup dried green split peas
¾ cup chopped onion
1 teaspoon nondairy margarine
2 cups UnBeef Broth (page 155) or UnChicken Broth (page 155)
¼ teaspoon cayenne pepper

Pressure-cook the split peas. Sauté the onion in the margarine. Combine all ingredients and simmer for 1 hour.

Three Sisters Soup

The American I ndians understood the nutritive value of combining dried beans, corn, and squash—so much so that they referred to them as "the three sisters."

3 tablespoons chopped onion
1½ teaspoons corn oil
2 cups cooked beans
2 cups corn
2 cups chopped squash
½ teaspoon sea salt
⅛ teaspoon cayenne pepper
3 cups UnBeef Broth (page 155)

Sauté the onion in the oil. Combine with rest of ingredients and cook.

Tofu Gumbo

2 cups diced yellow onion
1 cup sliced celery, ¼ inch thick
4½ teaspoons sliced garlic
1 tablespoon corn oil
1½ cups canned crushed tomatoes
½ cup sliced carrots, ¼ inch thick
4 cups sliced okra, ¼ inch thick
1 cup diced red bell pepper
1 cup diced green bell pepper
1 cup sliced yellow squash
¾ cup corn
1 tablespoon Cajun spice
1 teaspoon paprika
½ teaspoon fenugreek
¼ teaspoon hot pepper flakes
½ teaspoon sea salt
¼ teaspoon freshly ground black pepper
10 ounces tofu, frozen, pressed, and cubed

Sauté the onion, celery, and garlic in the oil until soft. Combine everything but the tofu, bring to a boil, and simmer for 20 minutes. Add the tofu and simmer 10 more minutes.

Tofu Stew

12 ounces tofu, frozen, pressed, and cubed
1 cup chopped onion
½ cup chopped celery
3 tablespoons corn oil
1 tablespoon sliced garlic
2¾ cups Heavenly Broth (page 158)
2 cups cut potatoes, in ½-inch chunks
½ cup quartered button mushrooms
½ cup cut turnip, in ½-inch chunks
½ cup cut parsnips, in ½-inch chunks
½ cup sliced carrot
½ cup soy sauce
½ teaspoon ground ginger
½ cup sliced yellow squash, ¼ inch thick
½ cup sliced zucchini, ¼ inch thick
½ teaspoon Szechuan peppercorns
⅛ teaspoon freshly ground black pepper
½ teaspoon sea salt
4 tablespoons chopped green onions

Sauté the tofu, onion, and celery in the oil until the onion is soft. Add the garlic and sauté 1 more minute. Add everything else but the green onions, bring to a boil, reduce heat, and simmer until the potatoes and turnip are very soft. Serve garnished with the green onions.

Tomato-Bean Corn Chowder

1 teaspoon minced garlic
½ cup diced onion, ¼-inch dice
¼ cup diced celery, ¼-inch dice
2 teaspoons corn oil
3¾ cups diced tomato, ¼-inch dice
4 cups water
1¼ cups peeled and diced potatoes, ¼-inch dice
1 cup cooked white beans
1 cup corn
3 dashes of Tabasco sauce
Pinch freshly ground black pepper
¾ teaspoon sea salt

Sauté the garlic, onion, and celery in the oil until soft. Combine everything, bring to a boil, reduce heat, and simmer 30 minutes.

Tomato Consommé

Unusual—and unusually good!

1 pound tomatoes, quartered
3 cups tomato juice
1 tablespoon corn oil

¾ cup chopped celery
¾ cup chopped onion
½ cup chopped fresh parsley
1 whole clove
1 clove garlic
½ bay leaf
1½ tablespoons tomato paste
¼ teaspoon thyme
½ teaspoon coriander seeds
2 cups UnBeef Broth (page 155)
¼ teaspoon cayenne pepper
½ teaspoon sea salt

Put the tomatoes, tomato juice, oil, celery, onion, parsley, clove, garlic, bay leaf, tomato paste, thyme, and coriander seeds in a blender and puree thoroughly. Pour into a nonreactive pot and add the broth, cayenne, and salt. Bring to a boil, reduce heat, and simmer, covered, for 15 minutes. Uncover and simmer 10 more minutes.

Tomato Soup 1

This is fabulous the first day and legendary a day or so later when the flavors have blended to perfection.

1 teaspoon nondairy margarine
¼ teaspoon rosemary
¼ teaspoon basil
¼ teaspoon sea salt
⅛ teaspoon cayenne pepper
2 cups chopped tomato
1 cup tomato sauce
⅓ cup chopped onion
1 teaspoon minced garlic
½ bay leaf
1 cup frozen lima beans, thawed
2 cups water

Combine all ingredients and cook for 30 minutes.

Tomato Soup 2

¼ cup chopped onion
1 teaspoon nondairy margarine
1½ teaspoons unbleached white flour
2½ cups water
2 cups chopped tomato
1 cup chopped carrot
½ teaspoon basil
2 tablespoons minced fresh parsley
1 teaspoon sea salt
¼ teaspoon black pepper or cayenne pepper

Sauté the onion in the margarine until it is soft. Add the flour and stir in well. Gradually add the water, stirring constantly. Add the rest of the ingredients and cook together for 30 minutes.

Tomato Soup 3

1½ cups chopped onion
⅛ teaspoon thyme
½ teaspoon basil
¼ teaspoon oregano
¼ teaspoon freshly ground black pepper
2 teaspoons nondairy margarine
5 cups diced tomato
3 tablespoons tomato paste
¼ cup unbleached white flour
3¾ cups UnChicken Broth (page 155)
1 teaspoon Sucanat
1 cup Cashew Kreem (page 93)

Sauté the onion, thyme, basil, oregano, and pepper in the margarine until the onion is soft. Add the tomato and tomato paste, blending well. Simmer for 10 minutes. Put the flour and ¼ cup of the broth in a blender, blend thoroughly, and stir into the tomato mixture. Add the rest of the broth and simmer 30 more minutes, stirring frequently. Let this cool, then puree in a blender or food processor. Return to the pot and add the Sucanat and Kreem. Heat through, stirring occasionally.

Tomato Soup 4

4 cups chopped tomato
1¼ cups peeled and diced potatoes
2 teaspoons Sucanat
1 teaspoon sea salt
¼ teaspoon freshly ground black pepper
1 tablespoon basil
1 cup UnChicken Broth (page 155)
½ cup Cashew Sour Kreem (page 94) or Tofu Sour Kreem (page 97)

In a saucepan put the tomatoes, potatoes, Sucanat, salt, pepper, and basil. Cook, covered, for 20 minutes until the potatoes are tender, stirring frequently. Add the broth and cook for another 2 to 3 minutes. Put through a sieve or food mill, and return to the pan. Just before serving take out 1 cup of the soup and mix it with the Sour Kreem, then put it back into the soup and mix it in well.

Tomato Soup with Rice

1/2 cup chopped bell pepper
1/3 cup chopped onion
1/2 teaspoon minced garlic
2 teaspoons corn oil
5 cups chopped tomato
1 1/2 cups sliced okra, or green beans, cut in 1-inch pieces
3/4 teaspoon sea salt
1/2 teaspoon basil
1/8 teaspoon dill
1/4 teaspoon cayenne pepper
1 1/2 cups cooked rice or barley
1 cup UnBeef Broth (page 155) or UnChicken Broth (page 155)

Sauté the bell pepper, onion, and garlic in the oil. Combine with rest of ingredients and cook.

Tomato-Mushroom Soup

First Class!

1 cup chopped onion
3/4 teaspoon minced garlic
1 tablespoon nondairy margarine
4 cups sliced mushrooms (fresh only)
2 1/2 cups UnChicken Broth (page 155)
1/4 cup water
6 tablespoons tomato paste
1/2 teaspoon sea salt
1/4 teaspoon freshly ground black pepper

Sauté the onion and garlic in the margarine until the onion is soft. Add the mushrooms and cook, covered, about 5 minutes or until the mushrooms are tender. Stir in the broth, water, tomato paste, salt, and pepper. Bring to a boil, reduce the heat, and simmer, covered, for 20 minutes.

Tomato Vegetable Cream Soup

3 tablespoons chopped onion
1/2 teaspoon minced garlic
1 teaspoon nondairy margarine
1 cup chopped tomato
1 1/2 cups mixed vegetables, chopped if need be
2 cups Thin White Sauce (page 262)
1/8 teaspoon basil
Pinch dill
1 1/2 teaspoons corn flour (not meal, though it can be used)
1/4 teaspoon sea salt

Sauté the onion and garlic in the margarine. Combine all ingredients and cook.

VARIATION: *Make the White Sauce with UnBeef Broth (page 155) or UnChicken Broth (page 155) and cut the salt in half.*

UnBeef Minestrone Soup

2 cups cubed UnBeef (page 109)
1/2 cup chopped onion
1 cup sliced celery
2 tablespoons corn oil
1 teaspoon sea salt
1/4 teaspoon freshly ground black pepper
2 cups canned tomato sauce
2 1/2 cups UnBeef Broth (page 155)
2 cups cooked kidney beans
1/4 teaspoon oregano
Pinch thyme
1/4 cup uncooked macaroni
1/4 cup chopped fresh parsley

Sauté the UnBeef, onion, and celery together in the oil until the gluten is browned and the vegetables are soft. Add everything else except the macaroni and parsley. Cover and simmer for 20 minutes. Add the macaroni and cook for 10 more minutes, until tender. Stir in the parsley.

UnChicken Noodle Soup

1 cup chopped onion
1 teaspoon minced garlic

2 tablespoons chopped bell pepper
1½ teaspoons corn oil
1 cup UnChicken (page 137) or Soy Grits UnChicken (page 140)
3 cups mixed vegetables, chopped if need be
3 cups UnChicken Broth (page 155)
¼ teaspoon freshly ground black pepper
½ cup spaghetti or other noodles

Sauté the onion, garlic, and bell pepper in the oil. Combine with the rest of the ingredients, except for the pasta, and cook together for 30 minutes. Meanwhile cook the pasta and drain it. At the end of the 30 minutes, add the pasta and cook for 5 more minutes.

VARIATION: *For UnChicken Rice Soup use 2½ cups of cooked rice instead of pasta.*

UnFish Soup

1 cup finely chopped green onions
⅓ cup finely chopped celery
1½ teaspoons corn oil
1 cup unbleached white flour
3 quarts UnChicken Broth (page 155)
1 cup canned tomato sauce
1 tablespoon lemon juice
2 cups cubed UnFish (page 149), cut into 1-inch cubes
1 bag Zatarain's Crab Boil
½ teaspoon cayenne pepper

Sauté the onions and celery in the oil. Brown the flour and add it to the onions and celery. Combine everything and cook for 20 to 30 minutes. Remove the bag of crab boil before serving.

UnShrimp and Corn Soup

3½ cups water
3½ cups UnShrimp Broth (page 150; can be the broth used in making the UnShrimp)
½ teaspoon cayenne pepper
1 cup finely chopped onion
½ cup finely chopped fresh parsley
1½ teaspoons minced garlic
1½ teaspoons nondairy margarine
2 cups chopped or mashed tomato
2 cups corn
4 cups UnShrimp (page 150)

Combine the water, broth, and pepper in a pot and bring it to a boil. Sauté the onion, parsley, and garlic in the margarine until the onion is soft. Add this along with the tomato and corn to the broth and bring it back to a boil. Lower heat to a simmer and add the gluten. Cook on low heat for 30 to 40 minutes, stirring occasionally.

UnShrimp Soup

2 quarts UnChicken Broth (page 155)
1 cup chopped green onions
½ cup chopped celery
1 tablespoon diced garlic
1 cup chopped fresh parsley
2 cups water
2 teaspoons Louisiana Hot Sauce, or ½ teaspoon cayenne pepper
2 tablespoons Lea and Perrins Steak Sauce
3 cups UnShrimp (page 150)

Put all of the ingredients, except for the UnShrimp, in a pot. Bring to a boil and lower the heat. Cover and simmer for 45 minutes. Add the UnShrimp and simmer for 30 more minutes.

UnShrimp Stew 1

Eat it up and call for more!

2½ teaspoons olive oil
¼ cup unbleached white flour
3 cups chopped onion
½ cup chopped bell pepper
½ cup chopped celery
½ teaspoon minced garlic
1 cup chopped fresh parsley, or ½ cup dried
4 cups water
4 cups UnShrimp (page 150)
¼ teaspoon sea salt
¼ teaspoon cayenne pepper

Heat the oil, add the flour, and cook to a dark brown over low heat, stirring constantly. Add the onion, bell pepper, celery, garlic, and parsley and cook for 10 minutes. Slowly add the water, stirring, and simmer over low heat for 30 minutes.

Add the UnShrimp, salt, and pepper. Cover and simmer for 30 more minutes, keeping the heat low. Serve over rice or pasta.

VARIATION: *Instead of the water, use 6 cups of canned tomatoes, crushed (without the liquid).*

UnShrimp Stew 2

1½ cups minced onion
2 tablespoons minced garlic
1¼ cups chopped bell pepper (half red and half green, if possible)
1 tablespoon olive oil
½ teaspoon freshly grated lemon peel
4½ cups cubed or chopped UnShrimp (page 150)
4 cups chopped tomato, or 2 cups canned, drained and chopped
1 bouquet garni made of 5 parsley sprigs, 3 thyme sprigs, and 2 bay leaves tied in cheesecloth
⅛ teaspoon cayenne
2 cups UnShrimp Broth (page 150; can be the broth used in making the UnShrimp)
1 tablespoon capers, drained
1 teaspoon freshly ground black pepper

Sauté the onion, garlic, and bell pepper in the oil. Combine everything and cook for 30 minutes. Remove the bouquet garni.

Vegetable Consommé

1 quart cold water
2 teaspoons corn oil
2½ cups chopped onion
1 cup diced celery
1½ cups peeled, seeded, and diced tomato
1 cup diced carrot
2 teaspoons coarsely chopped garlic
3 fresh parsley sprigs
1½ teaspoons basil leaves
2 cups chopped mushrooms
⅛ teaspoon thyme
2 bay leaves
2 pinches of chervil
¼ teaspoon freshly ground black pepper
1 teaspoon sea salt

Combine everything in a pot. Bring to a boil, reduce heat, and simmer lightly, covered, for 20 minutes. Turn off the heat, keep covered, and set aside to steep for 20 more minutes. Strain carefully through a fine strainer.

White Bean and Tomato Soup

1 cup chopped onion
1 teaspoon minced garlic
½ cup chopped celery
¼ cup chopped bell pepper
1 tablespoon corn oil
5 cups cooked white beans
2 teaspoons sea salt
¼ teaspoon basil
¼ teaspoon freshly ground black pepper or cayenne pepper
1 cup chopped tomato
1 cup chopped or sliced carrot
2 cups water

Sauté the onion, garlic, celery, and bell pepper in the oil until soft. Combine everything, bring to a boil, reduce heat, and simmer 20 to 30 minutes, adding more water if needed.

Winter Hot Pot

⅓ cup chopped onion
1½ teaspoons nondairy margarine
5 cups mixed vegetables, chopped if need be
¼ cup barley, soaked
3¾ cups UnBeef Broth (page 155)
1 bay leaf
½ teaspoon sea salt
¼ teaspoon cayenne pepper

Sauté the onions in the margarine until transparent. Add the rest of the ingredients. Bring to a boil, reduce heat, and simmer 15 to 20 minutes or until the vegetables are just tender.

Zucchini Soup

3 cups UnChicken Broth (page 155)
2 cups scrubbed, trimmed, and chopped zucchini
1½ cups thinly sliced onion
2 teaspoons corn oil
1 tablespoon curry powder
Salt
Pepper

Bring the broth to a boil. Add the zucchini, reduce heat, and simmer until the zucchini is tender, 12 to 15 minutes. Sauté the onion in the oil until soft, then add the curry powder and sauté for 3 more minutes. In a blender or food processor, puree the onion and zucchini mixtures, combine, and season with salt and pepper. Serve hot, chilled, or at room temperature.

VARIATION: *Use other types of squash.*

Zucchini-Carrot Soup

3 cups zucchini, quartered lengthwise and then sliced
1 cup carrot, quartered lengthwise and then sliced
1 cup potatoes, cut in eighths lengthwise and then sliced
2 tablespoons nondairy margarine
3¼ cups UnChicken Broth (page 155) or UnBeef Broth (page 155)
½ cup thinly sliced green onions

Sauté the zucchini, carrot, and potatoes in the margarine for 5 minutes. Add the broth and onions and bring to a boil, lower the heat, and simmer 5 to 7 more minutes.

Zucchini-Tomato Stew

¾ cup sliced onion
¾ teaspoon minced garlic
¾ cup chopped bell pepper
1½ teaspoons corn oil
¼ cup UnChicken Broth (page 155) or water (add ½ teaspoon salt if water)
2 cups sliced zucchini, in ½-inch slices
2½ cups chopped tomato
1 teaspoon basil
¼ teaspoon cayenne pepper

Sauté the onion, garlic, and bell pepper in the oil. Combine everything and cook over low heat, covered, 20 minutes or until the squash is tender.

Chili

Black Bean Chili 1

2 cups dried black beans
2 cups chopped onion
2 teaspoons minced garlic
1 tablespoon corn oil
1 tablespoon minced jalapeño
1 teaspoon cumin seeds
½ teaspoon cayenne pepper
½ teaspoon paprika
1 teaspoon oregano
1 teaspoon sea salt
4 cups chopped canned tomatoes

Pressure-cook and drain the beans, reserving the cooking water. Sauté the onion and garlic in the oil until onion is transparent. Add the jalapeño and spices and sauté for 1 more minute. Add rest of ingredients and simmer for 1 hour, adding bean water if more liquid is needed. Serve with vinegar on the side to be added to taste.

Black Bean Chili 2

2 cups dried black beans
1½ teaspoons cumin seed
1½ teaspoons oregano
1 teaspoon paprika
½ teaspoon cayenne pepper
1½ cups chopped onion
2 teaspoons corn oil
½ cup diced bell pepper
1½ teaspoons minced garlic
1½ cups chopped Italian tomato
1 cup tomato juice
½ teaspoon sea salt
¼ cup chopped green onions (including the tops)

Wash the beans thoroughly and pressure-cook them. in a small dry skillet, heat the herbs, and toss them until they are fragrant and set aside. Sauté the onion in the oil for 2 to 3 minutes. Stir in the bell pepper, garlic, and herbs until the onion is soft and golden. Add to the cooked beans, along with the tomato, juice, and salt. Simmer for 30 or more minutes. Serve with the green onions on top.

Chili

More than you can eat at one sitting, but the rest is terrific the second day in Chili-Mac (page 267)!

2 cups UnBeef (page 109) or UnBeef Soy Grits (page 109)
1½ cups coarsely chopped onion
3 tablespoons chili powder
1 teaspoon garlic powder
1 tablespoon corn oil
3¼ cups UnBeef Broth (page 155)
1 cup tomato paste
5 cups cooked kidney beans (other beans may be used)
1 quart chopped tomato

½ teaspoon cayenne pepper
½ teaspoon sea salt

Sauté the gluten (or grits), onion, chili powder, and garlic powder in the oil. Combine the broth and tomato paste. (You might want to blend the paste in a blender with some of the broth.) Combine with all ingredients and cook for 1 hour.

Chili Supreme

What else? Supreme!

3 cups chopped onion
1 tablespoon minced garlic
2 tablespoons minced jalapeños (with the seeds)
2 tablespoons corn oil
7 cups canned tomatoes, drained (keep the juice)
½ cup tomato paste
1 cup chopped bell pepper
¾ cup chopped carrot
1 tablespoon ground cumin
¾ teaspoon sea salt
½ teaspoon cayenne pepper
2 cups kidney beans, cooked
2 cups pinto beans, cooked
2 cups diced zucchini

Sauté the onion, garlic, and jalapeños in the oil until the onion is translucent, about 6 minutes. Add the tomatoes, 1 cup of the reserved tomato juice, tomato paste, bell pepper, carrots, cumin, salt, and cayenne. Simmer for 20 minutes, stirring frequently. Add the beans and cook 15 more minutes, thinning with more tomato juice if needed so the chili will not be too thick. Add the zucchini and cook 5 more minutes, stirring occasionally.

Chili with Mushrooms

Distinctively good. But be sure you use Mexican oregano, not Italian. It is not the same at all.

2 cups coarsely chopped onion
½ cup chopped bell pepper
1 tablespoon corn oil
2 teaspoons minced garlic
1½ cups shredded mushrooms
¾ teaspoon powdered cumin
1½ teaspoons sea salt
5 cups chopped tomato
½ cup canned tomato sauce
2 teaspoons coriander
¾ teaspoon powdered Mexican oregano
1 teaspoon cayenne pepper
4 cups cooked dried kidney beans, cooking liquid reserved

Sauté the onion and bell pepper in the oil. When the onion is transparent add the garlic and mushrooms and cook a little bit longer. Add the rest of the ingredients except for the beans but including the bean cooking liquid. Simmer together for 45 minutes. Add the beans and simmer 30 more minutes.

Countryside Chili

For those who like mild chili—and for everybody else, too!

4 teaspoons corn oil
3 cups ground UnBeef (page 109)
2 cups chopped onion
¾ cup chopped bell pepper
¼ cup chopped celery
6 cups canned whole tomatoes, undrained
½ cup canned tomato paste
1 tablespoon dried parsley flakes
2 tablespoons chili powder
½ teaspoon sea salt
½ teaspoon cayenne pepper
½ teaspoon garlic powder
2 cups cooked kidney beans
1 cup cooked pinto beans

Heat the oil in a large skillet and brown the UnBeef. Add the onion, bell pepper, and celery, and sauté until the onion is soft. Add the rest of the ingredients except for the beans, reduce heat, cover, and simmer for 1 hour. Stir in the beans (if needed, add tomato juice at this point to make it soupy) and cook, uncovered, for 30 more minutes.

Denver Chili

2 cups ground UnBeef (page 109)
1 cup diced onion
1 cup sliced celery
1 cup sliced carrot
1½ teaspoons minced garlic
2 tablespoons corn oil
2 cups canned tomatoes
2 cups tomato sauce
2 cups cooked kidney beans, drained
2 cups UnBeef Broth (page 155)
1 tablespoon dried parsley flakes
½ teaspoon oregano
½ teaspoon basil
½ teaspoon sea salt
¼ teaspoon black pepper
2 cups shredded cabbage
1 cup green beans, cut into 1-inch pieces
½ cup small elbow macaroni

Sauté the UnBeef, onion, celery, carrot, and garlic in the oil until the vegetables are soft. Combine everything except the cabbage, green beans, and macaroni. Bring to a boil, lower heat, cover, and simmer 20 minutes. Add the cabbage, green beans, and macaroni. Bring back to a boil, lower the heat, and simmer until the vegetables are tender.

Half-Hour Chili

3 cups chopped onion
⅓ cup chopped carrot
1 tablespoon minced jalapeño
1½ teaspoons minced garlic
1 tablespoon corn oil
4 teaspoons chili powder
1 teaspoon ground cumin
3½ cups chopped canned tomatoes, with juice
1 teaspoon Sucanat
4 cups cooked kidney beans, drained and rinsed
⅓ cup fine or medium-grain bulgur

Sauté the onion, carrot, jalapeño, and garlic in the oil until the onion is soft. Combine everything but the beans and bulgur and cook for 15 minutes. Stir in the beans and bulgur and cook 15 more minutes.

Pinto Bean Chili

2 cups chopped onion
½ cup chopped jalapeños
1 tablespoon minced garlic
1 tablespoon corn oil
5 cups cooked pinto beans, drained
2 cups diced tomato
2 teaspoons ground cumin
1 teaspoon oregano
½ teaspoon thyme
¼ teaspoon chili powder
⅛ teaspoon hot pepper flakes
1 bay leaf
Pinch Sucanat
1 cup corn
¼ cup finely diced UnBeef (page 109) or UnSausage (page 132)
1 tablespoon soy sauce
1½ teaspoons balsamic vinegar
1½ teaspoons lemon juice
1 tablespoon chopped fresh parsley
5 cups water or UnBeef Broth (page 155)

Sauté the onion, jalapeños, and garlic in the oil until soft. Combine everything and cook for 30 minutes.

UnChicken Chili

1 cup chopped onion
1 cup chopped bell pepper
1½ teaspoons minced garlic
1 tablespoon corn oil
4½ cups diced UnChicken (page 137)
4 cups canned stewed tomatoes
2 cups cooked pinto beans
⅔ cup salsa or Piquante Sauce (page 259)
2 teaspoons chili powder
1 teaspoon ground cumin
½ teaspoon sea salt

Sauté the onion, bell pepper, and garlic in the oil until the onion is soft. Add the rest of the ingredients and bring to a boil. Reduce the heat and simmer for 20 minutes.

Dairy Substitutes

The milk substitutes given here will keep only for two to three days, so it is best to make only as much as you need for a recipe or make sure to use the rest later that day or the next day.

Any other dairy substitutes that have vinegar or lemon juice in them will keep well for five days.

When storing these substitutes, use containers that will not have much air space. This will ensure that they keep better and longer.

Almond Milk

This is very thin, but that is necessary to obtain the right flavor.

1 cup almonds
Boiling water to cover
1/8 teaspoon salt
1 1/2 teaspoons vegetable oil
2 tablespoons Sucanat

Drop the almonds into boiling water. Boil for 10 seconds. Turn off the heat and let the almonds stand for 2 to 3 minutes. Drain water. Remove the skins and discard. Combine the almonds with the rest of the ingredients in a blender. Blend for 1 to 2 minutes. Strain through a cheesecloth.

Cashew Buttermilk

For 1 cup of "buttermilk," put 1 tablespoon of lemon juice or vinegar (white or cider) in a cup measure and add enough Cashew Milk (see below) to make 1 cup. Stir and let stand about 5 minutes.

Cashew Kreem

Make Cashew Milk, as below, but with only 2 cups of water.

Cashew Milk

1 cup raw cashew nuts
4 cups water
1/4 teaspoon salt
1 1/2 teaspoons Sucanat

In a blender put the cashews and 1 cup of the water. Blend until smooth. Add the rest of the ingredients and blend for 30 more seconds.

Note

If the "milk" is to be used in a dessert or other sweet dish, or even on breakfast cereal, make it with double the Sucanat (1 tablespoon of Sucanat).

VARIATION: *For use in some "salty" dishes, use UnBeef Broth (page 155) or UnChicken Broth (page 155) instead of water and leave out the Sucanat altogether.*

Cashew Sour Kreem

2 cups water
6 tablespoons cornstarch or arrowroot powder
1 cup hot water
2 cups raw cashews
1/3 cup lemon juice
1 teaspoon garlic powder
1 tablespoon sea salt
2 teaspoons onion powder

Mix the 2 cups of water with the cornstarch or arrowroot and boil on the stove until it thickens. Cool slightly. Blend the hot water and cashews well. Add the lemon juice, garlic powder, salt, and onion powder to the cashew liquid. Add this to the starch mixture and combine thoroughly. Cool before using.

Cashew Yogurt

Make Cashew Sour Kreem (page 94), using 1 1/2 teaspoons more lemon juice, and add 1/3 cup of water.

Notzarella Cheez

I saw this adaptation of my Mozzarella Cheez in Vegetarian Voice. *Bravo!*

2 cups water
2 1/4 teaspoons lemon juice
1/3 cup nutritional yeast
1/3 cup rolled oats
1/4 cup arrowroot
1/4 teaspoon garlic powder
1/4 teaspoon Italian herb seasoning
1 1/2 teaspoons onion powder
3 tablespoons tahini
1 1/2 teaspoons sea salt

Put everything in a blender and blend for 1 minute. Pour into a saucepan and heat, stirring constantly, until thickened. Blend with electric mixer to remove any clumps.

Note

This can be frozen, then quickly grated and sprinkled over dishes such as pizza.

Parmesan Cheez 1

This is somewhat like Parmesan cheese, but it adds a lot to a recipe where Parmesan cheese is needed. It is very strong in flavor, so be cautious in its use. Refrigerated, this keeps at least one month.

1 cup sesame seeds
1/4 cup lemon juice
1 1/4 cups nutritional yeast
2 teaspoons garlic powder
1 tablespoon onion powder
3 tablespoons Schilling's Vegetable Supreme Seasoning

Mix all together. Sprinkle on a cookie sheet. Cover with a piece of waxed paper. Roll out thin. Remove the waxed paper. Put in a 200°F oven for 2 hours. Grind fine and store in a covered container in a cool place.

Parmesan Cheez 2

This is for those who find the previous recipe too salty. To my taste this is more like powdered Yeast Cheez than Parmesan Cheese, but you may prefer it. Refrigerated, this keeps at least one month.

1 cup sesame seeds
2 teaspoons sea salt
1 cup nutritional yeast
2 teaspoons onion powder
1/2 teaspoon garlic powder
2 tablespoons Special Seasoning (page 304)
2 tablespoons lemon juice

Toast the sesame seeds in a dry skillet on medium-high heat, stirring constantly until they are slightly browned and beginning to crackle, about 5 minutes. Remove from heat, put in a blender, and blend on high until it is ground fine. Pour into a bowl, add the rest of the ingredients, and mix together well. Keep refrigerated.

Pimiento Cheez 1

This Cheez should not be grainy from the ground (blended) cashews. If this happens to yours, then you did not blend long enough or your blender lacks the power to do the job. We use a Vita-Mix, and it works perfectly.

1/4 cup agar
1 cup water
3/4 cup cashews
1/4 cup pimientos
1 teaspoon salt
1 teaspoon onion powder
1/2 teaspoon corn oil
2 tablespoons lemon juice

Soak the agar in water about 5 minutes and boil gently until clear. While the agar is boiling, place the nuts, pimientos, salt, onion powder, and oil in a blender and whirl until smooth. Add the hot agar and whirl 1/2 minute. Add the lemon juice and mix for only a second. Pour immediately into a mold and set in the refrigerator to cool.

VARIATIONS: *For a Cheez sauce or spread, use only half the agar. Use cooked potatoes instead of cashews.*

Pimiento Cheez 2

As stated above, this Cheez should not be grainy from the ground (blended) cashews. Make sure you blend it long enough.

1/4 cup agar
1 cup water
3/4 cup cashews
1/4 cup pimientos
1 1/4 teaspoons salt
1 teaspoon onion powder
2 tablespoons sesame seed
3 tablespoons nutritional yeast
Dash garlic powder
Dash dill seed
1/2 teaspoon corn oil
2 tablespoons lemon juice

Soak the agar in water about 5 minutes and boil gently until clear. Place the other ingredients, except the oil and lemon juice, in a blender with the agar and whirl. Slowly add the oil. Add the lemon juice last. Pour immediately into a mold and set in the refrigerator to cool.

VARIATIONS: *For a Cheez sauce or spread, use only half the agar. Use cooked potatoes instead of cashews.*

Pizza Cheez

1/2 cup nutritional yeast
1/4 cup cornstarch
1 teaspoon sea salt
1/2 teaspoon garlic powder
2 cups water
1 tablespoon corn oil
1 teaspoon prepared mustard

Mix the dry ingredients in a saucepan. Whisk in the water. Cook over medium heat while whisking until it thickens and bubbles. Cook 30 seconds more and remove from heat. Whip in the oil and mustard. Add 1 cup or more of water to make a thick, smooth sauce that will pour easily. Pour on pizza, and for the last few minutes of baking, broil the pizza until the Cheez is speckled.

Rice Kreem

1 cup white rice, cooked according to Basic Rice recipe (page 242)
2 cups water
3/4 teaspoon Sucanat
1/8 teaspoon vanilla

Put all in a blender and blend on high speed for 5 minutes. Do not strain.

Note

For use in desserts, double the Sucanat.

Rice Milk

1 cup white rice, cooked according to Basic Rice recipe (page 242)
2 cups water
3/4 teaspoon Sucanat
1/8 teaspoon vanilla

Put all in a blender and blend on high speed for 3 minutes. Strain through a cheesecloth. Squeeze liquid out of pulp remaining in the cheesecloth.

Note

For use in desserts, double the Sucanat.

Soy Milk Basic

Sort dried soybeans and wash in cold water. Soak the beans until they double in size, about 4 hours. In warm weather, soak them in the refrigerator so they will not ferment and spoil. Using 2½ cups of water to 1 cup of beans, liquefy in a blender or grind in a food grinder. Heat the mixture to a boil in a double boiler or heavy pot. Simmer for 40 minutes, stirring occasionally. Strain through a clean cloth (nylon, folded cheesecloth, etc.) placed in a colander or strainer. This only lasts a couple of days.

Soy Milk

4 cups Soy Milk Basic (see above)
1 teaspoon corn oil
¼ plus ⅛ teaspoon sea salt
¼ cup plus 3 tablespoons Sucanat

Blend together in a blender.

Soy Whipped Kreem

¾ cup Soy Milk (see above)
1 tablespoon cornstarch
½ cup corn oil
¼ cup Sucanat
⅛ teaspoon sea salt
2 teaspoons vanilla

Put the Soy Milk and cornstarch in a blender. While running on high, slowly add the oil in a thin stream until the spinning funnel of Soy Milk closes and the mixture stops blending—the blender blades will change speed. Add the Sucanat, salt, and vanilla to the blender and blend again until the mixture thickens as before. If necessary, add a small amount of oil. Allow to set in the refrigerator for at least one hour before using. This lasts only two or three days.

Tofu Buttermilk

Make Tofu Sour Kreem (page 97) and add ⅔ cup of water.

Tofu Cottage Cheez

1½ cups firm tofu
¼ cup Miraculous Whip (page 17) or other "mayonnaise" recipe (see Salad Dressings chapter)
2 tablespoons plus 1½ teaspoons lemon juice
2 teaspoons soy sauce
¼ teaspoon garlic powder
Pinch paprika

Mash all together.

Tofu Kreem Cheez 1

1½ cups tofu, squeezed
2 tablespoons corn oil
½ teaspoon sea salt
Dash white pepper
2 teaspoons lemon juice
Pinch onion powder

Puree in a blender until smooth and thick.

Tofu Kreem Cheez 2

1 cup Tofu Cottage Cheez (see above)
¼ cup nondairy margarine

Blend in a blender until smooth.

Tofu Ricotta Cheez

6 cups firm tofu, pressed to remove excess water
½ cup lemon juice
4 teaspoons Sucanat
2 teaspoons sea salt
¼ cup corn oil
4 teaspoons basil
1 teaspoon garlic powder

Mash the tofu. Mix the other ingredients into the mashed tofu, mixing well.

Tofu Sour Kreem

1 cup tofu
1/4 teaspoon corn oil
1 tablespoon lemon juice
1/2 teaspoon sea salt
1/4 teaspoon Sucanat

Combine and blend till smooth. Can be used in place of mayonnaise.

Tofu Whipped Kreem

1 1/2 cups tofu
3 tablespoons maple syrup
1/8 teaspoon sea salt
1/2 teaspoon vanilla
1 tablespoon corn oil

Puree in a blender until smooth.

Tofu Yogurt

Make Tofu Sour Kreem (see above), using 1 1/2 teaspoons more lemon juice, and add 1/3 cup of water.

Yeast Cheez

This is a bit like process cheese, but is distinctively different. Make it and see what I mean.

1/2 cup nutritional yeast
1/2 cup unbleached white flour
1 teaspoon sea salt
1/2 teaspoon garlic powder
2 cups water
1 tablespoon nondairy margarine
1/2 teaspoon prepared mustard

Mix the dry ingredients in a saucepan. Whisk in the water. Cook over medium heat while whisking until it thickens and bubbles. Cook 30 seconds more and remove from heat. Whip in the margarine and mustard. This thickens when it cools and thins when heated. Water can be added to thin it more. This keeps about five days.

Gluten: For Goodness' Sake!

Gluten is the protein of wheat (flour) that remains when the starch is washed away in water. Gluten is sometimes referred to as *seitan*, although that is a Japanese term properly applied only to gluten that has been flavored with soy sauce.

Gluten can be made into a variety of meat substitutes that are an ideal means of supplying healthful protein to the diet—something all vegetarians need just as much as nonvegetarians. Two-thirds of a cup of raw gluten supplies 56 grams of protein—a little more than the recommended daily allowance for a 167-pound man. Gluten is a boon for those of us who are frustrated with the way so many commercial meat substitutes contain egg albumen. And it is much less expensive than the commercial substitutes.

Gluten is usually to be preferred to textured vegetable protein (TVP), because TVP is made using a chemical process to separate the soy flour from the soybeans. I was told by the owner of a health food store (who refused to sell TVP) that Hexane—a poison—is used in the process. Organic TVP made in a nonchemical manner is available from The Farm, Summertown, TN 38483.

Many vegetarians who have an aversion to meat dislike the idea of eating nonmeat substitutes that look or taste like meat. This is quite understandable, yet meat substitutes can be of great value. For one thing they can demonstrate to meat eaters that there is an alternative to animal flesh. They also make it very easy for people to make the transition to vegetarianism, since they can keep on eating the kind of dishes they have been used to for much of their lives.

Meat substitutes are often the only tactic a person has to convince a spouse or children that vegetarianism does not mean grazing out in the back yard. For no matter how delicious and creative vegetarian dishes can be, there are some who just cannot believe they are eating "real food" if it does not include meat, or something very much like it. Through the years we have helped many individuals and families to become vegetarian by means of these meat substitutes. Although our personal motives for diet are based on what we feel are bedrock principles of health and spiritual development, not many share those ideals, at first. But serve them up a "meat" dish that is even better than the real thing and you have them more than halfway to taking what a friend of ours called the first step to wisdom, a vegetarian diet. It is results that count.

With these recipes vegetarians can continue using the dishes they liked when they ate meat. As

I have said, they are also excellent means of convincing nonvegetarians that they can live without meat, and they can help beginning vegetarians make the transition to a nonmeat diet.

By using these meat substitutes the family cooks can also keep right on using the same recipes and the same cookbooks they have all along. When meat is called for, no problem!

Don't forget to look for other excellent recipes in the "beef," "pork," "poultry," and "seafood" sections as well as in this one.

Here are a few guidelines for working with gluten:

- Raw gluten, unflavored and uncooked, will keep only one day. It should not be frozen.
- Once gluten is cooked, any that is not going to be used right away should be frozen. It will keep indefinitely and can also be refrozen.
- Unfrozen cooked gluten can be kept, refrigerated, for up to one week.
- Dishes containing gluten can only be kept as long as the life of the other ingredients.
- Gluten should be stored in airtight containers.

Basic Gluten

Don't let this intimidate you. It is easy after you have done it once. Do not use pastry flour in this because it does not contain enough gluten to work.

8 cups whole wheat flour
8 cups white flour
6 cups cold, not chilled, water

Mix the flours and water together and knead it for about 10 to 15 minutes, adding water or flour if needed, until you have a very smooth ball of dough with no cracks in it. Kneading is what develops the gluten. It should bounce back when you punch it.

Put this ball of dough in a bowl large enough to hold it and add enough cold water to cover the ball completely. Let it soak under water for one-half hour at least, preferably one to two hours.

Then begin kneading it under water, kneading out all the starch and being careful to hold the gluten together. Change the water when it gets quite milky from the starch, and keep changing it until the water stays almost clear. The last part of the kneading should be done in a colander (not a strainer) under running water.

If the dough disintegrates in the kneading-washing you must try another brand of flour.

Cook according to one of the methods given below.

Cooking Method 1

Oil a loaf pan. Place the raw gluten in the pan and bake at 450°F for 45 minutes. The gluten will rise just like a loaf of bread and when done will have a shiny golden brown "skin."

Slice the gluten "loaf" into slices 3/8 inch to 1/2 inch thick. If chunks are desired, cut the slices into cubes or strips.

Place the slices or cubes in boiling gluten broth (see chapter of specific gluten you're making for broth recipe), not flavoring broth, and boil for 30 minutes. A weight may be required to keep the gluten submerged while boiling.

If possible, let the cooked gluten soak overnight for best flavor, though it can be used right away if need be.

Cooking Method 2

The long, slow cooking time of this method permits the seasoning to penetrate the gluten and gives it a texture that enables it to be sliced very thin.

Shape 2 cups of raw gluten into an oval loaf and place it in an oiled loaf pan.

Pour 2 1/2 cups of the prescribed Gluten Broth (not Flavoring Broth) over the gluten.

Cover tightly with aluminum foil and bake in a 250°F oven for 10 hours or overnight, turning the gluten over after 5 hours of baking so the flavoring will be evenly absorbed.

For a larger quantity of gluten, increase the amounts of raw gluten and broth proportionately. You may need to increase the baking time to give the increased amount of gluten adequate time to absorb the broth. Be sure to bake it in a pan or dish that will be of a size that ensures that the broth covers the gluten at the beginning of the baking.

Cooking Method 3

We have found that pressure-cooking gluten is by far the best method. Not only is it much quicker, and therefore easier, the texture is perfect. Also, gluten cooked by other methods may have a "raw" taste even when cooked with other things in well-seasoned dishes. But pressure-cooking eliminates this problem completely.

I have still given the other methods of cooking gluten in case someone does not have a pressure cooker or would rather not use one.

To Pressure-Cook Gluten:

Put 2 cups of gluten in a pressure cooker with 6 cups of liquid (water for plain unflavored gluten, and one of the broths for flavored gluten) and a little sea salt and cook at 15 pounds for 45 minutes.

"Instant" Gluten

I have good news for those who would like to cook with gluten but don't want to make it the old-fashioned way. All you need do is obtain Vital Wheat Gluten (Instant Gluten Flour) from your local health foods store or order it from The Farm, Summertown, TN 38483. Vital Wheat Gluten is pure gluten powder, not "high gluten flour." Don't mistake it!

Important: *Gluten made in this way and immediately used will be somewhat less soft or tender than gluten made the regular way, but if you have time, put the gluten in a bowl and cover it with warm water and let it sit for 30 minutes and then bake it.*

Here is the formula for making one "loaf" of gluten from Vital Wheat Gluten.

1 cup Vital Wheat Gluten
14 tablespoons water (this is 7/8 cup—measure out 1 cup of water [16 tablespoons] and then remove 2 tablespoons)

Mix the gluten and water by hand until it forms a spongy "dough"—no kneading is required. Put into an oiled loaf pan and bake at 375°F until dark brown on top, 1 hour and 15 minutes. The gluten will rise just like a loaf of bread and when done will have a shiny golden brown "skin." However, after about 30 minutes of baking, check the gluten, and if it is starting to puff up more than 2 inches above the sides of the pan, pierce the top in 3 places with a knife. when it is done, slice the gluten "loaf" into slices 3/8 inch to 1/2 inch thick. If chunks are desired, cut the slices into cubes or strips.

Place the slices or cubes in boiling gluten broth (see the chapter of the specific gluten you're making for broth recipe), not Flavoring Broth, and boil for 30 minutes. A weight may be required to keep the gluten submerged while boiling.

If possible, let the cooked gluten soak overnight for best flavor, though it can be used right away if need be.

Baked Gluten

2 cups finely chopped onion
1 cup chopped bell pepper
1 teaspoon minced garlic
1 tablespoon corn oil
1 teaspoon sea salt
1 teaspoon dried mint
1/2 teaspoon cayenne pepper
4 cups crushed canned tomatoes
2 tablespoons chopped fresh parsley
1/4 teaspoon chopped fresh thyme
6 cups sliced flavored gluten

Sauté the onion, bell pepper, and garlic in the oil until the onion and pepper are tender. Put in the salt, mint, cayenne, tomatoes, parsley, and thyme. Cook for 15 minutes. Put the gluten in a casserole and pour this mixture over it. Cover the casserole tightly and bake at 325°F for 45 minutes. Serve with rice.

Fig. 1. Mix the flour and water together.

Fig. 2. Knead the flour and water for about 10 to 15 minutes.

Fig. 3. Add water or flour as (if) needed.

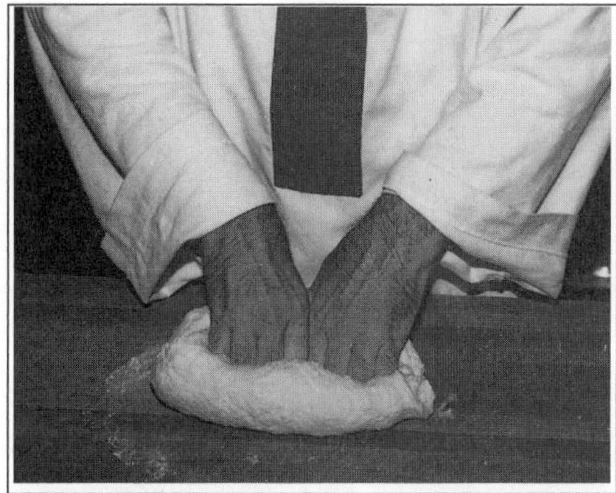
Fig. 4. …until you have a very smooth ball of dough with no cracks in it.

Fig. 5. Put this ball of dough in a bowl large enough to hold it and add enough cold water to cover the ball completely.

Fig. 6. Let it soak under water for one-half hour at least, preferably one to two hours.

Fig. 7. Then begin kneading it under water, kneading out all the starch and being careful to hold the gluten together. Change the water when it gets quite milky from the starch, and keep changing it until the water stays almost clear.

Fig. 8. The last part of the kneading should be done in a colander (not a strainer) under running water.

Fig. 9. During the washing process—towards the end of gluten development—the gluten will separate into small pieces. Just continue to wash, and the gluten will soon come together.

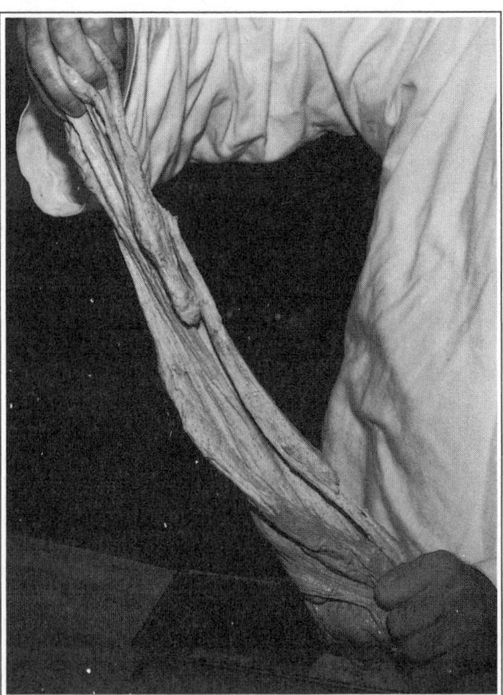

Fig. 10. (Left) Continue to wash in a colander until the water around the gluten becomes clear.

Fig. 11. (Above) When the gluten is finished it will be in one piece with a somewhat elastic consistency.

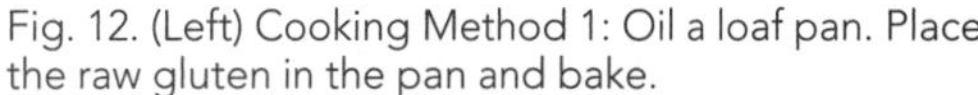

Fig. 12. (Left) Cooking Method 1: Oil a loaf pan. Place the raw gluten in the pan and bake.

Fig. 13. (Below Left) Slice the gluten "loaf" into slices ⅜-inch to ½-inch thick. If chunks are desired, cut the slices into cubes or strips.

Fig. 14. (Below) To pressure cook gluten: Put 2 cups of gluten in a pressure cooker with 6 cups of liquid (water for plain unflavored gluten, and one of the broths for flavored gluten) and a little sea salt and cook at 15 lbs. for 45 minutes.

Fig. 15. (Bottom) Sliced gluten "UnBeef," made with the Pressure Cooker Method.

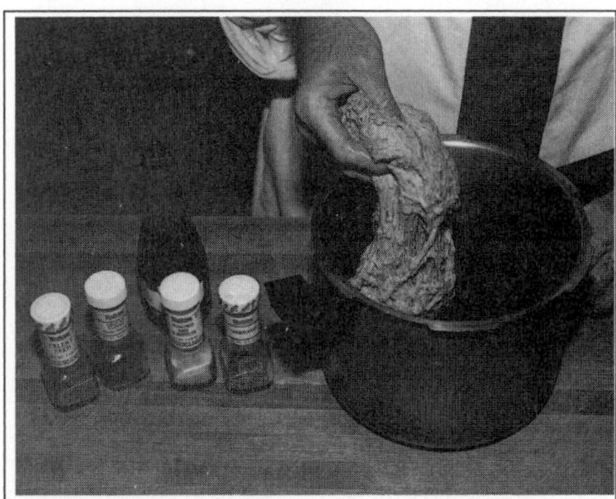

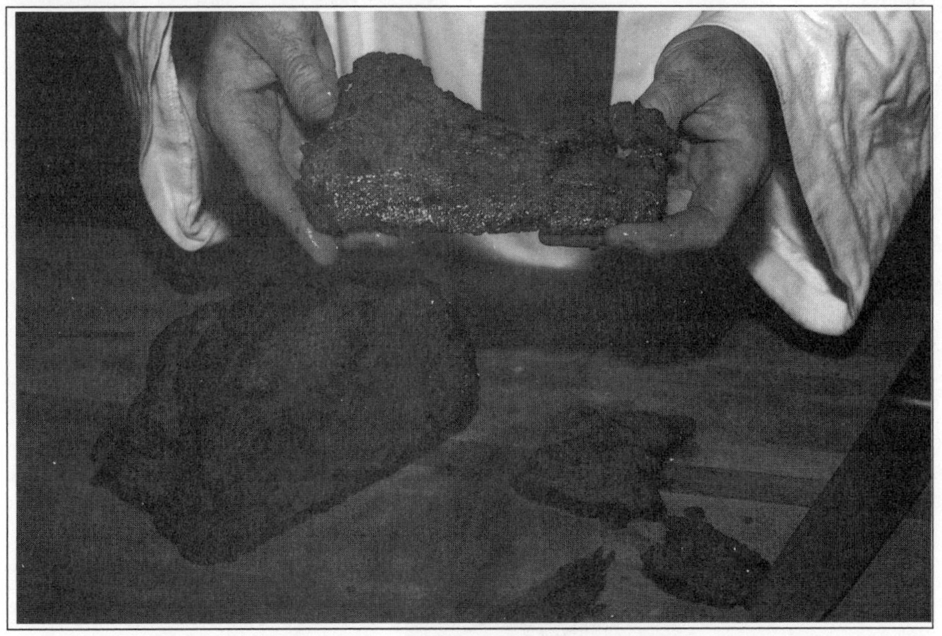

Baked Cubed Gluten

Fantastic is the word for this recipe. And don't worry about the hot sauce—it blends into the rest of the flavors and loses its bite.

5 cups flavored gluten, cooked by Method 2 or 3, and cut in 1-inch cubes
2 tablespoons corn oil
2 tablespoons unbleached white flour
1/2 teaspoon Kitchen Bouquet
3/4 cup chopped onion
3/4 teaspoon minced garlic
1 1/2 cups flavoring broth according to type of gluten being used
1/4 teaspoon sea salt
1 tablespoon Lea and Perrins Steak Sauce
1 1/2 teaspoons Louisiana Hot Sauce

In a skillet brown the gluten in the oil and put it in a baking dish or pan. Stir the flour into the oil remaining in the skillet and turn the heat down so it will cook slowly. Add the Kitchen Bouquet and keep stirring the flour constantly, adding more oil if the mixture is too dry, until the mixture is a rich brown. Add the onion and garlic, stirring constantly. Add the broth and keep stirring until it starts to form a thick gravy. Add the salt, steak sauce, and hot sauce. Add more water if you need to, and bring all to a boil. Pour the sauce over the gluten cubes. Bake at 400°F for 30 to 45 minutes, basting frequently and adding water if needed. This is good served on a bed of mashed potatoes.

Barbecue Gluten

This is something special!

2 cups chopped onion
3/4 cup chopped bell pepper
1/3 cup chopped celery
2 teaspoons minced garlic
2 1/2 teaspoons corn oil
6 cups thinly sliced flavored gluten
6 cups barbecue sauce of choice
1 teaspoon hot pepper flakes

Sauté the onion, bell pepper, celery, and garlic in the oil until the onion just starts to get soft. Add the gluten and continue to sauté until the gluten begins to brown. Add the barbecue sauce and pepper flakes and simmer for 20 more minutes. If it gets too dry, add more barbecue sauce or some water.

Gluten and Green Beans Stir-Fry

2 cups flavored gluten of choice
1/2 plus 1/8 teaspoon sea salt
1/3 teaspoon black pepper
2 teaspoons corn oil
1 cup green beans, cut into 1-inch lengths
1 cup chopped onion
1 teaspoon minced garlic
3/4 cup flavoring broth according to the type of gluten being used
1 teaspoon basil
1 tablespoon cornstarch
2 tablespoons water
1 1/2 cups chopped tomato
1/2 teaspoon Kitchen Bouquet

Thinly slice the gluten into 2 1/2 x 1/2-inch strips and season them with the 1/2 teaspoon salt and the pepper. Heat the oil in a skillet over medium heat until hot. Add the gluten and stir-fry 3 to 5 minutes. Remove the gluten from the skillet and put in 1 more teaspoon of oil and heat it until hot. Put the green beans, onion, and garlic in the skillet and sauté for a few minutes. Add the broth, basil, and 1/8 teaspoon salt. Cover and simmer for 15 minutes or until the beans are tender. Combine the cornstarch and water in a small bowl and stir until blended. Add the cornstarch mixture, gluten, and tomatoes to the skillet. Stir in the Kitchen Bouquet. Cook, stirring constantly, until the mixture boils and thickens, about 2 minutes.

Gluten and Potato Hash

1 1/2 cups ground flavored gluten
1 1/2 teaspoons nondairy margarine
1 cup chopped onion
1 teaspoon minced garlic

2 tablespoons browned flour
1 cup flavoring broth according to the type of gluten being used
3 cups diced cold, boiled potatoes
1/8 teaspoon freshly ground black pepper

Sauté the gluten in the margarine until it is browned. Just before the gluten is done, add the onions and garlic and sauté until the onion is soft. Add the flour. Gradually add the broth, stirring constantly. Add potatoes, gluten, and pepper and cook for 5 minutes. Transfer to a baking dish and bake at 375°F for about 30 minutes.

Gluten Chow Mein

1 1/2 cups chopped celery
1/2 cup chopped onion
1/2 cup chopped bell pepper
1/2 cup snow peas
1 teaspoon hot pepper flakes
4 teaspoons corn oil
1/3 cup cold water
1/3 cup cornstarch
1 cup flavoring broth according to the type of gluten being used
1/3 cup soy sauce
1 cup bean sprouts, blanched for 10 seconds
1/2 cup bamboo shoots
1/2 cup sliced water chestnuts
1 1/2 cup cubed flavored gluten

Sauté the celery, onion, bell pepper, peas, and pepper flakes in the oil until they are crisp-tender. Blend the water, cornstarch, broth, and soy sauce together. Add the blended liquid to the vegetables along with the sprouts, bamboo shoots, water chestnuts, and gluten. Cook until thick, about 15 minutes.

Gluten Curry

The aristocrat of curries!

1/2 cup finely chopped onion
1 tablespoon minced garlic
1/2 teaspoon powdered ginger
1 teaspoon corn oil
1 1/2 teaspoons garam masala
2 teaspoons chili powder
3/4 teaspoon turmeric
2 cups coconut milk
3/4 cup chopped tomato
1 1/2 teaspoons lemon juice
1/4 teaspoon sea salt
2 cups cubed flavored or unflavored gluten

Sauté the onion, garlic, and ginger in the oil until the mixture is golden. Add the garam masala, chili powder, and turmeric, and sauté for 2 more minutes. Stir in the coconut milk, tomato, lemon juice, and salt. Boil, stirring occasionally, until thickened. Add the gluten and cook together for 1 minute.

Gluten Dumplings

Unflavored gluten can often add a great deal to dishes that contain a lot of liquid, for it will absorb the flavors of the vegetables and seasonings. When the dish is fully assembled or boiling, take the raw (uncooked) gluten, break off 1/2-inch pieces, roll each between your thumb and fingers, and drop them in. After dropping in 10 pieces, stir so the gluten pieces will not stick to one another.

Gluten Enchiladas

You're always on target with this dish!

2 teaspoons minced garlic
2 cups chopped onion
2 teaspoons minced jalapeño
1 tablespoon corn oil
3 tablespoons chili powder
3/4 cup chopped black olives
1/4 teaspoon sea salt
4 cups ground flavored gluten
10 cups Spanish Tomato Sauce (page 260)
1 recipe of Corn Tortillas (page 52) or Flour Tortillas (page 52)
Yeast Cheez (page 97) or Pimiento Cheez (page 94) to cover

Sauté the garlic, onion, and jalapeños in the oil until the onion is transparent. Add the chili powder and sauté for 2 more minutes, stirring constantly. Add olives, salt, gluten, and 3 cups of the tomato sauce and cook for another 5 minutes. Dip a tortilla in the remaining tomato sauce, put some of the filling on it and roll it up and put it in a casserole pan. Do this with all the tortillas until the filling is used up. Cover the enchiladas with the remaining sauce. Spread a layer of Cheez over that. Bake at 350°F for 30 minutes.

VARIATION: *Use flavored soy grits instead of gluten.*

Gluten Hash

Don't think this is just a way of using up leftovers—it can stand on its own.

1 tablespoon nondairy margarine
3 cups chopped onion
2 cups sliced mushrooms
½ cup unbleached white flour
2 cups flavoring broth according to the type of gluten being used
½ cup Cashew Kreem (page 93)
3 cups diced flavored gluten
⅓ cup finely chopped fresh parsley
2 tablespoons Lea and Perrins Steak Sauce
⅛ teaspoon cayenne pepper

Melt the margarine and sauté the onion until it is soft. Add the mushrooms and cook until most of the liquid is evaporated. Stir in the flour and then the broth and Kreem, stirring constantly. Cook until thickened. Stir in the gluten, parsley, steak sauce, and pepper. Heat through. Serve over Toast Points (page 57).

Gluten Jambalaya

This is worth swimming the bayou for! Even if you are not a rice fan you will love it in this dish, I guarantee!

3 cups chopped onion
1 tablespoon finely chopped bell pepper
1 tablespoon finely chopped celery
1 tablespoon corn oil
4 cups sliced flavored gluten, ¼ inch thick
1 cup finely chopped Mexican Chorizo UnSausage (page 134)
3 cups uncooked rice
1½ teaspoons sea salt
Freshly ground black pepper
Cayenne pepper
2½ cups flavoring broth according to the type of gluten being used
2½ cups water
⅛ teaspoon liquid smoke
2 teaspoons finely chopped garlic

Sauté the onion, bell pepper, and celery in the oil until the onion is transparent. Add the glutens, rice, salt, and pepper. Cook over low heat for 15 minutes, stirring often. Add the broth, water, liquid smoke, and garlic. Stir and cover. Do not stir any more. Simmer over low heat for 20 or 30 minutes until the rice is done. Keep covered until served.

Gluten Loaf

2½ cups ground flavored gluten
1 cup rolled oats
1 cup bread crumbs
1 cup ground nuts
1 cup finely chopped onion
1¼ cups Kreem of Mushroom Soup (page 74)
½ teaspoon sea salt
¼ teaspoon minced garlic
2 tablespoons water
2 teaspoons corn oil

Mix the gluten, oats, bread crumbs, nuts, onion, soup, salt, and garlic together and form into a loaf. Put the loaf in a well-oiled baking dish or pan. Mix the water and oil and baste the loaf. Bake at 350°F until the loaf is brown and firm.

VARIATION: *Instead of gluten, use flavored soy grits.*

Gluten Paprika

You haven't lived until you've tried this.

1 cup chopped onion
¾ teaspoon chopped garlic
1 tablespoon corn oil
3 teaspoons paprika
5 cups cubed flavored gluten, in 1-inch cubes
2 cups cubed tomato
¾ cup chopped bell pepper

3 tablespoons water
1 teaspoon sea salt
1/4 teaspoon cayenne pepper
3 tablespoons unbleached white flour
1 1/2 cups Cashew Sour Kreem (page 94) or Tofu Sour Kreem (page 97)
1 cup Cashew Milk (page 93)

Sauté the onion and garlic in the oil until transparent. Stir in the paprika and cook a few more seconds. Add the gluten and sauté over high heat, lightly tossing, until it is lightly browned, about 15 minutes. Add the tomatoes and bell pepper along with the water, salt, and pepper. Mix well and cook over moderate heat for 12 to 15 minutes, stirring occasionally. Whisk in the flour. Combine the Sour Kreem and Cashew Milk. Add to the gluten and stir. Cook for a few more minutes, stirring, until thickened.

Gluten Piquant

This is a somewhat Cajun recipe adapted for use by vegetarians from some recipes of Justin Wilson, the famous television Cajun cook.

2 teaspoons olive oil
1/4 cup unbleached white flour
1 cup chopped mushrooms
1 cup chopped onion
1 cup chopped green onions
1/4 cup chopped bell pepper
2 tablespoons chopped celery
1/2 cup chopped fresh parsley
1 1/2 teaspoons minced garlic
3 cups cold flavoring broth according to the type of gluten being used
3 cups cubed flavored gluten, cooked by Method 2 or 3, and cut in 1-inch cubes
2 tablespoons olive oil
2 tablespoons Louisiana Hot Sauce
1 1/2 cups canned tomato sauce
1/4 cup mashed canned tomatoes
1 teaspoon dried mint, or 1 bay leaf
1 tablespoon lemon juice
2 tablespoons Lea and Perrins Steak Sauce
1/2 teaspoon sea salt

Heat the oil in the skillet, stir in the flour, and turn the heat down so it will cook slowly, stirring constantly, adding more oil if the mixture is too dry, until it is a rich brown. Add the mushrooms, onions (both kinds), and bell pepper, and sauté until they are tender. Add the celery and parsley, and sauté until the celery is tender. Add the garlic and sauté a bit longer. Add the broth, which should be cold, not heated, and stir in well. Let simmer. While the above is simmering, brown the gluten in the oil and put it in a cooking pot. Add all the rest of the ingredients and mix well. Cover and bring to a boil. Lower the heat and simmer for 2 1/2 hours, adding more water if needed. Serve over spaghetti, rice, or potatoes.

Gluten Pot Pie

This is a regular standby, but not dull!

1/2 cup chopped pimientos or bell pepper
1/2 cup sliced mushrooms
1/2 cup minced onion
1 tablespoon nondairy margarine
1/2 cup unbleached white flour
3 cups flavoring broth according to the type of gluten being used
6 cups mixed vegetables, cooked
3 cups flavored gluten
1 teaspoon minced garlic
1/4 teaspoon cayenne pepper

Sauté the pimientos (or pepper), mushrooms, and onion in the margarine. Stir in the flour. Gradually add the broth. Add rest of ingredients and cook until it is thick and bubbly. Serve over biscuits.

VARIATIONS: *With ham gluten use UnChicken Broth (page 155). Serve over rice instead of biscuits.*

Hearty Gluten Bake

A sure thing.

2 cups mashed potatoes
2 teaspoons nondairy margarine, melted
Corn oil
2 cups finely cubed flavored gluten of choice
1/2 cup chopped onion
4 teaspoons Lea and Perrins Steak Sauce
1/2 teaspoon sea salt
1/8 teaspoon cayenne pepper
1 cup Tofu Cottage Cheez (page 96)
2 medium tomatoes, sliced
1 cup Pimiento Cheez (page 94)

Mix the potatoes and margarine. Spread 1 1/2 cups of this in the bottom of a casserole and set aside. In some corn oil, sauté the gluten and onion until the gluten begins to brown. Add the steak sauce, salt, and pepper. Spoon the gluten mixture onto the potatoes in the casserole. Spread the Cottage Cheez over the gluten mixture. Cover with the tomato slices. Spread the Cheez over all. Spread the remaining potatoes over that. Bake at 350°F for 20 to 30 minutes.

Oven-Fried Gluten

Good the first day but better the next. When cold, it is very much like cold fried chicken.

Dry Mixture
1 3/4 cups cracker crumbs
1 teaspoon garlic powder
1/2 teaspoon sea salt
1/4 teaspoon freshly ground black pepper

1 cup finely chopped onion
1 1/2 teaspoons crushed garlic
1 1/2 teaspoons nondairy margarine, melted
4 cups raw gluten, made from all white flour
1/2 teaspoon sage
1 cup nutritional yeast
4 1/2 teaspoons sea salt
1 teaspoon freshly ground black pepper
1 teaspoon paprika
1/4 cup tahini
Nondairy margarine for rolling
2 tablespoons corn oil

Combine dry mixture ingredients and set aside. Sauté the onion and garlic in the margarine. Add all the other ingredients along with the hot sautéed onion and garlic to the raw gluten and work them through with your fingers. Take about a 1/3-cup piece of gluten and pull and flatten it out until it is about 1/4 inch thick and 3 to 4 inches long. Spread about 1 1/2 teaspoons of margarine on this stretched piece and roll it up like a jelly roll, then flatten it out with your fingers. Next, roll it in the dry mixture. Pour 2 tablespoons of corn oil on a baking sheet or in a baking pan. Put the gluten pieces rolled in the crumbs on it. Bake at 375°F for about 45 minutes, turning once when golden brown on the bottom. Be sure not to overcook.

Santa Fe Gluten

4 cups cubed flavored gluten
2 tablespoons corn oil
1 cup cooked Tomato Salsa (page 296)
1/2 teaspoon ground cumin

Sauté the gluten in the oil until browned. Add everything else and simmer, covered, 5 or 6 minutes.

UnBeef Substitutes and Dishes

UnBeef

If you have regular soy sauce instead of low-sodium soy sauce to use in this broth, then cut the amount you use in half. Cook 2 cups of raw gluten according to Method 1, 2, or 3 (pages 99–100) in:

¼ cup soy sauce
2 teaspoons Kitchen Bouquet
2 tablespoons nutritional yeast
½ cup chopped onion
¼ teaspoon rubbed sage
1 teaspoon corn oil
2 cups water

Combine everything and simmer for 5 minutes.

UnBeef Soy Grits

½ cup soy grits
1 cup boiling UnBeef Broth (page 155)

Stir grits into the broth and cook for 5 minutes.

Barbecued UnBeef

½ cup chopped onion
2 teaspoons corn oil
1 cup catsup
3 tablespoons cider vinegar
4 teaspoons lemon juice
1 tablespoon Louisiana Hot Sauce
1⅓ cups Lea and Perrins Steak Sauce
6 cups sliced UnBeef (see above)

Sauté the onion in the oil until transparent. Add everything else except the UnBeef and simmer for 10 minutes, stirring occasionally. Meanwhile brown the UnBeef in some oil. Pour half of the sauce into a baking dish or pan large enough so the UnBeef slices will make a single layer. Put in the UnBeef, pour the remaining sauce over it, and bake at 350°F for 20 minutes.

Chimichangas

2 cups chopped UnBeef (see above)
1 cup diced onion
1½ teaspoons minced garlic
1½ cups chopped tomato
Two 4-ounce cans of green chiles, chopped
1¼ cups peeled, boiled, and diced potatoes
3 tablespoons corn oil
1 teaspoon sea salt
1½ teaspoons oregano
2 teaspoons chili powder
1 tablespoon powdered coriander seed
12 flour tortillas, warmed

Sauté the UnBeef, onion, garlic, tomato, chiles, and potatoes in the oil until the onion is soft. Add the salt, oregano, chili powder, and coriander. Simmer 2 to 3 minutes. Place ½ cup of filling on each tortilla, and fold into "envelopes." Fry, seam side down, in hot (360°F to 375°F) oil until crisp and brown on both sides. Drain on paper towels. Serve with Cheez (page 94), Sour Kreem (page 97), Guacamole (page 32), salsa, shredded lettuce, chopped tomatoes, and sliced black olives on the side for topping.

Chinese Pepper UnSteak

Simple as this is, it delivers.

3 cups unflavored gluten cooked by Cooking Method 2 or 3 (pages 99–100)
2 teaspoons corn oil
1 teaspoon sea salt
1 cup sliced celery
1 cup sliced bell pepper
1 cup sliced onion
2 teaspoons minced garlic
2 cups sliced tomato

Cut the gluten in thin strips. Deep-fry (this is best) or sauté it in the oil until slightly brown. Remove from the pan. Sauté the vegetables and seasonings in the skillet, mixing gently but thoroughly. Cook until just tender. Add the gluten. Serve over rice. You can season this with soy sauce or some other condiment.

VARIATION: *Use gluten made with UnBeef Broth (page 155) or UnChicken Broth (page 155). Add 1 tablespoon of minced or sliced jalapeños.*

Company Pride Hash

Worthy of serving to guests—not just family.

1 teaspoon nondairy margarine
1 cup chopped or ground UnBeef (page 109)
1 cup cooked and diced potatoes
1 cup diced onion
1 tablespoon minced fresh parsley
½ cup Cashew Milk (page 93)
¼ teaspoon sea salt
⅛ teaspoon freshly ground black pepper

In a skillet (or on a griddle) melt the margarine. Add all the ingredients and mix well. Cover and cook until the mixture is crisp on the bottom. Then turn and brown the other side.

Continental Stroganoff

2½ cups UnBeef (page 109), cut into strips
¼ cup chopped onion
1 teaspoon nondairy margarine
3 tablespoons unbleached white flour
⅛ teaspoon freshly ground black pepper
1 cup Cashew Milk (page 93)
½ cup Cashew Sour Kreem (page 94) or Tofu Sour Kreem (page 97)

Sauté the gluten and onion in the margarine until the gluten is browned. Add the flour and pepper and gradually stir in the "milk." Add the Sour Kreem and heat through. Serve over rice or pasta with more Sour Kreem on the side.

Goulash

2 cups cubed UnBeef (page 109), cut into ½-inch cubes
1 cup diced bell pepper
1 cup chopped onion
1 teaspoon minced garlic
1 cup spaghetti sauce
½ teaspoon paprika
¼ teaspoon sea salt
Pinch caraway seed, crushed
⅓ cup Cashew Sour Kreem (page 94) or Tofu Sour Kreem (page 97)

Brown the gluten and set aside. Sauté the bell pepper, onion, and garlic until tender-crisp. Combine everything but the Sour Kreem in a casserole and bake at 400°F for 20 minutes. Stir in the Sour Kreem and serve.

VARIATION: *Use UnChicken (page 137).*

Oriental Marinated UnSteak

2 tablespoons corn oil
2 tablespoons oriental sesame oil
¼ cup Sucanat
⅓ cup low-sodium soy sauce
⅓ cup balsamic vinegar
3 tablespoons chopped green onions
½ teaspoon powdered ginger

1 tablespoon minced garlic
3 tablespoons lemon juice
½ teaspoon hot pepper flakes
⅓ cup water
4 cups sliced UnBeef (page 109)

In a blender or food processor, blend everything but the gluten until smooth. Put the gluten in a shallow dish and pour the marinade over it, turning it to coat it well. Cover and refrigerate for at least 6 hours or overnight. Discard the marinade and grill or broil the gluten on each side. Let it stand for 10 minutes.

Oriental UnBeef and Tomatoes

1 tablespoon cornstarch
2 tablespoons low-sodium soy sauce
1 tablespoon UnBeef Broth (page 155)
2½ teaspoons Sucanat
2 cups cubed UnBeef (page 109)
2 teaspoons corn oil
1 cup coarsely chopped onion
2 teaspoons minced garlic
¼ teaspoon sea salt
1½ cups diced tomato
1 teaspoon chili paste, or ¼ teaspoon of cayenne pepper
3 tablespoons tomato sauce
2 tablespoons UnFish Broth (page 155)

Combine the cornstarch, soy sauce, UnBeef Broth, and Sucanat. Add the UnBeef, toss well, and let marinate for 20 minutes. In 1 teaspoon of the oil sauté the onion for 1 minute and transfer to a plate. Add the other teaspoon of oil and sauté the garlic until it is golden. Add the UnBeef and salt and sauté for 1 minute. Sprinkle the tomato with the Sucanat, add it to the UnBeef along with the chili paste (or cayenne), and sauté just until the tomato is heated through. Add the tomato sauce and bring to a boil. Add the onion and UnFish Broth. Sauté for 1 minute. Serve with rice.

Reuben Casserole

4 cups mashed potatoes, warm
2 cups sauerkraut, rinsed and drained
4 tablespoons sliced green onions
2 cups diced UnBeef (page 109) or other gluten of choice, browned in oil
1 cup Notzarella Cheez (page 94) or Yeast Cheez (page 97)
Paprika

Combine the potatoes, sauerkraut, and onions. Mix well. Spoon ⅔ of this into a nonstick casserole. Put the UnBeef over this. Spread the Cheez over that. Top with the rest of the potato mixture. Sprinkle paprika over the top. Bake, uncovered, at 350°F for 30 minutes or until heated through.

Roast UnBeef 1

A favorite. Excellent cold, and gets better with age. Chopped or ground this is a superb hamburger substitute.

6 cups raw gluten
2 teaspoons plus additional corn oil (for covering gluten)
¾ cup plus additional soy sauce (for covering gluten)
1½ teaspoons sea salt
1½ teaspoons garlic powder
1 tablespoon onion powder
¼ plus ⅛ teaspoon freshly ground black pepper
1½ cups ground roasted unsalted peanuts

Combine all the ingredients well. Put in an oiled casserole, and spread out to about 1 inch thick. Blend together equal parts of corn oil, soy sauce, and water, enough to cover the gluten well. Pour this into the loaf pan. Bake at 350°F, covered, for 45 minutes. Uncover, and continue to bake until the gluten becomes dark brown on top.

Roast UnBeef 2

Make UnBeef (page 109) cooked according to Method 3 (page 100)

Salisbury UnSteak

2 cups sliced UnBeef (page 109)
2 N'eggs (page 302)
⅓ cup dried bread crumbs
Oil
2 tablespoons nondairy margarine
1½ cups sliced mushrooms
¼ cup finely chopped onion
1 teaspoon minced garlic
1¼ cup Kreem of Mushroom Soup (page 74)

Coat gluten slices with the N'eggs and coat with the crumbs. Brown on both sides in some oil (or grill on both sides) and set aside. Melt the margarine and sauté the mushrooms, onion, and garlic until soft. Add the soup and cook for 5 minutes. Cover the bottom of a casserole with a small amount of the sauce. Place the gluten in a single layer. Cover with rest of the sauce. Bake, uncovered, at 400°F for 20 minutes.

Saucy Ground UnBeef Casserole

You'll call for more!

1 cup ground UnBeef (page 109)
1 cup coarsely chopped onion
2 tablespoons corn oil
3 cups cubed eggplant, browned in oil
1½ teaspoons minced garlic
¾ teaspoon oregano
½ teaspoon sea salt
¼ teaspoon freshly ground pepper
1¼ cups zucchini, cut into 1-inch chunks
2 cups canned stewed tomatoes
¼ cup tomato paste

Sauté the UnBeef and onion in the oil until soft. Add the rest of the ingredients and continue to cook until the vegetables are almost tender, stirring occasionally. Bake at 375°F for 30 minutes.

VARIATION: *Use some type of UnSausage (page 132) instead of UnBeef.*

Saucy Meatless Loaf

2⅓ cups chopped mushrooms
1½ cups finely chopped onion
¾ teaspoon minced garlic
2 tablespoons olive oil
3½ cups crushed canned tomatoes
¾ cup tomato paste
1 teaspoon sea salt
⅛ teaspoon freshly ground black pepper
2 teaspoons Sucanat
½ cup tomato juice
1 bay leaf
2 teaspoons basil
4 cups ground UnBeef (page 109) (or a combination of UnBeef (page 109) and UnPork (page 122))
1 cup seasoned dried bread crumbs
3 tablespoons Cashew Milk (page 93)
2 N'eggs (page 302)

In a skillet sauté the mushrooms, onion, and garlic in the oil. Add the tomatoes, tomato paste, salt, pepper, and Sucanat. Take out 1½ cups of this mixture and set aside. To the skillet add the tomato juice, bay leaf, and basil. Simmer, uncovered, for 45 minutes, stirring occasionally. Meanwhile, combine the gluten, crumbs, "milk," N'eggs, and the 1½ cups of the sauce that was set aside. Press into a loaf or casserole pan. Bake at 350°F for 45 minutes. Take from the oven and spread the tomato-herb sauce over the top of the loaf. Return to the oven and bake 15 more minutes. Discard the bay leaf.

Saucy UnSteak Skillet

2 cups UnBeef (page 109), cut into large pieces
½ cup unbleached white flour mixed with ¼ teaspoon of freshly ground black pepper
2 teaspoons corn oil
1 cup chopped onion
2 teaspoons minced garlic
1 cup potato water
¼ cup catsup
1 tablespoon Kitchen Bouquet
2 tablespoons bell pepper flakes
1 teaspoon soy sauce
½ teaspoon marjoram
¼ teaspoon black pepper

2 cups cut potatoes, peeled, boiled whole, and cut in chunks (reserving the cooking water)
1¼ cups green beans
¼ cup sliced pimiento

Coat the gluten pieces with flour-pepper and pound it into the gluten. Brown the gluten in the oil. Add the onion and garlic and sauté until they are tender. Mix the potato water, catsup, Kitchen Bouquet, bell pepper flakes, soy sauce, marjoram, and pepper and pour it over the gluten and onion. Heat this to the boiling point, reduce heat, cover, and simmer 1 hour and 15 minutes to an hour and a half. Add potatoes, beans, and pimiento. Heat to boiling, reduce heat, cover, and simmer until the beans are tender, 10 to 15 minutes.

Spiced UnBeef Polenta

5 cups water
½ teaspoon sea salt
1 tablespoon nondairy margarine
1 cup cornmeal
1½ cups finely chopped onion
3 tablespoons corn oil
½ cup finely chopped bell pepper
2 cups ground UnBeef (page 109)
1½ teaspoons minced garlic
2 cups canned tomato sauce
1 teaspoon Sucanat
1 teaspoon chili powder
1 tablespoon cider vinegar
1 tablespoon peanut butter
1 teaspoon prepared mustard
2 teaspoons low-sodium soy sauce

Bring 4 cups water and salt to a boil and stir in the margarine and cornmeal. Lower the heat and simmer, stirring frequently, until it becomes thick, about 10 minutes. Sauté the onion in the oil for 2 minutes. Add the bell pepper and sauté 3 more minutes. Add the gluten and cook for 5 more minutes. Add the garlic and sauté 1 more minute. Stir in the remaining 1 cup water and rest of the ingredients and cook, stirring frequently, until much of the liquid has evaporated. Spread the cornmeal on a platter and top with the gluten mixture.

Stir-Fry UnBeef

Good on rice or pasta.

2 cups thinly sliced UnBeef (page 109)
1½ teaspoons plus 1 tablespoon corn oil
2 cups broccoli flowerets
½ cup sliced green onions
½ cup sliced mushrooms
1½ teaspoons soy sauce
¼ teaspoon powdered ginger
¼ teaspoon freshly ground black pepper

Sauté the gluten in 1½ teaspoons oil, take out, and set aside. Add tablespoon of oil to the skillet. Add the broccoli and sauté for 1 minute. Add the onions and sauté for 1 more minute. Add the mushrooms and sauté for 1 more minute. Add the gluten and the rest of the ingredients and sauté 2 or more minutes.

Stuffed Meatless Loaf

Stuffing

2 cups chopped or diced mixed vegetables of choice, cooked
1 N'egg (page 302)
2 tablespoons dried bread crumbs

Meatless Loaf

3 cups ground, UnBeef (page 109)
½ cup chopped onion
¼ cup corn oil
¼ cup catsup
¼ cup rolled oats
¼ cup dried bread crumbs
1 N'egg (page 302)
2 tablespoons Lea and Perrins Steak Sauce
1 teaspoon freshly ground black pepper
1 teaspoon sea salt
½ teaspoon garlic powder

Combine stuffing ingredients and set aside. Sauté the gluten and onion in the oil until the onion is soft. Combine with the rest of the loaf ingredients and spread half of it in a loaf pan. Spread the stuffing over that and top with the rest of the loaf mixture. Bake at 375°F for 45 to 55 minutes.

Swiss UnSteak

This is an all-time favorite, the one that has won over the most meat-eaters to the idea that there is an alternative to meat. It's easy, too!

2 teaspoons minced garlic
2 cups chopped onion
1½ cups chopped celery
2 tablespoons corn oil
2 quarts pureed tomato
½ teaspoon cayenne pepper (black, if you prefer)
1 teaspoon basil
1 teaspoon sea salt
2 cups UnBeef Broth (page 155)
6 cups sliced UnBeef (page 109) cooked and flavored according to Method 2 (page 99), and deep-fried
4 cups peeled and sliced potatoes, sliced ½ inch thick, and boiled

Sauté the garlic, onion, and celery in the oil until the onion is transparent. Add the tomato, pepper, basil, salt, and broth, and simmer together for 1 hour. Cover the bottom of a casserole with a small amount of this sauce. Place the gluten in a layer, covering the bottom of the casserole. Layer the potatoes over the gluten. Top with the remaining sauce. Bake at 375°F for 30 to 45 minutes.

Tamale Pie

Oh, yes!

2 cups ground UnBeef (page 109)
1 cup chopped onion
1 cup chopped bell pepper
1 tablespoon corn oil
2½ cups tomato sauce
1½ cups corn
½ cup chopped black olives
1½ teaspoons Sucanat
1 teaspoon sea salt
1 tablespoon plus 1 teaspoon chili powder
½ teaspoon minced garlic
Dash cayenne pepper
1 cup Yeast Cheez (page 97)
¾ cup cornmeal (yellow)
½ teaspoon sea salt
2 cups cold water
1 tablespoon nondairy margarine

In a large skillet, sauté the gluten, onion, and bell pepper in the corn oil until tender. Stir in the tomato sauce, corn, olives, Sucanat, salt, chili powder, garlic, and pepper. Simmer 20 to 25 minutes, or until thick. Stir in the Cheez and mix thoroughly. Put in an oiled 9x9x2-inch baking dish. Stir the cornmeal and salt into the cold water. Cook and stir until it is thick. Add the margarine and mix well. Spoon this over the UnBeef mixture in the dish and bake at 375°F for about 40 minutes.

Tangy UnMeatballs

Flavoricious!

2 cups ground UnBeef (page 109)
1 All-Purpose N'egg (page 302)
¼ cup chili sauce
¼ cup finely chopped onion
½ teaspoon sea salt
¼ teaspoon cayenne pepper
1½ cups Cheez Cracker crumbs (page 59)
Corn oil

Combine the gluten, N'egg, chili sauce, onion, salt, pepper, and 1 cup of the cracker crumbs and mix thoroughly. Shape into small balls and roll in the remaining crumbs. Put ½ inch of corn oil in a skillet and heat. Sauté the gluten balls 3 to 5 minutes, turning to brown on all sides.

UnBeef and Broccoli

1½ cups UnBeef (page 109), cut into very thin strips
1½ teaspoons corn oil
1 teaspoon minced garlic
1 medium onion, cut into wedges
2 cups Kreem of Broccoli Soup (page 73)
1 tablespoon soy sauce
¼ teaspoon sea salt
½ teaspoon cayenne pepper
2 cups broccoli florets
1 cup Pimiento Cheez (page 94)

Brown the gluten in the oil. Combine everything but the Cheez and cook until the broccoli is tender. Stir in the Cheez and serve over noodles or rice.

UnBeef and Mushroom Étouffée

4 cups cubed UnBeef (page 109)
4 teaspoons corn oil
½ cup unbleached white flour
3½ cups tomato juice
3 cups chopped onion
6 cups thickly sliced mushrooms
1 cup chopped bell pepper
1 tablespoon chopped garlic
3 tablespoons chopped fresh parsley
¼ teaspoon cayenne pepper
4½ teaspoons Louisiana Hot Sauce
⅓ cup Lea and Perrins Steak Sauce
1 teaspoon sea salt

Deep-fry the gluten and set it aside. Combine the oil and flour and cook until dark brown. Add the tomato juice and mix until it is absorbed by the flour-oil mixture. Add the onion, mushrooms, bell pepper, and garlic and cook for 10 minutes or until the onion is soft. Add the rest of the ingredients, including the gluten, and cook for 15 more minutes, adding more tomato juice if necessary to keep it from getting too thick. Transfer to a casserole and bake, uncovered, at 350°F for 30 minutes. Serve with rice, spaghetti, or mashed potatoes.

UnBeef Parmesan

1 N'egg (page 302)
2 teaspoons water
Pinch freshly ground black pepper
1 cup finely crushed crackers
½ cup Parmesan Cheez (page 94)
4 UnBeef (page 109) slices
Nondairy margarine
2 cups pizza sauce of choice

Combine the N'egg, water, and pepper. Put the crumbs and Cheez on a plate. Dip each gluten slice into the N'egg mixture and then into the crumb mixture. Melt some margarine in a skillet and brown the gluten on both sides, adding more margarine to keep from burning. (Or broil or grill until brown on both sides). Put a thin layer of the pizza sauce in a casserole. Cover with the gluten slices. Add the rest of the sauce. Sprinkle the remaining crumb mixture over all. Bake, uncovered, at 400°F for 20 minutes.

UnBeef Pot Roast

6 cups sliced or cubed UnBeef (page 109)
Unbleached white flour
⅔ cup nondairy margarine
1½ cups chopped onion
1½ teaspoons minced garlic
¼ cup Lea and Perrins Steak Sauce
¾ cup tomato sauce
2 cups UnBeef Broth (page 155)
1 teaspoon paprika
1½ teaspoons oregano, crumbled
½ teaspoon thyme, crumbled
½ teaspoon sea salt
½ teaspoon freshly ground black pepper

Coat the gluten with the flour, shaking off any excess. In the margarine brown the gluten and set aside. Add the onion and garlic and sauté until they are soft. Put the gluten back in and add the steak sauce, tomato sauce, broth, paprika, oregano, thyme, salt, and pepper. Bring to a boil, reduce heat, and simmer, covered, for 15 minutes. Turn the gluten and simmer 10 more minutes.

UnBeef Rouladen

As good as it is unusual. The pickle will surprise you.

4 UnBeef (page 109) slices, 1/4 inch thick
Coarse-ground prepared mustard
Sea salt
Cayenne pepper
1 medium dill pickle, quartered lengthwise
2 carrots, cut into sticks
1 small onion, cut into wedges
2 tablespoons unbleached white flour
1 tablespoon corn oil
3 cups UnBeef Broth (page 155)
6 tablespoons canned tomato sauce
2 teaspoons minced garlic

On one side of each gluten slice spread the mustard and sprinkle on the salt and pepper. On each one, top one edge with a piece of pickle, carrot, and a wedge of onion. Roll up and secure with a toothpick. Coat each roll with flour. In a skillet brown the gluten rolls evenly in the oil and remove from the skillet. Put the remaining flour in the oil and cook, stirring, until it browns. Stirring constantly, add the broth, tomato sauce, and garlic. Cook, stirring, until it thickens. Put the gluten rolls in a nonstick casserole and cover with the sauce. Bake at 400°F for 30 minutes, basting occasionally.

UnBeef Steaks with Peperonata Tomato Sauce

1/4 cup dried bread crumbs
1/4 cup Parmesan Cheez (page 94)
1 tablespoon chopped fresh parsley
Dash freshly ground black pepper
4 N'eggs (page 302)
6 UnBeef (page 109) slices, 1/2 inch thick
2 teaspoons minced garlic
3 cups thinly sliced onion, separated into rings
1 1/2 cups strips of bell pepper, cut into bite-size strips
1/4 teaspoon rosemary
3 tablespoons olive oil
6 cups chopped canned tomatoes, with liquid
2 tablespoons balsamic vinegar
1 tablespoon nondairy margarine

Combine the crumbs, Cheez, parsley, and pepper. Dip the gluten slices in the N'eggs and then coat with the crumb mixture. Set aside. In 2 tablespoons of the oil cook the garlic, onion, bell pepper, and rosemary until the onion is tender, stirring occasionally. Add the tomatoes and cook for 30 more minutes. Stir in the vinegar. Remove from heat and keep warm. Melt the margarine and rest of the oil. Brown the gluten slices, turning once. Cover the bottom of a casserole with a small amount of the tomato mixture. Place the gluten in a single layer. Cover with rest of tomato mixture. Bake, uncovered, at 400°F for 20 minutes.

UnBeef Stroganoff

A more than pleasant surprise.

2 cups UnBeef (page 109), cut into very thin strips
1/2 cup chopped onion
1 tablespoon nondairy margarine
1 1/4 cup Kreem of Mushroom Soup (page 74)
1/2 teaspoon paprika
1/4 teaspoon sea salt
1/2 cups Cashew Sour Kreem (page 94) or Tofu Sour Kreem (page 97)

In a skillet sauté the gluten and onion in the margarine until the onion is soft. Stir in the soup, paprika, and salt and heat through, stirring occasionally. Reduce the heat to very low and stir in the Sour Kreem. Gently heat through. Serve over noodles.

UnBeef with Rice and Tomatoes

6 UnBeef (page 109) slices, cut 1 inch thick
6 large bell pepper rings
2 cups rice, cooked
6 medium onion slices
6 tomato slices
6 cups canned tomatoes with juice
1/2 teaspoon sea salt
1/4 teaspoon cayenne pepper
1 teaspoon Louisiana Hot Sauce

Sprinkle the gluten on both sides with some salt and pepper, and brown it in a skillet. Put the gluten slices in a large baking dish so they do not overlap. Put a bell pepper ring on each gluten slice. With an ice cream scoop or large spoon take some of the rice and put it in the pepper ring, patting to make it firm. Put an onion slice on each mound of rice. Put a tomato slice on each onion slice. Empty the canned tomatoes into a bowl and chop or squeeze them until they are all broken up fine. Season the tomatoes with the salt, pepper, and hot sauce and pour them around the gluten slices. Cover and bake 1 hour at 375°F.

UnSteak and Onion Pie

1 cup sliced onion
2 cups cubed UnBeef (page 109)
2 teaspoons corn oil
¼ cup unbleached white flour
2 teaspoons sea salt
½ teaspoon freshly ground black pepper
½ teaspoon paprika
Pinch ground ginger
Pinch ground allspice
2 cups peeled and diced potatoes
1 cup diced carrot
1 cup peas
2 cups UnBeef Broth (page 155)
1 unbaked pie shell
1 unbaked top crust

Sauté the onion and gluten in the oil until the onion is soft. Stir in the flour. Add rest of ingredients but the crusts, and cook until the potatoes are almost tender. Spoon the filling into the pie shell and top with the crust. Seal the edges. Bake at 450°F until golden brown, 20 to 25 minutes.

UnSteak Étouffée

7 UnBeef (page 109) "steaks"
1 tablespoon corn oil
1½ cups Mushroom Gravy (page 253)
1 cup UnBeef Broth (page 155)
1 cup chopped onion
¼ cup chopped pimiento
1 tablespoon minced garlic
½ teaspoon celery seed
1 tablespoon minced fresh parsley
1 tablespoon soy sauce
½ teaspoon angostura bitters
½ teaspoon sea salt
¼ teaspoon freshly ground black pepper
1½ teaspoon Louisiana Hot Sauce or
¾ teaspoon Tabasco

Sauté the gluten in the oil. Combine the rest of the ingredients and pour over the gluten. Cover and let cook over low heat for 45 minutes.

Burgers

Barbecue Burgers

4 cups ground UnBeef (page 109)
4 slices of bread, crumbed
2 N'eggs (page 302)
½ cup Cashew Milk (page 93)
2 teaspoons sea salt
1 tablespoon minced onion
1 tablespoon minced celery
½ teaspoon chili powder
1 cup Barbecue Sauce (page 256)
2 teaspoons corn oil

Combine everything and shape into patties. Brown in oil or bake at 400°F for 30 minutes, turning after 15 minutes.

Bean Burgers 1

6 cups pressure-cooked dried beans
3 cups rice cooked in UnBeef Broth (page 155)
2 cups chopped tomato
1 cup tomato sauce
1 cup chopped bell pepper
⅓ cup chopped onion
1 teaspoon minced garlic
3 tablespoons soy sauce
1½ teaspoons sea salt
½ teaspoon basil
¼ teaspoon oregano
1 tablespoon minced fresh parsley
1 tablespoon corn oil

Mash the cooked beans. Mix all ingredients together. Form into patties. Brown in oil, or place on an oiled sheet pan and bake at 400°F until light brown, turning once, or cook on a griddle.

Bean Burgers 2

1¼ cups chopped red onion
1 cup grated carrot
1¼ cups chopped celery
¾ cup chopped bell pepper
1½ teaspoons minced garlic
4 teaspoons corn oil
6 cups cooked beans
3 cups rice, cooked
1½ teaspoons sea salt
¾ teaspoon basil
¾ teaspoon parsley
½ teaspoon garlic powder
½ cup soy sauce

Sauté onion, carrot, celery, bell pepper, and garlic in the oil. Mix well with rest of ingredients. Form into patties and brown in oil or place on a nonstick sheet pan and bake at 375°F for 35 minutes or until light brown.

Bean Burgers 3

2 cups bread crumbs
2 cups refried beans
1 cup cooked rice
¼ cup quick rolled oats
¼ cup tomato paste
½ teaspoon garlic powder
½ teaspoon sea salt
1 tablespoon arrowroot powder
3 tablespoons finely minced onion, or parsley
2 teaspoons corn oil
⅓ cup water

Combine everything, form into patties, and brown on both sides in some corn oil or place on a nonstick sheet pan.

Burgers Supreme

¼ cup chopped onion
1 tablespoon corn oil
8 tablespoons minced UnBacon (page 136)
1¼ cups finely chopped mushrooms
2 cups ground UnBeef (page 109)
2 cups ground UnPork (page 122)
¼ cup Parmesan Cheez (page 94)
½ teaspoon freshly ground black pepper
¼ teaspoon garlic powder
2 tablespoons Lea and Perrins Steak Sauce
⅓ cup unbleached white flour

Sauté the onion in the oil until soft. Combine everything and shape into patties. Brown in oil, broil, or grill.

Eggplant Burgers

This will surprise you! We know how to make a lot of "burgers," but this is far and away my favorite.

Sea salt
1 eggplant, peeled and cut into ½-inch-thick slices
4 cups unbleached white flour
¼ teaspoon garlic powder
¼ teaspoon onion powder
¼ teaspoon basil
¼ teaspoon freshly ground black pepper
Corn oil

Sprinkle a layer of sea salt on a counter top or other large surface, and lay the eggplant slices out on that. Sprinkle sea salt over the top of the slices. Let them sit for 20 minutes to draw out the moisture. Take each slice and pat it dry with paper towels and set aside. Mix the flour with the garlic powder, onion powder, basil, and black pepper. Lightly dust each slice of eggplant in the flour mixture, shaking off any excess. Deep fry in a skillet that has ¾ inch of hot corn oil until golden brown. Drain on paper towels. Put in buns just as you would "burgers."

Garbanzo Burgers

2 tablespoons finely chopped green onions
¾ cup finely chopped mushrooms
½ teaspoon curry powder
2 teaspoons corn oil
2½ teaspoons minced garlic
1 cup garbanzo beans, cooked and drained (keep liquid)
¾ cup garbanzo liquid
¼ teaspoon sea salt
¾ cup bread crumbs

Sauté the onions, mushrooms, and curry powder in the oil until soft. Put the garlic, garbanzos, garbanzo liquid, and salt in a blender and blend until smooth. Combine everything and mix well. Shape into patties and brown in oil, grill, or broil.

Gluten Burgers

2 cups ground flavored gluten of choice (page 99)
½ cup bread crumbs
⅓ cup finely chopped fresh parsley
1 N'egg (page 302)
1 tablespoon unbleached white flour
½ teaspoon sea salt
½ teaspoon freshly ground black pepper
½ cup finely chopped onion
1 teaspoon corn oil
1 teaspoon minced garlic

Combine the gluten, crumbs, parsley, N'egg, flour, salt, and pepper well. Cover and refrigerate. Sauté the onion in the oil until soft. Stir in the garlic, and take from the heat and let cool to room temperature. Stir into the gluten mixture. Shape into patties and brown in oil, grill, or broil.

Oat Burgers

These are as good as they sound insipid. Try them.

4 1/3 cups water
1 teaspoon corn oil
1/2 cup low-sodium soy sauce
1 1/2 cups chopped onion
1 teaspoon garlic salt
1/4 teaspoon Italian herb seasoning
1/4 cup nutritional yeast
4 1/2 cups rolled (not quick) oats

Combine everything but the oats and bring to a boil. Reduce the heat and add the oats. Stir in well. Cook about 5 minutes. Set aside to cool. Form or cut into patties and brown in oil or put them on a baking sheet and bake at 400°F for 45 minutes, turning every 15 minutes.

Oat Burgers with Mushrooms

You will not be ashamed of these.

1/2 pound mushrooms, diced
1 1/2 cups diced onion
1/2 teaspoon sea salt
2 tablespoons corn oil
4 cups water
1/3 cup low-sodium soy sauce
1 teaspoon garlic powder
1/4 teaspoon oregano
1/2 teaspoon basil
1/2 teaspoon thyme
1/4 cup nutritional yeast
5 cups rolled oats

Sauté the mushrooms, onion, and salt in the oil. While sautéing, bring all the other ingredients, except for the oats, to a boil. Lower the heat, add the sautéed vegetables, and add the oats, 1 cup at a time, allowing each cupful to sink a little before stirring gently. Cook up to 5 minutes, until the mixture starts to stick to the bottom of the pot. Set aside to cool. Form into patties and brown in oil or place on a nonstick baking sheet and bake at 350°F for 45 minutes, turning once after 20 minutes.

VARIATION: *Instead of the mushrooms, use bell pepper or celery, or a combination.*

Soyburgers

1 1/2 cups chopped onion
1 cup carrot, grated
1 1/4 cup finely chopped celery
3/4 cup finely chopped bell pepper
1 1/2 teaspoons minced garlic
4 teaspoons corn oil
6 cups cooked soybeans (save the cooking water)
3 cups cooked rice
1 1/2 teaspoons sea salt
3/4 teaspoon basil
3/4 teaspoon parsley
1/2 teaspoon garlic powder
1/2 cup soy sauce
1/3 cup tahini

Sauté onion, carrot, celery, bell pepper, and garlic in the oil. Mash beans, combine everything, and mix well. If too dry, add bean water or tomato juice. Form into patties and place on an oiled sheet pan. Bake at 400°F until light brown, turning once, or fry on a griddle.

Sunburgers

3 cups water
1/2 cup soy sauce
2 teaspoons corn oil
1 onion, chopped, or 1/8 cup of dried onion flakes
1/8 teaspoon garlic powder
1 teaspoon thyme
1/4 teaspoon liquid smoke
1/4 cup sunflower seeds
3 cups quick oats

Put all the ingredients except the oats in a large saucepan and bring to a boil. Add the oats slowly, stirring constantly and gently, until it is mixed. Turn the heat to low and simmer for a few minutes, being careful that the oats do not burn. Remove from heat, cover, and set aside until the mixture is cool enough to handle. Form into patties about ½ inch thick and 3½ inches in diameter. Bake at 350°F on an oiled baking sheet for 20 minutes. Turn the patties over and bake for 20 more minutes.

VARIATION: *Fry on a griddle.*

Tofu-Pepper Burgers

1 pound tofu, drained
1 cup finely chopped bell pepper
½ cup finely chopped red onion
1 tablespoon low-sodium soy sauce
1 garlic clove, minced
½ teaspoon powdered ginger
1 tablespoon corn oil
½ teaspoon lemon juice
3 tablespoons unbleached white flour

Wrap the tofu in a towel and place it under a weighted cutting board for 15 minutes. Combine all ingredients except the lemon juice and flour. Sauté in the oil until the vegetables begin to brown. Add the lemon juice and flour. Form into patties and brown in oil, broil, or grill on both sides.

UnBeef and Zucchini Burgers

2 cups ground UnBeef (page 109)
⅔ cup shredded zucchini
⅓ cup minced onion
¼ cup unbleached white flour
½ cup dried bread crumbs
½ teaspoon sea salt
1 N'egg (page 302)
2 teaspoons corn oil
¼ teaspoon freshly ground black pepper
⅔ cup Notzarella Cheez (page 94)
⅛ teaspoon garlic powder
½ teaspoon basil
¼ cup Cashew Milk (page 93)

Combine everything well. Shape into patties. Brown in oil, grill, or broil.

Vegeburgers

2 cups cooked soybeans, ground (reserve cooking water)
1 cup cooked garbanzos, ground (reserve cooking water)
1½ cups rice, cooked in UnChicken Broth (page 155)
1½ cups chopped onion
1½ teaspoons sage
¾ teaspoon celery salt
½ teaspoon garlic powder
1½ teaspoons corn oil

Combine all ingredients, adding bean water if too dry, or crumbs or oatmeal if too wet. Form patties and brown in oil or bake, covered with foil, for 25 minutes at 350°F, then turn and bake 10 minutes or more.

Vegetable Burgers

1 cup minced onion
1 cup grated carrot
1 cup grated turnip
1 cup grated zucchini
1 cup grated beets
1½ teaspoons chopped garlic
½ teaspoon ground cumin
1 teaspoon dill
¼ teaspoon tarragon
2 tablespoons corn oil
¼ cup instant rolled oats
¼ cup water
1½ cups mashed potatoes
⅔ cup cooked rice
½ teaspoon sea salt
½ teaspoon freshly ground black pepper

Sauté the onion, carrot, turnip, zucchini, beets, garlic, cumin, dill, and tarragon in the oil until the vegetables begin to wilt, about 5 minutes. Let them cool slightly. Soak the oats in the water for 5 minutes, drain, and press out excess water. Combine all the ingredients and mix well. Shape into patties and brown in oil, grill, or broil.

UnPork Substitutes and Dishes

UnPork 1

½ cup chopped onion
4½ teaspoons monosodium glutamate (MSG)
1 teaspoon sea salt
⅓ cup nutritional yeast
½ teaspoon hot pepper flakes
¼ teaspoon freshly ground black pepper
¾ teaspoon sage
1 teaspoon corn oil
2 cups water
2 cups raw gluten

Combine everything but raw gluten and simmer for 5 minutes. Cook raw gluten according to Method 1, 2, or 3 (pages 99–100) in broth.

UnPork 2

½ cup chopped onion
4½ teaspoons monosodium glutamate (MSG)
1 teaspoon sea salt
1 teaspoon poultry seasoning
⅓ cup nutritional yeast
1 teaspoon corn oil
2 cups water
½ teaspoon freshly ground black pepper
½ teaspoon mace
2 cups raw gluten

Combine everything but raw gluten and simmer for 5 minutes. Cook raw gluten according to Method 1, 2, or 3 (pages 99–100) in broth.

UnPork 3

½ cup chopped onion
4½ teaspoons monosodium glutamate (MSG)
1 teaspoon sea salt
1 teaspoon poultry seasoning
⅓ cup nutritional yeast
1 teaspoon corn oil
2 cups water
½ teaspoon freshly ground black pepper
1 teaspoon crushed garlic
¼ teaspoon powdered marjoram
2 cups raw gluten

Combine everything but raw gluten and simmer for 5 minutes. Cook raw gluten according to Method 1, 2, or 3 (pages 99–100) in broth.

UnPork Chops

½ cup chopped onion
4½ teaspoons monosodium glutamate (MSG)
1 teaspoon sea salt
⅓ cup nutritional yeast
½ teaspoon freshly ground black pepper
¼ teaspoon paprika
1 bay leaf
½ teaspoon ground sage
1 teaspoon corn oil
2 cups water
2 cups raw gluten

Combine everything but raw gluten and simmer for 5 minutes. Cook raw gluten according to Method 1, 2, or 3 (pages 99–100) in broth. Cut the gluten into "chops."

Barbecue "Spare Ribs"

1 cup chopped onion
1½ teaspoons nondairy margarine or corn oil
⅓ cup nutritional yeast flakes
½ cup tahini
2 tablespoons paprika
2 teaspoons sea salt
4 cups raw gluten
2 tablespoons corn oil
1 to 2 cups Barbecue "Spare Rib" Sauce (see below)

Sauté the onion in the margarine (or oil) until soft. Combine the nutritional yeast, tahini, paprika, and salt in a bowl. Add the onion along with the sautéing margarine (or oil) to this and combine well. Take half of this seasoning mixture and half (2 cups) of the gluten (broken into several pieces) and blend together in a food processor using the metal blade, gradually adding the gluten. Set aside and repeat with the other half of the seasoning mixture and ingredients. Spread the corn oil over the bottom of a baking sheet. Form into 2x3-inch patties 1 inch thick and place in rows on the baking sheet. Bake, uncovered, at 350°F for 45 minutes. Pour 1 to 2 cups of barbecue sauce over them. Put back in the oven and bake at 375°F for 20 minutes or until well done. Serve with extra barbecue sauce on the side.

Barbecue "Spare Rib" Sauce

½ cup chopped onion
1 teaspoon minced garlic
2 teaspoons corn oil or nondairy margarine
2½ cups canned tomato sauce
¼ cup water
1 cup Sucanat
2 tablespoons Barbados molasses
½ cup prepared mustard
1½ teaspoons sea salt
1 teaspoon allspice
2 teaspoons hot pepper flakes
1 sprig fresh parsley, chopped, or 1½ teaspoons dried
¼ cup water
1 tablespoon soy sauce
2 tablespoons lemon juice
1 teaspoon liquid smoke

Sauté the onion and garlic in oil or margarine until the onion becomes clear and golden. Add tomato sauce, the first ¼ cup of water, Sucanat, molasses, mustard, salt, allspice, pepper flakes, and parsley. Bring to a boil, reduce heat, and let simmer for about an hour. Add second ¼ cup of water, soy sauce, lemon juice, and liquid smoke. Cook 10 to 15 minutes longer.

Chili UnPork Chop Casserole

4 UnPork (page 122) slices, ¾ to 1 inch thick
Corn oil
1 cup chopped onion
¼ cup chopped jalapeños, or chopped canned chiles
½ cup chopped celery
2½ cups cooked rice
3½ cups Kreem of Mushroom Soup (page 74)
3 tablespoons low-sodium soy sauce

Brown the gluten on both sides in the oil. Remove and set aside. Sauté the onion, jalapeños, and celery until the onion is tender, adding more oil if needed. Stir in the rice, soup, and soy sauce. Blend well. Put into a nonstick casserole. Top with the gluten and bake, covered, at 400°F for 30 minutes.

Making your own Barbecue "Spare Ribs"

Left: Combine the sautéed onions, nutritional yeast, tahini, and spices with the gluten in a bowl and mix well (see recipe on page 123 for details).

Right: Form into 2 x 3-inch patties 1 inch thick, and place in rows on an oiled baking sheet. Bake, uncovered, at 350°F for 45 minutes.

Below: Pour 1 to 2 cups of Barbecue "Spare Rib" Sauce (recipe on page 123) over them. Put back in the oven and bake at 375°F for 20 minutes or until well done. Serve with extra barbecue sauce on the side.

Chinese UnPork with Water Chestnuts and Mushrooms

2 teaspoons corn oil
2 cups finely minced UnPork (page 122)
¼ cup minced mushrooms
10 water chestnuts, drained and minced
⅓ cup sliced green onions
2 teaspoons sliced jalapeños
½ teaspoon Sucanat
½ teaspoon powdered ginger
2 tablespoons soy sauce
1 tablespoon cornstarch, mixed in 3 tablespoons of cold water

In the oil, sauté the gluten, mushrooms, water chestnuts, onions, jalapeños, Sucanat, and ginger until the gluten browns. Add the soy sauce and cornstarch–cold water mixture and cook for 5 more minutes. Serve with rice.

Fried UnPork

½ cup unbleached white flour
¼ teaspoon white pepper
4 cups sliced UnPork (page 122), ¼ inch thick
¼ cup corn oil
1½ cups UnChicken Broth (page 155)
1 tablespoon white vinegar
2 tablespoons thinly sliced green onions
1 teaspoon fresh rosemary, or ¼ teaspoon dried
Nondairy margarine
½ teaspoon freshly ground black pepper

Combine the flour and white pepper. Lightly dredge the gluten in this, shaking off the excess. Heat 2 tablespoons of the oil in a skillet, put in ⅓ of the gluten and brown it well, then set it aside on a platter arranged in a single layer. Do the same with another ⅓ of the gluten, adding 1 tablespoon of the oil. Repeat this with the final ⅓ of the gluten, setting it aside on the platter. To the skillet add the broth, vinegar, onions, and rosemary. Bring to a boil and cook until slightly thickened, about 2 minutes. Return the gluten to the skillet briefly to heat it through, about 30 seconds. Put the gluten back on the platter. Stir the margarine into the sauce in the skillet and stir in the freshly ground black pepper. Spoon this over the gluten.

Ginger-Peach UnPork

Top of the class. You must try this!

1 tablespoon sea salt
½ teaspoon freshly ground black pepper
1 teaspoon ground ginger
2 tablespoons water
2 tablespoons cider vinegar
½ cups Sucanat
3 tablespoons chili sauce
3½ cups sliced peaches
4 cups UnPork (page 122)

Combine everything but the UnPork in a blender and blend until smooth. Marinate the gluten, in this overnight in the refrigerator. Coat the bottom of a baking pan with oil, put in the gluten, and pour in enough of the marinade just to cover the gluten. Bake at 425°F for 45 minutes.

Glorified UnPork Chops

6 UnPork (page 122) "chops"
1 tablespoon corn oil
1 cup sliced onion
1½ cups Kreem of Mushroom Soup (page 74)

Brown the chops three at a time in the oil. Stir in the onion and soup, transfer to a casserole, and bake, uncovered, at 350°F for 20 minutes.

Kraut-Stuffed UnPork Chops

Twelve ½-inch-thick slices of UnPork (page 122)
2 tablespoons corn oil
2 bell peppers
1 cup chopped onion
1½ cups peeled and shredded carrot
1 teaspoon sea salt
¼ teaspoon cayenne pepper
¼ teaspoon dried mint
1 tablespoon Sucanat
4 cups sauerkraut, drained

In a skillet brown the gluten slices on both sides in the oil. Remove and set aside. Slice 4 rings from the peppers and set aside. Dice the rest. Sauté the diced pepper and onion in the remaining oil until the onion is transparent. Stir in the carrot and sauté 1 minute. Add seasonings, Sucanat, and sauerkraut. Toss until combined. Layer 1/3 of this mixture in the bottom of a nonstick casserole. Put half the gluten over this in a layer. Layer another 1/3 of the sauerkraut mixture, and top with the rest of the gluten. Put the remaining sauerkraut mixture over all. Top with the pepper rings. Cover and bake at 400°F for 45 minutes.

Mexican UnPork Chops and Beans

2 tablespoons unbleached white flour
1 cup salsa
2 tablespoons lime juice
3/4 teaspoon chili powder
1/2 teaspoon garlic powder
2 cups kidney beans, cooked and drained
1 cup cubed bell pepper
4 UnPork (page 122) slices, 1/2 inch thick

Blend the flour, salsa, lime juice, chili powder, and garlic powder in a blender. Combine this with the beans and bell pepper. Put the gluten slices in a baking dish, pour the other ingredients over them. Cover and bake at 350°F for 30 minutes.

Orange UnPork Chops

6 UnPork (page 122) "chops," 1/2 inch thick
1 tablespoon corn oil
3/4 cup water
1/2 teaspoon paprika
1/2 teaspoon freshly ground black pepper
1 1/4 teaspoons sea salt
1 orange
1/3 cup Sucanat
1 tablespoon cornstarch
1/2 teaspoon cinnamon
4 or 6 whole cloves
1 cup orange juice

Brown the gluten on both sides in the oil. Add the water, paprika, pepper, and 1 teaspoon of the salt. Bring to a boil, reduce the heat, cover, and simmer about 35 minutes, turning once. Grate 1 tablespoon of the orange peel from the stem end. Cut 6 slices from the other end. Set aside. In a saucepan combine the grated peel, Sucanat, cornstarch, cinnamon, cloves, and rest of the salt. Stir in the juice, cook, stirring until thickened. Top the gluten with the sauce and serve.

Oriental UnPork Chops

1 cup unbleached white flour
1/2 teaspoon sea salt
1/4 teaspoon cayenne pepper
6 UnPork (page 122) "chops," cut thick
1/2 cup UnPork Broth (page 156)
1 cup chopped bell pepper
1 cup chopped onion
1 cup sliced mushrooms
3/4 teaspoon minced garlic
3 tablespoons low-sodium soy sauce
One 15-ounce can pineapple chunks, drained, reserving the juice

Combine the flour, salt, and pepper in a bag. Toss the gluten in this until coated. Take out the gluten and shake off excess flour. Broil or grill on both sides. Set aside in a casserole dish. Put the UnPork Broth, bell pepper, onion, mushrooms, and garlic in a skillet. Cover and simmer for 25 to 30 minutes. Add the soy sauce and juice from the pineapple. Stir until somewhat thickened. Add the pineapple chunks and bring to a boil. Pour over the gluten and serve.

Oven-Barbecued UnPork Chops

6 to 8 UnPork (page 122) slices, 3/4 inch thick
2 tablespoons Lea and Perrins Steak Sauce
2 tablespoons balsamic vinegar
2 teaspoons genuine maple syrup
1/2 teaspoon freshly ground black pepper
1/2 teaspoon chili powder
1/2 teaspoon paprika
3/4 cup catsup
1/3 cup hot water

Put the gluten in a baking dish (single layer) or cast-iron skillet. Combine the rest of the ingredients and pour over the gluten slices. Bake, uncovered, at 375°F for 1 hour.

Sautéed UnPork Chops with Tomato and Eggplant Sauce

4 UnPork (page 122) "chops," cut 1 inch thick
4 cups peeled and cubed eggplant
2 teaspoons olive oil
1 cup chopped onion
1½ teaspoons minced garlic
2 cups chopped canned tomatoes, with the juice
⅓ cup water
½ teaspoon sea salt
¼ teaspoon freshly ground black pepper
⅓ cup chopped fresh parsley

Deep-fry the gluten and set aside. Deep-fry the eggplant and set it aside. In the oil sauté the onion and garlic for 9 minutes. Stir in the tomatoes, water, salt, pepper, and parsley. Bring to a boil and add the eggplant. Cook for about 20 minutes. Cover the bottom of a casserole with half of the sauce. Put the gluten over that. Cover with the rest of the sauce. Cover the casserole tightly and bake at 400°F for 20 minutes.

Sweet and Sour UnPork 1

Batter

¾ cup unbleached white flour
¾ cup cornstarch
4½ teaspoons baking powder
¼ teaspoon sea salt
1 cup cold water
4½ teaspoons peanut oil

Sauce

⅔ cup white vinegar
½ teaspoon sea salt
6 tablespoons canned tomato sauce, or 1 tablespoon tomato paste mixed with 5 tablespoons of water
2 tablespoons Lea and Perrins Steak Sauce
¾ cup Sucanat
1 tablespoon cornstarch

To complete the dish

4 cups peanut oil for deep-frying
1½ cups cubed UnPork (page 122), cut into 1-inch cubes
1 tablespoon unbleached white flour
1 teaspoon minced garlic
4 green onions, white part only, cut ½ inch thick diagonally
½ cup bamboo shoots, cut into ¾x1-inch pieces
½ cup diced bell pepper (red preferred), cut into ¼-inch dice

For the Batter: Combine the flour, cornstarch, baking powder, and salt. Slowly add the water, stirring with a fork until the batter is smooth. Stir in the oil very well. This should make the batter the consistency of pancake batter. If it is too thick, add up to 2 tablespoons more water, a bit at a time. Set aside.

For the Sauce: Combine everything and set aside.

To Complete the Dish: Preheat the oven to 250°F. Heat the oil to between 350°F and 375°F. Coat the gluten cubes with the flour. Coat ⅓ of the gluten with the batter and transfer them, using tongs, to the hot oil. Fry for 5 seconds and turn them over. Fry for a total of 3 minutes, turning several times, until light brown. Transfer with a slotted spoon to a strainer set over a bowl to drain. In two batches, repeat this process with the other ⅔ of the gluten. Make sure the oil has come back up to temperature, put all the gluten back in, and fry about 3 more minutes until a deep golden brown. With a slotted spoon, put the gluten on a warm platter and put it in the warm oven.

Sauté the garlic and onions for 30 seconds on high heat. Add the bamboo shoots and bell pepper and sauté for 30 more seconds. Pour the sauce into this and, stirring, bring it to a boil and turn off the heat. Pour the sauce over the gluten.

Sweet and Sour UnPork 2

2 tablespoons unbleached white flour
3 tablespoons corn oil
2 cups UnPork Broth (page 156)
1⁄3 cup vinegar
1⁄3 cup low-sodium soy sauce
1⁄3 cup catsup or chili sauce
1⁄2 cup chopped celery
3⁄4 teaspoon sea salt
1⁄4 teaspoon cayenne
1 cup sliced carrot, in rounds
1 cup bell pepper, cut into strips
1 cup pineapple chunks, drained
6 cups UnPork (page 122), cut in strips or cubes

Brown the flour in 1 tablespoon of the oil in a small saucepan. Stir in the broth, vinegar, soy sauce, catsup, celery, salt, and cayenne, and cook, stirring frequently, until thick. Set aside. Heat the rest of the oil in a skillet and sauté the carrot for 1 minute, stirring constantly, then add the bell pepper and pineapple and heat through. Put everything together and simmer for 20 minutes. Serve over rice.

UnPork and Sauerkraut Casserole

3 cups cubed UnPork (page 122)
2 tablespoons corn oil
1 cup chopped onion
1 cup chopped celery
1 cup sliced fresh mushrooms
One 16-ounce can of sauerkraut, undrained
8 ounces noodles, cooked and drained
2 cups Kreem of Mushroom Soup (page 74), made with Cashew Kreem (page 93)
1⁄4 teaspoon sea salt
1⁄4 teaspoon freshly ground black pepper

Sauté the gluten in the oil until light brown. Add the onion, celery, and mushrooms and sauté until the onion is soft. Stir in the rest of the ingredients. Put into a casserole. Bake, uncovered, at 400°F for 30 minutes.

UnPork Chops with Crumb Crust

Crunchy and delicious!

1⁄4 cup dried bread crumbs
1 teaspoon basil
1⁄4 teaspoon sea salt
1⁄4 teaspoon freshly ground black pepper
4 N'eggs (page 302)
4 UnPork (page 122) slices, 1 inch thick
Oil

Combine the crumbs, basil, salt, and pepper. Dip the gluten in the N'eggs, then in the crumb mixture, coating both sides well. Oil a baking pan well and put the gluten on it. Broil until golden brown on both sides.

UnPork with Sauerkraut

3 cups chopped onion
1 tablespoon corn oil
3 cups cubed UnPork (page 122)
1 1⁄2 teaspoons paprika
1⁄2 teaspoon caraway seeds (optional)
5 tablespoons tomato paste
1⁄2 cups UnPork Broth (page 156)
1 cup water
2 cups sauerkraut, drained and washed
2 1⁄2 cups grated potatoes
1 cup Cashew Sour Kreem (page 94) or Tofu Sour Kreem (page 97)

Lightly sauté the onion in the oil in a heavy pot. Add the gluten and sauté it until it is light brown. Add the paprika, caraway seeds, tomato paste, broth, and water. Cover and simmer over low heat for 30 minutes. Add the sauerkraut and potatoes, cover, and simmer for 1 hour, adding extra water if you need it. Just before serving, stir in the Sour Kreem.

UnSausage and Sauerkraut Casserole

2 cups macaroni, uncooked
3 tablespoons corn oil
2 cups chopped or ground UnSausage (page 132) of choice
1 cup chopped onion
2 cups chopped canned tomatoes, with liquid
1 cup sauerkraut
1 teaspoon Sucanat
1/4 teaspoon sea salt
1/4 teaspoon cayenne
1 cup Yeast Cheez (page 97)

Cook the macaroni. Heat the oil in a skillet or pan and sauté the gluten and onion until the onion is soft. Add everything else but the Cheez and macaroni and cook for 10 minutes. Drain the macaroni and stir it into vegetables along with the Cheez. Put into a casserole and bake, uncovered, at 400°F for 30 minutes.

Zesty Grilled UnPork Chops

1/2 cup low-sodium soy sauce
1/4 cup water
1/4 cup lemon juice
1 tablespoon chili sauce
3 teaspoons Sucanat
1 teaspoon Barbados molasses
3/4 teaspoon minced garlic
Six 3/4-inch-thick slices of UnPork (page 122)

Combine the ingredients except for the gluten. Put the gluten slices in a baking dish and pour the marinade over them. Cover and refrigerate several hours or overnight. Remove the gluten from the marinade and grill or broil 4 inches from the heat until they are done, brushing occasionally with the marinade.

UnHam Substitutes and Dishes

UnHam

¼ cup low-sodium soy sauce
2 teaspoons Kitchen Bouquet
2 tablespoons nutritional yeast
½ cup chopped onion
¼ teaspoon rubbed sage
½ teaspoon freshly ground black pepper
½ teaspoon oregano
1 teaspoon garlic powder
1¼ teaspoons liquid smoke
1 teaspoon corn oil
2 cups water
1 teaspoon sea salt
2 cups raw gluten

Combine everything but raw gluten and simmer for 5 minutes. Cook raw gluten according to Method 1, 2, or 3 (pages 99–100) in remaining ingredients.

Baked UnHam

½ cup chopped onion
4½ teaspoons monosodium glutamate (MSG)
1 teaspoon sea salt
1 teaspoon poultry seasoning
⅓ cup nutritional yeast
2 tablespoons All-Purpose Seasoning (page 303)
1 teaspoon corn oil
2 tablespoons low-sodium soy sauce
2 tablespoons liquid smoke
2 tablespoons barley malt syrup
2 cups water
2 cups raw gluten

Combine everything but raw gluten and simmer for 5 minutes. Cook raw gluten according to Method 3 (page 100) in remaining ingredients.

Soy Grits UnHam

½ cup soy grits
1 cup boiling UnHam Broth (page 156)

Stir grits into the broth and cook for 5 minutes.

UnHam Loaf

1½ tablespoons cornstarch
1 cup UnHam Broth (page 156), cold
½ cups Sucanat
2 tablespoons Barbados molasses
¼ cup white vinegar
1 tablespoon dried mustard
3 cups ground UnPork (page 122)
2 cups ground UnHam (page 130)
1 cup Cashew Milk (page 93)
1 cup fine dried bread crumbs
¾ teaspoon prepared mustard
2 N'eggs (page 302)
2 tablespoons finely chopped bell pepper

In a saucepan, dissolve the cornstarch in the cold broth. Mix in the Sucanat, molasses, vinegar, and dried mustard. Bring to a boil, stirring often. Remove from the heat when it begins to thicken and set aside. Combine the glutens, "milk," crumbs, prepared mustard, N'eggs, and bell pepper. Press into a nonstick casserole or loaf pan. Pour a thin layer of sauce over it and bake at 325°F for 2 hours. Serve the rest of the sauce with the loaf.

UnSausage Substitutes and Dishes

A note on cooking UnSausage that applies to all the types of UnSausage recipes that are given here: If the UnSausage is to be used in a dish, the recipe will tell you if it needs any prior preparation. If you are going to eat it "straight," you can either fry it, using a small amount of oil, or spray or brush on a small amount of oil (both sides) and lightly broil.

Breakfast UnSausage

Nice and mild, yet flavorful.

1/2 cup chopped onion
4 1/2 teaspoons monosodium glutamate (MSG)
1 teaspoon sea salt
1 teaspoon poultry seasoning
1/3 cup nutritional yeast
1 teaspoon dried crushed sage leaves
1/2 teaspoon ground ginger
1/4 teaspoon freshly ground black pepper
1 teaspoon liquid smoke
1 teaspoon corn oil
2 cups water
2 cups raw gluten

Combine everything but the gluten and simmer for 5 minutes. Cook raw gluten according to Method 1, 2, or 3 (pages 99–100) in the broth.

Cajun UnSausage

This bites back!

1/2 cup chopped onion
4 1/2 teaspoons monosodium glutamate (MSG)
1 teaspoon sea salt
1 teaspoon cayenne pepper
1/8 teaspoon garlic powder
1 teaspoon cumin
1 teaspoon poultry seasoning
1/8 teaspoon sage
1/8 teaspoon curry powder
1 teaspoon dried mint
1/3 cup nutritional yeast
1 teaspoon corn oil
2 cups water
2 cups raw gluten

Combine everything but raw gluten and simmer for 5 minutes. Cook raw gluten according to Method 1, 2, or 3 (pages 99–100) in the broth.

Farmer's UnSausage

Flavor galore!

1/2 cup chopped onion
4 1/2 teaspoons monosodium glutamate (MSG)
1 teaspoon sea salt
1 teaspoon poultry seasoning
1/3 cup nutritional yeast
3/4 teaspoon fennel seed

½ teaspoon freshly ground black pepper
2 tablespoons soy sauce
1½ teaspoons oregano
¼ teaspoon cayenne
1 tablespoon Sucanat
1 tablespoon garlic powder
1 tablespoon prepared mustard
1 teaspoon allspice
1 teaspoon corn oil
2 cups water
2 cups raw gluten

Combine everything but raw gluten and simmer 5 minutes. Cook raw gluten according to Method 1, 2, or 3 (pages 99–100) in the broth.

Garlic UnSausage

A garlic lover's delight.

1 cup chopped onion
4½ teaspoons monosodium glutamate (MSG)
1 teaspoon sea salt
1 teaspoon poultry seasoning
⅓ cup nutritional yeast
⅓ cup garlic powder
½ teaspoon freshly ground black pepper
1 teaspoon corn oil
2 cups water
2 cups raw gluten

Combine everything but raw gluten and simmer 5 minutes. Cook raw gluten according to Method 1, 2, or 3 (pages 99–100) in the broth.

Herb UnSausage

This has been formulated for those who find the spices in regular UnSausage too hard to digest easily. But everybody will like it.

½ cup chopped onion
4½ teaspoons monosodium glutamate (MSG)
⅓ cup nutritional yeast
½ teaspoon garlic salt
1 teaspoon dried parsley
1 teaspoon dried sage
⅛ teaspoon thyme leaves
½ teaspoon freshly ground black pepper
1 teaspoon corn oil
2 cups water
¼ teaspoon ground allspice
2 cups raw gluten

Combine everything but raw gluten and simmer 5 minutes. Cook raw gluten according to Method 1, 2, or 3 (pages 99–100) in the broth.

Italian UnSausage

Pizza delight!

½ cup chopped onion
4½ teaspoons monosodium glutamate (MSG)
1 teaspoon sea salt
1 teaspoon poultry seasoning
⅓ cup nutritional yeast
½ teaspoon Sucanat
¼ teaspoon garlic powder
¼ teaspoon fennel seed
¼ teaspoon lemon pepper seasoning
¼ teaspoon paprika
⅛ teaspoon celery salt
⅛ teaspoon dried crushed sage leaves
⅛ teaspoon cayenne pepper
1½ teaspoons soy sauce
1 teaspoon Lea and Perrins Steak Sauce
1 teaspoon corn oil
2 cups water
2 cups raw gluten

Combine everything but raw gluten and simmer 5 minutes. Cook raw gluten according to Method 1, 2, or 3 (pages 99–100) in the broth.

Mexican Chorizo UnSausage

Good and spicy.

½ cup chopped onion
4½ teaspoons monosodium glutamate (MSG)
1 teaspoon sea salt
1 teaspoon poultry seasoning
⅓ cup nutritional yeast
1½ teaspoons paprika
½ teaspoon freshly ground black pepper
¾ teaspoon hot pepper flakes
¼ teaspoon Sucanat
¼ teaspoon garlic powder
¼ teaspoon dried oregano leaves
⅛ teaspoon powdered cumin seed
1 tablespoon white vinegar
1 teaspoon corn oil
2 cups water
2 cups raw gluten

Combine everything but raw gluten and simmer 5 minutes. Cook raw gluten according to Method 1, 2, or 3 (pages 99–100) in the broth.

Pizza UnSausage

This is a milder version of Italian UnSausage for those who prefer it.

½ cup chopped onion
4½ teaspoons monosodium glutamate (MSG)
1 teaspoon sea salt
1 teaspoon poultry seasoning
⅓ cup nutritional yeast
¼ teaspoon freshly ground black pepper
¼ teaspoon red pepper flakes
½ teaspoon fennel seed
1 teaspoon corn oil
2 cups water
2 cups raw gluten

Combine everything but raw gluten and simmer 5 minutes. Cook raw gluten according to Method 1, 2, or 3 (pages 99–100) in the broth.

Rosemary UnSausage

Different and delicious. Mild, too.

½ cup chopped onion
4½ teaspoons monosodium glutamate (MSG)
1 teaspoon sea salt
1 teaspoon poultry seasoning
⅓ cup nutritional yeast
½ teaspoon freshly ground black pepper
¾ teaspoon powdered rosemary
¼ teaspoon thyme
¼ teaspoon marjoram
¼ teaspoon freshly grated nutmeg
1 teaspoon corn oil
2 cups water
2 cups raw gluten

Combine everything but raw gluten and simmer 5 minutes. Cook raw gluten according to Method 1, 2, or 3 (pages 99–100) in the broth.

UnSausage and Cabbage

Not for food snobs, but the rest of us love it.

1½ cups cubed UnSausage (pages 132–35) of choice, cut into 1-inch cubes
2 teaspoons corn oil
4 cups chopped cabbage
2 cups thinly sliced onion
1½ cups broth of type of UnSausage used

Brown the gluten in the oil. Add the cabbage and onion and cook, stirring occasionally, until the cabbage is browned. Add the broth and simmer, partly covered, for 15 to 20 minutes, until the cabbage is tender. Serve over mashed potatoes.

Simple UnSausage

2 tablespoons soy sauce
1 teaspoon Kitchen Bouquet
1 tablespoon nutritional yeast
1/4 cup chopped onion
1/8 teaspoon rubbed sage
1/4 teaspoon freshly ground black pepper
1/4 teaspoon oregano
1/2 teaspoon garlic powder
1 teaspoon liquid smoke
2 tablespoons sausage seasoning
1 teaspoon corn oil
2 cups water
2 cups raw gluten

Combine everything but raw gluten and simmer 5 minutes. Cook raw gluten according to Method 1, 2, or 3 (pages 99–100) in the broth.

Soy Grits UnSausage

1/2 cup soy grits
1 cup boiling flavoring broth of UnSausage type desired (page 132)

Stir grits into the broth and cook for 5 minutes.

Watkins UnSausage

1/4 cup soy sauce
2 teaspoons Kitchen Bouquet
2 tablespoons nutritional yeast
1/2 cup chopped onion
1/4 teaspoon rubbed sage
1/2 teaspoon freshly ground black pepper
1/2 teaspoon oregano
1 teaspoon garlic powder
2 teaspoons liquid smoke
4 tablespoons Watkins Sausage Seasoning
1 teaspoon corn oil
2 cups water
2 cups raw gluten

Combine everything but raw gluten and simmer 5 minutes. Cook raw gluten according to Method 1, 2, or 3 (pages 99–100) in the broth.

UnBacon Substitutes and Dishes

UnBacon

Use in recipes as indicated. For crispy bacon, slice thinly, spray or coat lightly with oil, and broil until it starts to turn brown. It gets crisp as it cools, so do not overbroil, having it get crispy under the broiler.

UnBacon 1

¼ cup soy sauce
2 teaspoons Kitchen Bouquet
2 tablespoons nutritional yeast
½ cup chopped onion
¼ teaspoon rubbed sage
½ teaspoon freshly ground black pepper
½ teaspoon oregano
1 teaspoon garlic powder
1¼ teaspoons liquid smoke
1 teaspoon corn oil
2 cups water
1 teaspoon sea salt
2 cups raw gluten

Combine everything but raw gluten and simmer for 5 minutes. Cook raw gluten according to Method 3 (page 100) in broth.

UnBacon 2

½ cup chopped onion
4¼ teaspoons monosodium glutamate (MSG)
1 teaspoon sea salt
1 teaspoon poultry seasoning
⅓ cup nutritional yeast
½ teaspoon freshly ground black pepper
1 teaspoon minced garlic
1 teaspoon ground coriander seed
¼ teaspoon mace
1 teaspoon liquid smoke
1 teaspoon corn oil
2 cups water
2 cups raw gluten

Combine everything but raw gluten and simmer for 5 minutes. Cook raw gluten according to Method 3 (page 100) in the broth.

UnChicken Substitutes and Dishes

UnChicken

½ cup chopped onion
4½ teaspoons monosodium glutamate (MSG)
1 teaspoon sea salt
1 teaspoon poultry seasoning
⅓ cup nutritional yeast
1 teaspoon corn oil
2 cups water
2 cups raw gluten

Combine everything but raw gluten and simmer for 5 minutes. Cook raw gluten according to Method 1, 2, or 3 (pages 99–100) in the broth.

Braised UnChicken and "Chorizo"

1 tablespoon corn oil
3 cups cubed UnChicken (see above)
1 tablespoon curry powder
1 cup chopped onion
1 tablespoon minced garlic
2½ cups cubed potatoes
1¼ cups minced tomato
¼ cup unbleached white flour
2 tablespoons Lea and Perrins Steak Sauce
2 tablespoons tomato paste
3½ cups UnChicken Broth (page 155)
¼ cup cubed UnHam (page 130)
½ cup cubed Mexican Chorizo UnSausage (page 134)
½ cup chopped green olives
½ cup thick coconut milk
¼ teaspoon cayenne pepper

In the oil brown the UnChicken, transferring it to a bowl as it is browned. To the remaining oil add the curry powder and stir for about 30 seconds. Then add the onion, garlic, potatoes, and tomato, and cook, stirring, until the vegetables are softened. Stir in the flour and cook, stirring for 3 more minutes. Stir in the steak sauce, tomato paste, broth, UnHam, "chorizo," olives, coconut milk, and pepper. Add the UnChicken, and simmer, stirring occasionally, for 45 to 60 minutes.

Cajun UnChicken Bake

Sea salt
Cayenne pepper
Freshly ground black pepper
6 cups sliced UnChicken (see above), ¼ inch thick
Corn oil
3 cups chopped onion
½ cup chopped green onions
½ cup chopped bell pepper
½ cup chopped celery
1 cup chopped fresh parsley
¼ cup pimientos, cut in strips
4 cups water
¼ cup Lea and Perrins Steak Sauce
2 teaspoons Louisiana Hot Sauce

Sprinkle the salt and peppers on both sides of each gluten slice. Fry the gluten in the oil until it begins to brown. Pour a small amount of oil into the bottom of a baking pan. Put the gluten in the pan in a layer. On top of the gluten put the onions (both types), bell pepper, celery, and parsley. Put the pimiento strips over that. Mix the water, steak sauce, and hot sauce together and pour over all. Bake, covered, at 375°F for 1 hour. Just before serving, take off the cover and broil for a few minutes.

Chickaritos

Make plenty, for these are good!

3 cups finely chopped UnChicken (page 137)
1/4 cup minced jalapeños
1/2 cup finely chopped green onions
1 1/2 cups Yeast Cheez (page 97)
1 teaspoon Louisiana Hot Sauce
1 teaspoon garlic salt
1/4 teaspoon freshly ground black pepper
1/4 teaspoon ground cumin
1/4 teaspoon paprika
Enough Convent Pie Crust (page 328) for two 10-inch pie crusts
Water
Salsa
Guacamole (page 32)

Combine the gluten, jalapeños, onions, Cheez, and seasonings, and mix well. Roll out half of the crust into a 9 x 12-inch rectangle. Cut into 9 small rectangles. Put about 2 tablespoons of the filling across the center of each rectangle. Wet the edges of the pastry with water and roll it around the filling, crimping the ends with a fork to seal. Repeat with the rest of the pastry and filling. Place, seam side down, on an oiled or nonstick cookie sheet. Bake at 425°F until golden brown, 20 to 25 minutes. Serve with salsa and guacamole.

VARIATION: *Use UnBeef (page 109) instead for "Beefaritos."*

Creamed UnChicken with Mushrooms and Herbs

Amazingly flavorful.

1 cup sliced mushrooms
2 tablespoons minced onion
1/8 teaspoon thyme leaves
1 teaspoon corn oil margarine
2 cups UnChicken (page 137)
1/3 cup Ritz-style cracker crumbs (Hi-Hos are best—they do not contain animal fat)
1 cup Cashew Sour Kreem (page 94) or Tofu Sour Kreem (page 97)
1/2 cup Cashew Kreem (page 93)
Pinch sea salt
Pinch cayenne pepper

Sauté the mushrooms, onion, and thyme in the margarine until the mushrooms are tender. Stir in the remaining ingredients until blended.

Glorified UnChicken

4 cups sliced UnChicken (page 137)
1 tablespoon corn oil
2 cups Kreem of UnChicken Soup (page 75)
1/8 teaspoon pepper
Pinch thyme

Brown the gluten on both sides in the oil. Combine the soup, pepper, and thyme. Put half of this in the bottom of a casserole. Put the gluten over that in a layer. Pour the rest of soup mixture over the gluten. Bake, uncovered, at 400°F for 30 minutes.

Hungarian UnChicken

6 tablespoons unbleached white flour
1/2 teaspoon sea salt
1/2 teaspoon freshly ground black pepper
7 cups UnChicken (page 137), cubed or in pieces or slices
1/4 cup nondairy margarine
1 1/2 cups chopped onion
2 cups tomato juice
2 tablespoons paprika
1/4 teaspoon cayenne pepper
1 teaspoon Sucanat

1 teaspoon sea salt
1 bay leaf
2 cups UnChicken Broth (page 155)
Cooked noodles
1 cup Cashew Sour Kreem (page 94) or Tofu Sour Kreem (page 97)

Combine the flour, salt, and pepper, and toss with the gluten until it is well coated and set aside. In 1 tablespoon of the margarine sauté the onion until soft. Take out the onion and set aside. In the same pan, melt the rest of the margarine and brown the gluten well. Combine the tomato juice, paprika, cayenne, Sucanat, and salt. Pour over the gluten. Add the bay leaf and broth, and simmer 45 minutes. Remove the gluten and put it on a platter of noodles. Take out the bay leaf and stir in the Sour Kreem. Heat through for 2 or 3 minutes (do not boil). Pour this sauce over the gluten.

Italian UnChicken Casserole

2 tablespoons olive oil
4 UnChicken (page 137) slices
1 cup sliced mushrooms
1/2 cup finely chopped onion
1/4 teaspoon rosemary
1/4 teaspoon sea salt
1/4 teaspoon cayenne pepper
2 cups canned stewed tomatoes
3 tablespoons unbleached white flour

In half the oil brown the gluten on both sides. Heat the remaining oil in a skillet and sauté the mushrooms, onion, rosemary, salt, and pepper until the onions are soft. Add the tomatoes and cook 5 minutes. Blend in the flour well. Put half of this sauce over the bottom of a casserole. Layer the gluten over this. Pour the rest of the sauce over all and bake, uncovered, at 400°F for 20 minutes. Good as is, or served over pasta or rice.

Jambalaya

2 cups UnChicken (page 137), cut into pieces
2 cups rice, cooked
3 cups canned tomatoes
1 1/2 cups chopped onion
1/3 cup chopped green pepper
2/3 cup chopped celery
1 tablespoon nondairy margarine
1/2 teaspoon sea salt
1/2 teaspoon basil
1 1/2 cups bread crumbs

Mix the gluten, rice, and tomatoes. Sauté the onion, green pepper, and celery in the margarine. Add to the gluten mixture along with the salt and basil. Pour into a nonstick 2-quart casserole. Melt the rest of the margarine and toss with the bread crumbs. Spread the crumbs on top and bake, uncovered, for 1 hour at 350°F.

Note

Other flavors of gluten may also be used in this dish.

Moroccan UnChicken

1/4 cup minced onion
1 teaspoon olive oil
1/2 cup zucchini, unpeeled, coarsely grated, squeezed dry in a paper towel, and packed tightly
2 tablespoons chopped pimiento
1/2 cups Yeast Cheez (page 97)
1/4 teaspoon sea salt
1/4 teaspoon cayenne pepper
1 1/2 cups cubed UnChicken (page 137)
1 tablespoon olive oil
1/2 cup UnChicken Broth (page 155)

Sauté the onion in the teaspoon of oil until soft. Add the zucchini and cook, stirring, until tender. Stir in the pimiento, Cheez, salt, and cayenne. Mix well. Transfer to a small bowl and let cool slightly. Sauté the gluten in the tablespoon of oil until lightly browned. Combine everything and mix well.

Omelets

2½ cups unbleached white flour
2 tablespoons baking powder
2 tablespoons Sucanat
1 teaspoon sea salt
2¾ cups nutritional yeast
1 N'egg (page 302)
2 teaspoons corn oil
2 cups Cashew Milk (page 93)
½ cup chopped onion
½ teaspoon minced garlic
½ cup chopped bell pepper
¾ cup Pimiento Cheez (page 94)
¼ cup finely chopped UnBacon (page 136)

Mix the flour, baking powder, Sucanat, salt, and yeast. Add the N'egg, oil, and "milk" to that. This should be the consistency of pancake batter. Add water if needed to obtain this. Add onion, garlic, bell pepper, Cheez, and gluten and mix well. Using ⅓ cup of mixture for each omelet, cook on an oiled griddle at about 350°F, turning once, until golden brown on both sides. Serve with salsa, Tomato Sauce (page 261), Mushroom Gravy (page 253), or Onion Sauce (page 259).

Roasted UnChicken with Potatoes and "Chorizo"

4 cups potatoes, peeled and halved (or quartered, if large)
1 tablespoon olive oil
2 cups coarsely chopped onion
1 cup bell pepper (red preferred), cut into 1-inch squares
2 cups finely chopped Mexican Chorizo UnSausage (page 134), or other spiced sausage-type gluten
1 tablespoon minced garlic
4 cups UnChicken Broth (page 155)
½ teaspoon freshly ground black pepper
3 cups sliced UnChicken (page 137), coated with oil and broiled until brown

Heat a little olive oil in a skillet and cook the potatoes until golden brown all over, about 20 minutes. Pour off the oil and set the potatoes aside in the skillet. Heat the tablespoon of oil in another skillet and sauté the onion and bell pepper until soft and starting to brown, 12 or 15 minutes. Add the "sausage" and garlic and cook 5 more minutes. Add this to the potatoes. Add the broth and pepper and bring to a simmer. Cook, uncovered, until the potatoes are tender and the broth has reduced by half, about 10 minutes. Arrange the gluten slices in a baking dish, pour the potato mixture over them, and bake at 400°F for 10 to 15 minutes to heat through.

Soy Grits UnChicken

½ cup soy grits
1 cup boiling UnChicken Broth (page 155)

Stir grits into the broth and cook for 5 minutes.

Spanish UnChicken au Gratin

2 cups sliced fresh mushrooms
1½ cups chopped onion
1 tablespoon minced garlic
2 teaspoons corn oil
4 cups sliced UnChicken (page 137)
3 cups Kreem of Mushroom Soup (page 74)
¼ teaspoon cayenne pepper
2 tablespoons Parmesan Cheez (page 94)

Sauté the mushrooms, onion, and garlic in the oil until the onion is soft. Add the gluten and cook 5 more minutes. Add the mushroom soup and cayenne and cook for another 5 minutes. Put in a casserole dish and sprinkle with the "Parmesan." Bake at 400°F for 20 minutes.

Spanish UnChicken with Rice

1½ cups finely chopped onion
¾ teaspoon crushed clove garlic
½ cup finely chopped bell pepper
1 tablespoon olive oil
4 cups canned tomatoes
½ teaspoon Sucanat
1 tablespoon sea salt
2 tablespoons paprika
½ bay leaf
¼ teaspoon basil (ground)
3 cups water
2 cups rice, uncooked
3 cups UnChicken (page 137), cut in pieces

Sauté the onion, garlic, and bell pepper in the oil until soft. Add the tomatoes and seasonings and cook for 15 minutes. Add the water, rice, and gluten. Cook or bake until the rice is done, about 40 minutes.

Sunday Unfried UnChicken

Crunchy and delicious!

2 cups unbleached white flour
1/2 cup cornmeal
1 tablespoon sea salt
2 tablespoons dried mustard
2 tablespoons paprika
2 tablespoons garlic salt
1 tablespoon celery salt
1 tablespoon freshly ground black pepper
1 teaspoon ground ginger
1/2 teaspoon thyme
1/2 teaspoon oregano
6 cups UnChicken (page 137), cut into frying-size pieces
Corn oil, optional

Combine everything except the gluten and oil. Put 1 cup of this mixture in a bag and shake a few pieces of the gluten at a time to coat them well. Heat 1/4 inch of corn oil in a large skillet and brown the gluten on all sides and put into a shallow baking pan. Or you can broil or grill it until brown.

UnChicken à la King

Truly worthy of a king!

4 cups cubed UnChicken (page 137)
2 cups chopped onion
4 cups thickly sliced mushrooms
2 1/2 teaspoons nondairy margarine
4 1/2 teaspoons crushed garlic
1 tablespoon unbleached white flour
2 tablespoons chopped pimientos
3/4 cup thinly sliced carrot, steamed
4 cups UnChicken Broth (page 155) made with Cashew Milk (page 93)
1/8 teaspoon coarse freshly ground black pepper
1/8 teaspoon cayenne pepper

Deep-fry the gluten and set it aside. Sauté the onion and mushrooms in the margarine until they are soft. Add the garlic and cook 2 more minutes. Add the flour, and stir it in well. Add the rest of the ingredients and simmer for 10 minutes, adding more broth if it gets too thick. Serve on toast points or biscuits, rice, too.

UnChicken and Cheez Pot Pie

1 1/2 cups UnChicken Broth (page 155)
2 cups peeled and cubed potatoes
1 cup sliced carrot
1 cup peas
1/2 cup sliced celery
1/2 cup chopped onion
1/3 cup chopped pimientos
1/4 cup unbleached white flour
1 1/2 cups Cashew Milk (page 93)
1 cup Yeast Cheez (page 97)
4 cups cubed UnChicken (page 137)
1/4 teaspoon Watkins Poultry Seasoning
1/2 teaspoon sea salt
1/4 teaspoon freshly ground black pepper
1 recipe Convent Pie Crust (page 328), chilled

Bring the broth to a boil and add the vegetables. Simmer 10 to 15 minutes until tender. Blend the flour with the "milk" and stir into the broth mixture. Cook and stir over medium heat until slightly thickened and bubbly. Stir in the Cheez, gluten, poultry seasoning, salt, and pepper. Mix well. Put into a casserole and set aside. Roll out the dough on a lightly floured surface to a size that will fit the casserole, trimming the edges as needed. Put in the casserole over the filling and seal the edges. Make a few slits in the center for steam to escape. Bake at 425°F until the crust is golden brown, about 40 minutes.

UnChicken and Dumplings

6 cups cubed UnChicken (page 137)
4½ cups UnChicken Broth (page 155)
1 cup chopped onion
1⅓ cups sliced celery
1 cup sliced carrot
1 teaspoon sage
1 teaspoon sea salt
¼ teaspoon freshly ground black pepper
3 cups Biscuit Mix (page 50)
¾ cup plus 2 tablespoons Cashew Milk (page 93)
1 tablespoon minced fresh parsley

Simmer the gluten, broth, onion, celery, carrot, ½ teaspoon of the sage, salt, and pepper together until the vegetables are tender, about 45 minutes. Combine the Biscuit Mix, "milk," parsley, and rest of the sage to make a stiff batter. Drop by tablespoons into the simmering gluten mixture. Cover and simmer for 15 more minutes.

UnChicken and Pasta Toss

1½ cups UnChicken (page 137), cut into thin strips
½ cup sliced celery
½ cup bell pepper, cut into thin strips
¾ cup chopped onion
½ teaspoon minced garlic
4 teaspoons nondairy margarine
¾ cup UnChicken Broth (page 155)
¼ teaspoon dried tarragon
¼ cup chopped fresh parsley
¼ teaspoon freshly ground black pepper
8 ounces pasta, cooked

Sauté the gluten, celery, bell pepper, onion, and garlic in the margarine for 2 minutes. Add the broth, tarragon, parsley, and pepper. Simmer 15 minutes. Toss the pasta and gluten together to mix well.

UnChicken and Potato Sauté

Home food!

4 cups cubed UnChicken (page 137)
3 tablespoons nondairy margarine
1 cup chopped onion
¾ teaspoon minced garlic
2 tablespoons unbleached white flour
¼ teaspoon thyme
¼ teaspoon sea salt
⅛ teaspoon pepper
1¼ cups UnChicken Broth (page 155)
2 cups cooked, peeled, and cubed potatoes

Sauté the gluten in the margarine until browned. Add the onion and garlic and cook 5 minutes. Combine the flour and seasonings, stir in the broth, pour it over the gluten, cover, and simmer for 20 minutes. Add the potatoes and heat through.

UnChicken and UnSausage Gumbo

This is the real thing—I gar-on-tee it!

4½ teaspoons corn oil
¾ cup unbleached white flour
5 cups chopped onion
½ bell pepper, chopped
1 tablespoon chopped celery
6 UnChicken (page 137) slices, cut 1 inch thick
2 cups sliced UnSausage (page 132), ¼ inch thick
5 cups crushed and drained canned tomatoes
3 cups water
3 cups tomato juice
1 teaspoon minced garlic
1 tablespoon finely chopped fresh parsley
¾ cup finely chopped green onions
½ teaspoon cayenne pepper
½ teaspoon sea salt
2 cups chopped okra

Heat the oil in a large heavy pot, stir in the flour and cook, stirring constantly, until the flour is very dark brown but not burned. Lower the heat and add the onion, bell pepper, and celery. Cover and simmer until the onion is transparent, stirring occasionally. Add all the gluten, the tomatoes, water, tomato juice, garlic, parsley, green onions, pepper, and salt. Cover, and simmer stirring frequently. While that is cooking, sauté the okra in a skillet until soft, then add it to the rest of ingredients. Bring to a boil, reduce the heat, and simmer, covered, until most of the water is evaporated, 30 to 40 minutes. Serve on rice.

UnChicken Cacciatore 1

6 cups cubed UnChicken (page 137)
1 cup unbleached white flour
Corn oil
2 cups chopped onion
1 tablespoon minced garlic
2 cups sliced mushrooms
1½ cups UnChicken Broth (page 155)
3 cups canned tomato puree
1 teaspoon oregano
¼ cup chopped fresh parsley
¾ teaspoon sea salt
⅛ teaspoon freshly ground black pepper
⅛ teaspoon cayenne pepper

Toss the gluten with the flour until coated and brown it in a skillet in the oil. Remove and set aside. In the same skillet sauté the onion until soft (add more oil if needed). Combine everything, cover, and simmer 30 minutes. Serve over spaghetti.

UnChicken Cacciatore 2

5 cups cubed UnChicken (page 137)
1 cup unbleached white flour
2 cups sliced onion, separated into rings
1 cup bell pepper, cut into strips
2 cups sliced mushrooms
2 tablespoons nondairy margarine
2 teaspoons minced garlic
3 cups chopped tomato
¾ cup Cashew Milk (page 93)
1 teaspoon oregano
½ teaspoon freshly ground black pepper
¼ teaspoon cayenne
½ teaspoon sea salt
¾ cup Yeast Cheez (page 97)

Toss the gluten and flour together in a bag. Deep-fry and set aside. Sauté the onion, bell pepper, and mushrooms in the margarine until the onion is soft. Add everything else but the Cheez and gluten. Bring to a boil, reduce heat, and simmer 15 minutes. Add the gluten and simmer until thick. Stir in the Cheez and serve over spaghetti.

UnChicken Diane

4 large slices of UnChicken (page 137)
½ teaspoon sea salt
½ teaspoon freshly ground black pepper
1 tablespoon corn oil
1 tablespoon nondairy margarine
3 tablespoons chopped green onions
4½ teaspoons lemon or lime juice
3 tablespoons chopped fresh parsley
2 teaspoons Dijon-style mustard
¼ cup UnChicken Broth (page 155)

Sprinkle the gluten slices on both sides with the salt and pepper. Heat the oil and margarine in a skillet and cook the gluten, 2 minutes on each side. Put on a warm serving platter. Add to the skillet the onions, juice, parsley, and mustard, and cook for 15 seconds, stirring constantly. Stir in the broth and continue to stir until the sauce is smooth. Pour the sauce over the gluten and serve right away.

UnChicken Gumbo

Wonderful flavor.

2 teaspoons corn oil
⅔ cup unbleached white flour
1½ cups finely chopped onion
¾ teaspoon finely chopped garlic
4 cups UnChicken Broth (page 155)
¼ cup Lea and Perrins Steak Sauce
1 teaspoon Louisiana Hot Sauce or ½ teaspoon Tabasco
4 cups cubed UnChicken (page 137)
2 cups cubed UnSausage (page132) or UnHam (page 130)

Heat the oil in a skillet, stir in the flour, and cook until it is dark brown but not burned. Add all the ingredients and simmer for 30 minutes.

UnChicken Paella

1½ cups chopped onion
¾ teaspoon minced garlic
½ cup bell pepper, cut in strips
2½ teaspoons olive oil
1½ cups chopped tomato
2 tablespoons tomato paste
1 bay leaf
1 teaspoon thyme
1 teaspoon paprika
2 cups uncooked rice
4 cups UnChicken Broth (page 155), boiling
5 cups cubed UnChicken (page 137)

Sauté the onion, garlic, and bell pepper in the oil until the onion is transparent. Add the tomato, tomato paste, bay leaf, thyme, and paprika. Cook 10 minutes. Stir in the rice. Add the broth and cook for 5 or 6 minutes, stirring occasionally. Mix in the gluten. Put in a casserole and bake at 325°F until the broth is absorbed, 20 to 25 minutes.

UnChicken Paprika 1

2 teaspoons corn oil
1½ teaspoons minced garlic
1 tablespoon paprika
1 cup chopped tomato
½ cup thinly sliced bell pepper
1 cup UnChicken Broth (page 155)
¼ teaspoon sea salt
¼ teaspoon cayenne pepper
4 UnChicken (page 137) slices, browned in a small amount of oil
1 cup Cashew Sour Kreem (page 94) or Tofu Sour Kreem (page 97)

Put everything but the gluten and Sour Kreem in a skillet and cook, stirring occasionally, until the tomatoes are soft. Add the gluten, turning the pieces over to coat them. Simmer 2 more minutes. Stir in the Sour Kreem. Serve with noodles or rice.

UnChicken Paprika 2

3 cups sliced or chopped onion
2 tablespoons corn oil
2 tablespoons paprika
½ teaspoon cayenne pepper
6 cups sliced UnChicken (page 137), browned in a small amount of oil
½ teaspoon sea salt
3 tablespoons chopped fresh parsley
2½ cups UnChicken Broth (page 155)
2 cups Cashew Sour Kreem (page 94) or Tofu Sour Kreem (page 97)
4 teaspoons capers with juice

In a skillet sauté the onion in the oil until soft. Add the paprika, cayenne, gluten, salt, parsley, and broth. Cover and cook over low heat for 10 minutes. Stir in the Sour Kreem and capers with their juice and gently heat through.

VARIATION: *UnBeef (page 109) may be used instead of UnChicken.*

UnChicken Pot Pie

Almost beyond superb!

¼ cup unbleached white flour
¼ teaspoon sea salt
½ teaspoon freshly ground black pepper
½ teaspoon garlic powder
3 cups cubed UnChicken (page 137), cut into ½-inch cubes
2 tablespoons corn oil
1½ cups chopped onion
1 cup sliced carrot
1 cup sliced celery
2 tablespoons water
1 cup peas
4 cups sliced mushrooms
3 tablespoons nondairy margarine
¼ cup unbleached white flour
1 teaspoon sea salt
¼ teaspoon powdered sage
1 teaspoon garlic powder
¼ teaspoon thyme
½ teaspoon paprika
¼ teaspoon freshly ground black pepper

3½ cups UnChicken Broth (page 155)
1 unbaked Convent Pie Crust shell, and a top crust (page 328)

Combine the flour, salt, pepper, and garlic powder. Toss the gluten cubes in this and coat them well. Sauté the gluten in the oil until golden. Stir in the onion and cook 3 more minutes. Add the carrot, celery, and water. Cover and cook, stirring frequently, until the carrot is just tender. Remove from the heat and stir in the peas. In a saucepan sauté the mushrooms in the margarine until they are soft. Stir in the flour, salt, sage, garlic powder, thyme, paprika, and freshly ground black pepper, and cook 3 minutes more. Whisk in the broth and simmer, uncovered, for 10 minutes or until thickened.

Mix the gravy into the gluten and vegetable mixture and put the rest aside. Put the gluten-vegetable mixture into the pie shell, put on the top crust, seal it, and cut several slits in the top so the steam can escape. Bake at 400°F for 20 minutes, reduce the heat to 350°F, and bake until the crust is well browned, 20 to 30 more minutes.

UnChicken Tetrazzini

Something to sing about.

½ pound spaghetti
1 tablespoon nondairy margarine
¼ cup unbleached white flour
2 cups sliced mushrooms
½ cup bell pepper (red or green)
¾ teaspoon minced garlic
3½ cups UnChicken Broth (page 155) made with Cashew Milk (page 93)
⅛ teaspoon Tabasco sauce
½ teaspoon freshly ground black pepper
½ cup finely chopped fresh parsley
2 cups cubed UnChicken, (page 137; made by Method 3 [page 100] is best), browned in oil
1 cup Parmesan Cheez (page 94)

Cook the spaghetti, drain and blanch it. Set aside. Melt the margarine in a skillet, add the flour, and cook it, stirring, until it is dark brown but not burned. Add the mushrooms and bell pepper and sauté for 5 minutes. Add the garlic and sauté 2 more minutes. Add the broth, Tabasco, pepper, parsley, gluten, and ½ cup of the "Parmesan." Cook until the mixture begins to thicken. Mix in the pasta, put in a casserole, sprinkle the rest of the "Parmesan" on top, patting lightly to press it in. Cover and bake at 350°F for 20 minutes. Uncover and broil until the top is brown.

UnChicken with Mushrooms, Tomatoes, and Rice

2 cups chopped onion
2 teaspoons mashed garlic
1 tablespoon corn oil margarine
2⅓ cups chopped mushrooms
1 cup rice
2 cups coarsely chopped tomato
2 cups UnChicken Broth (page 155)
¼ cup pimiento strips
1 teaspoon sea salt
½ teaspoon cayenne pepper
3 cups UnChicken (page 137)
1¼ cups frozen green peas

Sauté onion and garlic in margarine until onion is transparent. Add mushrooms and continue sautéing until the mushrooms are tender. (Add a little more margarine, if necessary.) Add the rice and sauté for 5 minutes, tossing and turning. Now add the remaining ingredients and stir until blended. Simmer mixture until rice is cooked and liquid is absorbed. Stir and serve hot.

Yankee Unfried UnChicken

Good as is, but better with Mushroom Gravy (page 253) or Sour Kreem–Mushroom Gravy (page 254).

1 N'egg (page 302)
3 tablespoons Cashew Milk (page 93)
1 cup finely crushed soda crackers
1 teaspoon thyme
½ teaspoon paprika
⅛ teaspoon pepper
6 cups sliced UnChicken
3 tablespoons corn oil
1 cup Cashew Milk (page 93)

Combine the N'egg and 3 tablespoons of "milk." In a separate bowl, combine the crackers, thyme, paprika, and pepper and set aside. One at a time, dip the gluten slices in the N'egg mixture and then roll them in the cracker mixture. Heat the oil in a large skillet and evenly brown the gluten on both sides. Add the cup of "milk," reduce heat, cover tightly, and cook for 35 minutes. Uncover and cook 10 more minutes.

UnTurkey Substitutes and Dishes

UnTurkey

Cook 2 cups of raw gluten according to Method 1, 2, or 3 in:

UnTurkey Gluten Broth

2 tablespoons soy sauce
1 teaspoon Kitchen Bouquet
1/8 teaspoon rubbed sage
1/2 cup chopped onion
2 1/4 teaspoons monosodium glutamate (MSG)
1/2 teaspoon sea salt
1/2 teaspoon poultry seasoning
3 tablespoons plus 2 teaspoons nutritional yeast
1 teaspoon corn oil
2 cups water

Combine everything and simmer for 5 minutes.

Lisbon UnTurkey

2 tablespoons unbleached white flour
1/2 teaspoon ground cumin
1 teaspoon paprika
1/2 teaspoon cayenne pepper
1/4 teaspoon sea salt
3 cups UnTurkey (see above), in strips or cubes (or 4 slices of UnTurkey, 1/4 inch thick)
Corn oil
1/2 cup chopped bell pepper
1/4 cup chopped celery
1/4 cup sliced green onions
1 teaspoon minced garlic
1/4 cup black sliced olives
1/4 cup sliced green pimiento-stuffed olives
1/2 cup UnTurkey Broth (see above)
1/2 teaspoon cornstarch

Combine the flour, cumin, paprika, cayenne, and salt. Coat the gluten with this mixture and brown in a skillet in the oil. (Or broil or grill until brown on both sides.) Remove and set aside, keeping warm. In the same skillet, adding more oil if needed, sauté the bell pepper, celery, onions, and garlic until almost tender. Stir in the olives. Combine the broth and cornstarch. Add this and cook and stir until bubbly, then continue to cook, stirring for 1 more minute. Pour over the gluten and serve.

UnTurkey Cutlets Piccata

Something different.

1 N'egg (page 302)
1 tablespoon Cashew Milk (page 93)
Margarine
4 UnTurkey (see above) "cutlets" 1/4 inch thick
2 cups fresh bread crumbs
1 teaspoon lemon juice
1/2 cup UnTurkey Gluten Broth (see above)
Dash freshly ground black pepper

Combine the N'egg and "milk." Melt some margarine in a skillet. Dip each cutlet into the N'egg mixture and then into the bread crumbs. Fry the cutlets, 2 at a time, until lightly browned on both sides, adding more margarine if needed. Set the cutlets aside. Put the lemon juice into the skillet. Add the broth and pepper. Return the cutlets to the skillet, cover, and simmer 10 to 15 minutes.

UnTurkey Cutlets with Mushrooms and Tomatoes

2 tablespoons nondairy margarine
3 cups thickly sliced mushrooms
1 tablespoon lemon juice
2 tablespoons prepared mustard
1 teaspoon cornstarch
½ teaspoon sea salt
⅛ teaspoon freshly ground black pepper
2 cups UnTurkey (page 147), sliced ¼ inch thick
1½ cups coarsely chopped tomato
2 tablespoons chopped green onions, or chives

Melt the margarine and sauté the mushrooms. Add the lemon juice, mustard, cornstarch, salt, and pepper, stirring until smooth. Put into a nonstick casserole, arrange the gluten slices over it. Sprinkle the tomato and onions or chives over all. Bake at 350°F for 30 minutes.

UnTurkey Holiday Casserole

You can't do without it!

2 recipes UnTurkey (page 147)
Oil
1 recipe Bread Dressing (page 193)
3 recipes Mushroom Gravy (page 253), made with UnTurkey Gluten Broth (page 147)

Slice the gluten thin. Spray both sides of the slices lightly with oil and broil lightly, not letting it get crisp. Set aside. Put the dressing ingredients in a large casserole and cook according to the instructions given in the Bread Dressing recipe. When the dressing is done, cover it with ⅓ of the gravy. Put ½ of the gluten slices over that. Cover that with another ⅓ of the gravy. Cover with the rest of the gluten slices. Pour the rest of the gravy over all. Bake at 400°F for 30 minutes.

UnTurkey Meatless-Balls with Caper Sauce

3 cups ground UnTurkey (page 147), browned in corn oil
½ cup grated onion
1 N'egg (page 302)
1 tablespoon unbleached white flour
½ cup dried bread crumbs
Nondairy margarine
2 tablespoons unbleached white flour
⅛ teaspoon freshly ground black pepper
½ teaspoon sea salt
3 cups Cashew Milk (page 93)
2 tablespoons capers, drained
1 tablespoon chopped fresh parsley

Combine the gluten, onion, N'egg, flour, and crumbs. Shape into 1-inch balls. In the margarine brown the gluten balls, half at a time, removing them as they brown. Stir the flour, pepper, and salt into the remaining oil and cook 1 minute. Gradually stir in the "milk" and capers. Cook until slightly thickened, stirring constantly. Return the gluten to the skillet and bring to a boil. Reduce heat to low, cover, and simmer 10 minutes, stirring occasionally. Sprinkle with the parsley.

UnTurkey Salad Burritos

A masterpiece!

2 cups chopped UnTurkey (page 147)
2 tablespoons finely chopped celery
½ cup finely chopped onion
¼ cup sliced black olives (add up to ¼ cup more if you like)
1 cup Yeast Cheez (page 97), Pimiento Cheez (page 94), or Notzarella Cheez (page 94)
½ cups Miraculous Whip (page 17)
⅓ cup Tomato Salsa (page 296)
⅛ teaspoon sea salt
6 flour tortillas, 7 to 8 inches in diameter

Combine the gluten, celery, onion, olives, and Cheez. Whisk together the Miraculous Whip, salsa, and salt. Pour this sauce over the gluten mixture and blend well. Spoon this filling onto the tortillas and wrap them burrito-style. Put in a baking dish or pan and bake at 350°F for 20 minutes, until thoroughly warmed. Serve with extra salsa and olives.

UnSeafood Substitutes and Dishes

UnFish

Feed them to fish lovers and turn them into gluten lovers!

1 recipe Basic Gluten (page 99) using unbleached white flour

Broth
4 cups water
2 tablespoons monosodium glutamate (MSG)
1 tablespoon sea salt
2 teaspoons corn oil

Dip Mixture
2 cups Cashew Milk (page 93)
1/4 teaspoon cayenne pepper
1/4 teaspoons sea salt

Crumb Mixture
2 cups corn flour, cornmeal, Cream of Wheat (Farina), Malt-O-Meal, or powdered cracker crumbs
1/4 teaspoon cayenne pepper
1/4 teaspoon sea salt

Cook gluten according to Cooking Method 2 (page 99). Slice gluten 1/4 to 1/2 inch thick. Combine broth ingredients and simmer for 5 minutes. Boil the gluten in the broth for 30 minutes. Then let it soak overnight in the broth. Drain well. Dip each piece in dip mixture and roll in crumb mixture. Deep fry at 350°F until light brown.

VARIATION: *Coat in Deep-Frying Batter (page 338) and deep-fry at 400°F.*

Deep-Fried UnFish

Dip Mixture
2 cups Cashew Milk (page 93)
1/4 teaspoon cayenne pepper
1/4 teaspoon sea salt

Crumb Mixture
2 cups cracker crumbs or corn flour
1/4 teaspoon cayenne pepper
1/4 teaspoon sea salt

Take slices of UnFish (see above) cooked by Method 2 (page 99). Dip each slice in the dip mixture and then in the crumb mixture, coating well, but gently shaking off excess crumbs or flour. Deep fry.

UnSalmon Loaf

Unlikely as this recipe looks, it works beautifully.

1 cup tomato juice
1 cup water
1 cup soy flour
1½ teaspoons onion salt
1 tablespoon oil

Whirl everything in a blender until smooth and pour into an oiled baking dish. Bake at 400°F until a tan crust forms, about 40 minutes. Cool and turn onto a platter. Serve hot or cold.

UnScallops

These are so much better than either the real thing or the dreary canned imitations!

1 recipe Basic Gluten (page 99) using unbleached white flour

Broth
4 cups water
2 tablespoons monosodium glutamate (MSG)
1 tablespoon sea salt
2 teaspoons corn oil

Dip Mixture
4 cups Cashew Milk (page 93)
¼ teaspoon cayenne pepper
1 teaspoon sea salt

Crumb Mixture
4 cups powdered cracker crumbs, corn flour, cornmeal, Cream of Wheat (Farina), or Malt-O-Meal
½ teaspoon cayenne pepper
½ teaspoon sea salt

Cook gluten according to Cooking Method 1 (page 99), tearing the gluten into ¾-inch chunks. Combine broth ingredients and simmer for 5 minutes. Boil the gluten in the broth for 30 minutes. Then let it soak overnight in the broth. Drain well. Dip each piece in dip mixture and roll in crumb mixture. Deep fry at 350°F until light brown.

VARIATION: *Coat in Deep-Frying Batter (page 338) and deep-fry at 400°F.*

UnShrimp

When I became a vegetarian thirty years ago the only thing I missed was shrimp, which I loved heartily. Now I can enjoy it again, and so can you. This makes a lot of UnShrimp, but you can freeze it and it keeps just fine. Be sure you use the Zatarain's Crab Boil, which is whole spices in a bag.

1 recipe Basic Gluten (page 99)
1 gallon water
½ cup monosodium glutamate (MSG)
¼ cup sea salt
1 bag Zatarain's Crab Boil
1 tablespoon corn oil

Cook gluten according to Cooking Method 2 (page 99). Slice the cooked gluten ¼ inch thick and then cut into 1 x 2-inch pieces (or into shrimplike shapes). Combine rest of ingredients and simmer for 5 minutes. (If you want to make less broth, break open the Crab Boil bag and use the quantity of spices proportionate to the amount of water you are using, tying them in a piece of cheesecloth. Or, if you do not have Zatarain's Crab Boil, use the broth given above for UnScallops (see above) and UnFish (page 149).

Boil the gluten in the broth for 30 minutes. Then let it soak overnight in the broth, keeping the crab boil bag in the broth as well. Drain before using.

Broiled UnShrimp

3 tablespoons olive oil
3 tablespoons nondairy margarine
4 teaspoons Lea and Perrins Steak Sauce
1 teaspoon Louisiana Hot Sauce
6 cups UnShrimp (see above)
Cayenne pepper
1 cup water

Put the oil in a baking pan, slice the margarine into it, and heat it in an oven until the margarine is melted. Take the pan from the oven and add the steak sauce and hot sauce, mixing well. Put the gluten in a single layer into the mixture and sprinkle them generously with cayenne pepper.

Pour the water into the pan, using just as much as is needed to half-cover the gluten. Bake at 350°F for 20 minutes, then place in a broiler, basting frequently and turning, until the gluten is well browned and dark around the edges.

French Fried UnShrimp

You won't believe how wonderful these are.

6 cups UnShrimp (page 150)
3 cups Cashew Milk (page 93)
½ cup Parmesan Cheez (page 94)
2 cups sliced onion
1 teaspoon sliced garlic
½ cup sliced bell pepper
2 tablespoons Lea and Perrins Steak Sauce
2 teaspoons Louisiana Hot Sauce

Crumb Mixture

2 cups powdered cracker crumbs, corn flour, cornmeal, Cream of Wheat (Farina), or Malt-O-Meal
¼ teaspoon cayenne pepper
¼ teaspoon sea salt

Place the UnShrimp in a large bowl. Combine the "milk," "Parmesan," onion, garlic, bell pepper, steak sauce, and hot sauce, and blend in a blender. Pour this over the gluten, adding more milk if needed to cover it. Stir a bit to mix everything evenly, and marinate in the refrigerator overnight or at least 12 hours. Put the crumb mixture in a brown paper bag. Drain the UnShrimp a bit at a time, shake in the bag, and deep fry at 400°F. (Or coat in Deep-Frying Batter [page 338] and fry.)

Garlic UnShrimp Español

1 cup olive oil
1½ cups UnFish Broth (page 155)
½ cup water
3 tablespoons crushed garlic
1 teaspoon basil
1 teaspoon oregano
¼ teaspoon cayenne pepper
6 cups UnShrimp (page 150)

Whisk together the oil, broth, water, garlic, herbs, and pepper. Add the gluten and let it marinate, turning them, for at least 4 hours or overnight. Broil, in the marinade, about 4 inches from the heat, turning them once, for 5 minutes or until pale golden.

Marinated UnShrimp

This is delicious breaded and deep-fried, too.

6 cups UnShrimp (page 150)
3 cups UnShrimp Broth (see UnShrimp, page 150)
3 cups water
2 teaspoons Tabasco Sauce, or 4 teaspoons of Louisiana Hot Sauce
2 tablespoons dry mustard
¼ cup vinegar
2 cups sliced onion
3 tablespoons Sucanat
½ teaspoon angostura bitters

Combine everything, bring to a boil, let cool, and marinate for several hours.

Mexican UnShrimp

This is quite similar to UnShrimp Creole (page 152), but distinctive enough for me to include here for you to try. But be warned: This dish is hot.

¾ cup chopped onion
½ cup chopped bell pepper
½ cup chopped celery
1½ teaspoons corn oil
¾ cup canned tomatoes
2 teaspoons minced garlic
½ teaspoon cayenne pepper
½ teaspoon sea salt
1 teaspoon paprika
½ cup water
1 tablespoon unbleached white flour
2 cups UnShrimp (page 150)

Sauté the onion, bell pepper, and celery in the oil. Add the tomatoes, garlic, pepper, salt, paprika, water, and flour. Blend well and simmer for 45 minutes. Add the UnShrimp and simmer 15 more minutes. Serve over rice and top with Yeast Cheez (page 97) if desired.

UnOysters Baton Rouge

5 cups fresh mushrooms
1/4 cup nondairy margarine
1/2 cup unbleached white flour
1/4 cup water
1/2 cup chopped green onions
1 tablespoon minced garlic
2 cups Cashew Milk (page 93)
1 1/2 cups UnFish Broth (page 155)
1/2 cup minced fresh parsley
4 artichoke hearts, minced
1/8 teaspoon sea salt
1/8 teaspoon cayenne pepper
2 teaspoons Louisiana Hot Sauce

Stem the mushrooms, mince the stems, and set aside. Melt the margarine in a skillet, stir in the flour gradually, and cook until medium brown. Add the water, stir in the green onions and garlic, and cook until the onions are soft, stirring constantly. Add the "milk" and broth, a little at a time, stirring constantly. Cook until thick, adding a little more broth if needed. Add the mushroom stems, parsley, artichoke hearts, salt, pepper, and hot sauce. Simmer for 20 minutes, stirring occasionally. Put the mushroom tops in a shallow baking dish. Cover with the sauce and bake at 400°F for 20 minutes.

UnShrimp Creole

You can't eat this just once!

1/2 cup chopped onion
1/2 cup chopped celery
1/2 cup chopped fresh parsley
1/3 cup chopped bell pepper
2 teaspoons olive oil
2 cups water
2 cups sliced okra
2 cups chopped tomato
1 cup tomato puree or sauce
3/4 teaspoon minced garlic
1 teaspoon Lea and Perrins Steak Sauce
1/2 teaspoon Louisiana Hot Sauce
1/3 teaspoon sea salt
2 cups UnShrimp (page 150)
3 cups cooked rice

Sauté the onion, celery, parsley, and bell pepper in the oil until they are tender. Add the water, okra, tomato, tomato puree (or sauce), and garlic. Simmer for 5 minutes. Add the steak sauce, hot sauce, and salt. Cook for 30 minutes. Add the gluten and cook 30 more minutes until the mixture is thick. Serve over the rice.

UnShrimp Curry 1

1 1/2 cups unsweetened shredded coconut
1 1/2 teaspoons powdered coriander
1 1/4 cups warm water
3/4 cup finely chopped onion
1 tablespoon minced garlic
1 1/2 teaspoons corn oil
3/4 teaspoon powdered ginger
1 teaspoon turmeric
1/2 teaspoon ground cumin
1/4 teaspoon cayenne pepper
1/4 teaspoon freshly ground black pepper
2 1/2 cups UnShrimp (page 150)

Put the coconut, coriander, and water in a blender and puree on high. Sauté the onion and garlic in the oil until the onion is soft. Add the ginger, turmeric, cumin, cayenne, and black pepper, and sauté for 30 seconds. Add the gluten, stirring to coat well with the oil and spices. Add the coriander-coconut mixture, bring to a simmer, and cook for 10 minutes. Serve over rice.

UnShrimp Curry 2

3/4 cup chopped onion
2 teaspoons nondairy margarine
2 teaspoons minced garlic
1 tablespoon curry powder
1 1/4 cup carrot, cut 1/4 inch thick diagonally
1/2 cup UnChicken Broth (page 155)
1 1/2 cups Cashew Milk (page 93)
3/4 cup Tofu Buttermilk (page 96)
3 tablespoons cornstarch
2 tablespoons lemon juice
1/4 teaspoon sea salt
1/4 teaspoon cayenne pepper
1/8 teaspoon freshly ground black pepper

4 cups UnShrimp (page 150)
1/2 cup chopped bell pepper

Sauté the onion in the margarine until soft. Stir in the garlic and curry powder, and sauté for 1 minute. Stir in the carrot and broth. Bring to a boil and cook, uncovered, about 10 minutes, or until the carrot is just tender. In a separate bowl, combine the "milk," "buttermilk," and cornstarch. Add to the carrot mixture. Stir in the lemon juice, salt, and pepper. Cook and stir till thickened and bubbly. Add the gluten and bell pepper. Return to boiling. Cook, stirring, for 2 more minutes. Serve over rice or toast.

UnShrimp Gumbo

1 cup olive oil
1 1/2 cups unbleached white flour
3 cups chopped onion
1 1/2 cups chopped bell pepper
1 cup canned tomato sauce
3 tablespoons minced garlic
1 cup chopped green onions
3/4 cup finely chopped fresh parsley
10 cups water
1/4 cup Lea and Perrins Steak Sauce
1 teaspoon sea salt
1 teaspoon cayenne pepper
1 cup UnShrimp Broth (see UnShrimp, page 150)
6 cups UnShrimp (page 150)

Heat the oil in a skillet, stir in the flour, and cook until it is dark brown but not burned. Add the onion and bell pepper and sauté until the onion is transparent. Add the tomato sauce, garlic, and green onions and cook until the mixture is back to its original dark brown color. Add the parsley, water, steak sauce, salt, pepper, and broth. Cook for 45 minutes. Add gluten and cook for 30 minutes. Serve over rice.

UnShrimp Imperial

2 tablespoons finely chopped green onions
2 tablespoons finely chopped celery
2 tablespoons finely chopped carrot
2 teaspoons nondairy margarine
2 tablespoons unbleached white flour
1 1/4 cups Cashew Kreem (page 93)
1/4 teaspoon white pepper
1/4 cup UnFish Broth (page 155)
Dash Tabasco sauce
1 N'egg (page 302)
2 cups chopped or ground UnShrimp (page 150)
2 tablespoons finely chopped fresh parsley (leaves only)
1/2 cup finely chopped bell pepper (red preferred)
1/4 teaspoon grated orange peel
1 cup fine bread crumbs
1/2 teaspoon paprika

Sauté the green onions, celery, and carrot in the margarine for 1 minute. Stir in the flour and cook, stirring, for 3 minutes. Whisk in 1 cup of Kreem in a stream, add the pepper, and simmer, whisking, for 5 minutes. Take off the heat and stir in the broth and Tabasco. Separately, whisk together the N'egg and 1/4 cup of Kreem. Stir this into the vegetable mixture and combine well. Fold in the gluten, parsley, bell pepper, and orange peel. Put into a nonstick baking dish. Sprinkle with the bread crumbs and paprika, pressing in lightly. Bake at 425°F until the bread crumbs are golden and the casserole is heated through, 12 to 15 minutes.

UnShrimp Mold

1 can Campbell's Tomato Soup
1 1/2 cups Tofu Kreem Cheez (page 96)
2 package unflavored kosher (nonanimal) gelatin
1/2 cup water
1 cup Miraculous Whip (page 17) or other "mayonnaise" (pages 11, 12, 13, 19, 22, or 23)
4 or 5 green onions
1/4 teaspoon sea salt
1/2 teaspoon cayenne pepper
1/2 teaspoon Tabasco sauce
2 cups UnShrimp (page 150)

Heat the soup, directly from the can, without adding milk or water, to a boil. Stir in the Kreem Cheez. Dissolve the gelatin in the water and add it to the soup mixture. Let it cool. Add all other ingredients except the gluten. In a mold place alternating layers of sauce and gluten. Chill until the mold is set.

UnShrimp Pie

Remember the song about crawfish pie? UnShrimp Pie works just as well—maybe better.

¼ cup unbleached white flour
4 teaspoons corn oil
4 teaspoons olive oil
½ cup chopped onion
½ cup chopped mushrooms
½ cup chopped green onions
1 teaspoon minced garlic
1 cup water
½ cup peas, cooked and drained
½ cup diced carrot, cooked
¼ teaspoon sea salt
1½ teaspoons Louisiana Hot Sauce
2 cups UnShrimp (page 150)
1 recipe Convent Pie Crust (page 328)

Combine the flour and oils in a skillet and cook, stirring, until the flour is dark brown but not burned. Add the onion, mushrooms, green onions, and garlic, stirring. Add the water and bring to a boil. Add the peas, carrot, salt, hot sauce, and UnShrimp. Cook for 5 more minutes until it thickens. Put everything in a pie pan with crust and top it with more crust, cutting holes in top to let out the steam. Bake at 350°F until the crust is golden brown, about 45 minutes.

UnShrimp with Caper Sauce

Memorable is the word for this dish.

1 cup finely chopped onion
½ cup chopped fresh parsley
1½ teaspoons olive oil
1 tablespoon minced garlic
½ teaspoon dried mint, crumbled
¼ cup Lea and Perrins Steak Sauce
1 teaspoon Louisiana Hot Sauce, or ¼ teaspoon cayenne pepper
1 cup water
4 cups UnShrimp (page 150)
¾ cup Miraculous Whip (page 17)
1 tablespoon lemon juice
1 tablespoon creole or poupon mustard
2 tablespoons capers, drained

Sauté the onion and parsley in the oil until the onion is tender. Add garlic, mint, steak sauce, hot sauce, water, and gluten. Cook, stirring constantly, for 20 minutes. Combine the Miraculous Whip, lemon juice, mustard, and capers, and mix well. Serve UnShrimp over rice or spaghetti and top with the sauce. Do not mix the sauce with the UnShrimp before serving.

Flavoring Broths

I think this is one of the most valuable sections in this cookbook. By using these formulas you can impart a richer taste to the food you cook.

These broths are also used for flavoring the various dishes that need a meatlike taste without any actual gluten imitations. (They are not used for flavoring the gluten substitutes. The recipes for those broths are given in the sections for those meat substitutes. Some formulas are the same as these, however.)

Not only is the flavor given by these broths superior to any of the various powdered or cubed forms of "beef" or "chicken" flavoring, they are immensely more healthful.

UnChicken Broth

¼ cup chopped onion
2¼ teaspoons monosodium glutamate (MSG)
½ teaspoon sea salt
½ teaspoon poultry seasoning
2 tablespoons plus 2½ teaspoons nutritional yeast
1 teaspoon corn oil
2 cups water

Combine and simmer for 5 minutes.

UnBeef Broth

2 tablespoons soy sauce
1 teaspoon Kitchen Bouquet
1 tablespoon nutritional yeast
¼ cup chopped onion
⅛ teaspoon rubbed sage
1 teaspoon corn oil
2 cups water

Combine and simmer for 5 minutes

UnFish Broth

2 cups water
1 tablespoon monosodium glutamate (MSG)
1½ teaspoons sea salt
1 teaspoon corn oil

Combine and simmer for 5 minutes.

VARIATION: *Add ⅛ teaspoon of powdered kelp for 2 cups of broth and ¼ teaspoon for 4 cups of broth.*

UnHam Broth

¼ cup soy sauce
2 teaspoons Kitchen Bouquet
2 tablespoons nutritional yeast
½ cup chopped onion
¼ teaspoon rubbed sage
½ teaspoon freshly ground black pepper
½ teaspoon oregano
1 teaspoon garlic powder
1¼ teaspoons liquid smoke
1 teaspoon corn oil
1 teaspoon sea salt
2 cups water

Combine and simmer for 5 minutes.

UnPork Broth

¼ cup chopped onion
2¼ teaspoon monosodium glutamate (MSG)
½ teaspoon sea salt
½ teaspoon poultry seasoning
3 tablespoons nutritional yeast
1 teaspoon corn oil
2 cups water
¼ teaspoon freshly ground black pepper
½ teaspoon crushed garlic
⅛ teaspoon powdered marjoram

Combine and simmer for 5 minutes.

UnSausage Broth

2 tablespoons soy sauce
1 teaspoon Kitchen Bouquet
1 tablespoon nutritional yeast
¼ cup chopped onion
⅛ teaspoon rubbed sage
¼ teaspoon freshly ground black pepper
¼ teaspoon oregano
½ teaspoon garlic powder
2 tablespoons Watkins Sausage Seasoning
1 teaspoon liquid smoke
1 teaspoon corn oil
2 cups water

Combine and simmer for 5 minutes.

Heavenly Broth

This is one of the most valuable recipes in this book, not only because it works very well for sautéing in oilless cooking, but because it is incredibly nutritious, and is especially good for those who are ill to give a boost to the body as it battles the baddies. This is the vegan answer to chicken soup, which, in my opinion, has never been good for anybody!

Watch the amount of jalapeños, as they vary in hotness from season to season. You might want to work up to the level best for your taste. But don't leave them out, as they have valuable nutrients and antiseptics, including a natural form of quinine.

I give three ways of making Heavenly Broth after the list of ingredients, but there is a much, much better way: by using a Mehu-Maija Juicer. I had heard of these juicers many years ago and was intrigued at the idea, but my interest in raw juices deflected me from following up and getting information about it. When I discovered Heavenly Broth, my memory revived and I tracked it down.

The Mehu-Maija Juicers are not the juicers we are used to. They consist of three parts: a basket for the cut-up vegetables; a reservoir to collect their juice; and another reservoir that holds boiling water. By means of a double-boiler effect, the pure juice flows out of the vegetables (or fruits) and into the top reservoir. The result is marvelous and extremely easy to digest.

Although the instructions speak of "soft" fruits and vegetables being used in the juicer, we have tried "hard" vegetables and found that it works just as well on them. By using this method no water is mixed into the juice—you get 100%, the real thing. The taste of Heavenly Broth made in this way is simply heavenly.

Also excellent is tomato juice extracted this way (put in some onions with the tomatoes and it is really delicious). This, too, is especially good-tasting and easy on digestion.

Mehu-Maija juicers can be obtained from Lehman's Hardware Store and Appliances (wonderful people), 1 Lehman Circle, P.O. Box 41, Kidron, OH 44636. Phone 216/857-5757.

Heavenly Broth

4 cups potatoes (about 3)
2 cups carrots (about 4)
2 cups cauliflower
2 cups summer squash
2 cups cabbage
2 cups green beans
2 cups celery
3 cups onions (about 1 to 2)
2 cups bell peppers (about 2)
6 cups tomatoes (about 5)
1 cup parsley
¼ cup jalapeños
2 teaspoons sea salt
14 cups water

Do one of the following:

1. Chop all vegetables. Combine everything, bring to a boil, reduce heat, and simmer for 3 hours. Strain.
2. Shred or mince all vegetables in a food processor. Combine everything, bring to a boil, reduce heat, and simmer for 1½ hours. Strain.
3. Chop all vegetables. Combine everything and pressure-cook at 15 pounds for 35 minutes. Strain.

Vegetables

Anandamayi Kitchuri

This recipe was formulated by Sri Sri Anandamayi Ma, a leading religious teacher of India. She recommended it to all her students, saying that if a person ate this dish always, varying the vegetables, he or she would never be ill. I have personally known many people who ate this every day. The Ajwan, a small black seed with a slightly sour tang that is available in most Indian grocery stores, was not in the original recipe, but was recommended to me by one of those who cooked it daily. In the original there were no onions or garlic, either. This is very good served with Puris (page 56) or Flat Bread (page 52).

1 cup rice, uncooked
1 tablespoon corn oil
1 cup chopped onion
1 tablespoon sliced jalapeños
1½ teaspoons ground turmeric
1 teaspoon powdered ginger or 1 tablespoon grated fresh ginger
1 teaspoon ground cumin
1 teaspoon ground fenugreek
1 teaspoon ground anise
½ teaspoon ground ajwan
1¼ teaspoons sea salt
¼ teaspoon garlic powder
1 quart chopped vegetables of your choice
2½ cups tomato, fresh or canned (if canned drain well, and use the juice as part of the boiling water measure)
3 cups boiling water (and juice from canned tomatoes, if used)

Wash the rice repeatedly, changing the water, until there is no more starch in the water, and drain it well. Heat the oil until very hot. Sauté the onion and jalapeños, then add the spices and stir constantly as it all fries to a rich brown color and gives off a heavenly fragrance. Add the vegetables, tomato, and rice and stir continually until all is covered with the hot oil/spice mixture. Add the boiling water and stir. Bring to a boil, cover and simmer until all vegetables are done.

VARIATION: *Include 1½ cups of cooked dal, garbanzos, or other beans. Leave out the tomatoes. Include 2 cups of chopped UnBeef (page 109), UnChicken (page 137), or unflavored gluten. Fry the gluten in the spices until it browns before you add the vegetables and rice.*

Baked Mashed Potatoes

6 cups potatoes, peeled and cut into 1-inch pieces
1½ cups thinly sliced green sliced onions
¾ cup chopped onion
1¼ teaspoons minced garlic
2 teaspoons nondairy margarine
⅔ cup Cashew Milk (page 93)
1½ cups Yeast Cheez (page 97), Pimiento Cheez (page 94), or Notzarella Cheez (page 94)
1 teaspoon dried chives
½ teaspoon sea salt
⅛ teaspoon cayenne pepper

Cook the potatoes. While the potatoes are cooking, sauté the onions and garlic in the margarine until the onions are soft. Force the potatoes through a ricer or food mill, stir in the "milk," onion mixture, half the Cheez, the chives, salt, and pepper. Put this in a nonstick baking dish, spread the rest of the Cheez on top, and bake at 400°F for 20 minutes.

Boiled Cabbage

Take the outer leaves off a head of cabbage, cut it into sections, and remove the core. Shred or chop it finely. Drop it into rapidly boiling UnBeef Broth (page 155) or UnChicken Broth (page 155). Cook until it is barely tender, 7 or 8 minutes.

Boiled Cabbage Dinner

This is real frontier log cabin food not to be confused with the bland New England version.

2 tablespoons olive oil
1 medium cabbage, quartered
4 large onions, quartered
4 medium whole potatoes, peeled and quartered
4 large carrots, peeled and cut in large pieces
3 cups UnHam Broth (page 156)
3 cups water
1 tablespoon Louisiana Hot Sauce
1 teaspoon sea salt
4 cups cubed UnHam (page 130) or UnSausage (page 132)

In a pot large enough to hold all the ingredients put everything except the gluten and bring to a boil. After it boils add the gluten, and more water if necessary. Cook until the potatoes are done.

Boiled Okra

Sounds dull, but it's good!

4 cups okra, whole
1 teaspoon corn oil
2 cups flavoring broth of choice (pages 155–56)
1 cup water
2 teaspoons Louisiana Hot Sauce
2 teaspoons sea salt

Wash the okra. Cut off most of the okra stems but keep a small bit on each one so the okra "glue" will not leak out and make the dish slimy. Combine everything in a pot, bring to a strong boil, turn down the heat, and simmer slowly until the okra is tender.

Broccoli

1 teaspoon nondairy margarine
1½ teaspoons olive oil
2 cups coarsely chopped onion
1 teaspoon minced garlic
¼ teaspoon red pepper flakes
¾ cup chopped celery
6 cups broccoli, the stems chopped and the tops broken into small flowerets
¾ cup chopped bell pepper
1½ cups UnChicken Broth (page 155)
½ teaspoon sea salt

Melt the margarine in the oil. Sauté the onion, garlic, pepper flakes, and celery until transparent. Add the broccoli and bell pepper and sauté briefly. Then add the broth and salt and stir well. Cover and cook until tender, but do not overcook.

VARIATION: *Add 2 tablespoons of curry powder when sautéing.*

Broccoli Divan

1 tablespoon cornstarch
1 cup cold Cashew Milk (page 93)
1 teaspoon nondairy margarine
1/4 teaspoon sea salt
1/8 teaspoon freshly ground black pepper
1/2 cup Cashew Sour Kreem (page 94) or Tofu Sour Kreem (page 97)
1/2 cup Yeast Cheez (page 97), Pimiento Cheez (page 94), or Notzarella Cheez (page 94)
3/4 teaspoon prepared mustard
4 cups broccoli, cooked tender-crisp

Bring the cornstarch, "milk," margarine, salt, and pepper to a boil, stirring constantly. Boil until thickened. Remove from heat and stir in the Sour Kreem, Cheez, and mustard. Pour over the broccoli. Broil 4 inches from the heat for 3 to 5 minutes.

Broccoli, Mushrooms, and Tomatoes

4 2/3 cups mushrooms, halved
1/4 teaspoon sea salt
2 tablespoons nondairy margarine
5 cups broccoli, cut into 2 1/2 x 1-inch pieces and steamed
2 cups chopped tomato
3/4 teaspoon lemon-pepper seasoning salt

Sauté the mushrooms and salt in 1 tablespoon margarine until tender and golden. Stir in the broccoli, tomato, lemon-pepper seasoning salt, and remaining tablespoon of margarine. Heat through.

Browned Potatoes

Peel and boil potatoes in UnBeef Broth (page 155) or UnChicken Broth (page 155) until they are nearly tender. Drain. Melt 2 tablespoons of nondairy margarine in a pan and cook and turn the potatoes until they are light brown. Season with salt and pepper. Bake them in a 400°F oven, turning the potatoes to brown them evenly, until they are crisp and brown. Add more margarine if required.

Cabbage, Tomatoes, and Cheez

3 cups finely shredded cabbage, cooked and drained
3/4 teaspoon sea salt
1/4 teaspoon cayenne pepper
1 1/2 cups crushed or chopped canned tomatoes
1 cup Yeast Cheez (page 97) or Pimiento Cheez (page 94)
2 cups bread crumbs
2 teaspoons nondairy margarine

Cook the cabbage with the salt and pepper. In a nonstick casserole put alternating layers of tomatoes and cabbage, beginning with tomatoes. Spread with the Cheez and then with the bread crumbs, pressing in lightly. Bake at 325°F for about 30 minutes or until the crumbs are brown.

Cabbage Goulash

This may be the first time you taste anything like this, but you won't let it be the last!

1 1/2 cups chopped onion
5 teaspoons corn oil
2 cups ground UnSausage (page 132)
2 cups ground UnBeef (page 109)
3 1/2 cups chopped canned tomatoes, drained, reserving liquid
3/4 cup tomato paste
2 tablespoons balsamic vinegar
1 tablespoon chili powder
1 teaspoon garlic powder
1/4 teaspoon hot pepper flakes
10 cups shredded cabbage

Sauté the onion in the oil until soft. Add the rest of the ingredients except the cabbage. Mix well. Stir in the cabbage and simmer 15 to 20 minutes, or until the cabbage is tender.

Cajun Peas or Fresh Beans

Without a doubt, this is a winner.

1 cup chopped UnHam (page 130)
2 teaspoons nondairy margarine
6 cups peas, or fresh (not dried) beans
2 cups UnHam Broth (page 156)
1½ cups chopped onion
¾ teaspoon minced garlic
1 teaspoon Louisiana Hot Sauce

Sauté the gluten in the margarine for 5 minutes. Add everything else and cook until the peas are tender. Then salt to taste.

Carrots and Peas

In salted water, cook some chopped carrots and peas separately, in any proportions desired. Drain well. Combine. Season with salt and pepper. Pour melted margarine (¼ teaspoon to 1 cup of vegetables) over them, or heat together in Thin White Sauce (page 262) or Medium White Sauce (page 262). Use half as much sauce as vegetables.

Chili Corn and Zucchini

1 cup sliced onion
1½ teaspoons minced garlic
2 teaspoons corn oil or nondairy margarine
2 cups UnChicken Broth (page 155)
4 cups thinly sliced zucchini
1½ cups corn
2 tablespoons minced jalapeños
1 teaspoon sea salt
⅛ teaspoon freshly ground black pepper
½ cups Yeast Cheez (page 97)

Sauté the onion and garlic in the oil until soft. Combine everything but the Cheez and cook until the vegetables are tender. Drain off most of the liquid and stir in the Cheez.

Colonial Green Beans

Quietly special.

¼ cup chopped UnBacon (page 136)
2 cups green beans
2 cups thinly sliced carrot
1½ teaspoons minced garlic
½ teaspoon pepper
⅛ teaspoon sea salt
2 teaspoons nondairy margarine

Sauté everything in the margarine until the vegetables are crisp-tender.

Coponatini Eggplant

1 tablespoon sea salt
6 cups peeled and cubed eggplant
3 tablespoons olive oil
1 cup canned tomato sauce
¾ cup chopped onion
⅔ cup chopped celery
½ teaspoon minced garlic
3 tablespoons plus 1 teaspoon green olives, quartered
1 teaspoon vinegar
1 teaspoon sea salt

Sprinkle the tablespoon of salt over the cubed eggplant and let it sit for 30 minutes, then squeeze out the moisture lightly. Cook the eggplant in the oil until it is tender. Add the tomato sauce. Separately sauté the onion, celery, garlic, and olives in a little olive oil, then add the vinegar to the mixture. Combine all ingredients with the salt. Cook together until the flavors are blended. Serve with rice.

Copper Pennies

This unusual dish can be a salad, an appetizer, or a main course.

2 teaspoons corn oil
1 cup Sucanat
¾ cup vinegar
1½ cups tomato soup
1 tablespoon powdered mustard
2 tablespoons Lea and Perrins Steak Sauce

4 cups sliced carrot
1 cup sliced onion
1 small bell pepper, sliced

In a saucepan simmer the oil, Sucanat, vinegar, tomato soup, mustard, and steak sauce. Boil the carrot until it is tender. In a casserole alternately layer the carrot, onion, and pepper slices. Pour the sauce over all and refrigerate.

Corn à la King

3 tablespoons minced onion
1/2 cup chopped bell pepper
2 tablespoons chopped pimiento
1 teaspoon nondairy margarine
2 1/2 cups corn
1/2 cup Medium White Sauce (page 262) made with UnChicken Broth (page 155)
3/4 teaspoon sea salt
1/8 teaspoon cayenne pepper

Sauté the onion, bell pepper, and pimiento in the margarine. Add the rest of the ingredients and cook.

VARIATION: *Use squash instead of corn.*

Corn and Peppers

3/4 cup chopped bell pepper
3 tablespoons chopped onion
1/8 teaspoon cayenne pepper
1 1/2 teaspoons nondairy margarine
4 cups corn
1/2 teaspoon sea salt

Sauté the bell pepper, onion, and cayenne in the margarine. Combine with rest of ingredients and cook.

Corn Special

2 tablespoons chopped bell pepper
3 tablespoons chopped onion
1 teaspoon nondairy margarine
2 cups corn
1/4 teaspoon sea salt

Sauté the bell pepper and onion in the margarine. Add the corn and salt and cook.

Cottage Mashed Potatoes

1/4 cup chopped onion
1 1/2 teaspoons margarine, melted
3 cups mashed potatoes
1 1/2 cups Tofu Cottage Cheez (page 96)
1 1/2 cups peas
1/8 teaspoon cayenne pepper
3/4 teaspoon sea salt

Sauté the onion in margarine. Combine with rest of ingredients and serve.

Country Corn

Never ordinary!

2 teaspoons nondairy margarine
1/2 cup UnHam Broth (page 156)
1/2 teaspoon salt
6 cups corn
1 1/2 cups finely cubed UnSausage (page 132), any flavor

Melt the margarine and add the broth and salt. Heat through. Add the corn and gluten. Cook for 5 minutes, stirring occasionally.

Country Corn and Okra

Even more so!

2 1/2 teaspoons nondairy margarine
1/2 cup chopped onion
1 1/2 cups finely cubed UnSausage (page 132), any flavor
3 cups corn
3 cups okra
2 cups mashed canned tomatoes
1/2 cup UnHam Broth (page 156)
1/2 teaspoon salt

Melt the margarine and sauté the onion and gluten until the onion is soft. Add the rest of the ingredients, bring to a boil, and cook until the okra is done, stirring occasionally.

Country Corn Creole 1

This has character!

½ cup diced bell pepper
3 tablespoons minced onion
2½ teaspoons nondairy margarine
2½ cups chopped tomato
3 cups sliced okra
1 teaspoon sea salt
½ teaspoon oregano
3 cups corn
⅛ teaspoon cayenne pepper

Sauté the bell pepper and onion in the margarine. Combine with rest of ingredients and cook.

Country Corn Creole 2

1 tablespoon corn oil
2 cups sliced onion
¼ cup minced jalapeños
1½ cups diced bell pepper
2½ cups chopped tomato
3 cups sliced fresh okra
1 teaspoon sea salt
1 teaspoon oregano
½ teaspoon cumin seed
⅛ teaspoon cayenne pepper
3 cups corn

In the oil sauté the onion, jalapeños, and bell pepper until the onion is transparent. Add the rest of the vegetables and seasonings. Add just enough water to not quite cover the vegetables. Cook for 20 minutes over medium-low heat.

VARIATION: *Instead of water, cook with UnBeef Broth (page 155) or UnChicken Broth (page 155).*

Cream-Style Corn

Who can do without it?

1½ teaspoons nondairy margarine
5 cups corn
¼ teaspoon sea salt

Melt the margarine, put in a blender with the corn and salt, and blend, using two or three short spurts to get the corn to begin to break up. Be careful not to liquefy the corn. Heat and serve.

Creamed Carrots

¾ cup chopped onion
½ teaspoon minced garlic
1½ teaspoons nondairy margarine
4 cups cooked and chopped carrot
1 cup Cashew Milk (page 93)
½ teaspoon sea salt

Sauté the onion and garlic in the margarine. Place the carrot and "milk" in a blender and process. Add sautéed onion and salt to the blender and blend until smooth.

Creamed Green Peas

In a way, no big deal, but oh, so good!

3 tablespoons chopped onion
1 teaspoon nondairy margarine
2 cups green peas, cooked
½ teaspoon sea salt
⅔ cup Thin White Sauce (page 262) made with UnChicken Broth (page 155)

Sauté the onion in the margarine, then combine all ingredients and heat.

Creamed Potatoes

3 tablespoons chopped onion
½ teaspoon minced garlic
1 teaspoon nondairy margarine
3 cups boiled, cooled, and diced potatoes
1½ cups Medium White Sauce (page 262)
1½ teaspoons dried parsley
1 cup bread crumbs

Sauté the onion and garlic in the margarine. Combine the onion, potatoes, sauce, and parsley. Put in an oiled baking dish. Cover with bread crumbs, pressing in lightly. Bake at 400°F until the crumbs are brown.

VARIATION: *Add ½ cup of Yeast Cheez (page 97) or Pimiento Cheez (page 94) to the White Sauce and stir in well.*

Creamy Potatoes and Peas

1⁄4 cup chopped onion
1⁄2 teaspoon minced garlic
1 1⁄2 cups peas
1 1⁄2 teaspoons nondairy margarine
1 1⁄4 cup Thick White Sauce (page 262) made with UnChicken Broth (page 155)
Pinch cayenne pepper
1⁄4 teaspoon sea salt
3 cups hot cooked potato slices

Sauté the onion, garlic, and peas in the margarine. Combine the white sauce, pepper, and salt, and cook over low heat, stirring until the sauce is smooth. Combine with the potatoes and peas.

Creole Okra

Heaven on earth.

1⁄2 cup diced bell pepper
1 cup minced onion
2 1⁄2 teaspoons nondairy margarine
4 cups sliced okra
1 teaspoon minced garlic
1⁄8 teaspoon cayenne pepper
4 cups diced tomato
1 tablespoon parsley
1⁄4 teaspoon basil
1⁄4 teaspoon sea salt
3⁄4 cup UnBeef Broth (page 155)
1 cup cooked Tomato Salsa (page 296)

Sauté the bell pepper and onion in the margarine. Combine with rest of ingredients, except the salsa, and cook until the okra is tender. Stir in the salsa.

Creole Tomatoes

1⁄3 cup finely chopped onion
1⁄2 cup finely chopped bell pepper
1⁄8 teaspoon minced garlic
1⁄4 teaspoon minced jalapeños
1 teaspoon nondairy margarine
1 tablespoon chopped fresh parsley
3 cups chopped tomato
1 1⁄2 teaspoons sea salt
1⁄8 teaspoon white pepper
1 tablespoon nondairy margarine
2 tablespoons unbleached white flour
1 cup Cashew Milk (page 93)

Sauté the onion, bell pepper, garlic, and jalapeños in the margarine until the vegetables are soft but not brown. Add the parsley, tomato, salt, and pepper and cook for 10 minutes. In a separate pan melt the tablespoon of margarine and stir in the flour. Stirring constantly with a whisk, pour in the "milk" in a slow, thin stream. Cook over high heat until the sauce comes to a boil, thickens slightly, and is smooth. Reduce heat and simmer for 2 or 3 minutes to remove the raw taste of the flour. Stir into the tomato mixture.

Curried Broccoli

2 cups chopped onion
2⁄3 cup chopped bell pepper
2⁄3 cup chopped celery
1 teaspoon minced garlic
2 1⁄2 teaspoons nondairy margarine
2 tablespoons curry powder
6 cups broccoli, the stems chopped and the tops broken into small flowerets
1 cup UnChicken Broth (page 155)
3⁄4 teaspoon sea salt

Sauté the onion, bell pepper, celery, and garlic in the margarine until the onion is transparent. Add the curry powder and sauté for 30 seconds, stirring constantly. Add the broccoli and stir until all is coated with the hot oil. Add the broth and the salt.

Curried Green Beans

Everybody here calls for more!

2 cups chopped onion
1 1⁄2 teaspoons minced garlic
1⁄4 teaspoon hot pepper flakes
2 teaspoons corn oil
1 1⁄2 teaspoons curry powder
1 1⁄2 cups water
3⁄4 teaspoon sea salt
1 tablespoon lemon juice
6 cups green beans

Sauté onion, garlic, and pepper flakes in the oil until transparent. Add the curry powder and sauté 1 minute more, stirring constantly. Add the water, salt, and lemon juice and stir well. Stir in the beans. Cover and cook.

Curried Peas

Whenever someone feels hungry around here, two times out of three they say, "How about some curried peas?"

1/2 cup chopped onion
1 teaspoon nondairy margarine
1 tablespoon curry powder
1 tablespoon unbleached white flour
3 cups Cashew Milk (page 93)
1/8 teaspoon cayenne pepper
1/2 teaspoon sea salt
3 cups peas (if frozen, thawed; if fresh, lightly steamed)

Sauté the onion in margarine until transparent. Add the curry powder and sauté 30 seconds longer, stirring constantly. Add the flour and stir it in. Slowly add the "milk" as you stir continually. Add the cayenne and salt. Simmer for 10 minutes, stirring occasionally so it will not stick. Add the peas and cook for 5 more minutes. Serve with rice.

Curried Peas, Carrots, and Potatoes

1 cup chopped onion
3/4 teaspoon minced garlic
1 1/2 teaspoons curry powder
1 1/2 teaspoons nondairy margarine
3 cups cooked and cubed potatoes
1 cup peas
1 cup carrot, cooked
1/2 cup boiling water
1/2 cup coconut milk

Sauté the onion, garlic, and curry powder in the margarine until the onion is transparent. Add the potatoes, peas, and carrots and stir until coated with the hot oil. Add the water and cook for 5 minutes. Add the coconut milk and cook for 5 more minutes.

Curried Potatoes and Peas

When I was starving in India nearly thirty years ago, some Kashmiri friends made this for me and watched in awe as I ate their shares as well as mine!

1 1/2 teaspoons nondairy margarine
1/2 teaspoon powdered ginger
1 teaspoon minced garlic
1/3 cup chopped onion (red preferred)
1 teaspoon sea salt
1 teaspoon ground cumin
1/2 teaspoon turmeric
1 teaspoon powdered coriander
1/4 teaspoon Garam Masala (page 303)
1/4 teaspoon cayenne pepper
1 1/2 cups chopped tomato
2 cups green peas
1 1/2 cups potatoes, peeled and cut into 1/2-inch cubes
1/2 cups water

Heat the margarine over high heat until a drop of water flicked into it splutters instantly. Stir in the ginger and garlic. Add the onion and salt. Lower the heat to moderate and, stirring constantly, sauté the onion for 7 or 8 minutes, until it is soft and golden brown. Add cumin, turmeric, coriander, Garam Masala, and cayenne pepper. Stir in the tomato. Still stirring, cook briskly for 5 minutes until most of the liquid in the pan evaporates and the mixture is thick enough to draw away from the sides and bottom of the pan in a dense mass. Drop in the peas and potatoes and turn them about with the spoon until they are evenly coated with the tomato mixture. Stir in the water, bring to a boil over high heat, cover tightly, and reduce the heat to low. Simmer for 10 minutes, or until the peas and potatoes are tender but still intact.

Deep-Fried Okra

If your only acquaintance with okra is from those strange little "wheels" in Campbell's soup, or if you have only had okra cooked until it is mushy, be sure to try this.

5 cups Cashew Milk (page 93)
1 tablespoon Louisiana Hot Sauce

1 tablespoon soy sauce
3 cups corn flour
1 teaspoon garlic powder
1 teaspoon onion powder
1 teaspoon sea salt
8 cups okra, cut into 1/2-inch pieces

Combine the "milk," hot sauce, and soy sauce and set aside. Combine the corn flour, garlic and onion powders, and salt. Dip the okra in the Cashew Milk mixture, remove, and roll it in the corn flour mixture. Deep-fry at 350°F to 365°F until it is brown. Drain on paper towels and serve immediately.

Deep-Fried Squash

This tastes a lot like fried oysters, but is so much nicer to chew.

Dip Mixture
1 cup water
1/2 teaspoon garlic powder
1/2 teaspoon onion powder
1/2 teaspoon cayenne pepper
1 teaspoon sea salt

4 to 6 yellow squash, cut into 1/4-inch slices

Crumb Mixture
2 cups corn flour
1/4 teaspoon sea salt
1/4 teaspoon cayenne pepper

Parmesan Cheez (page 94)

Combine the dip mixture ingredients. Dip the squash in the mixture and then in the crumb mixture. Deep-fry for 1 minute at 350°F. Sprinkle with Parmesan Cheez after frying. Serve immediately.

Dutch Succotash

1/2 cup diced bell pepper
1/3 cup chopped onion
2 1/2 teaspoons nondairy margarine
3 cups cubed and cooked potatoes
2 cups corn, cooked
1 1/2 cups lima beans, cooked
2 1/4 cups chopped tomato
1/4 teaspoon cayenne pepper
1/2 teaspoon basil
1 teaspoon sea salt

Sauté the bell pepper and onion in the margarine. Combine with rest of ingredients and cook.

Eggplant and Tomatoes

4 cups sliced eggplant, 1/8 to 1/4inch thick
1 tablespoon olive oil
1 1/2 cups chopped onion
1 1/2 teaspoons minced jalapeños
1 1/2 teaspoons minced garlic
3 cups chopped tomato
1 1/2 teaspoons sea salt
1/8 teaspoon cayenne pepper

Heavily salt both sides of the eggplant slices. Let sit for 1 hour and wipe off the salt and liquid. Press between absorbent towels, squeezing out as much liquid as possible. Sauté the eggplant in half the oil until it becomes soft. Set aside on paper towels to drain. In the rest of the oil sauté the onion and jalapeños until the onion is soft. Add the garlic and tomato and cook for 2 minutes. Add the eggplant, salt, and cayenne. Cook until most of the liquid is evaporated.

French-Fried Potatoes

These are not particularly healthful, yet sometimes we get a yen for "junk" food, and it is better to make our own not-so-junk versions. This recipe is based on the McDonald's method of making french fries, and although it is somewhat tedious, I think you will find the results worth the extra trouble. The best type of potatoes for french fries is Russet Burbanks from Idaho.

1 quart cold water
1/2 cup white vinegar
4 cups sliced potatoes, 1/4-inch-thick sticks
2 quarts water
1 tablespoon sea salt
Iced water
Corn oil
Onion salt

Combine the quart of cold water and the vinegar. Put the potatoes in this, cover, and refrigerate for 2 hours. Drain in a colander. Bring the 2 quarts of water and salt to a boil. When the water is boiling hard, drop the potatoes into the water and cook for 1 minute. Put into the colander again and drain, and immediately plunge them into ice water. Drain them on paper towels as best you can to remove as much water as possible. Put corn oil in a heavy 2- to 3-quart saucepan to a depth of 4 inches. Using a french-frying basket, fry the potatoes at 400°F for only 1 minute. Remove and turn into a paper towel–lined bowl or basket. Repeat until all the potatoes have been fried, making sure the oil temperature never goes below 375°F and can quickly come back up to 400°F.

Now start all over again and refry the potatoes until they are crisp and golden brown. Sprinkle with onion salt while they are hot and serve before they get cold. If you are frying a good number of potatoes and do not want the first ones to get cold, after salting a batch of fries transfer them to a pan lined with a double thickness of paper towels and put them in a 250°F oven to keep them warm while you proceed with the remaining batches.

Note

Use only long white potatoes. The thicker the skin of the potato, the better the quality for frying.

Fried Green Tomatoes

After seeing the movie, we had to try them ourselves. Firm ripe tomatoes work very well as a variation.

3 tablespoons nondairy margarine
1 tablespoon corn oil
1 tablespoon Sucanat
1 cup unbleached white flour
1 N'egg (page 302)
1/4 cup Cashew Milk (page 93)
4 to 6 medium green tomatoes, sliced 1/2 inch thick
1 cup dried bread crumbs mixed with 1/8 teaspoon garlic powder, 1/4 teaspoon onion powder, 1/4 teaspoon freshly ground black pepper, 1/4 teaspoon powdered basil, and 1/4 teaspoon sea salt

Melt the margarine together with the oil in a skillet. Combine the Sucanat and flour. Combine the N'egg and "milk." Dip the tomato slices into the flour mixture, then into the "milk" mixture, and then into the crumbs. Fry on both sides until brown but firm enough to hold their shape.

To make gravy for these if you wish: Combine the leftover "milk" mixture with the leftover flour and the remaining bread crumbs. Add 1 more cup of Cashew Milk and 1 cup of UnBeef Broth (page 155). Blend together in a blender. Put in a skillet and cook until thickened. Add extra broth if it gets too thick.

Fried Mashed Potato Balls

3 tablespoons cornstarch
1/4 cup cold water
2 cups mashed potatoes, hot
1/4 teaspoon onion powder
1/4 teaspoon garlic powder
1 teaspoon baking powder
1/4 teaspoon sea salt
1/8 teaspoon cayenne pepper
Corn oil

Dissolve the cornstarch in the cold water. Add the other ingredients, except oil, and mix well. Form into balls and fry in the oil until brown. Place them to drain on paper towels in a colander. If needed, keep them hot in a 425°F oven.

Fried Taters 'n' Onions

Just what it is. Yum!

Corn oil
2 cups thinly sliced onion
1 quart sliced potatoes, medium thick
Garlic salt
Pepper (black or cayenne), or curry powder

Heat oil, put in onion and potatoes, and fry, turning regularly, until the potatoes brown. Toward the end of the frying, as you continue to fry, sprinkle with garlic salt and black or cayenne pepper, or garlic salt and curry powder.

Ginger Curry

1 pound firm tofu, frozen, thawed, and pressed
1/2 teaspoon powdered ginger
1 1/2 teaspoons minced garlic
6 tablespoons water
2 tablespoons almond butter or peanut butter
1 tablespoon low-sodium soy sauce
2 teaspoons curry powder
1/4 teaspoon cayenne pepper
1 tablespoon corn oil
1 cup chopped onion
2 cups Cashew Milk (page 93)
3/4 teaspoon sea salt
1/4 teaspoon freshly ground black pepper
2/3 cup peas
1/3 cup almonds, toasted

Cut the tofu into thin strips about 1/4 x 3/4 x 1 1/2 inches and set aside. Put the ginger, garlic, water, nut butter, soy sauce, 1 teaspoon of the curry powder, and the cayenne in a blender and blend. Pour this over the tofu strips. Gently turn and press the tofu until the mixture is absorbed. Heat the oil and sauté the onion until translucent. Add the other teaspoon of curry powder and sauté for about 1 minute. Add the tofu and continue to sauté until the tofu starts to brown. Add the "milk," salt, and pepper. Bring to a simmer and add the peas. Cook until the peas are tender, about 3 minutes. Just before serving stir in the almonds.

Golden Vegetable Layer

2 cups chopped potatoes
2 cups chopped carrot
1 1/2 teaspoons nondairy margarine
1/2 teaspoon sea salt
1/4 teaspoon cayenne pepper
2 cups Tomato Sauce (page 261), cooked down into a thick puree and kept warm

Steam or boil the potatoes and carrot until they are just tender. Mash them coarsely with the margarine, salt, and pepper, without letting them become smooth as in mashed potatoes. Put the mixture into a serving dish, top with the Tomato Sauce, and serve at once.

Greek Green Beans

1 cup onion, chopped or thinly sliced
3/4 teaspoon minced garlic
2 teaspoons corn oil
1/2 teaspoon oregano
3/4 cup diced tomato
1 tablespoon tomato paste
1/2 teaspoon sea salt
1/4 teaspoon freshly ground black pepper
3 cups green beans, trimmed, cut into 2-inch lengths, and cooked

Sauté the onion and garlic in the oil until soft. Combine everything but the beans and simmer 5 minutes. Add the beans and simmer until tender and some of the sauce is absorbed.

Greek Potatoes

Distinctive!

3 tablespoons chopped onion
1 1/2 teaspoons corn oil
1 bay leaf
1/2 teaspoon oregano
1/4 teaspoon thyme
1/2 teaspoon basil
2 tablespoons chopped fresh parsley
1 1/2 cups tomato, fresh or canned
1/2 cup tomato paste
1/2 cup water or UnBeef Broth (page 155)
1/4 teaspoon sea salt
1 teaspoon minced garlic
3 cups chopped potatoes, cut into 1-inch chunks

Sauté the onion in the oil. Put all the ingredients, except for the potatoes, in a pot, stir and simmer for 15 minutes. Place the potatoes in an oiled baking dish or pan. Pour the sauce over the potatoes and toss until well covered. Bake at 375°F until the potatoes test done when pierced with a fork, at least 1 hour. Check the potatoes near the end of the cooking time for moistness—the potatoes should soak up most of the sauce and be rather dry, but not blackened. Add a little water if necessary.

Green Bean, Potato, and Tomato Combo

This is always welcome. Try olive oil as a variation.

3 tablespoons chopped onion
1/2 teaspoon minced garlic
1 1/2 teaspoons corn oil
1 1/4 cups green beans (if fresh, stem and cut them into 1-inch sections)
1 1/4 cups chopped potatoes, cut into 1-inch chunks and cooked
2 1/2 cups pureed tomato (pureed in blender)
1/8 teaspoon basil
1/8 teaspoon oregano
1/8 teaspoon cayenne pepper
3/4 teaspoon sea salt
1/2 cups UnBeef Broth, page 155 (omit if you are using canned tomatoes)

Sauté the onion and garlic in the oil. Combine with rest of ingredients and cook until the beans are done, about 25 minutes. During the cooking time, you may have to add additional water to keep the mixture at a consistency of a thick stew.

Green Bean Succotash

Combine equal parts of cooked corn and finely shredded and cooked green beans. Season with salt, paprika, and nondairy margarine.

Green Beans

String and shred green beans lengthwise. Drop the beans into boiling water into which onion salt (1 1/2 teaspoons per quart) has been added. Cook the beans until they are barely tender, no longer, about 20 minutes. Drain the beans. Return to the pot and reheat them in melted nondairy margarine or Thin White Sauce (page 262) (half as much sauce as there are beans) into which Yeast Cheez (page 97) or Pimiento Cheez (page 94) may be added.

Green Beans and UnHam

1 cup cubed baked UnHam (page 130)
1 1/2 teaspoons olive oil
4 cups green beans
1 1/2 cups chopped onion
3/4 teaspoon chopped garlic
2 1/2 cups water
2 tablespoons Lea and Perrins Steak Sauce
2 teaspoons Louisiana Hot Sauce
1 teaspoon sea salt

In a pot, sauté the UnHam in the oil. Add the beans, onion, garlic, water, steak sauce, hot sauce, and salt. Cook until the beans are tender.

VARIATION: *Use UnBacon (page 136) or UnSausage (page 132) instead of the UnHam.*

Green Beans and Mushrooms

1 cup sliced mushrooms
1/4 cup sliced green onions
2 teaspoons corn oil
2 cups green beans, cut into 2-inch pieces
3/4 cup UnBeef Broth (page 155) or UnChicken Broth (page 155), or water
1/4 teaspoon sea salt
1/8 teaspoon pepper
1/8 teaspoon dried basil

Sauté the mushrooms and onions in the oil a few minutes, add the rest of the ingredients, and cook 10 to 15 minutes until the beans are done.

Green Beans Stir Fry

1 cup green beans, cut into 1-inch pieces
3/4 cup chopped onion
1/2 teaspoon minced garlic
2 teaspoons corn oil
1 cup UnBeef Broth (page 155) or UnChicken Broth (page 155)
1 teaspoon basil
1/4 teaspoon sea salt
1 1/2 cups chopped tomato
1 N'egg (page 302)

Sauté the beans, onion, and garlic in the oil for 1 minute. Add the broth, basil, and salt. Cover and simmer until the beans are tender, about 15 minutes. Add the tomato and N'egg. Cook, stirring constantly, until the mixture boils and thickens.

Green Beans Supreme

3 tablespoons chopped onion
1/2 teaspoon minced garlic
1 1/2 teaspoons nondairy margarine
4 cups green beans
1/2 cup UnBeef Broth (page 155) or UnChicken Broth (page 155)
1/4 teaspoon lemon peel
1/8 teaspoon cayenne pepper
1/8 teaspoon dill
1/4 teaspoon sea salt
1 cup Cashew Sour Kreem (page 94) or Tofu Sour Kreem (page 97)

Sauté the onion and garlic in the margarine. Combine all ingredients, except the Sour Kreem, and cook until beans are cooked but not too soft. Mix in the Sour Kreem.

Green Beans with Green Onion Dressing

1 pound green beans, ends removed
Ice water
1 recipe Green Onion Salad Dressing (page 15)

Cook the beans in plenty of rapidly boiling salted water until tender-crisp. Drain and plunge into ice water to chill. Drain well, wrap in a towel, and refrigerate. When ready to serve, slice at an angle and mix well with the chilled dressing.

Green Beans with Hazelnuts

This is blue-ribbon cuisine!

1/4 cup hazelnuts
2 cups UnChicken Broth (page 155)
3 cups green beans
2 tablespoons olive or corn oil
1 tablespoon balsamic vinegar
1/4 teaspoon sea salt
1/4 teaspoon freshly ground black pepper

Heat the oven to 350°F. Spread the nuts on a baking sheet and toast in the oven for about 8 minutes, until fragrant. Transfer to a kitchen towel and rub them together vigorously to remove most of the skins. Finely chop them and set aside. Bring the broth to a boil, add the beans, and cook until tender, about 6 minutes. Drain. Whisk the oil and vinegar together and pour over the beans and toss with the salt and pepper. Serve sprinkled with the hazelnuts.

Green Beans with UnBacon

1 1/2 teaspoons nondairy margarine
1 1/2 teaspoons corn oil
2 cups chopped onion
1 1/2 teaspoons minced garlic
1/4 teaspoon hot pepper flakes
6 cups green beans
1/3 cup finely chopped UnBacon (page 136)
1 quart UnChicken Broth (page 155) or UnBeef Broth (page 155)

Put the margarine and oil together and melt the margarine. Sauté the onion, garlic, and pepper flakes until the onion is transparent. Add the green beans and stir well until they are coated with the hot oil. Add the UnBacon. Add the broth and cook until the beans are done.

Green Beans with Garlic

2 cups green beans, trimmed and broken in half
2 tablespoons minced garlic
2 teaspoons olive oil
1/2 teaspoon sea salt
1 tablespoon soy sauce

Sauté the beans and garlic for 5 minutes in the oil. Keep heat high to singe the beans. Add the salt and soy sauce. Cover, lower heat, and cook for 5 minutes.

VARIATION: *Use broccoli instead of beans, the broccoli having been pared and sliced into thin sticks.*

Green Beans with Summer Savory

3 cups green beans, cut into 1½-inch pieces
Salted boiling water
2 tablespoons olive or corn oil
1 teaspoon minced garlic
1 tablespoon chopped fresh summer savory
½ teaspoon freshly ground black pepper
¼ teaspoon sea salt

Blanch the beans in salted boiling water for 3 minutes. Drain and run cold water over them. Drain and set aside. Heat the oil in a skillet. Stir in the garlic. Add the beans. Cook, stirring frequently, until the beans are quite tender and the garlic is translucent, 12 to 14 minutes. Stir in the savory, pepper, and salt.

Green Beans with Tomatoes

2 cups chopped onion
1½ cups chopped bell pepper
1½ cups chopped celery
1½ teaspoons minced garlic
¼ teaspoon hot pepper flakes
2 tablespoons olive oil
6 cups green beans
3 cups drained and chopped canned tomatoes, reserving the juice
2 tablespoons soy sauce
Tomato juice as needed

Sauté the onion, bell pepper, celery, garlic, and pepper flakes in the olive oil until the onion is transparent. Add the green beans and stir until they are coated well with the hot oil. Add the tomatoes and soy sauce. Cook until the beans are done, adding tomato juice if it seems to be getting too dry.

Green Lima Beans with Fines Herbes

2½ cups lima beans, cooked in a little UnChicken Broth (page 155) until tender
1 teaspoon nondairy margarine
1 teaspoon lemon juice
3 tablespoons chopped onion
1 tablespoon minced fresh parsley
½ teaspoon Fines Herbes (page 303)
½ teaspoon sea salt

Combine everything and cook together for 5 minutes.

Green Peas and Onions

3 tablespoons chopped onion
1 teaspoon nondairy margarine
2 cups green peas, cooked
⅛ teaspoon garlic powder
½ teaspoon sea salt

Sauté the onion in the margarine, then combine all ingredients and heat.

Hash Brown Waffles

4 cups shredded raw potatoes
2 tablespoons corn oil
3 teaspoons onion powder
½ teaspoon garlic powder
1 teaspoon sea salt
4 teaspoons nutritional yeast
2 tablespoons dried parsley
1 N'egg (page 302)
1 tablespoon unbleached white flour

Combine everything well. Press into a preheated and oiled waffle iron. Close and bake 12 to 15 minutes until browned.

VARIATION: *Use crumbled or chopped cooked potatoes.*

Hominy and Bell Pepper Sauté

1½ tablespoons olive or corn oil
1 cup thinly sliced onion
1 cup diced red bell pepper, cut into ½-inch dice
1 cup diced yellow bell pepper, cut into ½-inch dice
Two 16-ounce cans cooked hominy, drained
¼ cup water
½ teaspoon sea salt
¼ teaspoon freshly ground black pepper

Heat the oil in a saucepan, add the onion and bell peppers. Cover and cook over low heat, stirring, until tender, about 8 minutes. Stir in the hominy and 2 tablespoons of the water, cover, and cook 5 minutes. Stir in the rest of the water, cover, and cook 5 more minutes, or until the hominy is tender. Stir in the salt and pepper.

Jamaica Rice and "Peas"

3 cups chopped onion
1½ teaspoons minced garlic
1 tablespoon corn oil
3 cups red kidney beans, cooked and drained
1 tablespoon sea salt
1 tablespoon lemon juice
1 teaspoon basil
1 teaspoon oregano
2⅓ cups rice, cooked
2 cups UnChicken Broth (page 155)

Sauté the onion and garlic in the oil. Combine all ingredients, turn into a large casserole, and bake at 350°F for 1 hour, adding a little more broth if necessary.

Jamaican Vegetables

Marinade

½ cup diced green onions
1 cup diced onion
2 tablespoons seeded and minced jalapeño peppers
¾ cup low-sodium soy sauce
½ cup balsamic vinegar
¼ cup corn oil
⅓ cup Sucanat
1 teaspoon thyme
½ teaspoon ground cloves
½ teaspoon ground nutmeg
½ teaspoon ground allspice or cinnamon

Vegetables

8 cherry tomatoes, halved
1 bell pepper, seeded and cut into 8 pieces
8 large mushrooms
8 broccoli flowerets
1 onion, cut into 8 pieces

Combine the marinade ingredients in a food processor and process for 15 to 20 seconds at high speed. Pour this over the vegetables in a casserole and refrigerate 3 to 4 hours, occasionally spooning the marinade over the vegetables. Broil.

Kentucky Fried Green Beans

My Kentucky grandmother Burge used to make these in a nonvegetarian version. The memory clung to me through the years until one day I went into the kitchen determined to duplicate them. I did!

4 cups green beans, steamed
2 tablespoons corn oil
¾ cup chopped onion
1 tablespoon finely chopped UnBacon (page 136)
⅛ teaspoon freshly ground black pepper
¼ teaspoon garlic powder
½ teaspoon sea salt (or ½ teaspoon salt and ½ teaspoon monosodium glutamate [MSG])

Sauté the beans in the oil until nearly cooked. Add the rest of the ingredients and sauté until the beans are completely cooked.

Lazy Kitchuri

1 cup rice, uncooked
1 tablespoon corn oil
1 cup chopped onion
1 tablespoon sliced jalapeños
¼ cup curry powder (madrasi style is best)
1¼ teaspoons sea salt
¼ teaspoon garlic powder
1 quart chopped vegetables of choice
2½ cups chopped tomato, fresh or canned (drained well, using juice as part of the water measure)
3 cups boiling water (and tomato juice if canned tomatoes are used)

Wash the rice over and over, changing the water, until there is no more starch in the water, and drain it well. Heat the oil until very hot. Sauté the onion and jalapeños, then add the curry powder, salt, and garlic powder, and stir constantly as it all fries to a rich brown color with a heavenly fragrance. Add the vegetables, tomato, and rice and stir continually until all is covered with the hot oil/spice mixture. Add the boiling water and stir. Bring to a boil, cover, and simmer until all vegetables are done.

VARIATION: *Include 1½ cups of cooked dal, garbanzos, or other beans. Leave out the tomatoes. Include 2 cups of chopped flavored or unflavored gluten, frying the gluten in the spices until it browns before you add the vegetables and rice.*

Lima Beans

1 quart lima beans
Enough boiling UnBeef Broth (page 155) or UnChicken Broth (page 155) to cover beans
1 tablespoon nondairy margarine
1 teaspoon sea salt
1½ tablespoons lemon juice
1 tablespoon chopped fresh parsley

Cover lima beans with boiling UnBeef Broth or UnChicken Broth. Add nondairy margarine. Simmer for 15 minutes. Add sea salt. Cook the beans over a good flame until the water evaporates and add remaining ingredients.

VARIATION: *Instead of the last three ingredients, add ½ cup Cashew Milk (page 93) and heat thoroughly, but do not boil.*

Lima Beans and Tomatoes

¾ cup chopped onion
¼ cup chopped bell pepper
½ teaspoon minced garlic
1½ teaspoons corn oil
2 cups lima beans, dried, cooked, fresh, or frozen and thawed
¼ teaspoon cayenne pepper
2 teaspoons sea salt
1½ cups chopped tomato
¼ cup chopped celery

Sauté the onion, bell pepper, and garlic in the oil. Add the rest of the ingredients and cook gently until all are well done.

Lima Beans in Cheez Sauce

Add to cooked lima beans one-half as much Cheez Sauce (page 257).

Lima Beans in Piquante Sauce

¼ cup chopped onion
¼ cup chopped celery
½ teaspoon minced garlic
2 teaspoons nondairy margarine
2½ tablespoons unbleached white flour
1½ cups UnBeef Broth (page 155) or UnChicken Broth (page 155) made with Cashew Milk (page 93)
½ cups Yeast Cheez (page 97), Pimiento Cheez (page 94), or Notzarella Cheez (page 94)
2½ cups lima beans, cooked and drained
¼ teaspoon sea salt
⅛ teaspoon cayenne pepper
¼ teaspoon dried mustard
⅛ teaspoon basil

Sauté the onion, celery, and garlic in the margarine until the onion is light brown. Stir in the flour until it bubbles. Slowly stir in the broth. Reduce the heat and stir in the Cheez. Add the rest of the ingredients and stir.

Lima Beans with Cheez

More than a touch of class!

⅓ cup chopped onion
½ teaspoon minced garlic
1 teaspoon nondairy margarine
1 cup Yeast Cheez (page 97), Pimiento Cheez (page 94), or Notzarella Cheez (page 94)
4 cups lima beans, cooked
1 teaspoon soy sauce
½ teaspoon sea salt
¼ teaspoon cayenne pepper
Bread crumbs
Nondairy margarine

Sauté the onion and garlic in the margarine. Stir in the Cheez and stir over low heat until it melts. Add the rest of the ingredients except bread crumbs and margarine. Put in a baking dish, cover with bread crumbs, dot with margarine, and bake at 350°F until crumbs are brown, about ½ hour.

Lima-Corn Succotash

The ultimate succotash, I guarantee.

1½ cups chopped onion
½ cup chopped bell pepper
1½ teaspoons minced garlic
¼ teaspoon red pepper flakes
2 teaspoons nondairy margarine
3 cups corn (if fresh, cooked, if frozen, thawed)
3 cups green lima beans, cooked
¾ teaspoon sea salt

Sauté the onion, bell pepper, garlic, and pepper flakes in the margarine until the onion is transparent. Then add the corn, limas, and salt, and cook 5 minutes more.

VARIATION: *Add ½ cup finely chopped UnBacon (page 136), and cut the salt in half.*

Louisiana Corn and Tomatoes

1¼ cups coarsely chopped onion
⅛ teaspoon minced garlic
2 teaspoons corn oil
4 cups corn
½ cup coarsely chopped bell pepper
3 cups coarsely chopped tomato
1½ cups water
½ teaspoon cayenne pepper
1½ teaspoons sea salt

Sauté the onion and garlic in the oil until the onion is soft and translucent but not brown. Stir in the corn, bell pepper, tomato, water, cayenne, and salt. Bring to a boil over high heat. Reduce heat to low, cover partially, and simmer until the corn is tender, about 10 minutes.

Mashed Carrots

A worthy change from mashed potatoes.

Cook carrots, drain, and mash. Add nondairy margarine, salt, and pepper to taste.

Mashed Potatoes 1

Peel potatoes and cut them in large chunks. Boil in salted water until they can be broken apart with a fork but have not started to fall apart. Mash the potatoes with enough potato water to give a good consistency. For each quart of potatoes, mash in ¼ stick of nondairy margarine and ½ teaspoon of salt.

VARIATION: *Use Cashew Milk (page 93) instead of the potato water in the mashing. Use UnBeef Broth (page 155) or UnChicken Broth (page 155) as the mashing liquid. Cook the potatoes in UnBeef Broth or UnChicken Broth.*

Mashed Potatoes 2

2 pounds potatoes, unpeeled, cut into large pieces, cooked until tender, and drained
¼ cup Cashew Kreem (page 93)
½ cup Tofu Yogurt (page 97), made without the water
½ teaspoon sea salt
½ teaspoon paprika
¼ teaspoon white pepper

Put the potatoes through a sieve or ricer. Mash with the rest of the ingredients.

Mediterranean Ragout

Couscous

2 cups medium-grain couscous
3 cups water
1 teaspoon sea salt

Ragout

1½ cups chopped onion
1 tablespoon corn oil
2 cups water
1 cup sliced carrot
1 cup green beans
1 tablespoon minced garlic
1 tablespoon ground coriander
1 tablespoon paprika
2 teaspoons ground cumin
1½ teaspoons freshly ground black pepper
½ teaspoon cayenne pepper
6 tablespoons chopped fresh parsley
1 cup chopped tomato
1 cup chopped zucchini
4 cups chopped spinach
1½ teaspoons sea salt
3 tablespoons lemon juice

Put the couscous in a shallow baking pan. Bring the water and salt to a boil and pour over couscous. Cover the pan with foil and let sit 5 to 10 minutes. Sauté the onion in the oil until soft. Combine everything and cook until done. Serve over the couscous.

Mushroom Stroganoff

2 cups sliced onion
2 teaspoons corn oil
4 cups sliced mushrooms
1 teaspoon paprika
Pinch cayenne pepper
¼ teaspoon lemon zest
1 tablespoon low-sodium soy sauce
½ teaspoon Kitchen Bouquet
1½ teaspoons nutritional yeast
⅛ teaspoon rubbed sage
½ cup water
½ teaspoon sea salt
¼ teaspoon freshly ground black pepper
½ cup Cashew Sour Kreem (page 94) or Tofu Sour Kreem (page 97)
2 tablespoons chopped fresh dill or parsley

Sauté the onion in the oil until soft. Add the mushrooms and sauté 5 more minutes. Stir in the rest of the ingredients except for the Sour Kreem and dill. Simmer for 10 minutes. Take from the heat and let sit for 5 minutes. Stir in the Sour Kreem. Sprinkle with the dill or parsley. Serve with polenta, rice, or noodles.

Mushrooms in Kreem Sauce

Marvelous on toast, biscuits, or rice.

1 cup chopped onion
1½ teaspoons nondairy margarine
6 cups mushrooms, cleaned, stemmed, and sliced (save stems to use later in soup)
¾ teaspoon sea salt
⅛ teaspoon freshly ground black pepper
⅛ teaspoon nutmeg
Pinch paprika
2½ cups Thin White Sauce (page 262)
½ cup chopped fresh dill
½ cup chopped fresh parsley, chopped

Sauté the onion in the margarine until the onion is soft. Add the mushrooms, salt, pepper, nutmeg, paprika, and White Sauce, and cook together for 10 minutes. Add dill and parsley and cook for 2 more minutes.

VARIATION: *Add 1 tablespoon of chopped garlic. Add 1 tablespoon of minced jalapeños.*

Okra and Tomatoes

1 tablespoon olive oil
2 cups cubed UnBacon (page 136)
2 cups finely chopped onion
¾ teaspoon minced garlic
6 cups sliced okra
3 cups diced tomato
1 cup water or tomato juice
2 teaspoons Louisiana Hot Sauce
2 tablespoons Lea and Perrins Steak Sauce
½ teaspoon sea salt

In the oil sauté the UnBacon, onion, and garlic for 10 minutes. Add the okra and tomato. Pour water or juice over all. Add the hot sauce, steak sauce, and salt. Cook until the okra is tender and no longer tastes "green."

Okra with Cumin

Tastes like you are in India.

3 cups okra
1 teaspoon corn oil
1⁄3 cup onion (red preferred), sliced lengthwise into paper-thin slivers
1 teaspoon sea salt
2 teaspoons cumin
1⁄4 teaspoon white pepper

Wash the okra under cold running water. With a small, sharp knife scrape the skin lightly to remove any surface fuzz. Pat dry with paper towels. In a heavy skillet heat the oil over moderate heat until a drop of water flicked into it splutters instantly. Add the onion and salt and stir for 7 to 8 minutes, or until they are golden brown. Add the okra, cumin, and pepper, and continue to sauté, lifting and turning the vegetables constantly, until the okra is tender and most of the liquid in the pan has evaporated (frozen okra will still be somewhat sticky), about 25 minutes.

Oriental Eggplant and Mushrooms in Garlic Sauce

4 cups eggplant, peeled and cut into small cubes
3 cups thickly sliced mushrooms
2 cups coarsely chopped onion
3 tablespoons crushed garlic
1⁄4 teaspoon garlic powder
1 tablespoon olive oil
1 1⁄4 cups canned tomato sauce
4 1⁄2 teaspoons soy sauce or Maggi
4 1⁄2 teaspoons red chili paste with garlic
1⁄4 teaspoon sea salt

Deep-fry the eggplant and set aside. Sauté the mushrooms, onion, garlic, and garlic powder in the oil until soft. Add the rest of the ingredients including the eggplant. Cook until most of the liquid is evaporated, about 15 minutes. Serve with rice.

Oven-Fried Potatoes

These are superb!

2⁄3 cup corn oil
8 cups chopped potatoes, cut into 1-inch chunks
1 1⁄2 teaspoons dill
1 1⁄2 teaspoons oregano
1 1⁄2 teaspoons onion salt

Preheat oven to 450°F. Put the oil in a baking pan. Put the potato chunks in the pan and roll them around to coat them with the oil. Sprinkle generously with dill, oregano, and onion salt. Bake until done, about 1 hour, basting and turning every 10 minutes. Drain in a colander.

VARIATION: *Stir in 1⁄4 cup of finely chopped UnBacon (page 136), after 45 minutes. Use sea salt instead of onion salt with the dill and oregano, and stir in 1 cup of chopped onion after 45 minutes.*

Oven-Roasted Okra

At first this seems simple and bland, but then it reveals itself.

1⁄4 cup olive oil
1⁄2 teaspoon ground cumin
1⁄2 teaspoon oregano, crumbled
1⁄4 teaspoon sea salt
1⁄4 teaspoon white pepper
6 cups small whole okra, rinsed and patted dry

Combine oil and seasonings in a mixing bowl. Add the okra and toss to coat. Place okra in a heavy pan and roast at 500°F, stirring occasionally, until tender and evenly browned, 8 to 10 minutes. May be served with lemon wedges.

Oven UnFries

These nonoil fries are a surprise.

7 cups sliced potatoes, cut into thin "french-fry" strips
1 tablespoon soy sauce
1/4 teaspoon garlic powder
1/2 teaspoon onion powder
1 1/2 teaspoons paprika
3/4 teaspoon sea salt

Combine everything until the potatoes are evenly coated. Spread onto a nonstick baking sheet and bake at 400°F until browned, 35 to 45 minutes, turning once.

Paella-Limas

1 cup green limas, frozen
2 cups rice, uncooked
1 cup thinly sliced carrot
1 cup minced onion
1 teaspoon minced garlic
2 teaspoons corn oil
4 1/2 cups boiling water
1 3/4 teaspoons sea salt

Steam the lima beans and set aside. Sauté the rice, carrot, onion, and garlic in the oil until the vegetables are soft. Spoon into the boiling water, being careful not to get burned when the rice "explodes." (If it does not explode, something is wrong.) Put the rest of the ingredients into the water and boil for 30 minutes. Pour the paella into a casserole, cover and bake at 350°F for 1 hour, uncovering it for the last 5 minutes.

Peas and Carrots

1 1/4 cups chopped onion
1/2 teaspoon minced garlic
1/3 teaspoon hot pepper flakes
1 1/2 teaspoons corn oil
1 1/2 cups peas
1 cup carrot, sliced or diced
2/3 cup UnChicken Broth (page 155)
1/4 teaspoon sea salt
1 tablespoon nutritional yeast
1 tablespoon nondairy margarine
2 cups rice, cooked

Sauté the onion, garlic, and pepper flakes in the oil until onion is transparent. Add the peas and carrot and stir well until coated with the hot oil. Add the broth, salt, yeast, and margarine. Cover and cook. When done, add the rice and mix well.

VARIATION: *Add 1/2 cup of finely chopped UnBacon (page 136).*

Peperonata 1

1 1/2 cups sliced bell pepper, cut in strips
1 cup sliced onion
2 1/2 teaspoons corn oil
4 cups cubed and cooked potatoes
3 cups chopped tomato
1 teaspoon minced garlic
1/3 teaspoon sea salt
1/2 teaspoon basil
1 cup UnBeef Broth (page 155)
1/8 teaspoon cayenne pepper

Sauté the bell pepper and onion in the oil. Combine with rest of ingredients and cook.

Peperonata 2

Simple and heavenly!

Nondairy margarine
4 teaspoons olive oil
6 cups sliced onion, 1/8 inch thick
6 cups sliced bell pepper, cut in 1x1/2-inch strips
3 cups coarsely chopped tomato
1 teaspoon red wine vinegar
1 teaspoon sea salt
1/4 teaspoon white pepper

Melt the margarine in a skillet along with the olive oil. Sauté the onion for 10 minutes, or until it is soft and lightly browned. Stir in the pepper, reduce the heat, cover the skillet, and cook for 10 minutes. Add the tomato, vinegar, salt, and white pepper. Cover and cook for another 10 minutes. Cook the vegetables uncovered over high heat stirring gently, until almost all the liquid has boiled away. May be served hot or cold.

Pizza-Style Vegetables

4 teaspoons nondairy margarine
1 tablespoon olive oil
2⅔ cups sliced zucchini or yellow summer squash, ½-inch-thick slices
1 small onion, cut into ¼-inch-thick slices and separated into rings
¾ teaspoon minced garlic
½ teaspoon Italian seasoning, crushed
2 cups canned stewed tomatoes, undrained
½ cup Notzarella Cheez (page 94)
¼ cup Parmesan Cheez (page 94)

Heat the oil, add the zucchini, onion, garlic, and Italian seasoning, and cook, uncovered, for 5 minutes, stirring occasionally. Carefully add the undrained tomatoes. Cover and cook until the zucchini is crisp-tender, about 3 minutes. Take from the heat and stir in the Cheezes.

Potato Chips 1

These may not be real healthful, but there are times when a little splurge never hurts!

Take Idaho potatoes, slice them paper-thin, and put them directly into salted (1 teaspoon of sea salt per quart) cold water to remove the starch and prevent discoloration. Heat oil to 400°F. When ready to fry, take the potato slices, a batch at a time, drain in a colander, spread them out in a single layer on paper towels, and pat dry thoroughly with more towels. Then fry them in the hot oil, turning with a slotted spoon until crisp and golden brown, 2 or 3 minutes. Remove the chips from the oil, drain them in a colander, then transfer them to paper towels and, turning gently, sprinkle with onion salt.

Repeat until all the chips have been fried, making sure the oil temperature never goes below 375°F and can quickly come back up to 400°F. If you are frying a good number of chips and do not want the first ones to get cold, after salting a batch of chips transfer them to a pan lined with a double thickness of paper towels and put in a 250°F oven to keep warm while you proceed with the remaining batches. To serve, put the chips in a heated bowl.

An easier and better way: I happily recommend to you the Chip Factory made by West Bend. It makes marvelous potato chips automatically. All you do is peel the potatoes, trim them to fit into the machine, and wait for the goodies. The machine slices, fries, and empties the chips down the chute. The chips made by the Chip Factory are superthin and delicious. (Use baking potatoes for best results.) You will discover that they need no salt, no nothing—just the eating! If you put a paper towel on the chip chute any excess oil will be absorbed. Although they are great as they are being made, they are still good the next day or so. The Chip Factory makes a few chips at a time, but if you start making them about an hour before you will want chips, you will find that they add up in time. Get in the chips!

Potato Chips 2

1 tablespoon chili powder
¾ teaspoon sea salt
Pinch cayenne pepper

Combine all ingredients. Make potato chips as above, and sprinkle them with this instead of onion salt, or use onion salt instead of sea salt in this combination.

Potato Curry

½ cup chopped onion
¼ cup chopped bell pepper
½ teaspoon hot pepper flakes
½ teaspoon sea salt
½ teaspoon garlic salt
1½ teaspoons corn oil
1 tablespoon curry powder
4 cups cubed and boiled potatoes

Sauté the onion, pepper, pepper flakes, and salts in the oil. Add the curry powder and sauté for 30 seconds more. Add the potatoes. Simmer 10 minutes.

Potato Pancakes

Although these are good plain, they are outstanding with Cashew Sour Kreem (page 94), or Tofu Sour Kreem (page 97), salsa, Yeast Cheez (page 97), Pimiento Cheez (page 94), or Notzarella Cheez (page 94), Tofu Ricotta Cheez (page 96), or a gravy or sauce from the Gravies and Sauces chapters.

½ cup unbleached white flour
½ teaspoon sea salt
¼ cup Cashew Milk (page 93)
1½ tablespoons nondairy margarine, melted
½ teaspoon dill
⅛ teaspoon cayenne pepper
2 cups chopped potatoes, peeled and put in cold water to prevent discoloration

Stir together the flour, salt, "milk," melted margarine, dill, and pepper. Pat one of the potatoes dry and grate it coarsely into a sieve or colander. Press the grated potato firmly down into the sieve with the back of a large spoon to remove its moisture, then immediately stir the gratings into the flour and Cashew Milk mixture. Repeat this process with each potato until all have been grated and stirred into the Cashew Milk and flour. Heat a heavy skillet that has been lightly oiled. (After this initial oiling, the margarine in the pancake mixture will be sufficient for frying.)

For each pancake drop about ⅓ cup of mixture into the skillet. Let it fry for about a minute until a skin forms on the bottom and turn over and press flat, but not before the skin forms. Cook 3 or 4 pancakes at a time, leaving enough space between them so that they can spread into 3½- to 4-inch cakes. Fry them until they are golden brown and crisp around the edges, about 3 minutes on each side. Transfer the finished pancakes to a heated plate and cover them with foil to keep them warm while the rest are being cooked. Add more margarine whenever you need it.

Potato Pot Pie

⅓ cup chopped onion
1 teaspoon minced garlic
⅓ cup diced and steamed celery
1½ teaspoons corn oil
¼ cup sliced mushrooms
1 tablespoon unbleached white flour
½ cup UnChicken Broth (page 155)
2 cups diced and steamed potatoes
2 cups diced and steamed carrot

Sauté the onion, garlic, and celery in the oil until transparent. Add the mushrooms and sauté 2 to 3 more minutes. Add the flour. Slowly add the broth, letting the mixture cook and thicken. Stir in the potatoes and carrot, and heat through. Serve over biscuits.

Baked Potatoes

These are unparalleled in the baked potato world. I liked baked potatoes before eating these, but now I love them. The boiling enables you to bake them for the shortest time possible so the nutrients will not be destroyed by long baking. I think it markedly affects the flavor and texture, too, making them so good that you need not bother putting anything on them at all for flavoring.

Scrub the potatoes, but do not peel them. Put in water, bring to a boil and simmer lightly for 30 minutes. Take out of the water and bake in a 350°F oven for 30 more minutes.

Boiled Potatoes

6 cups cubed potatoes
6 cups UnBeef Broth (page 155) or UnChicken Broth (page 155)
½ cup chopped onion
1 teaspoon minced or sliced garlic
1 teaspoon minced or sliced jalapeño peppers
2 tablespoons nondairy margarine
½ teaspoon sea salt

Boil the potatoes in the broth and drain them, reserving the broth. Sauté the onion, garlic, and jalapeños in the margarine. Add this and the salt to the drained potatoes, plus 1 cup of the broth.

Potatoes and Green Onions

4 cups cubed potatoes, peeled and cut into 1-inch cubes
1½ teaspoons sea salt

2 tablespoons nondairy margarine
2 tablespoons finely chopped green onions
¾ teaspoon minced garlic
⅓ cup minced chives
¼ teaspoon freshly ground black pepper

In a saucepan, combine the potatoes and 1 teaspoon of the salt. Add enough water to cover the potatoes with 2 inches of water. Bring to a boil and cook until just tender, about 12 minutes. Drain in a colander. Heat the margarine in the saucepan, add the onions and garlic, and sauté until the onions are thoroughly softened but not browned. Increase the heat, add the potatoes, and toss them to coat well. Add the chives, pepper, and remaining ½ teaspoon of the salt. Cook, stirring occasionally, until heated through, about 5 minutes.

Potatoes and Greens

½ cup diced onion
2 teaspoons minced garlic
2 teaspoons hot pepper flakes
2 teaspoons corn oil
2 cups chopped potatoes, cut into 1-inch chunks and boiled
½ cup green beans, cooked
1½ cups diced tomato, or chopped canned tomatoes
½ cup tomato juice
¾ teaspoon sea salt
4 cups greens (one type or assorted)

Saute the onion, garlic, and pepper flakes in the oil until the onion is soft. Combine everything but the greens and cook until the vegetables are tender. Add the greens and cook until wilted.

Potatoes in Broth

4 large potatoes, peeled and cut in pieces
⅓ cup minced onion
3 cups UnBeef Broth (page 155) or UnChicken Broth (page 155)
1 tablespoon nondairy margarine
1 tablespoon flour
½ teaspoon sea salt
¼ teaspoon cayenne pepper

Simmer the potatoes with the onions in the broth until nearly tender. Drain, reserving the liquid, and set aside. Make a sauce of the liquid with the margarine and flour. Add seasonings. Combine potatoes and the sauce and simmer until tender.

VARIATION: *Add chopped chives to the sauce when it is finished.*

Potatoes in Their Own Gravy

5 cups diced potatoes
2½ cups flavoring broth of choice (page 155)
¼ teaspoon sea salt
½ cup chopped onion
½ cup sliced mushrooms
1½ teaspoons nondairy margarine
2 tablespoons unbleached white flour
1½ teaspoons nutritional yeast
½ teaspoon garlic powder
2 teaspoons soy sauce
⅛ teaspoon freshly ground black pepper

Cook the potatoes in the broth and salt until they are tender and drain them, retaining the liquid. Sauté the onion and mushrooms in the margarine until the onion is transparent. Stir in the flour, yeast, and garlic powder. Whisk in the potato liquid until all is smooth. Add the soy sauce and pepper and cook until thickened. Combine with the potatoes and serve.

Potatoes O'Brien

½ cup chopped bell pepper
1 teaspoon minced garlic
¾ cup chopped onion
1½ teaspoons nondairy margarine, plus more to dot casserole
1 tablespoon unbleached white flour
1 cup Cashew Milk (page 93)
½ teaspoon sea salt
¼ teaspoon cayenne pepper
¾ cup Yeast Cheez (page 97) or Pimiento Cheez (page 94)
4 cups boiled, chilled, and diced potatoes
Bread crumbs

Sauté the bell pepper, garlic, and onion in the margarine. Blend in the flour. Add the "milk" and bring to a boil. Add the salt, pepper, and Cheez. Add the potatoes. Place in an oiled baking dish. Cover with bread crumbs. Dot with nondairy margarine. Bake at 350°F until the crumbs are brown, about 15 minutes.

Potatoes Paprika

1 cup chopped onion
¾ teaspoon minced garlic
1½ teaspoons corn oil
1 tablespoon paprika
3 medium-size potatoes, peeled and cut into "french fries" 2 inches long
1½ teaspoons sea salt
2 cups water
½ cup bell pepper, cut in strips
1¼ cups chopped tomato

Sauté the onion and garlic in the oil until the onion is transparent. Stir in the paprika, add the potatoes and salt, and cook for a few seconds, stirring. Add the water, cover, and simmer for 10 minutes. Add the pepper strips and tomato. Cover and simmer until the potatoes are just tender, 10 to 15 minutes.

Quick Saucy Vegetables

4 cups raw or frozen vegetables, cooked
2 cups UnBeef Broth (page 155) or UnChicken Broth (page 155)
3 tablespoons minced onion
1 teaspoon minced garlic
1 teaspoon nondairy margarine
¼ teaspoon basil (if using UnBeef Broth)
¼ teaspoon dill (if using UnChicken Broth)
¼ teaspoon cayenne pepper
2 tablespoons cornstarch or arrowroot
¼ cup water

Cook the vegetables in the broth until tender, about 15 minutes, and drain. Sauté the onion and garlic in the margarine. Add the vegetables. Add the seasonings. Mix the cornstarch or arrowroot in the water and add to the vegetable mixture while stirring. Cook and stir until thickened. Serve over grains or pasta.

Quick Sauerkraut

I have a suspicion that this is a lot better for us than the canned stuff.

2 cups coarsely shredded cabbage
⅓ cup wine vinegar
1 teaspoon sea salt
2 cups plus 1 tablespoon water
1½ teaspoons unbleached white flour

Combine the cabbage, vinegar, salt, and 2 cups of water in a 2-quart pot. Bring to a boil and cook, partially covered, for 20 minutes. Mix the flour into a paste with 1 tablespoon of water. Stir into the hot cabbage and cook, stirring constantly, until thickened.

Ratatouille

Better than just good!

1 small eggplant, peeled and cubed
1 tablespoon olive oil
1½ cups cubed Italian tomato
¾ cup chopped zucchini
½ cup chopped bell pepper
⅔ cup chopped onion
2½ teaspoons minced garlic
½ teaspoon sea salt
⅛ teaspoon cayenne pepper

Sauté the eggplant in the oil until it is soft, then add all the ingredients, and cook on low heat for 10 to 20 minutes.

Red Cabbage 1

1 tablespoon nondairy margarine
3 tablespoons chopped onion
6 tablespoons Barbados molasses
3 tablespoons wine vinegar
¼ teaspoon sea salt
12 cups shredded red cabbage

Melt the margarine and sauté the onion lightly. Add the molasses, vinegar, and salt. Add the cabbage and cook for 25 minutes, stirring frequently.

Red Cabbage 2

10 cups shredded red cabbage
1 teaspoon caraway seeds
5 tablespoons lemon juice
2 tablespoons balsamic vinegar
4 tablespoons corn oil
3 tablespoons Sucanat
½ cup finely chopped onion
2 tablespoons apple juice
1 cup grated apple (Granny Smith is best because of its tartness)
1½ teaspoons sea salt

In a large bowl, combine the cabbage, caraway seeds, 3 tablespoons of the lemon juice, and vinegar. Marinate overnight, or at least 10 hours, in the refrigerator. Put the oil and Sucanat in a heavy saucepan on the stove, turn the heat to medium, and cook, stirring, until the Sucanat dissolves. Add the onion and stir it in. Add the cabbage and marinating liquid, apple juice, lemon juice, and apple. Stir and season with the salt. Lower the heat, cover, and simmer for one hour, stirring occasionally.

Roasted Eggplant, Onion, and Garlic in Tomato Sauce

1 pound eggplant, cut in ¾-inch slices
3 cups sliced onion (yellow preferred), ½ inch thick
Olive oil
6 garlic cloves, peeled
1 cup finely diced onion
2 teaspoons minced garlic
2 tablespoons basil
1 tablespoon oregano
1½ teaspoons cumin
¼ teaspoon thyme
1 bay leaf
4½ cups chopped canned tomato
¼ teaspoon sea salt
¼ teaspoon cayenne pepper

Salt the eggplant slices and let them sit 30 minutes. Brush the eggplant and onion slices with olive oil. Put them on separate baking sheets. Toss the garlic cloves in enough olive oil to coat them, put them in a baking dish, and cover with foil. Bake everything at 375°F. The garlic should be done when tender and slightly brown, 20 to 30 minutes. Allow the eggplant and onion to get brown as well, 25 to 40 minutes. Meanwhile, sauté the diced onion in olive oil with a pinch of salt. Add the minced garlic and the herbs, and stir together. Add the tomato, salt, and cayenne. Simmer for 45 to 60 minutes. When the vegetables are roasted, cube the eggplant and onion and add to the sauce along with the whole cloves of roasted garlic. Stir the sauce and adjust the seasonings if necessary.

Note

If you have any of this left over, cook up some lasagna noodles and use this for a filling. Great!

Roasted Potatoes and Onions

3 cups potatoes, peeled and cut into chunks
3 cups chopped onion (red preferred)
½ cup olive oil
3 tablespoons cider vinegar
⅛ teaspoon dried thyme
1 tablespoon minced garlic
1½ teaspoons sea salt
¾ teaspoon freshly ground black pepper

Combine everything and mix well. Put on a baking sheet and bake at 450°F, turning occasionally, until the potatoes are soft and brown on the edges. Put in a colander and drain the excess oil.

Sautéed Eggplant in Tomato Sauce with Basil

2 pounds eggplant
1 tablespoon plus 1 teaspoon sea salt
¼ cup corn oil
¼ teaspoon freshly ground black pepper
1 tablespoon minced garlic
1¼ cups crushed tomato
¼ cup fresh basil, shredded

Cut off the stem and bottom end of the eggplants. Cut them crosswise into 3/4-inch slices, then cut the slices into 3/4-inch strips. Put them into a colander, sprinkle with the tablespoon of salt, and toss. Set the colander over a bowl or in the sink and let it stand for at least 1 1/2 hours (2 to 3 hours is better), stirring a couple of times. Rinse the eggplant under cold, running water, rubbing the strips lightly in your hands. Shake the colander to drain.

Put the strips 1 inch apart on a triple thickness of paper towels. Cover with another triple layer of towels. With your palms press each eggplant strip very firmly until it looks green and translucent and feels firm and leathery when pressed between your fingertips. Repeat the pressing on fresh toweling if the eggplant has not yet reached this stage. Repeat with the rest of the eggplant strips. (After this step you can refrigerate the eggplant up to 3 hours before cooking.)

Heat the oil in a skillet. Add the eggplant strips and cook, stirring occasionally, until the eggplant is fully tender. Stir in the salt, pepper, and garlic. Cook 1 more minute. Stir in the tomato and basil and simmer until they thicken slightly.

Sautéed Spinach

1 pound fresh spinach
2 tablespoons olive oil
1/3 cup finely chopped onion
1/8 teaspoon ground sage
1/2 teaspoon sea salt

Wash the spinach and pat dry with paper towels. Trim off and discard the stems. In a heavy saucepan, heat the oil and sauté the onion, stirring frequently, until soft and transparent, but not brown, about 5 minutes. Add the spinach, sage, and salt and, stirring, turning the leaves about constantly, cook over moderate heat for 2 minutes or until tender.

Sautéed Vegetables

2 tablespoons corn oil
6 cups sliced vegetables of your choice
1 1/2 cups chopped onion
1 teaspoon minced garlic
1/4 teaspoon cayenne pepper
1/3 cup soy sauce

Heat the oil in a pan or skillet, add the rest of the ingredients, stir, and cook.

Scalloped Cabbage

4 cups cabbage, chopped, cooked, and drained
2 tablespoons chopped bell pepper
2 tablespoons chopped pimiento
1 cup Yeast Cheez (page 97) or Pimiento Cheez (page 94)
1 1/2 cups Medium White Sauce (page 262)
1 cup bread crumbs, tossed in 2 tablespoons of melted nondairy margarine

Place the cabbage in an oiled baking dish. Sprinkle the bell pepper and pimiento over the cabbage. Spread the Cheez over that. Cover with the White Sauce. Top with the bread crumbs. Bake at 365°F until the crumbs are browned, about 40 minutes.

Slumgullian

This is real down-home food, and I have adored it since the first time I ate it as a child!

1/3 cup chopped onion
2 teaspoons minced garlic
1/2 cup chopped bell pepper
1/8 teaspoon cayenne pepper
1 teaspoon nondairy margarine
1 1/2 cups drained and chopped canned tomatoes
1 cup UnBeef Broth (page 155)
1 1/2 cups corn

Sauté the onion, garlic, bell pepper, and cayenne in the margarine. Add the tomatoes and broth and continue to cook until the tomatoes break up. Add the corn and cook 5 minutes more.

VARIATION: *Use water instead of broth, and add 1/2 teaspoon of sea salt.*

Spanish Vegetables

Tomato Sauce

½ teaspoon minced garlic
1 teaspoon corn oil
2 cups chopped tomato
¼ teaspoon Sucanat
1 teaspoon sea salt

Peppers and Onions

½ cup chopped bell pepper
¾ cup chopped onion
1½ teaspoons corn oil

Vegetables

1 teaspoon corn oil
1 cup chopped or sliced vegetables of your choice
⅛ teaspoon cayenne pepper

For the tomato sauce, sauté the garlic in the oil until it browns. Add the rest of the ingredients, cook until done, and set aside. Sauté the bell pepper and onion in the corn oil until tender. Add to the tomato sauce. Sauté the vegetables and pepper until all are tender. Add to the tomato sauce. Stir well.

Spinach au Gratin

Put a thin layer of cooked and drained spinach in a baking dish. Cover it with a layer of Yeast Cheez (page 97), Pimiento Cheez (page 94), or Notzarella Cheez (page 94). Season with pepper and salt. Pour 3 tablespoons of Cashew Milk (page 93) over it. Broil until the Cheez is spotted brown.

Spinach, Tomatoes, and Rice

I adapted this Greek dish, which is a real staple. In my much younger days I used to cook up a huge pot of this and feast on it the rest of the week. It was never boring!

1 tablespoon olive oil
2 tablespoons corn oil
1½ cups chopped onion
1 tablespoon minced garlic
⅓ cup chopped bell pepper
2 cups spinach
4 cups chopped tomato
2 cups rice, uncooked
4 cups water
¾ cup tomato paste
2 teaspoons sea salt

Combine the oils in a pan and sauté the onion, garlic, and bell pepper. Add the remaining ingredients and simmer until cooked and of the proper consistency.

Spinach with Tomatoes

¼ cup chopped onion
1½ teaspoons minced garlic
1½ teaspoons corn oil
4 cups spinach, cooked, drained, and chopped or pureed
1 cup tomato paste or puree
½ teaspoon sea salt
¼ teaspoon cayenne pepper

Sauté the onion and garlic in the corn oil. Add the rest of the ingredients and mix.

Squash au Gratin

1½ teaspoons nondairy margarine
4 cups thinly sliced squash
¼ cup chopped onion
1 teaspoon sea salt
⅛ teaspoon cayenne pepper
1 cup sliced tomato
¼ cup Yeast Cheez (page 97) or Pimiento Cheez (page 94)

Melt the margarine. Add the squash, onion, salt, pepper, and tomato. Cover and cook for 15 minutes or until tender, stirring occasionally. Add the Cheez and heat through. Serve with rice.

Squash, Beans, and Corn

Just plain goodness!

3 cups cubed squash
1 cup chopped onion
3/4 teaspoon minced garlic
2 jalapeño peppers, minced
2 1/2 cups chopped tomato, or 1/2 cup chopped canned tomatoes
2 cups lima beans, fresh or frozen
2 cups green beans, sliced
2 1/2 teaspoons corn oil
1 cup water
3 cups corn
1 teaspoon sea salt
1/4 teaspoon freshly ground black pepper

Sauté the squash, onion, garlic, jalapeños, tomatoes, and beans in the oil until the onion is transparent. Add the water and simmer until the beans are done, stirring frequently. Add the corn, salt, and pepper, and cook 10 minutes more.

Squash, Green Beans, and Tomatoes

1/3 cup chopped onion
1 teaspoon minced garlic
1 1/2 teaspoons nondairy margarine
2 cups sliced and chopped squash
2 cups green beans
2 cups pureed tomato
1/2 teaspoon sea salt
Pinch cayenne pepper
1/4 teaspoon basil
1/4 teaspoon savory
1 cup UnBeef Broth (page 155)

Sauté the onion and garlic in the margarine. Combine with rest of ingredients and cook.

Squash and Peas

3 cups sliced and chopped squash
3 cups peas
1 1/2 teaspoons nondairy margarine
1/4 teaspoon sea salt
3 tablespoons minced onion
1/2 teaspoon minced garlic
Pinch cayenne pepper
1/4 teaspoon basil
1 cup UnChicken Broth (page 155)

Cook over medium heat until the squash is done.

Squash, Mushroom, and Pasta Pie

1 tablespoon nondairy margarine
3 tablespoons unbleached white flour
2 tablespoons minced onion
4 cups sliced mushrooms
1 1/2 teaspoons minced garlic
2 cups Cashew Milk (page 93)
1/2 teaspoon sea salt
1/4 teaspoon freshly ground black pepper
2 tablespoons UnHam Broth (page 156)
1 3/4 cups cubed UnHam (page 130), in 1/2-inch cubes
1/4 cup minced fresh parsley
1/4 teaspoon thyme
1/2 teaspoon basil
1/2 teaspoon dried mint leaves
4 cups sliced or chopped squash
10 ounces spinach pasta
2 cups Notzarella Cheez (page 94)
1 Basic Pie Crust recipe for 2 crusts (page 328)
Corn oil

In a heavy saucepan melt the margarine, add the flour, and cook, whisking, for 3 minutes. Add the onion, mushrooms, and garlic and cook until they are soft. Add the "milk" and bring to a boil, whisking, and simmer it, still whisking, until it is of the consistency of a sauce, about 5 minutes. Add the salt, pepper, broth, UnHam, parsley, thyme, basil, and mint. Cook for 5 more minutes, adding more broth if it becomes too dry.

Cut the squash lengthwise into 1/4-inch-thick slices. Deep-fry the squash at 380°F until golden, transferring the fried slices to paper towels to drain. Cook the spinach pasta according to the package instructions, drain it in a colander, and briefly rinse it with cold water. Combine the mushroom sauce, squash, and Cheez, and mix well. Put half of this into the unbaked pie shell.

Cover with all the pasta. Put the rest of the sauce-filling on top of the pasta. Put on the top crust and seal it all around. Mist the dough with oil and prick the top crust several times with a fork. Bake at 425°F until the top is golden, 20 to 30 minutes.

Squash with Tomatoes

¾ cup chopped bell pepper
¼ cup chopped onion
1 teaspoon minced garlic
1½ teaspoons corn oil
3 cups chopped squash, cut in half lengthwise and then cut into 1-inch chunks
⅛ teaspoon cayenne pepper
3 cups chopped tomato
4½ teaspoons soy sauce
¼ teaspoon basil
¼ teaspoon sea salt

Sauté the bell pepper, onion, and garlic in the oil. Combine with rest of ingredients and cook.

Stewed Squash

½ cup cubed UnHam (page 130), cut in ½-inch cubes
1 tablespoon corn oil
8 cups chopped squash
2 teaspoons Louisiana Hot Sauce
3 cups coarsely chopped onion
2 cups UnChicken Broth (page 155)
1 cup water
2 teaspoons minced garlic

Sauté the UnHam in the oil, but do not brown. Put in everything else, and bring to a vigorous boil. Lower the heat and simmer slowly until the squash is well cooked.

Super Okra

1 cup thinly sliced onion
1½ teaspoons corn oil
2½ teaspoons minced garlic
¼ teaspoon powdered ginger
1 teaspoon minced jalapeños
¼ teaspoon turmeric
2 tablespoons ground almonds
1 cup chopped tomato
10 okra "fingers" cut into ¾-inch-thick rounds
¼ teaspoon sea salt
1 tablespoon chopped fresh parsley

Sauté the onion in the oil until it turns reddish brown, 10 to 12 minutes. Stir in the garlic, ginger, jalapeños, turmeric, and almonds. Add the tomato and cook for 1 minute. Add the okra, mix well, and simmer, covered, until the okra is barely tender, 6 to 7 minutes. Stir in the salt. Sprinkle with the parsley just before serving.

Sweet-and-Sour Cabbage

As a cooked-cabbage hater, I recommend this wholeheartedly. It is simply delicious and demands seconds.

¼ cup thinly sliced onion
1 tablespoon olive oil
8 cups chopped cabbage, cut into ¼-inch strips
2 cups coarsely chopped Italian tomato
2 tablespoons wine vinegar
1½ teaspoons sea salt
¼ teaspoon cayenne pepper
1 tablespoon Sucanat

Sauté the onion in the oil for 2 or 3 minutes until it is transparent but not brown. Stir in the cabbage, tomato, vinegar, salt, and pepper. Simmer uncovered, stirring frequently, until the cabbage is tender, about 20 minutes. Stir the Sucanat into the cabbage and cook 1 or 2 minutes more.

Szechwan Braised Eggplant

This is the breath of the dragon!

4 teaspoons corn oil
4 cups eggplant, peeled and chopped into bite-size pieces
3 teaspoons minced garlic
¼ teaspoon powdered ginger
⅔ cup minced green onions
2 tablespoons chili paste with garlic (from an Asian grocery store)
⅓ cup UnChicken Broth (page 155)
2 tablespoons soy sauce
½ teaspoon Sucanat
1 teaspoon red wine vinegar

Heat the oil to very hot and sauté the eggplant, coating thoroughly with the oil. Add the garlic, ginger, and onions, and stir in well. Add all the rest of the ingredients, mix well, and cook for 3 minutes, stirring occasionally. Cover and let simmer until tender, 10 to 15 minutes.

Thai-Style Vegetables

This is not for the faint-hearted. It was cooked for me by two friends from Thailand. I ate it up and demanded more. So they made me more. I ate that and demanded even more. So they gave me this recipe, and I went into their kitchen and made more!

1/4 cup sliced garlic
1/3 cup sliced jalapeño peppers
2 teaspoons corn oil
1/3 cup soy sauce
6 cups thinly sliced vegetables of your choice
2 cups sliced onion

Sauté the garlic and jalapeños in the oil, but do not let the garlic brown. Add the soy sauce and vegetables and cook.

> **Note**
> Frying the jalapeños takes away some of the "bite." So for their full effect, do not sauté them, but add them along with the rest of the vegetables.

Tomatoes and Okra

3/4 cup finely chopped onion
2 teaspoons nondairy margarine
1 1/2 teaspoons minced garlic
4 cups sliced okra
2 1/2 cups chopped canned tomatoes
1 1/4 teaspoons sea salt
1/4 teaspoon cayenne pepper

Sauté the onion in the margarine until brown. Add and sauté the garlic and okra for 5 minutes. Add the rest of the ingredients and simmer, covered, until the okra is tender.

VARIATION: *Add 1/2 cup of chopped bell pepper and/or 2 cups of corn.*

Tomatoes and Vegetables

1 cup chopped bell pepper
3 tablespoons chopped onion
2 teaspoons nondairy margarine
4 cups chopped tomato
2 cups vegetables of your choice, chopped if need be
1/4 teaspoon cayenne pepper
1 teaspoon sea salt
1/3 teaspoon basil
1/3 teaspoon oregano

Sauté the bell pepper and onion in the margarine. Combine with rest of ingredients and cook.

Tomatoes, Corn, and Cheez

1/2 cup chopped bell pepper
1/3 cup chopped onion
1 teaspoon nondairy margarine
1 cup chopped canned tomatoes
2/3 cup corn
1/8 teaspoon cayenne pepper
1/2 teaspoon sea salt
1 1/3 cups Yeast Cheez (page 97), Pimiento Cheez (page 94), or Notzarella Cheez (page 94)

Sauté the bell pepper and onion in the margarine until they are browned. In a pan, heat the tomatoes and corn. Add the sautéed vegetables and the rest of the ingredients except the Cheez. Cook for 7 minutes, stirring frequently. Add the Cheez, stir in well, and heat through.

Tomatoes Creole

Perfect on rice.

1 cup chopped bell pepper
1½ cups chopped onion
2 teaspoons nondairy margarine
3 cups chopped canned tomatoes, or 4 large tomatoes, sliced
¾ teaspoon sea salt
¼ teaspoon cayenne pepper
2 tablespoons Barbados molasses

Sauté the bell pepper and onion in the margarine. Add the remaining ingredients and cook until all is tender.

Vegetable Curry

½ cup chopped onion
1¼ cups chopped UnBeef (page 109), UnChicken (page 137), or unflavored gluten
1 teaspoon curry powder
2 teaspoons corn oil
2½ cups Cashew Milk (page 93)
½ cup coconut milk
1 tablespoon cornstarch
¼ cup water
1⅓ cups diced potatoes
1½ cups diced carrot
⅔ cup green beans or green peas
1 teaspoon sea salt

Sauté the onion, gluten, and curry powder in the oil until the onion is soft and the gluten is browned. Add the Cashew Milk and coconut milk. Dissolve the cornstarch in the water and add to the sauce. Cook until slightly thickened. Cook the vegetables in water with the salt until tender. Drain them and add to the curry sauce. Serve over rice.

Vegetable Pie

2 cups peeled and thinly sliced potatoes
2 cups thinly sliced carrot
2½ cups coarsely chopped broccoli
3 tablespoons nondairy margarine
¼ teaspoon freshly ground black pepper
3 tablespoons unbleached white flour
1½ teaspoons sea salt
1¾ cups Cashew Milk (page 93)
1 cup Notzarella Cheez (page 94)
2 recipes Convent Pie Crust (page 328), divided into a top and bottom crust, the bottom put into a casserole dish or deep baking dish (not a pie pan or dish)

Cook the potatoes in boiling salted water until tender. Remove with a slotted spoon to a bowl. In the same water that you cooked the potatoes, heat the carrot to boiling, reduce heat, cover, and simmer for 10 minutes or until it is tender. Remove it with a slotted spoon to its own bowl. In the same water heat the broccoli to boiling, reduce heat, and simmer for 5 minutes, or until tender. Drain. In a saucepan melt the margarine, and stir in the pepper, flour, and salt until blended. Cook 1 minute. Gradually stir in the "milk." Cook, stirring constantly, until the mixture boils and thickens. Reduce heat to low and stir in the Cheez well. Remove from heat.

Spoon the potatoes into the unbaked crust. Spoon ⅓ of the Cheez sauce over that. Spread the carrot over all. Spoon ½ of the remaining sauce over the carrot. Top with the broccoli, then the rest of the sauce. Top with the crust and cut slits in the top for steam to escape. Bake at 425°F until the filling is bubbly and the crust is golden, 35 to 40 minutes.

Vegetable Pot Pie

1½ cups chopped onion
2 teaspoons corn oil
⅔ cup diced carrot
1¼ cups diced potatoes
½ teaspoon paprika
½ teaspoon basil
½ teaspoon marjoram
½ cup diced bell pepper
1 cup sliced mushrooms
½ cup peas
½ cup corn
1 teaspoon sea salt
½ teaspoon freshly ground black pepper
2 tablespoons nondairy margarine
2 tablespoons unbleached white flour
1 cup Cashew Milk (page 93)
1 teaspoon Dijon-style mustard
¼ teaspoon nutmeg
1 recipe Convent Pie Crust (page 328)

Sauté the onion in the oil until soft. Add the carrot, potatoes, paprika, basil, and marjoram. Cook, covered, on medium heat, stirring frequently, for about 10 minutes. Stir in the bell pepper, mushrooms, peas, corn, salt, and pepper. Cover and cook until the carrot is tender, 5 to 10 minutes. In a saucepan melt the margarine, add the flour, and stir constantly over low heat for 3 to 5 minutes. Whisk in the "milk," mustard, and nutmeg. Continue to stir over low heat until hot and slightly thickened, but do not boil. Remove from heat. If there is liquid in the sautéed vegetables, drain it off. Add the sauce, and combine well. Put the vegetables into the unbaked pie shell. Cover with the top crust and cut slits for steam to escape. Bake at 375°F for 40 minutes.

Yellow Squash Creole

1 cup chopped onion
1½ teaspoons minced garlic
¼ teaspoon hot pepper flakes
1½ teaspoons corn oil
3 cups sliced yellow squash
1 cup Creole Sauce (page 258)
½ cup water

Sauté the onion, garlic, and pepper flakes in the oil until onion is transparent. Add the squash and stir well until all is coated with the hot oil. Stir in the Creole Sauce and water. Cover and cook until the squash is tender.

Zucchini Plain

1 teaspoon nondairy margarine
1 teaspoon olive oil
2 cups coarsely chopped onion
1 teaspoon minced garlic
¼ teaspoon hot pepper flakes
¾ cup chopped celery
3 cups zucchini, cut in half lengthwise and then cut into 1-inch chunks
¾ cup chopped bell pepper
1½ cups UnChicken Broth (page 155)
¼ teaspoon sea salt

Melt the margarine in the olive oil. Sauté the onion, garlic, pepper flakes, and celery until transparent. Add the zucchini and bell pepper and sauté briefly. Then add the broth and salt and stir well. Cover and cook until tender, but do not overcook.

VARIATION: *Use other kinds of squash.*

Zucchini Supreme

Sauce

1 tablespoon cornstarch
1 cup cold Cashew Milk (page 93)
1 teaspoon nondairy margarine
¼ teaspoon sea salt
⅛ teaspoon freshly ground black pepper
4 teaspoons lemon juice
3 tablespoons fresh dill, or 1 teaspoon dried
1 tablespoon chopped fresh parsley

Vegetables

3 cups sliced zucchini, cut into 3-inch strips
1½ cups sliced onion
2 teaspoons corn oil

Bring the cornstarch, "milk," margarine, salt, and pepper to a boil, stirring constantly. Boil for 1 minute. Mix with the rest of the sauce ingredients. Sauté the zucchini and onion in the oil until tender-crisp. Toss with the sauce.

Zucchini with Mustard-Dill Sauce

4 cups Cashew Milk (page 93) or Cashew Kreem (page 93)
1/4 teaspoon cayenne pepper
1/2 cup unbleached white flour
Pinch plus 1/2 teaspoon sea salt
Pinch plus 1/2 teaspoon freshly ground black pepper
Corn oil
3 whole zucchini, ends cut off, and sliced lengthwise into 1/4-inch to 1/2-inch-thick slices
1/2 cup diced onion
2 cups water
1/4 cup plus 1 tablespoon chopped fresh dill
2 tablespoons grainy mustard
2 tablespoons Dijon-style mustard

Combine the "milk" and cayenne, and set aside. Mix together the flour, pinch of salt, and pepper, and set aside. Heat some corn oil in a large skillet. Dip the zucchini slices in the "milk"-cayenne mixture and dredge them in the flour, shaking off any excess. Brown the zucchini on both sides. Add the rest of the ingredients except the tablespoon of dill, and bring to a boil. Reduce heat, and simmer, covered, until thickened, about 20 minutes. Remove from heat and add tablespoon of dill.

Zucchini with Tomatoes

2 cups coarsely chopped onion
1/2 teaspoon minced garlic
1/2 teaspoon minced jalapeños, or 1/2 teaspoon red pepper flakes
3/4 cup chopped celery
2 1/2 teaspoons olive oil
3 cups chopped zucchini, cut in half lengthwise and then cut into 1-inch chunks
3/4 cup chopped bell pepper
3 cups chopped tomato
1 tablespoon soy sauce

Sauté the onion, garlic, jalapeños, and celery in the oil until transparent. Add the zucchini and bell pepper and sauté briefly. Then add the tomato and soy sauce and stir well. Cover and cook until tender, but do not overcook.

VARIATION: *Use other kinds of squash.*

Casseroles

Apulian-Style Baked Potatoes, Onions, and Tomatoes

2 cups thinly sliced onion
1½ teaspoons olive oil
1½ teaspoons nondairy margarine
2 teaspoons minced garlic
2 teaspoons minced jalapeños
6 cups chopped potatoes, peeled and sliced crosswise ¼ inch thick
3 cups diced tomato, cut into ⅓-inch dice
1¼ cups Yeast Cheez (page 97)
1 teaspoon oregano
1 teaspoon sea salt
½ teaspoon freshly ground black pepper
¾ cup UnChicken Broth (page 155)

Sauté the onion in the oil and margarine until soft. Add the garlic and jalapeños and cook 1 more minute. Combine with the rest of the ingredients and put into an oiled or nonstick casserole. Cover and bake at 400°F until the potatoes are done, about 1 hour. Uncover and bake 15 more minutes for the extra moisture to evaporate.

Baked Cubed UnBeef Casserole

This cannot fail to be appreciated!

3 tablespoons corn oil
5 cups cubed UnBeef (page 109), cooked by Method 1, 2, or 3 (pages 99–100), cut in 1-inch cubes
3 cups sliced potatoes, cut into ½-inch slices and boiled
1 cup sliced and boiled carrot
1⅓ cups sliced onion, cut into ½-inch slices
¼ cup unbleached white flour
1¼ teaspoon Kitchen Bouquet
3 cups thickly sliced fresh mushrooms
1½ cups chopped onion
1½ teaspoons minced garlic
3 cups UnBeef broth (page 155)
3 tablespoons Lea and Perrins Steak Sauce
1 tablespoon Louisiana Hot Sauce

Heat the oil in a skillet and fry the UnBeef cubes until they are browned on all sides. Take the gluten and put it in a baking dish along with the potatoes, carrot, and onion slices. Stir the flour into the oil in the skillet and turn the heat down so it will cook slowly. Add the Kitchen Bouquet and keep stirring the flour constantly, adding more oil if the mixture is too dry, until the mixture is a rich brown. Add the mushrooms and onion, stirring constantly, and cook until the onion is soft. Add the garlic and cook a little bit more. Add the broth and keep stirring until it starts to form a thick gravy. Add the steak sauce and hot sauce. Add more water if you need to, and bring all to a boil. Pour the sauce over the gluten and vegetables in the casserole. Cover and bake at 400°F for 30 to 45 minutes, basting frequently and adding water if needed.

Baked Curry

Don't judge by appearances. This is one of those recipes that looks stupid on paper but cooks up a genius!

2 teaspoons corn oil
2 teaspoons curry powder
2 tablespoons unbleached white flour
1½ cups broth of type of gluten being used (see Flavoring Broths chapter)
1½ cups cubed gluten, any flavor
¼ cup chopped onion
2 cups broccoli, cut into flowerets with peeled and sliced stem, steamed
2 cups cauliflower, cut into flowerets
1 cup cubed potatoes
1½ teaspoons lemon juice
1 tablespoon soy sauce
¼ teaspoon sea salt
¼ teaspoon paprika
1 cup dried bread crumbs

Heat the oil, add the curry powder, and stir for 1 minute over medium heat. Add the flour and stir for 1 more minute. Stir in the broth and cook until thickened, about 5 minutes. Add the rest of the ingredients except the crumbs and cook until the onion is soft. Put in a nonstick casserole and sprinkle the bread crumbs over all, pressing in lightly. Bake, covered, at 350°F for 10 to 15 minutes. Uncover and bake until the crumbs begin to brown.

Bread and Cheez Pudding

Surprising goodness!

½ cup minced onion
1 teaspoon nondairy margarine
1 cup Yeast Cheez (page 97) or Notzarella Cheez (page 94)
2 N'eggs (page 302)
2½ cups UnChicken Broth (page 155)
¼ teaspoon cayenne pepper
¼ teaspoon freshly ground black pepper
½ teaspoon sea salt
8 thick slices of bread, toasted, and cut or torn into small pieces

Sauté the onion in the margarine until soft. Combine everything and let sit for 15 minutes. Put into a nonstick casserole. Bake at 375°F until the top is puffed up and golden brown and it tests done when a knife is inserted into it, about 45 minutes.

Bread Dressing

There's always room for this—forget Jell-O!

1 cup grated carrot
½ cup chopped fresh chopped fresh parsley
¾ cup chopped onion
1½ pounds bread cut in ½-inch cubes
1 cup chopped celery
¼ cup finely chopped bell pepper
½ cup sliced mushrooms or black olives
¼ teaspoon freshly ground black pepper
2 teaspoons nondairy margarine, melted
5½ cups UnBeef Broth (page 155)

Mix the dry ingredients together. Combine the melted margarine and broth and pour over the dry ingredients gradually, stirring well. Pack into a casserole dish. Cover with aluminum foil and bake at 350°F for 45 minutes. Uncover and bake for 15 minutes more to brown the top.

Broccoli and Corn Scallop

2 teaspoons nondairy margarine
⅔ cup chopped onion
½ teaspoon minced garlic
2 tablespoons unbleached white flour
¾ cup water
2 cups Yeast Cheez (page 97), Pimiento Cheez (page 94), or Notzarella Cheez (page 94)
1 cup corn
1 cup cracker crumbs
5 cups broccoli, cooked and drained
2 tablespoons nondairy margarine, melted

Melt the margarine, sauté the onion and garlic, and blend in the flour. Gradually add the water and cook until thickened. Add the Cheez and stir until it melts. Stir in the corn and ½ cup of the cracker crumbs. Arrange the broccoli in a nonstick casserole and pour the Cheez sauce over it. Toss the remaining crumbs with 2 tablespoons of melted margarine and sprinkle them over the casserole. Bake at 350°F for 30 minutes.

VARIATION: *Omit the broccoli and add 5 cups more corn, or omit the corn and add 1 cup more broccoli.*

Broccoli and Potato Casserole with Chives and Cheez

2 cups chopped broccoli
2 cups cubed and boiled potato
¾ cup Cashew Milk (page 93)
1 cup Yeast Cheez (page 97) or Pimiento Cheez (page 94)
½ cup Parmesan Cheez (page 94)
3 tablespoons chives, chopped
½ teaspoon minced garlic
2 tablespoons chopped fresh parsley
1 cup tofu, crumbled
½ cup fresh bread crumbs
¾ teaspoon sea salt
⅛ teaspoon cayenne pepper

Combine all the ingredients in a bowl and stir until thoroughly mixed. Place the mixture into a nonstick 9x9-inch pan and spread evenly. Bake in a 350°F oven for 40 minutes.

Broccoli Casserole

½ cup chopped onion
½ cup chopped celery
2 teaspoons corn oil
1¼ cups Kreem of Mushroom Soup (page 74)
4½ cups frozen chopped broccoli, thawed
¾ cup Yeast Cheez (page 97) or Notzarella Cheez (page 94)
1½ cups cooked rice
½ teaspoon sea salt
¼ teaspoon freshly ground black pepper

Sauté the onion and celery in the oil until soft. Combine everything in a casserole. Bake at 350°F for 30 minutes.

Cabbage, Tomatoes, and Cheez

3 cups finely shredded cabbage, cooked and drained
¾ teaspoon sea salt
¼ teaspoon cayenne pepper
1½ cups crushed or chopped canned tomatoes
1 cup Yeast Cheez (page 97), Pimiento Cheez (page 94), or Notzarella Cheez (page 94)
2 cups bread crumbs

Combine the cabbage, salt, pepper, and tomatoes. Put in a nonstick casserole. Top with the Cheez and then with the bread crumbs, pressing down lightly. Bake at 325°F until the crumbs are brown, about 30 minutes.

Corn Bread Dressing

6 cups crumbled corn bread
2 cups Cream-Style Corn (page 164)
1 cup seeded and chopped jalapeños
½ cup chopped mushrooms or black olives
¾ cup Yeast Cheez (page 97), Pimiento Cheez (page 94), or Notzarella Cheez (page 94)
½ cup finely chopped onion
½ cup chopped bell pepper
1 tablespoon chopped fresh parsley
1 N'egg (page 302)
1 tablespoon nondairy margarine, melted

Put the crumbled corn bread in a large baking pan and bake at 350°F until toasted, about 30 minutes, stirring every 10 minutes. Take from the oven and set aside to cool. Combine the other ingredients. Mix well. Add the corn bread and toss to mix. Bake, covered, in a nonstick casserole at 325°F for 45 to 60 minutes or until heated through.

Cabbage Un-Rolls Casserole

1 cabbage head
4 cups ground flavored gluten of choice (see specific gluten chapters)
4 teaspoons corn oil
2 cups chopped onion
2 teaspoons minced garlic
1⁄4 teaspoon cayenne pepper
1 cup broth of the flavor of gluten used (see Flavoring Broths chapter)
2 cups cooked rice
2 cups Yeast Cheez (page 97) or Pimiento Cheez (page 94)
21⁄2 cups canned tomato sauce

Separate the cabbage into leaves, trimming away the tough part of the stem on each leaf. Put the leaves in a pan of salted boiling water and boil them until they are slightly soft. Drain and set aside. Sauté the gluten in the oil until it just begins to brown. Add the onion, garlic, pepper, and broth, and continue cooking until the onion is soft and the liquid has been absorbed or evaporated so the mixture is not mushy. Add the rice to the gluten mixture and cook for 2 more minutes. In a casserole put a layer of cabbage leaves. Spread the gluten mixture over the leaves. Cover with the remaining cabbage. Cover that with a layer of Cheez. Pour the tomato sauce over the Cheez. Bake at 375°F for 30 minutes.

Cajun Eggplant

This was originally a recipe for an appetizer. It was so good everybody demanded more, so it became a main dish, as it deserves to be.

3 small eggplants, peeled and sliced 1⁄4 inch thick and put in salted water
3 tablespoons olive oil
3 tablespoons unbleached white flour, sifted
11⁄2 tablespoons tomato paste
11⁄4 cups canned tomato sauce
1⁄4 cup finely chopped celery
2 tablespoons chopped fresh parsley
1 cup finely chopped onion
1⁄3 cup finely chopped bell pepper
1 teaspoon minced garlic
11⁄2 cups water
1 tablespoon Lea and Perrins Steak Sauce
1 teaspoon Louisiana Hot Sauce
11⁄4 teaspoons sea salt
2 to 21⁄2 cups Pimiento Cheez (page 94)
Parmesan Cheez (page 94)

Let the eggplant slices marinate in the salted water for 2 hours. Meanwhile, put 11⁄2 tablespoons of the olive oil in a skillet or heavy pot, heat it well, and stir in the flour. Cook the flour, stirring frequently, until it is a very dark brown, but not burned. (This can take some time.) Add the tomato paste to the flour and, stirring constantly, cook it until it returns to the dark color it was before the sauce was added. Add the tomato sauce and, stirring constantly, cook it until it again returns to the dark color.

Add the celery, parsley, onion, bell pepper, and garlic, and cook over very low heat for 20 to 30 minutes, stirring constantly. Add the water, Lea and Perrins, hot sauce, and salt. Add more water if the mixture is too thick. Cook over low heat for 1 hour. When the sauce is nearly done, rinse the eggplant and drain it in a colander. Put the remaining olive oil in a skillet and fry the drained eggplant slices to a deep brown, adding more oil if needed.

Place the slices in a casserole and spread some Pimiento Cheez over them. Sprinkle some "Parmesan" over that. Spread some of the sauce liberally over all. Add another layer of eggplant and repeat. Do this until all the eggplant is used up, finishing with a layer of sauce. Bake at 375°F for 20 minutes. Serve hot over rice or chill it in the refrigerator, cut it into squares, and serve.

Carrot Roast

4 cups grated carrot
4 cups cooked rice, or garbanzo beans, cooked
1 cup bread crumbs
1⁄2 cup water
21⁄2 teaspoons corn oil
1⁄3 cup chopped onion
1⁄4 teaspoon thyme
1⁄2 teaspoon sea salt

Mix all together and bake, covered, at 350°F for 45 minutes, and uncovered for 15 minutes. Serve with gravy (see Gravies chapter).

Cauliflower au Gratin

6 cups cauliflower flowerets
2 tablespoons plus 2 teaspoons nondairy margarine
½ cup diced onion
1½ cups Yeast Cheez (page 97), Pimiento Cheez (page 94), or Notzarella Cheez (page 94)
1 cup Cashew Sour Kreem (page 94) or Tofu Sour Kreem (page 97)
¼ teaspoon sea salt
½ cup dried bread crumbs

Cook the cauliflower flowerets in boiling salted water for 10 minutes. Drain well. Combine the cauliflower with 2 tablespoons of the margarine, the onion, Cheez, Sour Kreem, and salt. Put into a casserole. Melt the rest of the margarine and toss with the crumbs. Sprinkle the crumbs over the cauliflower mixture. Bake at 350°F for 30 minutes.

Cauliflower Bake

Sauce

1 tablespoon cornstarch
½ cup cold Cashew Milk (page 93)
¾ teaspoon sea salt
⅛ teaspoon freshly ground black pepper
¼ teaspoon paprika
1 cup Yeast Cheez (page 97), Pimiento Cheez (page 94), or Notzarella Cheez (page 94)

Vegetables

½ cup chopped celery
⅓ cup chopped bell pepper
1 cup chopped onion
2 teaspoons nondairy margarine
1½ teaspoons minced garlic
4 cups cauliflower flowerets, cooked
2 tomatoes, sliced

For the sauce, bring the cornstarch, "milk," salt, pepper, and paprika to a boil, stirring constantly. Boil until it thickens. Add the Cheez and stir over low heat until combined and set aside. Sauté the celery, bell pepper, and onion in the margarine until the onion is soft. Add the garlic and sauté 1 more minute. Add to the sauce. Put the cauliflower into a nonstick casserole. Cover with the tomato slices. Pour the sauce over all. Bake at 400°F for 20 minutes.

Cheez and Potato Bake

½ cup onion, sliced or chopped
1 teaspoon minced garlic
1 teaspoon corn oil
4 cups peeled and sliced potatoes, boiled in salted water
1 teaspoon celery salt
¼ teaspoon cayenne pepper
¼ teaspoon dill
2½ cups Thin White Sauce (page 262) made with UnChicken Broth (page 155)
1 cup Yeast Cheez (page 97), Pimiento Cheez (page 94), or Notzarella Cheez (page 94)

Sauté the onion and garlic in the oil until the onion is soft. In a nonstick casserole pan put a layer of onion. Add a layer of potatoes. Add another layer of onion. Mix the seasonings with the White Sauce and add it to the casserole. Top with the Cheez. Cover and bake at 400°F for 30 minutes, removing the cover for the last 10 minutes.

Cheez Enchilada Casserole

¾ cup chopped onion, plus more to top casserole
¼ cup chopped bell pepper
2 tablespoons corn oil
6 cups tomato sauce
¾ cup Tomato Salsa (page 296), plus more to top casserole
¼ teaspoon paprika
⅛ teaspoon sage
15 corn tortillas
9 cups Yeast Cheez (page 97)

Sauté the onion and bell pepper in the oil. Add the tomato sauce, salsa, paprika, and sage. Dip the tortillas in hot oil to make them soft. Layer in a casserole starting with tomato sauce mixture, then tortillas, and then Cheez. Repeat the layers two more times. Spread a thin layer of salsa and chopped onion on top. Bake for 15 minutes at 400°F.

Cheez Enchiladas 1

Plenty good and good and plenty!

- 2 teaspoons corn oil
- 3 tablespoons minced onion, plus 1/2 cup thinly sliced onion
- 3 tablespoons minced bell pepper, plus 1/2 cup thinly sliced bell pepper (red preferred)
- 3 tablespoons minced celery
- 2 teaspoons minced garlic
- 3 cups drained and crushed canned tomatoes
- 1/2 teaspoon ground cumin
- 1/2 teaspoon Sucanat
- 1 1/2 teaspoons paprika
- 3/4 teaspoon oregano, dried and crumbled
- 1/2 bay leaf
- 1/2 teaspoon sea salt
- 1/4 teaspoon cayenne pepper
- 8 corn tortillas
- 2 1/2 cups Yeast Cheez (page 97), Pimiento Cheez (page 94), or Notzarella Cheez (page 94)

In 1 teaspoon of the oil sauté the minced onion, bell pepper, celery, and garlic until all is softened. Add the tomatoes, cumin, Sucanat, paprika, oregano, bay leaf, salt, and pepper. Bring to a boil, reduce the heat, and simmer, stirring occasionally, for 20 minutes. Discard the bay leaf and set aside. In the other teaspoon of the oil sauté the sliced onion and bell pepper until they are softened, and transfer them with a slotted spoon to paper towels to drain. Dip the tortillas in the tomato sauce and set aside. To assemble, on each tortilla put some pepper and onion on the bottom third, top with 3 tablespoons of the Cheez, and roll up. As each is done, put it in a nonstick casserole. When all are in the dish, spoon the sauce over them and spread the remaining Cheez over all. Bake at 400°F for 20 minutes.

Cheez Enchiladas 2

Sauce

- 2 tablespoons cornstarch
- 3 cups UnChicken Broth (page 155)
- 3 tablespoons chili powder
- 1/4 teaspoon garlic powder
- 1/8 teaspoon ground cumin
- 1/8 teaspoon cayenne pepper
- 1/2 teaspoon sea salt
- 1/4 teaspoon onion powder
- 1 teaspoon corn oil

Filling

- 3/4 cup chopped onion
- 1 teaspoon corn oil
- 4 cups Pimiento Cheez (page 94)
- 1/4 cup chopped black olives

To complete the recipe

- 12 corn tortillas

To make the sauce, dissolve the cornstarch in the broth. Add the chili powder, garlic powder, cumin, pepper, salt, onion powder, and 1 teaspoon of the oil, and simmer together for 10 minutes. For the filling, sauté the onion in the remaining teaspoon of oil. Add the Cheez and olives to the onion. Put a small amount of the sauce in the bottom of a casserole pan or dish. Put a small amount of the filling in a tortilla, roll it up, and put it in the casserole. Do the same with the rest of the tortillas. Fifteen minutes before serving, put the rest of the sauce on the enchiladas and heat in a 350°F oven for 15 minutes.

Cheez Pie

1 cup finely chopped onion
1 teaspoon minced garlic
1/2 cup finely chopped bell pepper
2 1/2 teaspoons nondairy margarine
3 tablespoons cornstarch
2 cups Cashew Milk (page 93)
4 cups Pimiento Cheez (page 94) or Yeast Cheez (page 97)
4 cups Tofu Cottage Cheez (page 96)
4 cups drained and chopped canned tomatoes
1 recipe Basic Pie Crust (page 328) for two crusts

Sauté the onion, garlic, and bell pepper in the margarine. Mix the cornstarch with the "milk." Combine all ingredients. Put in unbaked pie shell and cover with top crust, perforating it with a fork or making slits with a knife for steam to escape. Bake at 425°F for 1 hour.

VARIATION: *Use other vegetables.*

Cheezy Onion Casserole

4 1/2 cups sliced onion
2 tablespoons nondairy margarine
1 cup Yeast Cheez (page 97)
1 cup Notzarella Cheez (page 94)
1/4 teaspoon pepper
1 3/4 cup Kreem of UnChicken Soup (page 75)
1 teaspoon low-sodium soy sauce
Enough slices of bread, "buttered" on both sides, to cover the casserole

Sauté the onion in the margarine until transparent and slightly brown. Combine the Cheezes and pepper thoroughly. Layer the onion and Cheez mixture in a nonstick casserole. Combine the soup and soy sauce and pour in the casserole and stir gently. Top with the bread slices. Bake at 350°F for 15 minutes. Push the bread slices under the sauce. Bake for 15 more minutes.

Chili-Cheez Bake

1 cup chopped onion
1 1/2 teaspoons minced garlic
1/3 cup chopped jalapeños
1 tablespoon corn oil
3 cups cooked rice
1 tablespoon chili powder
1/2 teaspoon sea salt
2 cups cooked kidney beans, drained
2 teaspoons ground cumin
1 teaspoon oregano
2 cups Yeast Cheez (page 97) or Notzarella Cheez (page 94)

Sauté the onion, garlic, and jalapeños in the oil until the onion is soft. In a casserole combine everything but the Cheez. Top with the Cheez. Bake, covered, at 400°F for 25 to 35 minutes.

Company Casserole

1 1/2 cups cubed baked UnChicken (page 137)
1 cup cubed baked UnHam (page 130)
Oil
2 1/2 cups cooked rice
1 1/4 cup chopped broccoli
1 1/4 cups Yeast Cheez (page 97)
1/2 cup sliced mushrooms
1 1/4 cups Miraculous Whip (page 17) or other "mayonnaise" (see Salad Dressings chapter)
1 1/4 teaspoons prepared mustard
2 cups Curried Mushroom Soup (page 70)
2 tablespoons Parmesan Cheez (page 94)

Fry the gluten (both kinds together) in a small amount of oil until browned and set aside. Spread the rice over the bottom of a nonstick casserole. Layer with the broccoli, then the gluten, the Cheez, and then mushrooms. Combine the mayonnaise, mustard, and soup, and spread over the mushroom layer. Sprinkle with the Parmesan Cheez. Bake at 350°F until the top is light golden brown, 45 to 60 minutes.

VARIATION: *If you don't care for the taste of curry powder, just substitute a plain Kreem of Mushroom Soup (page 74).*

Corn and Lima Stew Casserole

Filling

2 cups chopped onion
1 1/2 cups diced celery

½ cup chopped bell pepper
2 tablespoons corn oil
2 teaspoons finely minced jalapeños
1½ teaspoons minced garlic
1 teaspoon ground cumin
3 tablespoons chili powder
2 cups lima beans (not dried)
2 tablespoons minced fresh parsley
3 cups chopped fresh or canned tomato (with juice, if canned)
1 cup water
½ teaspoon sea salt
¼ teaspoon cayenne pepper
2 cups corn

Crust
5 cups water
1 teaspoon sea salt
1½ cups cornmeal
2 tablespoons corn oil
1½ teaspoons cayenne pepper or chili powder
2 cups Yeast Cheez (page 97)

For the filling, sauté the onion, celery, and bell pepper in the oil in a large pan or Dutch oven until soft. Add the jalapeños, garlic, cumin, and chili powder and sauté 1 more minute. Add the rest of the filling ingredients except the corn and simmer, covered, for 15 minutes. When the beans are tender, add the corn. Turn off the heat.

For the crust, bring the water to a boil. Add the salt and pour in the cornmeal in a steady stream, whisking constantly. Cook, stirring frequently at first, until the cornmeal is cooked, about 30 minutes. Stir in the oil, cayenne or chili powder, and the Cheez. This should be thick but pourable, add more water if it is not.

Put ⅔ of crust mixture into an oiled or nonstick casserole and spread over the bottom. Let sit about 5 minutes to get firm. Spoon the vegetables over the cornmeal mixture. Pour the remaining batter over the top. Set on a tray and bake at 375°F for 25 minutes.

Corn and Spinach Casserole

¼ cup minced onion
½ teaspoon minced garlic
1 teaspoon nondairy margarine
2 cups Cream-Style Corn (page 164)
1½ cups frozen spinach, chopped
1 teaspoon vinegar
½ teaspoon sea salt
¼ teaspoon black pepper or cayenne pepper
¼ cup fine dried bread crumbs
2 tablespoons Parmesan Cheez (page 94)

Sauté the onion and garlic in the margarine. Add the corn, spinach, vinegar, salt, and pepper. Put in a nonstick casserole. Blend the crumbs and Cheez, and spread over the vegetables. Bake at 400°F for 20 minutes.

Corn Bake

3 cups corn, cooked and drained
¼ cup Cashew Milk (page 93)
2 tablespoons finely chopped onion
1 teaspoon corn oil
½ teaspoon sea salt
½ teaspoon paprika
¾ cup Yeast Cheez (page 97), Pimiento Cheez (page 94), or Notzarella Cheez (page 94)
½ cup bread crumbs tossed in 2 tablespoons melted nondairy margarine

Combine the corn, Cashew Milk, onion, oil, salt, paprika, and Cheez. Turn into a nonstick casserole. Top with the bread crumbs, pressing down lightly. Bake at 350°F for 25 minutes.

Corn Chip Casserole

1½ cups chopped onion
¾ cup chopped bell pepper
4½ teaspoons chili powder
¼ teaspoon garlic powder
2 tablespoons corn oil
3 cups ground UnBeef (page 109)
1½ cups salsa
1½ cups canned tomatoes with juice
¼ teaspoon sea salt
6 cups corn chips
4 cups Notzarella Cheez (page 94)

Sauté the onion, bell pepper, chili powder, and garlic powder in the oil. Add the UnBeef and sauté until slightly brown. Combine everything but the chips and Cheez in a skillet and cook until most of the liquid is evaporated. Layer the bottom of a casserole with half the chips. Spread half the Cheez over that. Spread the gluten mixture over that. Repeat the chips and Cheez layers. Bake at 400°F for 30 minutes.

Corn Tamale Pie

More than worth the trying!

1/2 cup chopped bell pepper
3 tablespoons chopped onion
2 teaspoons corn oil
3/4 cup cornmeal
2 cups corn
3 cups canned tomatoes
1/2 cup chopped ripe olives
1/4 teaspoon cayenne pepper
1/2 cup tomato sauce
1 teaspoon sea salt
3 cups Yeast Cheez (page 97) or Pimiento Cheez (page 94)

Sauté the bell pepper and onion in the corn oil. Add the rest of the ingredients except the Cheez and simmer, covered, for 5 minutes, stirring occasionally and adding a little water (up to 3/4 cup) if it gets too thick. Put in a nonstick casserole. Bake at 350°F for 45 minutes. Within the last 10 minutes put the Cheez on the top and let it brown slightly.

Corn-Bean Pie

Simple goodness!

Crust
2 tablespoons corn oil
2 cups cornmeal
1/2 cup UnBeef Broth (page 155)

Filling
1/2 cup chopped bell pepper
1/3 cup chopped onion
1 teaspoon minced garlic
1 1/2 teaspoons corn oil
2 cups cooked and cubed potatoes
3 cups cooked dried beans
1 cup chopped tomato
Pinch cayenne pepper
1 cup UnBeef Broth (page 155)
1/4 teaspoon sea salt
Yeast Cheez (page 97) or Pimiento Cheez (page 94)

For the crust, in a small mixing bowl, stir the oil into the cornmeal with a fork. Add enough broth to make a stiff batter. Pat into a nonstick casserole or pie plate. To make the filling, sauté the bell pepper, onion, and garlic in the oil. Combine with the rest of the ingredients, except for the Cheez, in a pot. Cook for 2 minutes. Pour the filling into the prepared crust and bake at 350°F for about 30 minutes. Remove the pie and cover with the Cheez. Bake 10 more minutes.

VARIATION: *Use squash instead of potatoes.*

Country Casserole

3 cups chopped onion
4 teaspoons corn oil
1 tablespoon crushed garlic
1 cup UnChicken Broth (page 155)
2 cups chopped stewed tomatoes
1/4 teaspoon thyme
1/2 teaspoon sea salt
1/4 teaspoon cayenne pepper
2 cups cubed UnBeef (page 109)
2 cups cubed UnPork (page 122)
5 cups cooked white beans, drained

Sauté the onion in the oil until soft. Add the garlic and sauté 2 more minutes. Add the broth, tomatoes, thyme, salt, and pepper. Bring to a boil, reduce heat, and simmer, covered, for 10 minutes. Add the gluten and beans. Mix all together well. Transfer to a nonstick casserole and bake at 350°F, uncovered, for 30 minutes.

VARIATION: *Any type of flavored gluten can be used singly or in combination.*

Creamed Broccoli

2 tablespoons nondairy margarine
1/4 cup unbleached white flour
1 cup Cashew Milk (page 93) made with UnChicken Broth (page 155)
1/4 teaspoon sea salt
Pinch cayenne pepper
1/2 teaspoon paprika
1/2 cup minced onion
1/2 teaspoon minced garlic
4 cups broccoli, cooked, drained, and chopped very fine
1 cup bread crumbs tossed in 2 tablespoons of melted nondairy margarine

Melt the margarine and stir in the flour until well blended. Slowly stir in the Cashew Milk and add the salt, pepper, paprika, onion, and garlic. Add the broccoli and put in a nonstick casserole. Sprinkle with bread crumbs. Bake at 425°F for 15 to 20 minutes.

Creamed Cabbage Casserole

8 cups shredded cabbage
Salted water
1 1/2 cups sliced onion
1/2 teaspoon minced garlic
1 tablespoon nondairy margarine, plus more to dot casserole
1/8 teaspoon freshly ground black pepper
2 cups Yeast Cheez (page 97), Pimiento Cheez (page 94), or Notzarella Cheez (page 94)
1 1/2 cups Thin White Sauce (page 262) made with UnChicken Broth (page 155), boiling
2 cups bread crumbs

Boil cabbage in salted water. Sauté the onion and garlic in the margarine and mix with the cabbage and pepper. In a small nonstick casserole put a layer of half the cabbage. Spread 1 cup of Cheez over that. Layer the rest of cabbage, with the rest of Cheez over that. Pour the White Sauce over all. Top with bread crumbs and dot liberally with nondairy margarine. Bake at 400°F until the crumbs are brown.

Creamed Potatoes with Cheez

6 cups diced and boiled potatoes
3 cups Thin White Sauce (page 262), made with UnChicken Broth (page 155)
3/4 cup chopped onion
1 teaspoon minced garlic
2 teaspoons nondairy margarine, plus more to dot casserole
3 tablespoons chopped fresh parsley
3 cups Yeast Cheez (page 97) or Pimiento Cheez (page 94)
3/4 teaspoon sea salt
1 1/2 cups bread crumbs

Combine the potatoes and sauce. Sauté the onion and garlic in the margarine. Combine all ingredients except the bread crumbs. Put in a nonstick casserole. Cover with bread crumbs. Dot with nondairy margarine. Bake at 400°F until the crumbs are brown.

Creamed Spinach, Mushrooms, and Onions in Cheez Sauce

1 cup chopped onion
1 tablespoon minced garlic
1 cup sliced mushrooms
1 1/2 teaspoons nondairy margarine
3 cups Cheez Sauce 1 (page 257)
3 1/2 cups frozen spinach, defrosted, drained, and chopped
1/4 teaspoon sea salt
1/8 teaspoon freshly ground black pepper

Combine everything in a casserole, top with bread crumbs, pressing them down lightly, and bake at 350°F for 20 minutes or until the crumbs have browned.

Creole Rice Casserole

1 cup chopped onion
2 teaspoons minced garlic
2½ teaspoons corn oil
6 cups rice, cooked in UnChicken Broth (page 155)
3 cups sliced okra
¼ teaspoon cayenne pepper
4 cups Creole Sauce (page 258)
½ teaspoon sea salt
Yeast Cheez (page 97) or Pimiento Cheez (page 94)

Sauté the onions and garlic in the corn oil. Combine with all other ingredients, except Cheez, put in a casserole, and bake for 25 minutes at 350°F. Top with Cheez and bake for 5 more minutes.

Crunch-Top Potatoes

Try this!

3 tablespoons nondairy margarine
3 cups potatoes, peeled, cut in ½-inch slices, and boiled in UnBeef Broth (page 155)
¾ cup crushed corn flakes
1½ cups Yeast Cheez (page 97) or Pimiento Cheez (page 94)
½ teaspoon sea salt
1½ teaspoons paprika

Melt the margarine in a pan in a 375°F oven. Add a single layer of potatoes, turning them once in the margarine. Mix the remaining ingredients and sprinkle over the potatoes. Bake until done and the top is crisp, about ½ hour.

Curried Potato and Onion Casserole

1 cup Tofu Yogurt (page 97)
2 teaspoons corn oil
1 teaspoon cayenne pepper
1 tablespoon chopped garlic
½ teaspoon ground ginger
1 tablespoon curry powder
3 cups sliced onion, ¼ inch thick
6 cups sliced potatoes, ¼ inch thick
1 cup UnChicken Broth (page 155)

Combine the yogurt, oil, cayenne, garlic, ginger, and curry powder and set aside. Toss the onions and potatoes together. Add the yogurt mixture and spread the vegetables in an even layer in a shallow baking dish. Pour the broth over all. Bake at 350°F until thoroughly cooked and browned on top, about 1½ hours.

Eggplant and Cheez

This can be either a main dish (good on rice) warm, or an appetizer, cold.

2 cups cubed UnBacon (page 136) or UnHam (page 130)
Oil for deep-frying
¼ teaspoon sea salt
⅛ teaspoon cayenne pepper
1 cup unbleached white flour
6 cups sliced eggplant
2 teaspoons soy sauce
1½ cups Notzarella Cheez (page 94)
2 tablespoons Parmesan Cheez (page 94)

Deep-fry the gluten in the oil and drain on paper towels. Salt, pepper, and flour the eggplant, then deep-fry it and drain well on paper towels. Put a layer of eggplant in a casserole dish. Sprinkle soy sauce over the eggplant, then spread the Notzarella. Sprinkle a layer of gluten and "Parmesan" over that. Keep repeating this layering until all the eggplant is used up, finishing with a layer of "Parmesan." Bake at 350°F for 20 minutes.

Eggplant Casserole with Tomatoes, Garlic, and Rice

Oil for deep-frying
1 small eggplant, peeled and cut into ¼-inch slices
4 cups sliced zucchini, unpeeled and cut into ½-inch slices
2 cups chopped onion
4 teaspoons crushed garlic
1¼ cups sliced bell pepper, cut into strips
2 tablespoons olive oil
6 cups drained and chopped canned tomatoes
¼ cup chopped fresh parsley

1/4 teaspoon basil
1/4 teaspoon thyme
1/2 teaspoon sea salt
1/4 teaspoon cayenne pepper
3 cups rice, cooked in UnChicken Broth (page 155)
Yeast Cheez (page 97), Pimiento Cheez (page 94), or Notzarella Cheez (page 94) to cover
1/4 cup Parmesan Cheez (page 94)

Deep-fry the eggplant and set aside. Steam the zucchini. Sauté the onion, garlic, and bell pepper in the olive oil until the onion is soft. Add the tomatoes, herbs, and seasonings and simmer the mixture for 25 minutes, adding water if the sauce gets too thick. Stir in the cooked rice and vegetables. Place the mixture in a casserole and top with the Cheezes. Bake at 350°F for 20 minutes.

Eggplant Lasagna

A good idea and even better eating!

3 cups eggplant, peeled and sliced 1/3 inch thick
Corn oil for frying
4 cups Spanish Tomato Sauce (page 260)
2 cups chopped canned tomatoes
1/2 teaspoon Sucanat
1 teaspoon garlic salt
1/2 teaspoon basil
1/4 teaspoon oregano
1 cup frozen tofu, thawed and crumbled
1 1/4 cups chopped mushrooms
3/4 cup chopped onion
1 tablespoon olive oil
1/2 cup Cashew Sour Kreem (page 94) or Tofu Sour Kreem (page 97)

Fry eggplant slices in a small amount of corn oil. Drain well on paper towels. Simmer the tomato sauce, canned tomatoes, and seasonings for about 5 minutes. Meanwhile, sauté the tofu, mushrooms, and onion in the olive oil. Add the Sour Kreem and 1 cup of the tomato sauce. Layer ingredients in an 11x7x2-inch nonstick casserole starting with the tomato sauce, then eggplant slices, then tofu mixture. Repeat, ending with tomato sauce. Bake at 350°F for 30 minutes.

Eggplant Parmesan 1

A specialty of the house!

3 cups eggplant, peeled and cut in 1/2-inch slices
Sea salt
Unbleached white flour
Corn oil
2 cups Italian Pasta Sauce (page 263)
Notzarella Cheez (page 94), Pimiento Cheez (page 94), or Yeast Cheez (page 97)
Parmesan Cheez (page 94)

Sprinkle both sides of the eggplant slices with salt to draw out their moisture and spread them out in a single layer on a platter or board. After 20 to 30 minutes, pat the eggplant dry with paper towels. Dip each slice in flour, shaking or brushing off any excess. Heat the oil in a skillet and brown the eggplant a few slices at a time, working quickly to prevent them from soaking up too much oil. (If the oil cooks away, add more.) As the eggplant browns, transfer the slices to fresh paper towels to drain.

Pour 1/2 cup of the tomato sauce into a nonstick casserole pan. Layer the eggplant slices over the sauce. Cover with Cheez, and sprinkle the "Parmesan" over that. Repeat 1 or 2 more layers, finishing with tomato sauce, Cheez, and "Parmesan." Cover with foil and bake at 400°F in the middle of the oven for 30 minutes. Remove the foil and bake, uncovered, for 10 minutes. Watch closely to avoid overcooking.

Eggplant Parmesan 2

1 tablespoon olive oil
1 cup chopped onion
2½ teaspoons minced garlic
½ cup chopped bell pepper
½ teaspoon cayenne pepper
6 cups chopped tomato
½ teaspoon sea salt
1 tablespoon minced fresh basil
1 teaspoon minced fresh oregano
½ teaspoon minced fresh thyme
1 tablespoon minced fresh parsley (Italian preferred)
1 large eggplant, peeled, sliced ½ inch thick, and slightly browned in olive oil
4 cups Yeast Cheez (page 97)
1 cup Parmesan Cheez (page 94)
1 cup dried bread crumbs

Heat the oil in a large heavy pot and sauté the onion for several minutes. Add the garlic and bell pepper and sauté until all are soft. Add the cayenne and sauté briefly. Add the tomato, cover, and cook over low heat until the juice has come out, 5 to 10 minutes. Uncover, stir in the salt, and simmer gently until the sauce thickens, about 1 hour. Add the herbs and simmer a few more minutes. Take from the heat.

In an oiled or nonstick 8-inch casserole spread a thin layer of sauce on the bottom and arrange half the eggplant slices on top. Spread ⅓ of the Yeast Cheez over the eggplant. Spread on a thicker layer of sauce than the first one, and sprinkle ½ cup of the "Parmesan" over all. Repeat the layers, beginning with the eggplant and ending with the rest of the Yeast Cheez and "Parmesan." Sprinkle the bread crumbs over the top and press down lightly. Bake at 350°F, covered, until heated through, about 30 minutes. Uncover and bake until the bread crumbs brown.

English Wartime "Goose"

This was developed during World War II in England and is delicious!

4½ cups thinly sliced potatoes
2 cups thinly sliced apple
½ teaspoon sage
¼ teaspoon sea salt
¼ teaspoon freshly ground black pepper
1½ cups Yeast Cheez (page 97) or Notzarella Cheez (page 94)
1½ cups UnChicken Broth (page 155)
1 tablespoon unbleached white flour

Put a layer of potatoes in an oiled or nonstick casserole. Cover with a layer of apple and a little sage. Sprinkle lightly with salt and pepper. Spread with a layer of Cheez. Repeat the layers, ending with a layer of potatoes and a layer of Cheez over that. Pour in 1 cup of the broth and bake at 350°F for 45 minutes. Blend the flour with the rest of the broth, pour it into the casserole, and cook 15 more minutes.

Fresh Corn and Tomato Casserole

This favorite has endured the test of time!

5 cups corn
1 N'egg (page 302)
1½ teaspoons corn oil
1 cup water
1 cup bread crumbs
¾ teaspoon sea salt, plus more for sprinkling
¼ teaspoon cayenne pepper
3 tablespoons chopped onion
Sliced tomatoes

Blend together 1 cup of corn, N'egg, corn oil, and water to make "corn milk." Combine this with the rest of the ingredients except the tomatoes and cook until it begins to bubble. Turn out into a casserole and bake at 350°F until firm, about 1 hour. Place the sliced tomatoes on top and sprinkle lightly with salt. Bake an additional 15 minutes.

Genoese Squash

⅓ cup chopped onion
2 tablespoons corn oil
2 cups sliced squash, lightly steamed
1 cup Notzarella Cheez (page 94)
2 cups tomato, slightly pulverized in a blender
¼ teaspoon dill
¼ teaspoon sea salt

½ cup bread crumbs tossed with ¼ cup melted nondairy margarine.

Sauté the onion in the oil, then combine everything but the bread crumbs, top with the bread crumbs, and bake at 350°F for 30 minutes.

Gluten and Cabbage Casserole

1 cup chopped celery
½ cup chopped onion
½ teaspoon minced garlic
½ cup chopped bell pepper
1½ cups flavored gluten of choice (see specific gluten chapters)
1 tablespoon corn oil
½ cup canned tomato sauce
1 tablespoon parsley
¼ teaspoon oregano
¼ teaspoon sea salt
¼ teaspoon Italian herb seasoning
5 cups chopped cabbage, parboiled until it is tender
½ cup Pimiento Cheez (page 94) or Yeast Cheez (page 97)

Sauté the celery, onion, garlic, bell pepper, and gluten in the oil. Add the tomato sauce, parsley, oregano, salt, and Italian seasoning. In a nonstick casserole alternate layers of cabbage and sauce mixture. Top with the Cheez. Bake uncovered at 350°F for 30 minutes.

Gluten and Corn Casserole

½ cup chopped bell pepper
¼ cup chopped onion
1 teaspoon corn oil
1 cup flavored gluten or flavored soy grits
2 cups Medium White Sauce (page 262)
1 teaspoon prepared mustard
2 cups corn
½ cup Pimiento Cheez (page 94) or Yeast Cheez (page 97)

Sauté the bell pepper and onion in the oil until tender. Add the gluten (or grits) and cook for 5 minutes. Blend the White Sauce, mustard, and gluten mixture. Add the corn. Place in a casserole and top with Cheez. Bake at 350°F for 30 minutes.

Gluten and Eggplant Casserole

1½ cups ground flavored gluten of choice (see specific gluten chapters)
2 cups cubed eggplant, peeled and cut into 1-inch cubes
1½ cups chopped onion
1½ teaspoons minced garlic
1 tablespoon corn oil
2 cups canned tomatoes, including the juice
1 bay leaf
¼ teaspoon rosemary
Pinch ground cloves
¾ cup broth of type of gluten being used
½ teaspoon sea salt
¼ teaspoon cayenne
½ pound pasta
2 cups Yeast Cheez (page 97) or Notzarella Cheez (page 94)

Sauté the gluten, eggplant, onion, and garlic in the oil until the onion is soft. Stir in the tomatoes with the juice, bay leaf, rosemary, cloves, broth, salt, and pepper. Bring to a boil, reduce the heat, and simmer, covered, stirring occasionally and breaking up the tomatoes, for 20 minutes. Discard the bay leaf. Cook the pasta and stir it into the gluten mixture. Spoon half of this into a nonstick baking dish and top it with half of the Cheez. Spoon the remaining gluten mixture over that and top with the rest of the Cheez. Bake at 350°F until it is bubbling, 25 to 30 minutes.

Gluten and Rice Casserole

2 cups chopped onion
2 cups chopped celery
1 tablespoon corn oil
4½ cups rice, cooked
3 cups tomato paste
4 cups Pimiento Cheez (page 94) or Yeast Cheez (page 97)
2½ cups ground flavored gluten of your choice (see specific gluten chapters)
1 teaspoon bell pepper flakes
1 teaspoon garlic powder

Sauté the onion and celery in the oil. Combine with rest of ingredients and bake in a nonstick casserole at 400°F for 45 minutes, covered.

VARIATION: *Use flavored soy grits instead of gluten.*

Gluten-Vegetable Casserole

2 cups cubed potatoes, peeled and cut into 3/4-inch cubes
1 cup coarsely grated carrot
1 cup peas
3 cups flavoring broth (see Flavoring Broths chapter) of the type of gluten being used
2 tablespoons corn oil
3 tablespoons unbleached white flour
1/4 cup Lea and Perrins Steak Sauce
1 tablespoon Louisiana Hot Sauce
2 tablespoons nondairy margarine
2 cups cubed flavored gluten, cooked according to Method 2 or 3 (pages 99–100)
2 cups coarsely chopped onion
3 cups mushrooms
2 teaspoons minced garlic
1/4 cup finely chopped fresh parsley

In a saucepan combine the potatoes, carrot, peas, and broth. Simmer until the potatoes are done, about 10 minutes, and drain and set aside, reserving the broth. Put the oil in a skillet, stir in the flour, and cook, stirring constantly, until the flour is dark brown but not burned. Slowly stir in the reserved broth. Add the steak sauce and hot sauce. Melt the margarine in a skillet and fry the gluten, onion, and mushrooms until the gluten starts to brown, adding more oil if necessary. Add the garlic and parsley and sauté 2 more minutes. Combine everything and simmer over low heat for 10 minutes. Put in a casserole and bake at 375°F for 20 minutes.

Golden Vegetable Bake

2 tablespoons nondairy margarine, melted
2 tablespoons unbleached white flour
1 cup Cashew Milk (page 93), scalded
1 teaspoon sea salt
1/8 teaspoon black pepper or cayenne pepper
3/4 teaspoon paprika
1 1/2 cups shredded carrot
2 cups Cream-Style Corn (page 164)
2 tablespoons chopped onion
1/3 cup chopped bell pepper

Blend the melted margarine and flour. Gradually add the Cashew Milk. Cook, stirring constantly, until thickened. Add seasonings. Cool slightly. Stir in rest of ingredients. Pour into a nonstick casserole dish. Bake at 350°F 50 to 55 minutes.

Green Bean Casserole

2 cups green beans
Salted water
1 cup chopped bell pepper
1 1/2 cups chopped onion
1 teaspoon minced garlic
1 tablespoon nondairy margarine, plus more to "butter" casserole
1/4 teaspoon paprika
2 tablespoons soy sauce

Cook the green beans in salted water and drain. Sauté the bell pepper, onion, and garlic in the margarine. Mix with the beans, paprika, and soy sauce and put in a nonstick casserole "buttered" with margarine. Cover and bake at 350°F for about 30 minutes.

Green Beans in Tomato Sauce

2 cups green beans
Salted water
2 tablespoons nondairy margarine
2 tablespoons unbleached white flour
2 cups tomato juice
2 tablespoons soy sauce
1/4 teaspoon sea salt
1/4 teaspoon paprika
1/2 cup bread crumbs tossed in 1 tablespoon margarine

Cook the green beans in salted water. While the beans are cooking melt the margarine and stir in the flour. Gradually add the tomato juice, stirring constantly. Add the soy sauce, salt, and paprika, and cook for 5 more minutes. Drain the beans and place them in a nonstick casserole.

Pour the sauce over the beans. Bake at 350°F for about 20 minutes. Cover the top with the bread crumbs. Bake at 450°F until the crumbs are brown, about 10 more minutes.

VARIATION: *Instead of the bread crumbs tossed in margarine, use Yeast Cheez (page 97) or Pimiento Cheez (page 94) and dried bread crumbs dotted with margarine. Good over rice or toast.*

Green Beans Supreme 1

Just what the name says!

3⁄4 cup sliced onion
1⁄2 teaspoon minced garlic
1 tablespoon minced fresh parsley
2 teaspoons nondairy margarine, melted
2 tablespoons unbleached white flour
1⁄2 teaspoon sea salt
1⁄4 teaspoon paprika
4 cups green beans, julienned and steamed
1 cup Cashew Sour Kreem (page 94) or Tofu Sour Kreem (page 97)
1⁄2 cup Yeast Cheez (page 97) or Pimiento Cheez (page 94)
1⁄2 cup dried bread crumbs

Sauté the onion, garlic, and parsley in half of the margarine. Add flour, salt, and paprika and mix well. Stir in the beans and heat. Take off the heat and mix in the Sour Kreem. Put all into a nonstick casserole. Top with Cheez and bread crumbs, pressing down the crumbs lightly. Bake in a 325°F oven until the crumbs brown.

Green Beans Supreme 2

3 tablespoons chopped onion
3⁄4 cup chopped mushrooms
1⁄2 teaspoon minced garlic
2 teaspoons nondairy margarine
6 cups green beans, cooked
1⁄4 teaspoon lemon peel
1⁄4 teaspoon cayenne pepper
1⁄8 teaspoon dill
1⁄2 teaspoon sea salt
1 1⁄2 cups Yeast Cheez (page 97), Pimiento Cheez (page 94), or Notzarella Cheez (page 94)
1 1⁄2 cups bread crumbs

Sauté the onion, mushrooms, and garlic in the margarine. Combine everything except the Cheez and the bread crumbs. Put in a nonstick casserole and cover with Cheez. Top with bread crumbs, pressing down lightly. Bake at 400°F until the bread crumbs brown.

Green Chili Corn Casserole

Filling
3 cups diced onion
1 tablespoon corn oil
3 cups rice, cooked
2 1⁄4 cups corn kernels (thawed, if frozen)
2⁄3 cup diced red bell pepper
2⁄3 cup diced green bell pepper
1⁄2 teaspoon oregano
1 teaspoon coriander
1 teaspoon salt
3 teaspoons chili powder
2 tablespoons soy sauce
1⁄2 teaspoon curry powder
1⁄2 teaspoon ground cumin

Sauce
4 cups chopped and steamed potatoes
1 1⁄2 cups diced mild green chiles
1⁄2 tablespoon salt
3 cups water

To complete the recipe
12 tortillas

Sauté the onion in the oil until transparent. Mix the onion and all the filling ingredients together and set aside. Blend together all the sauce ingredients and set aside. To assemble, dip 4 corn tortillas into the sauce and layer them on the bottom of a 9x12-inch pan. Spread 4 cups of filling over the tortillas. Spread 1 cup of sauce over the filling. Repeat this assembly procedure, ending with 4 tortillas. Pour 2 cups of sauce over the top. Cover the pan and bake at 350°F for 50 minutes.

Harvest Vegetable Casserole

2 tablespoons nondairy margarine
3 cups sliced onion
1 cup sliced bell pepper, cut into 1-inch strips
1/2 cup uncooked barley
1 cup UnBeef Broth (page 155)
3/4 cup cut carrot, in chunks
2 large tomatoes, quartered
1 1/2 cups cut zucchini, in 1 1/2-inch chunks
2 1/2 cups green beans (each bean cut in half)
1 cup peas
1 1/2 cups cauliflower, separated into flowerets
2 tablespoons lemon juice
1 1/2 teaspoons crushed garlic
1 tablespoon sea salt
1 teaspoon paprika
2 tablespoons chopped fresh parsley

Sauté the onion and bell pepper in the margarine until browned. In a nonstick casserole, combine the barley, UnBeef Broth, carrot, tomatoes, zucchini, beans, peas, cauliflower, and onion mixture. Combine the lemon juice and garlic and pour over all. Sprinkle with salt and paprika. Cover and bake at 400°F until the barley is tender, about 1 1/2 hours. Stir in the parsley and serve.

Hot UnChicken Salad Casserole

2 1/2 cups diced UnChicken
1 cup diced celery
1 cup sliced mushrooms
1/2 cup minced onion
1 teaspoon lemon juice
1/8 teaspoon rosemary, crushed
1/4 teaspoon freshly ground black pepper
3/4 cup water chestnuts, drained and sliced
2 cups cooked rice
3/4 cup Cashew Mayonnaise (page 12) or Tofu Mayonnaise (page 22), or Miraculous Whip (page 17)
2 1/2 cups Kreem of UnChicken Soup (page 75)
3 tablespoons nondairy margarine, melted
3/4 cup cornflakes, crushed into crumbs
3/4 cup almonds, slivered

Combine the first nine ingredients. Blend the mayonnaise with the soup and toss with the gluten mixture. Put into an oiled or nonstick casserole. Combine the margarine with the cornflakes and almonds and sprinkle on top casserole. Bake at 350°F for 30 minutes.

Italian Eggplant Casserole

3 cups thinly sliced eggplant
Olive oil for frying, plus 2 teaspoons
1 1/2 cups chopped onion
1/2 teaspoon chopped garlic
1 cup chopped black olives
1 cup tofu, crumbled
1 1/2 cups canned tomato sauce
1 cup Golden Sauce (page 258)

Fry the eggplant in a small amount of olive oil. Drain well on paper towels. Sauté the onion and garlic in the 2 tablespoons of olive oil. Mix the onion with the olives and tofu. Layer in a nonstick casserole, starting with the eggplant, then tofu mixture, tomato sauce, and Golden Sauce. Bake for 30 to 45 minutes at 350°F.

Italian UnSausage Dressing

1/2 cup chopped onion
2 teaspoons corn oil
1/2 cup chopped mushrooms
1 cup Italian UnSausage (page 133)
1/2 teaspoon oregano
1/4 teaspoon sea salt
3/4 teaspoon minced garlic
2 slices of bread
3/4 cup Cashew Sour Kreem (page 94) or Tofu Sour Kreem (page 97)
1/2 cup Notzarella Cheez (page 94)
1/4 teaspoon thyme
1/2 teaspoon rosemary

Sauté the onion in the oil. Mix with next six ingredients (up to bread) very quickly in a food processor, or finely chop and blend them by hand. Set aside. Mix remaining ingredients in a bowl. Combine everything, put into a casserole, and bake, covered, at 350°F for 45 minutes. Uncover and bake 10 more minutes.

Italian UnSausage, Pasta, and Bean Casserole

2 cups ground Italian UnSausage (page 133)
2 cups ground UnBeef (page 109)
1½ cups chopped onion
1 tablespoon chopped garlic
1 teaspoon oregano
½ teaspoon thyme
2 tablespoons corn oil
3½ cups drained and chopped canned tomatoes
2 tablespoons tomato paste
½ teaspoon sea salt
½ teaspoon freshly ground pepper
2 cups cooked kidney beans, drained
¾ pound macaroni, cooked and drained
⅓ cup Parmesan Cheez (page 94)
¼ cup chopped fresh parsley
2 cups Yeast Cheez (page 97), Pimiento Cheez (page 94), or Notzarella Cheez (page 94)

Sauté the two types of gluten, onion, garlic, oregano, and thyme in the oil until the gluten is browned well. Add the tomatoes, tomato paste, salt, pepper, and beans, and heat through. Add the macaroni, "Parmesan," and parsley and toss together well. Put into a nonstick casserole. Spread the Cheez on top and bake, uncovered, at 375°F for 30 minutes.

Layered Casserole

Plain goodness!

3 cups green beans, cooked in UnChicken (page 155) or UnBeef Broth (page 155)
4 cups sliced potatoes, cooked with salt
¼ cup chopped onion
½ teaspoon minced garlic
2½ teaspoons corn oil
3 cups corn
1 cup water
2 tablespoons nondairy margarine, melted
Cracker crumbs for topping, tossed in some melted margarine

Place the cooked green beans in a nonstick casserole. Cover with the potato slices. Sauté the onion and garlic in the oil. Blend with the corn, water, and margarine, and pour over all. Top with cracker crumbs, pressing down lightly. Bake at 350°F until the cracker crumbs brown.

VARIATION: *Instead of green beans use green peas, squash, pumpkin, or cooked dried beans. Put a layer of Yeast Cheez (page 97) or Pimiento Cheez (page 94) on top of the corn and top with the cracker crumbs.*

Leftover Vegetables with Cheez

Always the same but different!

Moisten vegetables of your choice with one of the flavoring broths (see Flavoring Broths chapter), soups, or tomato juice. Place them in a nonstick casserole. Cover them with Notzarella Cheez (page 94), Pimiento Cheez (page 94), or Yeast Cheez (page 97). Top with bread crumbs and press them down lightly. Bake at 375°F until well heated.

Lima Beans with Cheez

½ teaspoon paprika
¾ cup UnBeef Broth (page 155)
1 teaspoon nondairy margarine
2½ cups lima beans, fresh, cooked (or frozen, thawed, and cooked)
½ cup Yeast Cheez (page 97) or Pimiento Cheez (page 94)
½ cup bread crumbs

Heat the paprika, broth, and margarine together until the margarine is melted. Mix in the lima beans. Place alternating layers of beans and Cheez in a nonstick casserole. Cover the top with bread crumbs and press down lightly. Bake at 350°F for 30 minutes.

Mexican Lasagna

Si! Si!

1 cup chopped onion
1 teaspoon minced garlic
2 teaspoons corn oil
2 cups cooked pinto, red, pink, or kidney beans
2 cups corn
4 cups canned tomato sauce
¼ cup cooked Tomato Salsa (page 296)
½ teaspoon oregano
1 teaspoon sea salt
20 corn tortillas
3 cups Yeast Cheez (page 97) or Pimiento Cheez (page 94)

Sauté the onion and garlic in the oil. Combine all the ingredients except the tortillas and Cheez. In a nonstick casserole pan, place a layer of tortillas. Over that put a layer of the filling. Over that spread 1 cup of the Cheez. Repeat one more time. Cover with another layer of tortillas. Top with the third cup of Cheez. Bake at 350°F for 20 minutes.

Mexican Lima Bean Casserole

⅓ cup chopped onion
¼ cup chopped bell pepper
Pinch cayenne pepper
1½ teaspoons nondairy margarine
½ teaspoon minced garlic
2 tablespoons Barbados molasses
2 cups canned tomatoes
1 teaspoon sea salt
2 cups lima beans, cooked

Sauté the onion, bell pepper, and cayenne pepper in the margarine. Combine all ingredients and bake in a nonstick casserole dish at 375°F for 45 minutes.

VARIATION: *Add Yeast Cheez (page 97), Pimiento Cheez (page 94), or Notzarella Cheez (page 94).*

Mushroom and Artichoke Pie

½ pound mushrooms, sliced (if fresh, clean first)
Two 10-ounce packages frozen artichoke hearts, thawed and chopped
3 tablespoons lemon juice
2 tablespoons olive oil
2 cups chopped onion
1½ teaspoons minced or mashed garlic
¼ cup water
1 tablespoon nutritional yeast
½ teaspoon monosodium glutamate (MSG)
¼ teaspoon poultry seasoning
½ cup chopped fresh parsley
1½ teaspoons sea salt
½ teaspoon freshly ground black pepper
15 ounces Tofu Ricotta Cheez (page 96)
3 N'eggs (page 302)
Convent Pie Crust (page 328)

Combine the mushrooms and artichokes. Sprinkle with the lemon juice. Heat the oil in a skillet, add the onion and garlic, and cook until lightly browned. Add the artichokes and mushrooms and cook 25 minutes, stirring occasionally. Add remaining ingredients except pie crust. Place ½ of crust in the bottom of a 9x9-inch baking dish. Cover with filling and top with rest of crust. Bake at 425° until the crust is browned, about 45 minutes.

Mushroom and Bell Pepper Quiche

3 tablespoons corn oil
3 tablespoons nondairy margarine
2 pounds medium-firm tofu, mashed
1 cup chopped onion
½ cup chopped bell pepper
2½ cups sliced mushrooms
2 cups chopped tomato
½ teaspoon minced garlic
¼ teaspoon sea salt, plus more to sprinkle on casserole
½ cup Yeast Cheez (page 97)
Sliced tomatoes
Freshly ground black pepper

Heat the oil and margarine together in a skillet and sauté the tofu until it begins to brown. Remove from the skillet with a slotted spoon and set aside. Add the onion, bell pepper, and mushrooms to the skillet, along with extra oil if needed, and sauté until they are soft. Add the tomato, garlic, and salt and sauté 5 more minutes. Put the tofu and Cheez in a blender and blend until smooth. Combine everything well, except for the tomato slices, and press into a nonstick casserole. Cover with a layer of tomato slices. Sprinkle some salt and pepper over the tomato slices, cover, and bake at 350°F for 30 to 40 minutes. Uncover and broil for a few minutes.

Noodle Casserole with Zucchini, Tomatoes, and Cheez

2 cups grated zucchini, sprinkled with 1/2 teaspoon of salt, drained in a strainer and pressed dry
3/4 cup chopped onion
1 1/2 teaspoons minced garlic
1 tablespoon olive oil
3 cups drained, and finely chopped canned tomatoes
1/2 teaspoon sea salt
1/8 teaspoon cayenne pepper
One 8-ounce package of noodles, cooked, drained, and tossed in 1/4 cup melted nondairy margarine
1 cup Yeast Cheez (page 97) or Pimiento Cheez (page 94)
1/2 cup Parmesan Cheez (page 94)

Sauté the zucchini, onion, and garlic in the oil until the zucchini and onion are tender. Add the tomatoes, salt, and pepper and simmer until the sauce is thick, about 10 minutes. Toss the cooked noodles with the Cheezes until blended. Toss with the sauce. Place in a casserole and heat in a 350°F oven until heated through.

Onions in Tomato Sauce

2 tablespoons nondairy margarine
2 tablespoons unbleached white flour
2 cups tomato juice
2 tablespoons soy sauce
1/4 teaspoon sea salt
1/4 teaspoon paprika
2 cups sliced onion
1/2 cup dried bread crumbs

Melt the margarine and stir in the flour. Gradually add the tomato juice, stirring constantly. Add the soy sauce, salt, and paprika, and cook for 5 more minutes. Put the sliced onion in a nonstick baking dish. Pour the sauce over the onion. Bake at 350°F for about 20 minutes. Cover the top with the bread crumbs. Bake at 450°F until the crumbs are brown, about 10 more minutes.

VARIATION: *Instead of only crumbs as a topping, use Yeast Cheez (page 97) or Pimiento Cheez (page 94) with crumbs over that. Good over rice or toast.*

Paella-Limas

1 cup green limas, frozen
5 teaspoons nondairy margarine
2 cups rice, uncooked
1 cup minced onion
1 cup thinly sliced carrot
4 1/2 cups boiling water
1 teaspoon sea salt

Steam the lima beans and set aside. Melt 3 teaspoons of the margarine in a heavy skillet, and stir in the rice. Continue stirring until the rice is slightly brown and popping (some rice does not pop). Sauté the onion and carrot together in the other 2 teaspoons of margarine for 3 minutes. Pour all the ingredients into the boiling water with the salt and boil for 30 minutes. Pour the paella into a casserole, cover, and bake at 350°F for 1 hour. Leave uncovered the last 5 minutes.

Piffel

I made this up, but couldn't think of a name for it. In disgust I said, "Piffel," and it had a name!

3⁄4 cup chopped onion
1⁄2 cup chopped bell pepper
2 teaspoons corn oil
6 cups vegetables of your choice, chopped or sliced, fresh or frozen (thawed well)
1 1⁄2 cups chopped tomato
1⁄2 teaspoon oregano
1⁄2 teaspoon basil
3 cups Yeast Cheez (page 97) or Pimiento Cheez (page 94)
1⁄4 teaspoon garlic powder
1 1⁄2 cups UnChicken Broth (page 155)

Sauté the onion and bell pepper in the oil. Combine all ingredients in a casserole dish and bake at 400°F for 45 minutes.

Cream of Piffel

I wanted a variation on Piffel—and succeeded!

3⁄4 cup chopped onion
1⁄4 cup chopped bell pepper
2 1⁄2 teaspoons corn oil
4 cups Thick White Sauce (page 262) made with UnChicken Broth (page 155)
6 cups vegetables of your choice, chopped or sliced, fresh or frozen (thawed well)
1⁄2 teaspoon Italian herb seasoning
1⁄4 teaspoon garlic powder
1⁄2 teaspoon cayenne pepper
3 cups Yeast Cheez (page 97) or Pimiento Cheez (page 94)
2 cups dried bread crumbs

Sauté the onion and bell pepper in the oil. Combine with the sauce, vegetables, herb seasoning, garlic powder, and pepper, and pour into a casserole dish. Cover with the Cheez. Top with bread crumbs, pressing down lightly. Bake at 400°F for 30 minutes.

Pimiento Cheez Loaf

1 cup Pimiento Cheez (page 94)
1 teaspoon cornstarch or arrowroot flour
2 cups cooked lima beans, mashed
1⁄4 cup chopped onion
2 tablespoons chopped fresh parsley
1⁄2 teaspoon sea salt
3⁄4 cup dried bread crumbs

Mix all ingredients except the bread crumbs and shape into a loaf, adding a little water if needed. Put in a pan and sprinkle with the crumbs. Bake at 325°F for 1 hour.

VARIATION: *Instead of the Pimiento Cheez, use 1 cup of Tofu Kreem Cheez (page 96) and 3 tablespoons of chopped pimientos.*

Polenta Casserole

1 cup cornmeal
4 cups UnBeef Broth (page 155)
1⁄2 teaspoon sea salt
3 tablespoons chopped onion
1 teaspoon minced garlic
1 tablespoon nondairy margarine
2 cups vegetable(s) of your choice, cooked
1⁄2 cup Yeast Cheez (page 97) or Pimiento Cheez (page 94)
1 teaspoon nondairy margarine
2 cups Tomato Sauce (page 261)

Mix the cornmeal with 1 cup of the broth until blended. Bring the remaining 3 cups of broth to a boil in a heavy saucepan. Add salt, then stir in the cornmeal paste and return to a boil, stirring continuously. Reduce heat to low and simmer, stirring occasionally with a wooden spoon, until the mixture is very thick. Add a little water if needed. Cook 15 to 20 minutes, depending on how fine or coarse the cornmeal is. Sauté the onion and garlic in the margarine and add them to the cooked vegetables. Add the vegetables to the cooked cornmeal. Stir in the Cheez and the margarine. Put the cornmeal mixture into a nonstick casserole. Top with the Tomato Sauce. Bake at 375°F for about an hour.

Potato-Broccoli Casserole

1 cup chopped onion
2 teaspoons minced garlic
2 teaspoons nondairy margarine, softened
2½ cups cubed potatoes, cooked in UnChicken Broth (page 155)
1½ cups broccoli, chopped and steamed
⅔ cup Yeast Cheez (page 97)
4 tablespoons Parmesan Cheez (page 94)
¼ teaspoon sea salt
⅛ teaspoon freshly ground black pepper
⅛ teaspoon cayenne pepper
¼ cup Cashew Kreem (page 93)
¼ cup chopped fresh parsley

Sauté the onion and garlic in the oil until the onion is soft. Mash the potatoes. Stir in the broccoli, ⅓ cup of the Yeast Cheez, 1 tablespoon of the Parmesan Cheez, salt, pepper, Kreem, parsley, onion, and garlic. Put in a nonstick baking dish. Spread the rest of the Yeast Cheez on top, sprinkle with the remaining "Parmesan," and bake at 350°F for 30 minutes. Broil, 4 inches from the heat until the top is golden, 1 to 2 minutes.

VARIATION: *Use carrots instead of broccoli.*

Potato-Cheez Bake

¼ cup chopped onion
½ cup nondairy margarine
6 cups mashed potatoes
3 cups Yeast Cheez (page 97), Pimiento Cheez (page 94), or Notzarella Cheez (page 94)
¼ teaspoon cayenne pepper
1½ teaspoons sea salt
½ teaspoon paprika

Saute the onion in the margarine. Combine everything well and put in a 1-inch layer in a casserole. Brush the top with melted margarine. Broil.

Potato and Tomato Gratin

1 cup chopped onion
1½ teaspoons minced garlic
2 teaspoons corn oil
2 cups diced tomato
½ teaspoon thyme, or 1 tablespoon basil
2 cups UnChicken Broth (page 155)
2½ cups sliced potatoes, peeled, sliced ⅛ inch thick, and cooked
½ teaspoon sea salt
¼ teaspoon freshly ground black pepper

Sauté the onion and garlic in the oil until soft. Add the tomato, thyme, and broth. Cook, covered, stirring occasionally, until the onion is soft and translucent. Put ⅓ of this sauce on the bottom of a casserole. Top with potato slices and sprinkle them with a little salt and pepper. Spoon over another ⅓ of the sauce, and add a layer of potatoes, also sprinkled with salt and pepper. Spoon over the rest of the tomato sauce and top with a layer of potatoes sprinkled with salt and pepper. Bake, covered, at 400°F until the potatoes are cooked through, about 60 minutes.

Potato Gratin

1½ cups finely chopped onion
1½ teaspoons minced garlic
1½ teaspoons nondairy margarine
4½ cups peeled and grated potatoes
2 tablespoons cornstarch
¾ teaspoon sea salt
¾ teaspoon freshly ground black pepper
1½ cups Cashew Kreem (page 93)
1 cup Yeast Cheez (page 97) or Notzarella Cheez (page 94)

Sauté the onion and garlic in the oil until soft. Add the rest of the ingredients except the Kreem and Cheez. Put into a nonstick casserole and pat it down. Drizzle the Kreem evenly over the top, sprinkle with the Cheez, and bake at 400°F until the potatoes are done and the top is golden, 25 to 30 minutes.

Potato Stuffing

1½ cups finely chopped onion
1 cup finely chopped celery
1 tablespoon corn oil
1 cup UnBeef Broth (page 155)
1 cup white bread cubes
3 cups mashed potatoes
2 tablespoons minced fresh parsley
¼ teaspoon garlic powder
¼ teaspoon sea salt
¼ teaspoon cayenne pepper

Sauté the onion and celery in the oil until soft. Take from heat. Add the rest of ingredients and mix well. Put into a casserole. Bake, uncovered, at 350°F until the top is lightly browned, about 45 minutes.

Potatoes and Carrots au Gratin

2½ cups peeled and sliced potatoes
1½ cups thinly sliced carrot
½ cup chopped bell pepper
¼ cup chopped onion
¾ cup Yeast Cheez (page 97), Pimiento Cheez (page 94), or Notzarella Cheez (page 94)
½ teaspoon sea salt
½ teaspoon dried mustard
⅛ teaspoon freshly ground black pepper
2 cups Kreem of Celery Soup (page 74)

Put the potatoes, carrot, bell pepper, and onion in a nonstick casserole. Combine half the Cheez with the rest of the ingredients. Pour this over the vegetables. Toss gently. Bake at 350°F, covered, until the potatoes are tender, 35 to 40 minutes. Spread the rest of the Cheez on top and bake, uncovered, for 10 to 15 more minutes.

Potatoes au Gratin

2 cups thinly sliced onion
1 teaspoon minced garlic
1 tablespoon nondairy margarine
⅛ teaspoon cayenne pepper
⅛ teaspoon freshly ground black pepper
¼ teaspoon sea salt
6 cups sliced potatoes, sliced ½ inch thick and boiled in salted water
3 cups Yeast Cheez (page 97), Pimiento Cheez (page 94), or Notzarella Cheez (page 94)
Parmesan Cheez (page 94) for sprinkling on top
⅔ cup UnChicken Broth (page 155), UnBeef Broth (page 155), or UnHam Broth (page 156)

Sauté the onion and garlic in the margarine until the onion is soft. Stir in the peppers and salt. Layer ½ of the boiled potato slices in a nonstick casserole, then a layer of ½ of the onion-garlic mixture, and a layer of ½ of the Cheez. Repeat the layering as above. Sprinkle some "Parmesan" over that. Pour the broth over it. Bake at 375°F until brown on top, about 45 minutes.

VARIATION: *Use cauliflower or broccoli instead of potatoes.*

Potatoes Scalloped in Margarine

Wash and peel the potatoes and cut them in slices ⅛ inch thick. Put them in cold water to cover for 15 minutes. Drain the potatoes and dry them between towels. Generously "butter" a baking dish with nondairy margarine and sprinkle it with fine dried bread or cracker crumbs. Cover the bottom carefully with a layer of potato slices. Dot them generously with margarine and sprinkle them lightly with salt and paprika. Repeat this layering until the dish is filled. Cover and bake at 375°F until the potatoes are tender, about 1 hour.

Potluck Potatoes

7½ cups peeled and chopped potatoes
1¼ cups Kreem of UnChicken Soup (page 75)
½ cup Cashew Sour Kreem (page 94) or Tofu Sour Kreem (page 97)
1 cup Tofu Kreem Cheez (page 96)

2 teaspoons nondairy margarine
3/4 cup Yeast Cheez (page 97)
1/4 cup sliced green onions
1/4 cup Cashew Milk (page 93)
1 tablespoon parsley flakes
1/4 teaspoon garlic salt
1/4 teaspoon freshly ground black pepper

Cook the potatoes in boiling water until tender, 10 to 12 minutes. Drain. Rinse with cold water. Drain again. Combine the soup, Sour Kreem, Kreem Cheez, and margarine. Add 1/4 cup of the Yeast Cheez, 3 tablespoons of the green onions, "milk," parsley, garlic salt, and pepper. Stir to combine. Put into a nonstick casserole and bake, uncovered, at 350°F until heated through, 30 to 35 minutes. Spread the rest of the Cheez on top and bake 5 more minutes. Sprinkle with the rest of the green onions.

Ratatouille

3 tablespoons olive oil
1 cup chopped onion
1 1/2 teaspoons minced garlic
1 1/4 cups sliced bell pepper, lengthwise 1/4 inch thick (a mixture of green, red, and yellow, if possible)
1 medium eggplant, sliced 1/4 inch thick
1 cup thinly sliced mushrooms
3/4 teaspoon sea salt
1/2 teaspoon freshly ground black pepper
1/3 cup fresh basil leaves (lightly packed), chopped
4 cups tomato, halved lengthwise and sliced crosswise 1/3 inch thick
2/3 cup Yeast Cheez (page 97), Pimiento Cheez (page 94), or Notzarella Cheez (page 94)

Heat the oil in a skillet and sauté the onion, garlic, bell pepper, eggplant, and mushrooms, adding more oil if needed, until softened (about 15 minutes). Add the salt, pepper, and basil. Stir in the tomato and cook for 1 more minute. Transfer to a nonstick casserole and spread the Cheez on top. Cover with foil and bake at 400°F until the vegetables are very tender, about 30 minutes. Can be served hot, warm, or cold.

Rice Dressing

1/4 cup chopped onion
1/3 cup chopped bell pepper
2 teaspoons nondairy margarine
4 cups rice cooked in UnChicken Broth (page 155)
1 cup dried bread crumbs
2/3 cup chopped black olives
3/4 teaspoon sea salt
1 cup Thin White Sauce (page 262) made with UnChicken Broth (page 155)

Sauté the onion and bell pepper in the margarine. Combine all ingredients in a casserole dish. Bake, uncovered, at 350°F for 30 minutes.

Rumbledethumps

A pity someone does not write a fairy story with this as a title! It is actually colcannon, a Scottish dish, adapted from an American version given in Gourmet *magazine.*

6 cups potatoes, peeled, diced, and cooked
1 tablespoon nondairy margarine, melted
2 tablespoons fresh chives or minced green onions
1/2 cup Cashew Milk (page 93)
4 cups diced and cooked cabbage
1 teaspoon sea salt
1/4 teaspoon freshly ground black pepper
1 1/2 cups Yeast Cheez (page 97), Pimiento Cheez (page 94), or Notzarella Cheez (page 94)

Mash the potatoes, stir in the margarine, chives (or green onions), "milk," cabbage, salt, and pepper. Put into a baking dish, spread the Cheez over the top, and bake at 400°F until heated through, about 30 minutes. Just before serving broil until the top browns lightly.

Sauerkraut Casserole

2 tablespoons corn oil
3 cups cubed UnPork (page 122)
1 cup chopped onion
1 cup chopped celery
One 16-ounce can of sauerkraut, undrained
8 ounces noodles, cooked and drained
1 1/4 cup Kreem of Mushroom Soup (page 74)
1/2 cup mushrooms
1/2 teaspoon sea salt
1/4 teaspoon freshly ground black pepper

Heat the oil in a skillet and brown the gluten. Add the onion and celery and sauté until the onion is transparent. Stir in the rest of the ingredients, put into a casserole, cover, and bake at 350°F for 1 hour, stirring occasionally.

Scalloped Broccoli 1

3 cups Cashew Milk (page 93)
2 teaspoons nondairy margarine
1/2 cup chopped onion
1 teaspoon minced garlic
2 tablespoons unbleached white flour
1 1/2 teaspoons sea salt
1/8 teaspoon black pepper or cayenne pepper
1 1/2 cups Pimiento Cheez (page 94) or Yeast Cheez (page 97)
6 cups broccoli, steamed and chopped

Preheat the "milk." Melt the margarine in a saucepan over low heat and sauté the onion and garlic. Blend in the flour, salt, and pepper. Add the "milk" slowly. Cook quickly, stirring constantly, until the mixture thickens and bubbles. Add the Cheez and stir it in well. Put half the broccoli in a nonstick casserole. Cover with half of the sauce. Repeat this layering. Cover and bake at 350°F for 1 hour. Uncover and bake 30 minutes longer.

Scalloped Broccoli 2

1 cup sliced mushrooms
1/2 cup chopped onion
2 teaspoons corn oil
1 1/2 teaspoons minced garlic
1/2 teaspoon crushed red pepper
4 cups UnChicken Broth (page 155)
6 cups broccoli, steamed and chopped
3 cups Notzarella Cheez (page 94)
1 1/2 cups bread crumbs

Sauté the mushrooms and onion in the oil until the onion is soft. Combine everything but the Cheez and bread crumbs and cook until the broccoli is tender. Drain off and discard 3 cups of the broth. Mix in the Cheez and put in a nonstick casserole. Top with the crumbs, pressing down lightly. Bake, uncovered, at 350°F until brown on top, about 45 minutes.

Scalloped Cabbage

4 cups chopped cabbage
3 tablespoons corn oil
3 tablespoons unbleached white flour
1/2 teaspoon sea salt
Dash freshly ground black pepper
1 cup Cashew Milk (page 93)
1 cup Yeast Cheez (page 97)
3/4 cup bread crumbs

Put cabbage in a casserole and set aside. Heat the oil in a saucepan. Stir in the flour, salt, and pepper, and cook until bubbly. Gradually stir in the "milk." Cook and stir until thickened. Fold in the Cheez. Pour over the cabbage. Sprinkle the bread crumbs on top and press lightly into the Cheez. Bake, uncovered, at 350°F until bubbly, 20 to 30 minutes.

Scalloped Carrots and Potatoes

1 cup sliced onion
1 teaspoon minced garlic
2 teaspoons nondairy margarine, melted
4 cups potatoes, peeled, sliced, and boiled in salted water
2 cups carrot, peeled, sliced, and boiled in salted water
2 tablespoons minced UnBacon (page 136)
1/2 teaspoon sea salt
1/8 teaspoon freshly ground black pepper

1/8 teaspoon rosemary leaf, crumbled
1/4 cup minced fresh parsley
2 cups Thin White Sauce (page 262)

Sauté the onion and garlic in the margarine and mix with the cooked potatoes. Put a layer of the potato-onion mixture in a nonstick casserole. Top with a layer of carrot. Combine the UnBacon, salt, pepper, rosemary, and parsley, and sprinkle 1/2 of that over the carrots. Pour 1/2 the White Sauce over all. Repeat. Bake at 350°F for 20 minutes.

Scalloped Corn

1/2 cup finely chopped bell pepper
1/2 cup chopped onion
2 1/2 cups Cheez Sauce of choice (page 257)
10 cups corn

Combine the bell pepper, onion, and Cheez Sauce. Stir in the corn. Put into a casserole and bake at 350°F until light brown on top.

Scalloped Eggplant

1 teaspoon sea salt
3 cups peeled and sliced eggplant
2 tablespoons chopped bell pepper
2 tablespoons chopped onion
1/2 teaspoon minced garlic
1 tablespoon nondairy margarine
2 cups tomato, cooked or canned
3/4 cup bread crumbs

Heavily salt both sides of the eggplant slices. Let sit for 1 hour and wipe off the salt and liquid. Press between absorbent towels, squeezing out as much liquid as possible. Cut into small pieces. Sauté the bell pepper, onion, garlic, and eggplant in 1/2 of the margarine, adding some corn oil if needed. Add the tomato and salt. Simmer 20 to 30 minutes or until tender. Pour into a nonstick baking dish. Melt the remaining margarine, mix with bread crumbs, and spread over the top of the eggplant mixture. Bake at 350°F until the eggplant is tender and the bread crumbs are brown, about 20 minutes.

Scalloped Peas and Squash

1/3 cup chopped onion
1 teaspoon nondairy margarine
2 cups sliced or cubed squash
2 cups peas (if frozen, partially thawed)
3 cups Medium White Sauce (page 262)
1 cup Yeast Cheez (page 97), Pimiento Cheez (page 94), or Notzarella Cheez (page 94)

Sauté the onion in the margarine. Combine the squash and peas. Place in a nonstick baking dish. Pour the sauce over the vegetables. Top with the Cheez. Bake at 375°F for 45 minutes.

VARIATION: *Use pumpkin instead of squash.*

Scalloped Potatoes 1

Fill a nonstick casserole with layers of peeled and very thinly sliced raw potatoes, sprinkling each layer generously with unbleached white flour, salt, and soy sauce, and spraying it with vegetable oil. Heat Cashew Milk (page 93) that has been seasoned with salt and paprika. Pour it over the potatoes until it can be seen through the top layer. Bake at 350°F for 75 minutes. (You may turn the potatoes with a spoon while cooking to ensure even baking.)

Scalloped Potatoes 2

3 cups Cashew Milk (page 93)
2 teaspoons nondairy margarine
1/2 cup chopped onion
1 teaspoon minced garlic
2 tablespoons unbleached white flour
1 1/2 teaspoons sea salt
1/8 teaspoon black or cayenne pepper
1 1/2 cups Yeast Cheez (page 97), Pimiento Cheez (page 94), or Notzarella Cheez (page 94)
6 cups peeled and thinly sliced potatoes

Preheat the "milk." Melt the margarine in a saucepan over low heat. Sauté the onion and garlic. Blend in the flour, salt, and pepper. Add the "milk" slowly. Cook quickly, stirring constantly, until the mixture thickens and bubbles. Add the Cheez and stir it in well. Put half the potatoes in a nonstick casserole. Cover with half of the sauce. Repeat this layering. Cover and bake at 350°F for 1 hour. Uncover and bake 30 minutes longer.

Scalloped Potatoes 3

1/2 cup Miraculous Whip (page 17)
2 tablespoons unbleached white flour
1 cup Cashew Milk (page 93)
1/4 teaspoon sea salt
1/8 teaspoon freshly ground black pepper
1 cup Yeast Cheez (page 97), Pimiento Cheez (page 94), or Notzarella Cheez (page 94)
4 cups sliced potatoes

Combine the Miraculous Whip and flour. Gradually stir in the "milk," salt, and pepper. Cook, stirring constantly, until the mixture thickens and comes to a boil. Add the Cheez and stir in well. Remove from heat. Put the potatoes in a baking dish and pour the liquid over them. Cover and bake at 350°F for 45 minutes. Uncover and bake until the potatoes are tender, about 15 more minutes.

Scalloped Potatoes and Mushrooms

1 1/2 cups chopped onion
2 1/2 cups mushrooms, stemmed and chopped coarsely
1 tablespoon plus 1 1/2 teaspoons finely chopped jalapeños
2 teaspoons minced garlic
2 tablespoons nondairy margarine
4 cups Medium White Sauce (page 262) made with UnChicken Broth (page 155)
6 cups potatoes, peeled, sliced 1 inch thick, and boiled in salted water

Sauté the onion, mushrooms, jalapeños, and garlic in the margarine. Add to the White Sauce and cook for 5 minutes. Add the sauce to the potatoes and stir well. Place in a casserole pan and bake at 375°F for 45 minutes.

Scalloped Potatoes and Spinach

1/3 cup chopped onion
2 teaspoons nondairy margarine
3 tablespoons unbleached white flour
2 cups Cashew Milk (page 93)
1/4 teaspoon sea salt
3/4 cup Yeast Cheez (page 97) or Notzarella Cheez (page 94)
5 cups potatoes, peeled and sliced 1/4 inch thick, cooked with 1/8 teaspoon of sea salt until just tender, and drained
1/2 10-ounce package frozen spinach, thawed and drained well
1 tablespoon chopped pimiento
Paprika

Sauté the onion in the margarine until tender. Stir in the flour. Stir in the "milk" and salt. Cook over medium heat until thickened and bubbly, stirring occasionally. Add the Cheez and stir in well. Combine this with the potatoes, spinach, and pimiento in a nonstick casserole and bake at 350°F for about 40 minutes. Sprinkle with the paprika and serve.

Shepherd's Pie 1

I never tire of this.

2 cups peas or dried beans, cooked
2 cups corn
2 cups green beans, cooked
1 tablespoon nondairy margarine, melted
1/2 teaspoon sea salt
2 cups UnBeef Gravy 1 or 2 (page 254)
2 1/2 cups mashed potatoes

Combine the peas, corn, beans, and margarine together in a deep casserole. Sprinkle them with the salt. Pour the gravy over the vegetables. Spread the mashed potatoes on top. Before serving, heat in oven until the peaks of the mashed potatoes are light brown, about 30 minutes.

Shepherd's Pie 2

This merits a blue ribbon!

2 cups cubed potatoes
½ cup UnBeef Broth (page 155), plus just enough to cover the potatoes
⅓ cup chopped onion
2 teaspoons corn oil
1 cup chopped tomato
1 cup chopped vegetable(s) of your choice
2 tablespoons chopped fresh parsley
1 teaspoon arrowroot
¼ teaspoon sea salt
1 cup Pizza Cheez (page 95)
1 recipe Basic Pie Crust for 2 crusts (page 328)
Oil

Boil the potatoes in the broth for 5 to 10 minutes. Sauté the onion in the corn oil. Add the potatoes, tomato, vegetable(s), and parsley. Cover and cook 5 more minutes. Dissolve the arrowroot and salt in the half cup of broth, then add it and the Cheez to the vegetables. Cook for 10 minutes, stirring occasionally. Oil a pie pan and put one of the unbaked crusts in it. Pour in the filling. Lay the other crust over the vegetable mixture. Seal the top. Cut slits in the top and brush it with oil. Bake at 350°F until the pastry is lightly browned, about 30 minutes.

Simple Garden Casserole

½ cup chopped onion
1 teaspoon minced garlic
1 teaspoon nondairy margarine
1 cup chopped zucchini
1 cup chopped tomato
½ teaspoon sea salt
¼ teaspoon freshly ground black pepper
½ cup Cashew Milk (page 93)
½ cup Biscuit Mix (page 50)
2 N'eggs (page 302)
⅓ cup Parmesan Cheez (page 94)

Sauté the onion and garlic in the margarine until soft. Add the zucchini, tomato, salt, and pepper and cook until the zucchini is soft. Put into a nonstick casserole. Beat the "milk," Biscuit Mix, N'eggs, and Cheez together until smooth. Pour evenly over the vegetables. Bake at 400°F until a knife inserted in the center comes out clean, 30 to 35 minutes. Let stand for at least 5 minutes before cutting.

Soy Grits Casserole

1 cup uncooked rice
1½ cups UnBeef Broth (page 155)
¼ cup chopped bell pepper
1½ teaspoons nondairy margarine
2 cups soy grits, soaked in 4 cups of UnBeef Broth (page 155)
2½ cups chopped tomato
¼ cup tomato paste
4 cups Yeast Cheez (page 97) or Pimiento Cheez (page 94)
¼ teaspoon sea salt

Cook rice in the broth. Sauté the bell pepper in margarine. Combine all ingredients and put in baking dish. Bake at 350°F until brown, about 20 minutes.

Soy Grits Enchilada Casserole

Hold on to your sombrero—this is good.

1 cup soy grits
2 cups UnBeef Broth (page 155), boiling hot
⅓ cup chopped onion
2 tablespoons chopped bell pepper
½ teaspoon minced garlic
4 teaspoons corn oil
⅛ teaspoon cayenne pepper
6 tablespoons cooked Tomato Salsa (page 296)
8 corn tortillas
3 cups Tomato Sauce (page 261)
1 cup Yeast Cheez (page 97), Pimiento Cheez (page 94), or Notzarella Cheez (page 94)

Soak the grits in the broth for at least 10 minutes, adding more if needed for the grits to absorb. Sauté the onion, bell pepper, and garlic in the oil. Add the grits and pepper and fry a few minutes more. Add the salsa. Dip the tortillas in hot oil to make them limp. Layer in a casserole pan starting with Tomato Sauce, then tortillas, Cheez, and then grits filling. Repeat layering again, and then top with Tomato Sauce, tortillas, Cheez, salsa, and chopped onion. Bake for 15 minutes at 400°F.

Spicy Potatoes

2 cups thinly sliced potatoes
1 tablespoon olive oil, plus more for coating potato slices
1/2 teaspoon minced garlic
1 tablespoon chopped red onion
1/4 cup chopped fresh parsley, or 2 tablespoons dried
1 teaspoon unbleached white flour
1/4 teaspoon cayenne pepper
1/2 cup chopped tomato
1/2 bay leaf
1/4 teaspoon Sucanat
1/4 teaspoon sea salt

Brush or spray the potato slices with olive oil. Place on a nonstick baking sheet and bake until lightly browned and tender, about 20 minutes. Set aside. Heat the tablespoon of oil in a heavy skillet. Add garlic, onion, and parsley. Cook until the onion is transparent but not browned. Whisk in the flour and cayenne. Add the rest of the ingredients. Cook over low heat for 10 minutes, stirring occasionally. Remove bay leaf. Pour sauce over potatoes, and bake, uncovered, at 350°F for 15 minutes.

Spinach and Herb Potato Casserole

I call this a "politician dish"—it stands on its record!

6 cups potatoes, peeled, boiled, and mashed
1 cup Tofu Kreem Cheez (page 96)
1 cup Cashew Sour Kreem (page 94) or Tofu Sour Kreem (page 97)
1 tablespoon nondairy margarine, softened or melted
2 teaspoons sea salt
1 1/2 teaspoons dill
1/4 teaspoon freshly ground black pepper
One 10-ounce package frozen chopped spinach, cooked and well drained

Whip the potatoes, Kreem Cheez, Sour Kreem, and margarine together until smooth. Add all the rest and beat until well mixed. Put into a nonstick casserole and bake at 375°F for 20 minutes.

Squash and Macaroni Bake

2 cups finely chopped squash
1/2 cup chopped onion
1/2 teaspoon minced garlic
1 1/2 teaspoons nondairy margarine
1/4 cup unbleached white flour
1/4 teaspoon sea salt
1/2 teaspoon oregano
1 3/4 cups water
3 cups Yeast Cheez (page 97) or Pimiento Cheez (page 94)
2 cups macaroni, cooked and drained
1 cup chopped tomato

Sauté the squash, onion, and garlic in the margarine. Blend in the flour and seasonings. Gradually add the water. Cook, stirring, until thickened. Stir in 1 1/2 cups of the Cheez. Stir in the macaroni and tomato. Pour into a nonstick casserole. Top with remaining Cheez and bake at 350°F for 25 minutes.

VARIATION: *Use pumpkin instead of squash.*

Squash Bake

8 cups sliced yellow squash
1/2 cup chopped onion
3/4 cup shredded carrot
1 tablespoon corn oil
1 1/2 cups Kreem of UnChicken Soup (page 75)
1/2 cup Cashew Sour Kreem (page 94) or Tofu Sour Kreem (page 97)
2 cups herb-flavored croutons

Cook the squash in lightly salted boiling water for 3 to 4 minutes, or until crisp-tender. Drain well. Sauté the onion and carrot in the oil until tender. Combine the onion, carrot, soup, Sour Kreem, and 1 1/2 cups of the croutons. Add the squash and mix lightly. Put into a nonstick casserole. Sprinkle with the remaining croutons.

Bake, uncovered, at 350°F until heated through, about 25 minutes.

Squash Casserole with Tomatoes, Cheez, and Rice

1/4 cup chopped onion
1 tablespoon nondairy margarine
2 cups sliced squash
2 cups chopped tomato
1/8 teaspoon cayenne pepper
1 1/2 cups Yeast Cheez (page 97) or Pimiento Cheez (page 94)
1/2 teaspoon sea salt
2 1/2 cups cooked rice

Sauté the onion in the margarine. Combine all the ingredients and stir until nicely blended. Place the mixture in a nonstick casserole and bake at 350°F for 45 minutes.

Squash Creole

You can rely on this.

2 1/2 cups sliced squash
2 teaspoons corn oil
1/4 cup chopped bell pepper
1/3 cup chopped onion
1 teaspoon minced garlic
3 tablespoons unbleached white flour
1 cup UnBeef Broth (page 155)
2 cups chopped canned tomatoes
1 tablespoon Barbados molasses
1/4 teaspoon cayenne pepper
1 teaspoon sea salt
1/2 bay leaf
3/4 cup Yeast Cheez (page 97), Pimiento Cheez (page 94), or Notzarella Cheez (page 94)
1 1/2 cups dried bread crumbs

Steam the sliced squash until tender and put in a nonstick baking dish. Heat the oil, add bell pepper, onion, and garlic and sauté. Add flour and stir until blended. Add broth, tomatoes, molasses, and spices to this mixture. Cook these ingredients until the pepper is tender, about 5 minutes. Pour this sauce over the squash. Cover with the Cheez and top with the bread crumbs, pressing down lightly. Bake at 350°F for until crumbs are well browned, about 30 minutes.

Squash Tamale Bake

So easy and so good.

1/2 cup chopped bell pepper
1 teaspoon minced garlic
1/3 cup chopped onion
2 teaspoons corn oil
2/3 cup cornmeal
3 cups canned tomatoes
2 cups cubed squash
1/4 teaspoon cayenne pepper
1/2 teaspoon sea salt
2 cups water

Sauté the bell pepper, garlic, and onion in the oil. Place all the ingredients together in a saucepan and stir until the squash has released its juice well, and the cornmeal has thickened. After partly cooking, turn out into a nonstick baking dish. Bake at 350°F for about 1 hour.

Tamale Pie

8 tablespoons chopped jalapeños
1 teaspoon cayenne pepper
1 3/4 cups cooked kidney beans, drained
3 cups thinly sliced onion, separated into rings
1 1/2 teaspoons minced garlic
1 cup chopped mushrooms
1 cup corn
2 cups Yeast Cheez (page 97)
2 cups Cashew Sour Kreem (page 94) or Tofu Sour Kreem (page 97)
2 cups water
1 cup masa harina
2 N'eggs (page 302)

Combine the jalapeños, cayenne, beans, onion, garlic, mushrooms, corn, Cheez, and Sour Kreem, and put into a casserole. Bring the water to a boil and gradually add the masa while stirring constantly. Reduce the heat and cook until it thickens, about 10 minutes. Take from the heat and stir in the N'eggs. Spread this over the casserole and bake at 375°F for 35 minutes.

Tomato and Corn Scallop

1 cup Yeast Cheez (page 97) or Pimiento Cheez (page 94)
1½ cups corn
¾ cup dried bread crumbs
Sliced tomatoes, enough to make two layers in the casserole

Combine the Cheez, corn, and ½ cup of the bread crumbs. In a nonstick casserole place half the corn mixture and cover with tomato slices. Repeat. Sprinkle the crumbs over the top and press down lightly. Bake at 350°F for 30 minutes.

Tomato Eggplant Bake

As delicious as it is simple!

3 cups cubed eggplant
Oil for deep-frying
1 cup chopped onion
½ cup finely chopped bell pepper
1 teaspoon minced garlic
2 teaspoons olive oil
2 cups stewed Italian tomatoes
⅛ teaspoon cayenne pepper
¼ teaspoon sea salt

Deep-fry the eggplant until it begins to brown and transfer it to paper towels to drain. Sauté the onion, bell pepper, and garlic in the olive oil. When the onion is soft, add the tomatoes, pepper, and salt and cook for 15 minutes. Mix in the eggplant. Transfer to a nonstick casserole and bake at 350°F for 20 minutes.

Tomato Rice with Cheez

2 tablespoons finely chopped bell pepper
3 tablespoons chopped onion
1 teaspoon nondairy margarine
1½ cups rice, cooked in UnBeef Broth (page 155)
1 cup chopped tomato
½ teaspoon Barbados molasses
½ teaspoon sea salt
¼ teaspoon paprika
1 cup Yeast Cheez (page 97) or Pimiento Cheez (page 94)
¼ cup dried bread crumbs
1 tablespoon nondairy margarine

Sauté the bell pepper and onion in the margarine. Mix everything together, except the bread crumbs, and put in a nonstick casserole dish. Cover with the bread crumbs. Dot with 1 tablespoon of margarine. Bake at 350°F for about 40 minutes.

Triple Layer Casserole

A potluck staple!

3 cups ground or cubed gluten of choice (see specific gluten chapters)
2 tablespoons corn oil
2 cups chopped onion
2 teaspoons minced garlic
1½ teaspoons minced jalapeños
3 cups potatoes, peeled, sliced, and boiled
¾ cup Cashew Milk (page 93)
Pinch freshly ground black pepper
5 cups Cream-Style Corn (page 164)
1 cup Cheez Cracker crumbs (page 59)

Brown the gluten in half the oil. Set aside. Sauté the onion, garlic, and jalapeños in the remaining oil. When the onion is soft, add the gluten and cook for 5 more minutes. Put the gluten on the bottom of a nonstick casserole. On top of that put the cooked potatoes. Stir the "milk" and pepper into the corn and pour that over the potatoes. Sprinkle the cracker crumbs on top. Bake at 375°F until the crumbs start to brown.

UnBacon and Cheez Potatoes

8 cups potatoes, peeled, cooked, and cubed
½ cup finely chopped onion
2 cups Yeast Cheez (page 97), Pimiento Cheez (page 94), or Notzarella Cheez (page 94)
1 cup Miraculous Whip (page 17)
1 cup finely chopped UnBacon (page 136)
¾ cup sliced black olives

Combine the potatoes, onion, Cheez, and Miraculous Whip. Put in a casserole. Sprinkle with the UnBacon and olives. Cover and bake at 350°F until heated through, about 30 minutes.

UnHam and Broccoli Casserole

3/4 cup cubed UnHam (page 130)
3/4 cup Yeast Cheez (page 97), Pimiento Cheez (page 94), or Notzarella Cheez (page 94)
1 3/4 cups cooked broccoli, drained and chopped
1 3/4 cups Kreem of Mushroom Soup (page 74)
3/4 cup Biscuit Mix (page 50)
1/3 cup Cashew Milk (page 93)
1 teaspoon nondairy margarine, melted
1 N'egg (page 302)

Combine the UnHam, Cheez, broccoli, and soup in a nonstick casserole. Stir the rest of the ingredients together until a dough forms. Drop by spoonfuls evenly over the broccoli mixture. Bake, uncovered, at 350°F until the top is golden brown, 40 to 45 minutes.

VARIATION: *Use another type of gluten.*

UnHam and Potato Casserole

Fundamentally good!

2 cups chopped onion
1 tablespoon minced garlic
1/2 teaspoon hot pepper flakes
1 tablespoon nondairy margarine
2 tablespoons unbleached white flour
4 cups UnPork Broth (page 156) made with Cashew Milk (page 93)
3 cups sliced UnHam (page 130), broiled on both sides
2 cups Pimiento Cheez (page 94)
6 cups sliced potatoes, 1/4 inch thick and boiled

Sauté the onion, garlic, and pepper flakes in the margarine. Add the flour and stir in well. Slowly add the broth and let it simmer for 15 minutes. Put a thin layer of this broth in a nonstick casserole pan, a layer of gluten, a layer of Cheez, and a layer of potatoes. Repeat the layering once more. Put any remaining broth over the top to cover the potatoes. Bake at 400°F for 30 minutes. Just before serving, broil for a few minutes to lightly brown the top.

UnHam and Potatoes au Gratin

2 cups potatoes, peeled, sliced, and cooked
1 cup diced UnHam (page 130)
1 tablespoon minced onion
1/3 cup nondairy margarine
3 tablespoons unbleached white flour
1 1/2 cups Cashew Milk (page 93)
1 cup Yeast Cheez (page 97), Pimiento Cheez (page 94), or Notzarella Cheez (page 94)
3/4 teaspoon sea salt
Dash white pepper

Combine the potatoes, UnHam, and onion in an oiled or nonstick casserole and set aside. In a saucepan melt the margarine and stir in the flour until smooth. Gradually add the "milk," stirring constantly until it thickens and bubbles. Add the Cheez, salt, and pepper. Stir until well combined and heated through. Pour over the mixture in the casserole and stir gently to mix. Bake at 350°F until bubbly, 35 to 40 minutes.

Vegetable Casserole with Tomatoes and Rice

1/2 cup chopped bell pepper
1/4 cup chopped onion
1 teaspoon minced garlic
2 1/2 teaspoons corn oil
4 cups vegetables of your choice, cut in pieces and cooked
3 cups drained and chopped canned tomatoes
1 tablespoon chopped fresh parsley
1/4 teaspoon basil
2 1/2 cups cooked rice
1 teaspoon sea salt
1 cup Yeast Cheez (page 97) or Pimiento Cheez (page 94)

Sauté the bell pepper, onion, and garlic in the oil. Combine all ingredients except Cheez in a nonstick casserole. Top with the Cheez and bake for 20 minutes at 400°F.

Vegetable Crumble

Crumble

2 tablespoons nondairy margarine
2 cups unbleached white flour
1 cup Yeast Cheez (page 97), Pimiento Cheez (page 94), or Notzarella Cheez (page 94)

Base

1/3 cup chopped onion
1/2 teaspoon minced garlic
1 1/2 teaspoons nondairy margarine
3 cups mixed vegetables, chopped if need be
1/4 cup unbleached white flour
1 1/2 cups chopped tomato
1 cup UnBeef Broth (page 155)
1/2 cup Cashew Milk (page 93)
3 tablespoons chopped fresh parsley
1/2 teaspoon sea salt
1/4 teaspoon paprika

For the crumble, rub the margarine into the flour until the mixture resembles fine crumbs. Add the Cheez and set aside. Sauté the onion and garlic in the margarine until the onion is transparent. Add the vegetables and cook over gentle heat, stirring occasionally, for 10 minutes. Stir in the flour, then add the rest of the ingredients. Bring to a boil, reduce the heat, cover, and simmer until the vegetables are just tender, about 15 minutes. Put in a nonstick casserole. Press the crumble topping over the vegetables. Bake at 375°F until golden brown, about 30 minutes.

Vegetable Enchiladas

1 1/4 cups potatoes, peeled and diced or cut into strips
1/4 cup olive or corn oil
1 1/2 cups finely chopped onion
1 tablespoon minced garlic
1 cup chopped zucchini
4 2/3 cups sliced mushrooms
4 cups drained and chopped canned tomatoes
1 tablespoon sliced jalapeños
1 1/4 teaspoons ground cumin
1 teaspoon sea salt
12 corn tortillas, steamed until soft
1 cup cooked Tomato Salsa (page 296)

Boil the potatoes in just enough water to cover until just tender, 15 to 20 minutes. Drain and set aside. Heat the oil in a skillet and sauté the onion until it begins to soften. Add the garlic, zucchini, mushrooms, tomatoes, and jalapeños, and sauté until tender. Stir in the cumin and potatoes, and sauté several minutes. Add the salt. Coat one side of each tortilla with salsa, spread some of the filling down the center and roll up quickly, then put in an oiled or nonstick baking pan. When all are in the pan, blend the rest of the filling and the rest of the salsa together and spread over the top. Bake at 350°F for 15 minutes.

Vegetable Pot Pie

What can I say but, Yum!

1 1/2 teaspoons corn oil
1 cup diced onion
1 cup thinly sliced celery
2/3 cup thinly sliced carrot
1 cup diced bell pepper
2/3 cup frozen green beans
1/3 cup frozen peas
1/3 cup unbleached white flour
1 cup Cashew Milk (page 93)
2 cups flavoring broth of choice (see Flavoring Broths chapter)
2 tablespoons minced fresh parsley
1 teaspoon sea salt
1/4 teaspoon sage
1/2 teaspoon thyme
1/4 teaspoon freshly ground black pepper
1/4 teaspoon cayenne
Convent Pie Crust (page 328)

Combine everything but the crust and cook, stirring often, until thickened. Put into a nonstick casserole. Lay the crust over the top of the mixture. Bake at 400°F until the crust is golden and the filling is bubbling, 20 to 30 minutes.

Vegetables and Cheez Casserole

1½ cups tomato sauce
1½ cups Yeast Cheez (page 97), Pimiento Cheez (page 94), or Notzarella Cheez (page 94)
4 cups vegetables of your choice, cut up and steamed
1 teaspoon sea salt
⅓ teaspoon cayenne pepper

Combine the tomato sauce and Cheez well. Combine everything, put into a casserole, and bake at 400°F for 15 to 20 minutes. Serve with rice or pasta.

Vegetables Parmesan 1

Excellent at all times!

⅓ cup chopped onion
1 teaspoon minced garlic
3 cups cut vegetables of your choice, in ½-inch slices
4 teaspoons corn oil
2 cups canned tomato sauce
1½ cups Yeast Cheez (page 97) or Pimiento Cheez (page 94)
½ cup Parmesan Cheez (page 94)

Sauté the onion, garlic, and vegetables in the oil. Oil a casserole dish. In the dish, pour ¼ inch of the tomato sauce. Over that put a layer of vegetables. Top with a layer of Cheezes. Repeat, ending with a layer of Cheez. Cover with foil and bake at 400°F for 30 minutes. Remove foil and bake uncovered for 10 minutes. Watch closely to avoid overcooking.

Vegetables Parmesan 2

Fancier than Number 1, but worth all the making!

2 cups chopped potatoes
1 tablespoon corn oil
2 cups vegetables of your choice, cut into pieces if needed
1 tablespoon nondairy margarine
⅓ cup chopped onion
1 teaspoon minced garlic
1 cup chopped tomato
2 tablespoons unbleached white flour
½ cup Cashew Milk (page 93)
½ teaspoon sage
½ teaspoon basil
½ teaspoon oregano
½ teaspoon sea salt
¼ teaspoon paprika
1 cup Parmesan Cheez (page 94)
1 cup bread crumbs

Boil the potatoes for about 10 minutes, or until just tender. Drain, reserving 1 cup of liquid. Heat the oil and sauté the vegetables until they are tender. Melt the margarine and sauté the onion and garlic until the onion is transparent. Add tomato to onion, stir in the flour, and cook 1 minute. Add the potato liquid, "milk," herbs, and seasonings to this. Bring to a boil, reduce heat, and simmer 15 to 20 minutes. Put the potatoes and vegetables in a nonstick casserole. Pour the tomato sauce over that. Sprinkle the "Parmesan" and then the bread crumbs over all, pressing down lightly. Put in the oven at 400°F until heated through, about 20 minutes.

VARIATION: *Instead of using 2 cups of potatoes plus 2 cups of vegetables, use 4 cups of vegetables, including or excluding potatoes as one of the vegetables.*

Zucchini Casserole 1

6 cups sliced zucchini
Salted water
2 cups chopped or cubed UnBeef (page 109)
½ cup chopped onion
1 teaspoon minced garlic
1 tablespoon corn oil
1 cup rice, cooked
1 teaspoon garlic salt
1 teaspoon oregano
2 cups Tofu Cottage Cheez (page 96)
2 cups Medium White Sauce (page 262) to which 3 tablespoons soy sauce has been added
1 cup Pimiento Cheez (page 94) or Yeast Cheez (page 97)

Cook the sliced zucchini in salted water for 2 to 3 minutes and drain well. Place half the zucchini in a nonstick casserole. Sauté the UnBeef, onion, and garlic in the oil until the onion is transparent. Pour over the zucchini in the baking dish. Sprinkle the cooked rice and seasonings over the gluten layer. Spoon the Cottage Cheez over the rice layer, and cover with the remaining zucchini. Spread White Sauce over all. Spread the Cheez over that. Bake at 300°F for 35 to 40 minutes.

Zucchini Casserole 2

½ cup chopped onion
¾ teaspoon minced garlic
5 tablespoons chopped jalapeños
1 tablespoon corn oil or nondairy margarine
1 cup chopped zucchini
½ cup chopped tomato
1 teaspoon chopped fresh basil
⅓ cup green peas
2 cups Yeast Cheez (page 97)
¼ cup fine bread crumbs

Sauté the onion, garlic, and jalapeños in the oil until the onion is soft. Combine everything but the Cheez and bread crumbs in a casserole and mix well. Spread the Cheez over all and top with the crumbs, pressing them down lightly. Bake at 375°F for 30 minutes.

Zucchini Casserole with Tomatoes, Cheez, and Rice

1 cup sliced mushrooms
½ cup chopped onion
1 teaspoon crushed garlic
2 cups zucchini, unpeeled, thinly sliced
4 teaspoons nondairy margarine
1½ cups chopped tomato
½ cup Cashew Sour Kreem (page 94) or Tofu Sour Kreem (page 97)
1 cup Yeast Cheez (page 97) or Pimiento Cheez (page 94)
¼ teaspoon sea salt
⅛ teaspoon cayenne pepper
3 cups cooked rice

Sauté the mushrooms, onion, garlic, and zucchini in the margarine until the zucchini is soft. Place in a large bowl and add the tomato. Beat together the Sour Kreem, Cheez, salt, and pepper. Combine all the ingredients and stir until nicely blended. Place the mixture in a casserole and bake at 350°F for 45 minutes.

VARIATION: *Cook the rice in UnBeef (page 155) or UnChicken Broth (page 155).*

Zucchini Creole

Always welcome!

3 tablespoons nondairy margarine
3 tablespoons unbleached white flour
1½ cups chopped tomato
¼ cup chopped bell pepper
¼ cup chopped onion
½ teaspoon sea salt
½ teaspoon Sucanat
½ bay leaf
Pinch powdered cloves
2½ cups sliced zucchini, steamed
¾ cup Yeast Cheez (page 97)
1 cup bread crumbs
Nondairy margarine

Melt the margarine and stir in the flour until blended. Add the tomato, bell pepper, onion, and spices and cook for 5 minutes. (If larger quantities are used, cook until the onion and pepper are tender.) Place zucchini in a nonstick baking dish and pour the tomato mixture over it. Cover with Cheez. Top with bread crumbs and dot with margarine. Bake at 350°F until the crumbs turn light brown.

Zucchini Parmigiana

4½ cups chopped tomato
½ cup minced onion
¼ cup minced fresh parsley
1 teaspoon basil
2½ teaspoons olive oil
½ teaspoon sea salt
¼ teaspoon cayenne pepper
Unbleached white flour
5 all-purpose N'eggs (page 302)
5 cups zucchini, sliced lengthwise into ¼-inch-thick slices
2½ cups Notzarella Cheez (page 94)

Cook the tomato over medium heat until it is falling apart, 15 to 25 minutes. Put them through a food mill (medium disk) into a bowl. Cook the onion, parsley, and basil in the oil over medium heat, stirring occasionally, for 15 minutes. Add the tomato, salt, and pepper, and simmer, stirring occasionally, until it is thickened slightly, 20 to 30 minutes.

Put the flour and N'eggs in two separate bowls. Dip the zucchini slices in the N'eggs, letting any excess drip off, and then dip them in the flour, shaking off any excess. Deep-fry the zucchini at 380°, turning, until they are golden, about 2 minutes. When done, transfer them to paper towels to drain. Spread a thin layer of the tomato sauce in a nonstick casserole. Put half of the zucchini in a layer. Over the zucchini pour half of the remaining tomato sauce. Spread a layer of half of the Cheez. Repeat this layering once more. Bake at 350°F for 20 to 30 minutes. Put under a broiler, about 6 inches from the heat, until the top is slightly browned, 2 to 4 minutes.

Dried Beans

Several years after the establishment of our monastery, which was always vegetarian, we all began feeling low in energy and out of sorts in general. I knew the problem was dietary, but did not know exactly what was wrong, and I began to wonder if we would have to modify our diet, a distasteful thought on all levels. Then it happened that a friend brought me a book on life in medieval English monasteries. Most significant to me was the section on monastic diet. Research had revealed that in all monasteries the monks ate cooked dried beans at every meal without exception. The usual menu was vegetable soup, bean soup, and bread.

Looking in books on nutrition I found that dried beans contained virtually all the needed amino acids. So we began eating beans every day, and in less than a week we were out of the slump.

I urge you to consider making beans a frequent, if not daily, item in your diet. This seems essential for vegans.

But what about beans and gas? The solution was found in the wonderfully wise and humorous *Carla Emery's Old Fashioned Recipe Book*. There was a whole section on beans. Carla Emery was what the English delicately called "a martyr to wind," and eating beans turned her into a holocaust! She tried all the recommended remedies, none of which worked. (I knew they wouldn't, for I had tried them all myself by the time I read her book.) Then some blessed and intelligent soul explained to her that when beans dry their nutrients become locked in something fierce, and only long cooking (or sufficient pressure-cooking) will unlock them. Otherwise they will be indigestible and the result will be evident to all. Since most people undercook beans they assume that it is just the nature of beans to produce internal cataclysms. Not true. So forget the Bean-O—just cook the beans thoroughly. They will take care of themselves.

To unlock the nutrients of beans it is best to pressure-cook them thoroughly. This applies to all dried beans, including lentils (whose "skins" will not clog the pressure cooker vent if enough water is used, as in the following instructions), soybeans, and whole dried peas. Cooking dried beans by boiling them the time required to fully release the nutrients is a tremendous waste of fuel energy. Even cooking them for twelve to fourteen hours in a Crock-Pot has not always proven to be sufficient, whereas pressure-cooking has proven completely effective.

Do not soak dried beans overnight before cooking as they will tend to ferment, especially in warm weather.

To cook beans/lentils in a pressure cooker use the following procedure.

1. Put the beans in the pressure cooker along with salt (1 teaspoon per quart of dried beans) and enough water to cover the beans with water at least 2 inches deep.
2. Add 1 tablespoon of corn oil (this is so the skins will not clog the pressure cooker vent).
3. Cover, without the weight, and bring them to a boil.
4. Continue to boil for 5 minutes.
5. Turn off the heat and let them rest for 1 hour.
6. Turn on the heat, put on the weight, and cook at 15 pounds of pressure.

Here is a list of times (minutes) recommended for pressure-cooking dried beans:

Black	35
Black-eyed peas	20
Garbanzos	25
Great northern (white)	25
Kidney	20
Lentils	5
Lima	25
Navy	25
Peas, whole	25
Pinto	25
Soy	45

Dal and split peas are cooked in water on the stove rather than pressure-cooked, as they foam up and tend to clog the cooker vent.

The amount that dried beans yield when cooked varies. Here is a listing of how much one cup of dried beans will yield according to type.

Black	2 cups
Black-eyed peas	2 cups
Garbanzos	2½ cups
Great northern (white)	2½ cups
Kidney	2½ cups
Lentils	2 cups
Lima	2½ cups
Navy	2½ cups
Peas, whole	2 cups
Pinto	2½ cups
Soy	2½ cups

Baked Beans 1

5 cups cooked dried beans
3 tablespoons minced onion
1 teaspoon minced garlic
2 teaspoons corn oil
⅛ teaspoon cayenne pepper
¾ cup Barbados molasses
2 cups canned tomato sauce
½ cup UnBeef Broth (page 155)
½ teaspoon savory
½ teaspoon sea salt
Yeast Cheez (page 97) or Pimiento Cheez (page 94)

Pressure-cook and drain the beans. Sauté the onion and garlic in the oil. Combine all ingredients except Cheez and simmer for 10 minutes, uncovered. Place in baking dish, cover with Cheez. Bake at 400°F 15 to 20 minutes.

Baked Beans 2

5 cups cooked dried beans
¾ cup chopped onion
2 teaspoons corn oil
¼ cup minced UnBacon (page 136)
½ cup Sucanat
¼ cup plus 2 tablespoons Barbados molasses
1 tablespoon dried mustard
1 teaspoon sea salt
2 cups canned tomato sauce

Pressure-cook the beans and drain them. Sauté the onion in the oil. Combine everything in a covered casserole dish and bake, covered, at 350°F for at least 90 minutes, the longer the better.

VARIATION: *Cut some Loma Linda Big Franks into pieces, and sauté with the onions.*

Baked Beans Boston Style

2½ cups dried navy or kidney beans, soaked 5 hours
⅓ cup Barbados molasses
¼ cup Sucanat
1 tablespoon dried mustard
¼ teaspoon cayenne pepper
2 teaspoons soy sauce
½ cup minced UnBacon (page 136)
1 tablespoon corn oil
2 cups coarsely chopped onion
2½ teaspoons minced garlic
2 bay leaves
1 teaspoon sea salt
¼ teaspoon freshly ground black pepper

Drain the beans, cover with fresh water, and bring to a boil for 5 minutes. Drain again. Whisk together the molasses, Sucanat, mustard, cayenne, and soy sauce in a bowl. Mix this with the beans. Add the rest of the ingredients. Put into a casserole and add enough water to cover the beans. Cover and bake at 300°F until the beans are very soft, 7 to 8 hours. Check periodically and add more water, if needed, to keep the beans from drying out. Uncover the last half hour of baking so a crust can form.

Baked Lentils

3 cups dried lentils
⅓ cup chopped onion
½ teaspoon minced garlic
2 teaspoons corn oil
2 teaspoons sea salt
2 cups tomato, blended until smooth
½ cup bread crumbs tossed in melted nondairy margarine

Pressure-cook the lentils. Sauté the onion and garlic in the oil. Combine all the ingredients except the bread crumbs and place in a baking dish. Top with the crumbs. Bake at 350°F until the crumbs are golden brown.

Barbecue Baked Beans

½ cup chopped bell pepper
½ cup chopped onion
2 teaspoons minced garlic
1 tablespoon corn oil
4 cups cooked dried beans
½ teaspoon cayenne pepper
3 cups Tomato Sauce (page 261)
¼ cup Barbados molasses
¼ cup wine vinegar
1 tablespoon Sovex or Vegex (dissolve in the vinegar)
1 teaspoon sea salt
Yeast Cheez (page 97) or Pimiento Cheez (page 94)

Sauté the bell pepper, onion, and garlic in the corn oil. Combine all ingredients except Cheez. Pour into a large oiled casserole. Add more tomato sauce if it is needed to cover the beans. Bake 30 minutes at 400°F, then cover with Yeast Cheez or Pimiento Cheez and bake 10 more minutes.

Barbecue Beans

Soybeans work well in this.

2¼ cups chopped onion
2 teaspoons minced garlic
1 tablespoon corn oil
1 cup tomato paste
3 cups water
½ cup Sucanat
1 tablespoon Barbados molasses
2 tablespoons soy sauce
½ teaspoon allspice
1 teaspoon sea salt
1½ teaspoons red pepper flakes
¼ cup vinegar or ½ cup lemon juice
4 cups beans, cooked and drained

Sauté the onion and garlic in the oil. Add the tomato paste and stir in well. Add the rest of the ingredients, except the beans, bring to a boil, and simmer for 15 minutes. Stir in the beans and cook for 15 to 20 more minutes.

Bean and Potato Loaf

4 cups cooked beans, without salt
2 cups hot mashed potatoes, cooked without salt
1 tablespoon nondairy margarine, melted
1¾ cups tomato juice

2 tablespoons tomato sauce
½ cup minced onion
1 teaspoon garlic
¼ teaspoon cayenne pepper
¼ teaspoon freshly ground black pepper
2 teaspoons sea salt
2 tablespoons chopped bell pepper
2 N'eggs (page 302)

Purée or mash the beans. Add rest of ingredients and mix lightly. Pour into an oiled or nonstick baking dish and bake slowly for 1 hour.

Bean Enchiladas

Sauce
1 cup chopped onion
1½ tablespoons minced garlic
2 teaspoons corn oil
6 cups crushed canned tomatoes
5 tablespoons chili powder
1½ teaspoons sea salt
1½ teaspoons Sucanat

Filling
4 cups cooked pinto beans, drained
2 teaspoons onion salt
¾ teaspoon garlic powder
½ teaspoon ground cumin
⅔ cup canned tomato sauce

Eight 6-inch Corn Tortillas (page 152)

Topping
2 cups Pimiento Cheez (page 94) or Yeast Cheez (page 97)
½ cup chopped onion
½ cup chopped black olives

For the sauce, sauté the onion and garlic in the oil until the onion is soft, then add the rest of the ingredients and simmer for 45 minutes. To make the filling, partially mash the beans in a bowl. Mix the rest of filling ingredients together and add to the beans. Mix well. To assemble, cover the bottom of a casserole with some of the sauce. Put some of the filling in each tortilla, roll it up, and put in the casserole with the seam side down. Cover with the rest of the sauce. Spread the Cheez over all. Sprinkle the onion and olives over that. Bake, uncovered, at 350°F for 25 minutes.

Bean Loaf

2½ cups dried beans, cooked and mashed
1 teaspoon sea salt
½ cup finely chopped bell pepper
½ cup tomato pulp
½ cup corn flakes
⅓ cup chopped onion
½ teaspoon paprika
1 teaspoon soy sauce
2 teaspoons corn oil

Combine all ingredients in an oiled loaf pan. Bake at 350°F for about 1 hour. Serve with Yeast Cheez (page 97) or Pimiento Cheez (page 94) or Tomato Sauce (page 261).

Bean Pot 1

¾ cup chopped onion
2 teaspoons nondairy margarine
5 cups cooked dry beans
1½ teaspoons sea salt
½ teaspoon minced garlic
½ cup pimiento
½ teaspoon paprika

Sauté the onion in the melted margarine for 5 minutes. Combine all ingredients and cook for 20 to 30 minutes.

Bean Pot 2

¾ cup chopped onion
2½ teaspoons corn oil
2 teaspoons minced jalapeños
1½ teaspoons minced garlic
5 cups cooked dried beans (reserve cooking water)
4 cups water, including reserved bean cooking water
2 teaspoons sea salt
1 bay leaf
2 cups diced potatoes
1½ cups diced carrot
½ teaspoon basil
¼ teaspoon oregano
1 tablespoon soy sauce

Sauté the onion in the oil until soft. Add the jalapeños and garlic and sauté 2 more minutes.

Add everything else and cook until the potatoes are done, about 30 minutes, adding more water if it gets too thick.

Beans and Tortillas

Tortillas

1 cup rye flour
2 cups unbleached white flour
⅔ cup soy flour
⅓ cup wheat bran
1¼ cups boiling water
1 teaspoon sea salt
2 tablespoons genuine maple syrup
¼ cup corn oil

Filling

8 cups cooked dried beans
2 cups Tomato Salsa (page 296)
2 cups Cashew Sour Kreem (page 94) or Tofu Sour Kreem (page 97)
1⅓ cups chopped tomato
⅓ cup chopped onion
2 cups Yeast Cheez (page 97), Pimiento Cheez (page 94), or Notzarella Cheez (page 94)

To make the tortillas, put the flours and bran into a bowl. Mix everything else together and stir into the flour, adding only enough extra water to make a stiff dough. Knead well and roll out small pieces of dough to paper-thin rounds about 8 inches in diameter. Bake these directly on top of an ungreased griddle or place on an ungreased baking sheet and bake at 250°F until thoroughly dried and slightly brown. Combine the filling ingredients. Put about 1 cup of filling along one edge of a tortilla and roll up.

Beans Bourgignonne

¾ cup chopped onion
2 teaspoons corn oil margarine
½ cup carrot, sliced in half rounds
1¼ cups cubed potatoes
1 cup UnChicken Broth (page 155)
3 tablespoons Italian tomato paste
⅛ teaspoon thyme
1 bay leaf
2 cups sliced mushrooms
4 cups pinto beans, cooked
2 garlic cloves, crushed
1 teaspoon sea salt

In a soup pot, sauté the onion in 1 tablespoon of the margarine. Add the carrot and potatoes. Stir in the broth, tomato paste, thyme, and bay leaf. Bring to a boil and simmer briskly until the potatoes and carrots are cooked, about 20 minutes, adding extra broth to keep the vegetables covered if necessary. Toward the end of the cooking time, sauté the mushrooms in the other tablespoon of margarine over low heat, then add them to vegetables along with the beans, garlic, and salt. Return to a boil, lower the heat, and simmer, uncovered, for another 10 minutes. Remove and discard the bay leaf.

Beans with Tomatoes

¾ cup chopped onion
1 teaspoon minced garlic
2 teaspoons corn oil
2 cups dried beans, cooked and drained, reserving the liquid
3 cups chopped canned tomatoes
1 teaspoon sea salt
Pinch cayenne pepper

Sauté the onion and garlic in the oil. Combine all ingredients and cook for one hour, adding bean water if it gets too dry.

Black Beans with Tomatoes

2 cups dried black beans
2 cups canned tomatoes
1 cup chopped onion
1 cup chopped celery
2 teaspoons corn oil
½ teaspoon garlic powder
2 teaspoons sea salt
½ teaspoon freshly ground black pepper

Pressure-cook the beans. Blend the tomatoes in a blender. Sauté the onion and celery in the oil. Combine everything and cook 20 to 30 minutes.

Buckaroo Beans

I can't describe these, but I sure can eat them!

2 cups dried pinto beans
½ cup chopped onion
1 teaspoon minced garlic
½ cup chopped bell pepper
2 teaspoons corn oil
1 bay leaf (whole)
½ cup minced or finely chopped UnBacon (page 136)
2 cups canned tomatoes
2 teaspoons chili powder
½ teaspoon dried mustard
¼ teaspoon oregano
1 teaspoon sea salt

Pressure-cook the beans. Sauté the onion, garlic, and bell pepper in the oil. Combine everything and cook until well done. Add more water if necessary.

Campfire Red Beans

These taste more like they were cooked over a smoky hickory campfire than if they really were. Mexican Chorizo UnSausage (page 134) is especially good in this dish.

4 cups dried kidney beans
2 cups cubed UnHam (page 130) or UnSausage (page 132)
1 tablespoon corn oil
1 cup chopped onion
1 tablespoon chopped garlic
1 teaspoon liquid smoke
1 tablespoon Louisiana Hot Sauce
2 tablespoons Lea and Perrins Steak Sauce
2 tablespoons parsley flakes
1 tablespoon bell pepper flakes
3 cups UnHam Broth (page 156) or UnSausage Broth (page 156)
3 cups water

Pressure-cook the beans. Sauté the gluten in the oil. Add the onion and garlic and sauté until the onion is soft. Put everything together and cook for 15 minutes.

Chili Beans1

Good by themselves or with Cheez (page 94) and tortillas (page 52).

¾ cup chopped onion
1 cup chopped bell pepper
2 teaspoons corn oil
4 cups cooked dried beans
1 teaspoon minced garlic
2½ cups chopped tomato
¼ teaspoon cayenne pepper
1 teaspoon sea salt

Sauté the onion and bell pepper in the oil. Combine all ingredients with sufficient water and simmer together slowly for 45 minutes.

Chili Beans 2

4 cups cooked dried pinto or kidney beans
1½ cups chopped onion
1 teaspoon minced garlic
1½ teaspoons corn oil
2 teaspoons sea salt
2 tablespoons chili powder
2 teaspoons cumin

Pressure-cook the beans. Sauté the onion and garlic in the oil. Combine everything and cook 10 to 15 minutes, adding any needed water.

Chimichangas

Never fails!

5 cups Refried Beans (page 237)
1 recipe Flat Bread (page 52), uncooked

Put ½ cup of beans on an uncooked "bread." Fold in the two sides and then the top and bottom. Deep-fry at 375°F until light brown, being careful to prevent them from unfolding. If not served immediately, refry quickly to reheat and recrisp the chimichangas shortly before serving. Serve with Cashew Sour Kreem (page 94) or Tofu Sour Kreem (page 97), Miraculous Whip (page 17), or some other type of vegan "mayonnaise," chopped tomatoes, and chopped lettuce.

VARIATION: *Use Flour Tortillas (page 52) instead of Flat Bread.*

Cowboy Beans

These are addicting!

2 cups dried pinto or pink beans
2 teaspoons sea salt
¾ teaspoon crushed red pepper
½ cup chopped onion
2 teaspoons minced garlic
⅔ cup minced UnBacon (page 136)
1½ teaspoons corn oil

Pressure-cook the beans with the salt. Drain. Cover with water. Add rest of ingredients and bring to a boil. Simmer for 30 minutes.

Dried Bean Patties

2 cups cooked dried beans of choice, mashed
½ cup chopped tomato
¾ cup chopped onion
½ cup chopped bell pepper
⅛ teaspoon cayenne pepper
2 cups bread crumbs
2 teaspoons sea salt
1 tablespoon soy sauce
½ teaspoon sage

Combine ingredients. Shape into balls and flatten. Dip them in flour. Chill the patties for one hour or more. Fry them slowly until brown on both sides.

Garbanzo Creole

¾ cup chopped onion
1 teaspoon minced garlic
½ cup chopped bell pepper
1½ teaspoons corn oil
3 cups cooked garbanzos
Pinch cayenne pepper
2 cups canned tomatoes
½ teaspoon sea salt
1 bay leaf
½ cup Tomato Sauce (page 261)
½ cup UnChicken Broth (page 155)

Sauté the onion, garlic, and bell pepper in the oil. Combine everything and cook for 30 minutes.

VARIATION: *Use another type of dried bean.*

Garbanzos Bombay (Kabuli Channa)

4 cups dried garbanzos
4 cups chopped onion
4 teaspoons minced garlic
2 tablespoons minced jalapeños
4 teaspoons turmeric
2 tablespoons powdered coriander
¾ teaspoon powdered ginger
1 tablespoon garam masala
4½ teaspoons nondairy margarine
6 cups chopped tomato
¼ cup lemon juice
1 tablespoon sea salt

Pressure-cook the garbanzos, reserving the cooking water. Sauté the onion, garlic, jalapeños, turmeric, coriander, ginger, and garam masala in the margarine. Add the cooked garbanzos and stir well until coated with the hot oil. Add the tomato, lemon juice, and salt, stirring well. Add 1 quart of the garbanzo water (adding some plain water if there is less than a quart). Cover and cook for about one hour. You may want to add some more (garbanzo) water if it seems to be getting too dry.

Garbanzos

2 cups dried garbanzos
2 teaspoons sea salt
1½ cups chopped onion
2 teaspoons corn oil
1 teaspoon powdered gingerroot
½ teaspoon ground cumin
1 teaspoon turmeric
1 teaspoon ground coriander
¼ teaspoon garam masala
½ teaspoon chili powder
⅛ teaspoon cayenne pepper
3 cups canned tomatoes, crushed, with juice

Cook the garbanzos in 1 teaspoon of the salt and reserve the liquid. Sauté the onion in the oil until it is tender. Add the ginger and cumin, and sauté for 2 to 3 minutes more. Add the rest of the spices and stir to blend together. Combine everything, including the garbanzo liquid, and simmer for 30 minutes.

Herbed Beans

¾ cup chopped onion
1½ teaspoons corn oil
2 cups dried beans, pressure-cooked
2 teaspoons sea salt
¼ teaspoon Fines Herbes (page 303)
Pinch cayenne pepper

Sauté the onion in the oil. Combine everything and cook for 1 hour.

Hummus 1

1⅓ cups dried garbanzos
2 tablespoons olive oil
1 tablespoon sea salt
1 tablespoon minced garlic
¼ cup lemon juice
1 cup tahini
¼ teaspoon cayenne pepper

Pressure-cook the garbanzos, drain, and mash them, reserving the cooking water. Add the remaining ingredients except the garbanzo water. Using the garbanzo water, blend all in a blender until smooth and of the consistency of a medium-thick sauce.

Hummus 2

2¼ cups cooked and drained garbanzos
¼ cup plus 2 tablespoons tahini
1 tablespoon coarsely chopped garlic
1 pound tofu
½ cup lemon juice
1¼ teaspoons sea salt
½ teaspoon freshly ground black pepper
¼ cup plus 2 tablespoons sesame seeds
2 teaspoons ground cumin
3 tablespoons minced green onions
2 tablespoons minced green onion tops

In a food processor combine the garbanzos, tahini, and garlic. Purée until smooth and thick. Add the tofu, lemon juice, salt, and pepper, and process until creamy. Toast the sesame seeds in a heavy skillet over medium heat until they begin to pop, about 3 minutes. Cook, stirring, until lightly toasted and fragrant, about 3 more minutes. Add ¼ of the seeds to the food processor and pulse briefly to incorporate. Set the rest aside. Put the cumin in the skillet and cook over medium heat, stirring, until fragrant, about 1 minute. Add, along with the onions, salt and pepper to the food processor and pulse briefly to incorporate. Remove to a bowl and stir in the rest of the sesame seeds and onion tops.

Kerala Dal

Kerala is the state at the southernmost tip of India where Saint Thomas the Apostle established the Indian Orthodox Church in A.D. 54. I expect he ate this very dish. If so, I hope he liked it as much as I do!

1 cup masur dal (the tiny orange kind that turns yellow when cooked)
3 cups water
½ teaspoon sea salt
2 teaspoons corn oil
1 tablespoon black mustard seeds
½ teaspoon cumin seeds
1 tablespoon minced garlic
1 teaspoon turmeric
3 cups chopped tomato
¼ teaspoon hing (asafetida*), optional
¼ teaspoon ground cumin
¼ teaspoon cayenne pepper
½ teaspoon sea salt

Cook the dal in the water and salt until it just begins to fall apart. Remove from heat and drain. Heat the oil in a very heavy, small pan. Add the mustard seeds, spreading them over the bottom of the pan evenly, and cook, stirring, until they turn blacker and start to pop. Add the cumin and garlic and cook just one minute more. Stir in the turmeric and immediately remove pan from the heat. In a large saucepan, combine tomatoes, hing, cumin, cayenne pepper, salt, and the fried seed mixture. Bring to a boil and cook for 15 minutes. Add the dal and cook until it falls apart.

* *Note! Asafetida can be purchased in Indian markets.*

Lentil Loaf

2 cups lentils, cooked
1 cup bread crumbs
½ cup chopped squash
⅓ cup chopped onion
2 tablespoons corn oil
3 tablespoons low-sodium soy sauce
½ cup rice, cooked
1 teaspoon sage
½ teaspoon thyme
1 teaspoon curry powder
⅔ cup water from cooking the lentils
1 tomato, sliced
Sesame seeds for garnish

Mix all ingredients together except for tomato and sesame seeds. Bake in a nonstick pan for 15 minutes at 375°F. Remove loaf from oven and top with tomato slices and sesame seeds. Reduce heat to 350°F and bake for another 15 minutes.

Lentil Patties

These are really distinctive. Many who do not usually like lentils love these.

2 cups lentils cooked in UnBeef Broth (page 155), drained, and mashed
3 cups fine bread crumbs
¾ cup minced onion
1 teaspoon minced garlic
1 teaspoon sea salt
¼ cup UnBeef Broth (can be that left over from cooking the lentils)
2 tablespoons chopped fresh parsley

Mix the ingredients thoroughly and let sit for 15 minutes. Form into patties. Place on floured cookie sheet and bake at 350°F until browned, 20 to 30 minutes. Or dip the patties into flour and sauté in corn oil until brown. Good with Lentil Patty Sauce (recipe follows).

Lentil Patty Sauce

⅓ cup chopped onion
1 teaspoon corn oil
2½ cups cooked tomato
½ teaspoon sea salt
3 tablespoons cornstarch
3 tablespoons water

Sauté the onion in the oil. Add tomato and salt. Bring to a boil. Blend the cornstarch with the water and stir into the tomato. Bring to a boil again and remove from heat.

Lentil Pot

2 cups lentils
¾ cup chopped onion
1 teaspoon minced garlic
1½ teaspoons wine vinegar
1 cup tomato
¾ cup chopped bell pepper
1½ teaspoons corn oil
1½ teaspoons soy sauce
1 bay leaf
½ teaspoon sea salt

Pressure-cook the lentils. Add the rest of the ingredients, including sufficient water, and cook 30 more minutes.

Mexican Bean Pot

2 cups dried pinto beans
2 cups UnSausage of choice (page 132) (Mexican Chorizo [page 134] is best)
1½ cups chopped onion
1 teaspoon minced garlic
¼ cup chopped bell pepper
2½ teaspoons corn oil
2 cups chopped tomato
1 teaspoon sea salt
1 teaspoon oregano
½ teaspoon ground cumin
½ teaspoon freshly ground black pepper

Pressure-cook the beans and retain the cooking water. Sauté the UnSausage, onion, garlic, and bell pepper in the oil. Combine everything and cook for 60 minutes, using the bean water and any extra water (or tomato juice) if it gets too dry.

Mexican Garbanzos

¾ cup chopped onion
1 teaspoon minced garlic
1½ teaspoons corn oil
4 cups garbanzo beans, pressure-cooked
½ cup chopped bell pepper
1 tablespoon Barbados molasses
½ cup tomato paste
1 teaspoon sea salt

Sauté the onion and garlic in the oil. Combine all ingredients and cook slowly for 30 to 60 minutes.

Red Beans and Rice

3 cups sliced or cubed UnSausage (page 132)
2 tablespoons corn oil
4 cups cooked kidney beans
1 cup corn
½ cup chopped bell pepper
2 cups salsa

Sauté the gluten in the oil until browned. Add everything else and cook until the bell pepper is crisp-tender. Serve over rice.

Red Beans with UnSausage

4 cups chopped onion
1 cup chopped celery
1 cup chopped bell pepper
2 tablespoons corn oil
1 tablespoon minced garlic
7½ cups cooked kidney beans
1½ cups chopped UnHam (page 130)
2 bay leaves
½ teaspoon thyme
2 cups chopped Italian UnSausage (page 133) or Mexican Chorizo UnSausage (page 134), browned in some oil
1½ teaspoons white pepper
½ teaspoon freshly ground black pepper
½ teaspoon cayenne pepper
4 cups UnHam Broth (page 156)

Sauté the onion, celery, and bell pepper in corn oil until soft. Add the garlic and sauté 2 more minutes. Combine everything in a large pot and cook for 30 minutes.

Refried Beans 1

Cannot be equaled, much less surpassed, by the canned stuff!

3 cups dried pinto beans
3 cups chopped onion
¼ cup chopped jalapeños
2 tablespoons corn oil
1 cup tomato paste
½ teaspoon sea salt
4 teaspoons minced garlic

Cook the beans and drain them, reserving the water. Sauté the onion and jalapeños in the oil until the onion is transparent. While the onion is sautéing, put the beans through a food processor or mill and purée them, adding the tomato paste, salt, and enough bean water to get a smooth texture. Add the garlic to the onion and jalapeños and cook for 2 more minutes. Add the bean mixture and combine everything thoroughly. Continue cooking on high heat, stirring frequently, for 10 minutes. You may need to add more bean water if this gets too dry.

Refried Beans 2

1½ cups chopped onion
⅔ cup corn oil
¼ cup tomato paste
⅔ cup UnBeef Broth (page 155)
4 cups cooked kidney, pinto, or red beans, mashed
½ teaspoon cayenne pepper
½ teaspoon sea salt

Sauté the onion in the oil. Combine the tomato paste and broth well. Mix everything together and cook for 10 minutes.

Refried Beans 3

3/4 cup chopped onion
1/2 cup corn oil
1 1/2 cups chopped tomato
1/4 teaspoon ground sage
1/2 teaspoon cayenne pepper
1/4 teaspoon paprika
1 teaspoon sea salt
5 cups cooked kidney, pinto, or red beans, mashed

Sauté the onion in 1/4 cup of the oil until transparent. Add everything else but the beans and cook until well done, adding bean water if needed, but not too much. Fry the beans in a skillet with the rest of the oil, stirring frequently, adding more bean water if needed to keep the beans from getting too dry. Pour in the sauce and continue cooking and stirring until fairly dry again.

Simple Cassoulet

1/2 cup diced onion
1 cup diced carrot
1 cup diced potatoes
1 tablespoon minced garlic
1 tablespoon olive oil
1 cup cubed UnChicken (page 137), UnHam (page 130), or UnSausage (page 132)
1/4 teaspoon thyme
1/4 teaspoon basil
1/4 teaspoon marjoram
1/4 teaspoon rosemary
1/2 teaspoon white pepper
1 tablespoon prepared mustard
1/2 teaspoon sea salt
2 cups white beans, cooked
2 cups water, or broth of the type of gluten being used (see Flavoring Broths chapter)

Sauté the vegetables and garlic in the oil for about 5 minutes in a heavy ovenproof pot or casserole dish. Add the gluten, the seasonings, and the beans. Add enough of the water or broth to barely cover the mixture. Cover and bake at 350°F for 45 minutes. Stir before serving.

Southern Pinto Beans

This is what it's all about!

4 cups pinto beans, pressure-cooked and drained
1 1/2 cups Yeast Cheez (page 97) or Pimiento Cheez (page 94)
2 cups corn
2 cups sliced tomato (more if needed to complete layer)
1 1/2 teaspoons sea salt
1/2 cup dried bread crumbs

In a casserole pan layer beans, half of Cheez, corn, remaining Cheez, tomato, salt, and bread crumbs. Bake at 350°F until heated through and brown on top, about 30 minutes.

Soy Fritters

4 cups soybeans, cooked and drained
1 1/2 cups water from cooking the beans
2 cups unbleached white flour
1 1/2 tablespoons baking powder
1 teaspoon sea salt
1 1/2 teaspoons garlic powder
1 1/2 cups chopped onion

Mash 3 cups of the soybeans. Combine everything to make a thick paste-batter. Drop into hot oil from a spoon and fry, turning them so they will brown all over. (Add more flour if the batter does not hold together in the frying.) Serve with a sauce such as Tartar Sauce (page 261), Tomato Sauce (page 261), Cheez Sauce (page 257), or Cashew Sour Kreem (page 94) or Tofu Sour Kreem (page 97).

VARIATION: *Use some other type of beans.*

Soyteena

This is very much like some of the canned meat substitute commercially available, but I think it is better. It is very good fried, especially the next day.

1 cup dried soybeans
2 cups water
1 cup tomato juice

½ cup peanut butter
2 teaspoons sea salt
⅓ cup finely chopped celery
¼ cup nutritional yeast
½ cup finely chopped onion
¼ cup soy sauce
½ teaspoon garlic powder
1 cup cornmeal

Combine all the ingredients, except the cornmeal, and process them in a blender until smooth. Remove from the blender and mix in the cornmeal well. Pour into oiled Number 2 cans. Cover cans with metal foil and secure it with rubber bands. Steam for 2 hours or longer in a large kettle that is about ⅓ full of water when the cans are set in it. Keep the water simmering in the kettle with the lid on. When cooled, remove the cans.

Special Garbanzos

¾ cup chopped onion
2 teaspoons minced garlic
1½ teaspoons corn oil
3 cups garbanzo beans, cooked
⅔ cup sliced carrot or squash
1 cup chopped bell pepper
1 teaspoon sage
2 tablespoons chopped fresh parsley
½ teaspoon Louisiana Hot Sauce
1½ teaspoons sea salt
¼ teaspoon cayenne pepper

Sauté onion and garlic in the oil until soft. Combine everything and cook 10 minutes over low heat, stirring occasionally.

VARIATION: *Use other types of beans.*

Swedish Brown Beans

The only Swedish brown bean recipe I like—and I love it!

4⅔ cups dried pinto beans
¾ cup chopped onion
½ teaspoon sliced garlic
1 tablespoon corn oil
2 cups UnBeef Broth (page 155)
½ teaspoon sea salt
¼ cup finely chopped UnBacon (page 136)
¼ teaspoon black pepper or cayenne pepper
¼ cup Barbados molasses
1 cup catsup or tomato sauce
1 teaspoon Louisiana Hot Sauce
½ cup wine vinegar
¼ teaspoon dried mustard

Pressure-cook the beans and drain. Sauté the onion and garlic in the oil. Combine all ingredients and cook together for 30 minutes.

Three-Bean Pot Pie

1½ cups chopped onion
1 tablespoon corn oil
1 teaspoon minced garlic
3 cups sliced squash
½ cup chopped bell pepper
1 cup Italian chopped tomato
1 cup garbanzo beans, cooked
1 cup kidney beans, cooked
1 cup pinto beans, cooked
¼ cup minced jalapeños
1 cup UnBeef Broth (page 155)
1 teaspoon ground cumin
¼ cup Italian tomato paste
1 cup tomato sauce
2 tablespoons nutritional yeast
1¼ teaspoons sea salt
½ recipe Convent Pie Crust (page 328), rolled out to fit over top of casserole dish

Sauté the onion in the oil until soft. Add garlic, squash, bell pepper, and tomato, and cook, stirring often, for 10 minutes, or until the squash is very soft. Remove from heat and add rest of ingredients. Pour into a nonstick casserole dish. Top with the crust and cut a few slits in it to let steam escape. Bake at 400°F until the crust is golden brown.

Tortilla and Tostada Filling 1

4 cups pressure-cooked dried beans, drained
2 cups salsa
2 cups Cashew Sour Kreem (page 94) or Tofu Sour Kreem (page 97)
1 1/3 cups chopped tomato
1/3 cup chopped onion
2 cups Yeast Cheez (page 97) or Pimiento Cheez (page 94)

Combine. Good rolled up in tortillas or spread on them. Add shredded lettuce if desired.

Tortilla and Tostada Filling 2

1/3 cup chopped onion
1 teaspoon minced garlic
1 1/2 teaspoons corn oil
1 teaspoon sea salt
1/4 teaspoon cayenne pepper
1 cup tomato
4 cups cooked dried beans of choice, drained

Sauté the onion and garlic in the oil. Combine with the salt, pepper, and tomato and cook well. Blend with the beans.

Tuscan White Bean Casserole 1

1 cup dried white beans
1/2 cup chopped onion
1 teaspoon olive oil
2 cups chopped tomato
3 tablespoons tomato paste
1/2 teaspoon sage
1 bay leaf
3 tablespoons chopped fresh parsley
1/2 teaspoon sea salt
1/8 teaspoon freshly ground black pepper

Pressure-cook the beans. Sauté the onion in the olive oil until transparent. Add the tomato, tomato paste, sage, bay leaf, parsley, salt, and pepper. Simmer for 15 minutes. Put the beans in a casserole. Stir in the tomato mixture. Cover and bake in a moderate oven for 20 to 25 minutes.

Tuscan White Bean Casserole 2

1 cup UnHam (page 130), UnSausage (page 132), or UnBacon (page 136), cut into strips
1 cup chopped onion
2 1/2 teaspoons minced garlic
1/4 teaspoon freshly ground black pepper
2 1/2 teaspoons olive oil
3 cups cooked white beans
UnChicken Broth (page 155)
Garlic oil
4 tomatoes, peeled, sliced, and soaked in olive oil and pepper
1/8 teaspoon sage
1/8 teaspoon freshly ground black pepper
Bread Crumb Topping (page 337)

Sauté the gluten strips with the onion, garlic, and pepper in the oil until the gluten is browned. Put all this into a saucepan with the cooked beans and enough broth to cover everything. Simmer for 20 minutes. Oil a nonstick casserole with garlic oil (plain olive oil if you have none). Put half of the beans in a layer in the casserole. Put the gluten slices on top of the beans. Put a layer of tomato slices and sage on top of the UnSausages. Sprinkle with the pepper. Put the other half of the beans on top in a layer. Cover the beans with Bread Crumb Topping. Bake at 350°F for 20 minutes in the upper half of the oven.

White Beans with Tomatoes 1

1/3 cup chopped onion
1 1/2 teaspoons minced garlic
1 1/2 teaspoons corn oil
3 cups cooked white beans
2 cups chopped tomatoes
1/2 teaspoon sea salt
1/8 teaspoon cayenne pepper
1 tablespoon wine vinegar

Sauté the onion and garlic in the oil. Stir in the rest of the ingredients. Cover and simmer over low heat for 10 minutes.

White Beans with Tomatoes 2

2 cups dried white beans
1 cup chopped onion
1 teaspoon minced garlic
½ cup chopped celery
¼ cup chopped bell pepper
2 teaspoons corn oil
2 teaspoons sea salt
¼ teaspoon basil
¼ teaspoon black pepper or cayenne pepper
1 cup chopped tomato
1 cup chopped or sliced carrot

Pressure-cook the beans. Sauté the onion, garlic, celery, and bell pepper in the oil. Combine everything and cook together 20 to 30 minutes, adding any water as needed.

White Beans with UnBacon

2 cups dried white beans
1 cup chopped onion
½ teaspoon minced garlic
1½ teaspoons corn oil
½ teaspoon sea salt
1 cup chopped fine or ground UnBacon (page 136)
¼ teaspoon black pepper or cayenne pepper

Pressure-cook the beans. Sauté the onion and garlic in the oil. Combine everything and cook together 20 to 30 minutes, adding any water that might be needed.

Grains

Barley

Basic proportions for cooking barley are:

1 cup barley
2 cups water
¾ teaspoon sea salt

Wash the barley well under cold running water while the cooking water is coming to a boil. Add the salt and the barley to the water and stir. Turn the flame down very low. Cover and cook for about 45 minutes. (Poor quality barley will cook faster than good quality.)

Basic Rice

Basic proportions for cooking jasmine or basmati rice are:

1 cup rice
1½ cups water
1 teaspoon sea salt

Wash the rice well under cold running water while the cooking water is coming to a boil. Add the salt and the rice to the water and stir. Turn the flame down very low. Cover and cook for about fifteen minutes.

Broccoli Risotto

¾ teaspoon thinly sliced garlic
2 cups broccoli flowerets
1 tablespoon corn oil
3 cups UnChicken Broth (page 155), hot
¼ cup chopped fresh parsley
Sea salt
Freshly ground black pepper
¼ cup chopped onion
¾ cup uncooked rice
1 teaspoon lemon juice
¼ cup Parmesan Cheez (page 94)

Sauté the garlic and broccoli in 2 teaspoons of the oil until the garlic is soft, about 3 minutes. Add ⅓ cup of broth, 3 tablespoons of the parsley, and the salt and pepper. Simmer, uncovered, until the broccoli is just tender. Set aside. Sauté the onion in the rest of the oil until soft. Add the rice and stir until it is coated with the oil. Stir ⅔ cup of broth into the rice and cook, stirring constantly, until all the liquid is absorbed. Add the rest of the broth, ⅓ cup at a time, stirring constantly, allowing the liquid to absorb between additions. Cook, uncovered, until the rice is creamy and the grains are tender. Stir in the lemon juice and 3 tablespoons of the Cheez. Sprinkle with the rest of the parsley and Cheez.

Cheez Rice

1 cup rice that was cooked in UnBeef Broth (page 155) or UnChicken Broth (page 155)
½ cup Yeast Cheez (page 97) or Pimiento Cheez (page 94)
¼ teaspoon paprika

Cook the rice, and while it is still hot and in the pot, stir in the other ingredients.

VARIATION: *Add 1 cup of tomato juice. Add ½ cup of Cashew Sour Kreem (page 94) or Tofu Sour Kreem (page 97).*

Cracked Wheat

Cracked wheat should not be confused with tabouli wheat, which needs no cooking. Basic proportions for cooking cracked wheat are:

1½ teaspoons corn oil
1 cup cracked wheat
¾ teaspoons sea salt
1½ cups boiling water

Heat the oil until it begins to smoke. Add the cracked wheat and stir rapidly and continuously to avoid burning and coat all the wheat with oil. Fry on high heat about 5 minutes until it starts to brown. Add the salt, then the wheat to the boiling water and stir. Bring back to boil. Turn the heat down very low. Cover and cook for about 15 minutes.

VARIATION: *Use UnBeef Broth (page 155) or UnChicken Broth (page 155) instead of water, and use only ⅓ teaspoon of salt.*

Creole Rice

1 cup chopped onion
2 teaspoons minced garlic
2½ teaspoons corn oil
3 cups sliced okra
¼ teaspoon cayenne pepper
4 cups Creole Sauce (page 258)
½ teaspoon sea salt
6 cups rice, cooked in UnChicken Broth (page 155)

Sauté the onion and garlic in the corn oil. Combine with all other ingredients except the rice. Cook over medium heat for 20 minutes. Add the rice and cook for 10 minutes more, adding more Creole Sauce if it becomes too dry.

Dirty Rice

5 cups UnBeef (page 109), UnPork (page 122), UnSausage (page 132), UnHam (page 130), or UnChicken (page 137), or a combination
1 tablespoon olive oil
1 cup finely chopped onion
1 cup finely chopped green onions
½ cup finely chopped bell pepper
½ cup finely chopped fresh parsley
½ cup finely chopped celery
2 tablespoons finely chopped garlic
½ teaspoon dried mint, crushed
½ teaspoon cayenne pepper
1 teaspoon Louisiana Hot Sauce
4½ teaspoons Lea and Perrins Steak Sauce
1 cup flavoring broth (see Flavoring Broths chapter) of the type of gluten used
3 cups cooked rice

Combine everything except the rice and cook together for 20 minutes, covered, stirring occasionally. Add the cooked rice and mix thoroughly. Cook over low heat for another 20 minutes.

Flavored Rice

1 cup rice
1½ cups flavoring broth of choice (see Flavoring Broths chapter)
½ teaspoon sea salt

Wash the rice well under cold running water while the broth is coming to a boil. Add the salt and the rice to the water and stir. Turn the heat down very low. Cover and cook for about 15 minutes.

Fried Rice

3 cups rice, uncooked
1 tablespoon nondairy margarine
1 tablespoon corn oil
4½ cups UnBeef Broth (page 155) or UnChicken Broth (page 155)
½ teaspoon sea salt

Wash rice thoroughly and drain. Combine the margarine and oil in a skillet and melt the margarine. Add the washed rice and stir frequently until the rice becomes light brown. This takes quite a while, so don't give up. (Some of the rice kernels may even "pop" like popcorn.) If the rice becomes too dry add more margarine or oil to keep it shiny as it fries. Bring broth to a boil. Add the salt. Then add the rice, which must come directly from the skillet and be hot and frying, to the boiling water a little bit at a time, taking care because it will "explode." Cover the pot and turn the heat down. Simmer for 10 minutes.

Gazpacho with Couscous

6 ounces quick-cooking or instant couscous
¼ teaspoon freshly ground black pepper
¼ cup chopped fresh parsley
2⅔ cups canned tomatoes
¾ cup tomato juice
1 cup cucumber, peeled, seeded, and sliced
1 cup diced bell pepper (half red and half green, if possible)
½ cup chopped onion
1 tablespoon chopped garlic
2 tablespoons balsamic vinegar
1 tablespoon jalapeños, seeded and diced
½ cup chopped green onions

Cook the couscous and mix in the pepper and parsley. Set aside. Put everything else in a blender or food processor and process just until coarse and chunky in texture. Refrigerate until cold. Mix in the couscous and serve.

Green Rice 1

1 cup rice that was cooked in UnChicken Broth (page 155)
½ cup Yeast Cheez (page 97) or Pimiento Cheez (page 94)
½ cup finely chopped fresh parsley
1 cup tomato juice
Pinch cayenne pepper
⅓ cup minced onion

Cook the rice, and while it is still hot and in the pot, stir in the other ingredients.

VARIATION: *Add Cashew Sour Kreem (page 94) or Tofu Sour Kreem (page 97).*

Green Rice 2

¾ cup sliced mushrooms
¾ cup chopped celery
¾ cup chopped onion
½ teaspoon minced garlic
1 tablespoon nondairy margarine
2 cups broccoli, chopped and steamed
1½ cups rice, cooked

Sauté the mushrooms, celery, onion, and garlic in the margarine until the onion and celery are transparent. Carefully stir in the broccoli and rice until all is heated through.

Millet

Basic proportions for cooking millet are:

1 cup millet
1½ cups water
¾ teaspoon sea salt

Wash the millet well under cold running water while the cooking water is coming to a boil. Add the salt and the millet to the water and stir. Turn the heat down very low. Cover and cook for about 30 minutes. (Poor quality millet will cook faster than good quality.)

VARIATION: *Use UnBeef Broth (page 155) or UnChicken Broth (page 155) instead of water, and use only ⅓ teaspoon of salt.*

Oven-Baked Rice with UnPork and Garbanzos

2 teaspoons olive oil
1½ cups tomato, peeled
1 tablespoon minced garlic
1 tablespoon paprika
1½ cups UnChicken Broth (page 155)
1½ cups UnPork Broth (page 156)
1½ cups uncooked rice, washed well
1¼ cups cooked garbanzo beans, drained and rinsed
2 cups UnPork (page 122), cut into ½-inch cubes and deep-fried
1¼ cups potatoes, peeled, sliced ¼ inch thick, and deep-fried

Heat the oil in a large skillet. Add the tomato and garlic and sauté until the tomato releases its liquid and becomes "saucy." Stir in the paprika and broths. Bring to a boil and add the rice. Cook until the rice begins to soften. Add the garbanzos and gluten. Transfer to a nonstick casserole. Layer the potatoes on top, cover tightly with foil, and bake at 400°F for 30 minutes.

Pilaf Imperial

3 cups cracked wheat
4½ cups UnBeef Broth (page 155) or UnChicken Broth (page 155), boiling
¼ cup soy sauce
1 teaspoon paprika
1½ cups chopped onion
1 teaspoon minced garlic
1½ cups chopped celery
1½ cups sliced water chestnuts
⅓ cup chopped bell pepper
2 tablespoons nondairy margarine

Combine the wheat, broth, soy sauce, and paprika and bake in a covered casserole at 350°F for 45 minutes. Sauté the onion, garlic, celery, chestnuts, and bell pepper in the margarine until tender. Combine all and serve with Cashew Sour Kreem (page 94) or Tofu Sour Kreem (page 97).

Rice Jambalaya

½ cup chopped bell pepper
¾ cup chopped onion
1 teaspoon minced garlic
1 cup sliced squash or pumpkin
2 tablespoons chopped pimientos
1 cup cubed tomato
1 tablespoon corn oil
1 cup rice, uncooked
2 cups UnChicken Broth (page 155)
¼ teaspoon cayenne pepper
1 teaspoon sea salt

Sauté the vegetables in the oil until just tender. Add rice, broth, pepper, and salt. Cook until rice is tender.

Rice with Peas

¼ cup finely chopped onion
¾ teaspoon minced garlic
2 teaspoons nondairy margarine or corn oil
2 cups plus 2 tablespoons UnChicken Broth (page 155)
½ teaspoon basil
1 cup rice
1 teaspoon sea salt
½ teaspoon freshly ground black pepper
4 cups peas

Sauté the onion and garlic in the oil until soft. Combine everything but the peas. Cook, covered, for 5 minutes. Stir in the peas and cook until done, about 5 minutes more.

Simple Risotto

⅓ cup chopped onion
1 teaspoon minced garlic
¼ cup chopped bell pepper
½ cup chopped mushrooms or black olives
1½ teaspoons nondairy margarine
1½ teaspoons corn oil
1 cup chopped tomato
1⅓ cups rice that was cooked in UnChicken Broth (page 155)
¼ teaspoon sea salt
¼ teaspoon paprika

Sauté the onion, garlic, bell pepper, and mushrooms (or olives) in the margarine and oil until the bell pepper is just tender. Add the tomato, rice, salt, and paprika. Continue stirring until the rice is heated through.

Spanish Rice 1

1/2 cup chopped bell pepper
3/4 cup chopped onion
1 tablespoon minced garlic
2 1/2 teaspoons corn oil
5 cups chopped tomato
1/4 teaspoon cayenne pepper
1 teaspoon sea salt
1/2 teaspoon basil
Pinch dill
1 1/4 cups UnBeef Broth (page 155)
3 1/2 cups rice that was cooked in UnBeef Broth

Sauté the bell pepper, onions, and garlic in the corn oil. Combine with the rest of the ingredients except for the rice and cook until it gets thick, 20 to 30 minutes. Add the cooked rice and cook for 5 more minutes.

VARIATION: *Include 4 cups of eggplant, cubed, and sauté it along with the bell peppers and onion.*

Spanish Rice 2

1 cup chopped onion
1 teaspoon minced garlic
2 tablespoons minced jalapeños
1/2 cup finely chopped bell pepper
2 teaspoons olive oil
3/4 cup tomato paste
2 cups UnChicken Broth (page 155)
2 tablespoons unbleached white flour
1/4 teaspoon sea salt
3 cups rice that was cooked in UnChicken Broth
1 cup garbanzo beans, cooked

Sauté the onion, garlic, jalapeños, and bell pepper in the oil. Mix the tomato paste and the broth. Add the flour and salt to the sautéed vegetables. Add the tomato-broth mixture. Simmer gently until thickened, about 3 to 5 minutes. Add the rice and garbanzos. Bake in an oiled casserole 25 minutes at 350°F.

VARIATION: *Substitute other dried beans or dried green peas for the garbanzos.*

Spanish Rice 3

2 cups UnBeef (page 109) or UnBeef Soy Grits (page 109)
1 1/2 cups chopped onion
1/2 teaspoon minced garlic
1/4 cup finely chopped bell pepper
1 tablespoon corn oil
1 cup rice, cooked
4 1/2 cups canned tomatoes
1 1/2 teaspoons sea salt
2 teaspoons chili powder
1/2 cup salsa
1/2 cup sliced black olives
1/2 cup sliced mushrooms
1 cup Pimiento Cheez (page 94) or Yeast Cheez (page 97)

Sauté the gluten (or grits), onion, garlic, and bell pepper in the oil until tender. Add the rice, tomatoes, salt, chili powder, and salsa. Simmer at least 10 minutes. Stir in the rest of the ingredients, cover, and bake 75 minutes at 350°F.

Spanish Rice 4

1 cup chopped onion
4 teaspoons minced garlic
4 teaspoons corn oil
4 cups canned stewed tomatoes
1/2 cup tomato sauce
1 cup diced green bell pepper
1 cup diced red or yellow bell pepper
1 cup sliced mushrooms
2 cups corn
1 teaspoon basil
1/2 teaspoon Italian seasoning
1 teaspoon sea salt
1/2 teaspoon freshly ground black pepper
1/2 teaspoon cayenne pepper
4 cups cooked rice

Sauté the onion and garlic in the oil until soft. Combine with everything but the rice, bring to a boil, reduce heat, and simmer 15 minutes. Combine with the rice.

Spicy Bulgur Pilaf

2 teaspoons nondairy margarine
3/4 cup chopped onion
1 1/2 teaspoons crushed garlic
1 cup bulgur wheat
1/4 teaspoon cayenne pepper
1/4 teaspoon ground cumin
1/4 teaspoon celery seed
1/2 cup finely diced bell pepper
1/4 teaspoon sea salt
2 1/4 cups UnChicken Broth (page 155) or UnBeef Broth (page 155), boiling

Melt the margarine. Add the onion, garlic, and bulgur and cook 2 to 3 minutes, stirring occasionally. Stir in the cayenne pepper, cumin, and celery seed, and continue cooking for 3 to 5 more minutes. Add the bell pepper and salt. Pour in the boiling broth. Reduce to a simmer, cover, and cook until all liquid is absorbed.

Spinach Risotto

2 cups rice, uncooked
2 teaspoons nondairy margarine
10 ounces frozen spinach, thawed and drained
3 1/2 cups UnChicken Broth (page 155)
1/4 teaspoon freshly ground black pepper

Sauté the uncooked rice in the margarine. Combine the other ingredients and bring them to a boil. Add the rice, lower the heat, and simmer, covered, until the rice is done, about 15 minutes.

Tabouli Wheat

Put the wheat in a bowl and cover with warm water, about 2 inches above the top of the wheat. Spring water takes 15 minutes, distilled water takes about twice as long. Drain in a colander, pressing lightly to press out excess water.

Vegetable Fried Rice 1

This is as delicious as it is simple and quick. Although it is worthy of serving at any time it is great as "emergency rations"!

2 teaspoons corn oil
2 tablespoons nondairy margarine
2 cups coarsely chopped onion
1 cup coarsely chopped bell pepper
1/2 cup chopped celery
3 cups thickly sliced mushrooms
2 teaspoons minced garlic
1 1/2 teaspoons hot pepper flakes
4 cups fresh coarsely chopped tomato
1/2 teaspoon sea salt
5 cups cooked rice

Combine the oil and margarine. Sauté the onion, bell pepper, celery, mushrooms, garlic, and pepper flakes until the bell pepper is soft. Add the tomato and salt. Cook for 5 more minutes. Add the rice and continue to stir until most of the moisture is evaporated and the rice starts to brown.

Vegetable Fried Rice 2

3 cups rice, uncooked
4 teaspoons nondairy margarine
4 teaspoons corn oil
4 1/2 cups UnBeef Broth (page 155) or UnChicken Broth (page 155)
1/2 teaspoon sea salt
1 1/2 cups chopped onion
3 cups vegetables of your choice, chopped if need be
1 tablespoon corn oil

Wash rice thoroughly and drain. Combine the margarine and oil in a skillet and melt the margarine. Add the washed rice and stir frequently until the rice becomes light brown—this takes quite a while, so don't give up. (Some of the rice kernels may even "pop" like popcorn.) If the rice becomes too dry add more margarine or oil to keep it shiny as it fries. Bring broth to a boil. Add the salt. Then add the rice, which must come directly from the skillet and be hot and frying, to the boiling water a little bit at a time, taking care because it will "explode."

Cover the pot and turn the heat down. Simmer for 10 minutes. While the rice is cooking, sauté the onion and vegetables in corn oil until softened. When the rice is done, add the rice to the vegetables and continue to sauté until all excess water is evaporated.

Vegetable Fried Rice 3

½ cup chopped onion
4 teaspoons corn oil
½ cup chopped bell pepper
⅓ cup chopped celery
1 cup chopped mushrooms
½ cup chopped squash
3 tablespoons soy sauce
1 cup rice, cooked

Sauté the onion in the oil until transparent, then sauté the rest of the ingredients for 15 minutes.

Tofu Dishes

Tofu, especially when it is frozen, thawed, and pressed, can be used in many of the recipes that call for gluten, and can be flavored by simmering or soaking the tofu in the same broths that are used to flavor the gluten.

Tofu

5 cups dried soybeans
2½ gallons boiling water
One of the following:
- 2 tablespoons nigari (see "Notes," page 250)
- 2 tablespoons Epsom salts
- 1 cup vinegar (any kind)
- 1 cup lemon juice

Wash the soybeans well and drain them. Put them in a bowl, cover them with 12 cups of cold water, and let them soak 8 to 12 hours. (If the room temperature is below 65°F then let them soak 16 to 20 hours.) Drain off the water and wash again.

Put ⅓ of the beans in a blender or food processor, add 5 cups of the boiling water, and grind into a puree. Set aside. Repeat this twice more. Put the water-bean mixture into a large pot on the stove, add 15 more cups of boiling water, bring to a boil, and boil slowly for 10 minutes, stirring constantly. Remove from the stove and strain through cheesecloth in a colander or large strainer, pressing hard to squeeze out all excess milk. (Use a rubber glove on your hand or the back of a large spoon for the pressing.)

Set the soy milk aside and return the soybean pulp to the pot. Add 10 cups of boiling water, put back on the stove, and bring to a boil again. As soon as it comes to a boil, remove from the heat and press out as before, adding the milk to the first batch. Let the milk cool to 185°F . This is important. A higher temperature will not work, and a cooler temperature will cause the tofu to be too soft.

Dissolve the 2 tablespoons of nigari in 2½ cups of hot water. Take ⅓ of the nigari mixture, hold it high above the surface of the soy milk, and while constantly stirring rapidly, add it all at once and continue stirring only 3 to 5 seconds more. Take the second ⅓ of the nigari mixture and sprinkle it over the top of the soy milk. Let it sit for 5 minutes. Take the last ⅓ of the nigari mixture and sprinkle it over the top of the soy milk.

Let it sit for 5 minutes, then as gently and slowly as possible stir the mixture once to circulate the milk.

Let it sit for 5 more minutes, then a second time as gently and slowly as possible stir the mixture once to circulate the milk. Let it sit for 5 more minutes, then a third time as gently and slowly as possible stir the mixture once to circulate the milk. Let it sit for 5 minutes more.

The mixture should by now have turned into curds and whey. (If this is not the case, then something has gone wrong, and you should mix up 1 tablespoon of nigari in 1 cup of hot water and sprinkle it on the top of the soy milk, stirring very slowly for 3 seconds. Then let it sit for 10 to 15 minutes, stirring every 5 minutes as previously described. But if the directions are followed correctly this should not be necessary.)

Pour or ladle the curds and whey slowly into a colander or large strainer lined with cheesecloth. Transfer the curds in the cheesecloth to a tofu press and press lightly with a weight for 5 minutes. Remove the weight and lift up the curds in the cheesecloth, and shake around gently to remove any folds that may have formed in the cheesecloth. Put all back into the tofu press and press with heavy weights for 15 minutes for soft tofu and 30 minutes for firm tofu. Cut into convenient size blocks.

For storage in the refrigerator, cover with cold water and put in an airtight container. Change the water every 24 hours. The tofu will keep for 7 to 10 days.

Notes

Nigari (bittern) is the best coagulant to use in making your own tofu, both for flavor and for efficiency (amount of curds obtained). It is extracted from sea water.

Nigari and Epsom salts make firm tofu. Vinegar and lemon juice make soft tofu.

If you want to use vinegar or lemon juice and yet get firmer tofu, then you must stir the curds for a few minutes longer.

Oven Method Tofu

This recipe looks pretty silly, but it really works quite well. As you can see, the advantage of this method is the ability to add flavorings to the tofu beforehand. You can add other flavorings not given in this recipe, but some flavorings may keep the tofu from solidifying very well. So you must be willing to experiment.

4 cups water
2¼ cups soy flour
⅔ cup pimientos
2½ teaspoons salt
2½ tablespoons nutritional yeast
½ cup flour
⅓ cup lemon juice
¼ tablespoon garlic salt
3 tablespoons corn oil

Place everything in a blender and whirl until smooth. Pour into a small, greased loaf pan. Bake 2 hours at 275°F . Turn off the oven, but keep it in the oven for one more hour. Chill before turning out of the pan. Peel off the brown skin on the top and trim the loaf to shape. Slice or cube for serving.

Indonesian-Style Baked Tofu

You will love this!

1½ teaspoons sesame oil (corn, if you do not have sesame)
½ teaspoon minced garlic
½ teaspoon powdered ginger
Pinch cayenne pepper (more, if you like)
¾ cup UnChicken Broth (page 155) or UnPork Broth (page 156)
3½ tablespoons peanut butter
1 tablespoon low-sodium soy sauce
1 tablespoon lemon juice
1½ teaspoons vinegar
8 ounces tofu, frozen, thawed, and pressed
2 tablespoons minced green onions

Heat the oil and sauté the garlic for 1 to 2 minutes. Add the ginger and cayenne and sauté 1 more minute. Add the broth and bring to a simmer. Cover and simmer 10 minutes. Take from heat. Add the peanut butter and soy sauce and whisk until smooth. Bring back to a simmer and cook, stirring, for about 10 minutes until the sauce thickens. Whisk in the lemon juice and vinegar. Cook 5 more minutes. Take from heat. Cut the tofu lengthwise into ¼- to ⅜-inch-thick slices. Arrange in a lightly oiled baking dish. Drizzle the sauce evenly over the tofu, cover, and bake at 400°F for 30 to 45 minutes. Sprinkle on the minced green onions and broil for 1 to 2 minutes.

Stir-Fry Tofu and Vegetables

A standby you can count on.

2 cups tofu, cut into 1-inch cubes
Corn oil
1½ cups onion, cut in wedges
2 teaspoons corn oil
1 cup thinly sliced carrot
½ cup green beans, cut in 1-inch pieces
½ cup sliced mushrooms
½ cup UnChicken Broth (page 155)
¾ teaspoon minced garlic
½ teaspoon basil
⅛ teaspoon freshly ground black pepper

Deep-fry the tofu in corn oil and put on paper towels to drain. Sauté the onion in the 2 teaspoons of oil for 1 minute. Add the carrot and sauté for 1 more minute. Add the green beans and sauté for 1 more minute. Add the mushrooms and sauté for 1 more minute. Add the tofu and the rest of the ingredients and sauté 5 minutes, or until the vegetables are soft.

Tofu UnBeef

This sauce for this magnificently simple dish can be used to flavor four cups of gluten as well.

2 cups coarsely chopped onion
1 teaspoon minced garlic
2 teaspoons chopped jalapeños
1 tablespoon corn oil
3 tablespoons cornstarch
1½ cups cold water
¼ cup soy sauce
1 teaspoon Kitchen Bouquet
1 teaspoon monosodium glutamate (MSG)
1½ cups water
4 cups frozen tofu that has been thawed and pressed

Sauté the onion, garlic, and jalapeños in the oil. Mix the cornstarch and water together and add it, stirring constantly. Add the rest of the ingredients, except the tofu, and simmer until it starts to thicken. While this sauce is cooking, cut or slice the tofu into pieces about ½ inch thick. Deep-fry the tofu in corn oil, making sure the oil is very hot, until the tofu is brown. Drain in a colander and put on paper towels to absorb excess oil. When the sauce is done, add the tofu to it and cook for 5 minutes.

Tofu UnChicken

2 cups coarsely chopped onion
2 teaspoons chopped jalapeños
3 tablespoons corn oil
1 tablespoon cornstarch
1½ cups cold water
¼ teaspoon poultry seasoning
1½ tablespoons nutritional yeast
½ teaspoon salt
1 teaspoon monosodium glutamate (MSG)
1½ cups water
4 cups firm tofu, or frozen tofu that has been thawed and pressed

Sauté the onion and jalapeños in the oil. Mix the cornstarch and water together and add, stirring constantly. Add the rest of the ingredients, except the tofu, and simmer until it starts to thicken. While this sauce is cooking, cut or slice the tofu into pieces about ½ inch thick. Deep-fry the tofu in corn oil, making sure the oil is very hot, until the tofu is brown. Drain in a colander and put on paper towels to absorb excess oil. When the sauce is done, add the tofu to it and cook for five minutes.

Tofu Hummus

Just as good as the chick pea type.

4 cups tofu
⅔ cup lemon juice
¼ cup olive oil
1⅓ teaspoons sea salt
⅓ cup soy sauce
⅔ cup tahini
2 tablespoons minced garlic

Blend all in a blender or food processor.

Tofu "Scrambled Eggs"

Extraordinary!

1 tablespoon corn oil
½ cup chopped onion
1 tablespoon soy sauce
½ teaspoon sea salt
¼ teaspoon garlic powder
¼ teaspoon turmeric powder
1 drop liquid smoke
2 tablespoons finely chopped UnBacon (page 136)
1 tablespoon nutritional yeast
2 teaspoons chopped jalapeños
2 cups soft tofu, crumbled

Put everything but the tofu in a skillet and stir well. Add the tofu and mix well with a fork until the seasonings are evenly distributed. Cook together until the water in the tofu evaporates and the mixture resembles scrambled eggs.

VARIATION: *Add ¼ cup chopped bell pepper. Add ½ cup sliced mushrooms or other vegetables. Try green onions instead of regular onions. Serve with salsa or some kind of tomato sauce.*

Tofu "Scrambled Eggs" Breakfast Casserole

1 recipe of Tofu "Scrambled Eggs" (see above) made with bell pepper and mushrooms
1 cup ground UnHam (page 130) or UnSausage (page 132), browned in corn oil
1 cup Yeast Cheez (page 97) or Pimiento Cheez (page 94)

Put the Tofu "Scrambled Eggs" in a casserole dish or a loaf pan, spread the gluten over that, and spread the Cheez over the gluten. Bake at 350°F for 10 minutes.

UnBeef Enchiladas

4 cups tofu, frozen, thawed, pressed, and crumbled (or cut in small pieces)
2 tablespoons corn oil
2 teaspoons minced garlic
2 cups chopped onion
2 teaspoons minced jalapeños
3 tablespoons chili powder
¾ cup chopped black olives
¼ teaspoon sea salt
10 cups Spanish Tomato Sauce (page 260)
1 recipe Corn Tortillas (page 52) or Flour Tortillas (page 52)
Yeast Cheez (page 97) or Pimiento Cheez (page 94) to cover

Sauté the tofu in 1 tablespoon of the oil until the edges begin to brown. Set aside. in the other tablespoon of oil, sauté the garlic, onion, and jalapeños until the onion is transparent. Add the chili powder and sauté for 2 more minutes, stirring constantly. Add olives, salt, tofu, and 3 cups of the Tomato Sauce and cook for another 5 minutes. Dip a tortilla in the Tomato Sauce, put some of the filling on it and roll it up and put it in a casserole pan. Do this with all the tortillas until the filling is used up. Cover the enchiladas with the remaining sauce. Spread a layer of Cheez over that. Bake at 350°F for 30 minutes.

Gravies

Brown Gravy

4 teaspoons nondairy margarine
3 tablespoons sliced onion
½ teaspoon minced garlic
2 tablespoons unbleached white flour
1 cup pureed tomato
¾ cup UnBeef Broth (page 155)
¼ teaspoon sea salt
¼ teaspoon paprika

Melt the margarine and sauté the onion and garlic until the onion is light brown. Remove the onion and stir in the flour and cook until it turns brown as well. Slowly stir in the pureed tomato. Add the onion, broth, salt, and paprika. Stir and cook until the sauce is smooth and boiling.

Cajun UnBeef Gravy

Get adventurous!

2 tablespoons corn oil
1 cup ground UnBeef (page 109)
¼ cup unbleached white flour
1¼ teaspoons Kitchen Bouquet
¼ cup corn oil
3 cups mushrooms (fresh preferred), stemmed and halved
1 cup chopped onion
2 teaspoons minced garlic
4 cups UnBeef Broth (page 155)
3 tablespoons Lea and Perrins Steak Sauce
4 teaspoons Louisiana Hot Sauce

In a skillet heat 1 tablespoon of the oil and fry the UnBeef until it is browned on all sides. Remove the gluten and set aside. Put the other tablespoon of oil in the skillet and heat. Stir the flour into the oil and turn the heat down so it will cook slowly. Add the Kitchen Bouquet and keep stirring the flour constantly, adding more oil if the mixture is too dry, until the mixture is a rich brown. Add the mushrooms, onion, and garlic, stirring constantly. Continue to cook for 10 minutes, adding up to ½ cup of the broth if needed to keep it from sticking. Add the rest of the broth, steak sauce, and hot sauce, turn the heat down, and continue cooking until it starts to thicken, about 20 minutes, stirring occasionally.

Mushroom Gravy

Don't pass this by.

2 cups sliced mushrooms
1 teaspoon crushed garlic
1 tablespoon corn oil
¼ cup unbleached white flour
4 cups UnBeef Broth (page 155) or UnChicken Broth (page 155)

Sauté the mushrooms and garlic in the oil. Blend in the flour. Slowly add the broth. Cook for 15 minutes.

Nutritional Yeast Gravy

⅓ cup unbleached white flour
⅓ cup nutritional yeast
2 tablespoons nondairy margarine or corn oil
2 cups water
1 tablespoon soy sauce
¼ teaspoon sea salt
⅛ teaspoon freshly ground black pepper or cayenne pepper

Toast the flour over medium low heat until it starts to smell "toasty." Stir in the yeast. Add the margarine or oil and cook for a few minutes until it is bubbly. Add the water and cook, whisking until it thickens and bubbles. Add the soy sauce, salt, and pepper.

Sour Kreem–Mushroom Gravy

2 tablespoons nondairy margarine
1 cup sliced mushrooms
¼ cup chopped onion
½ cup Tofu Sour Kreem (page 97)
2 tablespoons unbleached white flour
¾ cup Cashew Milk (page 93)
¼ teaspoon sea salt
¼ teaspoon black or white pepper

Heat the margarine in a saucepan. Add the mushrooms and onion. Sauté for 5 minutes, or until tender. Combine the Sour Kreem and flour, then stir in the Cashew Milk, salt, and pepper. Add to the mushroom mixture. Cook, stirring, till thickened and bubbly. Stir and cook 1 more minute.

UnBeef Gravy 1

¼ cup unbleached white flour
4 teaspoons corn oil
2 cups UnBeef Broth (page 155)

In a skillet blend the flour in the heated oil. Slowly add the broth. Cook for 10 minutes.

Note

If potatoes have been boiled, use the potato water in making the UnBeef Broth.

UnBeef Gravy 2

4 teaspoons corn oil
¼ cup unbleached white flour
1 teaspoon Kitchen Bouquet
1½ cups chopped onion
1½ teaspoons minced garlic
3 cups UnBeef Broth (page 155)
½ teaspoon sea salt
2 tablespoons Lea and Perrins Steak Sauce
1 tablespoon Louisiana Hot Sauce

Heat the oil in a skillet and stir in the flour. Turn the heat down so it will cook slowly. Add the Kitchen Bouquet and keep stirring the flour constantly, adding more oil if the mixture is too dry, until it is a rich brown. Add the onion and garlic, stirring constantly. Add the broth and keep stirring until it starts to form a thick gravy. Add the salt, steak sauce, and hot sauce. Add more water if you need to, and bring all to a boil and simmer for 10 minutes.

UnChicken Gravy

¼ cup unbleached white flour
1 tablespoon corn oil
2 cups UnChicken Broth (page 155)

In a skillet blend the flour in the heated oil. Slowly add the broth. Cook for 10 minutes.

> **Note**
>
> If potatoes have been boiled, use the potato water in making the UnChicken Broth.

UnHam Gravy 1

⅓ cup chopped onion
1⅓ ground cups UnHam (page 130) or UnBacon (page 136)
2 tablespoons corn oil
⅓ cup unbleached white flour
1 quart Cashew Milk (page 93)
¼ teaspoon freshly ground black pepper

Sauté the onion and "ham" in the oil. Add the flour and blend well. Gradually add the Cashew Milk, and then the rest of the ingredients. Cook for 10 minutes.

UnHam Gravy 2

1 tablespoon corn oil
¼ cup unbleached white flour
2 cups UnHam Broth (page 156)

In a skillet blend the flour in the heated oil. Slowly add the broth. Cook for 10 minutes.

> **Note**
>
> If potatoes have been boiled, use the potato water in making the UnHam Broth.

UnHamburger Gravy

We like this on mashed potatoes, though it goes just as well on bread and biscuits—even rice!

2 cups UnBeef (page 109), ground or chopped small, or soy grits soaked in UnBeef Broth (page 155)
¼ cup chopped onion
½ teaspoon minced garlic
1 tablespoon corn oil
6 tablespoons unbleached white flour
4 cups Cashew Milk (page 93) made with UnBeef Broth (page 155)

Sauté the gluten (or grits), onion, and garlic in the oil until it is lightly browned. Add the flour and mix well. Gradually add the "milk," stirring constantly. Cook and stir over medium heat until thickened.

Sauces

Get creative with these sauces. Use them in many ways: over bread, biscuits, grains, pasta, vegetables, as dips—whatever!

Barbecue Sauce 1

1 cup chopped onion
1 tablespoon corn oil
6 tablespoons tomato paste
1 1/4 cups water
1/4 cup Sucanat
1 tablespoon Barbados molasses
1/4 cup lemon juice
2 tablespoons prepared mustard
2 teaspoons sea salt
1/4 teaspoon cayenne pepper

Put all together and cook for 1 hour.

Barbecue Sauce 2

1 tablespoon corn oil
2 cups chopped onion
2 garlic cloves
1/2 cup chopped fresh parsley
3/4 teaspoon Louisiana Hot Sauce
1 cup water
1 tablespoon lemon juice
4 tablespoons Lea and Perrins Steak Sauce
1 1/2 teaspoons sea salt
1 1/2 cups canned tomato sauce
1 teaspoon liquid smoke

Heat the oil in a large saucepan. Blend the onion, garlic, parsley, and hot sauce in a blender with just enough water so it will blend. Pour this into the saucepan and simmer for 30 minutes. Add the rest of the ingredients and simmer for 30 more minutes, covered, adding more water if it is needed.

Brown Sauce

4 teaspoons nondairy margarine
3 tablespoons sliced onion
1/2 teaspoon minced garlic
2 tablespoons unbleached white flour
1 cup puréed tomato
3/4 cup UnBeef Broth (page 155)
1/4 teaspoon sea salt
1/4 teaspoon paprika

Melt the margarine and sauté the onion and garlic until the onion is light brown. Remove the onion and stir in the flour and cook until it turns brown as well. Slowly stir in the puréed tomato. Add the onion, broth, salt, and paprika. Stir and cook until the sauce is smooth and boiling.

"Butter" Sauce with Herbs

1 tablespoon unbleached white flour
1 tablespoon nondairy margarine
2 tablespoons Cashew Milk (page 93)

2 tablespoons minced onion
½ teaspoon minced garlic
1½ teaspoons basil
1½ teaspoons parsley
⅛ teaspoon sea salt

Place all ingredients in a double boiler, cook, and stir until smooth.

Cajun Catsup

This is delightful—I guarantee it!

4 cups chopped onion
1 cup chopped celery
1 cup chopped bell pepper
1 cup chopped fresh parsley
2 tablespoons corn oil
2 tablespoons chopped garlic
3 cups Lea and Perrins Steak Sauce
½ cup Louisiana Hot Sauce
3 cups tomato sauce
3 teaspoons sea salt

In a large skillet, sauté the onion, celery, bell pepper, and parsley in the oil until the onion is soft and transparent. Add the garlic and cook a little longer. Add the steak sauce, hot sauce, tomato sauce, and salt, and bring to a boil. Lower the heat and cover, and cook for 2 to 3 hours. This can be kept refrigerated for a few weeks.

Catsup

1 cup tomato puree
2 teaspoons corn oil
2 teaspoons molasses
1 teaspoon sea salt
2 tablespoons wine vinegar
3 tablespoons chopped onion

Combine all the ingredients and cook for 15 to 30 minutes. While still warm, pour into a blender and blend until smooth as possible.

Cheez Sauce 1

1 tablespoon corn oil
½ cup flour
3 cups water
1½ teaspoons sea salt
⅛ teaspoon cayenne pepper
3 cups Yeast Cheez (page 97) or Pimiento Cheez (page 94)

Heat the oil. Slowly add the flour, blending it with a whisk. Slowly add the water, continuously blending with the whisk. Cook until bubbly and thick. Add the salt, pepper, and Cheez.

VARIATION: *Use UnBeef Broth (page 155) or UnChicken Broth (page 155) instead of water, and cut the salt in half.*

Cheez Sauce 2

1 tablespoon nondairy margarine
2 tablespoons unbleached white flour
1½ cups Cashew Milk (page 93)
1 cup Yeast Cheez (page 97) or Pimiento Cheez (page 94)
½ teaspoon sea salt
⅛ teaspoon paprika
Dash cayenne pepper
½ teaspoon dried mustard

Melt the margarine in a saucepan. Stir in the flour until it is blended. Slowly stir in the "milk." When the sauce is smooth and boiling, reduce the heat and add the rest of the ingredients, stirring in well.

VARIATION: *Make the "milk" with UnChicken Broth (page 155), and cut the salt in half.*

Cheez Sauce 3

1 cup Cashew Sour Kreem (page 94) or Tofu Sour Kreem (page 97)
⅔ cup Yeast Cheez (page 97) or Pimiento Cheez (page 94)
2 tablespoons chopped onion
2 tablespoons lemon juice
¼ teaspoon sea salt

Combine everything well. Use over broccoli, brussels sprouts, spaghetti, etc.

Cheez Sauce 4

½ cup Yeast Cheez (page 97) or Pimiento Cheez (page 94)
¼ cup Miraculous Whip (page 17)
½ cup Cashew Sour Kreem (page 94) or Tofu Sour Kreem (page 97)
¼ teaspoon paprika

Combine everything well. Use over broccoli, brussels sprouts, spaghetti, etc.

Cheez and Onion Sauce

1½ cups chopped onion
1 teaspoon minced garlic
2 teaspoons nondairy margarine
2 tablespoons unbleached white flour
2 cups Cashew Milk (page 93), warm
1 teaspoon sea salt
¼ teaspoon paprika
½ cup Yeast Cheez (page 97) or Pimiento Cheez (page 94)

Sauté the onions and garlic in the margarine. Add the flour and blend. Add the "milk" slowly while stirring. Stir in the salt, paprika, and Cheez.

Chili Sauce

1 cup catsup
2 tablespoons prepared horseradish
2 tablespoons lemon juice
1 teaspoon chopped fresh parsley
1 teaspoon chopped chives

Combine all the ingredients and stir to blend. Put in a container and refrigerate.

Cocktail Sauce 1

1½ cups catsup
2½ tablespoons lemon juice
1 tablespoon plus 1½ teaspoons horseradish
2 tablespoons Lea and Perrins Steak Sauce
1 teaspoon grated onion
2 dashes Louisiana Hot Sauce

Combine all the ingredients and stir to blend. Put in a container and refrigerate.

Cocktail Sauce 2

½ cup Miraculous Whip (page 17)
1 tablespoon olive oil
2 teaspoons Louisiana Hot Sauce
2 cups catsup
1 teaspoon sea salt
2 tablespoons Lea and Perrins Steak Sauce
3 tablespoons lemon juice
1 tablespoon creamed-style horseradish

Put the Miraculous Whip in a bowl, and while beating constantly with a fork, add the oil. Continuing to beat, add the hot sauce and then the catsup. Add the salt, steak sauce, lemon juice, and horseradish, mixing well. Cover and chill for at least 30 minutes. Beat just before serving.

Creole Sauce

Good over rice.

2 teaspoons nondairy margarine
⅓ cup chopped onion
½ cup chopped bell pepper
⅓ cup chopped mushrooms
1 teaspoon minced jalapeños
1½ cups chopped tomato
⅓ teaspoon sea salt
1 teaspoon Barbados molasses
1 tablespoon unbleached white flour
⅓ cup water

Melt the margarine, and sauté the onion, bell pepper, mushrooms, and jalapeños for 2 minutes. Add the rest of the ingredients and cook until the sauce is thick.

Golden Sauce

½ cup chopped onion
½ teaspoon minced garlic
2 teaspoons corn oil
¾ cup water
½ cup cooked chopped potatoes
¼ cup cooked chopped carrot
3 tablespoons nutritional yeast
½ teaspoon sea salt
1 tablespoon lemon juice

Sauté the onion and garlic in the oil. Liquefy all the ingredients together in a blender until smooth. Heat to serving temperature.

Maître d'Hôtel Butter Sauce

1/4 cup nondairy margarine
1/2 teaspoon sea salt
1/8 teaspoon paprika
1/2 tablespoon chopped fresh parsley
1 1/2 teaspoons lemon juice

Cream the margarine until it is very soft. Add the salt, paprika, and parsley. Very slowly add the lemon juice, stirring the sauce constantly.

Olive Sauce 1

1 tablespoon nondairy margarine
3 tablespoons sliced onion
1/2 teaspoon minced garlic
2 tablespoons unbleached white flour
1 cup pureed tomato
12 black olives, sliced
3/4 cup UnBeef Broth (page 155)
1/4 teaspoon sea salt
1/4 teaspoon paprika

Melt the margarine and sauté the onion and garlic until the onion is light brown. Remove the onion and stir in the flour and cook until it turns brown as well. Slowly stir in the pureed tomato. Add the onion, olives, broth, salt, and paprika. Stir and cook until the sauce is smooth and boiling.

Olive Sauce 2

1/4 cup sliced green onions
1/4 cup sliced mushrooms
2 teaspoons nondairy margarine
1 cup sliced black olives
2 tablespoons liquid from the olives
1 cup Cashew Sour Kreem (page 94) or Tofu Sour Kreem (page 97)
1/2 teaspoon garlic powder
1/2 teaspoon soy sauce

Sauté the onions and mushrooms in the margarine for 1 minute. Stir in the rest of the ingredients and heat just until hot, but not boiling.

Onion Sauce 1

3/4 cup chopped onion
2 teaspoons nondairy margarine
1 teaspoon soy sauce
1/2 teaspoon sea salt
1/2 teaspoon paprika

Sauté onion for 5 minutes in margarine. Add rest of ingredients.

VARIATION: *Use chives instead of onions.*

Onion Sauce 2

3 cups chopped onion
2 cups boiling water, plus more to cover onion
UnBeef Broth (page 155)
2 tablespoons nondairy margarine
3 tablespoons unbleached white flour

Cover the onion with boiling water and cook for 5 minutes. Drain and cover with 2 more cups of boiling water. Boil them until they are soft. Rub through a sieve. Add enough broth to make 2 1/2 cupfuls. Melt the margarine and stir in the flour until blended. Stir in the onion puree.

Piquante Sauce

2 tablespoons nondairy margarine
5 tablespoons sliced onion
1/2 teaspoon minced garlic
2 tablespoons unbleached white flour
1 cup pureed tomato
1 tablespoon lemon juice
1 tablespoon minced bell pepper
1/8 teaspoon cayenne pepper
1/4 teaspoon sea salt
1/4 teaspoon paprika
3/4 cup UnBeef Broth (page 155)

Melt the margarine and sauté the onion and garlic until the onion is light brown. Remove the onion and stir in the flour and cook until it turns brown as well. Slowly stir in the pureed tomato. Add the onion, lemon juice, bell pepper, cayenne, salt, paprika, and broth. Stir and cook until the sauce is smooth and boiling.

Sour Kreem and Chive Sauce

1 cup Cashew Sour Kreem (page 94) or Tofu Sour Kreem (page 97)
4 teaspoons chives
1/4 teaspoon Louisiana Hot Sauce

Combine well.

Spanish Tomato Sauce

Truly special!

1/2 teaspoon minced garlic
2 teaspoons olive oil
1 quart chopped tomato
3/4 cup tomato paste
1 bay leaf
2 teaspoons sea salt
1/2 teaspoon oregano
1/2 teaspoon basil
1 cup chopped onion
1/2 cup chopped bell pepper
1/2 teaspoon ground cumin

Sauté the garlic in the oil. Puree the tomato in a blender and add to the oil. Put all together, adding water if needed, and simmer until thick.

Spicy Barbecue Sauce 1

4 1/2 cups tomato sauce
3/4 cup tomato paste
1/3 cup Barbados molasses
1/2 cup water
1/3 cup white wine vinegar
2 tablespoons lemon juice
2 tablespoons prepared mustard
2 tablespoons Lea and Perrins Steak Sauce
2 teaspoons hot pepper sauce
1/2 cup finely chopped onion
1 teaspoon minced garlic
1/2 teaspoon freshly ground black pepper
1/2 teaspoon ground cloves
1/2 teaspoon allspice
1/4 teaspoon ground ginger
1 tablespoon corn oil

Combine all the ingredients in a large saucepan. Cook over medium heat for about 30 minutes, stirring frequently to prevent sticking.

Spicy Barbecue Sauce 2

This is the sauce given for Barbecue "Spare Ribs" (page 123), but it is good for everything.

1/2 cup chopped onion
1 teaspoon minced garlic
1 tablespoon corn oil or margarine
2 1/2 cups tomato sauce
1/4 cup water
1 cup Sucanat
2 tablespoons Barbados molasses
1/2 cup prepared mustard
1 tablespoon plus 1 teaspoon sea salt
1 teaspoon allspice
1 1/2 teaspoons crushed red pepper
1 sprig fresh parsley, or 1 1/2 teaspoons dried
1/4 cup water
2 tablespoons lemon juice
1 teaspoon liquid smoke
1 tablespoon soy sauce

Sauté the onion and garlic in oil or margarine until the onion becomes clear and golden. Add tomato sauce, water, Sucanat, molasses, mustard, salt, allspice, pepper, and parsley. Bring to a boil, reduce heat, and let simmer for about an hour. Add water, lemon juice, liquid smoke, and soy sauce. Cook 10 to 15 minutes longer.

Taco Sauce

5 cups chopped tomato
2 1/2 teaspoons minced garlic
1 teaspoon crushed red pepper flakes
2 teaspoons sea salt
1 tablespoon minced bell pepper
1 1/2 cups finely chopped onion
1 teaspoon chili powder
1 teaspoon oregano
1 teaspoon thyme
1 tablespoon Sucanat
1 tablespoon unbleached white flour
1 tablespoon corn oil
1 tablespoon wine vinegar

Blend in blender or food processor and cook for 1 hour.

Tartar Sauce

Never make UnFish (page 149) without making some of this, too.

1 cup Cashew Mayonnaise (page 12) or Tofu Mayonnaise (page 22), or Miraculous Whip (page 17)
1 tablespoon minced onion
1½ teaspoons prepared mustard
1 tablespoon horseradish
¼ cup dill pickles (or sweet pickles, if you prefer)

Combine well and refrigerate for a while to let the flavor develop.

Tomato Sauce 1

⅓ cup chopped onion
1 teaspoon minced garlic
2 teaspoons corn oil
6 cups coarsely chopped tomato
½ cup plus 1 tablespoon tomato paste
1 tablespoon basil
1¼ teaspoons sea salt
⅛ teaspoon cayenne pepper
1 tablespoon Barbados molasses

Sauté the onion and garlic in the oil. Combine with rest of ingredients and cook.

Tomato Sauce 2

⅓ cup chopped onion
1 teaspoon minced garlic
2 teaspoons corn oil
6 cups coarsely chopped tomato
½ cup plus 1 tablespoon tomato paste
1½ teaspoons Italian seasoning
1½ teaspoons fennel seed
1¼ teaspoons sea salt
⅛ teaspoon cayenne pepper
1 tablespoon Barbados molasses

Sauté the onion and garlic in the oil. Combine with rest of ingredients and cook.

Tomato Sauce 3

½ teaspoon minced garlic
1 teaspoon olive oil
1 quart chopped tomato
¾ cup tomato paste
1 bay leaf
2 teaspoons sea salt
½ teaspoon oregano
½ teaspoon basil
1 teaspoon Sucanat (optional)

Sauté the garlic in the olive oil. Puree the tomato in a blender and add to the oil. Put all together, adding water if needed, and simmer until thick.

Tomato and Cheez Sauce

2 teaspoons nondairy margarine
¾ cup chopped onion
3 cups chopped tomato
½ cup Cashew Milk (page 93)
1 teaspoon finely chopped fresh basil, or ¼ teaspoon dried
¼ teaspoon oregano
Pinch ground cumin
½ teaspoon sea salt
¼ teaspoon paprika
1 cup Yeast Cheez (page 97), Pimiento Cheez (page 94), or Notzarella Cheez (page 94)

In a skillet heat the margarine over moderate heat. Sauté the onion until transparent, but not brown. Add everything else but the Cheez and cook, stirring, for 5 minutes. Then, stirring constantly, add the Cheez.

Tomato and Onion Sauce

A tremendous thunderstorm punctuated with hurricane-strength winds once kept me from going out to get dinner ingredients. So, I had to use what was on hand. That turned out to be tomatoes, onions, and rice. This is excellent over rice or pasta.

4 cups chopped onion
1 tablespoon minced garlic
1 cup chopped bell pepper
1 cup chopped celery
1 tablespoon minced jalapeños
3 tablespoons corn oil
4 cups chopped tomato
1 teaspoon sea salt
½ teaspoon cayenne pepper
3 tablespoons soy sauce
1 cup water

Sauté the onion, garlic, bell pepper, celery, and jalapeños in the oil until the onion is soft and transparent, but not brown. Add the rest of the ingredients and cook with the onion thoroughly until the consistency is thick, but not dry.

VARIATION: *Sauté 2 tablespoons of curry powder along with the onion, etc.*

UnBeef and Tomato Sauce

1½ teaspoons minced garlic
1 cup chopped onion
2 teaspoons corn oil
2 cups ground UnBeef (page 109)
3 cups finely chopped tomato
⅔ cup tomato paste
2 tablespoons Sucanat
1 teaspoon Italian herb seasoning
1 bay leaf
½ teaspoon sea salt
⅛ teaspoon black pepper or cayenne pepper

Sauté the garlic and onion in the oil until the onion is soft. Add the gluten and sauté it well. Add the remaining ingredients. Simmer the sauce uncovered for about 20 to 30 minutes.

White Sauce

Thin
2 teaspoons nondairy margarine
2 teaspoons unbleached white flour
¼ teaspoon sea salt
1½ cups Cashew Milk (page 93)

Medium
1 tablespoon nondairy margarine
1 tablespoon unbleached white flour
¼ teaspoon sea salt
1 cup Cashew Milk (page 93)

Thick
4 teaspoons nondairy margarine
2 tablespoons unbleached white flour
¼ teaspoon sea salt
1 cup Cashew Milk (page 93)

Melt the margarine in a saucepan over low heat. Blend in the flour and salt. Add the "milk" all at once. Cook quickly, stirring constantly, until the mixture thickens and bubbles, then remove the sauce from the heat. Add other flavorings, if any, at this point, stirring until smooth.

If sauce cooks too long, it becomes too thick and the margarine separates out. To correct this, stir in a little more "milk" and cook quickly, stirring constantly, until the sauce bubbles again.

Pasta Sauces

Kreem Cheez Spaghetti Sauce

Forget modesty. This is another wonderful "invention" of mine!

4 cups Tofu Cottage Cheez (page 96), blended smooth
4 cups Cashew Milk (page 93) made with UnChicken Broth (page 155)
1 teaspoon nondairy margarine
¼ teaspoon garlic powder
¼ teaspoon freshly ground black pepper
¼ cup Parmesan Cheez (page 94)

Combine the Cottage Cheez and "milk" and heat in a double boiler. Combine the other ingredients and stir into the "milk" mixture. Cook for 30 minutes.

Italian Pasta Sauce

1 cup chopped bell pepper
1½ cups chopped onion
1 tablespoon corn oil
6 cups chopped tomato
½ teaspoon sea salt
3 cups chopped squash
½ teaspoon basil
½ teaspoon oregano
½ teaspoon cayenne pepper
2 teaspoons minced garlic
3 cups UnBeef Broth (page 155)

Sauté the bell pepper and onion in the oil. Combine all ingredients and cook.

Mary Krieger's Sure-to-Please Spaghetti Sauce

This is heavenly simple and simply heavenly. It never fails. Thanks, Mary!

2 quarts canned tomato sauce
2 tablespoons dried minced onion
1 teaspoon dried minced garlic
½ teaspoon freshly ground black pepper
1½ teaspoons Italian seasoning
1 cup sliced or chopped mushrooms
2 tablespoons olive oil

Combine everything. Bring to a low boil, reduce the heat, and simmer, cooking until thickened, stirring occasionally, 1 to 1½ hours.

Onion Sauce for Spaghetti

Reliable!

2 cups chopped onion
1 teaspoon minced garlic
1½ teaspoons nondairy margarine
1½ teaspoons olive oil
½ teaspoon sea salt
½ teaspoon black pepper or cayenne pepper
1 teaspoon Sucanat
2 cups tomato sauce
1 cup UnBeef Broth (page 155)

Sauté the onion and garlic in the margarine and oil until soft. Mix and simmer all ingredients for 30 minutes.

Pasta Sauce Neapolitan

2 tablespoons minced garlic
2 teaspoons olive oil
1 cup sliced black olives
¼ cup fresh basil (firmly packed in the measure), chopped, or 1 tablespoon dried
1 teaspoon hot pepper flakes
2 cups canned tomato sauce
1 cup Yeast Cheez (page 97), Pimiento Cheez (page 94), or Notzarella Cheez (page 94)
Parmesan Cheez (page 94)

Sauté the garlic in the oil slowly until it is softened but not browned. Add the olives, basil, pepper flakes, and tomato sauce. Heat through. Stir in the Cheez and mix well until heated through. Serve over pasta. Sprinkle with Parmesan Cheez.

Sour Kreem Spaghetti Sauce

3 cups Cashew Sour Kreem (page 94) or Tofu Sour Kreem (page 97)
1 cup UnChicken Broth (page 155)
2 teaspoons sea salt
Two 4-ounce jars of pimientos
¼ cup corn oil
3 tablespoons minced onion

Put the Sour Kreem, broth, salt, and pimientos in a blender and blend until smooth. While the blender is still going, slowly add the corn oil. Put into a bowl and mix in the onion.

Spaghetti Sauce

This never fails to please.

1 cup coarsely chopped onion
¾ cup chopped celery
¾ teaspoon minced garlic
1 tablespoon olive oil
6 cups chopped tomato
1½ cups UnBeef (page 109) or UnBeef Soy Grits (page 109)
½ teaspoon hot pepper flakes
1½ teaspoons sea salt
1½ teaspoons Italian seasoning
¼ cup UnBeef Broth (page 155)
½ cup tomato paste

Sauté the onion, celery, and garlic in the olive oil. Combine everything and cook for 1 hour or more.

Tomato-Mushroom Marinara Sauce

1½ cups coarsely chopped onion
1½ teaspoons minced garlic
4 cups sliced mushrooms, ¼ to ½ inch thick
2 tablespoons corn oil
5 cups chopped canned tomatoes, with their juice
1 teaspoon oregano
½ teaspoon fennel seed
2 tablespoons basil
¼ teaspoon hot pepper flakes
1¼ teaspoons sea salt

Sauté the onion, garlic, and mushrooms in the oil until the onion is soft. Combine everything and simmer for 1 hour, adding more water or tomato juice if it gets too thick.

UnBeef and Tomato Sauce

1½ teaspoons minced garlic
1 cup chopped onion
2 teaspoons corn oil
2 cups ground UnBeef (page 109)
3 cups finely chopped tomato
⅔ cup tomato paste
2 tablespoons Sucanat
1 teaspoon Italian herb seasoning
1 bay leaf

½ teaspoon sea salt
⅛ teaspoon black pepper or cayenne pepper

Sauté the garlic and onion in the oil until the onion is soft. Add the gluten and sauté it well. Add the remaining ingredients. Simmer the sauce, uncovered, for about 20 to 30 minutes.

UnBeef Pasta Sauce

4 cups cubed UnBeef (page 109), cut into 1-inch cubes
¼ cup olive oil
1 cup chopped onion
2½ cups UnChicken Broth (page 155)
2 bay leaves
⅓ cup finely chopped celery
⅓ cup shredded carrot
2 tablespoons finely chopped fresh parsley
1 tablespoon tomato paste
¼ teaspoon sea salt
¼ teaspoon freshly ground black pepper
1 cup drained and chopped canned tomatoes
1 cup chopped mushrooms

Brown the gluten in the oil. Add the onion and cook until golden. Add the broth, bay leaves, celery, carrot, parsley, tomato paste, salt, and pepper. Cook for 3 minutes. Stir in the tomatoes and mushrooms. Cover partially and cook, stirring occasionally, for 45 minutes.

UnChicken Pasta Sauce

½ cup minced onion (red preferred)
2 teaspoons olive oil
1 teaspoon minced garlic
¼ cup diced bell pepper, cut into ¼-inch dice
½ teaspoon chili powder
¼ teaspoon ground cumin
⅛ teaspoon cayenne pepper
1½ cups ground UnChicken (page 137)
2 cups canned tomatoes (Italian preferred) with the juice
¼ cup tomato paste
¼ teaspoon basil
¼ teaspoon oregano
¼ teaspoon hot pepper flakes
¼ teaspoon sea salt

Sauté the onion in the oil until soft. Add the garlic, bell pepper, chili powder, cumin, and cayenne, and cook, stirring, for 1 minute. Add the gluten and cook, stirring, for 4 minutes. Stir in the tomatoes and juice, breaking the tomatoes up, along with the tomato paste, basil, oregano, pepper flakes, and salt. Simmer, stirring occasionally, until thickened, about 10 minutes.

VARIATION: *Use another type of flavored gluten.*

UnShrimp Pasta Sauce

¾ teaspoon minced garlic
2 green onions, minced
1 teaspoon corn oil
1½ cups chopped tomato
2 tablespoons chopped fresh basil
½ teaspoon hot pepper flakes
½ teaspoon sea salt
1 tablespoon capers
1 cup UnShrimp (page 150)
2 teaspoons nondairy margarine
2 tablespoons UnShrimp Broth (see Unshrimp, page 150)

Sauté the garlic and onions in the oil until the garlic is pale golden. Add the tomato, basil, pepper flakes, salt, and capers. Sauté the gluten in the margarine for 5 minutes, then add the broth and cook until most of the liquid is evaporated. Add the gluten to the sauce.

Zucchini Spaghetti Sauce

¾ cup chopped onion
1 teaspoon minced garlic
2 cups thinly sliced zucchini
1½ cups sliced bell pepper, cut into julienne strips
2 tablespoons corn oil
3 cups chopped tomato
⅓ cup UnChicken Broth (page 155)
2 teaspoons sea salt
⅛ teaspoon paprika

Sauté the onion, garlic, squash, and bell pepper in the corn oil. Add rest of ingredients and cook for 15 minutes.

VARIATION: *Use another type of squash, or even another type of vegetable.*

Pasta

A Note on Making and Cooking Pasta

Although pasta can be made by simply mixing and rolling it out, a pasta machine is invaluable. If you have a hand-operated machine, when ready for the "rolling out" step, put the dough through the machine at the thickest setting. Then narrow it down one point and run the dough through again. Keep repeating this until you run it through at the desired thickness (thinness, actually).

Whether you have a hand-operated or electric pasta maker, it will help keep your noodles from falling apart if you position an electric fan to blow on the noodles as they emerge from the machine, and thus rapidly dry them.

If you will not be using all of the pasta, dry it out in a 200°F oven. Then you can store it indefinitely in a sealed bag that is free from moisture.

Do not put oil in the water in which you cook pasta. It will make the pasta more likely to stick together and it will coat the pasta, so seasonings and sauces will not adhere to it as they should.

Basic Pasta

2 cups unbleached white flour
1/4 cup gluten flour
1/2 teaspoon sea salt
2 tablespoons corn oil
1/2 cup water
1/2 cup nutritional yeast

Mix all ingredients into a stiff dough, adding more water as needed. Knead briefly. Roll dough as thin as possible. Cut into size and shapes desired. Dry in the air overnight or in a 200°F oven on cookie sheets until all moisture is gone.

Basic N'egg Pasta

Make the Basic Pasta recipe (above), but add 3 N'eggs (page 302) to the ingredients.

Basic Semolina Pasta

Make the Basic Pasta recipe (see above), but in place of the 2 cups of unbleached white flour use 1 cup of flour and 1 cup of white semolina. For any additional "flouring" use semolina instead of regular flour.

Baked Macaroni with Tomatoes

4 cups macaroni, cooked
3½ cups Yeast Cheez (page 97), Pimiento Cheez (page 94), or Notzarella Cheez (page 94)
3 cups tomato juice
1 teaspoon sea salt
¼ cup chopped fresh chopped fresh parsley
2 teaspoons basil or thyme
½ teaspoon paprika
¼ teaspoon onion powder
¼ teaspoon garlic powder
1 cup bread crumbs

Mix the macaroni, 3 cups Cheez, tomato juice, salt, parsley, and basil in a casserole dish. Combine the ½ cup of Cheez, paprika, onion powder, garlic powder, and bread crumbs. Spread this over all and bake at 350°F for 30 minutes.

Baked Pasta with UnBeef

2 cups ground UnBeef (page 109)
2½ teaspoons crushed garlic
¾ cup Spaghetti Sauce (page 264)
¾ cup UnBeef Gravy (page 155)
½ cup Cashew Kreem (page 93)
1 teaspoon oregano
½ teaspoon rosemary
Cayenne pepper
¾ pound pasta
1 cup Yeast Cheez (page 97) or Notzarella Cheez (page 94)

Combine everything but the pasta and cup of Cheez. Simmer this together, and at the same time cook the pasta and drain it well. Mix the pasta with the sauce. Put into a casserole and spread the Cheez over the top. Bake, uncovered, at 350°F for 25 minutes.

Calzone

1 tablespoon Sucanat
1 cup lukewarm water
1 tablespoon dried yeast
2 cups unbleached white flour
1 tablespoon oil
½ teaspoon sea salt
Apple juice

Place the Sucanat, water, and yeast in a large bowl and stir until the yeast and Sucanat are dissolved. Let sit until it is foamy, 8 to 10 minutes. Stir in 1 cup of flour and mix well. Let rise 20 minutes. Stir down and add remaining flour, oil, and salt. Knead 5 to 10 minutes or until pliable and not sticky, adding more flour as needed. Place dough on a floured board, cover with a towel, and let it rise for 1½ hours.

Divide the dough into 8 balls and roll each into an even circle. Place a filling—such as from the recipes found in the chapters on Casseroles, Dried Beans, Gravies, Sauces, UnBeef Substitutes and Dishes, Pies, Square Meals, or Vegetables—in the center of each circle (if you like, include tomato sauce), spreading it 1 inch from the edge. Fold the circles into half-moon shapes and pinch the edges tightly closed. Pierce the tops three or four times with a fork to let out the steam. Brush the tops with apple juice. Place on an oiled baking sheet and bake at 400°F for 25 minutes.

Chili-Mac

This is great "kid food"—and am I ever a kid!

1 cup chopped onion
1 teaspoon minced garlic
1 teaspoon minced jalapeños
2 teaspoons corn oil
1 pound macaroni, cooked in salted water and drained
¼ teaspoon sea salt
6 cups chili recipe of choice (pages 90–92)

Sauté the onion, garlic, and jalapeños in the oil. Toss the macaroni with this along with the salt. Put the macaroni in a casserole, top with the chili, and bake at 350°F for 30 minutes. (If you are using leftover chili that has gotten thick overnight, dilute it with 1 cup of tomato juice and heat.)

VARIATION: *Top with Yeast Cheez (page 97) or Pimiento Cheez (page 94) before baking.*

Creole Spaghetti

2 tablespoons chopped onion
1/2 cup chopped bell pepper
2 teaspoons corn oil
2 cups UnBeef Soy Grits (page 109)
2 cups stewed tomatoes
2 cups spaghetti, cooked and drained
1/2 teaspoon sea salt
1/4 teaspoon cayenne pepper

Sauté the onion and bell pepper in the oil. Add soy grits, tomatoes, spaghetti, salt, and pepper. Cover and cook 15 to 20 minutes, stirring frequently.

Delicious Lasagna

The name tells it all!

1/2 pound uncooked lasagna noodles
2 cups ground UnBeef (page 109)
1/4 cup chopped onion
2 cups canned tomato sauce
Two 10-ounce packages frozen spinach, thawed and drained well
1 teaspoon parsley flakes
1/2 teaspoon oregano
1 teaspoon basil
1/2 teaspoon sea salt
1/4 teaspoon freshly ground black pepper
2 cups Tofu Ricotta Cheez (page 96)
2 1/2 cups Notzarella Cheez (page 94)

Cook the noodles and set aside. Combine the UnBeef, onion, tomato sauce, spinach, parsley, oregano, basil, salt, and pepper. Simmer, uncovered, for 10 minutes, stirring occasionally. Remove from heat and add the Tofu Ricotta. In a nonstick casserole layer half the noodles, half the gluten mixture, and half the Notzarella. Repeat. Bake at 375°F until the Cheez starts to brown, 20 to 30 minutes.

Eggplant Lasagna

1 medium eggplant, peeled and sliced 1/4 inch thick
1 cup chopped onion
1 1/2 teaspoons crushed garlic
1/2 cup olive oil
3 cups chopped tomato
1/2 cup tomato sauce
1/2 teaspoon basil
1/2 teaspoon oregano
1/2 teaspoon parsley
2 tablespoons unbleached white flour
Dash freshly ground black pepper
8 ounces lasagna noodles, cooked, drained, and set aside
1 pound tofu, frozen, thawed, pressed, crumbled, and browned in olive oil
2 tablespoons Parmesan Cheez (page 94) or soy Parmesan

Salt both sides of the eggplant slices and let sit for 1 hour, then press out the moisture. Sauté the onion and garlic in 2 tablespoons of the oil until soft. Add the tomato, tomato sauce, basil, oregano, and parsley. Simmer 10 to 15 minutes. While the sauce is simmering, combine the flour and pepper and coat the eggplant slices with the mixture. Brown the eggplant in the oil and set aside. Put enough sauce into a baking dish to just cover the bottom. Put in a layer of eggplant slices. Add a layer of noodles, top with a layer of tofu, and cover with sauce. Repeat the layers ending with the sauce. Sprinkle the Cheez over all. Cover and bake at 375°F for 30 minutes.

Fettucini with Spinach Pesto

12 ounces fettucini, uncooked
4 teaspoons corn oil
3/4 teaspoon basil leaves
1/8 teaspoon cayenne pepper
3 tablespoons chopped onion
1 teaspoon minced garlic
3 tablespoons corn oil
2 cups fresh spinach
2/3 cup Yeast Cheez (page 97), Pimiento Cheez (page 94), or Notzarella Cheez (page 94)
1 cup Cashew Sour Kreem (page 94) or Tofu Sour Kreem (page 97)

Cook the fettucini. Put 2 teaspoons of corn oil, basil, cayenne, onion, and garlic in a blender and blend until smooth. Add the rest of the oil, then the spinach, Cheez, and Sour Kreem, blending well and scraping down the sides of the blender when needed. Let sit a few minutes for the flavors to blend. Toss with the drained fettucini.

Fried Noodles

Make one of the Basic Pasta recipes (page 266), and cut dough into 1x3/4-inch strips and deep-fry. These can be used in various recipes, including Chinese dishes, and can also be a snack for hungry children. These may be lightly salted or sprinkled with garlic salt, onion salt, or soy sauce for more flavor.

Gnocchi

UnBeef Broth (page 155)
2 cups unbleached white flour
1/4 teaspoon sea salt
1 tablespoon corn oil
4 cups potatoes, mashed with UnChicken Broth (page 155) or UnBeef Broth (page 155)
Pasta sauce of choice (see Pasta Sauces chapter)

Heat a large pot of UnBeef Broth. Meanwhile mix the flour and salt and shape into a mound in the center of a breadboard. Make a well in the center and pour in the oil and add the mashed potatoes. Knead the mixture with your hands (use extra flour if it gets sticky). Divide the dough into 4 balls and roll into long cylinders no more than an inch thick. Cut into 1-inch pieces. Rub fork tines over each piece of dough to make an impression. Drop the gnocchi into boiling broth. They will sink, then rise to the surface as they cook. Remove with a slotted spoon as soon as they rise. Toss with pasta sauce.

Herbed Noodles

When you are in a hurry for something good, this is it!

12 ounces noodles of any type, cooked and tossed in 1/4 cup of melted corn oil margarine
2 cups Tofu Cottage Cheez (page 96)
1 cup Cashew Sour Kreem (page 94) or Tofu Sour Kreem (page 97)
1/3 cup finely chopped onion
1/4 teaspoon garlic powder
1/4 cup chopped fresh parsley
1/2 teaspoon Italian herb seasoning
1 tablespoon lemon juice
1 teaspoon sea salt
1/8 teaspoon cayenne pepper

Combine and let sit for a while to exchange flavors.

Herbed Noodles with Cheez, Lemon, and Green Onions

2 tablespoons nondairy margarine, melted
12 ounce noodles of any type, cooked
2 cups crumbled tofu
3/4 cup Yeast Cheez (page 97), Pimiento Cheez (page 94), or Notzarella Cheez (page 94)
1 cup Parmesan Cheez (page 94)
1/2 cups finely chopped green onions
1/4 cup chopped fresh parsley
1 1/2 teaspoons minced garlic
1/2 teaspoon Italian herb seasoning
3 tablespoons lemon juice
1/2 teaspoon sea salt
1/8 teaspoon cayenne pepper

In a 9x13-inch pan, toss the melted margarine with the cooked noodles. Beat together the remaining ingredients until thoroughly blended. Pour the mixture on the noodles and toss and turn until all is blended. Bake at 350°F until the top begins to brown, about 20 minutes.

VARIATION: *Add 10 ounces of chopped frozen spinach to the Cheez mixture.*

Hungarian Noodle Bake

1/4 pound spaghetti, uncooked
Boiling salted water
1/4 cup finely chopped onion
1/2 teaspoon minced garlic
1 teaspoon nondairy margarine
1 1/2 cups Tofu Cottage Cheez (page 96)
1 cup Cashew Sour Kreem (page 94) or Tofu Sour Kreem (page 97)
Dash Louisiana Hot Sauce
2 teaspoons poppy seeds
1/2 teaspoon sea salt
Dash paprika or cayenne pepper
Parmesan Cheez (page 94)

Cook the spaghetti in boiling salted water until tender. Drain. Sauté onion and garlic in margarine until soft. Combine all ingredients together, except paprika and Cheez, and put in an oiled baking dish. Bake at 350°F until hot, about 25 minutes. Sprinkle with paprika. Serve with Parmesan Cheez.

Lasagna

A leading favorite!

1/2 pound lasagna noodles, uncooked
1 1/2 cups sliced mushrooms
1 1/2 cups chopped onion
2 teaspoons minced garlic
1 tablespoon olive oil
3 cups ground UnBeef (page 109)
4 teaspoons Parmesan Cheez (page 94)
1/8 teaspoon cayenne pepper
9 cups Tomato Sauce 1 (page 261)
2 cups Tofu Cottage Cheez (page 96)
2 to 3 cups Yeast Cheez (page 97), Pimiento Cheez (page 94), or Notzarella Cheez (page 94)

Cook the noodles, drain, and set aside. Sauté the mushrooms, onion, and garlic in the rest of the oil until the onion is soft. Combine with the gluten along with the "Parmesan," cayenne, and 2 cups of the Tomato Sauce and cook for 5 more minutes. Layer a casserole dish starting with Tomato Sauce, then noodles, Cottage Cheez, the gluten mixture, and a thin layer of the Cheez. Repeat, and top with a layer of Tomato Sauce, noodles, Cottage Cheez, and more Tomato Sauce. Bake at 375°F 30 to 40 minutes.

Lasagna Noodles

Use Basic Pasta recipe (page 266). Roll out to 1/8-inch thickness. Cut into 1 1/2-inch strips. Dry in the air overnight or in a 200°F oven on cookie sheets until all moisture is gone.

Lasagna RoOll-Ups

One 10-ounce package frozen chopped spinach, thawed and squeezed dry
2 tablespoons minced green onions
2 teaspoons corn oil
2 cups Tofu Ricotta Cheez (page 96)
1/4 cup Parmesan Cheez (page 94)
5 1/2 cups Tomato Sauce 1 (page 261)
1/2 teaspoon sea salt
1 N'egg (page 302)
12 lasagna noodles, cooked and drained
1/2 cup water
2 cups Notzarella Cheez (page 94)

Cook the spinach and onions in the oil until tender, stirring frequently. Remove from heat and stir in the Cheezes, 1 1/2 cups of the Tomato Sauce, salt, and N'egg. Put the noodles in a single layer on waxed paper. Spread some of the Cheez mixture on each noodle and roll up each one jelly-roll fashion. Combine the spaghetti sauce and water and put about 3/4 of it into a casserole. Arrange the rolled noodles, seam side down, in the sauce. Top with the Notzarella and rest of the sauce. Cover loosely with foil. Bake at 375°F for 30 minutes or until hot and bubbly.

Macaroni and Cheez

3 cups elbow macaroni, uncooked
Boiling salted water
2 tablespoons nondairy margarine
1/3 cup chopped onion
1/3 cup unbleached white flour
3 cups Cashew Milk (page 93)
3/4 teaspoon sea salt
1/4 teaspoon cayenne pepper
3 cups Pimiento Cheez (page 94)
Sliced tomatoes

Cook the macaroni in boiling salted water as per package instructions. Drain and blanch. Set aside. In a saucepan melt the margarine and sauté the onion. Blend in the flour. While stirring, slowly add the "milk," salt, and pepper. Cook until thick and bubbly. Add the Cheez and stir in well, being careful it does not burn. Pour this sauce into the macaroni and stir until all is well mixed. Put in a casserole and top with the tomatoes. Bake at 350°F for about 30 minutes, until the top is slightly browned.

VARIATION: *Use fettucini noodles instead of macaroni. Add 4 cups of a cooked vegetable, cut into small pieces, and 1 teaspoon of basil to the sauce while it is cooking.*

Macaroni and Yeast Cheez Casserole

This is simple, but so flavorful that I could eat it just about every day.

1/4 cup chopped onion
2 tablespoons nondairy margarine
1/2 cup unbleached white flour
5 1/4 cups water
3 tablespoons soy sauce
2 1/4 teaspoons garlic powder
1/4 teaspoon turmeric
1 1/2 teaspoons sea salt
1/3 cup corn oil
1 1/2 cups nutritional yeast
8 1/2 cups cooked macaroni

Sauté the onion in the margarine. Whisk in the flour, and continue to beat until the mixture is smooth and bubbly. Then whisk in the water, soy sauce, garlic powder, turmeric, and salt, beating well until all is well mixed and smooth. Cook this until it thickens and bubbles. Finally whisk in the corn oil and yeast flakes. Mix 3/4 of the sauce with the macaroni and put in a casserole dish. Pour the rest of the sauce on top and sprinkle paprika over that. Bake at 350°F for 15 minutes. Put under the broiler for a few minutes until the Cheez is spotted brown.

VARIATION: *Use fettucini noodles instead of macaroni. Add 4 cups of a cooked vegetables, cut into small pieces, and 1 teaspoon of basil to the sauce while it is cooking.*

Macaroni Delight

2 cups uncooked macaroni
2 cups Kreem of Mushroom Soup (page 74)
1 cup Cashew Milk (page 93)
2 teaspoons Dijon-style mustard
1/4 teaspoon freshly ground black pepper
2 cups broccoli flowerets
1 cup cauliflowerets
1/2 cup bell pepper (red preferred), cut into 1-inch squares
1 1/2 cups cubed UnHam (page 130) or UnTurkey (page 147)
3/4 cup Yeast Cheez (page 97), Pimiento Cheez (page 94), or Notzarella Cheez (page 94)

Cook and drain the macaroni. Meanwhile heat the soup, "milk," mustard, and pepper to boiling. Add the vegetables, and bring back to a boil. Reduce the heat, cover, and simmer for 10 minutes or until the vegetables are tender, about 10 minutes, stirring occasionally. Stir in the gluten, Cheez, and macaroni. Heat through.

Mexican Bean and Pasta Dish

1/3 cup finely chopped bell pepper
1/3 cup chopped onion
1 tablespoon corn oil
6 cups chopped tomato
1/2 teaspoon cayenne pepper
1/2 teaspoon oregano
1 teaspoon sea salt
3 cups UnBeef Broth (page 155)
2 1/2 cups pasta broken into small pieces and cooked
1 1/2 cups corn
3 cups pinto or kidney beans, cooked

Sauté the bell pepper and onion in the corn oil. Combine the tomato, cayenne, oregano, salt, and broth in a pot, add the bell pepper and onion, and bring to a boil. Simmer for 15 minutes. Add the pasta, corn, and beans and simmer, uncovered, for 10 more minutes.

Mushroom Lasagna

1 eggplant (about 1¼ pounds)
1½ cups finely minced onion
½ cup bell pepper
2 tablespoons corn oil
5 cups coarsely chopped mushrooms
2 teaspoons minced garlic
5 cups canned crushed tomatoes with puree
2 tablespoons chopped fresh parsley
¼ teaspoon thyme
¼ teaspoon nutmeg
¼ teaspoon hot pepper flakes
3 cups Notzarella Cheez (page 94)
3 cups ground UnBeef (page 109)
½ pound lasagna noodles, cooked
1 cup tomato sauce
2½ cups thinly sliced tomatoes
1 teaspoon sea salt

On a nonstick baking sheet roast the eggplant for 1 hour. Peel and finely chop the pulp. Set aside. In a large pan sauté the onion and bell pepper in the oil until just translucent. Add the mushrooms and sauté over medium heat for 15 minutes, or until all the liquid has evaporated. (Add more oil if necessary.) Stir in the eggplant, garlic, and crushed tomatoes. Cook until the eggplant is very soft and the liquid has evaporated. Add the parsley, thyme, ground nutmeg, and pepper flakes. Set aside. Spread ⅓ of the mushroom mixture over the bottom of a casserole. Cover with ⅓ of the Notzarella and top with ⅓ of the UnBeef. Cover with a layer of noodles. Repeat layering with same proportions. Spread the tomato sauce over the top. Layer the sliced tomatoes over that. Sprinkle with salt and pepper. Bake at 350°F for 40 minutes. Take from the oven and let sit 15 minutes before serving.

Noodle Bake

¼ pound spaghetti, uncooked
¾ cup chopped onion
½ teaspoon minced garlic
1 teaspoon nondairy margarine
2 cups Yeast Cheez (page 97) or Pimiento Cheez (page 94)
¼ teaspoon sea salt
½ teaspoon paprika

Cook and drain the spaghetti. Sauté the onion and garlic in the margarine. Combine everything except paprika. Put into a nonstick baking dish. Bake at 350°F for 25 minutes. Sprinkle with paprika.

Noodles Romano

2 tablespoons dried parsley flakes
1 teaspoon basil
1 cup Tofu Cottage Cheez (page 96), blended smooth
⅛ teaspoon paprika
⅔ cup boiling water
8 ounces spaghetti, uncooked
1 teaspoon minced garlic
1 tablespoon nondairy margarine
½ cup Pimiento Cheez (page 94), Notzarella Cheez (page 94), or Yeast Cheez (page 97)

Combine the parsley flakes, basil, Cottage Cheez, and paprika. Stir in the boiling water. Blend the mixture well and keep warm over a pan of hot water or in a double boiler. Cook the spaghetti in salted water until just tender and drain. Sauté the garlic in the margarine for 1 to 2 minutes, then pour over the spaghetti and toss lightly and quickly to coat well. Sprinkle (or spread) the Cheez over the spaghetti. Add the Cottage Cheez sauce and mix well.

Noodles with UnBeef Sauce

4 teaspoons minced garlic
¼ teaspoon powdered ginger
¼ teaspoon crushed hot pepper flakes
1½ cups chopped onion
2 tablespoons corn oil
2 cups ground UnBeef (page 109)
½ cup UnChicken Broth (page 155)
⅓ cup UnFish Broth (page 156)
¼ cup UnBeef Broth (page 155)
¼ cup low-sodium soy sauce
2 tablespoons cornstarch
½ cup sliced green onions, sliced diagonally
2 tablespoons toasted sesame oil

16 ounces vermicelli noodles, cooked and drained
Chopped green onions

Sauté the garlic, ginger, pepper flakes, and onion in the oil until the onion is transparent. Add the UnBeef and sauté until it is light brown. Combine 1/4 cup of the UnChicken broth with the UnFish and UnBeef broths, and the soy sauce. Stir this into the gluten mixture. Cover, reduce the heat, and simmer for 10 minutes, stirring 1 or 2 times. Dissolve the cornstarch in the rest of the UnChicken broth. Slowly stir this into the gluten mixture. Add the green onions. Cook, stirring, until the sauce is thick. Combine the cooked noodles and the sesame oil. Pour the gluten sauce over this and toss gently. Serve topped with chopped green onions.

Pasta Primavera 1

1 cup onion, cut into thin wedges
1 teaspoon minced garlic
1 cup sliced mushrooms
1 tablespoon nondairy margarine
1 cup broccoli, flowerets and stem, sliced
2/3 cup matchstick carrot
1 cup thinly sliced zucchini
3/4 cup UnChicken Broth (page 155)
1/2 cup chopped fresh parsley
2 teaspoons lemon juice
3/4 teaspoon basil
1/4 teaspoon cayenne pepper
2 tablespoons Parmesan Cheez (page 94)
8 ounces pasta, cooked

Sauté the onion, garlic, and mushrooms in the margarine for 2 minutes. Add the broccoli, carrot, zucchini, and broth. Simmer until the carrot is done. Add the remaining ingredients except the Cheez and pasta, and cook for 1 minute. Toss everything together to mix well.

Pasta Primavera 2

1 tablespoon olive oil
1 1/4 cups diced onion
1 tablespoon chopped garlic
1 cup sliced zucchini
1 cup sliced yellow squash
1 cup sliced bell pepper, cut into strips
1 3/4 cups chopped and drained canned tomatoes, reserving the juice
2/3 cup tomato paste
3/4 cup warm water
1/2 teaspoon sea salt
1/4 teaspoon freshly ground black pepper
2 tablespoons fresh basil, chopped, or 1 teaspoon dried, crushed
One 9-ounce package linguine

Heat the oil in a skillet and sauté the onion and garlic for 1 minute. Add the zucchini, squash, and bell pepper. Sauté 3 to 4 more minutes. Stir in the reserved tomato juice, tomato paste, water, salt, and pepper. Simmer until the vegetables are tender. Stir in the tomatoes and basil and simmer 20 more minutes. Prepare the pasta and top with the sauce.

Pasta Shells with Broccoli

3 tablespoons chopped onion
1 teaspoon minced garlic
1 teaspoon olive oil
1 pound small pasta shells, cooked and drained
1 head broccoli
1 cup Tofu Cottage Cheez (page 96)
1/8 teaspoon cayenne pepper
1/2 teaspoon basil
1/2 teaspoon oregano
1/2 teaspoon sea salt
Tofu Sour Kreem (page 97)

Sauté the onion and garlic in the oil. Add the shells and set aside and keep warm. Cut the stems off the broccoli head and set aside. Cut the head into tiny flowerets and steam until just tender. Keep warm. Chop the broccoli stems into tiny pieces and cook until very tender. Cool and blend in a food processor or blender until smooth. Add the Cottage Cheez, cayenne, basil, oregano, onion, garlic, and salt. Combine well. Heat the Cottage Cheez mixture, but do not cook or boil. Pour over the warm pasta and toss until all is coated. Add the broccoli flowerets and toss lightly. Serve with Sour Kreem on the side.

Pasta Snacks

These can be made from leftover pasta, too.

After cooking the pasta, drain well, cool under cold running water, and pat dry. When pasta is dry, spray lightly with vegetable oil. Place on broiler trays and brown, turning a few times. These may be lightly salted or sprinkled with garlic salt, onion salt, or soy sauce for more flavor.

Pasta with Spicy Broccoli

12 ounces pasta
Salted boiling water
1 pound broccoli
1/2 teaspoon hot pepper flakes
1/4 teaspoon minced garlic
2 teaspoons olive oil
3 1/2 cups diced fresh tomato, or canned, diced, with 1/2 cup of the liquid
1/2 teaspoon sea salt

Cook the pasta in salted boiling water according to instructions. Cut broccoli into florets. Peel the stems and slice them into rounds. Steam the broccoli until tender-crisp (about 3 minutes), and set aside. Sauté the pepper flakes and garlic in the oil. Add the tomato and salt and cook over medium heat for 5 to 10 minutes. Add to broccoli. Serve over cooked pasta.

Piroshkis

Follow the recipe for Calzone (page 267), but roll out the entire dough as you would for a pie crust and then cut into rounds of the size you prefer. Bake at 400°F until they start to brown.

VARIATION: *Use pie crust dough instead of calzone dough.*

Quick Cheez Dumplings in Tomato Sauce

2 cups Biscuit Mix (page 50)
2/3 cup Yeast Cheez (page 97) or Pimiento Cheez (page 94)

Make biscuits with the mix, adding 2 tablespoons of the Cheez to the biscuit dough. Pat or roll out the dough 1/8 inch thick. Cut into 3-inch rounds. Place 1 teaspoon of Cheez in the center of each round. Wet the edges of the rounds with cold water. Gather up the edges to form a ball. Pinch them well. Drop the dumplings into thin tomato sauce, soup, or juice. Cover tightly and cook for 15 minutes. Do not lift the lid until the time is up!

Sesame Noodles

3 tablespoons low-sodium soy sauce
2 tablespoons rice vinegar and white wine vinegar
1/2 teaspoon hot pepper flakes
2 tablespoons Sucanat
1/2 cup creamy peanut butter
1 tablespoon oriental sesame oil
1/2 teaspoon powdered ginger
1/2 cup UnChicken Broth (page 155)
8 ounces linguine or lo mein noodles
Chopped green onions

In a saucepan combine the soy sauce, vinegar, pepper flakes, Sucanat, peanut butter, oil, ginger, and broth. Simmer, stirring, until thickened and smooth, and let cool slightly. Cook the noodles, drain them, rinse them under cold water, and drain again well. Put the noodles in a bowl and toss them well with the sauce. Serve at room temperature and garnish with the chopped green onions.

Simple Pasta

1/2 cup chopped onion
1 teaspoon minced or sliced garlic
1 1/2 teaspoons olive oil
6 cups pasta, cooked
1 teaspoon total of herbs of choice, such as basil, oregano, rosemary, thyme, savory, bay leaf, dill weed, or Italian herb seasoning
1/4 teaspoon cayenne pepper
1/2 teaspoon paprika
Nutritional yeast, optional

Sauté the onion and garlic in the oil for 5 minutes. Combine all ingredients except nutritional yeast and heat through for 5 minutes, stirring occasionally. Nutritional yeast may be stirred in at the end for added flavor and nutrition.

Spaghetti and Soy Grits

2/3 cup chopped onion
1 1/2 teaspoons minced garlic
1/4 cup chopped black olives
1/2 cup chopped bell pepper
1 cup chopped squash
1 tablespoon olive oil
2 cups UnBeef Soy Grits (page 109)
2 cups tomato paste
1/4 cup low-sodium soy sauce
1/2 teaspoon oregano
1 teaspoon paprika
3/4 teaspoon Italian herbs
1/2 teaspoon chili powder
1 teaspoon monosodium glutamate (MSG)
1/4 teaspoon sea salt
1/4 teaspoon freshly ground black pepper
8 ounces spaghetti, cooked and drained

Sauté the onion, garlic, olives, bell pepper, and squash in the oil until onion is clear. Add the grits and cook 5 minutes. Add the rest of the ingredients except the spaghetti. Cook slowly for 10 minutes. Mix sauce with the spaghetti.

Spaghetti Bolognese

Top of the line.

2 1/2 cups chopped onion
2 1/2 cups chopped mushrooms
2 tablespoons olive oil
1 1/2 teaspoons soy sauce
1 1/2 teaspoons Sucanat
1 tablespoon minced garlic
1 1/2 cups tomato paste
3 cups water
1 1/2 teaspoons basil
1/4 teaspoon fennel seed
1/4 teaspoon oregano
1 1/2 teaspoons sea salt
3/4 teaspoon black pepper or cayenne pepper
1/2 pound spaghetti, uncooked

Sauté the onion and mushrooms in the oil. Add the remaining ingredients, except the spaghetti, and cook for 30 minutes. Cook and drain the spaghetti. Combine with the sauce.

Special Spaghetti

6 ounces spaghetti, uncooked
Salted water
1/2 cup Yeast Cheez (page 97) or Pimiento Cheez (page 94)
1/4 cup chopped onion
1/2 teaspoon minced garlic
2 tablespoons chopped mushrooms or black olives
2 teaspoons corn oil
1 cup chopped tomato
1/2 teaspoon sea salt
1/4 teaspoon paprika

Cook the spaghetti in salted water. Drain, blanch, then rinse with hot water. Add the Cheez and mix. Sauté the onion, garlic, and mushrooms or olives in the oil. Add the tomato, salt, and paprika, and cook for 10 minutes. Toss the sauce with the spaghetti.

Spinach Lasagna

8 ounces lasagna noodles, uncooked (9 noodles)
1 1/2 cups chopped onion
2 1/3 cups sliced mushrooms
1 teaspoon minced garlic
1 tablespoon corn or olive oil
Two 10-ounce packages frozen spinach, thawed and squeezed dry
1 teaspoon oregano
1 teaspoon basil
1/4 teaspoon freshly ground black pepper
2 cups Tofu Cottage Cheez (page 96) or Tofu Ricotta Cheez (page 96)
3 1/2 cups Notzarella Cheez (page 94)
4 cups canned tomato sauce
1/4 cup Parmesan Cheez (page 94)

Cook the noodles. While they are cooking, sauté the onion, mushrooms, and garlic in the oil for 5 minutes. Take from the heat and stir in the spinach, oregano, basil, and pepper. Set aside. Combine the Tofu Cheez with 2 cups of the Notzarella. Line a nonstick baking dish with 3 noodles. Cover the noodles with half of the spinach mixture, half of the Cheez mixture, and half of the tomato sauce. Cover this with 3 more noodles and repeat the layering. Top with the last 3 noodles and spread the 1½ cups of the Notzarella over them. Sprinkle the "Parmesan" over all. Bake at 375°F for 45 minutes. Let stand 10 minutes before serving.

Thai-Style Pasta

Sesame oil can be used in this instead of corn oil, if you like.

1 cup chopped onion
1 teaspoon corn oil
1 pound pasta, cooked and drained
1 teaspoon Sucanat
¼ cup soy sauce
3 tablespoons fresh lemon juice
¼ teaspoon crushed red pepper
⅔ cup unsalted roasted peanuts, chopped
½ cup water

Sauté the onion in the oil until transparent. Add rest of ingredients and sauté for 5 more minutes.

UnBeef and Pasta Bake

4 ounces pasta
2 tablespoons corn oil
1 cup ground UnBeef (page 109)
½ cup chopped onion
⅓ cup sliced bell pepper, cut into strips
⅔ cup sliced zucchini or yellow straight-neck squash, ¼ inch thick
1 teaspoon minced garlic
½ teaspoon sea salt
¼ teaspoon oregano
⅛ teaspoon freshly ground black pepper
2 cups spaghetti sauce of choice
¾ cup diced tomato
1 cup Notzarella Cheez (page 94)

Cook the pasta. Meanwhile, heat the oil in a casserole and sauté the UnBeef, onion, bell pepper, zucchini, garlic, salt, oregano, and pepper until the onion is soft. Stir in the spaghetti sauce and cook, covered, until well heated through. Combine everything but the Cheez in the casserole, spread the Cheez over the top, and bake, uncovered, at 400°F for 30 minutes.

UnBeefy Macaroni and Cheez

1 pound uncooked macaroni
1 tablespoon sea salt
½ cup chopped onion
1 tablespoon dried parsley flakes
¼ teaspoon oregano
¼ teaspoon freshly ground black pepper
2 tablespoons corn oil
2 cups ground UnBeef (page 109)
3 cups Cashew Milk (page 93)
3 tablespoons unbleached white flour
2 cups Yeast Cheez (page 97) or Notzarella Cheez (page 94)
¾ cup diced tomato

Cook the macaroni in water with the salt and drain. While the pasta is cooking, sauté the onion, parsley flakes, oregano, and pepper in the oil until the onion is soft. Add the UnBeef. Combine the "milk" and flour until smooth and stir into the UnBeef mixture. Cook over high heat, stirring, until the mixture boils and thickens slightly. Boil for 1 more minute. Reduce heat to low and stir in the Cheez, tomato, and cooked macaroni. Bake uncovered at 400°F for 20 minutes.

UnChicken Lasagna

1½ cups diced onion
2½ teaspoons corn oil
¼ cup ground UnBacon (page 136)
4 cups ground UnChicken (page 137)
¼ teaspoon rosemary
1 teaspoon sea salt
1 teaspoon cayenne pepper
2 teaspoons tomato paste
2 cups UnChicken Broth (page 155)
2 bay leaves
2 cups sliced mushrooms
1 pound lasagna noodles, cooked
4 cups White Sauce (page 262) made with UnChicken Broth (page 155)
3 cups Yeast Cheez (page 97) or Notzarella Cheez (page 94), or a combination

Sauté the onion in the oil until soft. Add the gluten and continue to sauté until it begins to brown. Combine everything but the noodles, White Sauce, and Cheez. Cook for 20 minutes. Line a nonstick casserole with some of the cooked noodles. Mix the White Sauce thoroughly with the Cheez. Combine 1⅓ cups of the White/Cheez sauce and 3 tablespoons of the UnChicken mixture and set aside.

Layer, starting with ¼ of the White/Cheez sauce noodles, then ⅓ of the UnChicken mixture noodles. Repeat this twice, ending with a layer of White/Cheez sauce. Cover with any remaining noodles (if there are none, it is all right). Top with the reserved sauce combination. Bake at 450°F for 30 minutes.

White Lasagna

This is really special—I know you will agree! It is also a gourmet's way to use up leftovers.

½ pound lasagna noodles, uncooked
2 cups chopped onion
2 cups thickly sliced mushrooms
1 tablespoon minced garlic
1½ cups ground UnChicken (page 137)
2 cups broccoli, chopped fine, boiled, and drained
3 tablespoons olive oil
2 cups UnChicken Broth (page 155) made with Cashew Milk (page 93)
2 cups Notzarella Cheez (page 94)
⅛ teaspoon cayenne pepper
⅛ teaspoon freshly ground black pepper
Parmesan Cheez (page 94)

Cook the noodles in salted water and set aside. Sauté the onion, mushrooms, garlic, gluten, and broccoli in the oil until the onion is soft. Combine the broth, Notzarella Cheez, and peppers, and heat until it becomes a thick batter. In an oiled casserole put a layer of noodles. Spread half of the vegetable mixture over the noodles. Spread ⅓ of the Cheez sauce over the vegetables. Repeat these three layers. Make another layer of noodles. Spread the remaining third of the Cheez sauce over the noodles. Sprinkle the "Parmesan" over the sauce. Bake at 375°F until light brown on top, about 30 minutes.

VARIATION: *Instead of broccoli in the filling, use spinach or some other vegetables, or beans (green or dried).*

Pizza

Blender Pizza Sauce

I made this up in a pinch, and it was so good it became a permanent item in our repertoire.

7½ cups canned tomatoes
½ cup tomato paste
2 teaspoons onion powder
½ teaspoon garlic powder
1 teaspoon oregano
1 teaspoon sea salt
½ teaspoon cayenne pepper
1 tablespoon olive oil

Drain the tomatoes well in a colander, shaking them to drain fully. Put tomatoes into a blender and blend just until they are barely "scrambled." Pour them back into the colander and drain again, shaking to drain fully. Put the drained tomato pulp back into the blender and add the rest of the ingredients. Blend to mix everything well, but make sure the sauce does not become too liquid but remains thick and substantial.

Cheez-Only Pizza

Make Quick Pizza (page 280), but omit the tomato sauce. Omit the toppings, too, if you like.

Easy Pizza Crust

Make up the dough for the White Bread recipe (page 57), roll out, and use as crust for 2 pizzas.

"Meatza" Pie

This is an adapted version of a Middle Eastern dish that does not have Cheez, though it is good with Cheez.

4 cups unbleached white flour
1½ cups warm water
2 teaspoons yeast
1 tablespoon olive oil
1 teaspoon sea salt
2 cups chopped onion
½ cup chopped bell pepper
¼ cup olive oil
2 cups ground Italian UnSausage (page 133), with 2½ teaspoons minced garlic
1 cup chopped tomato
¼ cup tomato paste
¼ cup chopped fresh parsley
1 teaspoon fresh mint or ¼ teaspoon dried
Cornmeal
Garlic Oil (page 304)
1½ cups Notzarella Cheez (page 94)
Parmesan Cheez (page 94)

Put the flour in a bowl and make a "well" in the center. Pour the water in the "well," sprinkle the yeast on top of the water and stir it in lightly with your fingers. Let it rest for a few minutes until it becomes bubbly. Add the tablespoon of oil and the salt and mix it all together into a dough with your hands. Knead for a couple of minutes until you have a smooth dough. Let the dough rise for 1 to 1½ hours in a warm place.

Sauté the onion and bell pepper in the ¼ cup of oil. When the onion becomes transparent, add the UnSausage and sauté until it starts to brown. Mix in the tomato, tomato paste, parsley, and mint and cook for 10 to 15 minutes. Roll out the dough to any shape you desire for the pizza, making sure it is thicker around the edges. Put the dough in a pan that has been dusted with cornmeal. Wipe some Garlic Oil along the outer edges of the dough. Spread the Notzarella over the dough. Put on the gluten topping. Sprinkle "Parmesan" over the topping.

Bake at 450°F until the crust begins to brown. Take the pizza from the oven and brush more Garlic Oil around the edges of the crust. Continue to bake until the dough is golden brown and the bottom is brown (at least in spots) as well.

VARIATION: *Use other types of UnSausage (pages 132–35). Instead of gluten, use 4 cups of fresh mushrooms, and when sautéing them, add ¼ cup of soy sauce. Leave out the Cheezes.*

Onion-Garlic Pizza

This is an adaptation of the famous "Great White Pizza" that used to be made at Sadie's Saloon in Lincoln, Nebraska.

Crust

3 tablespoons yeast
1¾ cups water
1½ teaspoons Sucanat
5¼ cups unbleached white flour
1½ teaspoons sea salt
2 tablespoons oi
Cornmeal

Topping

6 cups sliced onion (sliced by being put through a food processor)
2 tablespoons minced garlic
¼ cup nondairy margarine
1 cup chopped fresh parsley
2 tablespoons soy sauce

Seasoning

2 teaspoons rosemary, crushed
2 teaspoons rubbed sage
2 teaspoons thyme, crushed
Sea salt
Paprika

To complete the recipe:

Notzarella Cheez (page 94)

For the crust, dissolve yeast in the water with the Sucanat. Allow to froth. Sift the flour into a bowl, add the salt and oil, and stir. Add yeast mixture and combine thoroughly. Knead until smooth and elastic. Sprinkle 1 tablespoon of cornmeal onto each pizza pan. Divide the dough into two equal parts. Roll out the dough and put it into the pizza pans, trimming off any excess dough.

To make the topping, sauté onion and garlic in melted margarine until soft. Add parsley and soy sauce and sauté 1 to 2 minutes. Spread evenly over two 14-inch pizzas. Bake at 350°F for 15 minutes, then take out.

Mix together the seasonings and sprinkle ⅔ of it over the partially baked pizzas. Top each pizza with Notzarella Cheez. Lightly sprinkle rest of the seasoning mixture over the Cheez. Return to the oven and continue to bake at 350°F for fifteen minutes more.

Pizza Bread

2½ cups water
2 tablespoons yeast
3 tablespoons plus 1½ teaspoons Sucanat
4 cups unbleached white flour
3 tablespoons oil
1 tablespoon sea salt

Combine ingredients and form into a dough. Spread out in a well-oiled casserole pan. Spread Pizza Sauce (page 280) thickly over it. Bake at 500°F until the sauce darkens.

Pizza Sauce 1

1 cup chopped onion
1 tablespoon minced garlic
1 tablespoon olive oil
6 cups chopped tomato
1 teaspoon sea salt
½ teaspoon basil
½ teaspoon oregano
½ teaspoon hot pepper flakes
2 cups chopped mushrooms
1 cup water

Sauté the onion and garlic in the oil. Combine with the rest of the ingredients and cook for 45 minutes, adding more water if it gets too thick.

Pizza Sauce 2

1½ cups chopped onion
1½ cups thickly sliced mushrooms
1½ teaspoons minced or sliced garlic
1½ teaspoons minced or sliced jalapeños
4 teaspoons corn oil
4 cups canned tomatoes with juice
½ teaspoon sea salt
½ teaspoon basil
¼ teaspoon oregano
¼ teaspoon fennel seed
Nutritional yeast, optional

Sauté the onion, mushrooms, garlic, and jalapeños in the oil. Combine everything except the nutritional yeast in a pot, bring to a boil, lower the heat, and simmer, uncovered, for 1 hour, adding more tomato juice if it gets too thick. Nutritional yeast may be stirred in at the end for added flavor and nutrition.

Quick Pizza

2 tablespoons cornmeal
1 recipe Cracker dough (page 59)
1 recipe Blender Pizza Sauce (page 278)
3 cups Notzarella Cheez (page 94)
Toppings of your choice, such as gluten, onions, bell pepper, mushrooms, green olives, black olives, sautéed in oil

Sprinkle 1 tablespoon of cornmeal onto each pizza pan. Divide the Cracker dough into two equal parts. Roll out the dough and put it into the pizza pans, trimming off any excess. Bake at 550°F for about 5 minutes. Spread the sauce on the crusts. Top with the Cheez. Sprinkle desired topping over the pizzas. Bake until the crust lightly browns on the bottom, about 10 to 15 minutes.

Taco Pizza

Since there are a lot of onions in the refried beans, none are put on the top, but if you are an onion lover, do so.

1 recipe "Meatza" Pie dough (page 278)
Garlic Oil (page 304)
6 cups Refried Beans (page 237)
4 cups Notzarella Cheez (page 94)
4 cups finely chopped lettuce
8 cups finely chopped tomato

Divide the dough in half and press it out onto 2 sheet pans oiled with garlic oil. Coat the tops of the dough with garlic oil. Spread the Refried Beans over the dough. Put the pizzas in the oven and bake at 450°F until the crust just begins to show color. Remove the pizzas from the oven and spread the Cheez over the beans. Brush Garlic Oil around the outer edges of the pizza dough. Return to the oven and bake until the crust is golden brown. Take out of the oven and put the lettuce and tomato on top.

VARIATION: *Put chopped black olives, pickled green tomatoes, pickled jalapeño slices, or Tomato Salsa (page 296) on top as well as lettuce and tomato.*

Tomato and Cheez Pizza

This is our version of the "Garden Pizza" that used to be available from Sadie's Saloon in Lincoln, Nebraska.

1 recipe White Bread dough (page 57)
1/4 cup chopped or sliced mushrooms
1/4 cup chopped onion
1 teaspoon minced garlic
2 tablespoons corn oil
2 cups chopped tomato
1/4 cup tomato paste
1/2 teaspoon sage
1/2 teaspoon basil
1/2 teaspoon oregano
1/4 teaspoon sea salt
1/4 teaspoon paprika
12 black olives, chopped
2 tablespoons chopped bell pepper
5 tomatoes, in slices or wedges
2 cups Notzarella Cheez (page 94)

Knead the dough lightly, then, on a lightly floured surface, roll out to a circle 12 inches in diameter, or make four 4-inch rounds. Place dough on an oiled baking sheet, cover with oiled plastic wrap, and leave in a warm place for 30 minutes to rise. Sauté the mushrooms, onion, and garlic in the oil until the onion is transparent. Add the chopped tomato, tomato paste, herbs, and seasonings. Simmer gently, stirring occasionally, until the mixture is pulpy. Spread the tomato mixture over the dough. Put the olives, bell pepper, and tomato slices (or wedges) over the top. Spread on the Cheez. Bake at 425°F for about 25 minutes (small pizzas will take about 15 minutes).

Focaccia

Focaccia

Focaccia is the granddaddy of pizza, and should not be neglected. In Italy it is often eaten for breakfast.

3½ teaspoons dried yeast
1 teaspoon Sucanat
1¾ cups lukewarm water
3½ cups unbleached white flour
1 teaspoon sea salt
5 tablespoons olive oil
Coarse salt for sprinkling on top

Combine the yeast, Sucanat, and water, and let it sit for 5 minutes. During that time mix the flour and salt together. Add the yeast mixture to the flour along with 3 tablespoons of the oil and knead it until the dough is soft and slightly sticky. Form the dough into a ball and put it into an oiled bowl, turning it to coat it with the oil. Let the dough rise, covered with plastic wrap, in a warm place until it is doubled in bulk, about 1½ hours. Press the dough evenly into a baking pan and let it rise, covered loosely, in a warm place until it is almost doubled in bulk, about 1 hour.

Dimple the dough, making ¼-inch deep indentations with your fingertips. Brush it with the remaining 2 tablespoons of oil, and sprinkle it with coarse salt (omit this if you like). Bake in the lower part of the oven at 400°F until it is golden brown, 30 to 40 minutes. Let it cool in the pan on a rack. Serve either warm or at room temperature. You can split this for sandwiches.

Onion Focaccia

3½ teaspoons dried yeast
½ teaspoon Sucanat
1 cup lukewarm water
3½ cups unbleached white flour
¾ teaspoon sea salt
½ cup olive oil
3 cups thinly sliced onion
1 large shallot, sliced thin
4 green onions, chopped fine
¼ teaspoon sage, crumbled
¼ teaspoon cayenne pepper
2 tablespoons Parmesan Cheez (page 94)
Olive oil (or Garlic Oil [page 304])

Combine the yeast, Sucanat, and water, and let it sit for 5 minutes. During that time mix the flour and salt together. Add the yeast mixture to the flour mixture, along with 3 tablespoons of the oil, and knead it until the dough is soft and slightly sticky. Form the dough into a ball and put it into an oiled bowl, turning it to coat it with the oil. Let the dough rise, covered with plastic wrap, in a warm place until it is doubled in bulk, about 1½ hours. Press the dough evenly into a baking pan and let it rise, covered loosely, in a warm place until it is almost doubled in bulk, about 1 hour.

Stir together the remaining 5 tablespoons of the oil with the onion, shallot, green onions, sage, and pepper. Sprinkle this evenly over the dough. Sprinkle the Cheez over all. Bake in the lower part of the oven at 400°F for 20 minutes. Remove from oven and brush some olive oil (use Garlic Oil [page 304] if you have it) on the outer crust. Return to oven and bake until it is golden brown, 15 to 25 minutes. Let it cool in the pan on a rack. Serve either warm or at room temperature.

VARIATION: *Include ½ to 1 cup of chopped or sliced black olives.*

Rosemary Focaccia

3½ teaspoons dried yeast
½ teaspoon Sucanat
1 cup lukewarm water
3½ cups unbleached white flour
1 teaspoon sea salt
5 tablespoons olive oil
½ teaspoon minced garlic
1 tablespoon finely chopped fresh rosemary, or 1 teaspoon dried, crumbled
Coarse salt for sprinkling on top

Combine the yeast, Sucanat, and water, and let it sit for 5 minutes. During that time mix the flour and salt together. Add the yeast mixture to the flour mixture along with 3 tablespoons of the oil and knead it until the dough is soft and slightly sticky. Form the dough into a ball and put it into an oiled bowl, turning it to coat it with the oil. Let the dough rise, covered with plastic wrap, in a warm place until it is doubled in bulk, about 1½ hours. Press the dough evenly into a baking pan and let it rise, covered loosely, in a warm place until it is almost doubled in bulk, about 1 hour.

Combine the remaining 2 tablespoons of oil with the garlic and rosemary. Dimple the dough, making ¼-inch-deep indentations with your fingertips. Brush it with the oil mixture and sprinkle it with coarse salt (omit this if you like). Bake in the lower part of the oven at 400°F until it is golden brown, 35 to 45 minutes. Let it cool in the pan on a rack. Serve either warm or at room temperature.

UnSausage Focaccia

3½ teaspoons dried yeast
½ teaspoon Sucanat
1 cup lukewarm water
3½ cups unbleached white flour
1 teaspoon sea salt
½ cup olive oil
2¼ cups UnSausage of choice (see UnSausage chapter)
¼ teaspoon freshly ground black pepper
¼ teaspoon dried oregano, crumbled
Coarse salt for sprinkling on top

Combine the yeast, Sucanat, and water, and let it sit for 5 minutes. During that time mix the flour and salt together. Add the yeast mixture to the flour mixture along with 3 tablespoons of the oil and knead it until the dough is soft and slightly sticky. Transfer it to a lightly floured surface and knead in the UnSausage, pepper, and oregano until they are incorporated completely. Form the dough into a ball and put it into an oiled bowl, turning it to coat it with the oil. Let the dough rise, covered with plastic wrap, in a warm place until it is doubled in bulk, about 1½ hours. Press the dough evenly into a baking pan and let it rise, covered loosely, in a warm place until it is almost doubled in bulk, about 1 hour.

Dimple the dough, making ¼-inch-deep indentations with your fingertips. Brush it with the remaining 5 tablespoons of the oil (use Garlic Oil [page 304] if you have it), and sprinkle it with coarse salt (omit this if you like). Bake in the lower part of the oven at 400°F until it is golden brown, 35 to 40 minutes. Let it cool in the pan on a rack. Serve either warm or at room temperature.

Square Meals

Really a variation on the piroshki (pierogi) and calzone, these are marvelous. They are great to take along on trips or to "potluck." When we visit someone and want to bring along the food as well, these are the favorite for both ease and outright good eating.

Feel free to use other fillings than those given here, such as those found in the Casseroles, Dried Beans, Sauces and Gravies, Meat Substitutes, or Vegetables chapters. The possibilities for variety are limited only by your imagination.

Square meals freeze very well for future use.

Square Meals

2 tablespoons yeast
1 cup warm water
1 teaspoon Sucanat
3 tablespoons corn oil
3 cups unbleached white flour
1½ teaspoons sea salt
¼ cup nutritional yeast
½ teaspoon onion powder
Corn oil

Mix the yeast, water, and Sucanat. Let stand in a warm place until risen and foamy, 10 to 15 minutes. Whisk in the oil. in another bowl sift together the flour, salt, nutritional yeast, and onion powder, and mix well. Add this, small amounts at a time, with a whisk, to the yeast mixture. Continue to mix it with a spoon until it is smooth.

Knead it for a while, just until it is a nice soft ball. Roll it out to ⅛-inch thickness. Cut into 4-inch squares. Moisten all 4 edges with water. Put ⅓ cup of filling (see recipes following) in the center of each square. Bring the corners up over the filling and pinch together. Pinch the four seams closed as well. Put on a lightly oiled cookie sheet, seam side down. Poke holes in the top several times (at least 4) with a fork. Brush the tops with corn oil. Bake in a 400°F oven until golden brown on top, about 8 to 10 minutes.

VARIATION: *Add ¼ teaspoon of garlic powder to the dough.*

Barbecue Filling 1

1½ cups chopped onion
2 teaspoons minced garlic
½ cup chopped bell pepper
¼ cup chopped celery
1 tablespoon corn oil
2 cups tomato sauce
½ cup tomato paste
⅓ teaspoon cayenne pepper
2 teaspoons chili powder

½ teaspoon sea salt
2 cups UnBeef (page 109) or UnBeef Soy Grits (page 109)

Sauté the onion, garlic, bell pepper, and celery in the oil until soft. Add the tomato sauce, tomato paste, and spices, and cook for 5 minutes. Add the gluten and cook 5 more minutes.

Barbecue Filling 2

1 cup chopped onion
1 teaspoon minced garlic
⅓ cup chopped bell pepper
3 tablespoons chopped celery
¼ teaspoon hot pepper flakes
2 teaspoons corn oil
3 cups sliced and chopped UnBeef (page 109)
1½ cups Barbecue "Spare Rib" Sauce (page 123)

Sauté the onion, garlic, bell pepper, celery, and pepper flakes in the oil until the bell pepper is soft. Add the gluten and barbecue sauce. Cook for 10 minutes. If it becomes too dry, add more barbecue sauce.

Broccoli and Cheez Filling

Two 16-ounce packages frozen cut broccoli, thawed
1 cup UnChicken Broth (page 155) made with Cashew Milk (page 93)
3 cups chopped onion
1 tablespoon corn oil
⅓ cup unbleached white flour
2 cups Yeast Cheez (page 97) or Pimiento Cheez (page 94)
1 teaspoon sea salt
¼ teaspoon cayenne pepper

Cook broccoli until tender in the broth. Sauté the onion in oil until transparent. Add flour, stirring until blended. Gradually add the broccoli, stirring constantly. Add Cheez, salt, and cayenne and mix well.

Broccoli-Mushroom Filling

1 cup sliced green onions
¼ cup chopped bell pepper
2 teaspoons minced garlic
2 tablespoons corn oil
4 cups sliced mushrooms
4 cups broccoli flowerets
2 cups Yeast Cheez (page 97)
3 tablespoons soy sauce
¼ teaspoon thyme
¼ teaspoon cayenne pepper
1 tablespoon cornstarch dissolved in 2 tablespoons cold water

While the dough is rising, sauté the onions, bell pepper, and garlic in the oil. Add the mushrooms and sauté 3 more minutes. Add the broccoli and sauté 2 more minutes. Add the Cheez, soy sauce, thyme, and cayenne. Stir in the dissolved cornstarch and simmer until thickened, about 3 minutes. Let this cool some before filling the pastry.

Cheez and Onion Filling

2⅓ cups coarsely chopped onion
4 teaspoons corn oil
½ teaspoon minced garlic
3½ cups drained and chopped canned tomatoes
½ teaspoon oregano
¼ teaspoon sea salt
⅛ teaspoon freshly ground black pepper
2 cups Yeast Cheez (page 97)

Sauté the onion in 3 teaspoons of the oil until soft. Set aside. Sauté the garlic in the remaining teaspoon oil until soft. Stir in the tomatoes, oregano, salt, and pepper. Cook until slightly thickened, about 10 minutes, stirring occasionally. Combine everything and heat through.

Dal Filling

3/4 cup red lentils
1 1/2 cups flavoring broth of choice (see Flavoring Broths chapter)
1 1/4 cups peeled and cubed potatoes, parboiled
1/4 teaspoon mustard seeds (black preferred)
3/4 teaspoon minced garlic
1/2 teaspoon ground ginger
1/3 teaspoon turmeric
1/4 teaspoon cumin
1/4 teaspoon sea salt
1 tablespoon corn oil
1/4 teaspoon ground coriander
1/4 teaspoon cayenne pepper

Wash the lentils in a fine mesh colander several times with cold water and pick out debris. Bring to a boil in a saucepan with broth. Reduce heat and simmer 20 minutes, stirring frequently. Skim off the froth that rises to the top. Cook uncovered until the liquid is almost absorbed and the lentils have turned a golden color. Add the potatoes and stir well. Sauté the mustard seeds, garlic, ginger, turmeric, cumin, and salt in the oil for 1 minute. Add this mixture to the lentils along with the coriander and cayenne. Simmer for 10 minutes. Let this cool some before filling the pastry.

Gluten and Vegetable Filling

1/4 teaspoon crushed hot pepper flakes
2 tablespoons corn oil
1 cup sliced green onions
2 teaspoons minced garlic
1/2 cup chopped bell pepper
2 cups grated carrot
2 cups chopped flavored gluten of choice (see specific gluten chapters)
3/4 cup peeled and grated potatoes
2 teaspoons Dijon-style mustard
1 cup Tomato Sauce (page 261) or Mushroom Gravy (page 253)
3 tablespoons parsley
1/2 teaspoon sea salt
1/4 teaspoon cumin

Sauté the pepper flakes in the oil for 2 minutes. Add the onions, garlic, bell pepper, and carrot and sauté for 3 minutes. Stir in the gluten, potatoes, and mustard. Sauté for 5 more minutes. Add the rest of ingredients, reduce heat, and simmer 10 minutes. Let this cool some before filling the pastry.

Hot Dog and Barbecued Bean Filling

Baked Beans

1/2 cup chopped bell pepper
2 teaspoons minced garlic
1/2 cup chopped onion
1 tablespoon corn oil
4 cups cooked dried beans, drained
1/2 teaspoon cayenne pepper
3 cups Tomato Sauce (page 261)
1/4 cup Barbados molasses
1/4 cup wine vinegar
1 tablespoon Sovex or Vegex (dissolve in the vinegar)
1 teaspoon sea salt

Hot Dogs

4 cups Loma Linda "Big Franks," drained and ground

To make the baked beans, sauté the bell pepper, garlic, and onion in the corn oil. Combine all ingredients. Pour into a large oiled casserole. Add more Tomato Sauce if it is needed to cover the beans. Bake 40 minutes at 400°F. Refrigerate for one day before using. This is important. Sauté the Big Franks in a small amount of corn oil. To assemble, mix the refrigerated beans and franks together.

VARIATION: *Use 4 cups of ground UnHam (page 130) or UnSausage (page 132) instead of Big Franks.*

Hot Dog and Sauerkraut Filling

2 cups chopped onion
1 tablespoon corn oil
4 cups sauerkraut, with juice squeezed out (not just drained)
1/2 teaspoon caraway seeds

1/8 teaspoon cayenne pepper
2 cups Loma Linda "Big Franks," ground

Sauté the onion in the oil until soft. Put everything together and cook for 10 minutes.

VARIATION: *Use 4 cups of ground UnSausage (page 132) instead of Big Franks.*

"Meat Pie" Filling

1/4 cup chopped bell pepper or pimientos
1/4 cup minced onion
1/8 teaspoon cayenne pepper
1 tablespoon nondairy margarine
1 tablespoon unbleached white flour
3 cups mixed vegetables, cooked
1 1/2 cups Medium White Sauce (page 262)
1 1/2 cups ground or chopped UnBeef (page 109), UnChicken (page 137), UnPork (page 122), UnHam (page 130), or UnSausage (page 132)

Sauté the bell pepper (or pimientos), onion, and cayenne in the margarine. Stir in the flour well. Add everything, including the gluten, and cook, stirring, until it is thick, about 10 minutes.

VARIATION: *Make the White Sauce with broth the flavor of the gluten (see Flavoring Broths chapter).*

Mexican Filling 1

1/2 cup coarsely chopped onion
2 teaspoons minced garlic
1/4 cup chopped bell pepper
1 tablespoon corn oil
3/4 cup coarsely chopped tomato
1 1/2 cups cooked pinto beans, drained and partially mashed
1/4 teaspoon cumin
1 1/2 teaspoons chili powder
1/2 teaspoon freshly ground black pepper
1 teaspoon sea salt

Sauté the onion, garlic, and bell pepper in the oil until they begin to brown, about 5 minutes. Add the tomato and cook another 2 minutes. Stir in the rest of the ingredients, lower the heat, and simmer for 20 minutes.

Mexican Filling 2

2 cups chopped UnBeef (page 109)
1 cup diced onion
1 1/2 teaspoons minced garlic
1 1/2 cups chopped tomato
Two 4-ounce cans green chiles, chopped
1 1/4 cups peeled, boiled, and diced potatoes
2 tablespoons corn oil
1 teaspoon sea salt
1 1/2 teaspoons oregano
2 teaspoons chili powder
1 tablespoon powdered coriander

Sauté the gluten, onion, garlic, tomato, chiles, and potatoes in the oil until the onion is soft. Add the salt, oregano, chili powder, and coriander. Simmer 2 to 3 minutes.

Pizza Filling

2 cups chopped onion
2 cups chopped mushrooms
2 teaspoons minced garlic
1 cup chopped bell pepper
2 tablespoons olive oil
2 cups Tomato Sauce 2 (page 261)
1/4 teaspoon hot pepper flakes
3/4 cup Notzarella Cheez (page 94)

Sauté the onion, mushrooms, garlic, and bell pepper in the oil until the onion and pepper are soft. Add the Tomato Sauce and pepper flakes and stir in the Cheez. If this seems too dry, add some more Tomato Sauce; if too wet, let it cool down.

Spanakopita Filling

1½ cups finely chopped onion
2 teaspoons garlic powder
1 tablespoon olive oil
1½ pounds frozen spinach, thawed and squeezed free of liquid
2 teaspoons sea salt
2 teaspoons oregano
1½ teaspoons freshly ground black pepper
2½ cups Tofu Cottage Cheez (page 96), crumbled

Sauté the onion and garlic in the olive oil for 5 minutes, or until the onion begins to brown. Add the spinach and the spices, and cook, stirring frequently, for 5 minutes. Let it cool and add the Cottage Cheez.

Spicy Garbanzo Filling

½ cup finely chopped onion
1 teaspoon minced garlic
2 teaspoons olive oil
¾ cup chopped tomato
1⅓ cups garbanzo beans, cooked
¼ cup chopped fresh parsley
2 teaspoons lemon juice
¾ teaspoon ground cumin
¾ teaspoon ground coriander
1½ teaspoons turmeric
⅛ teaspoon cayenne pepper
½ teaspoon sea salt

Sauté the onion and garlic in the oil until the onion begins to brown. Add the tomato and sauté for 2 or 3 minutes more. Add the rest of the ingredients, and cook together for 20 minutes.

Sweet Square Meals

⅔ cup Cashew Milk (page 93)
½ cup plus 1 teaspoon Sucanat
⅓ cup nondairy margarine
2 tablespoons yeast
¼ cup lukewarm water
1 N'egg (page 302)
4½ cups unbleached white flour
1 teaspoon grated lemon rind
½ teaspoon mace

Heat the Cashew Milk with the ½ cup Sucanat and margarine until the margarine melts. Allow this mixture to cool to lukewarm. Combine the yeast, water, and 1 teaspoon Sucanat until dissolved. Add the N'egg and the yeast mixture to the Cashew Milk mixture. Combine half the flour with lemon rind and mace, then add the liquid, beating until smooth. Mix in the remaining flour. Let it stand for 10 minutes. Knead for 5 minutes on a lightly floured board. Place dough in a lightly greased bowl, turning once to bring the greased side up.

Cover with a damp cloth and let rise in a warm place until double. Punch down, turn over, cover, and let rise until double again. Punch down, shape into a ball, and put on a lightly floured surface. Cover with a bowl and let it rest 10 minutes. Roll it out to ⅛-inch thickness. Cut into 4-inch squares.

Put ⅓ cup of filling (see recipes following) in the center of each square. Bring the corners up over the filling and pinch together. Pinch the four seams closed as well. Put on a lightly oiled cookie sheet, seam side down. Poke holes in the top several times (at least 4) with a fork. Brush the tops with corn oil. Bake in a 400°F oven until golden brown on top, 8 to 10 minutes.

Apple Filling 1

2½ cups peeled, cored, and sliced apple
1 tablespoon water
2 cups Sucanat
2 tablespoons Barbados molasses
Half lemon rind, grated
¼ teaspoon cinnamon

Put the apple, water, Sucanat, molasses, lemon rind, and cinnamon in a saucepan. Simmer 10 minutes, stirring occasionally. Do not allow the apple to become mushy. Cool.

VARIATION: *For a "mincemeat" flavor, use ground cloves instead of cinnamon.*

Apple Filling 2

6 cups peeled, cored, and finely chopped apple
1 1/4 cups Sucanat
1/2 teaspoon cinnamon
Dash nutmeg
4 teaspoons nondairy margarine
2 tablespoons unbleached white flour

Mix all ingredients together and simmer until the apple is soft, 10 to 15 minutes.

Blueberry Filling

1 3/4 cups canned blueberries
1/3 cup Sucanat
1/4 cup plus 2 tablespoons unbleached white flour
3/4 teaspoon sea salt
3/4 teaspoon cinnamon
2 tablespoons nondairy margarine

Drain berries and reserve liquid. Combine Sucanat, flour, salt, and cinnamon, and stir into the reserved berry liquid. Heat, stirring constantly, until thick and smooth. Add the margarine and berries.

Cherry Filling

1 1/3 cups liquid from canned cherries, or water if they are fresh
1/2 cup cornstarch
1 1/3 cups Sucanat
1 tablespoon nondairy margarine
1/4 teaspoon sea salt
4 cups cherries, pitted (if canned, reserve liquid for recipe)

Mix some of the cherry liquid (or water) with the cornstarch. Heat rest of liquid to boiling. Add cornstarch mixture, stirring with a wire whisk. Cook until thick and clear. Stir in the Sucanat, margarine, and salt. Bring to a boil, stirring. Remove from heat. Add cherries and mix gently. Cool thoroughly.

Dried Fruit Filling

1 cup coarsely chopped mixed dried fruit
1 cup apple juice, unsweetened
1/4 cup walnuts, chopped
1/2 cup Sucanat
1 1/4 teaspoons cinnamon
1/8 teaspoon brandy or rum extract, optional

Put dried fruit and apple juice in a saucepan. Let it soak for 1 hour. Bring to a boil, partially covered, and simmer until the liquid is absorbed and the fruit is soft, about 10 minutes. Add the walnuts, Sucanat, cinnamon, and extract (if used). Combine.

Peach Filling

1 tablespoon nondairy margarine
2 tablespoons unbleached white flour
4 cups sliced peaches
1 cup Sucanat
1/8 teaspoon cinnamon
1/8 teaspoon sea salt

Melt the margarine. Stir in the flour well. Add the rest of the ingredients and keep stirring until the Sucanat liquefies. Cook until the peaches turn darker.

Strawberry Filling

4 cups frozen strawberries
1 cup Sucanat
3 tablespoons unbleached white flour
1/2 teaspoon sea salt

Thaw and drain the berries and save the liquid. Combine the Sucanat, flour, and salt, and stir into the liquid. Heat, stirring constantly, until thick and smooth. Add berries.

Pickles, Relish, Salsa, Etc.

Anne Goldstein's Marinated Mushrooms

1 cup olive oil (or ½ cup olive oil and ½ cup corn oil)
¾ cup balsamic vinegar
½ cup chopped onion (red preferred)
⅓ cup chopped fresh parsley
1½ teaspoons sliced garlic
1 teaspoon Sucanat
Sea salt
Freshly ground black pepper
2 pounds white mushrooms, stems removed
½ cup sliced bell pepper (red preferred), cut into strips

Combine everything and marinate in the refrigerator for at least a full day, 2 or 3 days are even better.

Anne Goldstein's Caponata

This is a must!

1 large eggplant
1 large bell pepper
⅓ cup olive oil
1 large onion, cut into ½-inch squares
3 celery ribs, diced
2 teaspoons minced garlic
3½ cups coarsely chopped canned tomatoes
2 tablespoons tomato paste
¼ cup brine-cured olives
2½ tablespoons capers
2 tablespoons balsamic vinegar
2 teaspoons Sucanat
2 teaspoons sea salt
¾ teaspoon oregano
¼ teaspoon hot pepper flakes
1 tablespoon chopped fresh parsley
½ teaspoon freshly ground black pepper

Broil or grill the eggplant and bell pepper. Put them into a paper bag so the gathered moisture will soften them. Peel and cube the eggplant. Dice the bell pepper or cut it into strips. Heat the oil and sauté the onion for 3 to 5 minutes. Add the celery and sauté 5 more minutes. Add half of the garlic and sauté another minute. Add the eggplant, pepper, tomatoes, tomato paste, olives, capers, vinegar, Sucanat, salt, oregano, and pepper flakes. Cook, partially covered, until most of the liquid is evaporated, about 20 minutes. Stir in the parsley, black pepper, and the rest of the garlic.

Anne Goldstein's Corn Relish

2 pounds frozen or fresh corn
1½ cups chopped onion (red preferred)
½ cup chopped green bell pepper
½ cup chopped red bell pepper

3 cups balsamic vinegar
½ cup Sucanat
1 teaspoon mustard seed
1 teaspoon celery seed
1 tablespoon sea salt
1 tablespoon freshly ground black pepper

Combine everything in a saucepan and bring to a boil. Reduce heat and cook until it thickens slightly, about 40 minutes. Cool.

Aunt Lou Maxey's Tomato Relish

My great-aunt Lou Maxey could not cook to save her soul. But she sure could make relish!

7½ pounds tomatoes
1½ cups coarsely chopped onion
1 cup coarsely chopped bell pepper
3 tablespoons Sucanat
1 tablespoon sea salt
3 tablespoons cider vinegar
1½ teaspoons ground cinnamon
½ teaspoon ground allspice
½ teaspoon ground nutmeg (fresh preferred)
½ teaspoon ground cloves

Put the tomatoes, onion, and bell pepper in a food processor and chop to medium coarseness. Transfer to a heavy pot and stir in the Sucanat and salt. Bring to a boil over high heat. Stirring frequently, cook briskly, uncovered, until the mixture is reduced to about half its original volume and is thick enough to hold its shape almost solidly in a spoon. Add the vinegar, cinnamon, allspice, nutmeg, and cloves. Reduce the heat to low, partially cover, and simmer for 1 hour. Immediately ladle the relish into hot sterilized jars, filling them to ⅛ inch from the tops. Seal the jars at once.

Aunt May's Pepper Relish

The mildness of this is its virtue!

½ cup finely chopped red bell pepper
½ cup finely chopped green bell pepper
½ cup finely chopped yellow bell pepper
¼ cup chopped onion
2 tablespoons minced garlic
3 tablespoons chopped fresh parsley
3 tablespoons balsamic vinegar
3 tablespoons olive oil
1 teaspoon sea salt
1 teaspoon white pepper
½ teaspoon cayenne pepper

Whisk everything together in a bowl to combine thoroughly. Chill, covered, for at least 2 hours and up to 2 days. Stir before serving.

Bread and Butter Zucchini

12 cups sliced zucchini, ¼ inch thick
1½ cups thinly sliced onion
2 large cloves garlic
⅓ cup sea salt
2 quarts crushed ice or ice cubes
4 cups Sucanat
1½ teaspoons turmeric
1½ teaspoons celery seed
2 tablespoons mustard seed
3 cups white vinegar

Combine the zucchini, onion, and garlic. Add the salt and mix thoroughly. Cover with crushed ice or ice cubes. Let stand for 3 hours. Drain thoroughly. Remove garlic cloves. Combine Sucanat, spices, and vinegar. Heat just to boiling. Add the drained zucchini and onion slices and heat for 5 minutes. Pack hot pickles loosely into sterilized, hot pint jars ½ inch from the top. Seal and process in a boiling water bath for 5 minutes.

Cajun Catsup

This is a delicious Cajun-style recipe.

4 cups chopped onion
1 cup chopped celery
1 cup chopped bell pepper
1 cup chopped fresh parsley
3 tablespoons corn oil
2 tablespoons chopped garlic
3 cups Lea and Perrins Steak Sauce
½ cup Louisiana Hot Sauce
3 cups Tomato Sauce (page 261)
3 teaspoons sea salt

In a large skillet, sauté the onion, celery, bell pepper, and parsley in the oil until the onion is soft and transparent. Add the garlic and cook a little longer. Add the steak sauce, hot sauce, Tomato Sauce, and salt, and bring to a boil. Lower the heat and cover, and cook for 2 to 3 hours. This can be kept refrigerated for a few weeks.

Caponata

6 tablespoons olive oil
1 teaspoon hot pepper flakes
2 cups coarsely chopped celery
3 cups coarsely chopped onion
1 tablespoon minced garlic
2/3 cup coarsely chopped bell pepper (red preferred)
3 1/2 cups canned tomatoes with juice
8 cups diced eggplant, cut into 1/2-inch dice and deep-fried
10 black olives, chopped fine
5 green olives, chopped fine
2 tablespoons capers, rinsed and minced
1/3 cup minced fresh parsley
1/4 cup balsamic vinegar
2 tablespoons Sucanat
1/2 teaspoon sea salt
1/4 teaspoon freshly ground black pepper

Heat the oil in a large saucepan. Stir in the pepper flakes and celery, and cook, stirring occasionally, for 5 minutes. Add the onion, garlic, and bell pepper. Sauté until the onion is soft, about 5 more minutes. Add the tomatoes and liquid, breaking up the tomatoes. Reduce heat, cover, and simmer 10 minutes. Add the eggplant, olives, and capers, stir in well, cover, and simmer for 15 more minutes. Stir in the parsley, vinegar, and Sucanat. Cook just until the Sucanat is dissolved. Add the salt and pepper.

Chili Macho

Go ahead—I dare you to try this!

3 cups canned tomatoes
1 cup chopped onion
1 clove garlic, minced
1 cup chopped jalapeño peppers
1 1/2 teaspoons sea salt

Blend all in the blender, but only until coarsely chopped. Let sit until the flavors are well blended.

Chilipetin Sauce

1 cup chopped green chile peppers
1 cup chopped onion
1 clove garlic
1 green tomato
1 teaspoon flour
1 cup vinegar
2 tablespoons Sucanat
1 teaspoon sea salt

Grind finely or chop the peppers, onion, garlic and tomato. Put in a saucepan with the flour and stir well. Bring the vinegar, Sucanat and salt to a boil. Pour into the pepper mixture. Boil, stirring occasionally, uncovered, until it thickens slightly, about 30 minutes. Seal while hot in sterilized jars. The sauce will be thin, but it thickens with age.

Dill Pickles

If the angels in heaven make dill pickles they use this recipe.

4 pounds cucumbers
3 cups white vinegar
3 cups water
1/3 cup sea salt

For each pint jar

2 tablespoons dill seed
3 peppercorns
1 or 2 dried chile peppers
1 clove garlic

Wash the cucumbers. Either leave them whole or cut them in half or into spears. Combine the vinegar, water, and salt, and heat to the boiling point. Pack the cucumbers into hot, sterilized jars. Add the dill seed, peppercorns, peppers, and garlic. Fill the jars up to the mark (molded in the glass) with the boiling hot vinegar mixture. Seal the jars and process in a boiling water bath for 10 minutes.

Dilled Green Beans

8 cups whole green beans

For each pint jar

¼ teaspoon crushed hot pepper flakes
½ teaspoon mustard seed
½ teaspoon dill seed (or 1 dill head)
1 clove garlic
5 cups vinegar
5 cups water
½ cup sea salt

Wash beans thoroughly. Drain and cut into lengths that will fit into pint jars. Pack the beans in sterilized, hot jars. Add the hot pepper flakes, mustard seed, dill seed, and garlic. Combine the vinegar, water and salt; heat to boiling. Pour boiling liquid over the beans. Seal and process in a boiling water bath for 5 minutes.

Green Tomato Pickles

Simply beyond description. The tomatoes are exquisitely flavorful with a texture like butter. This recipe can be used to pickle any vegetables you wish, alone or in combination, including cucumbers. For a stronger dill taste, use fresh dill weed instead of seeds.

Green tomatoes
9 cups water
6 cups cider vinegar
¾ cup sea salt
3 cloves garlic, peeled and cut in half
1 teaspoon dill seed
3 red chile peppers, stemmed

Wash the tomatoes well. Sterilize the quart jars and lids. Combine the water, cider vinegar, and salt and bring to a boil. In each quart jar put enough green tomatoes cut in halves or quarters to fill the jar to its neck. As you are filling each jar with the tomatoes, intersperse garlic, dill seed, and chile peppers among them. Pour the boiling brine into the jars, making sure the tomatoes are completely covered. Seal and process in a boiling water bath for 20 minutes.

Green Tomato Salsa

This sneaks up on you and is hot! But is worth it.

2 cups finely chopped hot peppers
1½ cups finely chopped red onion
¼ cup finely chopped bell pepper
2½ cups finely chopped green tomato
2½ cups water
4 cups chopped ripe tomato, or drained and chopped canned tomatoes (reserve juice and replace some or all of the water)
1 tablespoon plus 1 teaspoon sea salt
2 tablespoons balsamic vinegar

Combine all and bring to a boil. Simmer for 1½ to 2 hours. For a bit more tang you can add 1 more tablespoon of vinegar.

Hot Herbed Carrots

4 hot peppers
4 cloves garlic
1 teaspoon rosemary
4 cups baby carrots, or 2 pounds larger carrots cut in 4-inch lengths
2 cups water
2 cups white vinegar
3 tablespoons Sucanat
3 tablespoons sea salt

Halve the peppers lengthwise. In each of 4 pint jars, put 1 pepper (2 halves), 1 clove garlic, and ¼ teaspoon of rosemary. Pack the jars full of carrots. Combine the water, vinegar, Sucanat, and salt, and bring to a boil. Reduce the heat and simmer for 5 minutes. Pour the liquid over the carrots. Seal and process in a boiling water bath for 10 minutes.

Hot Stuff

This is halfway between a simple salsa and a relish. It works well with dishes that are bland in both flavor and texture.

2 cups finely chopped onion
2 cups stemmed, seeded, and chopped hot peppers
Sea salt
¾ cup white vinegar
¼ cup water

Combine the onion and peppers in a bowl. Spoon into sterilized canning jars and add the salt, 1 teaspoon per quart jar, or ½ teaspoon per pint jar. In a small saucepan, heat the vinegar and water together, but do not bring it to a boil. When the liquid is too hot to touch with your finger, it is ready. Pour it into the jars, making sure to cover the peppers and onion. Seal, and let it sit for 3 to 4 days before using it.

Jalapeño and Bell Pepper Chutney

I can eat this by the spoonful!

3 red bell peppers, chopped
3 green bell peppers, chopped
3 jalapeños, seeded and minced
1 cup chopped onion
1½ cups Sucanat
1½ cups cider vinegar
1 teaspoon sea salt

Combine everything in a heavy saucepan. Bring to a boil and simmer, stirring occasionally, for 1½ hours or until the liquid is syrupy. Transfer to a bowl and chill, covered, overnight.

Louisiana Hot Sauce

This has the zing of the commercial version, yet is somehow milder. Because of the garlic it has more flavor, too.

3 cups stemmed and finely chopped hot peppers
1 cup white vinegar
½ cup water
1 tablespoon finely chopped garlic
1 tablespoon sea salt

Combine all the ingredients in a saucepan and simmer, covered, until the peppers are very soft, stirring occasionally. Take from the heat and mash with a potato masher. Press the mixture through a sieve so that only the skins and seeds remain in the sieve. Discard them. If the mixture is too thick to pour, add more salt and vinegar. Pour into sterilized jars and seal.

Marinated Mushrooms

Simply miraculous and simply a must!

12 ounces mushrooms
½ cup sliced green onions
¼ cup chopped bell pepper
2 tablespoons minced fresh parsley
½ cup Italian Dressing (page 16), or bottled (Wishbone is best)

Combine everything in a glass bowl and marinate several hours or overnight.

Marinated Tomatoes

Taste-full!

3 cups thickly sliced tomato
⅓ cup olive oil
¼ cup red wine vinegar
1 teaspoon sea salt
¼ teaspoon freshly ground black pepper
½ teaspoon minced garlic
2 tablespoons chopped onion
1 tablespoon chopped fresh parsley
1 tablespoon fresh basil, chopped, or 1 teaspoon dried

Put the tomato slices in a large shallow dish. Combine the rest of the ingredients in a blender and blend well. Pour over the tomato slices. Cover and refrigerate a few hours.

Mean Green

For those with the moxie.

3 cups very coarsely chopped green tomato or tomatillo
¾ cup chopped onion
1 cup coarsely chopped jalapeños (with seeds)

1½ teaspoons pressed garlic
2 teaspoons sea salt
¼ teaspoon oregano (crushed leaves)
⅛ teaspoon coriander
⅛ teaspoon Sucanat

Process everything in a food processor using the metal chopping blade. Cook, stirring, for 5 minutes.

Pickled Beans and Onions

6 cups green beans
Salted water
2 cups vinegar
2 cups Sucanat
1½ cups water
1 tablespoon pickling spice
1 tablespoon mustard seed
2 cups pearl onion, peeled

Wash beans and trim the ends. Parboil in salted water 5 to 6 minutes and drain well. Combine vinegar, Sucanat, water, and spices in a large saucepan. Simmer about 15 minutes. Pack the beans and onion into sterilized hot jars, leaving ¼-inch head space. Remove any air bubbles with a nonmetallic spatula. Adjust the caps. Seal and process for 10 minutes in a boiling water bath canner.

Pickled Calico Vegetables

6 cups cauliflower flowerets (1 large head)
1 cup chopped onion, cut in chunks
2 bell peppers, chopped into ½-inch pieces
2 cups sliced carrot
¼ cup pickling salt
Crushed ice
1 quart white vinegar
1½ cups Sucanat
2 teaspoons mustard seed
2 teaspoons celery seed
2 teaspoons Louisiana Hot Sauce

Combine the vegetables and salt in a large mixing bowl. Cover with crushed ice and let it stand for 3 hours. Drain the vegetables. Rinse them well. Combine the vinegar, Sucanat, mustard seed, celery seed, and hot sauce in a large saucepan or pot. Bring to a boil. Add the vegetables and simmer 5 to 7 minutes. Carefully pack into sterilized hot jars to ¼ inch from the top. Remove any air bubbles with a nonmetallic spatula. Seal and process 10 minutes in a boiling water bath canner.

Quick Tomato Relish

3 cups diced tomato
2 cups chopped bell pepper
¼ cup Italian Dressing (page 16)

Combine and refrigerate so flavor can develop.

Sweet Tomato Relish

12 cups seeded and chopped tomato
1 cup thinly sliced celery
1½ cups chopped bell pepper
3 cups thinly sliced onion
2 tablespoons prepared horseradish, drained
3 tablespoons sea salt
1 cup Sucanat
¼ teaspoon freshly ground black pepper
¼ teaspoon ground cloves
1 tablespoon mustard seeds
1 teaspoon cinnamon
1 cup cider vinegar

Thoroughly combine the tomato, celery, bell pepper, onion, horseradish, and salt. Chill, covered, overnight. Drain. Add the rest of the ingredients. Cover and chill, stirring occasionally, for at least 3 hours before serving.

Tomato Relish

Zesty!

1 quart finely chopped tomato
⅓ cup finely chopped onion
½ cups finely chopped celery
¼ cup finely chopped bell pepper
1 teaspoon sea salt
⅓ cup lemon juice
2 tablespoons olive oil

Combine and refrigerate so flavor can develop.

Tomato Salsa

This is a staple for us. Unbeatable!

1 cup chopped bell pepper
¼ cup chopped onion
1 tablespoon corn oil
1 cup chopped jalapeños, or 2 teaspoons of hot pepper flakes
4 cups blanched, peeled, and chopped tomato
1 teaspoon garlic powder
1½ teaspoons sea salt
1 tablespoon vinegar

Sauté the bell pepper and onion in the corn oil. Combine with rest of ingredients and cook.

VARIATION: *Instead of fresh tomatoes, use 2 cups of canned tomato sauce.*

Note

When made with jalapeños, this gets hotter in a few days, so you might want to use only ½ cup of jalapeños the first time around.

Tomato Salsa Cruda

Nothing crude about this sophisticated relish.

2 cups canned tomatoes
2 tablespoons minced onion
1 teaspoon hot pepper flakes
1 tablespoon minced fresh parsley
1 teaspoon lemon or lime juice
1 tablespoon olive oil
¼ teaspoon sea salt

Purée the tomatoes in a blender or processor until fairly smooth. Combine the purée with the remaining ingredients and let them stand for at least 15 minutes for the flavors to meld. Use as soon as possible.

Tomato Salsa Fresca

2 cups finely chopped canned tomatoes
3 tablespoons minced onion
½ cup minced bell pepper
1 teaspoon hot pepper flakes
1 tablespoon lemon or lime juice
1 tablespoon olive oil
1 teaspoon sea salt

Combine and let stand for 30 minutes to blend.

Zucchini Pickles

Try it and like it.

8 cups thinly sliced zucchini
2 cups thinly sliced onion
½ cup coarse salt
Water
1 quart white vinegar
2 cups Sucanat
2 teaspoons celery seeds
2 teaspoons mustard seeds
2 teaspoons dill seeds
1 teaspoon dried mustard

In a large bowl, combine the zucchini, onion, and salt with enough water to cover. Let it stand 1 hour. In a large saucepan, combine the vinegar, Sucanat, celery seeds, mustard seeds, dill seeds, and dried mustard. Bring to a boil and boil for 3 minutes. Drain the zucchini and onion. Pour the hot vinegar mixture over the zucchini and onion. Let stand 1 hour. Transfer to the saucepan, bring to a boil, and boil for 3 minutes. Pack into sterilized jars, seal, and process in boiling water, enough to cover the jars, for 10 to 15 minutes, according to the jar manufacturer's instructions. Cool and store in a cool, dry place.

Zucchini–Red Pepper Relish

2 cups cubed zucchini, cut in ½-inch cubes
2 cups chopped sweet red pepper, cut in ¼-inch squares
2 tablespoons sea salt
2½ cups water
1½ cups white vinegar
1¼ cups Sucanat
2 tablespoons minced onion
1 teaspoon cumin seed
1 teaspoon instant minced garlic
½ teaspoon hot pepper flakes

In a large bowl, place zucchini, pepper, and salt. Mix well. Cover and refrigerate 12 to 15 hours. Take from the refrigerator, drain off liquid, rinse vegetables well, and drain thoroughly. In a large saucepan, place the water, vinegar, Sucanat, onion, cumin, garlic, and pepper flakes. Bring to a boil. Reduce the heat and simmer, covered, for 10 minutes. Add the zucchini and pepper. Simmer, covered, stirring occasionally until the vegetables are tender, about 15 minutes. Ladle into eight ½-pint sterilized hot canning jars, leaving ¼-inch head space. Cover, following manufacturer's directions. Process for 10 minutes in a boiling water bath according to the jar manufacturer's directions.

Zucchini Relish

This is worth its weight in gold.

5 cups minced zucchini
½ cup sea salt
2½ cups minced onion
½ cup diced celery
¾ cup diced bell pepper
1 teaspoon turmeric
1½ teaspoons dried mustard
4½ teaspoons celery seed
3 cups Sucanat
2½ cups white vinegar
1½ tablespoons cornstarch

Combine the zucchini, salt, onion, celery, and bell pepper. Allow this to stand overnight to draw out the juices. Drain and rinse thoroughly. Drain again in a colander. While the vegetables are still in the colander, press out as much liquid as possible. Combine the pressed vegetables with the rest of the ingredients in a pot and bring to a rolling boil. Reduce the heat and simmer for 20 minutes. Ladle the relish into hot sterilized jars and seal, or put in refrigerator and keep.

Sandwiches and Spreads

Apple Butter

1 gallon pureed apple
3 cups Sucanat
1 orange, peeled and diced with all the juice
2 tablespoons lemon or lime juice
Pinch sea salt

Combine and cook on low heat, simmering, for six hours, or until it turns dark brown and is thick. This keeps very long in the refrigerator.

Barbecue Bean Sandwich Spread

Mix together 1 part of Barbecue Beans (page 228) and 1 part of Cheez Spread (see below).

Bean Sandwich Spread

8 cups cooked dried beans, mashed
½ cup finely chopped bell pepper
2 cups chopped tomato
½ cup minced onion
2 tablespoons lemon juice
1 tablespoon corn oil
1½ teaspoons sea salt

Combine everything.

Cheez Spread 1

6 cups Yeast Cheez (page 97) or Pimiento Cheez (page 94)
⅓ cup chopped onion
1 cup chopped black olives
1 cup finely chopped bell pepper
1½ cups Cashew Mayonnaise (page 12) or Tofu Mayonnaise (page 22), or Miraculous Whip (page 17)
¼ teaspoon cayenne pepper
½ teaspoon basil
⅛ teaspoon dill
1½ teaspoons sea salt

Combine everything.

VARIATION: *If this seems a bit too bland, put in a little wine vinegar or lemon juice.*

Cheez Spread 2

6 cups Yeast Cheez (page 97) or Pimiento Cheez (page 94)
½ cup chopped onion
1 cup finely chopped dill pickles or green olives
¼ cup finely chopped pimiento
1½ cups Cashew Mayonnaise (page 12) or Tofu Mayonnaise (page 22), or Miraculous Whip (page 17)
1 tablespoon prepared mustard
2 teaspoons Louisiana Hot Sauce
½ teaspoon sea salt

Cheez Toast

Spread slices of bread with melted margarine that has been mixed with onion or garlic powder, or just nondairy margarine. Bake on high, or broil until toasted. Take from oven. Lightly sprinkle each slice with finely chopped UnBacon (page 136). Cover each slice with Yeast Cheez (page 97) or Pimiento Cheez (page 94). Replace in oven and broil or bake until brown spots appear.

"Egg" Salad

½ cup finely chopped onion
¼ teaspoon turmeric
¼ teaspoon dill
¼ teaspoon sea salt
1½ teaspoons olive oil
1 cup crushed firm tofu
½ cup Cashew Mayonnaise (page 12) or Tofu Mayonnaise (page 22), or Miraculous Whip (page 17)
2 tablespoons chopped green onion tops
½ teaspoon Louisiana Hot Sauce
1 teaspoon nutritional yeast

Sauté the onion, turmeric, dill, and salt in the oil until the onion is soft, and set aside. When cool, combine with the rest of the ingredients.

VARIATION: *Add ¼ teaspoon garlic powder. Add 1 tablespoon minced jalapeños. When making sandwiches, add sliced lettuce and tomatoes.*

Eggplant Appetizer Spread

¼ cup corn oil
6 cups peeled and cubed eggplant, cut into ½-inch cubes
1 teaspoon cornstarch
⅔ cup UnChicken Broth (page 155)
1 teaspoon minced garlic
½ teaspoon powdered ginger
3 teaspoons red chili paste
1 tablespoon white wine vinegar or rice vinegar
3 green onions, sliced thin
2 tablespoons soy sauce
2 teaspoons Sucanat
1 bell pepper (red preferred), minced

In the corn oil sauté the eggplant until it is tender and browned. Transfer with a slotted spoon to paper towels to drain. Dissolve the cornstarch in the broth. In the oil sauté the garlic, ginger, chili paste, and vinegar for 30 seconds. Add the onions and sauté for 30 more seconds. Add the soy sauce, Sucanat, cornstarch mixture, bell pepper, and eggplant, and sauté until the eggplant has absorbed most of the liquid, about 1 minute.

Eggplant "Caviar"

2 large eggplants, baked at 400°F for 45 minutes (should yield about 3 cups of pulp)
¾ cup tomato paste
¾ cup UnBeef Broth (page 155)
2 teaspoons corn oil
1 teaspoon sea salt
½ teaspoon onion powder
¼ teaspoon garlic powder

Blend everything in a food processor and cook until most of the liquid evaporates. Refrigerate. Best served cold or at room temperature.

Grilled Cheez Sandwiches

Not exactly what Mom used to make, but plenty good!

2½ cups lightly salted and crumbled tofu
3 cups Yeast Cheez (page 97) or Pimiento Cheez (page 94)
Nondairy margarine

Stir the crumbled tofu into the Cheez. Spread between two slices of bread. Put nondairy margarine on the outsides of the bread and grill. Chopped onion, chopped bell pepper, chopped UnBacon (page 136), or slices or pieces of tomato can also be added to the Cheez before grilling.

Fruit Butter

This makes about 6 cups of "butter," which will go quickly once you taste it!

1 gallon pureed fruit
3 cups Sucanat (4 cups for peach butter)
1 orange, peeled and diced with all the juice
Pinch sea salt

Combine and cook on low heat, simmering, for six hours, or until it turns dark brown and is thick. This keeps very long in the refrigerator.

Gluten Sandwich Spread

3 cups coarsely ground flavored gluten (see specific gluten chapters)
3/4 cup Tofu Kreem Cheez (page 96)
1 teaspoon lemon juice
10 green onions, minced
1 cup Miraculous Whip (page 17)
4 teaspoons Louisiana Hot Sauce
3 tablespoons Lea and Perrins Steak Sauce

Combine everything.

Pimiento Cheez Spread

1/3 cup Cashew Mayonnaise (page 12) or Tofu Mayonnaise (page 22), or Miraculous Whip (page 17)
1/4 cup pimientos, drained
1 teaspoon prepared mustard
1 cup Yeast Cheez (page 97) or Pimiento Cheez (page 94)
1 teaspoon soy sauce

Process in a blender until smooth and creamy. Or chop the pimientos and mix with the rest of the ingredients by hand.

Reuben Sandwiches

Reliable goodness!

1/2 cup water
4 cups cabbage, shredded
3/4 cup chopped bell pepper, chopped
1/2 teaspoon dill
1/2 teaspoon sea salt
3/4 cup Cashew Sour Kreem (page 94) or Tofu Sour Kreem (page 97)
Italian Dressing (page16)
Bread
Tomato slices
Yeast Cheez (page 97) or Pimiento Cheez (page 94)

Pour the water in a wok and bring it to a boil. Add cabbage and bell pepper. Stir well, cover, and let steam until tender, 1 to 2 minutes. Remove the cabbage and pepper from the wok and put in a bowl. Add dill, salt, and Sour Kreem. Spread a slice of bread with Italian Dressing. Put 1/2 cup of cabbage mixture on the bread. Put tomato slices on the cabbage. Top with Cheez and broil until spotted brown.

VARIATION: *Try Quick Sauerkraut (page 182) instead of the cabbage–bell pepper mixture.*

Saturday Night Specials

Special is the word!

2 cups Pimiento Cheez (page 94), Yeast Cheez (page 97), or Notzarella Cheez (page 94)
1/2 cup finely chopped onion
1/4 cup finely chopped bell pepper
1/2 cup sliced or chopped green or black olives
1/8 teaspoon cayenne pepper
1/8 teaspoon garlic powder
1/4 cup catsup
1 tablespoon prepared mustard
3 tablespoons finely chopped UnBacon (page 136)

Mix all ingredients. Spread 1/4 inch thick over bread. Broil until the Cheez gets brown spots.

Sloppy Joes

Not just for kids!

1 cup soy grits
2 cups UnBeef Broth (page 155)
1 1/2 cups chopped onion
1/2 cup finely chopped bell pepper
1/4 cup finely chopped celery
4 teaspoons corn oil
2 cups Tomato Sauce (page 261)
1/4 teaspoon cayenne pepper
1 1/2 teaspoons chili powder
1/4 teaspoon sea salt

Soak the grits in one cup of the broth. Sauté the onion, bell pepper, and celery in the oil until the onion is transparent. Add the grits and sauté for 10 minutes. Add the rest of the ingredients, including the second cup of broth, and stir around, sautéing for another 10 minutes, adding more Tomato Sauce if needed.

VARIATION: *Instead of the soy grits, use 2 cups of ground UnBeef (page 109), leaving out the second cup of the UnBeef Broth. At the end, mix in 3 cups of Yeast Cheez (page 97), Pimiento Cheez (page 94), or Notzarella Cheez (page 94).*

Super Cheez Sandwiches

Nondairy margarine
Garlic salt
Hamburger buns (or other rolls)
Garlic "butter"
Parmesan Cheez (page 94)
Pimiento Cheez (page 94)
Notzarella Cheez (page 94)
Prepared mustard
Shredded lettuce
Sliced onion
Sliced tomato
Chopped black olives
Dill pickles, sliced
Pickled jalapeño slices

Melt nondairy margarine and add garlic salt. Spread halves of the buns with garlic "butter" and sprinkle with Parmesan Cheez. Spread the bottom halves with Pimiento Cheez and the top halves with Notzarella. Bake at 450°F until the Cheez starts to brown in spots. Take out of oven and top with mustard, lettuce, onion, tomato, olives, pickles, and pickled jalapeños. Sandwich top and bottom together and serve.

VARIATION: *Use a salad dressing, such as Thousand Island (page 21), instead of mustard. Use Guacamole (page 32) instead of mustard.*

N'eggs

Many nonvegetarian recipes call for eggs, and sometimes, the dish will come out just fine without them as you adapt the recipe for vegetarian use. However, when an egg is absolutely necessary for the recipe to work, but you don't want to use the real thing, a N'egg, a contraction of "no egg," can substitute.

There are two formulas: One is specifically used in baked goods and pastries, and the other is for everything else.

Pastry N'egg

One-third cup of this formula equals one egg.

1/4 cup flax seeds
3/4 cup water

Grind the seeds into a powder. Mix in a blender with the water. Refrigerate what you don't use, but use it within 24 hours, for it does not keep well.

All-Purpose N'egg

This formula equals one egg.

2 tablespoons gluten flour, or unbleached white flour
1 1/2 teaspoons corn oil
1/2 teaspoon baking powder
2 tablespoons water

Combine thoroughly. Use right away, because the baking powder loses its effectiveness within 2 hours.

Seasonings

All-Purpose Seasoning

Mix this up, taste it, and decide how you'd like to use it.

1/4 teaspoon hot pepper flakes
2 1/2 teaspoons rubbed sage
1/2 teaspoon ground nutmeg
1/2 teaspoon dried mustard
1/2 teaspoon freshly ground black pepper
4 teaspoons paprika
1 1/2 teaspoons sea salt

Put everything in a blender and blend on high until all is finely ground. Do not take the mixture out of the blender, but let it sit 3 minutes. Remove it and store it in a covered container.

Fines Herbes

1 part rosemary
1 part thyme
1/2 part oregano or summer savory
3 parts basil

Combine and store in an airtight container.

Garam Masala 1

This is one formula for the Garam Masala (hot mixture) that is used in Indian cooking. You might like to try it in other types of dishes as well, such as Anandamayi Kitchuri, or try substituting it for curry powder or even for black pepper or cayenne pepper.

3 tablespoons coriander seed
2 teaspoons cumin seed
8 whole cloves
One 2-inch stick cinnamon
1/2 teaspoon freshly ground black pepper
4 bay leaves

Roast the coriander and cumin seeds in a dry frying pan over medium heat, shaking often, until they are lightly browned, about 4 minutes. In a blender or nut grinder, grind all the ingredients together into a fine powder. Store in an airtight container.

Garam Masala 2

This is far more complex than the first formula, but well worth making.

1 tablespoon plus 1½ teaspoons cayenne pepper
2 tablespoons paprika
1 tablespoon onion salt
1 teaspoon garlic powder
1 teaspoon basil
½ teaspoon powdered ginger
¼ teaspoon freshly ground black pepper
⅛ teaspoon ground cloves
⅛ teaspoon ground cinnamon
⅛ teaspoon cardamom
⅛ teaspoon nutmeg
⅛ teaspoon allspice
⅛ teaspoon cumin
⅛ teaspoon fenugreek
⅛ teaspoon turmeric

Grind everything together in a blender or nut grinder into a fine powder and store in an airtight container.

Hot Oil

An ideal way to spice up food. Add some to cooking oil, even popcorn oil, for real effect.

2 cups corn oil
½ cup hot pepper flakes

Combine the oil and pepper flakes in a small heavy saucepan. Warm it until the oil almost begins to bubble, then reduce the heat. Cook over low heat until the pepper flakes darken but do not turn black. Let cool overnight at room temperature. Strain through cheesecloth. Store, tightly covered, in the refrigerator, and this will keep indefinitely. Serve at room temperature.

Note

Asian cooks prefer to cook this over the low heat until the pepper flakes blacken in the oil. You can try both ways and see which you like best. The first way produces a beautiful red oil that is plenty hot. The second will be quite a bit darker and somewhat heavier in taste.

Garlic Oil

Keep this always on hand. It has many uses, such as spreading on pizza or bread dough, sautéing vegetables, or mixing in with other oils to give a subtle garlic taste to dishes.

4½ teaspoons crushed garlic
1 cup olive oil

Stir the crushed garlic into the oil, and let it sit overnight in the refrigerator before using. Keep in refrigerator.

Special Seasoning

1⅓ cups nutritional yeast
1 tablespoon onion powder
2 teaspoons garlic powder
1 tablespoon paprika
½ teaspoon ground celery seed
½ teaspoon turmeric
1 teaspoon parsley
1 tablespoon barley malt powder
3 tablespoons sea salt

Put everything in a blender and blend on high until all is finely ground. Do not take the mixture out of the blender, but let it sit 3 minutes. Remove it and store it in a covered container.

Desserts

Apple Crisp

Fit for a king!

8 cups sliced apple
½ cup Cashew Milk (page 93)
½ cup nondairy margarine
¾ cup rolled oats
½ cup unbleached white flour
2 teaspoons cinnamon
½ teaspoon sea salt
2½ cups Sucanat

Grease a casserole dish with some nondairy margarine. Put in the apple and pour in the "milk" on top. Melt the ½ cup of margarine. As margarine is melting, mix all the other ingredients together. Add margarine and stir with a fork until all is moistened. Crumble this mixture over the apple. Bake at 350°F until the apple is done and topping is brown, about 45 minutes.

VARIATION: *Use other kinds of fruit.*

Apple Squares

Filling

½ cup Sucanat
¼ cup cornstarch
2 cups water
10 cups thinly sliced apple
1 teaspoon cinnamon
½ teaspoon nutmeg
2 tablespoons lemon juice

Pastry

2 cups unbleached white flour
½ teaspoon sea salt
⅔ cup nondairy margarine, chilled
2 N'eggs (page 302)
¼ cup cold water
1 tablespoon lemon juice

Glaze

½ cup Sucanat
1 tablespoon Cashew Milk (page 93)
1 tablespoon nondairy margarine
½ teaspoon vanilla

For the filling, combine the Sucanat, cornstarch, and water in a saucepan, mixing until well blended. Add the apple and heat to boiling, stirring constantly. Reduce the heat, and simmer 5 minutes, stirring frequently. Remove from the heat. Stir in the spices and lemon juice. Set aside.

To make the pastry, combine the flour and salt. Cut in the margarine until the mixture is crumbly. Combine the N'eggs, water, and lemon juice. Blend into the flour mixture, forming a ball. Divide this in half. On a lightly floured surface roll half of the dough between two pieces of waxed paper so it will fit into a 13x9x2-inch baking pan. Put into the pan and spread the filling over it. Roll the rest of the dough out to fit over the pan, and put it on top. Fold the bottom pastry over the top and press to seal. Cut a few small slits in the top crust. Bake at 400°F until lightly browned, about 40 minutes.

To make glaze, combine ingredients and drizzle over the warm pastry.

Banana Pudding

Luscious is the word for this!

4 cups Cashew Milk (page 93)
1 cup Sucanat
1/2 cup shredded dried coconut
1/2 cup cornstarch
1/4 teaspoon sea salt
2 teaspoons vanilla
4 ripe bananas
1 1/2 cups Tofu Whipped Kreem (page 97)

Put the "milk," Sucanat, coconut, cornstarch, salt, and vanilla in a saucepan and cook, stirring constantly, until thick, and remove from heat. Mash 2 bananas and add to mixture. Slice the other bananas and add. Pour into a dish and chill until set. Top with Tofu Whipped Kreem.

Cheezcake

Filling
3 cups Pimiento Cheez (page 94)
4 tablespoons chopped green olives
2 tablespoons chopped fresh chives, or
  1 tablespoon dried
1/2 teaspoon garlic powder
1 teaspoon lemon juice
1/2 teaspoon soy sauce
1/4 teaspoon paprika
1/2 teaspoon sea salt
1/4 teaspoon Louisiana Hot Sauce

Crust
1 1/4 cups Cheez Cracker crumbs (page 59)
1/4 cup nondairy margarine, melted

Combine all ingredients for filling and set aside. For crust, combine cracker crumbs and margarine and press into a pie pan and bake at 375°F for 6 to 8 minutes or until light brown. Put the filling in the crust and refrigerate until needed.

Blueberry Cheez Cake

So virtuous it's positively sinful!

1 cup Tofu Kreem Cheez (page 97)
1 cup Sucanat
1 teaspoon vanilla
1 cup Soy Whipped Kreem (page 96) or Tofu
  Whipped Kreem (page 97)
1 recipe Graham Cracker Crust (page 328)
1 recipe Blueberry Pie Filling (page 330)

Beat together the Kreem Cheez, Sucanat, and vanilla until smooth. Fold in Whipped Kreem, spoon into Graham Cracker Crust. Spoon blueberry filling on top. Chill to set.

Carob Custard

1/2 cup pecans
1/4 teaspoon vanilla
3 1/4 cup water
1/2 teaspoon sea salt
1/4 cup carob powder
1 1/2 cups Sucanat
6 tablespoons cornstarch
Shredded dried coconut

Blend ingredients, except coconut, together in a blender until the nuts are smooth. Heat until thick, stirring constantly. Pour into custard cups. Sprinkle with the coconut.

Carob Pudding

3 tablespoons cornstarch
2 tablespoons soy flour
3 tablespoons carob powder
1/4 teaspoon sea salt
1/2 cup Sucanat
2 cups Cashew Milk (page 93)
2 teaspoons vanilla
1 cup whole, lightly toasted peanuts

Mix all ingredients except the vanilla and the peanuts. Cook for 5 minutes, stirring constantly. Add the vanilla and peanuts. Pour into molds to cool.

Cherry Cobbler

You won't be sorry!

4 cups pitted cherries
2 tablespoons cornstarch
⅔ cup plus 2 tablespoons Sucanat
2 tablespoons lemon juice
¼ teaspoon almond extract
1 cup unbleached white flour
¼ cup nondairy margarine
1 teaspoon baking powder
½ teaspoon sea salt
¼ cup plus 3 tablespoons water
¼ cup boiling water

Into the cherries stir the cornstarch, ⅔ cup of the Sucanat, lemon juice, and almond extract, and set aside. Combine the flour, margarine, baking powder, salt, 2 tablespoons Sucanat, and water, blending them until it resembles coarse meal. Stir in the boiling water, stirring only until the batter is just combined. In an 8-inch skillet or a baking dish bring the cherry mixture to a boil. Drop the batter by heaping tablespoons onto it. Bake at 350°F until the top is golden, 45 to 50 minutes.

Coconut Rice Pudding

You will remember this long and lovingly!

2 cups Cashew Milk (page 93)
6 sticks cinnamon
1 teaspoon whole cloves
¼ teaspoon powdered ginger
1 quart water
1 cup rice, uncooked
2 cups coconut milk
1 cup Sucanat
1 teaspoon sea salt
½ cup raisins

Put the "milk," cinnamon sticks, cloves, and ginger in a saucepan. Bring to a boil over high heat, then lower the heat and simmer, uncovered, for 5 minutes. Remove from heat and set aside for at least 1 hour. Strain the "milk" through a fine sieve. Discard the cinnamon, cloves, and ginger. If there is less than 2 cups of "milk," add more to make 2 cups.

Bring the water to a boil and drop in the rice. Cook, uncovered, for 5 minutes, then drain the rice in a sieve and wash it under cold water. In a saucepan, combine the coconut milk, strained spiced "milk," Sucanat, and salt. Bring to a boil over high heat, then stir in the rice, cover the pan, and reduce the heat. Simmer for 30 minutes, then stir in the raisins, re-cover the pan, and cook until the liquid is completely absorbed and the rice is tender, about 10 minutes longer. Sprinkle with cinnamon and serve at room temperature.

Date and Apple Squares

2 cups chopped apple
1½ cups chopped pitted dates
1 cup unbleached white flour
1½ teaspoons baking powder
½ cup Sucanat
⅓ cup Barbados molasses
2 tablespoons nondairy margarine, melted
1 N'egg (page 302)
Pinch of sea salt

Mix all ingredients together to combine evenly. Spread mixture into a lightly oiled square cake pan. Bake at 400°F until golden brown and risen, about 30 minutes. Cut into squares.

French Silk Pie

There is a frozen commercial version of this that gave us a real sugar blitz. Still, good sense prevailed and we worked out our own that is truly even better. Bliss without blitz!

Cookie Crust

3 sticks nondairy margarine, cold
2½ cups Sucanat
1½ teaspoons vanilla
3 cups unbleached white flour
¾ cup unsweetened cocoa powder
½ teaspoon sea salt
½ teaspoon baking soda
1½ cups chopped semisweet chocolate, in ⅛-inch bits
2 sticks plus 2 tablespoons nondairy margarine

Filling
1 stick nondairy margarine
1 cup Sucanat
2 teaspoons vanilla
1½ squares unsweetened chocolate
2 teaspoons agar flakes
1 cup Cashew Milk (page 93)

Topping
Cool-Whip nondairy topping
Semisweet chocolate shavings

To make the crust, cream 3 sticks cold margarine and Sucanat together until smooth and light. Add rest of crust ingredients except remaining margarine and mix well. Gather the dough into a ball. On a floured surface roll out the dough to ¼-inch thickness and cut into squares. (It doesn't matter if they're even, just as long as they're small enough to process well in the food processor.) Put on greased cookie sheets and bake one sheet at a time in the middle of the oven at 350°F for 12 to 15 minutes. When cool, put the cookies in a food processor or blender and blend until they reach crumb consistency. For each crust, cut 3 tablespoons of margarine into ⅓ cup of cookie crumbs. Press this into a 9-inch pie pan or dish and bake at 375°F for 8 minutes.

For the filling, cream the margarine and Sucanat together until smooth. Add the vanilla. Melt the chocolate and beat it into the margarine mixture. Stir the agar flakes into the "milk" and bring to a boil, lower heat, and simmer 1 to 2 minutes, then beat into the margarine mixture. Pour into a cooled cookie crust and let it come to room temperature. Chill for several hours, then top with Cool-Whip nondairy topping and semisweet chocolate shavings.

Fruit and Almond Kreem Tart

1 recipe Convent Pie Crust (page 328)
2 cups sliced or chopped fruit of choice
⅓ plus ½ cup Sucanat
¼ teaspoon cinnamon
⅛ teaspoon nutmeg
5 tablespoons nondairy margarine in bits
2 N'eggs (page 302)
¼ cup plus 1 tablespoon unbleached white flour
1 cup Cashew Milk (page 93), hot
½ teaspoon vanilla
¼ teaspoon almond extract
¼ teaspoon rum flavoring
⅓ cup ground blanched almonds

Roll out the pie dough ⅛ inch thick on a floured surface and fit it into a 10-inch round tart pan with a removable bottom. Trim the dough, leaving a 1-inch overhang, and fold the overhang over the rim, pressing it onto and ¼ inch above the rim of the pan. Prick the shell lightly with a fork and chill it for 30 minutes. Line the shell with waxed paper, and fill the paper with uncooked rice (or something similar you have on hand) to weight it, and bake the shell at 425°F for 10 minutes. Remove the rice and paper carefully, and bake until it is pale golden, 5 to 10 more minutes. Cool in the pan or on a rack.

Put the fruit in a single layer in a baking dish, sprinkle with the ⅓ cup of Sucanat, cinnamon, and nutmeg, and dot with 2 tablespoons of margarine. Bake the fruit at 350°F until the fruit is just tender and has given off its juice, 20 to 30 minutes. Let the fruit cool completely, strain the cooking juice through a sieve into a small saucepan, and reserve it.

Beat the ½ cup of Sucanat and N'eggs together well. Sift in the flour and beat until smooth. Add the hot "milk" in a stream, beating, and beat until all is well combined. Transfer this to a heavy saucepan, bring it to a boil while stirring, and simmer, stirring, until it thickens, about 3 minutes. Take from the heat and stir in 3 tablespoons of margarine, the vanilla, almond extract, and rum flavoring. Strain this through a sieve set over another bowl.

Into the sieved mixture fold the almonds, and chill, covered with a "buttered" round of waxed paper, for 1 hour. Spoon the almond mixture into the shell and top with the fruit. Boil the reserved juice until it is reduced to a glaze, and spoon this over the fruit. Chill the tart for 1 to 3 hours.

Fruit Cocktail Bread Pudding

When you've got to have bread pudding, try this one.

10 slices stale bread
3 N'eggs (page 302)
2¾ cups Sucanat
¼ cup nondairy margarine
1 cup raisins
1 cup chopped pecans
One 16-ounce can low-calorie fruit cocktail sweetened with fruit juice
2½ cups Cashew Milk (page 93)
2 tablespoons vanilla

Mix all ingredients together in a large bowl, blending well. Turn into an oiled 9x13-inch pan. Bake at 400°F until it gets brown on top, about 55 minutes.

Fruit Shortcake

This gives a whole new meaning to the word heavenly!

Filling
One 3-inch cinnamon stick, crushed
4 whole cloves
2 cups sliced fruit of choice
1 cup water
1 cup Sucanat

Shortcakes
2 cups unbleached white flour
2 tablespoons Sucanat
1 tablespoon baking powder
½ teaspoon sea salt
¼ cup nondairy margarine
½ cup Cashew Kreem (page 93)
2 N'eggs (page 302)
1 teaspoon vanilla
Apple juice
2 cups Soy Whipped Kreem (page 96) or Tofu Whipped Kreem (page 97), well chilled

For the filling, tie the cinnamon and cloves into a small piece of cheesecloth. Put the fruit, water, Sucanat, and spice bag into a saucepan and simmer until the fruit is just tender, 5 to 7 minutes. Transfer the fruit with a slotted spoon to a bowl. Boil the cooking liquid until it is reduced by half. Add any fruit juice that may have accumulated in the bowl. Let the syrup cool to room temperature and discard the spice bag. Add the syrup to the fruit and chill, covered, until it is cold, at least 1 hour.

To make the shortcake, sift the flour, Sucanat, baking powder, and salt together into a bowl. Blend in the margarine until the mixture resembles coarse meal. Whisk together the Kreem, N'eggs, and vanilla, and add this to the flour mixture, stirring with a fork just until a soft dough is formed. Turn the dough out onto a floured surface and knead it gently for 20 seconds.

Pat the dough into an 8-inch round, transfer it to a "buttered" baking sheet, and cut it into 6 equal wedges without cutting all the way through. Brush the wedges with apple juice, and bake at 425°F until they are golden, 15 to 20 minutes. Transfer to a rack, cool, and separate the wedges. Split each wedge horizontally with a fork, arrange the bottom halves on 6 plates, and spoon the filling over them. Top the filling with the Whipped Kreem and then put on the top half of the wedge.

Fruit Squares

Crumble
2 tablespoons vegetable oil
½ cup Sucanat
⅓ cup water
1 cup unbleached white flour
1 teaspoon sea salt
1½ cups quick oats
½ cup finely ground blended oats

Filling
1 cup dates or raisins
1 cup water
1 teaspoon lemon juice
½ teaspoon vanilla
⅛ teaspoon sea salt
2 tablespoons cornstarch
¾ cup pineapple juice

To make the crumble, mix the oil, Sucanat, and water. In a separate bowl, mix the flour, salt, quick oats, and blended oats. Combine both mixtures, crumbling together.

For the filling, mix the fruit, water, lemon juice, vanilla, salt, and cornstarch. Boil until the fruit is soft. Press half of the crumble on the bottom of a greased pan. Spread the filling over it. Cover with the rest of the crumble. Bake at 375°F until browned, about 40 minutes. Cool. Wet the top layer by spooning 3/4 cup of pineapple juice over it. Cover the pan and keep in the refrigerator overnight. Cut into squares.

VARIATION: *Instead of dates (or raisins) and water, prepare the filling with 2 cups crushed, unsweetened pineapple, canned pears, or apples.*

Lemon Cheezcake

1 cup very fine graham cracker crumbs
3 tablespoons nondairy margarine
3½ cups Tofu Cottage Cheez (page 96), made without garlic power
2 lemons, juice and grated rind
1⅓ cups Powdered Sucanat (page 340)

Stir the crumbs into the margarine and press into the base of a round cake pan. Run the Cottage Cheez through blender until it is perfectly smooth. Beat the lemon juice and rind together with the Sucanat. Slowly add the blended Cottage Cheez, beating, until all is smooth. Spread the mixture over the crust and smooth the surface. Cover and refrigerate for several hours.

Lemon Cheezcake Deluxe

For the sophisticate in you!

2½ cups graham cracker crumbs
¼ plus 1½ cups Sucanat
10 tablespoons nondairy margarine, melted
3 cups Tofu Kreem Cheez (page 97), made without onion powder
3 N'eggs (page 302)
1½ cups Powdered Sucanat (page 340)
3 tablespoons plus ⅓ cup lemon juice
1 teaspoon vanilla
1 tablespoon grated lemon peel
1 lemon, sliced paper-thin
3 cups water
2 tablespoons plus 2 teaspoons cornstarch

Combine the graham cracker crumbs, ¼ cup Sucanat, and margarine, and press into the bottom and 2 inches up the sides of a 9-inch springform pan. Bake at 350°F for 5 minutes and cool. Beat together the Kreem Cheez and N'eggs. Gradually add the Powdered Sucanat, lemon juice, and vanilla, and mix well. Fold in the lemon peel. Pour into the crust. Bake at 350°F for 40 minutes. Cool to room temperature and refrigerate at least 4 hours.

Remove any seeds from the lemon slices, reserve 1 slice for garnish, and coarsely chop the rest of the slices. Place in a saucepan with 2 cups of the water, bring to a boil, reduce the heat, and simmer, uncovered, for 15 minutes. Drain and discard the liquid. In a saucepan combine the 1½ cups Sucanat and cornstarch, stir in the remaining water, lemon juice, and cooked lemon. Bring to a boil, stirring constantly, and boil for 3 minutes. Chill until cool, stirring occasionally. Pour over the Cheezcake and garnish with the lemon slice. Chill until ready to serve.

Lemon Custard

1 lemon, quartered, seeds removed
½ cup water
2 cups orange juice
2 tablespoons oil
1¼ cups Sucanat
¼ cup cornstarch
Pecans, raisins, or dates for topping

Place the lemon in a blender, peel and all, with all the other ingredients except topping and blend until it is finely ground. Place in a saucepan and bring to a boil. Simmer about 2 minutes, stirring constantly. Pour into serving dishes. Put a few pecans, a few raisins, or a date on top.

Use also as a pie filling.

VARIATION: *Use 3 oranges, peeled and with seeds removed, instead of the orange juice. They should be blended with the lemon until fine.*

Maple Pecan Cheezcake

A triumph!

2 cups Ginger Snaps (page 324), crushed into fine crumbs
6 tablespoons nondairy margarine, melted
4 cups Tofu Kreem Cheez (page 96), made without onion powder
1 cup Powdered Sucanat (page 340)
½ cup genuine maple syrup
3 N'eggs (page 302)
½ cup Cashew Sour Kreem (page 94) or Tofu Sour Kreem (page 97)
½ teaspoon sea salt
1 teaspoon vanilla
¾ teaspoon maple flavoring
1 cup pecans, toasted lightly and chopped fine

Make the crust by stirring together the ginger snap crumbs and margarine until well combined, and press this onto the bottom and halfway up the side of a 9-inch springform pan. With an electric mixer cream the Kreem Cheez and Powdered Sucanat together until light and fluffy. Beat in the syrup, N'eggs, Sour Kreem, salt, vanilla, maple flavoring, and pecans. Put the filling into the crust, and bake at 350°F for 1 hour. Turn off the heat and let the cake cool down thoroughly in the oven with the door slightly open, and then chill, covered, overnight.

Pears in "Custard"

An attention getter!

4 cups thinly sliced pears
⅓ plus ½ cup Sucanat
1 tablespoon lemon juice
2 tablespoons unbleached white flour
¾ plus ½ teaspoon cinnamon
½ plus ¼ teaspoon ground ginger
¼ teaspoon sea salt
⅓ cup orange juice concentrate
12 ounces tofu
¼ cup Cashew Milk (page 93)
1 teaspoon vanilla
1 teaspoon grated lemon peel

Combine the pears, ⅓ cup Sucanat, lemon juice, flour, ¾ teaspoon cinnamon, ½ teaspoon ginger, and salt, and put into a baking dish or pan. Put the rest of the ingredients into a blender and puree until smooth. Pour the puree over the pears and bake at 350°F for 40 to 50 minutes. Serve warm or cold.

Pears in Mustard Syrup

This goes well with gluten.

4 cups peeled, cored, and diced pears, cut into ⅓-inch dice
⅓ cup Sucanat
1 tablespoon finely grated lemon peel
¼ cup water
1 cup fresh or frozen (not thawed) cranberries
1 teaspoon minced candied ginger
1 tablespoon dried mustard

In a saucepan combine the pears, Sucanat, lemon peel, and water. Stir to mix well, bring to a boil, and simmer until the pears are just tender, about 8 minutes. Stir in the cranberries and ginger and cook until the cranberries pop, about 4 more minutes. With a slotted spoon transfer the fruits to a bowl. Boil the liquid in the saucepan over high heat until syrupy, about 2 minutes. Stir the syrup into the fruit and set it aside to cool for 15 minutes. Stir in the mustard until thoroughly combined. Serve at room temperature. (This can be made as much as 2 days ahead and kept, covered, in the refrigerator.)

Pineapple Pudding

4 cups unsweetened pineapple juice
1½ cups Sucanat
⅓ cup cornstarch
½ teaspoon mint flavoring
1 cup crushed unsweetened pineapple, drained
½ teaspoon salt

Bring 3 cups of the juice and Sucanat to a rolling boil. Mix the cornstarch with the other 1 cup of the juice and add gradually to the rest, stirring constantly. Add the remaining ingredients. Pour into dessert cups. Chill. Serve with Whipped Kreem (page 96), if desired.

Spiced Bread Pudding

8 slices of bread
1½ cups Cashew Milk (page 93)
⅔ cup raisins, soaked in 1 cup hot water and drained
2 tablespoons nondairy margarine
⅓ cup Sucanat
⅓ cup Barbados molasses
1 tablespoon allspice
1 N'egg (page 302)
Pinch nutmeg

Break up the bread and place it in a mixing bowl with the "milk." Let soak. Add the raisins, margarine, Sucanat, molasses, allspice, and N'egg. Beat well. Put in an oiled casserole dish, level the surface, sprinkle with nutmeg, and bake at 350°F until "set," about 45 minutes. Serve hot or cold.

Steamed Irish Raisin Pudding

1½ cups raisins
1¾ cups Cashew Milk (page 93)
½ cup Sucanat
1½ cups unbleached wheat flour
½ teaspoon salt
¼ teaspoon coriander
1 tablespoon grated lemon rind
1½ cups bread crumbs
1 cup peeled and grated apple

"Plump" the raisins by putting them loosely in a container and covering them with hot water. Let them sit overnight or until soft. (May be stored in the refrigerator until you need them.) Blend the "milk" and Sucanat together. Combine all the ingredients and turn into a well-greased 2-quart tube mold or large can. Steam for 2 hours. Cool and unmold. Slice and serve with a dessert sauce.

Summer Fruit Terrine

When you care enough to fix the very berry best!

Terrine

1 cup white grape juice
¾ cup Sucanat
3 tablespoons lemon juice
¼ teaspoon almond extract
4 large peaches, peeled and pitted
2 tablespoons agar flakes
⅓ cup water
18 strawberries, hulled and halved lengthwise
½ cup raspberries (fresh only)
½ cup blueberries
¾ cup seedless white (green) grapes, halved lengthwise

Sauce

½ cup Sucanat
3 tablespoons lemon juice
¼ cup water
¼ teaspoon almond extract
2 large peaches, peeled, pitted, and chopped
1½ cups fresh raspberries, or 10 ounces frozen in light syrup, drained

For the terrine, combine the grape juice, Sucanat, lemon juice, and almond extract in a saucepan. Bring to a boil, stirring, until the Sucanat is dissolved. Coarsely chop 2 of the peaches and add. Simmer for 10 to 15 minutes, or until they are very tender, and transfer them with a slotted spoon to a blender. Add 1 cup of the cooking liquid and blend until smooth.

In a small saucepan sprinkle the agar flakes over ⅓ cup of water and let it soften for 5 minutes. Heat this over low heat, stirring, until the gelatin is dissolved. With the blender running, add the gelatin mixture in a stream to the peach mixture and blend until it is combined well. (There will be about 2½ cups of puree.)

Line a terrine or loaf pan with plastic wrap and pour into it about ¼ cup of the puree, or enough to just cover the bottom. Arrange half the strawberries, cut sides down, in one layer on the peach puree. Pour enough of the peach puree over the strawberry layer to just cover it. Halve the remaining 2 peaches, slice them thin, and in a bowl toss them with ¼ cup of the peach puree. Arrange half of the peach slices, overlapping them slightly, over the strawberry layer and pour enough of the remaining peach puree over the peach layer to just cover it.

Toss the raspberries and blueberries with the $\frac{1}{4}$ cup of the peach puree. Arrange the berries in one layer over the peaches. Pour enough of the remaining peach puree into the terrine to just cover the berries. Toss the grapes with about 2 tablespoons of the remaining puree, and arrange them in one layer over the berries. Pour enough of the remaining puree into the terrine to just cover the grape layer.

Arrange the remaining peaches in one layer, overlapping them slightly, over the grapes and pour enough of the puree over them to just cover them. Arrange the remaining strawberries, cut sides up, in one layer over the peaches and cover them with the rest of the puree.

Chill the terrine until it is just set, about 1 hour. Cover it with plastic wrap and chill it overnight.

To make the sauce, combine the Sucanat, lemon juice, almond extract, and $\frac{1}{4}$ cup of water. Bring this to a boil, stirring until the Sucanat is dissolved. In a blender puree the peaches and the raspberries with the syrup until smooth. Force the mixture through a fine sieve set over a bowl. Discard the solids. Chill the sauce, covered, for at least 1 hour or overnight. Remove the plastic wrap from the top of the terrine, invert the terrine onto a serving plate, and peel off the plastic wrap carefully. Cut the terrine into $\frac{3}{4}$-inch slices with a serrated knife and serve it with the sauce.

Note

If fresh raspberries are not available for the terrine, omit them and add ½ cup more blueberries instead.

Vanilla Pudding 1

2¼ cups Cashew Milk (page 93)
½ cup Sucanat
⅛ teaspoon sea salt
2 teaspoons agar flakes
2 tablespoons arrowroot powder
1 teaspoon vanilla extract
1 tablespoon nondairy margarine

Combine 1¾ cups of the "milk" with the Sucanat and salt in a small saucepan. Sprinkle in the agar flakes and bring to a simmer over medium heat, without stirring. Simmer for one minute. Thoroughly dissolve the arrowroot in the remaining ¼ cup of Cashew Milk and add it to the pudding while stirring briskly. Return to a simmer and cook for 1 to 2 minutes. Remove from heat and mix in the vanilla and margarine. Chill.

Vanilla Pudding 2

3 tablespoons cornstarch
⅓ cup Sucanat
¼ teaspoon salt
2 cups Cashew Milk (page 93)
2 teaspoons vanilla

Mix cornstarch, Sucanat, and salt in top of a double boiler. Gradually add "milk" until smooth. Place over boiling water and cook, stirring constantly, until mixture thickens. Cover and continue cooking 10 minutes. Stir in vanilla and chill.

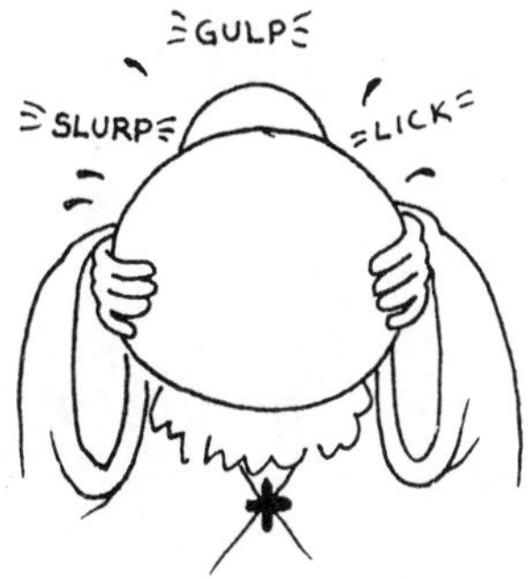

N'Ice Kreem

From the health standpoint, the major reason we "went vegan" was our realization that every bout of flu that swept through the monastery occurred the day after a big ice cream bash. (I had once had a private flu epidemic on my own when traveling that was also preceded by an ice cream orgy.) What, then, to do? Here is the answer. Freeze and enjoy!

Banana N'Ice Kreem

Simple and heavenly!

4 large frozen bananas
1 teaspoon Sucanat

Cut the frozen bananas into chunks. Place them in a food processor fitted with a steel blade. Pulse until chopped. Add the Sucanat. Process until the bananas are smooth and creamy. Serve immediately.

VARIATION: *Add one cup of frozen fruit when processing.*

Coconut N'Ice Kreem

Better than you-know-who's!

2 cups shredded coconut
3 cups coconut milk
1 cup raw cashew pieces
2 teaspoons vanilla
2½ cups tofu
1½ cups bananas
1 cup genuine maple syrup
⅔ cup coconut oil
¼ teaspoon sea salt

Put everything in a food processor in batches and purée until creamy and smooth. Freeze in an ice cream freezer.

Tahini N'Ice Kreem

This N'Ice Kreem has a character all its own.

1⅓ cups fruit puree
⅔ cup tahini
2 tablespoons Sucanat
½ teaspoon almond or vanilla extract

Mix fruit puree with tahini until smooth, stir in the remaining ingredients, and freeze.

Tofu N'Ice Kreem 1

You won't regret it.

2¼ cups tofu, well chilled
6 tablespoons genuine maple syrup
1 tablespoon corn oil
2 teaspoons vanilla
⅛ teaspoon sea salt

Combine 1½ cups of the tofu with the syrup, oil, vanilla, and salt in a blender and puree for 1 minute. Put in a covered container and place in the freezer overnight. Puree the other ¾ cup of tofu in a blender until smooth. Cut the frozen tofu into small chunks. While pureeing at high speed, add a few chunks of the frozen tofu at a time to the tofu in the blender until all has been added and the mixture is smooth and thick. Serve immediately.

VARIATION: *Toward the end of the pureeing add ½ cup (well-packed) frozen fruit. Replace 1 teaspoon of vanilla with 1 teaspoon of almond extract or 1 teaspoon of rum extract and, at the end, add ½ cup of chopped pecans. Add 2 teaspoons of peppermint or other extract.*

Tofu N'Ice Kreem 2

This is the deluxe model.

4 cups fruit
1 cup pineapple juice
1 cup very finely ground raw cashews
2 teaspoons vanilla
2½ cups tofu
1½ cups bananas
1 cup genuine maple syrup
⅔ cup corn oil
3 tablespoons lemon juice
¼ teaspoon sea salt

Put everything in a food processor in batches and purée until creamy and smooth. Freeze in an ice cream freezer.

Note

When making Peach or Mango N'Ice Kreem, use ½ teaspoon of almond extract and ½ teaspoon of vanilla.

Cake

Carob Cake

1 1/2 cups unbleached white flour
3 tablespoons carob powder
1/2 teaspoon sea salt
2 teaspoons baking powder
1/3 cup Sucanat
1/3 cup Barbados molasses
1 teaspoon vanilla
6 tablespoons nondairy margarine, melted
3/4 cup water

Sift the dry ingredients into a bowl. Mix the liquid ingredients, including the melted margarine, in a separate bowl. Pour the liquid ingredients into the dry, and stir until the batter is smooth. Pour the batter into an oiled, floured pan. Bake in a preheated 350°F oven for 35 to 45 minutes.

VARIATION: *Leave out the carob powder for a white cake.*

Christmas Fruitcake

1/3 cup coarsely chopped crystallized ginger
1 cup walnuts, coarsely chopped
1/2 cup almonds, coarsely chopped
3/4 cup golden raisins
1/3 cup currants
1/2 cup dried prunes, quartered
3/4 cup dried apricots, quartered
1 orange peel, grated
1 lemon peel, grated
1 teaspoon brandy extract in 1/3 cup water
1 1/4 cups Sucanat
1/2 cup nondairy margarine
2 N'eggs (page 302)
1 cup flour
1 1/2 teaspoons baking powder
1/4 teaspoon baking soda
1 teaspoon cinnamon
1/2 teaspoon nutmeg
Nuts and apricot halves

Combine the first 10 ingredients. Stir well. Cover and let rest for 30 to 60 minutes. Cream the Sucanat and margarine. Beat in the N'eggs. Sift the flour, baking powder, soda, cinnamon, and nutmeg, and add to the margarine mixture and beat until smooth. Combine with the fruit. Mix thoroughly by hand. Spoon into an oiled 1/2-quart cake pan that has been lined with waxed paper. Bake at 275°F for 2 hours. Remove and let rest for 5 minutes. Unmold. Decorate top with nuts and apricot halves. Cool.

Cottage Pudding

Simply indescribable as a "shortcake."

1/4 cup corn oil
1 3/4 cups unbleached white flour
2 teaspoons baking powder
1/2 teaspoon sea salt
3/4 cup Sucanat

¾ cup Cashew Milk (page 93)
1 N'egg (page 302)
1 teaspoon vanilla

Mix the oil, flour, baking powder, salt, and Sucanat. Add the "milk," N'egg, and vanilla and beat until smooth. Pour into an oiled and floured baking pan, cover and bake at 350°F for 45 to 60 minutes. Let stand 5 minutes before removing from pan.

Crazy Cake

3 cups unbleached white flour
2 cups Sucanat
½ cup carob powder
1 teaspoon sea salt
2 teaspoons baking soda
2 tablespoons white vinegar
2 teaspoons vanilla
2 cups water
¾ cup corn oil

Sift the dry ingredients together. Add the vinegar, vanilla, water, and oil. Bake at 350°F for 50 minutes, or until a toothpick inserted comes out clean.

Date-Nut Cake

Quietly good.

2¾ cups Sucanat
1 cup nondairy margarine
2 N'eggs (page 302)
1 cup walnuts, chopped
2 cups dates, chopped
1 teaspoon cinnamon
½ teaspoon allspice
½ teaspoon cloves
3 cups unbleached white flour, sifted
2 teaspoons baking soda
½ teaspoon sea salt
1½ cups water
½ cup liquid barley malt

Cream the Sucanat and margarine. Sir in the N'eggs, nuts, dates, and spices. In another bowl sift the flour, baking soda, and salt together and stir in the water and malt. Combine the mixture with the Sucanat/margarine and mix until well blended. Bake in a casserole pan at 350°F for 1 hour and 15 minutes.

Devon Apple Cake

2 cups unbleached white flour
3 teaspoons baking powder
¼ teaspoon sea salt
½ teaspoon ground cinnamon
½ teaspoon ground allspice
⅓ cup Sucanat
⅓ cup Barbados molasses
½ cup nondairy margarine
2 cups peeled, cored, and coarsely chopped apple
1 N'egg (page 302)

Oil and flour the base of a square cake pan. In a bowl combine the flour, baking powder, salt, cinnamon, allspice, Sucanat, and molasses. Rub in the margarine until the mixture resembles fine crumbs. Add apple and N'egg to mixture and stir quickly to combine. Spread evenly in the pan and bake at 375°F until risen and firm to the touch, about 30 minutes. Allow to cool in pan before cutting into squares.

Fruitcake 1

For me this is real fruitcake!

1½ cups dried apricots, chopped
1½ cups dates, chopped
1½ cups golden raisins
1 cup water
1 cup orange juice
½ cup corn oil
3 cups unbleached white flour
4½ teaspoons baking powder
1 cup pecans, broken
1 tablespoon Barbados molasses
1 tablespoon finely grated lemon rind
2 teaspoons ground allspice
1½ cups Sucanat
3 tablespoons rum flavoring (not extract)

Line two 9x5x3-inch loaf pans with waxed paper. Place all the ingredients in a bowl and beat well until evenly mixed. Pour into the pans and bake at 300°F until they test done, 1½ to 2 hours.

Fruitcake 2

1½ cups nondairy margarine
3 cups Sucanat
6 N'eggs (page 302)
1 cup Cashew Milk (page 93)
1 teaspoon brandy extract
1 teaspoon vanilla
½ teaspoon sea salt
½ teaspoon cream of tartar
1 cup water
3½ cups unbleached white flour
1 cup raisins
1 cup dried apricots, chopped and soaked
½ cup dried cherries, chopped and soaked
½ cup dried orange, chopped (can be made by chopping up an orange and letting it dry out)
½ cup dried lemon, chopped (see above)
1 cup pecans, chopped

Cream the margarine and Sucanat together. Add the N'eggs, "milk," brandy extract, vanilla, salt, cream of tartar, and water. Add the flour slowly and mix while doing so. Fold in the fruits and nuts. The batter should be stiff but not dry. If needed, add more water. Divide batter in half and place in two oiled loaf pans. Bake at 275°F for 2 to 2½ hours. Use a toothpick to tell if the cake is done. Also, the sides of the cake should not adhere to the pan when it is done.

Gingerbread

If the old witch had known this recipe, Hansel and Gretel would have truly eaten her out of house and home!

½ cup nondairy margarine
½ cup Sucanat
1 cup Barbados molasses
2½ cups unbleached white flour
2½ teaspoon baking soda
1 teaspoon cinnamon
2 teaspoons ground ginger
½ teaspoon ground cloves
½ teaspoon sea salt
1 cup boiling water

Cream margarine and Sucanat. Add molasses and dry ingredients. Blend well. Add boiling water and beat well. Pour batter into a well-greased and floured baking pan. Bake at 350°F until it passes the "toothpick test," 30 to 35 minutes.

Lemon Cake

½ cup nondairy margarine
¾ cup Sucanat
1 lemon, juice and rind, grated
1 N'egg (page 302)
1 cup unbleached white flour
1½ teaspoons baking powder

Oil and flour a square cake pan. Heat margarine and ½ cup of the Sucanat over low heat until the margarine is melted. Take off the heat and stir in the lemon rind. Beat the N'egg into the Sucanat mixture. Fold in the flour and baking powder and turn the mixture into the pan. Bake at 350°F until it is just firm to the touch, about 30 minutes. Warm the lemon juice and ¼ cup of Sucanat and mix together. Prick the cake all over with a fork or toothpick, and spoon the syrup over it. Leave in the pan to cool.

VARIATION: *Use a small orange, juice and rind, instead of lemon.*

Mexican Fruitcake

2 cups unbleached white flour
2 cups Sucanat
One 20-ounce can unsweetened crushed pineapple with the juice
2 N'eggs (page 302)
2½ teaspoon baking soda
⅔ cup shredded coconut
⅔ cup pecans, coarsely chopped
Whipped Kreem (page 96)

Mix all ingredients except Whipped Kreem together. Put in an oiled 9x13-inch pan (or in two 8x8-inch pans). Bake at 350°F for 40 minutes (if in the two pans, for 30 minutes). Top with Whipped Kreem.

Molasses Cake

¾ cup Barbados molasses
2 tablespoons nondairy margarine
1½ cups unbleached white flour
Pinch sea salt
½ teaspoon ground allspice
¼ teaspoon ground nutmeg
¼ teaspoon ground cinnamon
1 N'egg (page 302)
¾ teaspoon baking soda
3 tablespoons Cashew Milk (page 93)

Heat the molasses and margarine together until the margarine has melted. Remove from heat and beat in the flour, salt, spices, and N'egg. Blend the baking soda and "milk" together and stir into mixture. Put in an oiled cake pan. Bake at 350°F until golden brown and firm to the touch, 25 to 30 minutes. Cool slightly before turning out onto a wire rack.

Orange Gingercake

2 cups unbleached white flour
1½ teaspoons ground ginger
1½ teaspoons baking powder
½ teaspoon baking soda
½ teaspoon sea salt
1⅓ cups Sucanat
2 tablespoons Barbados molasses
6 tablespoons nondairy margarine
¼ cup Cashew Milk (page 93)
1 N'egg (page 302)
1 orange rind, grated
2 tablespoons orange juice

Oil and flour a cake pan. Put the flour, ginger, baking powder, baking soda, and salt in a mixing bowl. Heat together the Sucanat, molasses, and margarine until the margarine is melted. Combine all ingredients, beat well, and pour into the pan. Bake at 325°F until just firm to the touch, about ½ hour. Cool in the pan. Cut into squares.

Pineapple Upside-Down Cake

This truly bears repeating!

2 tablespoons nondairy margarine
1 cup Sucanat
2½ cups drained canned crushed pineapple
1½ cups unbleached white flour
2 teaspoons baking powder
½ teaspoon salt
¾ cup Sucanat
1 N'egg (page 302)
½ cup water
½ cup nondairy margarine

Melt the 2 tablespoons of margarine. Add the 1 cup of Sucanat and mix well. Put this in the bottom of a cake pan. Cover this with the pineapple and set aside. Sift the flour, baking powder, salt, and ¾ cup of Sucanat together. In a separate bowl, mix the N'egg, water, and ½ cup of margarine together. Combine well with the flour mixture until it is smooth. Spread over the pineapple. Bake at 400°F until brown and crusty, about 35 minutes. Let cool for 30 minutes and then turn out of the pan, fruit side up, onto a serving tray or platter.

VARIATION: *At the beginning mix in 1 cup of pecan pieces with the margarine and Sucanat.*

Shortcake

2⅓ cups Biscuit Mix (page 50)
½ cup Cashew Milk (page 93) or water
3 tablespoons Sucanat
3 tablespoons nondairy margarine, melted

Mix all together until a soft dough forms. Spread in an ungreased pan. Bake at 425°F until golden brown, 15 to 20 minutes. Cool for 10 minutes, cut into pieces, and split each horizontally.

Syrup Cake

2½ cups unbleached white flour
1½ teaspoons baking powder
½ teaspoon baking soda
1 teaspoon ground ginger
1 teaspoon cinnamon
¼ teaspoon ground nutmeg (fresh preferred)
¼ teaspoon ground cloves
½ teaspoon sea salt
¾ cup pecans, coarsely chopped
½ cup raisins
1 tablespoon unbleached white flour
⅔ plus ½ cup Sucanat
⅓ cup Barbados molasses
1¼ cup boiling water
⅔ cup nondairy margarine, softened
2 N'eggs (page 302)

Grease and flour a 9x13-inch cake pan. Combine the flour, baking powder, baking soda, ginger, cinnamon, nutmeg, cloves, and salt, and sift them together into a mixing bowl. In a separate bowl, mix the pecans, raisins, and flour. Combine the ⅔ cup Sucanat, molasses, and boiling water and set aside. Cream the margarine and ½ cup of Sucanat. Beat in the N'eggs. Add about ⅔ cup of the flour and spice mixture and, when it is well incorporated, beat in ½ cup of the syrup mixture.

Repeat three more times, alternating about ⅔ cup of the flour and spice mixture with ½ cup of the syrup mixture, beating well after each addition. Add the floured pecans and raisins, folding them in gently but thoroughly with a rubber spatula. Pour the batter into the pan, spreading it evenly and smoothing the top with the spatula. Bake at 350°F until a toothpick or cake tester inserted in the center comes out clean, 35 to 45 minutes.

Uncooked Fruitcake

¾ cup water
1 cup fruit juice or nectar
1 cup raisins, ground
1 cup dates, chopped
2 cups dried fruit (any kind), chopped
1 cup bread crumbs
1 cup sunflower seeds, or other nuts, broken small

Combine the water and fruit juice and soak the dried fruits for 2 hours. Add the crumbs and seeds, pack into an oiled mold, and set for one or more days in the refrigerator. Unmold, slice, and serve.

Vanilla Cake 1

1¾ cups unbleached white flour
1 teaspoon baking powder
½ teaspoon sea salt
¾ cup Sucanat
⅓ cup nondairy margarine, melted
⅔ cup water
2 teaspoons vanilla
1 tablespoon wine vinegar

Sift the dry ingredients in a mixing bowl. Whip together the liquid ingredients and pour them into the dry. Stir with a wooden spoon until smooth, with no lumps remaining. Pour the batter into an oiled cake pan or muffin tin (for cupcakes). Bake at 375°F for 30 to 40 minutes.

Vanilla Cake 2

3½ cups unbleached white flour
2 cups Sucanat
1 teaspoon sea salt
2 teaspoons baking soda
2 tablespoons white vinegar
4 teaspoons vanilla
2 cups water
¾ cup corn oil

Sift the dry ingredients together. Add the vinegar, vanilla, water, and oil. Bake at 350°F until a toothpick inserted comes out clean, about 50 minutes.

Velvet Crumb Cake

1½ cups Biscuit Mix (page 50)
½ cup Sucanat
1 N'egg (page 302)
½ cup Cashew Milk (page 93) or water
2 tablespoons nondairy margarine
1 teaspoon vanilla
½ cup flaked coconut
⅓ cup Powdered Sucanat (page 340), packed in well
¼ cup chopped nuts
3 tablespoons nondairy margarine, softened
2 tablespoons Cashew Milk (page 93) or water

Beat the first 6 ingredients together, at low speed, stirring constantly, for 30 seconds, then beat at medium speed, scraping the bowl occasionally, for 4 minutes. Pour into a greased and floured baking pan and bake at 350°F until a wooden pick inserted in center comes out clean, 30 to 35 minutes. Cool slightly. Combine the rest of the ingredients and spread over cake. Broil 3 inches from the heat until the topping is golden brown, about 3 minutes.

Cookies

Apple Cakes

A perfect soft cookie-cake.

2 cups unbleached white flour
Pinch sea salt
½ teaspoon ground cinnamon
1 teaspoon baking powder
¾ cup nondairy margarine
2 apples, peeled, cored, and diced
1 cup Sucanat
1 N'egg (page 302)

In a bowl combine flour, salt, cinnamon, and baking powder. Rub in the margarine until the mixture resembles fine crumbs. Add remaining ingredients and combine well together. Place heaping spoonfuls on a lightly oiled baking sheet and bake at 375°F until golden brown, 20 to 25 minutes. Cool slightly before transferring to a wire rack.

Butterscotch Shortbread

1 cup nondairy margarine
½ cup Sucanat
¼ cup Barbados molasses
2¼ cup unbleached white flour
¾ teaspoon sea salt

Beat the margarine, Sucanat, and molasses together. Combine well with rest of ingredients. Roll out ¼ inch thick. Cut into rounds or shapes. Bake on an ungreased baking sheet at 300°F for 20 to 25 minutes.

Canadian Shortbread

1 cup nondairy margarine
½ cup Sucanat
1 teaspoon vanilla
1 cup unbleached white flour
½ teaspoon baking soda
2 cups rolled oats

Beat the margarine, Sucanat, and vanilla until fluffy. Combine the flour, baking soda, and oats. Add to margarine mixture and mix well. Chill an hour or more (or freeze for later use). Roll out ¼ inch thick. Cut into rounds. Bake on an ungreased baking sheet at 350°F for 10 to 12 minutes.

VARIATION: *Form dough into 1½-inch balls and flatten them rather than roll out and cut out rounds.*

Carob Chip Cookies

Now this has enough chips to satisfy.

½ cup nondairy margarine
¾ cup Sucanat
1 N'egg (page 302)
1 teaspoon vanilla
1 cup unbleached white flour

½ teaspoon baking soda
¼ teaspoon sea salt
1½ cups carob chips

Let margarine stand at room temperature until soft. In a bowl, cream together the softened margarine, Sucanat, N'egg, and vanilla. In a separate bowl stir the flour, baking soda, and salt together. Add to creamed mixture and stir well. Stir in carob chips. Drop teaspoonfuls 2 inches apart onto a greased cookie sheet. Bake at 375°F until golden brown, 10 to 12 minutes.

Coconut Cookies

These are excellent for those who do not like overly sweet goodies. If Red Riding Hood had some of these in her basket the wolf might have taken them and been satisfied!

½ cup nondairy margarine
½ cup corn oil
⅓ cup water
¾ cup Sucanat
¼ teaspoon sea salt
½ teaspoon vanilla
⅔ cup coconut
1 teaspoon baking powder
1 tablespoon cornstarch
2 cups unbleached white flour

Whip together the margarine, oil, water, and Sucanat until creamy. Beat in the salt, vanilla, and coconut. Mix the baking powder, cornstarch, and flour and add to the creamed mixture to make a smooth drop batter. Drop the batter by heaping teaspoonfuls onto an oiled baking sheet. Bake at 350°F until set, 10 to 12 minutes. Remove immediately from the sheet and cool on a rack.

Colossal Cookies

The name says it all!

⅔ cup nondairy margarine
5 cups Sucanat
⅔ cup Tofu Mayonnaise (page 22), Cashew Mayonnaise (page 12), or Miraculous Whip (page 17)
1½ teaspoons vanilla
2½ cups chunky peanut butter
7½ cups rolled oats
1¼ cups carob chips
1 tablespoon baking soda

Cream the margarine and Sucanat. Add "mayonnaise" and vanilla. Add rest of ingredients. Drop by 2 tablespoonfuls on an oiled baking sheet. Bake at 375°F in the middle of the oven until golden brown.

Crunchies

½ cup nondairy margarine
⅔ cup Sucanat
1½ cups unbleached white flour
1¾ teaspoons baking powder
½ cup oatmeal
2 tablespoons currants
1 tablespoon Barbados molasses
½ teaspoon ground allspice

Melt the margarine in a saucepan. Remove from heat and stir in all the ingredients until evenly blended. Roll mixture into balls about the size of a walnut. Place well apart on a lightly greased baking sheet. Bake at 350°F 12 to 15 minutes. Allow to cool slightly on the baking sheet before transferring to a wire rack.

Fiery Ginger Snaps

¾ cup nondairy margarine
1¾ cups Sucanat
¼ cup Barbados molasses
1 N'egg (page 302)
2¼ cups unbleached white flour
2 teaspoons baking soda
½ teaspoon sea salt
1 tablespoon powdered ginger
1¼ teaspoons cinnamon
⅔ teaspoon ground cloves
½ teaspoon cayenne pepper
Powdered Sucanat (page 340)

Cream together the margarine, Sucanat, molasses, and N'egg until light and fluffy. Sift together the other ingredients except Powdered Sucanat and stir into the molasses mixture until blended. Form into small balls. Roll heavily in Powdered Sucanat and place 2 inches apart on an oiled cookie sheet. Flatten the cookies with the bottom of a glass. Bake at 375°F for about 10 minutes. Remove from the pan immediately.

Fig Bars

Filling
2 cups dried figs
2 teaspoons grated lemon peel
Pinch sea salt
1½ cups apple juice or cider

Crust
½ cup nondairy margarine
⅔ cup Sucanat
1 cup unbleached white flour
1 cup rolled oats
1 teaspoon baking powder
¼ teaspoon sea salt

To make filling, bring figs, lemon peel, salt, and juice (or cider) to a boil. Simmer, covered, until the figs are fairly tender, about 15 minutes. Mash figs thoroughly with a potato masher. If necessary, simmer 10 more minutes and mash again until the mixture is smooth.

For crust, combine the margarine and Sucanat in a mixing bowl. Add the flour, oats, baking powder, and salt, and mix well. Crust should be crumbly. Press half the crust into the bottom of an 8-inch square baking pan. Spread the fig mixture evenly over it. Press the remaining crust mixture evenly on top. Bake until the topping is lightly browned, about 40 minutes.

VARIATION: *Use other kinds of dried fruit.*

Frosted Apple-Date Bits

Cookies
¾ cup nondairy margarine
1 cup Sucanat
1 teaspoon vanilla
⅔ cup Cashew Milk (page 93)
2 cups unbleached white flour
½ teaspoon baking soda
½ teaspoon sea salt
1 teaspoon cinnamon
¼ teaspoon nutmeg
1 cup very finely chopped apple
1 cup dates, finely chopped

Frosting
2 tablespoons nondairy margarine
¼ cup water
1 teaspoon cinnamon
1½ cups Powdered Sucanat (page 340)

To make cookies, cream together margarine and Sucanat in a large bowl. Add vanilla and "milk" and mix well. Separately, mix the flour, baking soda, salt, and spices. Add flour mixture to creamed mixture. Stir until well blended. Stir in chopped apple and dates. Drop by large tablespoonfuls onto greased cookie sheet. Bake at 375°F until done, 8 to 10 minutes. Cool.

For frosting, heat together the margarine and water over low heat until the margarine melts. Transfer to a mixing bowl. Add cinnamon and Sucanat. Blend well. Let set until thickened, then spread on cooled cookies.

Fruit Bars

Truly elegant.

3 tablespoons corn oil
1 tablespoon Barbados molasses
⅔ cup Sucanat
¾ cup dates, chopped, or raisins
1 N'egg (page 302)
2 teaspoons vanilla
1½ cups unbleached white flour
¼ teaspoon sea salt
½ teaspoon baking powder
⅓ cup water

Beat together all ingredients except baking powder and water. Stir in the baking powder and water. Beat well, then pour into a greased and floured cake pan. Bake at 350°F until just firm to the touch, 25 to 30 minutes. Cut into bars while still warm.

Ginger Snaps

Yes, they do!

¾ cup nondairy margarine
1½ cups Sucanat
¼ cup Barbados molasses

1 N'egg (page 302)
2¼ cup unbleached white flour, sifted
2 teaspoons baking soda
½ teaspoon sea salt
1 teaspoon ground ginger
1 teaspoon cinnamon
½ teaspoon cloves
¼ cup Powdered Sucanat (page 340) for rolling

Cream together the margarine, Sucanat, molasses, and N'egg until light and fluffy. Sift together the other ingredients except Powdered Sucanat and stir into the molasses mixture until blended. Form into small balls. Roll in Powdered Sucanat and place 2 inches apart on an oiled cookie sheet. Bake at 375°F for about 10 minutes. Remove from the pan immediately.

Gingernuts

You may have read about these in Jane Eyre, *and if you haven't, cook a batch and read the book as you eat them!*

5 tablespoons nondairy margarine
1½ cups unbleached white flour
1¾ teaspoons baking powder
⅓ cup Sucanat
¼ cup Barbados molasses
¾ teaspoon baking soda
2 teaspoons ground ginger
¼ cup Powdered Sucanat (page 340) for rolling

Rub margarine into flour and baking powder until mixture resembles fine crumbs. Stir in Sucanat. Warm molasses in a saucepan and stir in baking soda and ginger. Add molasses mixture to dry ingredients, and knead well to form a soft dough. Roll mixture into balls about the size of a walnut. Place well apart on oiled baking sheets and flatten slightly. Bake at 350°F about 15 minutes. Allow to cool slightly on the baking sheet before transferring to a wire rack.

Maple Nut Chews

These have real style and rich flavor.

½ cup golden raisins
Apple juice
3 tablespoons nondairy margarine
½ cup Sucanat
½ teaspoon maple flavoring
1 N'egg (page 302)
½ cup unbleached white flour, sifted
¼ teaspoon sea salt
¼ teaspoon baking powder
½ cup pecans or walnuts, chopped

Place the raisins in a small saucepan and cover them with apple juice. Bring to a boil, turn off the heat, and let the raisins sit for 10 minutes. Drain the raisins and reserve the apple juice. In a saucepan, melt margarine and Sucanat, then cool slightly. Beat in the maple flavoring and N'egg. Sift in flour, salt, and baking powder. Stir in the margarine mixture and 3 tablespoons of the reserved apple juice. Stir in the raisins and nuts. Spread ½ to ¾ inch thick in a greased pan. Bake at 350°F for 25 to 30 minutes. Cool slightly and cut into bars. (The flavor is markedly better the next day.)

Molasses Cookies 1

A favorite cookie, one to which we often turn whenever the cookie hunger strikes.

¾ cup nondairy margarine
1 cup Sucanat
1 N'egg (page 302)
¼ cup Barbados molasses
2¼ cup unbleached white flour
2 teaspoons baking soda
¼ teaspoon sea salt
1 teaspoon ground ginger
1 teaspoon ground cinnamon
½ teaspoon ground cloves
¼ cup up Powdered Sucanat (page 340) for rolling

Cream together the margarine and Sucanat. Add N'egg and molasses and mix well. Separately combine the flour, baking soda, salt, and spices. Add flour mixture to creamed ingredients and blend well. Form dough into small or medium balls. Roll in Powdered Sucanat and place 2 inches apart on a greased cookie sheet. Bake at 375°F for 6 to 8 minutes.

Molasses Cookies 2

6 cups unbleached white flour
3/4 cup Sucanat
1 1/2 teaspoons sea salt
4 1/2 teaspoons baking powder
3/4 teaspoon baking soda
2 1/4 cups Barbados molasses
1 1/2 teaspoons wine vinegar
1 cup corn oil

Sift the dry ingredients together. Blend the liquid ingredients. Slowly add the dry into the wet ingredients while mixing with an electric hand mixer. Spoon out onto oiled cookie sheets. Bake at 350°F for 10 minutes.

Molasses Cookies 3

1 1/4 cups Sucanat
1/4 cup water
1 teaspoon white vinegar
1 cup nondairy margarine
1 3/4 cups Barbados molasses
3 cups unbleached white flour
2 teaspoons ground ginger
2 teaspoons cinnamon
1 teaspoon salt
1 tablespoon baking powder
1/2 teaspoon baking soda

Blend Sucanat, water, vinegar, margarine, and molasses together. Sift together all remaining ingredients. Combine blended and sifted ingredients, and mix together well. Roll into balls, each about 2 tablespoons. Place on greased cookie sheet. Bake at 350°F for about 10 minutes.

Monastery Shortbread

We serve this to every one of our visitors. Many have asked for the recipe, but we have kept it as a trade secret. Now I give it to you!

3 cups unbleached white flour
1/4 teaspoon sea salt
3/4 cup nondairy margarine
1/2 cup genuine maple syrup
1 teaspoon vanilla

Combine the flour and salt and set aside. Beat the margarine, syrup, and vanilla until smooth. Mix this into the flour, using your hands if necessary, until the dough is uniform and holds together. Pat into an oiled 9x13-inch pan. Bake at 350°F until the edges are lightly browned, 8 to 12 minutes. While still warm, cut into 2-inch squares. Cool completely in the pan and then remove.

Oatmeal Chewies

6 cups rolled oats
2 cups unbleached white flour
4 teaspoons soy flour
1 teaspoon baking soda
1/2 teaspoon sea salt
2 dashes cinnamon
2/3 cup corn oil
2/3 cup water
2 cups Barbados molasses
2 teaspoons vanilla
1 cup raisins

Sift the dry ingredients together. Add rest of ingredients and mix together. Place by 2 tablespoonfuls on an oiled cookie sheet. Bake at 375°F until light brown on the bottom.

Oatmeal-Raisin Cookies

If you missed these in childhood, then make up for it by eating plenty of them now.

3/4 cup nondairy margarine
3/4 cup Sucanat
1/4 cup Barbados molasses
2 teaspoons vanilla
1 1/2 cups unbleached white flour
1 teaspoon baking soda
1 1/2 cups rolled oats
1 cup raisins

Cream together the margarine, Sucanat, and molasses. Stir in vanilla. Separately, combine the flour and baking soda. Combine flour mixture and creamed mixture and blend thoroughly. Add oats and raisins and mix well. Drop by large spoonfuls onto greased cookie sheet. Bake at 375°F until done, 10 to 12 minutes.

Peanut Butter Cookies 1

I think that peanut butter cookies, not apple pie, have become the standard of Americanism. And these can set the standard.

1 1/4 cups unbleached white flour
3/4 teaspoon baking soda
1/4 teaspoon sea salt
1/2 cup nondairy margarine
1 cup Sucanat
1/2 cup peanut butter
1 N'egg (page 302)
1/2 teaspoon vanilla
1/2 teaspoon water
Powdered Sucanat (page 340)

Combine the flour, soda, and salt. Separately combine the margarine and Sucanat. Combine everything except Powdered Sucanat and mix thoroughly, adding more water if necessary to get a moist, but not sticky, consistency. Shape in 1-inch balls. Roll in Powdered Sucanat and place on a cookie sheet. Press on the tops of the balls in a crisscross pattern with a fork. Bake at 375°F for 15 minutes.

Peanut Butter Cookies 2

Although you may be able to eat just one, you cannot eat just two or three!

1 N'egg (page 302)
1 cup Sucanat
1 cup smooth peanut butter

Mix all together. Scoop out level tablespoonfuls and roll into balls. Put on an ungreased baking sheet and flatten with a fork. Bake at 350°F for 18 minutes. Cool on a wire rack.

Spicy Hermits

Not quickly forgotten!

1/2 cup nondairy margarine
1 1/2 cups Sucanat
1/4 cup Barbados molasses
1 N'egg (page 302)
1 1/2 cups unbleached white flour
1 tablespoon instant coffee powder
1/2 teaspoon baking soda
1/2 teaspoon cinnamon
1/4 teaspoon sea salt
1/4 teaspoon nutmeg
1/4 teaspoon cloves
3/4 cup raisins
1/2 cup walnuts, broken

Cream the margarine, Sucanat, molasses, and N'egg together. Sift the dry ingredients together and add to the creamed mixture. Stir in the raisins and nuts. Drop teaspoonfuls 2 inches apart on a lightly oiled cookie sheet. Bake at 375°F for 10 minutes. Makes about 3 1/2 dozen cookies.

Sucanat Health Cookies

1 1/2 cups Sucanat
1/2 cup corn oil
1 cup Cashew Milk (page 93)
2 N'eggs (page 302)
1 tablespoon vanilla
1 teaspoon almond extract
1/2 teaspoon sea salt
2 teaspoons cinnamon
2 cups rolled oats
1 1/2 cups unbleached white flour
2 teaspoons baking powder
1/2 cup sunflower seeds
1/2 cup almonds, chopped
1/2 cup walnuts or pecans, chopped
1 cup raisins

Combine the Sucanat, "milk," and N'eggs. Stir in the vanilla, almond extract, salt, and cinnamon. Add the oats, flour, baking powder, nuts, and raisins. Drop by tablespoons on a cookie sheet and flatten with fingers. Bake 12 to 15 minutes at 350°F.

Pies

Basic Pie Crust

The secret to this is that the margarine and water are as cold as possible.

6 cups unbleached white flour
1 tablespoon sea salt
1½ cups nondairy margarine, cold, and cut into bits
1 cup iced water

Sift the flour and salt together. Add the margarine and stir with a fork until all is crumbly. Add the water slowly while kneading until all holds together, then stop. Divide into balls. Roll out about ⅛ inch thick. Put in a pie pan or dish. Bake at 350°F for 35 minutes.

Convent Pie Crust

1½ cups unbleached white flour
⅛ teaspoon sea salt
2 tablespoons Sucanat
6 tablespoons nondairy margarine
½ teaspoon vanilla
3 to 4 tablespoons cold water

Put the flour, salt, and Sucanat in a food processor and process with the standard cutting blade for 1 minute. Add the margarine and process 30 more seconds. Add the vanilla and water through the tube and process until the dough forms into a ball. (If you do not have a processor, just combine the first three ingredients, cut in the margarine, add the vanilla and water, and stir to form a ball.) Wrap in waxed paper and chill at least 30 minutes. Roll out the dough and put into a 9-inch pie pan.

Note

For nonsweet dishes, omit the Sucanat and vanilla and increase the salt to ¼ teaspoon.

Graham Cracker Crust

1¼ cups ground Graham Crackers (page 60)
¼ cup Sucanat
¼ cup nondairy margarine
Pinch cinnamon
Pinch nutmeg

Combine all ingredients and press into a pie pan and bake at 375°F until browned, 6 to 8 minutes.

Graham Cracker–Walnut Crust

1½ cups very finely ground Graham Crackers (page 60)
1 cup walnuts, chopped
3 tablespoons nondairy margarine, softened

Mix everything together well and press into a pie pan.

Grape-Nuts Pie Crust

2 cups Grape-Nuts
1/3 cup apple juice concentrate, thawed
3 tablespoons water
1 teaspoon cinnamon
1 teaspoon grated dried lemon peel

Put the Grape-Nuts into a blender or food processor and process briefly until crushed, or put them in a plastic bag and crush with a rolling pin. Put everything in a bowl and combine thoroughly, adding more water if needed to make the mixture bind together. Press into a nonstick pie pan or dish.

Apple Pie

4 cups peeled, cored, and sliced apple
1 tablespoon water
3 cups Sucanat
2 tablespoons Barbados molasses
1/2 lemon rind, grated
1/4 teaspoon cinnamon
Basic Pie Crust (page 328), unbaked

Put apple, water, Sucanat, molasses, lemon rind, and cinnamon in a saucepan. Simmer 10 minutes, stirring occasionally. Do not allow the apples to become mushy. Cool. Line a 9-inch pie pan with dough. Fill with the apple mixture. Top with pie crust and seal edges well. Make a hole in the center of the top crust. Bake at 400°F until golden brown, about 25 minutes.

VARIATION: *For a "mincemeat" flavor, use ground cloves instead of cinnamon.*

Banana Kreem Pie

Luscious is the word for this!

4 cups Cashew Milk (page 93)
1 cup Sucanat
1/2 cup coconut
1/2 cup cornstarch
1/4 teaspoon sea salt
2 teaspoons vanilla
4 ripe bananas
Basic Pie Crust (page 328), baked
1 1/2 cups Soy Whipped Kreem (page 96) or Tofu Whipped Kreem (page 97)

Put the "milk," Sucanat, coconut, cornstarch, salt, and vanilla in a saucepan and stir constantly while cooking until thick. Remove from heat. Mash 2 bananas and add to mixture. Slice the other bananas and add. Pour into a baked pie crust and chill until set. Top with Whipped Kreem.

VARIATION: *Use Graham Cracker Crust (page 328).*

Berry Kreem Pie

Crust

1 1/2 cups ground Graham Crackers (page 60)
2 tablespoons Sucanat
1/4 cup almonds, ground to a meal in a blender
1 teaspoon cinnamon
1/2 teaspoon ground ginger
3 tablespoons oil

Glaze

1 cup apple juice or white grape juice
1 heaping tablespoon of agar flakes, or 1 1/2 tablespoons arrowroot powder dissolved in 1 1/2 tablespoons cold water

Filling

1 recipe Vanilla Pudding (page 313)
2 cups blueberries
1 1/2 cups sliced peaches or strawberries

For the crust, combine the cracker crumbs, Sucanat, almonds, cinnamon, and ginger in a medium-sized mixing bowl. Add the oil and mix well. Press the mixture onto the bottom and sides of an 8- or 9-inch pie pan. Bake at 375°F for 10 minutes. Cool before filling.

To make the glaze, pour the juice into a small saucepan and bring it to a simmer. If using agar, sprinkle the flakes over the juice without stirring and simmer gently 3 to 5 minutes, stirring if necessary to completely dissolve the agar. If using arrowroot, add the dissolved powder to the simmering juice while stirring briskly. Continue stirring until the mixture thickens, 1 to 2 minutes. Cool to lukewarm before using.

For the filling, allow the Vanilla Pudding to cool to lukewarm. Pour it into the prebaked crust. Cover with 1½ cups of the blueberries. Neatly arrange the sliced peaches or strawberries on top. Add the remaining ½ cup of blueberries. Spoon the glaze over the berries.

Blueberry Cobbler

2 cups fresh or canned blueberries
1½ cups Sucanat
1 cup unbleached white flour
1½ teaspoons baking powder
¼ teaspoon salt
1 N'egg (page 302)
1 cup Cashew Milk (page 93)
2 tablespoons nondairy margarine, melted

Place the berries in a buttered 9x9-inch baking pan. Sprinkle a little less than half the Sucanat over them evenly. In a bowl, mix together the flour, baking powder, and salt. Mix the rest of the Sucanat and the N'egg and stir it into the flour. Slowly add the "milk." Then add the melted margarine. Stir vigorously until it is smoothly blended. Pour this batter evenly over the berries. Bake at 400°F until the batter is golden brown, 30 to 35 minutes.

Blueberry Pie Filling

1¾ cups canned blueberries
⅓ cup Sucanat
¼ cup plus 2 tablespoons unbleached white flour
¾ teaspoon sea salt
¾ teaspoon cinnamon
¼ cup plus 2 tablespoons nondairy margarine

Drain berries and save liquid. Combine Sucanat, flour, salt, and cinnamon, and stir into the liquid saved from the berries. Heat, stirring constantly, until thick and smooth. Add margarine and berries.

Catherine Xenia's Pumpkin Pie Filling

Those who love pumpkin pie will love this even more!

Filling
One 16-ounce can pumpkin
1 cup plus 2 tablespoons Sucanat
¼ cup tapioca
1½ teaspoons cinnamon
½ teaspoon powdered ginger
¼ teaspoon ground cloves
½ teaspoon sea salt
1¾ cups Cashew Milk (page 93)
¼ cup genuine maple syrup

Convent Pie Crust (page 328)

Topping
¾ cup chopped walnuts
6 tablespoons Sucanat
3 tablespoons genuine maple syrup
2 tablespoons nondairy margarine, melted

For filling, mix pumpkin and the dry ingredients. Add the "milk" and syrup and heat. Pour into the pie shell. Bake at 400°F for 15 minutes. Turn down to 300°F and bake for 55 more minutes. Cover the edges of crust with foil after 35 minutes to prevent overbaking. Let the pie cool completely. Combine topping ingredients and spread over the top of the pie. Broil about 5 inches from the heat source until the topping is bubbly, about 3 minutes.

Cherry Cobbler

You won't be sorry.

4 cups cherries, pitted
2 tablespoons cornstarch
⅔ cup plus 2 tablespoons Sucanat
2 tablespoons lemon juice
¼ teaspoon almond extract
1 cup unbleached white flour
1 teaspoon baking powder
½ teaspoon sea salt
1 tablespoon water
6 tablespoons nondairy margarine, cold and cut into bits
¼ cup boiling water

Mix the cherries with the cornstarch, 2⁄3 cup Sucanat, lemon juice, and almond extract. Combine the flour, baking powder, salt, 2 tablespoons Sucanat, tablespoon of water, and margarine, blending them until all resembles coarse meal. Stir in the boiling water, stirring only until the batter is just combined. In an 8-inch skillet or baking dish bring the cherry mixture to a boil. Drop the batter by heaping tablespoons onto it. Bake at 350°F until the top is golden, 45 to 50 minutes.

Cherry Pie

1 1⁄3 cups liquid from canned cherries, or water if they are fresh
1⁄2 cup cornstarch
1 1⁄3 cups Sucanat
1⁄4 teaspoon sea salt
4 cups cherries, pitted
Convent Pie Crust (page 328)
2 tablespoons nondairy margarine

Mix some of the cherry liquid (or water) with the cornstarch. Heat rest of liquid to boiling. Add cornstarch mixture, stirring with a wire whisk. Cook until thick and clear. Stir in the Sucanat and salt. Bring to a boil, stirring. Remove from heat. Add cherries, mixing gently. Cool thoroughly. Put in unbaked pie shell. Dot the top with the margarine and put on the top crust, cutting ventilation slits in it. Bake at 425°F until well browned, about 1 hour.

Convent Caramel Apple Pie

Proof that you can always make a good thing better.

1⁄2 cup Sucanat
1⁄2 cup genuine maple syrup
2 tablespoons unbleached white flour
1 1⁄2 teaspoons lemon juice
1⁄2 teaspoon grated lemon peel
1⁄3 cup Cashew Milk (page 93)
1⁄2 teaspoon cinnamon
1⁄2 teaspoon vanilla
5 1⁄2 cups peeled and sliced apples, cut into about 16 slices per apple
Convent Pie Crust (page 328)

Combine all the filling ingredients except the apples, and stir to combine well. Add the apples and stir well again. Pour into the pie shell. Cover entire pie lightly with foil. Bake at 375°F until the apples are soft, about 1 hour. Remove the foil, bake to brown the crust, 10 to 15 more minutes. Take from the oven. Spoon the liquid that has settled at the bottom over the apples to coat them. Cool on a rack.

Fruit Pie 1

4 cups sliced fruit
1 1⁄2 cups Sucanat
3 tablespoons cornstarch
1⁄8 teaspoon sea salt
1⁄3 cup water for blending (only if needed)
2 tablespoons lemon juice (only if fruit is not naturally tart)
Basic Pie Crust (page 328)

Chop 1 cup of the fruit in medium-sized pieces. Blend the rest of the fruit with the Sucanat, cornstarch, salt, and water (if needed). Boil until thickened. Add the lemon juice, if needed. Cool slightly and mix in the chopped fruit. Pour into the baked pie crust and let cool.

Fruit Pie 2

4 cups sliced fruit
1 1⁄2 cups Sucanat
3 tablespoons cornstarch
1⁄8 teaspoon sea salt
1⁄3 cup water for blender (only if needed)
2 tablespoons lemon juice (only if fruit is not naturally tart)
Convent Pie Crust (page 328)

Set aside 3 cups of fruit. Chop and blend 1 cup of the fruit with the Sucanat, cornstarch, salt, and water (if needed). Add the 3 cups of sliced fruit to mixture. Boil until thickened. Add the lemon juice, if needed. Pour into unbaked pie crust. Cover with top crust and make slits to let out the steam. Bake at 400°F until brown, about 30 minutes.

Lemon Custard Pie

1 lemon, quartered, seeds removed
½ cup water
2 cups orange juice
1 tablespoon oil
1¼ cups Sucanat
¼ cup cornstarch
Basic Pie Crust (page 328)

Place the lemon in a blender, peel and all, with all the other ingredients and blend until it is finely ground. Place in a saucepan and bring to a boil. Simmer about 2 minutes, stirring constantly. Pour into baked pie shell and chill.

VARIATION: *Use 3 oranges, peeled and with seeds removed, instead of the orange juice. They should be blended until fine with the lemon.*

Peach Pie

4 cups sliced peaches
1 cup Sucanat
2 tablespoons unbleached white flour
⅛ teaspoon cinnamon
⅛ teaspoon sea salt
Convent Pie Crust (page 328)
2 tablespoons nondairy margarine

Combine the ingredients except for the margarine. Put in unbaked pie shell. Dot the top with the margarine and put on the top crust, making ventilation slits. Bake at 425°F until well browned, about 1 hour.

Pecan Pie

How I used to yearn for pecan pie, but since eggs seemed a necessary ingredient I had to keep on yearning! But now I can have all I want, and so can you!

¼ cup nondairy margarine, melted
¼ cup cornstarch or arrowroot
2 cups Cashew Milk (page 93)
½ cup genuine maple syrup
½ cup Sucanat
2 teaspoons vanilla
1 cup chopped pecans, toasted in 4 teaspoons margarine
½ cup pecan halves, toasted in 2 teaspoons margarine
Basic Pie Crust (page 328)

Combine the margarine, cornstarch (or arrowroot), "milk," syrup, Sucanat, and vanilla in a blender and blend until smooth. Cook in a saucepan until thickened, stirring constantly, about 5 minutes. Stir in the chopped pecans. Pour into the pie shell and top with the pecan halves. Let cool.

Pineapple Pie

2 cups crushed, unsweetened pineapple
⅓ cup cornstarch
1 teaspoon grated lemon or orange peel
¾ cup Sucanat
⅛ teaspoon salt
Basic Pie Crust (page 328)

Drain off the pineapple juice and mix the cornstarch into it. Combine all the ingredients and cook until thick. Pour into a baked pie crust.

Shoofly Pie

1 cup unbleached white flour
¾ cup Sucanat
1 teaspoon cinnamon
¼ teaspoon powdered ginger
¼ teaspoon ground cloves
¼ teaspoon sea salt
3 tablespoons nondairy margarine, softened and cut into bits
½ cup Barbados molasses
½ cup boiling water
½ teaspoon baking soda
Convent Pie Crust (page 328)

In a mixing bowl, combine flour, Sucanat, spices, and salt. With a fork, work the margarine into the dry ingredients until the mixture resembles a coarse meal. In another bowl, dissolve the molasses in the boiling water. Sprinkle in the baking soda and stir until it dissolves. Add about ⅔ of the crumb mixture and stir together until the crumbs are moistened (the mixture need not be smooth). Pour into the pie crust and top with the remaining crumbs. Bake at 375°F until the crust and crumbs are golden and the filling is set, 30 to 35 minutes. Serve warm or at room temperature.

Sister Mary Michael's Mincemeat Pie

Truly worth it!

1½ cups peeled, cored, and finely chopped Granny Smith apples
1 cup golden raisins, chopped
½ cup prunes, chopped
½ cup apple juice
¼ cup orange juice
3 tablespoons lemon juice
2 teaspoons grated lemon rind
2 teaspoons grated orange rind
1 cup Sucanat
½ teaspoon sea salt
1 teaspoon cinnamon
¼ teaspoon cloves
3 tablespoons unbleached white flour
½ teaspoon vanilla
Convent Pie Crust (page 328)

Combine all the other ingredients and put into pie shell. Cover the outer edges of the crust with foil. Bake at 350°F for 45 minutes. Remove the foil and bake 15 more minutes. Cool to room temperature before serving.

Note

If the lemon or orange peel is dyed, you should lightly shave off the outermost layer with a potato peeler before grating.

Strawberry Pie Filling

4 cups frozen strawberries
½ cup Sucanat
3 tablespoons unbleached white flour
½ teaspoon sea salt

Drain berries and save liquid. Combine the Sucanat, flour, and salt, and stir into the liquid. Heat, stirring constantly, until thick and smooth. Add berries.

Sweet Pastry

Cinnamon Rolls

Enjoy!

4 teaspoons cinnamon
½ cup Powdered Sucanat (page 340)
1 recipe Sweet Roll Dough (page 336)
½ cup nondairy margarine, melted
1 cup raisins or thick fruit jam
2 recipes Confectioner's Icing (see below)

Combine the cinnamon and Sucanat. Roll out the Sweet Roll Dough into an 8x14-inch rectangle. Brush with melted margarine. Sprinkle with cinnamon-Sucanat, and then the raisins or jam. Roll up like a jelly roll, starting at the wide end. Cut into 1-inch "slices." Place close together in an oiled pan and brush with melted margarine. Cover and let rise in a warm place until increased one-half in size. Bake at 375°F for 20 to 30 minutes. Let cool, then spread Confectioner's Icing over the rolls.

Confectioner's Icing

3 tablespoons water
1 teaspoon nondairy margarine
1⅔ cups Powdered Sucanat (page 340)
Pinch sea salt
1 teaspoon vanilla

Bring the water to a boil and immediately add the margarine, stirring. When the margarine is melted, add the Sucanat, salt, and vanilla. Stir until the Sucanat is melted. Add more boiling water drop by drop if necessary to produce a smooth, spreading consistency. Beat until very creamy, 2 or 3 minutes, scraping down the sides. Drizzle immediately on slightly warm baked goods.

VARIATION: *Add ⅓ cup of carob powder. Lemon or other fresh (strained) fruit juice may be substituted for the water and vanilla, if desired.*

Doughnut Squares

¼ cup lukewarm water
1 package dry yeast
¼ cup Sucanat
2 tablespoons nondairy margarine
½ teaspoon sea salt
½ cup boiling water
½ cup Cashew Kreem (page 93)
1 N'egg (page 302)
4½ cups unbleached white flour
Oil
Confectioner's Icing (see above)

Pour the water into a small bowl and sprinkle the yeast over it. Let it rest for 2 to 3 minutes, then mix well. Set in a warm, draft-free place until the yeast bubbles up and the mixture almost doubles in bulk, about 10 minutes.

Meanwhile combine the Sucanat, margarine, and salt in another bowl. Pour in the boiling water and stir with a wooden spoon until the ingredients are thoroughly blended and the mixture has cooled to lukewarm. Stir in the Kreem, yeast mixture, and N'egg. Add 2 cups of the flour and, when it is completely incorporated, beat in up to $2\frac{1}{2}$ more cups of flour, $\frac{1}{4}$ cup at a time. Add only enough flour to make the dough smooth but not sticky.

When the dough becomes too stiff to stir easily with the spoon, work in the additional flour with your fingers. Gather the dough into a ball, place it on a lightly floured surface, and pat it into a rectangle about 1 inch thick. Dust a little flour over and under the dough and roll it out from the center to within an inch of the edge of the dough. Lift the dough and turn it at right angles, rolling from the center as before.

Repeat the lifting, turning, and rolling until the rectangle is about $\frac{1}{4}$ inch thick and at least 25 inches long by 10 inches wide. (If the dough sticks to the surface, lift it with a wide metal spatula and sprinkle a little flour under it.)

With a pastry wheel or sharp knife, cut the dough into ten 5-inch squares. Immediately deep-fry them in 350°F oil, two or three at a time. Turn them over with a slotted spoon as they rise to the surface. Continue deep-frying, turning frequently, until they are crisp and golden brown on all sides, 3 to 5 minutes. Transfer to paper towel. When lukewarm, glaze with Confectioner's Icing.

Doughnuts

Make Sweet Roll Dough recipe (page 336). Roll out to $\frac{1}{2}$-inch thickness. Let rest 5 minutes. Dip a 3-inch doughnut cutter into flour and cut out doughnuts in dough. Let rise, uncovered, on floured pans in a warm place until light, about 45 minutes. Fry in deep-fryer at 370°F for about 3 minutes, turning once. (They should be golden brown on each side.) Drain on paper towels. Glaze with Confectioner's Icing (page 334).

Fruit Scones

2 cups unbleached white flour
3 teaspoons baking powder
Pinch of salt
6 tablespoons nondairy margarine
3 tablespoons Sucanat
$\frac{1}{2}$ cup golden seedless raisins, soaked in warm water for 30 minutes and drained
$\frac{1}{2}$ cup Cashew Milk (page 93)

Put flour, baking powder, and salt in a bowl. Rub in the margarine until mixture resembles fine crumbs. Stir in Sucanat and raisins, then add enough "milk" for a soft, manageable dough. Knead gently on a lightly floured surface, then roll out about $\frac{3}{4}$ inch thick. Cut out 3-inch rounds. Place fairly close together on a lightly greased baking sheet and bake at 425°F until golden brown, 10 to 15 minutes. Cool on a wire rack. Best to eat these the day they are made.

Jelly Filled Doughnuts

Follow Doughnuts recipe (see above), except cut into $2\frac{1}{2}$-inch rounds. After draining on paper towels, inject fruit filling. Glaze with Confectioner's Icing (page 334).

Raisin Dunkers

A treasure! We have relied on these through the years.

$2\frac{1}{3}$ cups unbleached white flour
$\frac{1}{4}$ cup Sucanat
1 tablespoon baking powder
1 teaspoon sea salt
$\frac{1}{4}$ teaspoon cinnamon
$\frac{1}{3}$ cup nondairy margarine
$\frac{3}{4}$ cup Cashew Milk (page 93)
$\frac{2}{3}$ cup raisins, chopped
1 cup nondairy margarine, melted
$\frac{3}{4}$ teaspoon cinnamon
$\frac{3}{4}$ cup Powdered Sucanat (page 340)

Sift the flour with the Sucanat, baking powder, salt, and cinnamon. Cut in the $\frac{1}{3}$ cup of margarine. Add the "milk" and raisins, stirring to a soft dough (add more Cashew Milk if necessary). Turn onto a lightly floured board. Roll out to ½-inch thickness. Cut into strips 2 inches wide and 5 inches long. Dip into the melted margarine and place on a baking sheet. Bake at 425°F until lightly browned, about 15 minutes. Mix the cinnamon and Powdered Sucanat together. Dip the strips again in melted margarine and roll in the cinnamon-Sucanat.

Raisin-Orange Coffee Cake

2 tablespoons plus 1 cup unbleached white flour
3 tablespoons plus ⅓ cup Sucanat
1 tablespoon nondairy margarine, softened
2 teaspoons baking powder
½ teaspoon sea salt
¼ cup nondairy margarine
2 teaspoons grated orange peel
⅓ cup orange juice
¼ cup Cashew Milk (page 93)
½ cup raisins

Mix together the 2 tablespoons flour, 3 tablespoons Sucanat, and 1 tablespoon softened margarine until crumbly and set aside for topping. Stir together the 1 cup of flour, baking powder, and salt, and set aside. In a small mixing bowl beat the margarine and ⅓ cup Sucanat until well combined. Add orange peel and beat well. Stir in orange juice, "milk," and raisins. Add flour mixture, stirring until just moistened. Spread batter evenly in a greased baking pan. Sprinkle with topping. Bake at 350°F until it tests done, about 25 minutes. Drizzle with a glaze made of Powdered Sucanat (page 340) and hot water.

Sweet Roll Dough

⅔ cup Cashew Milk (page 93)
Pinch sea salt
½ cup plus 1 teaspoon Sucanat
½ cup nondairy margarine
2 tablespoons yeast
¼ cup lukewarm water
1 N'egg (page 302)
4½ cups unbleached white flour
1 teaspoon grated lemon rind
½ teaspoon mace

Heat the "milk" with salt, ½ cup of Sucanat, and margarine until the margarine melts. Allow to cool to lukewarm. Combine yeast, water, and teaspoon of Sucanat, and allow to dissolve. Add the N'egg and the yeast mixture to the Cashew Milk solution. Combine half the flour with lemon rind and mace, then add the liquid, beating until smooth. Mix in the remaining flour. Let it stand for 10 minutes.

Knead for 5 minutes on a lightly floured board. Place dough in a lightly greased bowl, turning to coat. Cover with a damp cloth and let rise in a warm place until doubled in size. Punch down, turn over, cover, and let rise until double again. Punch down, shape into 2 balls on a lightly floured surface. Cover with a bowl and let rest 10 minutes. Dough is then ready for use in Doughnuts (page 335), Cinnamon Rolls (page 334), or other pastries.

Etc.

Baked Spring Rolls

2 ounces rice vermicelli
½ teaspoon sesame oil
¾ cup coarsely grated carrot
½ cup thinly sliced green onions
½ cup water chestnuts, cut into matchstick pieces
½ cup bamboo shoots, cut into matchstick pieces
½ cup snow peas, thinly sliced
½ cup savoy cabbage, very finely shredded
¼ cup sunflower seeds
1 tablespoon sesame seeds, toasted
1 teaspoon soy sauce
4 teaspoons corn oil
8 sheets rice paper (8½-inch diameter)

Cook the rice vermicelli in boiling water for 3 minutes, and drain. Place in a large bowl and toss with the sesame oil. Add the vegetables, sunflower seeds, sesame seeds, and soy sauce. Toss again and set aside. Place the oil in a small dish. Dip 1 sheet of the rice paper into warm water until soft, 15 to 30 seconds. Place on a dish towel. Brush the surface lightly with oil.

Spoon ⅛ of the filling onto the bottom half of the rice paper. Fold the bottom edge of the rice paper to just cover the filling. Brush the surface lightly with oil. Fold in the edges, then roll up, brushing the surfaces with oil as you roll. Repeat with the remaining rice paper sheets and filling. Place each roll seam-side down on a foil-lined cookie sheet. Bake at 450°F on the lowest oven rack, turning once, until lightly browned, 15 to 20 minutes.

Bread Crumb Topping

2 cups bread crumbs
1½ teaspoons minced garlic
2 tablespoons chopped fresh parsley
2 tablespoons corn oil
Freshly ground black pepper
Tomato puree or paste

Toss the crumbs, garlic, parsley, oil, and pepper together in a bowl. Mix in just enough tomato purée or paste to add a touch of color.

Breading Food for Frying

The breading material may be cracker crumbs, bread crumbs, cornmeal, or any "crunchy" form of grain. They may be used plain or combined with seasonings. Roll the food to be breaded in the crumbs, then dip it in N'egg (page 302) or "milk" (see Dairy Substitutes chapter), and again roll it in the crumbs. To avoid sticky hands, bread with one hand and dip with the other. If breading is done half an hour before the food is fried, the crumbs will adhere better. It is important to cover the entire surface of the food with N'egg or "milk" before the second "crumbing."

Carob Fudge

How sweet it really is!

3 tablespoons nondairy margarine
½ cup carob powder
¼ cup Powdered Sucanat (page 340)
⅔ cup ground almonds
1 teaspoon vanilla extract
3 tablespoons almonds, ground or finely chopped

Blend margarine and carob powder thoroughly. Add the Sucanat, ⅔ cup ground almonds, and vanilla, and mix thoroughly. Sprinkle ground almonds onto a clean, dry surface and shape the fudge into a roll, coating it with almonds. Cut into bite-size pieces. Keep in refrigerator until needed.

Cinnamon Toast

Mix one part cinnamon with three parts of Powdered Sucanat (page 340). Sprinkle on buttered toast. Place toast slices in a moderate oven or under a broiler to crisp them.

VARIATION: *Instead of one part cinnamon, use half nutmeg and half cinnamon.*

Coconut Milk

Break the coconut shell and remove the meat. Pare off the brown skin. Chop or break the meat into small chunks. Measure the meat and put it and an equal measure of hot (not boiling) water into a blender and blend at high speed for 1 minute. Stop the machine and scrape down the sides with a rubber spatula. Blend again until the coconut is reduced to a thick, fibrous liquid.

Scrape the entire contents of the blender into a fine sieve lined with a double thickness of dampened cheesecloth and set over a deep bowl. With a wooden spoon, press down hard on the coconut to extract as much liquid as possible. Bring the ends of the cheesecloth together to enclose the pulp and wring the ends vigorously to squeeze out the remaining liquid. Discard the pulp.

Deep-Frying Batter

This is excellent for frying gluten, but works for vegetables, too.

1 teaspoon powdered basil
1 teaspoon freshly ground black pepper
½ teaspoon garlic salt
3 cups unbleached white flour
2 tablespoons baking powder
2 to 3 cups club soda

Combine the basil, pepper, garlic salt, flour, and baking powder. Add the soda until you have a batter of the desired consistency. Dip whatever you wish to fry into the batter and then deep-fry at 400°F.

French Toast

1½ cups water
3 tablespoons soy flour
1 tablespoon cornstarch
1 tablespoon Sucanat
¼ teaspoon vanilla
Pinch sea salt
Pinch cinnamon
2 tablespoons nondairy margarine, melted
¼ teaspoon turmeric

Blend everything in a blender until perfectly combined and smooth. Heat together until it thickens into a "batter." Soak bread slices in the batter and then fry to golden brown on both sides.

Fried Cheez Balls

1 cup Biscuit Mix (page 50)
⅓ cup water
1½ cups Yeast Cheez (page 97) or Pimiento Cheez (page 94)
⅓ cup chopped onion
Oil

Mix everything together, form into 1-inch balls, and fry in oil.

Fruit Jam

3/4 cup plus 2 tablespoons cornstarch
6 cups Sucanat
6 cups fruit, mashed well

Mix the cornstarch with the Sucanat, and add to the fruit. Cook for 20 minutes. Allow to cool, and can or refrigerate.

Garlic Bread

1/2 cup nondairy margarine
1 tablespoon pressed garlic
1/4 cup Parmesan Cheez (page 94)
1/8 teaspoon freshly ground black pepper
Bread

Melt the margarine, add the garlic, and let it "steep" at very low heat for 2 minutes. Mix in the Cheez and pepper, and stir well. Spread generously on bread and toast it in the oven.

Garlic Olives

The taste only improves with age.

2/3 cup olive oil
1/3 cup lemon juice or vinegar
1 tablespoon minced garlic
1 1/4 cups ripe olives

Combine everything and refrigerate overnight or at least for several hours. Use whenever ripe olives are called for.

Hot Cheez and Cider Dip

Now this is really different!

1/2 cup apple cider
1 cup Yeast Cheez (page 97) or Pimiento Cheez (page 94)
1/2 teaspoon sea salt
1/8 teaspoon cayenne pepper
1/4 teaspoon finely chopped fresh parsley or chives
Pinch garlic salt

Heat the cider to the boiling point, then reduce to a simmer. Stir the Cheez gradually into the cider until all is well blended. Add the seasonings.

Instant Tomato Juice

1 cup tomato paste
4 cups water
1 teaspoon sea salt

Mix together thoroughly. You can put it through a blender, but will have to wait until the bubbles and froth subside.

Note

For a tomato juice cocktail, add pepper (or hot sauce), garlic powder, and a little lemon juice to this.

Instant Tomato Puree

1 cup tomato paste
1 cup water
1 teaspoon sea salt

Mix together thoroughly. You can put it through a blender, but will have to wait until the bubbles and froth subside.

Instant Tomato Sauce

1 cup tomato paste
2 cups water
1 teaspoon sea salt

Mix together thoroughly. You can put it through a blender, but will have to wait until the bubbles and froth subside.

"Maple" Syrup

2 cups Sucanat
1 cup water
1/2 teaspoon cream of tartar
1/2 teaspoon maple flavoring

Boil the Sucanat, water, and cream of tartar for 3 minutes. Remove from heat and add maple flavoring.

Mulled Cider

1 quart cider
3 whole cloves
3 whole allspice
One 3-inch cinnamon stick
1/4 lemon, unpeeled, thinly sliced
1/4 cup Sucanat

Boil together for 10 minutes. Strain and serve hot.

Orange-Grape Juice

Combine equal parts of white grape juice and orange juice.

Pancake Syrup 1

1 cup water
2 cups Sucanat
1 1/2 teaspoons maple flavoring

Combine all ingredients, bring to a boil, and immediately take off the heat and set to cool.

Pancake Syrup 2

1 cup Barbados molasses
2 cups Sucanat
1/2 cup water
1 1/2 teaspoons maple flavoring

Combine all ingredients, bring to a boil, and immediately take off the heat and set to cool.

Pancakes 1

2 cups Biscuit Mix (page 50)
1 cup Cashew Milk (page 93) or water
2 N'eggs (page 302)

Beat the ingredients until smooth and pour by scant 1/4 cupfuls onto a hot griddle (oiled if necessary). Cook until the edges are dry, then turn over and cook until golden brown.

Pancakes 2

1 1/4 cups flour
2 tablespoons Sucanat
2 teaspoons baking powder
1/2 teaspoon sea salt
2 tablespoons corn oil
1 1/4 cups water, or 1/2 cup Cashew Milk (page 93) plus 3/4 cup water

Combine the dry ingredients, creating a "well" in the center. Pour the liquids into the well. Stir together until just blended, the batter will be lumpy. (Do not overmix.) Cook on oiled griddle or skillet.

Party Cheez Dip

2 cups Tofu Kreem Cheez (page 96)
1 cup Pimiento Cheez (page 94) or Notzarella Cheez (page 94)
1 tablespoon chopped pimiento
1 tablespoon chopped bell pepper
1 tablespoon finely chopped onion
1 tablespoon lemon juice
4 teaspoons Lea and Perrins Steak Sauce
2 tablespoons Louisiana Hot Sauce
1/8 teaspoon sea salt

Combine all and let sit for a while to develop flavor.

Pecan Patties

1 cup pecans, ground to a cornmeal-like consistency
1 cup rice, cooked
1 cup Cashew Milk (page 93)
1 tablespoon soy flour
1 teaspoon sea salt
1 tablespoon dried parsley flakes
1 cup bread crumbs
1 tablespoon dried minced onion
1/4 teaspoon garlic powder

Combine all ingredients and shape into patties. Place on an oiled cookie sheet. Brush the tops with corn oil. Bake at 350°F until brown, about 30 minutes.

Powdered Sucanat

1/2 cup Sucanat
2 tablespoons cornstarch

Combine and process into a powder at high speed in a blender.

Self-Rising Flour

1 cup unbleached white flour with 2 teaspoons taken out
1½ teaspoons baking powder
½ teaspoon sea salt

Combine well.

Spicy Tomato Juice

7 cups tomato juice, made from fresh tomatoes
1 teaspoon sea salt
⅛ teaspoon cayenne pepper

Simmer together for 15 minutes. Cool and refrigerate.

UnShrimp Dip

Don't dilute the soup—use it directly from the can.

1 can Campbell's Tomato Soup
½ cup catsup
4 teaspoons Louisiana Hot Sauce, or 2 teaspoons Tabasco sauce
½ teaspoon onion juice
¼ teaspoon garlic salt
½ teaspoon minced celery
Dash paprika
Dash cayenne pepper
1 tablespoon nondairy margarine

Combine everything except the margarine, and beat together well. Chill. Just before serving, blend in the margarine until the mixture becomes smooth.

Uncooked Applesauce

This is a wonderful surprise! Having tried it, you will never want the canned goop.

8 cups peeled, cored, and quartered Granny Smith apples
2 tablespoons lemon juice
1 cup Sucanat
½ teaspoon cinnamon
⅛ teaspoon nutmeg

Puree the apples in a blender until just smooth. Add rest of ingredients, mix well, and chill.

Vegetarian Dog Food

This was formulated by a veterinarian for his dogs, and we have raised several healthy dogs using it as their basic food. However, you should read Dogs and Cats Go Vegetarian, *by Barbara Lynn Peden, for a full picture on vegetarian dogs and cats and their nutritional requirements.*

1 gallon leftover vegetables, including peels, ends, etc. (see note)
Water to cover
2 tablespoons baking yeast
4 cups soybeans
6 cups rolled oats

If you don't have any vegetable scraps, or not enough to make 1 gallon, just put in what extra vegetables you may have to make up the amount. If need be, cut the vegetables into chunks. The night before you are going to make the dog food, put the soybeans in water and let them soak overnight. The next day grind them in either a food mill or a blender. (If there is any corn among the vegetables, that should be ground, as well.) When ready to cook, put the vegetables, soybeans, and yeast in a large pot and cover with water. Bring to a boil and simmer for about 2 hours. Add the rolled oats and cook until they are done.

> ***Note***
>
> Save the peels, ends, etc., from vegetables when you prepare your food, and keep them refrigerated, uncooked.

Waffles

2 cups Biscuit Mix (page 50)
1½ cups Cashew Milk (page 93)
1 N'egg (page 302)

Beat the ingredients until smooth. Pour onto center of hot waffle iron. Bake until steaming stops. Remove carefully.

Index

A

Abbot George's Low-Calorie Soup, 61
Alfalfa Sprout Dressing, 10
All-Purpose N'egg, 302
All-Purpose Seasoning, 303
Almond Dressing, 10
Almond Milk, 93
Almost Instant Vegetable Soup (1, 2), 61
Anadama Bread, 49
Anandamayi, 159
Anne Goldstein's Caponata, 290
Anne Goldstein's Corn Relish, 290–91
Anne Goldstein's Marinated Mushrooms, 290
Anne Goldstein's Tabouli, 26
Apple
- about, 3
- and banana bread, 49
- butter, 298
- cakes, 322
- crisp, 305
- filling (1, 2), 288–89
- icing bread, 49–50
- pie, 329
- squares, 305–6

Applesauce, uncooked, 341
Apulian-Style Baked Potatoes, Onions, and Tomatoes, 192
Aunt Lou Maxey's Tomato Relish, 291
Aunt May's Pepper Relish, 291
Austrian Potato Salad, 42
Avocado
- -cashew dressing, 10
- dressing (1, 2, 3, 4, 5, 6), 10–11
- mayonnaise, 11
- -olive dressing, 11
- salad (1, 2), 26
- and tomato soup, 62

B

Baked Bean Soup, 62
Baked Beans (1, 2), 229
Baked Cubed Gluten, 104
Baked Cubed UnBeef Casserole, 192–93
Baked Curry, 193
Baked Gluten, 100
Baked Lentils, 230
Baked Macaroni with Tomatoes, 267
Baked Mashed Potatoes, 160
Baked Pasta with UnBeef, 267
Baked Potato, 180
Baked Spring Rolls, 337
Baked UnHam, 130
Baking Powder Biscuits, 50
Banana Kreem Pie, 329
Banana N'Ice Kreem, 314
Banana Pudding, 306
Barbecue
- baked beans, 230
- bean salad, 26
- bean sandwich spread, 298
- beans, 230
- burgers, 118
- filling (1, 2), 284–85
- gluten, 104
- sauce (1, 2), 256
- "spare ribs", 123, 124
- "spare ribs" sauce, 123
- UnBeef, 109

Barley, 242
Basic Gluten, 99–100
Basic N'egg Pasta, 266
Basic Pasta, 266
Basic Pie Crust, 328
Basic Rice, 242
Basic Semolina Pasta, 266
Basque Vegetable Soup, 62
Batter, deep-frying, 338
Bean. *See also* Black Bean recipes; Dried Beans
- Bourgignonne, 232
- burgers (1, 2, 3), 118–19
- enchiladas, 231
- green lima, with Fine Herbes, 172
- lima, 174
- lima, and garbanzo salad, 34
- lima, and tomatoes, 174
- lima, -corn succotash, 175
- lima, gazpacho salad, 34
- lima, in Cheez sauce, 174
- lima, in piquante sauce, 174
- lima, salad (1, 2), 34
- lima, soup, 76
- lima, with Cheez, 174–75, 209
- loaf, 231
- pot (1, 2), 231–32
- and potato loaf, 230–31

Bean, *continued*
salad, 26
sandwich spread, 298
sprout salad (1, 2), 26
and tortillas, 232
Berry Kreem Pie, 329–30
Biscuit(s), 50
baking powder, 50
drop, 52
dumplings, 50
yeast (1, 2), 58
Bitters Dressing, 12
Black Bean and Spinach Soup, 62
Black Bean Chili (1, 2), 90
Black Bean Soup (1, 2, 3), 62–63
Black Beans with Tomatoes, 232
Blender Pizza Sauce, 278
Blueberry Cheez Cake, 306
Blueberry Cobbler, 330
Blueberry Filling, 289
Blueberry Pie Filling, 330
Boiled Cabbage, 160
Boiled Cabbage Dinner, 160
Boiled Okra, 160
Boiled Potatoes, 180
Borscht (1, 2), 63
Braised UnChicken and "Chorizo", 137
Bread(s). *See also* Biscuits
Anadama, 49
apple and banana, 49
apple icing, 49–50
balls, fried Cheez, 53
breadsticks, 50–51
buns, hamburger, 54
buns, whole wheat, 58
and butter zucchini, 291
cakes, fried cornmeal, 53
Cheez, 51
and Cheez pudding, 193
chips, corn, 51–52
corn (1, 2, 3), 51
Cinnamon Toast, 338
cranberry, 52
croutons, garlic, 54
crumbs, "buttered," 51
crumb topping, 337
dressing, 193
flat, 52
French, 53
French Toast, 338
garlic, 54, 339
herb, 54
herb and onion, 54
hush puppies, 54
Mexican, 54
Mexican corn, 54–55
muffins, sweet, 57
oatcakes, 55
onion, 55
pocket, 55–56
pumpernickel, 56
puris, 56
raisin, 57
"sourdough," 57
soy, 57
toast points, 57
tortillas, corn, 52
tortillas, flour, 52–53
white, 57
whole wheat, 57
whole wheat, one-hour, 55
Breading food for frying, 337
Breadsticks, 50–51
Breakfast UnSausage, 132
Broccoli, 160
bean, and spaghetti soup, 63–64
casserole, 194
and Cheez filling, 285
and corn scallop, 193–94
curried, 165
divan, 161
-mushroom filling, 285
with mushrooms and tomatoes, 161
and potato casserole with chives and Cheez, 194
risotto, 242
salad, potato, and garbanzo, and, 27
Broiled UnShrimp, 150–51
Broths, 155–58
about, 157
heavenly, 158
UnBeef, 155
UnChicken, 155
UnFish, 155
UnHam, 156
UnPork, 156
UnSausage, 156
Brown Gravy, 253
Brown Sauce, 256
Browned Potatoes, 161
Buckaroo Beans, 233
Budapest Bean Soup, 64
Burgers
barbecue, 118
bean (1, 2, 3), 118–19
buns, hamburger, 54
eggplant, 119
garbanzo, 119
gluten, 119–20
oat, 120
oat, with mushrooms, 120
soyburgers, 120
sunburgers, 120–21
supreme, 119
tofu-pepper, 121
UnBeef and zucchini, 121
vegeburgers, 121
vegetable, 121
"Buttered" Bread Crumbs, 51
"Butter" Sauce with Herbs, 256–57
Butterscotch Shortbread, 322

C

Cabbage
boiled, 160
boiled, dinner, 160
borscht, 65
and Cheez soup (1, 2), 64
goulash, 161
and lima bean salad, 27
and pepper salad, 27
pineapple salad, 27
and potato soup, 64
scalloped, 184
slaw (1, 2), 27
soup (1, 2), 65
sweet-and-Sour, 187
tomatoes, and Cheez, 161, 194
and tomato soup, 65
Un-Rolls casserole, 195
Cajun Catsup, 257, 291–92
Cajun Cole Slaw, 28
Cajun Eggplant, 195
Cajun Peas or Fresh Beans, 162
Cajun Potato Salad, 42

Cajun UnBeef Gravy, 253
Cajun UnChicken Bake, 137–38
Cajun UnSausage, 132
Cakes, 316–21. *See also* Desserts
  apple, Devon, 317
  carob, 316
  crazy, 317
  date-nut, 317
  fruitcake (1, 2), 317–18
  fruitcake, Christmas, 316
  fruitcake, Mexican, 318
  fruitcake, uncooked, 320
  gingerbread, 318
  gingercake, orange, 319
  lemon, 318
  molasses, 319
  pudding, cottage, 316–17
  shortcake, 319
  syrup, 320
  upside-down, pineapple, 319
  vanilla (1, 2), 320
  velvet crumb, 321
Calsoup, 65
Calzone, 267
Campfire Red Beans, 233
Canadian Shortbread, 322
Caper French Dressing, 12
Caponata, 292
Caponata, Anne Goldstein's, 290
Caraway Dressing, 12
Carob Cake, 316
Carob Chip Cookies, 322–23
Carob Custard, 306
Carob Fudge, 338
Carob Pudding, 306
Carrot
  creamed, 164
  dressing, 12
  hot herbed, 293
  mashed, 175
  and peas, 162
  roast, 195–96
  soup, 66
Cashew Buttermilk, 93
Cashew Cheez Dressing, 12
Cashew Kreem, 93
Cashew Mayonnaise, 12
Cashew Milk, 93
Cashew Sour Kreem, 94
Cashew Yogurt, 94
Casseroles, 192–227
  beans, lima, casserole, Mexican, 210
  beans, lima, with Cheez, 209
  bread, corn, dressing, 194
  bread and Cheez pudding, 193
  bread dressing, 193
  broccoli, 194
  broccoli, creamed, 201
  broccoli, scalloped (1, 2), 216
  broccoli and corn scallop, 193–94
  broccoli and potato with chives and Cheez, 194
  cabbage, creamed, 201
  cabbage, scalloped, 216
  cabbage, tomatoes, and Cheez, 194
  cabbage Un-Rolls, 195
  carrot roast, 195–96
  carrots and potatoes, scalloped, 216–17
  cauliflower au gratin, 196
  cauliflower bake, 196
  Cheez and potato bake, 196
  Cheez enchilada, 196–97
  Cheez enchiladas (1, 2), 197
  Cheez loaf, pimiento, 212
  Cheez pie, 198
  Cheezy onion, 198
  chili-Cheez bake, 198
  company, 198
  corn, green chili, 207
  corn, scalloped, 217
  corn and lima stew, 198–99
  corn and spinach, 199
  corn and tomato, fresh, 204
  corn bake, 199
  corn-bean pie, 200
  corn chip, 199–200
  corn tamale pie, 200
  country, 200
  curry, baked, 193
  eggplant, Cajun, 195
  eggplant, Italian, 208
  eggplant, scalloped, 217
  eggplant, with tomatoes, garlic, and rice, 202–3
  eggplant and Cheez, 202
  eggplant lasagna, 203
  eggplant Parmesan (1, 2), 203–4
  gluten and cabbage, 205
  gluten and corn, 205
  gluten and eggplant, 205
  gluten and rice, 205–6
  gluten-vegetable, 206
  "goose," English wartime, 204
  green bean, 206
  green beans in tomato sauce, 206–7
  green beans supreme (1, 2), 207
  lasagna, Mexican, 210
  layered, 209
  mushroom and artichoke Pie, 210
  mushroom and bell pepper quiche, 210–11
  noodle, with zucchini, tomatoes, and Cheez, 211
  onions in tomato sauce, 211
  paella-limas, 211
  peas and squash, scalloped, 217
  piffel, 212
  piffel, cream of, 212
  polenta, 212
  potato and onion, curried, 202
  potato and tomato gratin, 213
  potato-broccoli, 213
  potato-Cheez bake, 213
  potatoes, crunch-top, 202
  potatoes and carrots au gratin, 214
  potatoes and mushrooms, scalloped, 218
  potatoes and spinach, scalloped, 218
  potatoes au gratin, 214
  potatoes, onions, and tomatoes, baked, Apulian-Style, 192
  potatoes, potluck, 214–15
  potatoes, scalloped (1, 2, 3), 217–18
  potatoes scalloped in margarine, 214
  potatoes, spicy, 220
  potatoes with Cheez, creamed, 201
  potato gratin, 213

Casseroles, *continued*
potato stuffing, 214
ratatouille, 215
rice, Creole, 202
rice dressing, 215
Rumbledethumps, 215
sauerkraut, 216
shepherd's pie (1, 2), 218–19
simple garden, 219
soy grits, 219
soy grits enchilada, 219–20
spinach, mushrooms, and onions in Cheez sauce, creamed, 201
spinach and herb potato, 220
squash, Genoese, 204–5
squash, with tomatoes, Cheez, and rice, 221
squash and macaroni Bake, 220
squash bake, 220–21
squash Creole, 221
squash tamale bake, 221
tamale pie, 221
tomato and corn scallop, 222
tomato eggplant bake, 222
tomato rice with Cheez, 222
triple layer, 222
UnBacon and Cheez potatoes, 222–23
UnBeef, baked cubed, 192–93
UnChicken salad, hot, 208
UnHam and broccoli, 223
UnHam and potato, 223
UnHam and potatoes au gratin, 223
UnSausage, dressing, Italian, 208
UnSausage, Italian, pasta, and bean, 209
vegetable, bake, golden, 206
vegetable, harvest, 208
vegetable, with tomatoes and rice, 223–24
vegetable crumble, 224
vegetable enchiladas, 224
vegetable pot pie, 224
vegetables, leftover with Cheez, 209
vegetables and Cheez, 225
vegetables Parmesan (1, 2), 225
zucchini (1, 2), 225–26
zucchini, with tomatoes, Cheez, and rice, 226
zucchini Creole, 226
zucchini parmigiana, 227
Catherine Xenia's Pumpkin Pie Filling, 330
Catsup, 257
Catsup, Cajun, 291–92
Cauliflower au Gratin, 196
Cauliflower Bake, 196
Cheese substitutes, about, 3
Cheez
balls, fried, 338
bread, 51
and cider dip, 339
crackers, 59
dip, party, 340
enchilada casserole, 196–97
enchiladas (1, 2), 197
and onion filling, 285
and onion sauce, 258
and onion soup, 66
-only pizza, 278
pie, 198
and potato bake, 196
rice, 243
sauce (1, 2, 3, 4), 257–58
soup (1, 2), 66
spread (1, 2), 298
toast, 299
Cheezcake, 306
Cheezy Onion Casserole, 198
Chef's Bean Salad, 28
Cherry Cobbler, 307, 330–31
Cherry Filling, 289
Cherry Pie, 331
Chickaritos, 138
Chili, 90–91
beans (1, 2), 233
black bean (1, 2), 90
-Cheez bake, 198
corn and zucchini, 162
countryside, 91
Denver, 92
half-hour, 92
-Mac, 267
macho, 292
pinto bean, 92
potato soup, 66
sauce, 258
supreme, 91
UnChicken, 92
UnPork Chop Casserole, 123
with mushrooms, 91
Chilipetin Sauce, 292
Chilled Tomato and Bell Pepper Soup, 66–67
Chimichangas, 109–10, 233
Chinese Pepper UnSteak, 110
Chinese UnPork with Water Chestnuts and Mushrooms, 125
Chive Dressing, 12
Christmas Fruitcake, 316
Chutney, Jalapeño and bell pepper, 294
Cider, 16, 339, 340
dip, hot Cheez and, 339
dressing, hot Cheez and, 16
mulled, 340
Cinnamon Rolls, 334
Cinnamon Toast, 338
Cocktail Sauce (1, 2), 258
Coconut
cookies, 323
crackers, 59
milk, 338
N'Ice Kreem, 314
rice pudding, 307
Cold Kreem of Squash Soup, 67
Cold Kreem of Tomato Soup, 67
Cold-As-A-Cucumber Soup, 68
Colonial Green Beans, 162
Colossal Cookies, 323
Company Casserole, 198
Company Pride Hash, 110
Confectioner's Icing, 334
Continental Stroganoff, 110
Convent Caramel Apple Pie, 331
Convent Pie Crust, 328
Cookies, 322–27
apple cakes, 322
apple-date bits, frosted, 324
bars, fig, 324
bars, fruit, 324
butterscotch shortbread, 322
Canadian shortbread, 322
carob chip, 322–23
coconut, 323

colossal, 323
crunchies, 323
ginger snaps, 324–25
ginger snaps, fiery, 323–24
gingernuts, 325
hermits, spicy, 327
maple nut chews, 325
molasses (1, 2, 3), 325–26
monastery shortbread, 326
oatmeal chewies, 326
oatmeal-raisin, 326
peanut butter (1, 2), 327
Sucanat health, 327
Coponatini Eggplant, 162
Copper Pennies, 162–63
Corn
à la king, 163
bake, 199
-bean pie, 200
bread (1, 2, 3), 51
bread, Mexican, 54–55
bread dressing, 194
chili, and zucchini, 162
Chip Casserole, 199–200
Chips, 51–52
Chowder (1, 2), 68
Chowder Deluxe, 69
country, 163
country, and okra, 163
country, Creole (1, 2), 164
cream-style, 164
green chili, casserole, 207
and Lima Stew Casserole, 198–99
Louisiana, and tomatoes, 175
and Peppers, 163
and Potato Chowder (1, 2), 68
relish, Anne Goldstein's, 290–91
Rice, and Bean Salad, 29
salad (1, 2), 28
salad, Mexican, 35
salad, Mexican bean and, 35
scalloped, 217
soup, 69
soup, Kreem of, 74
special, 163
and spinach casserole, 199
squash, beans, and, 186
tamale pie, 200
and tomato casserole, 204
and tomato chowder, 68
tortillas, 52
Cottage Cheez Salad (1, 2), 29
Cottage Mashed Potatoes, 163
Cottage Pudding, 316–17
Country Casserole, 200
Country Corn, 163
Country Corn and Okra, 163
Country Corn Creole (1, 2), 164
Country Rice Salad, 29
Countryside Chili, 91
Couscous Salad, 30
Cowboy Beans, 234
Cracked Wheat, 243
Crackers, 59
Crackers, 59–60
Cheez, 59
coconut, 59
crackers, 59
graham, 60
rye crisps, 60
Cranberry Bread, 52
Crazy Cake, 317
Cream of Piffel, 212
Cream-Style Corn, 164
Creamed Broccoli, 201
Creamed Cabbage Casserole, 201
Creamed Carrots, 164
Creamed Green Peas, 164
Creamed Lentil-Celery Soup, 69
Creamed Potatoes, 164
Creamed Potatoes with Cheez, 201
Creamed Spinach, Mushrooms, and Onions in Cheez Sauce, 201
Creamed UnChicken with Mushrooms and Herbs, 138
Creamy Onion Soup, 69
Creamy Potatoes and Peas, 165
Creole Okra, 165
Creole Rice, 243
Creole Rice Casserole, 202
Creole Sauce, 258
Creole Soup, 70
Creole Spaghetti, 268
Creole Tomatoes, 165
Crunchies, 323
Crunch-Top Potatoes, 202
Crunchy Kreem Dressing, 13
Cucumber Dressing, 13
Cucumber Salad (1, 2), 29–30
Curried Broccoli, 165
Curried Green Beans, 165–66
Curried Mushroom Soup, 70
Curried Peas, 166
Curried Peas, Carrots, and Potatoes, 166
Curried Potato and Onion Casserole, 202
Curried Potatoes and Peas, 166
Curried Split Pea Soup, 70
Curry Mayonnaise, 13
Curry Stew, 70–71

Dairy substitutes
about, 93
almond milk, 93
cashew buttermilk, 93
cashew Kreem, 93
cashew milk, 93
cashew sour Kreem, 94
cashew yogurt, 94
coconut milk, 338
notzarella Cheez, 94
parmesan Cheez (1, 2), 94
pimiento Cheez (1, 2), 94–95
pizza Cheez, 95
rice Kreem, 95
rice milk, 95
soy milk, 96
soy milk basic, 96
soy whipped Kreem, 96
tofu buttermilk, 96
tofu cottage Cheez, 96
tofu Kreem Cheez (1, 2), 96
tofu ricotta Cheez, 96
tofu sour Kreem, 97
tofu whipped Kreem, 97
tofu yogurt, 97
yeast Cheez, 97
Dal Filling, 286
Dal Soup, 71
Date and Apple Squares, 307
Date-Nut Cake, 317
Deep-Fried Okra, 166–67

Deep-Fried Squash, 167
Deep-Fried UnFish, 149
Deep-Frying Batter, 338
Delicious Lasagna, 268
Denver Chili, 92
Desserts. *See also* Cakes; Pies; Sweet pastry dishes
apple crisp, 305
apple squares, 305–6
banana pudding, 306
blueberry Cheez cake, 306
bread pudding, spiced, 312
carob custard, 306
carob fudge, 338
carob pudding, 306
Cheezcake, 306
cherry cobbler, 307
coconut rice pudding, 307
date and apple squares, 307
French silk pie, 307–8
fruit and almond Kreem tart, 308
fruit cocktail bread pudding, 309
fruit shortcake, 309
fruit squares, 309–10
fruit terrine, summer, 312–13
lemon Cheezcake, 310
lemon Cheezcake deluxe, 310
lemon custard, 310
maple pecan Cheezcake, 311
pears in "custard", 311
pears in mustard syrup, 311
pineapple pudding, 311
raisin pudding, steamed Irish, 312
vanilla pudding (1, 2), 313
Devon Apple Cake, 317
Dieter's Broth, 71
Dill Dressing, 13
Dill Pickles, 292
Dilled Cucumbers, 30
Dilled Green Beans, 293
Dilled Potato Salad, 42–43
Dip(s)
guacamole (1, 2, 3, 4, 5), 32
hot Cheez and cider, 339
party Cheez, 340
UnShrimp, 341
Dirty Rice, 243
Dog food, vegetarian, 341
Dogs and Cats Go Vegetarian, 341
Doughnut Squares, 334–35
Doughnuts, 335
Dressing. *See* Salad dressing
Dried beans, 228–41
about, 228
baked (1, 2), 229
baked, Boston style, 230
baked lentils, 230
barbecue, 230
barbecue baked, 230
Bean Enchiladas, 231
bean and potato loaf, 230–31
bean loaf, 231
bean pot (1, 2), 231–32
black beans with tomatoes, 232
Bourgignonne, 232
buckaroo, 233
campfire red, 233
chili beans (1, 2), 233
chimichangas, 233
cowboy, 234
dressing, 13
garbanzo Creole, 234
garbanzos, 234
garbanzos Bombay (kabuli channa), 234
herbed, 235
hummus (1, 2), 235
kerala dal, 235
lentil patties, 236
lentil pot, 236
Mexican bean pot, 236
Mexican garbanzos, 237
patties, 234
pressure-cooking, 229
red beans and rice, 237
red beans with UnSausage, 237
refried (1, 2, 3), 237–38
salad, 30
simple cassoulet, 238
southern pinto, 238
soy fritters, 238
Soyteena, 238–39
special garbanzos, 239
Swedish brown, 239
three-bean pot pie, 239
with tomatoes, 232
tortilla and tostada filling (1, 2), 240
and tortillas, 232
Tuscan white bean casserole (1, 2), 240
white with tomatoes (1, 2), 240–41
white with UnBacon, 241
Dried Fruit Filling, 289
Drop Biscuits, 52
Dumplings,
Baked Spring Rolls, 337
biscuit, 50
gluten, 105
quick Cheez, in tomato sauce, 274
UnChicken and, 142
Dutch Succotash, 167

E

Easy Days Vegetable Soup, 71
Easy Pizza Crust, 278
Eggplant
appetizer spread, 299
burgers, 119
Cajun, 195
casserole, Italian, 208
casserole with tomatoes, garlic, and rice, 202–3
caponata, 292
caponata, Anne Goldstein's, 290
"caviar", 299
and Cheez, 202
coponatini, 162
lasagna, 203, 268
Oriental, and mushrooms in garlic sauce, 177
parmesan (1, 2), 203–4
roasted, onion, and garlic in tomato sauce, 183
sauce, sautéed UnPork chops with tomato, 127
sautéed, in tomato sauce with basil, 183–84
scalloped, 217
Szechuan braised, 187–88
and tomatoes, 167
"Egg" Salad, 299
English Wartime "Goose", 204

Farmer's UnSausage, 132–33
Fettucini with Spinach Pesto, 268
Fiery Ginger Snaps, 323–24
Fig Bars, 324
Fillings, for Square Meals, 284–90
  apple (1, 2), 288–89
  barbecue (1, 2), 284–85
  blueberry, 289
  broccoli and Cheez, 285
  broccoli-Mushroom, 285
  Cheez and onion, 285
  cherry, 289
  dal, 286
  fruit, dried, 289
  garbanzo, spicy, 288
  gluten and vegetable, 286
  hot dog and barbecued bean, 286
  hot dog and sauerkraut, 286–87
  "meat pie", 287
  Mexican (1, 2), 287
  peach, 289
  pizza, 287
  spanakopita, 288
  strawberry, 289
Fines Herbes, 303
Flat Bread, 52
Flavored Rice, 243
Flour, about, 3
  self-rising, 341
  tortillas, 52–53
Focaccia, 282
  onion, 282–83
  rosemary, 283
  UnSausage, 283
French Bread, 53
French Dressing (1, 2, 3), 14
French-Fried Potatoes, 167–68
French Fried UnShrimp, 151
French Silk Pie, 307–8
French-Style Potato Salad (1, 2), 43
French Toast, 338
Fresh Corn and Tomato Casserole, 204
Fresh Herb Dressing, 14
Fresh Tomato Dressing, 14
Fresh Tomato Soup, 71
Fresh Vegetable Dressing, 14
Fried Cheez Balls, 53, 338
Fried Cornmeal Cakes, 53
Fried Green Tomatoes, 168
Fried Mashed Potato Balls, 168
Fried Noodles, 269
Fried Rice, 244
Fried Taters 'n' Onions, 168–69
Fried UnPork, 125
Frosted Apple-Date Bits, 324
Fruit and Almond Kreem Tart, 308
Fruit Bars, 324
Fruit Butter, 299–300
Fruitcake (1, 2), 317. *See also* Cakes
Fruit Cocktail Bread Pudding, 309
Fruit Jam, 339
Fruit Pie (1, 2), 331
Fruit Scones, 335
Fruit Shortcake, 309
Fruit Squares, 309–10
Fudge, carob, 338

Garam Masala (1, 2), 303–4
Garbanzo and Cabbage Salad, 30
Garbanzo and Cabbage Soup, 72
Garbanzo Bean Salad (1, 2), 30
Garbanzo Burgers, 119
Garbanzo Creole, 234
Garbanzo Salad (1, 2), 30–31
Garbanzo Soup, 72
Garbanzo-Tomato Salad, 31
Garbanzos, 234
Garbanzos Bombay (Kabuli Channa), 234
Garlic and Dill Dressing, 14–15
Garlic Bread, 54, 339
Garlic Croutons, 54
Garlic Dressing, 14
Garlic Oil, 304
Garlic Olives, 339
Garlic UnSausage, 133
Garlic UnShrimp Español, 151
Gazpacho
  Gazpacho (1, 2, 3), 72–73
  salad, 31
  with couscous, 244
  dressing, green, 15
  salad, with lima bean, 34
Genoese Squash, 204–5
German Potato Salad (1, 2, 3), 43–44
Ginger Curry, 169
Ginger Snaps, 324–25
Ginger-Peach UnPork, 125
Gingerbread, 318
Gingernuts, 325
Glorified UnChicken, 138
Glorified UnPork Chops, 125
Gluten
  about, 98–99
  baked, 100
  baked cubed, 104
  barbecue, 104
  basic, 99–100
  burgers, 119–20
  and cabbage casserole, 205
  and corn casserole, 205
  and eggplant casserole, 205
  chow mein, 105
  cooking methods, 99–100, 101–3
  curry, 105
  dumplings, 105
  enchiladas, 105–6
  and green beans stir-fry, 104
  hash, 106
  Hearty Gluten Bake, 108
  "instant", 100
  jambalaya, 106
  loaf, 106
  oven-fried, 108
  paprika, 106–7
  piquant, 107
  and potato hash, 104–5
  pot pie, 107
  and rice casserole, 205–6
  salad, 31
  sandwich spread, 300
  Santa Fe, 108
  substitute, 3
  -vegetable casserole, 206
  and vegetable filling, 286
Gnocchi, 269
Golden Corn Soup, 73
Golden Sauce, 258–59

Golden Vegetable Bake, 206
Golden Vegetable Layer, 169
Goulash, 110
Graham Cracker Crust, 328
Graham Cracker-Walnut Crust, 328–29
Graham Crackers, 60
Grains, 242–48. *See also* Rice
barley, 242
bulgar, pilaf, spicy, 247
cracked wheat, 243
gazpacho with couscous, 244
millet, 244
tabouli wheat, 247
Grandma's Potato Salad, 44
Grape-Nut Pie Crust, 329
Gravy(ies), 253–55
brown, 253
mushroom, 253–54
nutritional yeast, 254
Sour Kreem-mushroom, 254
unbeef (1, 2), 254
UnBeef, Cajun, 253
UnChicken, 255
UnHam (1, 2), 255
UnHamburger, 255
Greek Green Beans, 169
Greek Potatoes, 169–70
Green Bean(s)
casserole, 206
colonial, 162
curried, 165–66
dilled, 293
with garlic, 171
Greek, 169
Green Beans, 170
with green onion dressing, 171
with hazelnuts, 171
Kentucky fried, 173
and mushrooms, 170
potato, and tomato combo, 170
roast potato salad with, onions and, 47
squash, tomatoes, and, 186
stir fry, 170–71
stir-fry, gluten and, 104
succotash, 170
with summer savory, 172
supreme (1, 2), 207
supreme, 171
with tomatoes, 172
in tomato sauce, 206–7
with UnBacon, 171
and UnHam, 170
Green Chili Corn Casserole, 207
Green Dressing (1, 2), 15
Green Gazpacho Dressing, 15
Green Goddess Dressing, 15
Green Lima Beans with Fine Herbes, 172
Green Onion Salad Dressing, 15
Green Pea Salad (1, 2), 31–32
Green Pea Soup, 73
Green Peas and Onions, 172
Green Rice (1, 2), 244
Green Tomato Pickles, 293
Green Tomato Salsa, 293
Green Vegetable Salad, 32
Grilled Cheez Sandwiches, 299
Guacamole (1, 2, 3, 4, 5), 32

H

Half-Hour Chili, 92
Hamburger Buns, 54
Harvest Vegetable Casserole, 208
Hash Brown Waffles, 172
Hearty Gluten Bake, 108
Heavenly Broth, 158
Herb
bread, 54
dressing (1, 2), 15–16
mayonnaise dressing, 16
and onion bread, 54
UnSausage, 133
Herbed Beans, 235
Herbed Noodles, 269
Herbed Noodles with Cheez, Lemon, and Green Onions, 269
Herbed Potato Salad, 44
Hominy and Bell Pepper Sauté, 172–73
Hot Cheez and Cider Dip, 339
Hot Cheez and Cider Dressing, 16
Hot Dog and Barbecued Bean Filling, 286
Hot Dog and Sauerkraut Filling, 286–87
Hot Herbed Carrots, 293
Hot Oil, 304
Hot Potato Salad, 44
Hot Stuff, 294
Hot UnChicken Salad Casserole, 208
Hummus (1, 2), 235
Hummus Dressing, 16
Hungarian Noodle Bake, 269–70
Hungarian UnChicken Stew, 73
Hungarian UnChicken, 138–39
Hush Puppies, 54

I

Indonesian-Style Baked Tofu, 250
"Instant" Gluten, 100
Instant Tomato Juice, 339
Instant Tomato Puree, 339
Instant Tomato Sauce, 339
Italian Dressing (1, 2), 16
Italian Eggplant Casserole, 208
Italian Pasta Sauce, 263
Italian UnChicken Casserole, 139
Italian UnSausage, 133
Italian UnSausage, Pasta, and Bean Casserole, 209
Italian UnSausage Dressing, 208

J

Jalapeño and Bell Pepper Chutney, 294
Jam, fruit, 339
Jamaican Vegetables, 173
Jamaica Rice and "Peas", 173
Jambalaya, 139
Jelly Filled Doughnuts, 335
Juice, orange-grape, 340
Juice, tomato, instant, 339

K

Kentucky Fried Green Beans, 173
Kerala Dal, 235
Kidney Bean Salad (1, 2), 32–33
Kitchen Bouquet, about, 4
Kraut-Stuffed UnPork Chops, 125–26

Kreem Cheez Spaghetti Sauce, 263
Kreem French Dressing, 13
Kreem of Broccoli Soup, 73
Kreem of Carrot Soup, 73–74
Kreem of Cauliflower Soup, 74
Kreem of Celery Soup, 74
Kreem of Corn Soup, 74
Kreem of Mushroom Soup, 74
Kreem of Onion Soup, 74
Kreem of Pea Soup (1, 2), 74
Kreem of Pinto Bean and
Tomato Soup, 75
Kreem of Potato Soup (1, 2), 75
Kreem of UnChicken Soup, 75

L

Lasagna Noodles, 270
Lasagna Roll-Ups, 270
Lasagna, 270
Layered Casserole, 209
Lazy Kitchuri, 173–74
Leftover Vegetables with Cheez,
209
Lemon Cake, 318
Lemon Cheezcake, 310
Lemon Cheezcake Deluxe, 310
Lemon Custard, 310
Lemon Custard Pie, 332
Lemon Dressing, 16–17
Lemon Garlic Dressing, 17
Lentil and Tomato Soup, 75
Lentil Loaf, 236
Lentil Patties, 236
Lentil Pot, 236
Lentil Salad (1, 2, 3, 4), 33–34
Lentil Soup (1, 2, 3, 4), 75–76
Lima Bean(s), 174
with Cheez, 174–75, 209
in Cheez sauce, 174
-corn succotash, 175
and garbanzo salad, 34
gazpacho salad, 34
in piquante sauce, 174
salad (1, 2), 34
soup, 76
and tomatoes, 174
Liquid Smoke, about, 4
Lisbon UnTurkey, 147
Lorenzo Dressing, 17
Louisiana Corn and Tomatoes, 175
Louisiana Hot Sauce, 4, 294

M

Macaroni and Cheez Salad, 34
Macaroni and Cheez, 270
Macaroni and Yeast Cheez
Casserole, 271
Macaroni Delight, 271
Maître d'Hôtel Butter Sauce, 259
Maple Nut Chews, 325
"Maple" Syrup, 339
Maple Pecan Cheezcake, 311
Margarine, nondairy, about, 6
Marinade Dressing, 17
Marinated Mushrooms, 294
Marinated Tomatoes, 294
Marinated UnShrimp, 151
Marinated Zucchini Salad, 34–35
Mary Krieger's Sure-to-Please
Spaghetti Sauce, 263
Mashed Carrots, 175
Mashed Potato and Cheez Soup,
76–77
Mashed Potatoes (1, 2), 175
Mayonnaise Dressing, 17
Mean Green, 294–95
Measurements, about, 4
"Meat Pie" Filling, 287
"Meatza" Pie, 278–79
Mediterranean Ragout, 176
Mehu-Maija juicers, 157
Mexican
bean and corn salad, 35
bean and pasta dish, 271
bean pot, 236
bread, 54
chorizo UnSausage, 134
corn bread, 54–55
corn salad, 35
filling (1, 2), 287
fruitcake, 318
garbanzos, 237
lasagna, 210
lima bean casserole, 210
potato salad, 44–45
summer stew, 77
tomato dressing, 17
tomato vinaigrette, 17
UnPork chops and beans, 126
UnShrimp, 151
Milk substitutes, about, 5. *See also*
Dairy substitutes
Millet, 244
Minestrone (1, 2), 77
Miraculous Whip, 17–18
Mixed Vegetable Salad (1, 2), 35
"Mock" Cream of Mushroom
Soup, 78
Molasses, about, 5
Molasses Cake, 319
Molasses Cookies (1, 2, 3),
325–26
Monastery Potato Soup, 78
Monastery Shortbread, 326
Monastery Tomato Salad, 35
Monastery Vegetable Soup, 78
Monosodium glutamate, about,
5–6
Moroccan UnChicken, 139
Mulled Cider, 340
Mulligatawny Soup, 78
Mushroom(s)
Anne Goldstein's marinated,
290
and artichoke pie, 210
and bell pepper quiche, 210–11
gravy, 253–54
in Kreem sauce, 176
lasagna, 272
marinated, 294
salad, 35
Stroganoff, 176
substitute, about, 6

N

N'eggs, 266, 302
about, 302
all-purpose, 302
pasta, basic, 266
pastry, 302
N'Ice Kreem, 314–15
banana, 314
coconut, 314
tahini, 314
tofu (1, 2), 314–15
Nonoil cooking, about, 6
Noodle Bake, 272

Noodle Casserole with Zucchini, Tomatoes, and Cheez, 211
Noodles Romano, 272
Noodles with UnBeef Sauce, 272–73
Notzarella Cheez, 94
Nut Butter Dressing (1, 2, 3, 4), 18
Nutritional Yeast Dressing, 18
Nutritional Yeast Gravy, 254

O

Oat Burgers, 120
Oat Burgers with Mushrooms, 120
Oatcakes, 55
Oatmeal Chewies, 326
Oatmeal-Raisin Cookies, 326
Oil, about, 6–7
Oil and Lemon Juice Dressing, 18
Oil and Vinegar Dressing, 18
Okra
- boiled, 160
- Creole, 165
- with cumin, 177
- deep-fried, 166–67
- oven-roasted, 177
- super, 187
- and tomatoes, 176–77, 188

Old-Fashioned Boiled Dressing, 18–19
Olive Dressing, 19
Olive Sauce (1, 2), 259
Olives, garlic, 339
Omelets, 140
One-Hour Whole Wheat Bread, 55
Onion Bread, 55
Onion Focaccia, 282–83
Onion-Garlic Pizza, 279
Onions, about, 7
Onion Sauce (1, 2), 259
Onion Sauce for Spaghetti, 264
Onion Soup, 78–79
Onions in Tomato Sauce, 211
Orange Gingercake, 319
Orange-Grape Juice, 340
Orange UnPork Chops, 126
Oregano-Mint Dressing, 19
Oriental Eggplant and Mushrooms in Garlic Sauce, 177
Oriental Marinated UnSteak, 110–11
Oriental UnBeef and Tomatoes, 111
Oriental UnPork Chops, 126
Oven-Baked Rice with UnPork and Garbanzos, 245
Oven-Barbecued UnPork Chops, 126–27
Oven-Fried Gluten, 108
Oven-Fried Potatoes, 177
Oven Method Tofu, 250
Oven-Roasted Okra, 177
Oven UnFries, 178

P

Paella-Limas, 178, 211
Pancake Syrup (1, 2), 340
Pancakes (1, 2), 340
Parmesan Cheez (1, 2), 94
Parsley Dressing, 19
Parsleyed Potato Salad, 45
Party Cheez Dip, 340
Pasta, 266–77
- baked with UnBeef, 267
- basic, 266
- basic N'egg, 266
- basic semolina, 266
- bean and pasta dish, Mexican, 271
- calzone, 267
- chili-mac, 267
- fettucini with spinach pesto, 268
- gnocchi, 269
- lasagna, 270
- lasagna, delicious, 268
- lasagna, eggplant, 268
- lasagna, mushroom, 272
- lasagna noodles, 270
- lasagna roll-ups, 270
- lasagna, spinach, 275–76
- lasagna, UnChicken, 276–77
- lasagna, white 277
- macaroni and Cheez, 270
- macaroni and Cheez, UnBeefy, 276
- macaroni and yeast Cheez casserole, 271
- macaroni delight, 271
- macaroni with tomatoes, baked, 267
- making and cooking, 266
- noodle bake, 272
- noodle bake, Hungarian, 269–70
- noodles, fried, 269
- noodles, herbed, 269
- noodles, herbed, with Cheez, lemon, and green onions, 269
- noodles romano, 272
- noodles, sesame, 274
- noodles with UnBeef sauce, 272–73
- piroshkis, 274
- quick Cheez dumplings in tomato sauce, 274
- primavera (1, 2), 273
- shells with broccoli, 273
- simple pasta, 274
- snacks, 274
- spaghetti and soy grits, 275
- spaghetti Bolognese, 275
- spaghetti, Creole, 268
- spaghetti, special, 275
- with spicy broccoli, 274
- Thai-style, 276
- and UnBeef bake, 276

Pasta Salad Vinaigrette, 36
Pasta sauce(s), 263–65
- Italian, 263
- Neapolitan, 264
- onion, for spaghetti, 264
- spaghetti, 264
- spaghetti, Kreem Cheez, 263
- spaghetti, Mary Krieger's sure-to-please, 263
- spaghetti, Sour Kreem, 264
- tomato-mushroom marinara, 264
- UnBeef, 265
- UnBeef and tomato, 264–65
- UnChicken, 265
- UnShrimp, 265
- zucchini spaghetti, 265

Pastry N'egg, 302
Peach Filling, 289
Peach Pie, 332

Peanut Butter Cookies (1, 2), 327
Peanut Pasta Salad, 36
Pears in "Custard", 311
Pears in Mustard Syrup, 311
Peas
  and carrots, 178
  Cajun or fresh beans, 162
  carrots, and potatoes, curried, 166
  creamed green, 164
  curried, 166
  green, and onions, 172
  Jamaica Rice and "Peas", 173
Pease Porridge, 79
Pecan patties, 340
Pecan Pie, 332
Pecos Bean Salad, 36
Peperonata (1, 2), 178
Pepper(s)
  bell, quiche, mushroom and, 210–11
  bell, sauté, hominy and, 172–73
  bell, soup, chilled tomato and, 66–67
  burgers, tofu-, 121
  corn and, 163
  Jalapeño, about, 3
  Jalapeño and bell, chutney, 294
  red, about, 7
  relish, Aunt's May, 291
  UnSteak, Chinese, 110
Pickled Beans and Onions, 295
Pickled Calico Vegetables, 295
Pickles
  dill, 292
  green tomato, 293
  zucchini, 296
Pies, 320–33
  apple, 329
  banana Kreem, 329
  berry Kreem, 329–30
  Blueberry Cobbler, 330
  cherry, 331
  Cherry Cobbler, 330–31
  convent caramel apple, 331
  crust, basic, 328
  crust, convent, 328
  crust, graham cracker, 328
  crust, graham cracker-walnut, 328–29
  crust, Grape-Nut, 329
  filling, blueberry, 330
  filling, Catherine Xenia's pumpkin, 330
  filling, strawberry, 333
  fruit (1, 2), 331
  lemon custard, 332
  mincemeat, Sister Mary Michael's, 333
  peach, 332
  pecan, 332
  pineapple, 332
  shoofly, 332–33
Piffel, 212
Pilaf Imperial, 245
Pimiento Cheez (1, 2), 94–95
Pimiento Cheez Loaf, 212
Pimiento Cheez Spread, 300
Pineapple Pie, 332
Pineapple Pudding, 311
Pineapple Upside-Down Cake, 319
Pink Beans and Red Cabbage Salad, 36
Pinto Bean Chili, 92
Piquant Cauliflower, 36
Piquante Sauce, 259
Piroshkis, 274
Pizza, 278–81
  blender sauce, 278
  bread, 279
  Cheez, 95
  Cheez-only, 278
  crust, easy, 278
  filling, 287
  "Meatza", 278–79
  onion-garlic, 279
  quick, 280
  sauce (1, 2), 280
  -style vegetables, 179
  taco, 280
  tomato and Cheez, 281
  UnSausage, 134
Pocket Bread, 55–56
Polenta Casserole, 212
Portuguese Bean Soup, 79
Potato(es)
  -broccoli casserole, 213
  and carrots au gratin, 214
  -Cheez bake, 213
  -cucumber salad, 45
  and "Chorizo", roasted UnChicken with, 140
  and green onions, 180–81
  and greens, 181
  and mushroom soup, 79
  and tomato gratin, 213
  au gratin, 214
  au gratin, UnHam and, 223
  bake, Cheez and, 196
  baked mashed, 160
  baked, 180
  baked, Apulian-style, onions, and tomatoes, 192
  balls, fried mashed, 168
  boiled, 180
  browned, 161
  Cheez, UnBacon and, 222–23
  chips (1, 2), 179
  Corn and Potato Chowder (1, 2), 68
  creamed, 164
  creamed, with Cheez, 201
  creamy, and peas, 165
  crunch-top, 202
  curried peas, carrots, and, 166
  curried, and onion casserole, 202
  curried, and peas, 166
  curry, 179
  dressing (1, 2, 3), 19
  French-fried, 167–68
  gratin, 213
  Greek, 169–70
  green bean, and tomato combo, 170
  hash, gluten and, 104–5
  in broth, 181
  in their own gravy, 181
  Kreem of Potato Soup (1, 2), 75
  loaf, bean and, 230–31
  loaf, bean and, 230–31
  Mashed Potatoes (1, 2), 175
  mashed, and Cheez soup, 76–77
  mashed, cottage, 163
  mayonnaise, 19
  O'Brien, 181–82

Potato(es), *continued*
-onion soup, 80
oven-fried, 177
pancakes, 180
paprika, 182
potluck, 214–15
pot pie, 180
roasted, and onions, 183
salad, broccoli, and garbanzo, 27
sauté, UnChicken and, 142
scalloped, and mushrooms, 218
scalloped, and spinach, 218
scalloped carrots and, 216–17
scalloped in margarine, 214
Scalloped Potatoes (1, 2, 3), 217–18
soup, 79
soup, cabbage and, 64, 80
soup, chili, 66
soup, Monastery, 78
soup with garlic and greens, 80
spicy, 220
-spinach soup, 80
stuffing, 214
Potato Salad(s), 38, 42–48
Austrian, 42
Cajun, 42
dilled, 42–43
French-Style Potato Salad (1, 2), 43
German Potato Salad (1, 2, 3), 43–44
Grandma's, 44
herbed, 44
hot, 44
Mexican, 44–45
with mustard dressing, 46
parsleyed, 45
with peas, 46
Potato-Cucumber Salad, 45
Potato Salad (1, 2, 3, 4), 45–46
red, 46
roast, with green beans and onions, 47
Russian Potato and Beet Salad, 38
tangy, 47
Tunisian, 47
warm, with garlic UnSausage, 48
Powdered Sucanat, 340
Pumpernickel Bread, 56
Puree, tomato, instant, 339
Puris, 56

Q

Quick Cheez Dumplings in Tomato Sauce, 274
Quick Pizza, 280
Quick Saucy Vegetables, 182
Quick Sauerkraut, 182
Quick Tomato Relish, 295

R

Raisin Bread, 57
Raisin Dunkers, 335–36
Raisin-Orange Coffee Cake, 336
Ratatouille, 182, 215
Red Beans and Rice, 237
Red Beans with UnSausage, 237
Red Cabbage (1, 2), 182–83
Red Potato Salad, 46
Refried Beans (1, 2, 3), 237–38
Relish
caponata, 292
caponata, Anne Goldstein's, 290
corn, Anne Goldstein's, 290–91
hot stuff, 294
mean green, 294–95
pepper, Aunt May's, 291
quick tomato, 295
sweet tomato, 295
tomato, 295
tomato, Aunt Lou Maxey's, 291
zucchini, 297
zucchini-red pepper, 297
Reuben Casserole, 111
Reuben Sandwiches, 300
Rice, about, 7–8
and Avocado Salad, 37
basic, 242
and bean salad, 37
casserole, Creole, 202
casserole, gluten and, 205–6
Cheez, 243
Cheez, and, 226
Creole, 243
dirty, 243
dressing, 215
flavored, 243
fried, 244
fried, vegetable (1, 2, 3), 247–48
garlic, and, 202–3
green (1, 2), 244
Jamaica, and "peas", 173
jambalaya, 245
Kreem, 95
milk, 95
oven-baked with UnPork and garbanzos, 245
with peas, 245
pilaf imperial, 245
pudding, coconut, 307
red beans and, 237
risotto, broccoli, 242
risotto, simple, 245–46
risotto, Spinach, 247
salad (1, 2), 36–37
salad, corn, bean and, 29
salad, country, 29
salad Especial, 37
salad southern style, 38
salad with black-eyed peas, 38
salad with olives and capers, 38
soup, UnChicken, 87
Spanish (1, 2, 3, 4), 246
Spanish UnChicken with, 140–41
squash casserole with tomatoes, Cheez, and, 221
UnBeef with tomatoes and, 116–17
UnChicken with Mushrooms, Tomatoes, and, 145
vegetable casserole with tomatoes and, 223–24
Roast Potato Salad with Green Beans and Onions, 47
Roast UnBeef (1, 2), 111
Roasted Eggplant, Onion, and Garlic in Tomato Sauce, 183
Roasted Potatoes and Onions, 183

Roasted Tomato Soup, 80–81
Roasted UnChicken with Potatoes and "Chorizo", 140
Rosemary Focaccia, 283
Rosemary UnSausage, 134
Rumbledethumps, 215
Russian Dressing (1, 2), 19–20
Russian Potato and Beet Salad, 38
Russian Vegetable Soup, 81
Rye Crisps, 60

S

Salad dressings, 10–24
- alfalfa sprout, 10
- almond, 10
- avocado-cashew, 10
- avocado (1, 2, 3, 4, 5, 6), 10–11
- avocado-olive, 11
- avocado, simple, 11
- bitters, 12
- boiled, old-fashioned, 18–19
- caraway, 12
- carrot, 12
- cashew Cheez, 12
- chive, 12
- cucumber, 13
- dill, 13
- dried bean, 13
- French (1, 2, 3), 14
- French, caper, 12
- French, Kreem, 13
- French, tomato, 23
- French, zesty, 24
- garlic, 14
- garlic and dill, 14–15
- green (1, 2), 15
- green gazpacho, 15
- Green Goddess, 15
- green onion, 15
- herb (1, 2), 15–16
- herb, fresh, 14
- hot Cheez and cider, 16
- hummus, 16
- Italian (1, 2), 16
- Kreem, crunchy, 13
- lemon, 16–17
- lemon garlic, 17
- Lorenzo, 17
- marinade, 17
- mayonnaise, 17
- mayonnaise, avocado, 11
- mayonnaise, cashew, 12
- mayonnaise, curry, 13
- mayonnaise, herb, 16
- mayonnaise, potato, 19
- mayonnaise, tomato, 23
- Mexican tomato, 17
- Mexican tomato vinaigrette, 17
- miraculous whip, 17–18
- nut butter (1, 2, 3, 4), 18
- nutritional yeast, 18
- oil and lemon juice, 18
- oil and vinegar, 18
- olive, 19
- oregano-mint, 19
- parsley, 19
- potato (1, 2, 3), 19
- Russian (1, 2), 19–20
- sour Kreem (1, 2), 20
- sweet basil, 20
- tahini (1, 2, 3, 4, 5, 6), 20–21
- tahini oil, 21
- tartar, 21
- Thousand Island (1, 2, 3), 21
- Tofu Mayonnaise (1, 2, 3, 4, 5, 6, 7), 22–23
- tomato (1, 2), 23
- tomato, fresh, 14
- vegetable, fresh, 14
- tomato-cashew, 23
- vinaigrette (1, 2), 24

Salad(s), 25–42
- about, 25
- Anne Goldstein's Tabouli, 26
- avocado (1, 2), 26
- barbecue bean, 26
- bean, 26
- bean, dried, 30
- bean sprout (1, 2), 26
- broccoli, potato, and garbanzo, 27
- cabbage and lima bean, 27
- cabbage and pepper, 27
- cabbage-pineapple, 27
- cauliflower, piquant, 36
- chef's bean, 28
- corn (1, 2), 28
- corn, rice, and bean, 29
- cottage Cheez (1, 2), 29
- country rice, 29
- cucumber (1, 2), 29–30
- couscous, 30
- cucumbers, dilled, 30
- garbanzo (1, 2), 30–31
- garbanzo and cabbage, 30
- garbanzo bean (1, 2), 30
- garbanzo-tomato, 31
- gazpacho, 31
- gluten, 31
- green pea (1, 2), 31–32
- green vegetable, 32
- guacamole (1, 2, 3, 4, 5), 32
- kidney bean (1, 2), 32–33
- lentil (1, 2, 3, 4), 33–34
- lima bean (1, 2), 34
- lima bean and garbanzo, 34
- lima bean gazpacho, 34
- macaroni and Cheez, 34
- Mexican bean and corn, 35
- Mexican corn, 35
- mixed vegetable (1, 2), 35
- Mushroom Salad, 35
- Niçoise (1, 2), 38–39
- pasta, vinaigrette, 36
- peanut pasta, 36
- Pecos bean, 36
- pink beans and red cabbage, 36
- potato and beet, Russian, 38
- rice (1, 2), 36–37
- rice, Southern style, 38
- rice and avocado, 37
- rice and bean, 37
- rice especial, 37
- rice with black-eyed peas, 38
- rice with olives and capers, 38
- slaw, cabbage (1, 2), 27
- slaw, Cajun cole 28
- slaw, tomato, 40–41
- summer crock, 39
- sunshine, 39
- tabouli, 39
- three-bean (1, 2, 3), 40
- tomato, 40
- tomato, monastery, 35
- tomato, summer, 39
- tomato and bean, 40
- tossed, 41

Salad(s), *continued*
UnShrimp, 41
white bean (1, 2), 41
zucchini, marinated, 34–35
Salisbury UnSteak, 112
Salsa. *See also* Sauce(s)
chilipetin sauce, 292
cruda, tomato, 296
fresca, tomato, 296
green tomato, 293
hot stuff, 294
Louisiana hot sauce, 294
tomato, 296
Salt, sea, about, 8
Sandwiches, 298–301
cheese, grilled, 299
Cheez, super, 301
Cheez toast, 299
reuben, 300
Saturday night specials, 300
sloppy Joes, 300–301
Sante Fe Gluten, 108
Saturday Night Specials, 300
Sauces, 256–62. *See also* Pasta sauces
barbecue (1, 2), 256
barbecue, spicy (1, 2), 260
brown, 256
"butter" with herbs, 256–57
catsup, 257
catsup, Cajun, 257
Cheez (1, 2, 3, 4), 257–58
Cheez and onion, 258
chili, 258
chilipetin, 292
cocktail (1, 2), 258
Creole, 258
golden, 258–59
Louisiana Hot, 4, 294
Maître d'Hôtel Butter, 259
olive (1, 2), 259
onion (1, 2), 259
piquante, 259
sour Kreem and chive, 260
Spanish tomato, 260
taco, 260
tartar, 261
tomato (1, 2, 3), 261
tomato, instant, 339
tomato and Cheez, 261
tomato and onion, 262
UnBeef and tomato, 262
white, 262
Saucy Ground UnBeef Casserole, 112
Saucy Meatless Loaf, 112
Saucy UnSteak Skillet, 112–13
Sauerkraut, quick, 182
Sauerkraut Casserole, 216
Sautéed Eggplant in Tomato Sauce with Basil, 183–84
Sautéed Spinach, 184
Sautéed UnPork Chops with Tomato and Eggplant Sauce, 127
Sautéed Vegetables, 184
Savannah UnBeef and Okra Stew, 81
Scalloped Broccoli (1, 2), 216
Scalloped Cabbage, 184, 216
Scalloped Carrots and Potatoes, 216–17
Scalloped Corn, 217
Scalloped Eggplant, 217
Scalloped Peas and Squash, 217
Scalloped Potatoes (1, 2, 3), 217–18
Scalloped Potatoes and Mushrooms, 218
Scalloped Potatoes and Spinach, 218
Seasonings, 303–4
all-purpose, 303
fines herbes, 303
garam masala (1, 2), 303–4
garlic oil, 304
hot oil, 304
special, 304
Seitan. *See* Gluten
Self-Rising Flour, 341
Sesame Noodles, 274
Shchi (1, 2), 81–82
Shepherd's Pie (1, 2), 218–19
Shoofly Pie, 332–33
Shortcake, 319
Simple Avocado Dressing, 11
Simple Cassoulet, 238
Simple Garden Casserole, 219
Simple Pasta, 274
Simple Risotto, 245–46
Simple UnSausage, 135
Sister Mary Michael's Mincemeat Pie, 333
Sloppy Joes, 300–301
Slumgullian, 184
Smoky Black Bean and Vegetable Soup, 82
Soup(s), 61–89
Abbot George's Low-Calorie Soup, 61
avocado and tomato, 62
bean, baked, 62
bean, black, and spinach, 62
bean, black (1, 2, 3), 62–63
bean, black, and vegetable, smoky, 82
bean, Budapest, 64
bean, lima, 76
bean, Portuguese, 79
borscht (1, 2), 63
borscht, cabbage, 65
broth, dieter's, 71
broccoli, bean, and spaghetti, 63–64
broccoli, Kreem of, 73
cabbage (1, 2), 65
cabbage and Cheez (1, 2), 64
cabbage and potato, 64
cabbage and tomato, 65
calsoup, 65
carrot, 66
carrot, Kreem of, 73–74
cauliflower, Kreem of, 74
celery, Kreem of, 74
Cheez and onion, 66
Cheez Soup (1, 2), 66
chili potato, 66
chowder, corn (1, 2), 68
chowder, corn and potato (1, 2), 68
chowder, corn and tomato, 68
chowder, corn deluxe, 69
cold-as-a-cucumber, 68
consommé, vegetable, 88
corn, 69
corn, golden, 73
corn, Kreem of, 74
Creole, 70
dal, 71
garbanzo, 72

garbanzo and cabbage, 72
gazpacho (1, 2, 3), 72–73
gumbo, tofu, 84
hot pot, winter, 88
lentil (1, 2, 3), 75–76
lentil and tomato, 75
lentil-celery, creamed, 69
minestrone (1, 2), 77
Mulligatawny Soup, 78
mushroom, cream of, "mock", 70
mushroom, curried, 70
mushroom, Kreem of, 74
onion, 78–79
onion, creamy, 69
onion, Kreem of, 74
pea, green, 73
pea, Kreem of, (1, 2), 74–75
pinto bean and tomato, Kreem of, 75
porridge, pease, 79
potato, 79
potato, Kreem of (1, 2), 75
potato, mashed, and Cheez, 76–77
potato, monastery, 78
potato and mushroom, 79
potato-cabbage, 80
potato-onion, 80
potato-spinach, 80
potato with garlic and greens, 80
shchi (1, 2), 81–82
Sour Kreem tomato, 82
spinach, 83
split pea (1, 2, 3), 83
split pea, curried, 70
squash, Kreem of, cold, 67
stew, curry, 70–71
stew, Mexican summer, 77
stew, tofu, 84
stew, UnChicken, Hungarian, 73
stew, UnShrimp (1, 2), 87–88
thickener, 82
three sisters, 84
tomato (1, 2, 3, 4), 85–86
tomato, fresh, 71
tomato, Kreem of, cold, 67
tomato, roasted, 80–81
tomato, spicy, 82
tomato and bell pepper, chilled, 66–67
tomato-bean corn chowder, 84
tomato consommé, 84–85
tomato-mushroom, 86
tomato vegetable cream, 86
tomato with rice, 86
UnBeef and okra stew, Savannah, 81
UnBeef minestrone, 86
UnChicken, Kreem of, 75
UnChicken noodle, 86–87
UnChicken rice, 87
UnFish, 87
UnShrimp, 87
UnShrimp and corn, 87
vegetable, almost instant (1, 2), 61
vegetable, Basque, 62
vegetable, easy days, 71
vegetable, monastery, 78
vegetable, Russian, 81
vegetable, spicy, 82–83
white bean and tomato, 88
zucchini, 89
zucchini-carrot, 89
zucchini-tomato stew, 89
"Sourdough" Bread, 57
Sour Kreem-Mushroom Gravy, 254
Sour Kreem and Chive Sauce, 260
Sour Kreem Dressing (1, 2), 20
Sour Kreem Spaghetti Sauce, 264
Sour Kreem Tomato Soup, 82
Southern Pinto Beans, 238
Sovex and Vegex, about, 8
Soy Bread, 57
Soyburgers, 120
Soy Fritters, 238
Soy Grits Casserole, 219
Soy Grits Enchilada Casserole, 219–20
Soy Grits UnChicken, 140
Soy Grits UnHam, 130
Soy Grits UnSausage, 135
Soy Milk, 96
Soy Milk Basic, 96
Soy sauce, about, 8
Soyteena, 238–39
Soy Whipped Kreem, 96
Spaghetti, special, 275
Spaghetti and Soy Grits, 275
Spaghetti Bolognese, 275
Spaghetti Sauce, 264
Spanakopita Filling, 288
Spanish Rice (1, 2, 3, 4), 246
Spanish Tomato Sauce, 260
Spanish UnChicken au Gratin, 140
Spanish UnChicken with Rice, 140–41
Spanish Vegetables, 185
Special Garbanzos, 239
Special Seasoning, 304
Spiced Bread Pudding, 312
Spiced UnBeef Polenta, 113
Spices, about, 8
Spicy Barbecue Sauce (1, 2), 260
Spicy Bulgur Pilaf, 247
Spicy Garbanzo Filling, 288
Spicy Hermits, 327
Spicy Potatoes, 220
Spicy Tomato Juice, 341
Spicy Tomato Soup, 82
Spicy Vegetable Soup, 82–83
Spinach
au gratin, 185
casserole, corn and, 199
creamed, mushrooms, and onions in Cheez sauce, 201
and herb potato casserole, 220
lasagna, 275–76
pesto, fettucini with, 268
risotto, 247
sautéed, 184
scalloped potatoes and, 218
soup, 83
soup, black bean and, 62
soup, potato-, 80
tomatoes, and rice, 185
with tomatoes, 185
Split Pea Soup (1, 2, 3), 83
Spreads, 298–301
apple butter, 298
barbecue bean, 298
bean, 298
Cheez (1, 2), 298
eggplant appetizer, 299
eggplant "caviar", 299

Spreads, *continued*
"egg" salad, 299
fruit butter, 299–300
gluten, 300
pimiento Cheez, 300
Spring rolls, baked, 337
Square Meals, 284
Squash
au gratin, 185
bake, 220–21
beans, and corn, 186
casserole with tomatoes, Cheez, and rice, 221
Creole, 221
deep-fried, 167
green beans, and tomatoes, 186
and macaroni bake, 220
mushroom, and pasta pie, 186
and peas, 186
stewed 187
tamale bake, 221
with tomatoes, 187
yellow, Creole, 190
Steak sauce, Lea and Perrins, about, 4
Steamed Irish Raisin Pudding, 312
Stewed Squash, 187
Stir-Fry Tofu and Vegetables, 251
Stir-Fry UnBeef, 113
Strawberry Filling, 289
Strawberry Pie Filling, 333
Stuffed Meatless Loaf, 113
Sucanat Health Cookies, 327
Sucanat, powdered, 340
Summer Crock Salad, 39
Summer Fruit Terrine, 312–13
Summer Tomato Salad, 39
Sunburgers, 120–21
Sunday Unfried UnChicken, 141
Sunshine Salad, 39
Super Cheez Sandwiches, 301
Super Okra, 187
Swedish Brown Beans, 239
Sweet and Sour UnPork (1, 2), 127–28
Sweet Basil Dressing, 20
Sweet-and-Sour Cabbage, 187
Sweeteners, about, 8
Sweet Muffins, 57
Sweet pastry dishes, 334–36. *See also* Desserts
coffee cake, raisin-orange, 336
dough, sweet roll, 336
doughnut squares, 334–35
doughnuts, 335
doughnuts, jelly filled, 335
dunkers, raisin 335–36
icing, confectioner's, 334
rolls, cinnamon, 334
scones, fruit, 335
Sweet Roll Dough, 336
Sweet Square Meals, 288
Sweet Tomato Relish, 295
Swiss UnSteak, 114
Syrup, "maple", 339
Syrup, pancake (1, 2), 340
Syrup Cake, 320
Szechuan Braised Eggplant, 187–88

T

Tabasco sauce, about, 4
Tabouli, Anne Goldstein's, 26
Tabouli Salad, 39
Tabouli Wheat, 247
Taco Pizza, 280
Taco Sauce, 260
Tahini, about, 9
Tahini Dressing (1, 2, 3, 4, 5, 6), 20–21
Tahini N'Ice Kreem, 314
Tahini Oil Dressing, 21
Tamale Pie, 114, 221
Tamale pie, corn, 200
Tangy Potato Salad, 47
Tangy UnMeatballs, 114
Tartar Dressing, 21
Tartar Sauce, 261
Textured vegetable protein (TVP). *See* Gluten
Thai-Style Pasta, 276
Thai-Style Vegetables, 188
Thousand Island Dressing (1, 2, 3), 21
Three Sisters Soup, 84
Three-Bean Pot Pie, 239
Three-Bean Salad (1, 2, 3), 40
Toast Points, 57
Tofu dishes, 249–52
baked, Indonesian-style, 250
buttermilk, 96
cottage Cheez, 96
gumbo, 84
hummus, 251
Kreem Cheez (1, 2), 96
mayonnaise (1, 2, 3, 4, 5, 6, 7), 22–23
N'Ice Kreem (1, 2), 314–15
oven method, 250
-pepper burgers, 121
ricotta Cheez, 96
"scrambled eggs", 252
"scrambled eggs" breakfast casserole, 252
sour Kreem, 97
stew, 84
stir-fry, and vegetables, 251
tofu, 249–50
UnBeef, 251
UnBeef enchiladas, 252
UnChicken, 251
whipped Kreem, 97
yogurt, 97
Tomato(es). *See also* Pasta sauce; Salsa; Sauces
about, 9
Apulian-style baked potatoes, onions, and, 192
baked macaroni with, 267
-bean corn chowder, 84
and Bean Salad, 40
beans with, 232
black beans with, 232
broccoli, mushrooms, and, 161
cabbage, and Cheez, 161, 194
casserole, fresh corn and, 204
and Cheez Pizza, 281
and Cheez Sauce, 261
chowder, corn and, 68
and corn scallop, 222
consommé, 84–85
corn, and Cheez, 188
Creole, 165, 189
dressing (1, 2), 23
dressing, -cashew, 23
dressing, French, 23
dressing, fresh, 14
dressing, Mexican, 17

eggplant and, 167
eggplant bake, 222
eggplant casserole with garlic, rice and, 202–3
fried green, 168
gratin, potato and, 213
green bean, potato, and, 170
green beans with, 172
juice, instant, 339
juice, spicy, 341
lima beans and, 174
Louisiana corn and, 175
marinated, 294
mayonnaise, 23
-mushroom soup, 86
noodle casserole with zucchini, Cheez and, 211
okra and, 176–77, 188
and onion sauce, 262
Oriental UnBeef and, 111
pickles, green, 293
puree, instant, 339
relish, 295
relish, tomato, 295
relish, sweet, 295
relish, Aunt Lou Maxey's, 291
rice with Cheez, 222
salad, 40
salad, garbanzo-, 31
salad, monastery, 35
salad, summer, 39
slaw, 40–41
soup, cold Kreem of, 67
soup, fresh, 71
soup, Kreem of pinto bean and, 75
soup, lentil and, 75
soup, -mushroom, 86
soup, sour Kreem, 82
soup, spicy, 82
soup, tomato, roasted, 80–81
soup, white bean and, 88
spinach, rice, and, 185
spinach with, 185
squash, green beans, and, 186
squash casserole with Cheez, rice and, 221
squash with, 187
stew, zucchini-, 89
Tomato Sauce (1, 2, 3), 261
Tomato Soup (1, 2, 3, 4), 85–86
UnBeef with rice and, 116–17
UnChicken with mushrooms, rice, and, 145
UnTurkey cutlets with mushrooms and, 148
vegetable casserole with, and rice, 223–24
vegetable cream soup, 86
and vegetables, 188
vinaigrette, Mexican, 17
white beans with (1, 2), 240–41
zucchini casserole with Cheez, rice, and, 226
zucchini with, 191
Tortilla and Tostada Filling (1, 2), 240
Tossed Salad, 41
Triple Layer Casserole, 222
Tunisian Potato Salad, 47
Tuscan White Bean Casserole (1, 2), 240

U

UnBacon
and Cheez potatoes, 222–23
green beans with, 171
omelets, 140
UnBacon (1, 2), 136
white beans with, 241
UnBeef, 109
barbecued, 109
and broccoli, 114–15
broth, 155
casserole, baked cubed, 192–93
casserole, ground, saucy, 112
chimichangas, 109–10
company pride hash, 110
continental Stroganoff, 110
enchiladas, 252
goulash, 110
gravy (1, 2), 254
loaf, saucy meatless, 112
loaf, stuffed, meatless, 113
minestrone soup, 86
and mushroom étouffée, 115
Parmesan, 115
and pasta bake, 276
pasta sauce, 265
polenta, spiced, 113
pot roast, 115
Reuben casserole, 111
with rice and tomatoes, 116–17
roast (1, 2), 111
Rouladen, 116
soy grits, 109
steaks with peperonata tomato sauce, 116
stir-fry, 113
Stroganoff, 116
tamale pie, 114
and tomatoes, Oriental, 111
and tomato sauce, 262, 264–65
UnMeatballs, tangy, 114
and zucchini burgers, 121
UnBeefy Macaroni and Cheez, 276
UnChicken, 137
à la King, 141
au gratin, Spanish, 140
bake, Cajun, 137–38
braised, and "Chorizo", 137
broth, 155
cacciatore (1, 2), 143
casserole, Italian, 139
and Cheez pot pie, 141
Chickaritos, 138
chili, 92
creamed, with mushrooms and herbs, 138
Diane, 143
and dumplings, 142
glorified, 138
gravy, 255
gumbo, 143
gumbo, and UnSausage, 142–43
Hungarian, 138–39
jambalaya, 139
lasagna, 276–77
Moroccan, 139
with mushrooms, tomatoes, and rice, 145
noodle soup, 86–87
paella, 144
paprika (1, 2), 144
pasta sauce, 265

UnChicken, *continued*
and pasta toss, 142
and potato sauté, 142
pot pie, 144–45
rice soup, 87
roasted, with potatoes and "chorizo", 140
soy grits, 140
Spanish, with Rice, 140–41
tetrazzini, 145
UnFried, Sunday, 141
UnFried, Yankee, 146
and UnSausage gumbo, 142–43
UnCooked Applesauce, 341
Uncooked Fruitcake, 320
UnFish, 149
UnFish, deep-fried, 149
UnFish Broth, 155
UnFish Soup, 87
UnHam
baked, 130
and broccoli casserole, 223
broth, 156
gravy (1, 2), 255
loaf, 131
and potato casserole, 223
and potatoes au gratin, 223
soy grits, 130
UnHam, 130
UnHamburger Gravy, 255
UnOysters Baton Rouge, 152
UnPork
broth, 156
casserole, and sauerkraut, 128
casserole, chili UnPork chop, 123
casserole, UnSausage and sauerkraut, 129
chops, 122–23
chops, and beans, Mexican, 126
chops, glorified, 125
chops, grilled, zesty, 129
chops, kraut-stuffed, 125–26
chops, orange, 126
chops, Oriental, 126
chops, oven-barbecued, 126–27
chops, sautéed, with tomato and eggplant sauce, 127
chops with crumb crust, 128
fried, 125
ginger-peach, 125
sauce, barbecue "spare ribs", 123
with sauerkraut, 128
"spare ribs", barbecue, 123, 124
sweet and sour (1, 2), 127–28
UnPork (1, 2, 3), 122
with water chestnuts and mushrooms, Chinese, 125
UnSalmon Loaf, 150
UnSausage
about, 132
breakfast, 132
broth, 156
and cabbage, 134
Cajun, 132
chorizo, Mexican, 134
farmer's, 132–33
focaccia, 283
garlic, 133
herb, 133
Italian, 133
pizza, 134
rosemary, 134
and sauerkraut casserole, 129
simple, 135
soy grits, 135
Watkins, 135
UnScallops, 150
UnSeafood dishes. *See* UnFish; UnOysters; UnSalmon; UnScallops, UnShrimp
UnShrimp, 150
broiled, 150–51
with caper sauce, 154
and corn soup, 87
Creole, 152
curry (1, 2), 152–53
dip, 341
French fried, 151
garlic, Español, 151
gumbo, 153
imperial, 153
marinated, 151
Mexican, 151
mold, 153
pasta sauce, 265
pie, 154
salad, 41
soup, 87
stew (1, 2), 87–88
UnSteak
étouffée, 117
marinated Oriental, 110–11
and Onion Pie, 117
pepper, Chinese, 110
Salisbury, 112
skillet, saucy, 112–13
Swiss, 114
UnTurkey, 147
cutlets piccata, 147–48
cutlets with mushrooms and tomatoes, 148
holiday casserole, 148
Lisbon, 147
meatless-balls with caper sauce, 148
salad burritos, 148

V

Vanilla Cake (1, 2), 320
Vanilla Pudding (1, 2), 313
Vegeburgers, 121
Vegetable(s). *See also* individual vegetables
Anandamayi, 159
burgers, 121
casserole with tomatoes and rice, 223–24
and Cheez casserole, 225
consommé, 88
copper pennies, 162–63
crumble, 224
curry, 189
enchiladas, 224
fried rice (1, 2, 3), 247–48
ginger curry, 169
golden vegetable layer, 169
hash brown waffles, 172
hominy and bell pepper sauté, 172–73
Jamaican, 173
kitchuri, lazy, 173–74
Mixed Vegetable Salad (1, 2), 35

paella-limas, 178
parmesan (1, 2), 225
peperonata (1, 2), 178
pickled, 295
pie, 189
pizza-style, 179
pot pie, 190, 224
quick saucy, 182
ragout, Mediterranean, 176
ratatouille, 182
red cabbage (1, 2), 182–83
sauerkraut, quick, 182
sautéed, 184
Slumgullian, 184
Spanish, 185
succotash, Dutch 167
succotash, lima-corn, 175
taters 'n' onions, fried, 168–69
Thai-style, 188
UnFries, oven, 178
Vegetarian Dog Food, 341
Vegetarianism, about, 1–3
Velvet Crumb Cake, 321
Vinaigrette Dressing (1, 2), 24
Vinaigrette, Mexican tomato, 17
Vinaigrette, pasta salad, 36
Vitamin B12, about, 9

W

Waffles, 341
Warm Potato Salad with Garlic UnSausage, 48
Watkins UnSausage, 135
White Bean
salad (1, 2), 41
with tomatoes (1, 2), 240–41
and tomato soup, 88
with UnBacon, 241
White Bread, 57
White Lasagna, 277
White Sauce, 262
Whole Wheat Bread, 57
Whole Wheat Buns, 58
Winter Hot Pot, 88

Y

Yankee Unfried UnChicken, 146
Yeast, nutritional, about, 6
Yeast Biscuits (1, 2), 58
Yeast Cheez, 97
Yellow Squash Creole, 190

Z

Zatarain's Crab Boil, about, 9
Zesty French Dressing, 24
Zesty Grilled UnPork Chops, 129
Zucchini
bread and butter, 291
-carrot soup, 89
casserole (1, 2), 225–26
casserole with tomatoes, Cheez, and rice, 226
Creole, 226
with mustard-dill sauce, 191
parmigiana, 227
pickles, 296
plain, 190
-red pepper relish, 297
relish, 297
soup, 89
spaghetti sauce, 265
supreme, 190
with tomatoes, 191
-tomato stew, 89